UNITED KINGDOM

G.R. Hidderley, University of Central England, Birmingham

Jonathan Liebenau, London School of Economics and Political Science

UNITED STATES OF AMERICA

Kimberly Cass, Marquette University

P.C. Chu, Ohio State University, Columbus

Frank S. Davis, Jr, Bloomsburg University

William DeLone, American University

Vasant Dhar, New York University

Robert A. Fleck, Jr., Columbus College

Jeet Gupta, Ball State University

Vijay Gurbaxani, University of California, Irvine

Bart Hodge, Virginia Commonwealth University

Rob Kauffman, University of Rochester

Rob Kling, University of California, Irvine

Roger Letts, Fairleigh Dickinson University

Jane Mackay, Texas Christian University

Efrem G. Mallach, University of Lowell

Richard O. Mason, Southern Methodist University

Khris McAlister, University of Alabama, Birmingham

Sheizaf Rafaeli, University of Michigan

Brian Reithel, University of Mississippi

James Riha, Northern Illinois University

Edward M. Roche, Seton Hall University

Naveed Saleem, University of Houston, Clear Lake

Cort Schlichting, Spring Hill College

Ivan J. Singer, University of Hartford

Jill Y. Smith, University of Denver

William H. Starbuck, New York University

Kathy Stevens, Merrimack College

Dennis Strouble, Bowling Green State University

E. Burton Swanson, University of California, Los Angeles

Bernadette Szajna, Texas Christian University

Kranti Toraskar, Penn State University

Duane Truex, State University of New York, Binghamton

Patrick J. Walsh, State University of New York, Binghamton

Diane Walz, University of Texas, San Antonio

About the Authors

*Essentials of Management
Information Systems*

Kenneth C. Laudon is Professor of Information Systems at New York University's Stern School of Business. He holds a B.A. in Economics from Stanford and a Ph.D. from Columbia University. He has authored nine books dealing with information systems, organizations, and society. Professor Laudon has also written over forty articles concerned with the social, organizational, and management impacts of information systems, privacy, ethics, and multimedia technology.

Professor Laudon's current research is on the planning and management of large-scale information systems for the 1990s and multimedia information technology. He has received grants from the National Science Foundation to study the evolution of national information systems at the Social Security Administration, the IRS, and the FBI. A part of this research is concerned with computer-related organizational and occupational changes in large organizations, changes in management ideology, changes in public policy, and understanding productivity change in the knowledge sector. Ken Laudon is the Director of the Stern School Virtual Multimedia Facility.

Ken Laudon has testified as an expert before the United States Congress. He has been a researcher and consultant to the Office of Technology Assessment (United States Congress) since 1978, and to the Office of the President, several executive branch agencies, and Congressional Committees. Professor Laudon also acts as a consultant on systems planning and strategy to several Fortune 500 firms.

Ken Laudon's hobby is sailing.

Jane Price Laudon is a management consultant in the information systems area and the author of seven books. Her special interests include systems analysis, data management, MIS auditing, software evaluation, and teaching business professionals how to design and use information systems.

Jane received her Ph.D. from Columbia University, her M.A. from Harvard University, and her B.A. from Barnard College. She has taught at Columbia University and the New York University Graduate School of Business. She maintains a lifelong interest in Oriental languages and civilizations.

The Laudons have two daughters, Erica and Elisabeth.

Essentials of Management Information Systems reflects a deep understanding of MIS research and teaching as well as practical experience designing and building real world systems.

Essentials of Management Information Systems

Essentials of Management Information Systems:

Organization and Technology

Kenneth C. Laudon
New York University

Jane P. Laudon
Azimuth Corporation

PRENTICE HALL, Upper Saddle River, New Jersey 07458

Laudon, Kenneth C.
    Essentials of management information systems : organization and
technology / Kenneth C. Laudon, Jane P. Laudon.
        p. cm.
    Includes index.
    ISBN 0-02-368083-0
    1. Management information systems. I. Laudon, Jane Price.
II. Title.
T58.6.L3753 1995
658.4'038—dc20

94-9417
CIP

Editor: Charles E. Stewart, Jr.

Production Supervisor: John Travis

Production Manager: Nick Sklitsis and Francesca Drago

Text Designer: Patricia Smythe

Cover Designer: Maria Lange

Cover Art: Gino Severini

Sea = Dancer (Mare = Ballerina). January 1914. Oil on canvas, including artist's painted frame. 105.3 × 85.9 cm (41 ½ × 33 ¹³/₁₆ inches).

Solomon R. Guggenheim Museum, New York, The Peggy Guggenheim Collection, Venice, 1976

PHOTO: Carmelo Guadagno copyright The Solomon R. Guggenheim Foundation, New York

Photo Director: Chris Migdol

Photo Researcher: Dallas Chang

Printed in the United States of America

10 9 8 7 6 5 4 3

ISBN 0-02-368083-0

Prentice-Hall International (UK) Limited, *London*
Prentice-Hall of Australia Pty. Limited, *Sydney*
Prentice-Hall Canada Inc., *Toronto*
Prentice-Hall Hispanoamericana, S.A., *Mexico*
Prentice-Hall of India Private Limited, *New Delhi*
Prentice-Hall of Japan, Inc., *Tokyo*
Simon & Schuster Asia Pte. Ltd., *Singapore*
Editora Prentice-Hall do Brasil, Ltda., *Rio de Janeiro*

Preface

Essentials of Management Information Systems: Organization and Technology is based on the premise that professional managers in both the private and public sectors cannot afford to ignore information systems. In today's business environment, professional managers must learn how to use information technology to create competitive firms, manage global corporations, and provide useful products and services to customers. Briefly, it is difficult—if not impossible—to manage a modern organization without at least some grounding in the fundamentals of what information systems are and how they affect the organization and its employees. Accordingly, we have written this book to provide a concise introduction to management information systems (MIS) that undergraduate and MBA students will find vital for their professional success.

Essentials of Management Information Systems is an abridged 15-chapter version of the larger text, *Management Information Systems: Organization and Technology (Third Edition)*. The main features, conceptual framework and style of the larger text are presented here in a concise manner. The *Essentials* text is well-suited for courses lasting less than one semester, mini-courses and those requiring a smaller MIS text to combine with hands-on software, case studies or other projects.

The Contemporary Environment

The book reflects three related trends in the contemporary business environment of the 1990s. First, globalization of markets puts new emphasis on organizational design and management control. When your parts originate in Korea, your assembly occurs in Mexico, and your finance, marketing and general counsel are in New York, then you know you face tough challenges in designing the proper organization and managing the work.

Second, the transformation of the American and other advanced industrial economies into full-fledged knowledge and information economies puts new emphasis on time-based competition, productivity of knowledge workers, short product life cycles, and employee training. When 75% of the gross national product is an output of the information sector, then the productivity of information workers is a central societal concern. When your firm's future depends on having a new product in the marketplace in nine months, then you face a difficult challenge as a manager in speeding up the work of engineers and other knowledge workers. The demand for information, for communications, has never been so great.

Third, the development of powerful microprocessors and telecommunications networks has brought forth a new information architecture based on powerful desktop computers and communications networks. We can now put what used to be called a mainframe computer on every desktop, and we can now design organizations in which every desktop and information worker can be part of the firm's information network. A few years ago this was a dream.

The work of an organization—and its employees—depends increasingly on what its information systems are capable of doing. Increasing market share, becoming the high-quality or low-cost producer, developing new products, and/or increasing employee productivity, depend more and more on the kinds and quality of information systems in the organization.

One result of these trends is a change in the role of the modern manager. Today's managers are not only expected to use systems but are also expected to:

- Know how to use information technology to design competitive and efficient organizations.
- Understand the business and system requirements of a global environment.
- Use information systems to ensure quality throughout the firm.
- Manage the procurement of a variety of information technologies.
- Manage and control the influence of systems on employees and customers.
- Understand the ethical dilemmas and controversies which surround the use of advanced information systems.

In essence, contemporary managers are expected to know enough about information technology to use it in the design and management of their organizations. These new management responsibilities require a deeper understanding of information technology and systems than ever before. Although this book primarily deals with private organizations, public sector managers are no less susceptible to these trends and changes in management and organization.

Unique Features of This Text

Essentials of Management Information Systems has many unique features designed to create an active, dynamic learning environment.

- **Interactive Multimedia Edition:** This is the first MIS text with an interactive multimedia version on CD-ROM. The Multimedia Edition features the full 15 chapters of the printed text plus 15 additional videos explaining key concepts, audio clips, line art, research articles, and interactive exercises. The multimedia version can be used independently of the hard cover version or in conjunction with the hard cover text as an interactive study guide. All supplements for the printed version may be used with the Multimedia Edition.

- **An integrated framework for describing and analyzing information systems.** An integrated framework portrays information systems as being composed of management, organization and technology elements. This framework is used throughout the text to describe and analyze information systems and information system problems. A special diagram accompanying each chapter-opening vignette graphically illustrates how management, organization, and technology elements work together to create an information system solution to the business challenges discussed in the vignette. The diagram can be used as a starting point to analyze any information system problem.

- **Real-World Examples:** Real-world examples drawn from business and public organizations are used throughout to illustrate text concepts. Each chapter opens with a vignette illustrating the themes of the chapter by showing how a real-world organization meets a business challenge using information systems. More than 100 companies in the United States and over 75 organizations in Canada, Europe, Australia, and Asia are discussed (see the United States and Foreign Companies indexes.)

Each chapter contains three WINDOW ON boxes (WINDOW ON MANAGEMENT, WINDOW ON ORGANIZATIONS, WINDOW ON TECHNOLOGY) that present real-world examples illustrating the management, organization, and technology issues in the chapter. Each WINDOW ON box concludes with a section called *To Think About* which consists of a question or series of questions for students to apply chapter concepts to management problem solving. The themes for each box are:

WINDOW ON MANAGEMENT: Management problems raised by systems and their solution; management strategies and plans; careers and experiences of managers using systems.

WINDOW ON TECHNOLOGY: Hardware, software, telecommunications, data storage, standards, and systems-building methodologies.

WINDOW ON ORGANIZATIONS: Activities of private and public organizations using information systems; experiences of people working with systems.

- **Coverage of new leading-edge topics.** Full chapters address the challenges posed by today's competitive global business environment: Managing International Information Systems (Chapter 14); Ethical and Social Issues in Information Systems (Chapter 15); Building Successful Systems: Quality and Implementation (Chapter 9); and Knowledge and Information Work Systems (Chapter 10) address these themes. The text includes up-to-date coverage of topics such as:

  - The information superhighway
  - Business process redesign (redesigning organizations with information systems)
  - Case-based reasoning
  - Fuzzy logic
  - Outsourcing
  - Multimedia
  - Object-oriented systems development

- **A truly international perspective:** In addition to a full chapter on Managing International Information Systems, all chapters of the text are illustrated with real-world examples from 75 corporations in Europe, Asia, Latin America, Australia, and the Middle East. Each chapter contains at least one WINDOW ON box, case study or opening vignette drawn from a non-U.S. firm, and often more. The text concludes with six major international case studies contributed by leading MIS experts in Canada, Europe, and Australia—Andrew Boynton, International Institute for Management Development (Switzerland); Len Fertuck, University of Toronto (Canada), Helmut Krcmar and Bettina Schwarzer, Hohenheim University (Germany); Tapio Reponen, Turku School of Economics and Business Administration (Finland); Alan Underwood, Queensland University of Technology (Australia); and Peter Weill and J. B. Barolsky, University of Melbourne (Australia).

- **Activist pedagogy to teach management problem-solving.**

Essentials of Management Information Systems contains many features that encourage students to actively learn and to engage in management problem-solving.

Interactive learning: The CD-ROM version provides an interactive, computer-managed instruction component that lets students learn at their own pace. Students can select and access material using powerful electronic indexes for subjects, names, and organizations. They can review key terms with an electronic glossary. Each chapter of the text contains a bulletized summary of the key points for immediate on-line access and review through hot buttons and on-line glossaries and indexes. Videos and audio clips for each chapter illustrate real-world applications of key concepts. An interactive study guide provides helpful question-and-answer sessions, which can be automatically graded and handed to the professor.

Group projects: At the end of each chapter is a group project that encourages students to develop teamwork and oral and written presentation skills. The group project exercise asks students to work in groups of three or four to research a specific topic, analyze the pros and cons of an issue, write about it, and orally present the group's findings to the class. For instance, students might be asked to work in small groups to analyze a business and to suggest appropriate strategic information systems for that particular business or to develop a corporate ethics code on privacy that considers E-mail privacy and employers' use of information systems to monitor work sites.

Management Challenges Section: Each chapter concludes with two or three major challenges relating to the chapter topic that managers are likely to encounter. These challenges are multi-faceted and sometimes pose dilemmas. They make excellent springboards for class discussion. Some of these Management Challenges are the organizational obstacles to building a database environment, determining the right level of integration between different types of systems, and major risks and uncertainties in systems development.

To Think About questions concluding every WINDOW ON box require students to apply chapter concepts to real-world scenarios. These questions frequently ask students to assume the role of managers, use multiple perspectives, consider different alternatives, and think creatively. The questions can be used for class discussion or for short written projects.

Case Studies: Management problem-solving opportunities are also provided by case studies at the end of each chapter and by the six international case studies concluding the text.

Book Overview

The five parts of the book are designed to be relatively independent of each other. Each instructor may choose to emphasize different parts.

Part One is concerned with the organizational foundations of systems and their emerging strategic role. It provides an extensive introduction to real-world systems, focusing on how they are related to organizations and to management. This section is important for understanding the larger environment in which systems operate and for showing students how systems relate to organizational design, strategy, and operations.

Part Two provides the technical foundation for understanding information systems, describing hardware, software, storage, and telecommunications technologies. The section concludes by describing connectivity, standards, and the challenge of making all of the information technologies work together in a new information architecture based on enterprise-wide networks.

Part Three focuses on the process of redesigning organizations using information systems. Because information systems and organizations are so closely intertwined, we see systems analysis and design as an exercise in organizational design, one that requires great sensitivity to the right tools and techniques, quality assurance and change management.

Part Four describes the role of information systems in capturing and distributing organizational knowledge and intelligence and in enhancing management decision-making. It shows how knowledge creation and distribution, work group collaboration, and individual and group decision making can be supported by the use of knowledge work systems, decision support systems, and executive support systems. Organizational performance can also be enhanced by carefully chosen artificial intelligence applications.

Part Five concludes the text by examining the special management challenges and opportunities created by the pervasiveness and power of contemporary information systems: ensuring security and control, developing global systems, and coping with the ethical and social impact of information systems. Throughout the text emphasis is placed on using information technology to redesign the organization's products, services, procedures, jobs and management structures, with numerous examples drawn from multinational systems and global business environments.

CHAPTER OUTLINE

Each chapter contains the following:

- A detailed outline at the beginning to provide an overview.
- An opening vignette describing a real-world organization to establish the theme and importance of the chapter.
- A diagram analyzing the opening vignette in terms of the management, organization, and technology model used throughout the text.
- A list of learning objectives.
- Marginal glosses of key terms in the text.
- Management challenges.
- A chapter summary keyed to the learning objectives.
- A list of key terms that the student can use to review concepts.
- Review questions for students to test their comprehension of chapter material.
- A set of discussion questions that can be used for class discussion or for research topics.
- A group project to develop teamwork and presentation skills.
- A chapter-ending case study that illustrates important themes.
- A list of references for further research on topics.

Instructional Support Materials:

SOFTWARE

A series of optional management software cases called *Solve It! Management Problem Solving with PC Software* has been developed to support the text. *Solve it* consists of 10 spreadsheet and 10 database cases drawn from real-world businesses, plus a data diskette with the files required by the cases. The cases are graduated in difficulty. The case book contains complete tutorial documentation showing how to use spreadsheet and database software to solve the problems. A new version of *Solve it!* with all new cases is published every year. *Solve it!* can be purchased directly from the supplier, Azimuth Corporation, 124 Penfield Ave., Croton-on-Hudson, New York 10520 (Telephone 914-271-6321).

MULTIMEDIA MANUAL: INSTRUCTOR'S MANUAL/TEST BANK/TRANSPARENCY MASTERS AND VIDEO CASES

The *Instructor's Resource Manual,* written by Ken and Jane Laudon and Marshall R. Kaplan, has been fully revised and now includes lecture outlines as well as answers to review questions, discussion questions, group project exercises, case study questions, video cases, and To Think About questions. The Test Bank has been expanded to include of 25 true-false questions, 25 multiple choice questions, and 25 fill in the blank questions for each chapter. The Instructor's Resource Manual contains transparency masters.

VIDEO CASES

Video cases based on the real-world corporations and organizations used in the text are available to adopters. The five video cases illustrate the concepts in each section and can be used for class discussion or written projects. The video cases are analyzed in the Instructor's Resource Manual.

INSTRUCTOR'S RESOURCE MANUAL ON DISK

The Instructor's Resource Manual is available on disk to adopters wishing to put it on their computers.

COMPUTERIZED TEST BANK

All test bank questions are available in computerized form.

TRANSPARENCY ACETATES

A set of approximately 100 full-color transparency acetates is available to illuminate key concepts.

Acknowledgments

The production of any book involves many valued contributions from a number of persons. We would like to thank in particular our editors at Macmillan for encouragement, insight, and strong support for many years. We are grateful to Charles Stewart for his energy, enthusiasm, and insight in guiding the initial preparation of this text and to P. J. Boardman for her support of the final stages of the project. We commend Paul Smolenski, John Travis and the Macmillan and Prentice Hall production departments for guiding production of this text under a very ambitious schedule and Pat Smythe for her beautiful design work.

We are deeply indebted to Marshall R. Kaplan for his invaluable assistance in the writing of Chapters 9, 10, and 11 and for his work on the Instructor's Resource Manual and to Rachel Bunin for her developmental assistance.

The Stern School of Business at New York University and the Information Systems Department provided a very special learning environment, one in which we and others could rethink the MIS field. Special thanks to Vasant Dhar, Robert Kauffman, and Stephen Slade for providing critical feedback and support where deserved. Professor Norm White was especially helpful in commenting on the technical chapters in Part II and we thank him. Professor William H. Starbuck of the Management Department at NYU provided valuable comments and insights.

Professor Al Croker of Baruch College and NYU, Professor Kenneth Marr of Hofstra University, Professor Edward Roche of Seton Hall University, Jiri Rodovsky, and Russell Polo provided additional suggestions for improvement.

We are truly grateful to our colleagues in the MIS field who shared their expertise and comments with us. We want to thank Len Fertuck, Andrew Boynton, Helmut Krcmar, Tapio Reponen, Bettina Schwarzer, Alan Underwood, and Peter Weill for contributing case studies. They deeply enrich the text.

One of our goals for *Essentials of Management Information Systems* was to write a book which was authoritative, synthesized diverse views in the MIS literature, and helped define a common academic field. A large number of leading scholars in the field were contacted and assisted us in this effort. Reviewers and consultants for this text took considerable time and care to examine individual chapters as specialists and the entire manuscript as instructors in the MIS course. Insofar as time and space allowed, we tried to incorporate their ideas in the text. We deeply appreciate their work and their suggestions for improving the text. These consultants are listed in the front end papers of the book. It is our hope that this group endeavor contributes to a shared vision and understanding of the MIS field.

Contents
in Brief

Contents

Windows on MIS

CHAPTER

1

The Challenge of Information Systems

UPS Competes Globally with Information Technology

United Parcel Service, the world's largest air and ground package distribution company, started out in 1907 in a closet-sized basement office. Jim Casey and Claude Ryan—two teenagers from Seattle with two bicycles and one phone—promised the ''best service and lowest rates.'' UPS has used this formula successfully for nearly 90 years.

UPS still lives up to that promise today, delivering close to 3 billion parcels and documents each year to any address in the United States and to more than 180 countries and territories. The company not only excels at traditional package delivery but is competing against Federal Express in the overnight delivery business as well. Critical to the firm's success has been its investment in advanced information technology. Between 1992 and 1996, UPS expects to invest $3.2 billion on information technology that will keep it a worldwide market leader. Technology has helped UPS boost customer service while streamlining its overall operations.

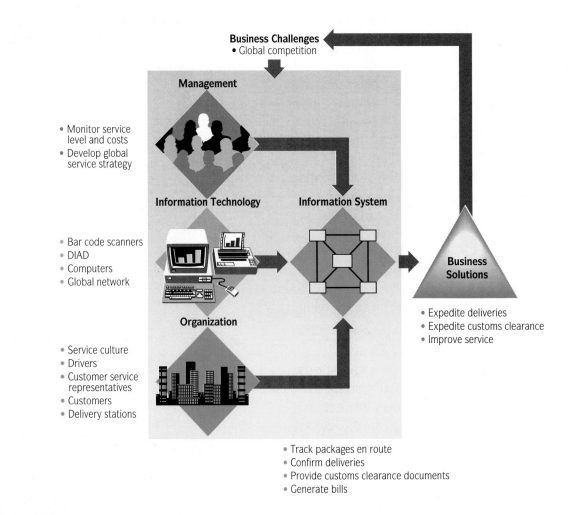

Using a handheld Delivery Information Acquisition Device (DIAD), UPS drivers automatically capture customers' signatures along with pickup, delivery, and timecard information. The drivers then transmit this information to UPS's computer network, where it is stored in UPS's Delivery Information Automated Lookup System (DIALS). If retrieved, the information can provide proof of delivery to the customer. The system can also generate a printed response to queries for the customer.

With its Package Tracking System (PTS), UPS can monitor packages throughout the delivery process. At various points along the route from sender to receiver, a bar code device scans shipping information on the package label; the information is then fed into a central computer. Customer service representatives can check the status of any package from desktop computers linked to the central computer and are able to respond immediately to inquiries from customers.

UPS's Inventory Express, launched in 1991, warehouses customers' products and ships them overnight to any destination the customer requests. Customers using this service can transmit electronic shipping orders to UPS by 1:00 A.M. and expect delivery by 10:30 that same morning.

In 1988, UPS moved aggressively into overseas markets and set up its own global communications network, UPSnet, as the information processing pipeline for worldwide operations. UPSnet extends the system's capabilities internationally by providing access to information for billing and delivery confirmation, tracking international shipments, and expediting customs clearance. UPS uses its network to transmit documentation electronically on each shipment directly to customs officials prior to the arrival of shipments. The customs officials clear the shipment or flag it for inspection. UPS recently contracted with GM Europe to provide just-in-time delivery of auto parts. Through these advances, UPS can compete globally.

Sources: Chuck Hawkins with Patrick Oster, "After a U-Turn, UPS Really Delivers," *Business Week* (May 31, 1993); Linda Wilson, "Stand and Deliver," *InformationWEEK* (November 23, 1992) and *UPS Public Relations,* "High Tech Advances Lead UPS into the Paperless Age" (April 1992).

U PS's reliance on information technology to drive its business illustrates the essential role that information systems have come to play in organizations and industries. The company's successes demonstrate how information systems can help businesses compete in today's global business environment.

Like UPS, most organizations will need information systems to survive and prosper. This chapter starts our investigation of information systems and organizations by explaining what an information system is and describing its management, organization, and technology dimensions.

After completing this chapter, you will be able to:

- Define an information system.
- Explain the difference between computer literacy and information systems literacy.
- Describe the information needs of different organizational levels.
- Explain why information systems are so important today.
- Identify the major conceptual approaches to information systems.
- Identify the major management challenges to building and using information systems in organizations.

1.1   Why Information Systems?

Until the 1980s, there was little need for this textbook or course. Managers generally did not need to know much about how information was collected, processed, and distributed in their organizations, and the technology involved was minimal. Information itself was not considered an important asset for the firm. In most organizations, information was viewed as an unfortunate, costly by-product of doing business—simply "red tape." The management process was considered a face-to-face, personal art and not a far-flung, global coordination process. But today few managers can afford to ignore how information is handled by their organization.

The Competitive Business Environment of the 1990s

Two very powerful worldwide changes have altered the environment of business. The first change is the emergence and strengthening of the global economy. The second change is the transformation of industrial economies and societies into knowledge- and information-based service economies. These changes in the business environment and climate, summarized in Table 1.1, pose a number of new challenges to business firms and their management.

Table 1.1	THE CHANGING BUSINESS ENVIRONMENT OF THE 1990s

Globalization

- Management and control in a global marketplace
- Competition in world markets
- Global work groups
- Global delivery systems

Transformation of Industrial Economies

- Knowledge- and information-based economies
- Productivity
- New products and services
- Leadership
- Time-based competition
- Shorter product life
- Turbulent environment
- Limited employee knowledge base

A growing percentage of the American economy—and other advanced industrial economies in Europe and Asia—depends on imports and exports. Foreign trade—both exports and imports—accounts for a little over 25 percent of the goods and services produced in the United States, and even more in countries like Japan and Germany. This percentage will grow in the future. The success of firms in the 1990s depends on their ability to operate globally.

Globalization of the world's industrial economies greatly enhances the value of information to the firm and offers new opportunities to businesses. Today, information systems provide the communication and analytic power that firms need for conducting trade and managing businesses on a global scale. To provide worldwide package delivery service, for instance, companies like UPS must develop global information systems that can trace specific packages, analyze information on package flow and costs, operate 24 hours a day in different national environments, and service local as well as international management reporting needs. In short, controlling the far-flung global corporation is a major business challenge that requires powerful information system responses.

Globalization and information technology also bring new threats to domestic business firms: Because of global communication and management systems, customers now can shop in a worldwide marketplace, obtaining price and quality information reliably, 24 hours a day. This phenomenon heightens competition and forces firms to play in open, unprotected worldwide markets. To become effective and profitable participants in international markets, firms need powerful information and communication systems.

TRANSFORMATION OF
INDUSTRIAL ECONOMIES

The United States—the world's largest single economy and marketplace—is going through its third economic revolution. In the first revolution, the nation had by 1890 transformed itself from a colonial backwater to an agrarian powerhouse capable of feeding large segments of the world population. In the second revolution, the United States had by 1920 transformed itself from an agrarian nineteenth-century society to a first-class industrial power. In the third revolution, now in progress, the country is transforming itself into a knowledge- and information-based service economy. Both Japan and Germany, and the other major industrial powers to varying degrees, are experiencing a similar revolution.

The knowledge and information revolution began at the turn of the twentieth century and has gradually accelerated. Figure 1.1 shows that by 1976 the number

Figure 1.1
The growth of the information economy. Since the turn of the century, the United States has experienced a steady decline in the number of farm workers and blue-collar workers who are employed in factories. At the same time, the country is experiencing a rise in the number of white-collar workers who produce economic value using knowledge and information. By 1976 the number of white-collar workers had surpassed the number of blue-collar, service, and farm workers. *Source: Adapted from "The Mechanization of Office Work," by Vincent Guiliano,* Scientific American, *September 1982. Copyright © 1982 by Scientific American, Inc. All rights reserved.*

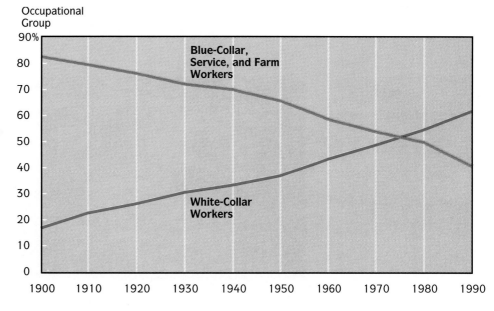

of white-collar workers employed in offices surpassed the number of farm workers, service workers, and blue-collar workers employed in manufacturing. Today, most people no longer work in farms or factories but instead are found in sales, education, health care, banks, insurance firms, and law firms; they also provide business services like copying, computer software, or deliveries. These jobs primarily involve working with, distributing, or creating new information and knowledge. In fact, knowledge and information work now accounts for a significant 75 percent of the American gross national product, and nearly 70 percent of the labor force.

In a knowledge- and information-based economy, information technology and systems take on great importance. For instance, information technology constitutes more than 70 percent of the invested capital in service industries like finance, insurance, and real estate. This means that for many managers—perhaps for most—decisions about information technology will be the most common investment decisions.

Because the productivity of employees will depend on the quality of the systems serving them, management decisions about information technology are critically important to the prosperity and survival of a firm. Consider also that the growing power of information technology makes possible new services of great economic value. Credit cards, overnight package delivery, and worldwide reservation systems are examples of services that are based on new information technologies. Over the next decade, information and the technology that delivers it will become critical, strategic resources for business firms and their managers.

What Is an Information System?

Information system:
Interrelated components that collect, process, store, and disseminate information to support decision making, control, analysis, and visualization in an organization.

An **information system** can be defined technically as a set of interrelated components that collect (or retrieve), process, store, and distribute information to support decision making and control in an organization. In addition to supporting decision making, coordination, and control, information systems may also help managers and workers analyze problems, visualize complex subjects, and create new products.

Information systems may contain information about significant people, places, and things within the organization or in the environment surrounding it (see Figure 1.2).

Three activities in an information system produce the information organizations need for making decisions, controlling operations, analyzing problems, and creating new products or services. These activities are input, processing, and

The sales clerk at this grocery store is able to capture the inventory control information by using a hand-held terminal and scanning gun. The clerk scans the Universal Product Codes and enters the quantity of each dairy product left on the shelf.

Figure 1.2
Functions of an information system. An information system contains information about an organization and its surrounding environment. Three basic activities—input, processing, and output—produce the information organizations need. Feedback is output returned to appropriate people or activities in the organization to evaluate and refine the input.

Input: The capture or collection of raw data from within the organization or from its external environment for processing in an information system.

Processing: The conversion of raw input into a form that is more meaningful to humans.

Output: The distribution of processed information to the people or activities where it will be used.

Feedback: Output that is returned to the appropriate members of the organization to help them evaluate or correct input.

Computer-based information systems (CBIS): Information systems that rely on computer hardware and software for processing and disseminating information.

output. **Input** captures or collects raw data from within the organization or from its external environment. **Processing** converts this raw input into a more meaningful form. **Output** transfers the processed information to the people or activities where it will be used. Information systems also require **feedback,** which is output that is returned to appropriate members of the organization to help them evaluate or correct the input stage. In the information system used by UPS, the raw input is the data on the shipping label. The central computer processes these data into reports that become output on the computer terminals of UPS customer service representatives, who use them to check the status of packages.

Our interest in this book is in formal, organizational computer-based information systems (CBIS) like those designed and used by UPS. Formal systems rest on accepted and fixed definitions of data and procedures for collecting, storing, processing, disseminating, and using these data. The formal systems we describe in this text are structured—that is, they operate in conformity with predefined rules that are relatively fixed and not easily changed. For instance, UPS's package delivery system requires that all packages be identified with both the sender's and recipient's name and address.

Informal information systems (such as office gossip networks) rely, by contrast, on implicit agreements and unstated rules of behavior. There is no agreement on what is information, or on how it will be stored and processed. They are essential for the life of an organization, but an analysis of their qualities is beyond the scope of this text.

Formal information systems can be either computer-based or manual. Manual systems use paper-and-pencil technology. These manual systems serve important needs, but they too are not the subject of this text. **Computer-based information systems (CBIS),** in contrast, rely on computer hardware and software technology to process and disseminate information. From this point on, when we use the term *information systems* we will be referring to computer-based information systems—formal organizational systems that rely on computer technology. The Window on Technology describes some of the typical technologies used in contemporary computer-based information systems.

The Difference Between Computers and Information Systems

Although computer-based information systems use computer technology to process raw data into meaningful information, there is a sharp distinction between a computer and a computer program on the one hand, and an information

TECHNOLOGY

The 'Rite' Approach to Inventory Management

A shoe store's stockroom is often a jumble of shoeboxes piled loosely together. Shoe store managers consequently do not know precisely what items they have in stock and may order the wrong items. Stride Rite, the children's footwear giant that makes Keds and Sperry topsiders, has changed that situation for its customers with telecommunications and bar code technology.

About 50 representatives in Stride Rite's children's shoe and Keds divisions make sales calls using an oversized briefcase with a scanning gun, a handheld terminal, and a miniature printer. The sales representatives use the scanning gun to take inventory of Stride Rite products rapidly in each retail shoe store by scanning the shelves. The handheld terminal captures that information. Then the reps plug the terminal into a telephone line, and dial up an electronic Universal Product Code catalog on a computer in a network. The portable printer puts out a precise snapshot of the retailer's inventory.

The technology has reduced the time required to take inventory from eight hours to less than two hours and eliminates some of the guesswork in writing orders. The sales representatives can write up more "intelligent orders"—orders that identify exactly what inventory items need to be replenished. Stride Rite plans to enhance this system in the future so that it can compare the store's stock against an inventory model specified by the retailer and can recommend what the retailer should order.

Stride Rite believes that with this system it can respond to retail stores more rapidly and accurately and that faster order turnaround gives the company an advantage over competitors.

Source: Paul Gillin, "The 'Rite' Approach," *Computerworld*, June 1, 1992.

To Think About: What are the inputs, processing, and outputs of this system? What technologies are used? What would happen if these technologies were not available?

system on the other. Electronic computers and related software programs are the technical foundation, the tools and materials, of modern information systems. Computers provide the equipment for storing and processing information. Computer programs, or software, are sets of operating instructions that direct and control computer processing. Knowing how computers and computer programs work is important in designing solutions to organizational problems, but the reason for using them comes from the information system of which computers are just a part.

Housing provides an appropriate analogy. Houses are built with hammers, nails, and wood, but these do not make a house. The architecture, design, setting, landscaping, and all of the decisions that lead to the creation of these features are part of the house and are crucial for finding a solution to the problem of putting a roof over one's head. Computers and programs are the hammer, nails, and lumber of CBIS, but alone they cannot produce the information a particular organization needs. To understand information systems, one must understand the problems they are designed to solve, their architectural and design elements, and the organizational processes that lead to these solutions. Today's managers must combine computer literacy with information system literacy.

A Business Perspective on Information Systems

From a business and management perspective, information systems are far more than just input–process–output machines operating in a vacuum. *From a business perspective, an information system is an organizational and management solution, based on information technology, to a challenge posed by the environment.* Examine this definition closely because it emphasizes the organizational and management nature of information systems: Information systems provide a major organizational solution to challenges and problems created in the business environment. To understand information systems—to be information systems literate as opposed to computer literate—a manager must understand the broader organization, management, and information technology dimensions of systems (see Figure 1.3) and their power to provide solutions to the business challenges that are described in this text.

Review the diagram at the beginning of the chapter, which reflects this expanded definition of an information system. The diagram shows how UPS's information systems provide a solution to the business challenges posed by intense global competition. The diagram also illustrates how management, technology, and organization elements work together to create these systems. We begin each chapter of the text with a diagram like this one to help you analyze the opening case. You can use this diagram as a starting point for analyzing any information system or information system problem you encounter.

To design and use information systems effectively, you must first understand the environment, structure, function, and politics of organizations, as well as the role of management and management decision making. Then you must examine the capabilities and opportunities provided by contemporary information technology to provide solutions. This text is organized to fulfill this plan.

ORGANIZATIONS   Information systems are a part of organizations. Indeed, for some companies, such as credit reporting firms, without the system there would be no business. The key elements of an organization are its people, structure and operating procedures, politics, and culture. We introduce these components of organizations here and describe them in greater detail in Chapter 3.

Formal organizations are composed of different levels and specialties. Their structures reveal a clear-cut division of labor. Experts are employed and trained for different functions, including sales, manufacturing, accounting, finance, and human resources. An organization coordinates work through a structured hierarchy and formal, standard operating procedures. The hierarchy arranges people in a pyramidal structure of rising authority and responsibility. The upper levels of the hierarchy consist of managerial, professional, and technical employees, while the lower levels consist of operational personnel.

Figure 1.3
Information systems are more than computers.
Using information systems effectively requires an understanding of the organization, management, and information technology shaping the systems. All information systems can be described as organizational and management solutions to challenges posed by the environment.

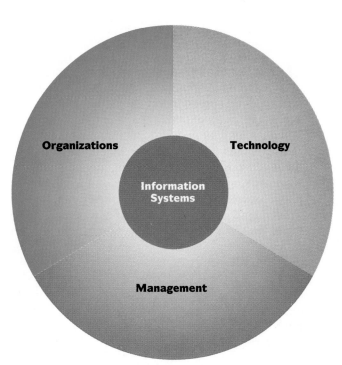

Standard operating procedures (SOPs): Precise, defined rules for accomplishing tasks that have been developed to cope with expected situations.

Rationalization of procedures: The streamlining of standard operating procedures to maximize the advantages of computerization and make information systems more efficient.

Knowledge workers: People such as engineers or architects who design products or services and create knowledge for the organization.

Data workers: People such as secretaries or bookkeepers who process and disseminate the organization's paperwork.

Production or service workers: People who actually produce the products or services of the organization.

Standard operating procedures (SOPs) are precise, defined rules for accomplishing tasks that have been developed to cope with expected situations; these rules guide employees in a variety of procedures, from writing an invoice to responding to complaining customers. Most standard operating procedures are formalized and written down, but some are informal work practices.

Many of a firm's SOPs are incorporated into information systems—such as how to pay a supplier or how to correct an erroneous bill. These procedures are often rationalized when they are computerized. **Rationalization of procedures** is the streamlining of standard operating procedures so that they can maximize the advantages of computerization and make information systems more efficient. For instance, before Stride Rite could automate its inventory information, it had to have a system that assigned standard codes and descriptions for every style of shoe it produced and sold. It also had to have a shipping network in place, with formal rules for placing and shipping orders from shoe stores. Without a certain amount of rationalization in Stride Rite's organization, its advanced technology would have been useless.

Organizations require many different kinds of skills and people. In addition to managers, **knowledge workers** (such as engineers, architects, or scientists) design products or services, and **data workers** (such as secretaries, bookkeepers, or clerks) process the organization's paperwork. **Production** or **service workers** (such as machinists, assemblers, or packers) actually produce the products or services of the organization.

Each organization has a unique culture, or fundamental set of assumptions, values, and ways of doing things, that have been accepted by most of its members. Parts of an organization's culture can always be found embedded in its information systems. For instance, the concern with putting service to the customer first is an aspect of the organizational culture of United Parcel Service that can be found in the company's package tracking systems.

Different levels and specialties in an organization create different interests and points of view. These views often conflict. Conflict is the basis for organizational politics. Information systems come out of this cauldron of differing perspectives, conflicts, compromises, and agreements that are a natural part of all organizations. In Chapter 3 we will examine these features of organizations in greater detail.

MANAGEMENT

Senior managers: People at the highest organizational level who are responsible for making long-range decisions.

Middle managers: People in the middle of the organizational hierarchy who are responsible for carrying out the plans and goals of senior management.

Operational managers: People who monitor the day-to-day activities of the organization.

Managers perceive business challenges in the environment; they set the organizational strategy for responding, and they allocate the human and financial resources to achieve the strategy and coordinate the work. Throughout, they must exercise responsible leadership. The business information systems described in this book reflect the hopes, dreams, and realities of real-world managers. These are managers' conventional responsibilities.

But less understood is the fact that managers must do more than manage what already exists. They must also create new products, services, and even re-create the organization from time to time. A substantial part of management is creative work driven by new knowledge and information. Information technology can play a powerful role in re-engineering the organization.

Chapter 3 describes the activities of managers and management decision making in detail. It is important to note that managerial roles and decisions vary at different levels of the organization. **Senior managers** make long-range strategic decisions about products and services to produce. **Middle managers** carry out the programs and plans of senior management. **Operational managers** are responsible for monitoring the firm's daily activities. All levels of management are expected to be creative: to develop novel solutions to a broad range of problems. Each level of management has different information needs and information system requirements.

TECHNOLOGY

Computer hardware: Physical equipment used for input, processing, and output work in an information system.

Computer software: Detailed, preprogrammed instructions that control and coordinate computer hardware components in an information system.

Storage technology: Physical media and software governing the storage and organization of data for use in an information system.

Telecommunications technology: Physical devices and software that link various computer hardware components and transfer data from one physical location to another.

Information systems technology is one of many tools available to managers for coping with change. More importantly today, information technology is the glue that holds the organization together. It is the instrument through which management controls and creates, and it is an arrow in the manager's quiver. CBIS utilize computer hardware, software, storage, and telecommunications technologies.

Computer hardware is the physical equipment used for input, processing, and output activities in an information system. It consists of the following: the computer processing unit; various input, output, and storage devices; and physical media to link these devices together. Chapter 4 describes computer hardware in greater detail.

Computer software consists of the detailed preprogrammed instructions that control and coordinate the computer hardware components in an information system. Chapter 5 explains the importance of computer software in information systems.

Storage technology includes both the physical media for storing data, such as magnetic disk or tape, and the software governing the organization of data on these physical media. More detail on physical storage media can be found in Chapter 4, whereas Chapter 6 treats data organization and access methods.

Telecommunications technology, consisting of both physical devices and software, links the various pieces of hardware and transfers data from one physical location to another. Chapter 7 covers telecommunications technology and issues.

Returning to the Stride Rite system in the Window on Technology, let us identify the management, organization, and technology elements. The organization element anchors the inventory analysis system in Stride Rite's sales function. It identifies the required procedures for taking inventory, such as counting the number of boxes in each retail store and providing reports for retail store managers and for higher-level managers in Stride Rite itself. The system must also satisfy the needs of Stride Rite managers and workers. Sales representatives need to be trained in both inventory counting procedures and in how to use the system so that they can sell more effectively. Stride Rite's management perceived it was losing sales by not having an up-to-date inventory control system to drive manufacturing. Management strategy, hence, was to achieve a closer coordination between shoe production and customer demand, thereby reducing manufacturing costs and increasing sales revenues. It needed to plan shoe production based on sales patterns and inventory turnover in its retail outlets. Retail shoe store managers needed some way of controlling their inventory to make sure that they were stocking the styles and sizes that they could sell. The technology supporting this system consists of scanning guns, handheld terminals, printers, telecommunications links, Stride Rite's central computer, and storage technology for the Universal Product Code catalog. The result is an information system solution to a business challenge.

Different Kinds of Systems

Operational-level systems: Information systems that monitor the elementary activities and transactions of the organization.

Because there are different interests, specialties, and levels in an organization, there are different kinds of systems. Figure 1.4 illustrates one way to depict the kinds of systems found in an organization. In the illustration, the organization is divided into strategic, management, knowledge, and operational levels and then is further divided into functional areas such as sales and marketing, manufacturing, finance, accounting, and human resources. Systems are built to serve these different organizational interests (Anthony, 1965).

Operational-level systems support operational managers by keeping track of the elementary activities and transactions of the organization, such as sales, receipts, cash deposits, payroll, credit decisions, and the flow of materials in a factory. The principal purpose of systems at this level is to answer routine

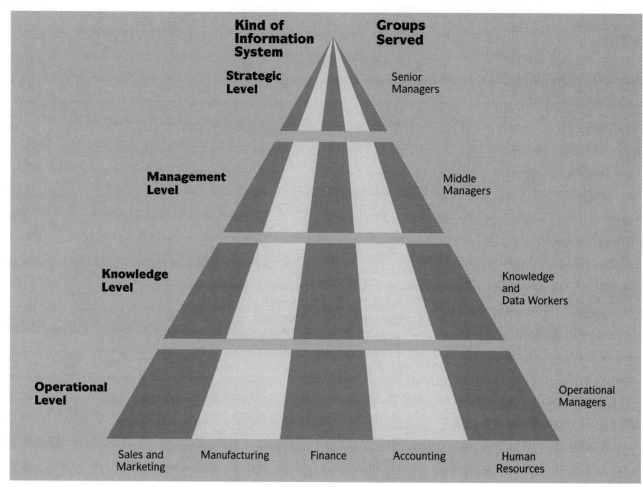

Figure 1.4
Types of information systems. Organizations and information systems can be divided into strategic, management, knowledge, and operational levels. They can be divided further into five functional areas: sales and marketing, manufacturing, finance, accounting, and human resources. Information systems serve each of these levels and functions. Strategic-level systems help senior managers with long-term planning. Management-level systems help middle managers monitor and control. Knowledge-level systems help knowledge and data workers design products, distribute information, and cope with paperwork. Operational-level systems help operational managers keep track of the firm's day-to-day activities.

questions and to track the flow of transactions through the organization. How many parts are in inventory? What happened to Mr. Williams's payment? What is the size of the payroll this month? To answer these kinds of questions, information generally must be easily available, current, and accurate. Examples of operational-level systems include a system to record bank deposits from automatic teller machines or one that tracks the number of hours worked each day by employees on a factory floor.

Knowledge-level systems:
Information systems that support knowledge and data workers in an organization.

Knowledge-level systems support knowledge and data workers in an organization. The Window on Organizations illustrates how knowledge-level systems can improve the productivity of engineers and designers. The purpose of knowledge-level systems is to help the business firm integrate new knowledge into the business and to help the organization control the flow of paperwork. Knowledge-level systems, especially in the form of workstations and office systems, are the fastest-growing applications in business today.

Management-level systems:
Information systems that support the monitoring, controlling, decision-making, and administrative activities of middle managers.

Management-level systems are designed to serve the monitoring, controlling, decision-making, and administrative activities of middle managers. The principal question addressed by such systems is: Are things working well? These systems compare the current day's output with that of a month or a year ago.

ORGANIZATIONS

Computers Speed Up Product Design

Manufacturers have long tried to use teams of design engineers to speed up the development of new products. Thanks to computer-aided design (CAD) systems, it is now possible to eliminate much of the manual drafting and building of physical prototypes that slowed down the design process.

For instance, Odense Steel Ship-yards, part of Denmark's huge Maersk shipping group, has developed a CAD system that can establish a three-dimensional topographic model of an entire ship with all components. Bath Iron Works Inc. in Bath, Maine, uses CAD workstations with three-dimensional solid modeling capabilities to help build naval destroyers, considered among the most complex pieces of equipment that can be manufactured. Up to 2000 design engineers collectively decide the locations for massive quantities of cables, plumbing equipment, and other structures inside the cramped confines of a destroyer. An object placed by one engineer that might interfere with one placed by another can be detected and corrected before the ship is built. Before, when designers relied solely on manual drafting, engineers could not detect such problems until the ship was under construction.

Engineers at the Greenville, South Carolina North American research center for Groupe Michelin S. A.— a French-based firm that is the largest tire manufacturer in the world—created and tested hundreds of tires before building any actual prototypes and doing any road testing. The engineers discovered that tires will last longer if the tire/ground contact stresses are evenly distributed throughout the contact area. This often produces a rectangular contact area, compared to a more oval contact area frequently obtained with older tire designs. The new computer techniques allow computation of contact stresses and contact area prior to prototype fabrication. Before engineers used computerized systems to design

and test tires, they would build prototypes, hire drivers to drive them for two months or more, and then change the design as needed. Developing a tire could take several years.

The prototyped designs from CAD systems can automatically feed the design specifications to many firms' computerized manufacturing systems, even if these systems are in different locations. For instance, the Ford Motor Company can transmit three-dimensional computerized design drawings from a design studio in Dunton, England, to Dearborn, Michigan, for review and revision on a computer screen. In a matter of hours, the revised 3-D design data can be transmitted through a network to a computerized milling machine in Turin, Italy. By designing with computers in a global network, Ford hopes to eventually cut the development time for a new car to as little as 24 months.

Sources: Julie Edelson Halpert, "One Car, Worldwide, with Strings Pulled from Michigan," *The New York Times*, August 29, 1993; *The New York Times*, "Computer Tests Pump More Miles Into Tires," April 1, 1992; and Paul Tate, "Maersk Spots LAN-Ho," *InformationWEEK*, January 27, 1992.

To Think About: What problems can such systems solve?

Management-level systems typically provide periodic reports rather than instant information on operations. There is less need for instant information, but periodic reports are still required. An example is a relocation control system that reports on the total moving, house-hunting, and home financing costs for employees in all company divisions, noting wherever actual costs exceed budgets.

Some management-level systems support nonroutine decision making (Keen and Morton, 1978). They tend to focus on less structured decisions for which information requirements are not always clear. These systems often answer "what if" questions: What would be the impact on production schedules if we were to double sales in the month of December? What would happen to our return on investment if a factory schedule were delayed for six months? Answers to these questions frequently require new data from outside the organization, as well as data from inside that cannot be drawn from existing operational-level systems.

Strategic-level systems:
Information systems that
support the long-range
planning activities of senior
management.

Strategic-level systems help senior management tackle and address strategic issues and long-term trends, both in the firm and in the external environment. Their principal concern is matching changes in the external environment with existing organizational capability. What will employment levels be in five years? What are the long-term industry cost trends, and where does our firm fit in? What products should we be making in five years?

The next chapter describes the types of information systems found at each organizational level. It also shows typical applications of each type of system.

Information systems may also be differentiated by functional specialty. Major organizational functions, such as sales and marketing, manufacturing, accounting, finance, and human resources, are each served by their own information systems. In large organizations, subfunctions of each of these major functions also have their own information systems. For example, the manufacturing function might have systems for inventory management, process control, plant maintenance, computer-aided engineering, and material requirements planning.

A typical organization has operational-, management-, knowledge-, and strategic-level systems for each functional area. For example, the sales function generally has a sales system on the operational level to record daily sales figures and to process orders. A knowledge-level system designs promotional displays for the firm's products. A management-level system tracks monthly sales figures by sales territory and reports on territories where sales exceed or fall below anticipated levels. A system to forecast sales trends over a five-year period serves the strategic level.

Finally, different organizations have different information systems for the same functional areas. Because no two organizations have exactly the same objectives, structures, or interests, information systems must be custom-made to fit the unique characteristics of each. There is no such thing as a universal information system that can fit all organizations, even in such standard areas as payroll or accounts receivable. Every organization does the job somewhat differently.

1.2 The Changing Management Process

Information systems cannot be ignored by managers because they play such a critical role in contemporary organizations. The first information systems of the 1950s were operational systems that automated such clerical processes as check processing. These were followed by management-level systems in the 1970s and strategic-level systems in the 1980s. Because early systems addressed largely technical operational issues, managers could afford to delegate authority and concern to lower-level technical workers. But because today's systems directly affect how managers decide, how senior managers plan, and in many cases what products and services are produced (and how), responsibility for information systems cannot be delegated to technical decision makers. Information systems today play a strategic role in the life of the firm.

The New Role of Information Systems in Organizations

Figure 1.5 illustrates the new relationship between organizations and information systems. There is a growing interdependence between business strategy, rules, and procedures, on the one hand, and information systems software, hardware, data, and telecommunications on the other. A change in any of these components often requires changes in other components. This relationship becomes critical when management plans for the future. What a business would like to do in five years is often dependent on what its systems will be able to do.

A second change in the relationship of information systems and organizations results from the growing complexity and scope of system projects and applica-

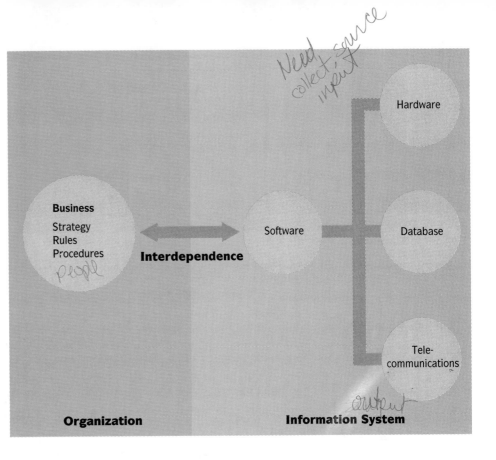

Figure 1.5
The interdependence between organizations and information systems. In contemporary systems there is a growing interdependence between organizational business strategy, rules, and procedures and the organization's information systems. Changes in strategy, rules, and procedures increasingly require changes in hardware, software, databases, and telecommunications. Existing systems can act as a constraint on organizations. Often, what the organization would like to do depends on what its systems will permit it to do.

tions. Building systems today involves a much larger part of the organization than it did in the past (see Figure 1.6). Whereas early systems produced largely technical changes that affected few people, contemporary systems bring about managerial changes (who has what information about whom, when, and how often) and institutional "core" changes (what products and services are produced, under what conditions, and by whom).

In the 1950s, a computerized payroll system involved employees in the treasurer's office, a few part-time programmers, a single program, a single machine, and a few clerks. The change from a manual to a computer system was largely technical. The computer system simply automated an existing procedure. In contrast, today's integrated human resource system (which includes payroll processing) may involve all major corporate divisions, the human resources department, dozens of full-time programmers, a flock of external consultants, multiple machines (or remote computers linked by telecommunications networks), and perhaps hundreds of end users in the organization who use payroll data to make calculations about benefits and pensions and to answer a host of other questions.

Figure 1.6
The widening scope of information systems. Over time, information systems have come to play a larger role in the life of organizations. Early systems brought about largely technical changes that were relatively easy to accomplish. Later systems affected managerial control and behavior; ultimately systems influenced "core" institutional activities concerning products, markets, suppliers, and customers.

The desktop manual adding machine was an early entry to the information system arena providing a simple number keypad to perform basic calculations.

The UNIVAC II computer represented a first step in the changing management process by automating clerical processes such as data entry and led the way for contemporary information systems.

The desktop microcomputer is the foundation of a contemporary information system.

The data, instead of being located in and controlled by the treasurer's office, are now available to hundreds of employees via desktop computers, each of which is as powerful as the large computers of the 1970s. This contemporary system embodies both managerial and institutional changes.

The Changing Nature of Information Technology

One reason why systems play a larger role in organizations, and why they affect more people, is the growing power and declining cost of information technology—the computers and peripheral devices that make up the core of information systems. Although the details are covered in later chapters, here it is sufficient to note that it is now possible to put the power of a large mainframe computer—which took up nearly an entire floor of a company in the 1970s—on every desktop in an organization of the 1990s. This new hardware capability makes powerful, easy-to-use software available to complete novices. In a few hours, relatively unskilled employees can be taught word processing, project scheduling, spreadsheet preparation, and telecommunications applications on a microcomputer. The skills needed for these activities once belonged exclusively to employees who had been through extensive specialized training. Now it is conceivable that everyone in an organization may be using a computer simultaneously in some way during the work day.

In addition, it is now possible for end users to design their own applications and simple systems without the help of professional programmers. A good manager cannot afford to ignore the fact that many of his or her employees are using information technology much of the time. Is this use productive? Could it be made more productive? Where are the major bottlenecks? How can we measure the benefits of investing in the technology? When should professional help be sought, and when can end users design their own solutions?

The Changing Character of Applications

Both the changing role of systems and the new technology have brought about new kinds of systems and applications. Whereas in the past massive systems were built to provide generic information on sales, inventory, production, finance, and marketing, it is now feasible and desirable to create custom-made, specialized applications that serve just one or a few people or groups in the organization. Whether they are microcomputer-based spreadsheet applications, collaborative group computing applications, or support systems for middle man-

MANAGEMENT

Send an Accountant to Cure Ailing Systems

When its information systems couldn't keep up with corporate growth plans, medical products maker McGaw Inc. chose an accountant to reshape its information systems department.

Previously, McGaw had been owned by a succession of parent corporations—American Hospital Supply, Colgate-Palmolive, and then the Kendall Company. It became an independent company in 1990. McGaw's managers never gave information systems much attention, and the owners didn't understand what systems could contribute to the business's bottom line. McGaw had two choices in its search for a new head of information systems. One choice was to find an experienced information systems executive who could appreciate business and finance. The alternative was to find an experienced business and finance executive who appreciated information systems. McGaw chose the latter course, and hired Rich Hirschberg, the former controller of Metwest,Inc., to head its information systems department.

Before hiring Hirschberg, McGaw did not take advantage of the potential in information technology. Its information systems were out-dated and they slowed down operations. Systems weren't properly designed to provide the information required by the business. For instance, sales and marketing staff had trouble obtaining information on specific accounts or on the market in general. Information systems were organized along departmental lines—manufacturing, sales, and so forth; they did not address the needs of the organization as a whole.

Hirschberg brought a "business view" to information systems, working toward making information systems a competitive tool. He reorganized his information systems staff to create one generic group of information systems professionals and created the firm's first cohesive information systems plan in years.

McGaw is not alone in choosing someone with business expertise to manage information systems. A significant number of top information systems executives actually started their careers in other business departments. Most have a broad base of experience in other areas. For instance, Al Hyland, director of worldwide systems for the Polaroid Corporation in Waltham, Massachusetts, started in research. Linda George, direc-tor of corporate information systems at Gencorp, Inc., in Akron, Ohio, originally studied to be a mathematics teacher.

Many believe it is ideal when an information systems specialist can take a tour of duty into business operations to see how the technology is applied—or when a business specialist has experience with information systems. According to a report prepared by the New York-based Open Users Recommended Solutions group and the Gartner Group Inc., a Stamford, Connecticut, consulting firm, the success of information systems in the firm will hinge on the ability to align information systems services with business needs and to shift from a product to a service orientation.

Sources: John P. McPartlin, "Generation Exasperated," *InformationWEEK*, October 25, 1993; Jim Nash, "Just What the Doctor Ordered," *Computerworld*, June 1, 1992; and Katie Crane, "Take Chances and Diversify on Your Journey to Upper Ranks," *Computerworld*, November 4, 1991.

To Think About: Many believe the ideal manager has both information systems and business experience. Do you agree? Why or why not?

agement, the new kinds of applications require direct, close interaction between technical support personnel and managers who will use the system, plus senior management support. Managers need some computer understanding to maximize the benefit from such applications.

One class of new applications—called expert systems, described in Chapter 12—requires technical experts known as *knowledge engineers* to capture the knowledge of skilled workers and managers. These kinds of systems illustrate the close cooperation and understanding required of both managers and information systems specialists.

The Need to Plan the Information Architecture of an Organization

It is not enough for managers to be computer literate. Systems today require that a manager have an understanding of major islands or constellations of technologies: data processing systems, telecommunications, and office technologies (see the articles by McKenney and McFarlan, 1982; McFarlan et al., 1983a, 1983b). As the scope of information systems widens, these previously separate islands of technology must be closely coordinated. Managers today must know how to track, plan, and manage the many islands of technology in a way best suited to their organization. This systems knowledge is important.

In addition, managers must know how to recognize organizational problems and find a systems solution. For this, knowledge of the organization is required. As corporations realize the need for conscious planning of the information architecture in a firm, they are placing MBAs and other generalists in charge of the information systems function. This phenomenon is illustrated by the Window on Management.

Together, systems knowledge and organizational understanding shape the information architecture of the organization. **Information architecture** is the particular form that information technology takes in an organization to achieve selected goals or functions. Information architecture includes the extent to which data and processing power are centralized or distributed. Managers increasingly play a critical role in determining the information architecture of their organizations. There is no one else to do the job.

Figure 1.7 illustrates the major elements of information architecture that a student will have to understand if he or she is to become an effective manager. Although the computer systems base is typically operated by technical personnel, general management must decide how to allocate the resources it has assigned to hardware, software, and telecommunications. Increasingly, the top managers of systems and communications departments are also general managers. Resting upon the computer systems base are the major business application systems, or the major islands of applications. Because managers and employees

Information architecture: The particular form that information technology takes in a specific organization to achieve selected goals or functions.

Figure 1.7
The information architecture of the firm. Today's managers must know how to arrange and coordinate the various computer technologies and business system applications to meet the information needs of each level of their organization, as well as the needs of the organization as a whole.

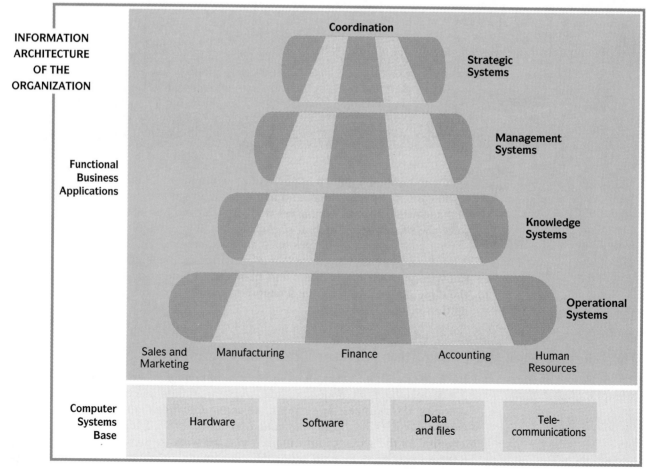

directly interact with these systems, it is critical for the success of the organization that these systems meet business functional requirements now and in the future. In many service industries—such as airlines, hotels, banks, insurance firms, and brokerages—the major business applications provide unique competitive advantages. Failure to develop these systems can lead to business failure.

The following are some typical questions regarding information architecture that today's managers should be able to answer: Should the corporate sales data and function be distributed to each corporate remote site, or should it be centralized at headquarters? Should the organization purchase stand-alone microcomputers or build a more powerful centralized mainframe environment within an integrated telecommunications network? Should the organization build its own data communications utility to link remote sites or rely on external providers like the telephone company? Although there is no one right answer to these questions (see Allen and Boynton, 1991), a manager today should at least have the knowledge to deal with them.

1.3 Contemporary Approaches to Information Systems

The study of information systems is a multidisciplinary field; no single theory or perspective dominates. Figure 1.8 illustrates the major disciplines that contribute perspectives, issues, and insights in the study of information systems. In general, the field can be divided into technical and behavioral approaches. Information systems are sociotechnical systems. Though they are composed of machines, devices, and "hard" physical technology, they require substantial social, organizational, and intellectual investments to make them work properly.

Technical Approach

Technical approaches to information systems dominated the field in its early years. The disciplines that contribute to the technical approach are computer science, management science, and operations research. Computer science is concerned with establishing theories of computability, methods of computation, and methods of efficient data storage and access. Management science emphasizes the development of models for decision making and management practices. Operations research focuses on mathematical techniques for optimizing selected parameters of organizations such as transportation, costs, inventory control, and transaction costs.

The technical approach to information systems emphasizes mathematically based, normative models to study information systems, as well as the physical technology and formal capabilities of these systems.

Figure 1.8
Contemporary approaches to information systems. The study of information systems deals with issues and insights contributed from technical and behavioral disciplines.

Examples of literature in these fields can be found in *Communications of the Association of Computing Machinery (CACM), Management Science,* and *Operations Research.* Articles from these three journals are excerpted and referenced throughout the text, and interested students should examine these sources to learn more about this approach to modern information systems.

Behavioral Approach

A growing part of the information systems field is concerned with behavioral problems and issues. Many behavioral problems, such as system utilization, implementation, and creative design, cannot be expressed with the normative models used in the technical approach. Other behavioral disciplines also play a role. Sociologists focus on the impact of information systems on groups, organizations, and society. Political science investigates the political impacts and uses of information systems. Psychology is concerned with individual responses to information systems and cognitive models of human reasoning. The leading journals in these areas are the *American Sociological Review, Administrative Science Quarterly, American Political Science Review,* and the *Journal of Psychology.*

The behavioral approach does not ignore technology. Indeed, information systems technology is often the stimulus for a behavioral problem or issue. But the focus of this approach is generally not on technical solutions; it concentrates rather on changes in attitudes, management and organizational policy, and behavior (Kling and Dutton, 1982).

Approach of This Text: Sociotechnical Systems

The study of management information systems (MIS) arose in the 1960s and focused exclusively on computer-based information systems aimed at managers (Davis and Olsen, 1985). The MIS discipline, and the first academic departments, emerged in business schools in the United States. MIS combines the theoretical work of computer science, management science, and operations research with a practical orientation toward building systems and applications. It also pays attention to behavioral issues. The leading journals in this field are *MIS Quarterly* and the *Journal of Management Information Systems.* Business journals such as the *Harvard Business Review* and the *Sloan Management Review* also contain articles relevant to MIS.

Our experience as academics and practitioners leads us to believe that no single perspective effectively captures the reality of information systems. Problems with systems—and their solutions—are rarely all technical or all behavioral. Our best advice to students is to understand the perspectives of all disciplines. Indeed, the challenge and excitement of the information systems field is that it requires an appreciation and tolerance of many different approaches.

A sociotechnical systems perspective helps to avoid a purely technological approach to information systems. For instance, the fact that information technology is rapidly declining in cost and growing in power does not necessarily or easily translate into productivity enhancement or bottom-line profits.

In this book, we stress the need to optimize the performance of the system as a whole. Both the technical and behavioral components need attention. This means that technology must be changed and designed in such a way as to fit organizational and individual needs. At times, the technology may have to be "deoptimized" to accomplish this fit. Organizations and individuals must also be changed through training, learning, and planned organizational change in order to allow the technology to operate and prosper (see, for example, Liker et al., 1987). Figure 1.9 illustrates this process of mutual adjustment in a sociotechnical system.

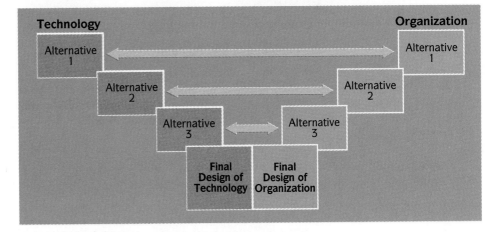

Figure 1.9
A sociotechnical perspective on information systems. In a sociotechnical perspective, the performance of a system is optimized when both the technology and the organization mutually adjust to one another until a satisfactory fit is obtained. Source: Tornatsky et al., 1983.

1.4 The Challenge of Information Systems: Key Management Issues

A senior executive was in charge of a $275 million software redevelopment project in the Social Security Administration; the project was three years behind schedule. The executive lamented that "senior management just did not understand the difficulty of rewriting over 10 million lines of programming code" (Laudon, 1989).

Increasingly, information systems are bringing about changes in business goals, relationships with customers and suppliers, and internal operations. Creating a new system now means much more than installing a new machine in the basement. Today, this process typically places thousands of terminals or microcomputers on the desks of employees who have little experience with them, connecting the devices to powerful communications networks, rearranging social relations in the office and work locations, changing reporting patterns and asking employees to achieve higher levels of productivity. Briefly, new systems today often require the development of a new information architecture.

One message of this text is that despite, or perhaps because of, the rapid development of computer technology, there is nothing easy or mechanical about building workable information systems. Building, operating, and maintaining information systems are challenging activities for a number of reasons. We believe there are five key challenges that managers should heed:

1. The Strategic Business Challenge: How can businesses use information technology to design organizations that are competitive and effective?

Investment in information technology amounts to over half of the annual capital expenditures of most large service-sector firms. Yet despite investing more in computers than any other country, the United States still faces a serious productivity challenge. America's productivity growth rate in the 1980s of just under 2 percent per year was far below that of other industrial countries. The product life cycle for Ford's Taurus is ten years, but Toyota redesigns its cars every five years. On average, the time to bring a new manufactured product to market in the United States is twice that of Japanese industry. The productivity lag has been especially pronounced in the service sector. Until recently, white-collar productivity increased at an annual rate of only .28 percent (Roach, 1991).

Technical change moves much faster than humans and organizations are changing. The power of computer hardware and software has grown much more

must redesign org to be competitive
Must eliminate unnecessary work

rapidly than the ability of organizations to apply and use this technology. To stay competitive, many organizations actually need to be redesigned. They will need to use information technology to simplify communication and coordination, eliminate unnecessary work, and eliminate the inefficiencies of outmoded organizational structures. If organizations merely automate what they are doing today, they are largely missing the potential of information technology. Organizations need to rethink and redesign the way they design, produce, deliver, and maintain goods and services.

2. The Globalization Challenge: How can firms understand the business and system requirements of a global economic environment?

The rapid growth in international trade and the emergence of a global economy call for information systems that can support both producing and selling goods in many different countries. In the past, each regional office of a multinational corporation focused on solving its own unique information problems. Given language, cultural, and political differences among countries, this focus frequently resulted in chaos and the failure of central management controls. To develop integrated multinational information systems, businesses must cope with restrictive transborder dataflow legislation in more than 25 countries, and must create cross-cultural accounting and reporting structures (Roche, 1992; Buss, 1982; Carlyle, 1988).

3. The Information Architecture Challenge: How can organizations develop an information architecture that supports their business goals?

While information technology can suggest some new ways of doing business, firms still need to have a clear idea of their business goals and how these can best be supported by information systems. Many organizations cannot meet their goals because they are crippled by fragmented and incompatible computer hardware, software, telecommunications networks, and information systems. Integrating these "islands of information" into a coherent architecture is now a priority.

4. The Information Systems Investment Challenge: How can organizations determine the business value of information systems?

A major problem raised by the development of powerful, inexpensive computers involves not technology but rather management and organizations. It's one thing to use information technology to design, produce, deliver, and maintain new products. It's another thing to make money doing it. How can organizations obtain a sizable payoff from their investment in information systems?

Engineering massive organizational and system changes in the hope of positioning a firm strategically is complicated and expensive. Is this an investment that pays off? How can you tell? Senior management can be expected to ask these questions: Are we receiving the kind of return on investment from our systems that we should be? Do our competitors get more? While understanding the costs and benefits of building a single system are difficult enough, it is daunting to consider whether the entire systems effort is "worth it." Imagine, then, how a senior executive must think when presented with a major transformation in information architecture, a bold venture in organizational change costing tens of millions of dollars and taking many years.

5. The Responsibility and Control Challenge: How can organizations design systems that people can control and understand? How can organizations ensure that their information systems are used in an ethically and socially responsible manner?

Information systems play such a critical role in business, government, and daily life that organizations must take special steps to ensure that they are accurate, reliable, and secure. Automated or semiautomated systems that malfunction or are poorly operated can have extremely harmful consequences. A firm invites disaster if it uses systems that don't work as intended, that don't deliver information in a form that people can interpret correctly and use, or that have control rooms where controls don't work or where instruments give false signals. The potential for massive fraud, error, abuse, and destruction is enormous.

Information systems must be designed so that they function as intended and so that humans can control the process. When building and using information systems, health, safety, job security, and social well-being should be considered as carefully as meeting an organization's business goals. Managers will need to ask: Can we apply high quality assurance standards to our information systems as well as to our products and services? Can we build information systems that respect people's rights of privacy while still pursuing our organization's goals? Should information systems monitor employees? What do we do when an information system designed to increase efficiency and productivity eliminates people's jobs?

This text is designed to provide future managers with the knowledge and understanding required to deal with these challenges. To further this objective, each chapter concludes with a Management Challenges box that outlines the key issues managers should be aware of.

Summary

Define an information system.

The purpose of a CBIS is to collect, store, and disseminate information from an organization's environment and internal operations for the purpose of supporting organizational functions and decision making, communication, coordination, control, analysis, and visualization. Information systems transform raw data into useful information through three basic activities: input, processing, and output.

Explain the difference between computer literacy and information systems literacy.

Information systems literacy requires an understanding of the organizational and management dimensions of information systems as well as the technical dimensions addressed by computer literacy.

Describe the information needs of different organizational levels.

To be useful, a CBIS must faithfully reflect the organization's requirements for information. It must fit the needs of the specific organizational level and the business function that it is intended to support.

Operational-level systems keep track of the firm's day-to-day activities. Knowledge-level systems support the integration of new knowledge throughout the firm; they also exist to manage paperwork. Management-level systems support the planning, controlling, and monitoring activities of middle management. Strategic-level systems support long-term planning. Each functional specialty, such as sales, manufacturing, accounting, finance, and human resources, typically has all four types of systems.

Explain why information systems are so important today.

In general, there is a much greater need to plan for the overall information architecture of the organization. The kinds of systems built today are more important for the overall performance of the organization, especially in today's highly globalized and information-based economy; technologies have become more powerful and more difficult to implement; and new applications require intense interaction between professional technical experts and general management.

Identify the major conceptual approaches to information systems.

There are both technical and behavioral approaches to studying information systems. Both perspectives can be combined into a sociotechnical approach to systems.

Identify the major management challenges to building and using information systems in organizations.

There are five key management challenges in building and using information systems: 1) designing systems that are competitive and efficient; 2) understanding the system requirements of a global business environment; 3) creating an information architecture that supports the organization's goals; 4) determining the business value of systems; and 5) designing systems that people can control, understand, and use in a socially and ethically responsible manner.

Key Terms

Information system	Senior managers
Input	Middle managers
Processing	Operational managers
Output	Computer hardware
Feedback	Computer software
Computer-based information systems (CBIS)	Storage technology
	Telecommunications technology
Standard operating procedures (SOPs)	Operational-level systems
Rationalization of procedures	Knowledge-level systems
Knowledge workers	Management-level systems
Data workers	Strategic-level systems
Production or service workers	Information architecture

Review Questions

1. Distinguish between a computer, a computer program, and an information system.

2. What activities convert raw data to usable information in information systems? What is their relationship to feedback?

3. What is the relationship between an information system, the organization, and the organizational environment?

4. What is information systems literacy?

5. What are the organization, management, and technology dimensions of information systems?

6. Identify and describe the four levels of the organizational hierarchy. What types of information systems serve each level?

7. Why should managers study information systems?

8. What is the relationship between an organization and its information systems? How is this relationship changing over time?

9. What do we mean by the information architecture of the organization?

10. Distinguish between a behavioral and a technical approach to information systems in terms of the questions asked and the answers provided.

11. What major disciplines contribute to an understanding of information systems?

12. What are the key management challenges involved in building, operating, and maintaining information systems today?

Discussion Questions

1. Some people argue that the creation of CBIS is fundamentally a social process. Hence, a person who is an expert in information technology may not be suited to design a CBIS. Discuss and comment.

2. Most of the problems we have with information systems will disappear when computers become faster and cheaper. Discuss and comment.

Group Project

In a group with three or four classmates, find a description in a computer or business magazine of an information system used by an organization. Describe the system in terms of its inputs, processes, and outputs and in terms of its management, organization, and technology features. Present your analysis to the class.

CASE STUDY

Writing the Book in the Year 2000

Publishing companies have avoided information technology in the same way that they have rejected bad manuscripts. Outside writers or artists created manuscripts. These were sent to outside designers, who designed the jackets and art work. Then the job was sent to outside typesetting shops, who set the art and manuscript into type. Finally the work went to a printer. The process took six to ten months for a book, sometimes a full two months for a brochure. Despite the time-consuming process, the book publishers have been slow to change.

In 1986, for instance, Simon & Schuster, the $1.5 billion publishing arm of Paramount Communications, didn't have a personal computer and was using decades-old filing and processing systems. Then in 1990 Simon & Schuster launched a six-year plan to incorporate information technology into all facets of the company.

Simon & Schuster hopes to become a "print/technology" company by the year 2000, converting a paper-bound publishing and distribution process into an electronic digital one. Everything from writing manuscripts to tracking royalties to warehousing and order management is being restyled with computer and telecommunications technology. Simon & Schuster has three goals for its information systems: cutting costs, speeding the delivery of products, and boosting efficiency. The firm hopes to boost its profit margins to 15 percent, well above the industry average, which is typically in the single digits. Simon & Schuster's management believes that publishing is process-oriented, and the winning firm is the one that processes the best, the fastest, and the most economically.

Simon & Schuster has installed more than 3000 personal computers and workstations, providing 65 percent of its employees—from editors to production people—with desktop computers. Soon more than 90 percent will have computers on their desktops. A typical desktop system is the forecasting system that creates models for book sales and inventory management. One of the great challenges of publishing is knowing how many books to print. The system will forecast demand, control the number of books the firm warehouses, and measure book levels in retail stores.

In book publishing, cutting costs in inventory and distribution isn't enough unless costs are also minimized while the books are actually being produced. During the pre-press part of the process, publishers have to determine advances on royalties to be paid to authors; they have to make budgets for editing and research; and they need to decide how many books to print. Often they have only a 20-page book proposal as a guideline. Educational book projects are especially tricky, since big curriculum projects such as a new reading program for kindergarten through sixth grade require up-front expenditures of tens of millions of dollars.

It may never be possible always to predict correct advances or sales, but Simon & Schuster feels it can reduce production costs using Electronic Manuscript Management (EMM). The traditional method of preparing a book for publication is tediously manual, entailing hard copies of marked-up manuscripts, page proofs, and illustrations passed back and forth between authors and editors. Simon & Schuster expects EMM to reduce the production process from two years to a matter of weeks and months. Authors' manuscripts will be prepared on computer diskettes and submitted directly to typesetters. Book pages can be composed entirely electronically. Art and design images will be prepared by computer or will be digitized and then integrated into the manuscript using computerized "composition page makers."

The EMM system enhances the creative process. Before, when Simon & Schuster pasted up hard copy, even simple changes cost hundreds of dollars. Now changes can be made using personal computers in-house, rather than being sent out to freelance designers.

Simon & Schuster has also installed a new royalty tracking system and a new order management system that speeds the processing of orders placed by retail bookstores and schools. A new automated warehousing system will improve inventory management.

Savings are already apparent—approximately $500 per book on typesetting alone. This amounts to companywide savings of $275,000 per year. By installing its own private network to transmit voice and data domestically and to international facilities in Europe and Australia, Simon & Schuster cut telecommunications costs by more than 60 percent in two years. That is important because the firm determined that its investment in information systems had to compete with other investments. If the technology investments don't return a payback, the expenditures won't be made.

Simon & Schuster is also using its new information technologies to diversify its products. In March 1990 the firm acquired Computer Curriculum Corporation, which develops software for integrated learning systems and custom "on-demand" books. A Technology Group oversees Computer Curriculum and three other divisions responsible for computerized business training, educational media projects, and consumer education services. Computer-based remedial, technical, and management training programs are being tested with major corporations such as General Motors.

The firm has some concerns that its 10,000 employees won't assimilate the new technology at the pace it is being introduced. How quickly, for instance, can an employee skilled in an age-old manual hard-copy tradition take advantage of the capabilities of a state-of-the-art design workstation?

Source: Bob Violino, "Writing the Book on Technology," *InformationWEEK*, March 16, 1992.

Case Study Questions

1. How large a role do information systems play at Simon & Schuster?

2. What management, organization, and technology issues do you think Simon & Schuster addressed when it put in its new information systems?

3. Simon & Schuster's information systems are used by people in many different functions who need different kinds of information. What kinds of organizational decisions and functions do they support? You may find it helpful to organize your answers in tabular form.
   Organizational Level   Function   Decision

4. Why do you think that book publishers have not more rapidly embraced information systems technology?

5. How much advantage do Simon & Schuster's information systems provide over more traditional publishers? What problems do they solve?

6. What are the costs and effects of not embracing this technology? Are there benefits to maintaining traditional book production methods?

7. How important are information systems in solving the problems of book publishing? What are some problems that technology cannot address?

References
Alavi, Maryam, and Patricia Carlson. "A Review of MIS Research and Disciplinary Development." *Journal of Management Information Systems* 8, no. 4 (Spring 1992).

Allen, Brandt R., and Andrew C. Boynton. "Information Architecture: In Search of Efficient Flexibility." *MIS Quarterly* 15, no. 4 (December 1991).

Anthony, R. N. *Planning and Control Systems: A Framework for Analysis.* Cambridge, MA: Harvard University Press, 1965.

Buss, Martin D. J., "Managing International Information Systems." *Harvard Business Review* (September 1982).

Carlyle, Ralph Emmett, "Managing IS at Multinationals." *Datamation* (March 1, 1988).

Cash, James I., F. Warren McFarlan, James L. McKenney, and Lynda M. Applegate. *Corporate Information Systems Management,* 3rd ed. Homewood, IL: Irwin, 1992.

Clark, Thomas D. Jr., "Corporate Systems Management: An Overview and Research Perspective." *Communications of the ACM* 35, no. 2 (February 1992).

Davis, Gordon B., and Margrethe H. Olson. *Management Information Systems: Conceptual Foundations, Structure, and Development,* 2nd ed. New York: McGraw-Hill, 1985.

Gorry, G. A., and M. S. Morton. "Framework for Management Information Systems." *Sloan Management Review* 13, no. 1 (Fall 1971).

Keen, Peter G. W. *Shaping the Future: Business Design Through Information Technology.* Cambridge, MA: Harvard Business School Press, 1991.

Keen, P. G. W., and M. S. Morton. *Decision Support Systems: An Organizational Perspective.* Reading, MA: Addison-Wesley, 1978.

Kling, Rob, and William H. Dutton. "The Computer Package: Dynamic Complexity," in *Computers and Politics,* edited by James Danziger, William Dutton, Rob Kling, and Kenneth Kraemer. New York: Columbia University Press, 1982.

Laudon, Kenneth C. "A General Model for Understanding the Relationship Between Information Technology and Organizations." Working paper, Center for Research on Information Systems, New York University, 1989.

Liker, Jeffrey K, David B. Roitman, and Ethel Roskies. "Changing Everything All at Once: Work Life and Technological Change." *Sloan Management Review* (Summer 1987).

McFarlan, F. Warren, James L. McKenney, and Philip Pyburn. "The Information Archipelago—Plotting a Course." *Harvard Business Review* (January–February 1983a).

McFarlan, F. Warren, James L. McKenney, and Philip Pyburn. "Governing the New World." *Harvard Business Review* (July–August 1983b).

McKenney, James L., and F. Warren McFarlan. "The Information Archipelago—Maps and Bridges." *Harvard Business Review* (September–October 1982).

Niederman, Fred, James C. Brancheau, and James C. Wetherbe. "Information Systems Management Issues for the 1990s." *MIS Quarterly* 15, no. 4 (December 1991).

Orlikowski, Wanda J., and Jack J. Baroudi. "Studying Information Technology in Organizations: Research Approaches and Assumptions." *Information Systems Research* 2, no. 1 (March 1991).

Roach, Stephen S. "Services Under Siege—The Restructuring Imperative." *Harvard Business Review* (September–October, 1991).

Roach, Stephen S. "Technology and the Services Sector: The Hidden Competitive Challenge." *Technological Forecasting and Social Change* 34 (1988).

Roche, Edward M. "Planning for Competitive Use of Information Technology in Multinational Corporations." AIB UK Region, Brighton Polytechnic, Brighton, U.K., Conference Paper, March 1992. Edward M. Roche, W. Paul Stillman School of Business, Seton Hall University.

Scott-Morton, Michael, Ed. *The Corporation in the 1990s.* New York: Oxford University Press, 1991.

Strassman, Paul. *The Information Payoff—The Transformation of Work in the Electronic Age.* New York: Free Press, 1985.

Tornatsky, Louis G., J. D. Eveland, Myles G. Boylan, W. A. Hertzner, E. C. Johnson, D. Roitman, and J. Schneider. *The Process of Technological Innovation: Reviewing the Literature.* Washington, D.C.: National Science Foundation, 1983.

CHAPTER

2

The Strategic Role of Information Systems

Information Systems Keep Gillette on the Cutting Edge

In the early 1900s, when Gillette introduced the first safety razor, it recognized right away that its products were vulnerable to competition. Anyone could obtain a piece of steel at a reasonable price. The way to stay ahead of the pack was to shape that same piece of steel into a sharper, sturdier blade at the lowest possible cost and to be the first to bring a superior product to market. The Gillette Company has pursued this strategy ever since.

Gillette has 64 percent of the U.S. wet-shaving market and is a market leader in the rest of the world as well. Gillette has 70 percent of the market share in Europe and 80 percent in Latin America. This is a cutthroat market where a price difference of a few pennies can spell the difference between success and failure.

Information systems have helped Gillette stay ahead as both a low-cost, high-quality producer and

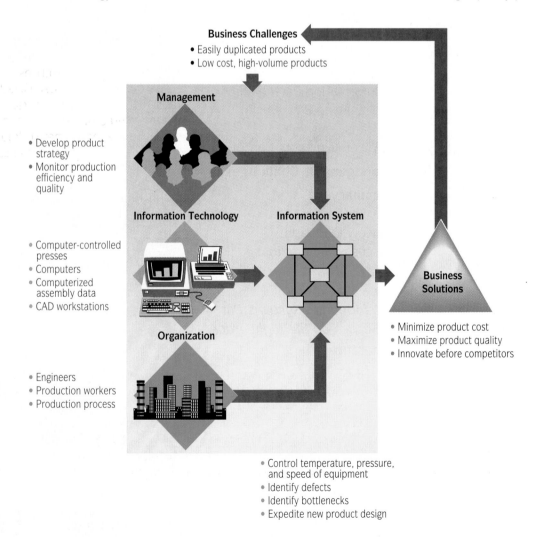

as an innovator of new shaving products. With advanced technology, Gillette can cut fractions of a cent off the cost of manufacturing a blade cartridge, yet produce a high-quality product. When you're making a billion razor blades a year, shaving a few tenths of a cent off the cost of each blade creates many millions of dollars in savings.

Virtually everything in Gillette's Boston manufacturing plant is automated. The firm's 3000 workers spend most of their time monitoring equipment, checking report printouts, or searching for bottlenecks in the production process.

With computerized process-control devices, Gillette can control temperature, pressure, and other machine settings more precisely while optimizing output. The result: Both blade cartridge and razor parts can be fashioned much faster and with higher quality than five or ten years ago. A "cycle" in the production process that used to take ten seconds is now down to seven or eight.

Gillette uses information systems to enforce scrupulous quality control standards. For instance, a high-resolution microscopic camera linked to a minicomputer examines every mounted twin blade for Gillette's Sensor razor. The minicomputer compares the images captured by the camera with the image of correctly mounted blades stored in its memory, rejecting blades that are not absolutely parallel. Since an infinitesimal change in angle will give an unsatisfactory shave, the system rejects blades that are off by a couple of microns.

Information systems help detect weak links in the production process as well. Gillette increased output of its Sensor razors by 4 percent by improving a small clip resembling a staple that anchors the cartridge assembly. Engineers found out that the gap in the clip was too narrow by analyzing computerized data from millions of cartridge assemblies.

Information systems have also helped Gillette capture market share with innovative new razors. Ten Gillette designers used three-dimensional computer-aided design software running on networked workstations to design the Sensor razor that uses independently suspended twin blades to deliver a closer shave. Sensor was an instant hit and became the top seller in the nondisposable razor market, with 43 percent of market share.

Sources: Lawrence Ingrassia, "The Cutting Edge," *The Wall Street Journal,* April 6, 1992; and "Gillette Holds Its Edge by Endlessly Searching for a Better Shave," *The Wall Street Journal,* December 10, 1992.

The Gillette Company's intensive use of information systems illustrates how critical they have become for supporting organizations' functions and goals and for enabling them to stay ahead of the competition. In this chapter we show how information systems serve different organizational levels and different business functions. We then look at the problems firms face from competition and the ways that information systems can provide competitive advantage. Gillette used information systems to pursue strategies to maximize the quality and innovation of its products while minimizing costs. Information systems can be used to pursue other competitive strategies as well.

The types of information systems discussed in this chapter are presented from a functional rather than a technical standpoint. They illustrate how systems work to serve the goals of the organization, what kinds of information they contain, who uses the results, and how they might be used to give a company a competitive advantage.

After completing this chapter you will be able to:

- Describe the role played by the six major types of information systems in organizations.
- Discuss the relationship between the various types of information systems.
- Describe the various ways that information systems can be used to create strategic advantage for firms.
- Describe how the competitive forces and value chain models can be used to identify opportunities for strategic information systems.
- Explain why strategic information systems are difficult to build and to sustain.

2.1 Describing Systems: Vocabulary and Symbols

Before exploring the contributions made by information systems in the organization, we must look at the special vocabulary and graphic symbols used to describe these systems. Systems designers and other computer professionals rely on these symbols and terminology to represent system functions and design. We use them later in the chapter to describe the various types of information systems in organizations.

Symbols Used to Describe Information Systems

To help you interpret system functions and design, this section introduces some of the more common symbols for representing information systems. Figure 2.1 shows the major graphic symbols used in this text to describe systems. Five kinds of symbols are important in most system descriptions:

- Input: keyboard input and digitizing devices
- Output: on-line display terminal, document, printer
- Processing: computers
- Storage: magnetic tape, on-line storage, database, optical disk
- Telecommunications: links such as cable, telephone line, or wireless transmission

Four of the symbols refer to different ways of storing information: on-line storage (usually a magnetic or optical disk), database (usually a magnetic disk), and magnetic tape. *On-line storage* refers to information that the computer and user can access immediately. An example might be a computerized file of your class list, which contains the names and identification numbers of all the members of your class and which you can access directly from a computer terminal. The computer, in other words, is directly connected to the computerized file. A *database* is simply (for now) a collection of files to which the user can gain access. *Magnetic tape* stores data much like audio tape and videotape store pictures and music—namely, in sequential order using magnetic impressions on a thin film.

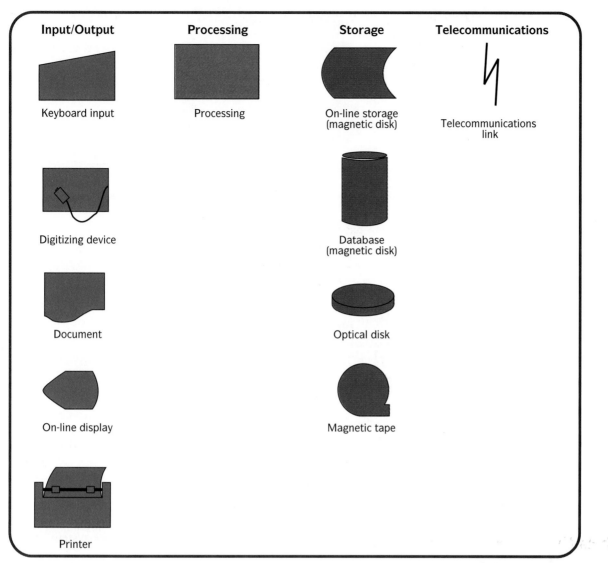

Figure 2.1
Common graphic symbols used to represent the major components of information systems.

Batch and On-Line Processing

Batch processing: A method of processing information in which transactions are accumulated and stored until a specified time when it is convenient or necessary to process them as a group.

Transaction file: In batch systems, the file in which all transactions are accumulated to await processing.

Master file: Contains all permanent information and is updated during processing by the transaction data.

On-line processing: A method of processing information in which transactions are entered directly into the computer system and processed immediately.

Most systems process information in one of two ways: through batch or through on-line processing. In **batch processing,** transactions such as orders or payroll timecards are accumulated and stored in a group or batch until the time when, because of some reporting cycle, it is efficient or necessary to process them. Transactions are accumulated in a **transaction file,** which contains all the transactions for a particular time period. Periodically this file is used to update a **master file,** which contains permanent information on entities. (An example is a weekly payroll master file that stores employee earnings and deductions data. It is updated with weekly timecard transactions.) Adding the transaction data to the existing master file creates an updated version of the master file.

In **on-line processing,** which is now very common, the user enters transactions into a device that is directly connected to the computer system. Transactions are entered directly into the system and are processed immediately. The master file is updated continuously.

Figure 2.2 compares batch and on-line processing. Batch systems often use tape as a storage medium, whereas on-line processing systems use disk storage, which permits immediate access to specific items of information. In on-line processing, there is a direct connection to the computer for input and output.

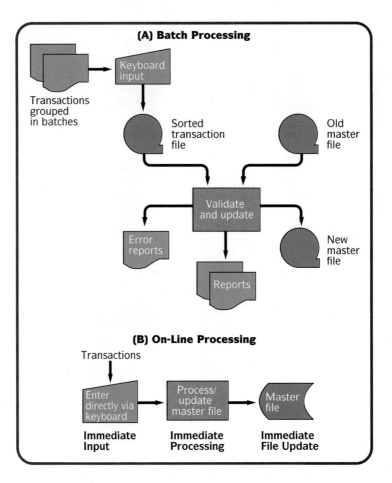

Figure 2.2
A comparison of batch and on-line processing. In batch processing, transactions are accumulated and stored in a group. Since batches are processed on a regular interval basis, such as daily, weekly, or monthly, information in the system will not always be up-to-date. A typical batch-processing job is payroll preparation. In on-line processing, transactions are input immediately and usually processed immediately. Information in the system is generally up-to-date. A typical on-line application is an airline reservation system.

The demands of the business determine the type of processing. If the user needs periodic or occasional reports or output, as in payroll or end-of-the-year reports, batch processing is most efficient. If the user needs immediate information and processing, as in an airlines reservation system, then the system should use on-line processing.

2.2 Major Types of Information Systems

No single system provides all the information an organization needs. Organizations have many information systems serving different organizational levels and functions. Thus, the typical systems found in organizations are designed to assist workers or managers at each level and in the functions of sales and marketing, manufacturing, accounting, finance, and human resources. In this section we describe the specific categories of systems serving each organizational level. The examples we give for each category will also illustrate the value that each category contributes to the organization.

Six Major Types of Systems

In Chapter 1 we explained why different types of systems are needed at different levels of the organization and by different functional specialties. Figure 2.3 shows the specific types of information systems that correspond to each organizational level. The organization has executive support systems (ESS) at the strategic level; management information systems (MIS) and decision support systems (DSS) at the management level; knowledge work systems (KWS) and office automation systems (OAS) at the knowledge level; and transaction pro-

Categories of Systems

	Sales and Marketing	Manufacturing	Finance	Accounting	Human Resources
Executive Support Systems (ESS)	Strategic-Level Systems				
	5-year sales trend forecasting	5-year operating plan	5-year budget forecasting	Profit planning	Manpower planning
Management Information Systems (MIS)	Management-Level Systems				
	Sales management	Inventory control	Annual budgeting	Capital investment analysis	Relocation analysis
Decision Support Systems (DSS)	Sales region analysis	Production scheduling	Cost analysis	Pricing/profitability analysis	Contract cost analysis
Knowledge Work Systems (KWS)	Knowledge-Level Systems				
	Engineering workstations		Graphics workstations		Managerial workstations
Office Automation Systems (OAS)	Word processing		Image storage		Electronic calendars
Transaction Processing Systems (TPS)	Operational-Level Systems				
		Machine control	Payroll	Auditing	Compensation
	Order tracking	Plant scheduling	Accounts payable	Tax reporting	Training & development
	Order processing	Material movement control	Accounts receivable	Cash management	Employee recordkeeping

Figure 2.3

The six major types of information systems needed for the four levels of an organization. Information systems are built to serve each of the four levels of an organization. Transaction processing systems (TPS) serve the operational level of an organization. Knowledge work systems (KWS) and office automation systems (OAS) serve the knowledge level of an organization. Decision support systems (DSS) and management information systems (MIS) serve the management level of the organization. Executive support systems (ESS) serve the strategic level of an organization.

cessing systems (TPS) at the operational level. Systems at each level in turn are specialized to serve each of the major functional areas.

Table 2.1 summarizes the features of the six types of information systems. It should be noted that each of the different kinds of systems may have components that are used by organizational levels and groups other than their main constituencies. A secretary may find information on an MIS, or a middle manager may need to extract data from a TPS.

TRANSACTION PROCESSING SYSTEMS

Transaction processing systems (TPS): Computerized systems that perform and record the daily routine transactions necessary to conduct the business; they serve the operational level of the organization.

Transaction processing systems (TPS) are the basic business systems that serve the operational level of the organization. A transaction processing system is a computerized system that performs and records the daily routine transactions necessary to conduct the business. Examples are sales order entry, hotel reservation systems, client information (for public agencies), payroll, employee record keeping, and shipping.

At the operational level, tasks, resources, and goals are predefined and highly structured. The decision to grant credit to a customer, for instance, is made by a lower-level supervisor according to predefined criteria. The decision, in that sense, has been "programmed." All that must be determined is whether the customer meets the criteria.

Figure 2.4 depicts an accounts receivable TPS, which is a typical transaction processing system found in most firms. An accounts receivable system keeps track of the money owed to the firm by its customers. The master file is composed of discrete pieces of information (such as a name, address, or customer

Table 2.1   CHARACTERISTICS OF INFORMATION PROCESSING SYSTEMS

Type of System	Information Inputs	Processing	Information Outputs	Users
ESS	Aggregate data; external, internal	Graphics; simulations; interactive	Projections; responses to queries	Senior managers
DSS	Low-volume data; analytic models	Interactive; simulations; analysis	Special reports; decision analyses; responses to queries	Professionals; staff managers
MIS	Summary transaction data; high-volume data; simple models	Routine reports; simple models; low-level analysis	Summary and exception reports	Middle managers
KWS	Design specifications; knowledge base	Modeling; simulations	Models; graphics	Professionals; technical staff
OAS	Documents; schedules	Document management; scheduling; communication	Documents; schedules; mail	Clerical workers
TPS	Transactions; events	Sorting; listing; merging; updating	Detailed reports; lists; summaries	Operations personnel; supervisors

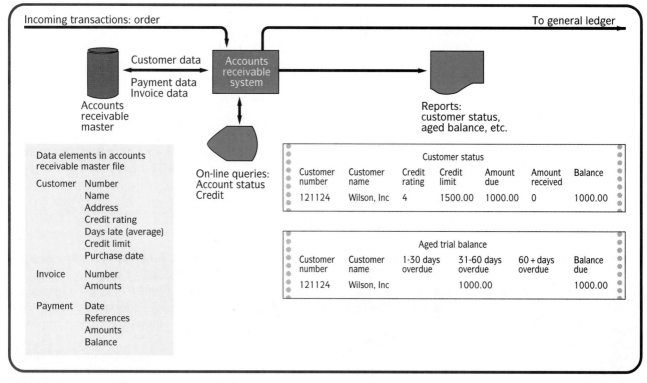

Figure 2.4
A symbolic representation for an accounts receivable TPS.

number) called *data elements*. Data are keyed into the system, updating the data elements. The elements on the master file are combined in different ways to make up reports of interest to management. These TPS can generate other report combinations of existing data elements.

The typical TPS applications are identified in Figure 2.5. The figure illustrates the five functional categories of TPS: sales/marketing, manufacturing/production, finance/accounting, human resources, and other types of TPS that are unique to a particular industry. The computerized process control manufacturing system used by The Gillette Company is an example of a manufacturing TPS.

All organizations have these five kinds of TPS (even if the systems are manual). It is difficult to imagine a modern organization without a transaction processing system. These systems are often so central to a business that in the 1960s it was estimated that organizations might only survive for a day without functioning computer systems. In the business environment of the 1990s, TPS failure for a few hours can spell the demise of a firm and perhaps other firms linked to it.

Two features of TPS are noteworthy. First, many TPS span the boundary between the organization and its environment. They connect customers to the firm's warehouse, factory, and management. If TPS do not work well, the organization fails either to receive inputs from the environment (orders) or to deliver outputs (assembled goods). Second, TPS are major producers of information for the other types of systems. Because TPS track relations with the environment, they are the only place where managers can obtain both up-to-the-minute assessments of organizational performance and long-term records of past performance. (See the discussion of MIS below.) TPS can be viewed as "organizational message processing systems" (Huber, 1982), informing managers about the status of internal operations and about the firm's relations with the external environment, and supporting other information systems that facilitate management decision making (Culnan, 1989).

Figure 2.5
Typical applications of TPS. There are five functional categories of TPS: Sales/marketing, Manufacturing/production, Finance/accounting, Human resources, and other types of systems specific to a particular industry. TPS support most business functions in most organizations. Within each of these major functions are subfunctions. For each of these subfunctions (e.g., sales management) there is a major application system.

	Type of TPS System				
	Sales/ marketing systems	Manufacturing/ production systems	Finance/ accounting systems	Human resources systems	Other types (e.g., university)
Major functions of system	Sales management	Scheduling	Budgeting	Personnel records	Admissions
	Market research	Purchasing	General ledger	Benefits	Grade records
	Promotion	Shipping/receiving	Billing	Compensation	Course records
	Pricing	Engineering	Cost accounting	Labor relations	Alumni
	New products	Operations		Training	
Major application systems	Sales order information system	Materials resource planning systems	General ledger	Payroll	Registration system
	Market research system	Purchase order control systems	Accounts receivable/payable	Employee records	Student transcript system
	Pricing system	Engineering systems	Budgeting	Benefit systems	Curriculum class control systems
		Quality control systems	Funds management systems	Career path systems	Alumni benefactor system
				Personnel planning systems	

Knowledge work systems (KWS) and **office automation systems (OAS)** serve the information needs at the knowledge level of the organization. Knowledge work systems aid knowledge workers, whereas office automation systems primarily aid data workers (although they are also used extensively by knowledge workers).

Knowledge work systems (KWS): Information systems that aid knowledge workers in the creation and integration of new knowledge in the organization.

In general, *knowledge workers* are people who hold formal university degrees and who are often members of a recognized profession, like engineers, doctors, lawyers, and scientists. Their jobs consist primarily of creating new information and knowledge. Knowledge work systems, such as scientific or engineering design workstations, promote the creation of new knowledge and ensure that new knowledge and technical expertise are properly integrated into the business. One example of a KWS is the computer-aided design system used by Gillette designers to develop the Sensor razor.

Office automation systems (OAS): Computer systems, such as word processing, electronic mail systems, and scheduling systems, that are designed to increase the productivity of data workers in the office.

Data workers typically have less formal, advanced educational degrees and tend to process rather than create information. They consist primarily of secretaries, accountants, filing clerks, or managers whose jobs are principally to use, manipulate, or disseminate information. Office automation systems are information technology applications designed to increase the productivity of data workers in the office by supporting the coordinating and communicating activities of the typical office. Office automation systems coordinate diverse information workers, geographic units, and functional areas. The systems communicate with customers, suppliers, and other organizations outside the firm and serve as a clearinghouse for information and knowledge flows.

Typical office automation systems handle and manage documents (through word processing, desktop publishing, digital filing), scheduling (through electronic calendars), and communication (through electronic mail, voice mail, or videoconferencing). **Word processing** refers to the software and hardware that create, edit, format, store, and print documents (see Chapters 5 and 10). Word processing systems represent the single most common application of information technology to office work, in part because producing documents is what offices are all about. **Desktop publishing** produces professional publishing-quality documents by combining output from word processing software with design elements, graphics, and special layout features.

Word processing: Office automation technology that facilitates the creation of documents through computerized text editing, formatting, storing, and printing.

Desktop publishing: Technology that produces professional-quality documents combining output from word processors with design, graphics, and special layout features.

One of the largest impediments to automating offices is the deluge of paper documents that must be preserved. Hundreds of billions of documents are produced annually by U.S. businesses. Many, such as marriage licenses, birth certificates, and contracts of all kinds, require a signature and the preservation of that signature for a long period. Many other basic documents, like purchase orders, invoices, approval sheets, remittance advice, and others, are also still stored manually in filing cabinets. One solution to paperwork management problems is **digital image processing,** the conversion of documents and images into computerized form so that they can be stored and accessed by computer systems. The Window on Technology illustrates how the United Services Automobile Association solved this problem with an imaging network that eliminated paper filing systems for its policy department. Chapter 10 contains a fuller discussion of this technology.

Digital image processing: Technology that converts documents and graphic images into computerized form so that they can be stored, processed, and accessed by computer systems.

Knowledge workers, who create and produce knowledge, have traditionally utilized office automation technology as well. Now, however, they also have knowledge work systems and technologies available to support their role in the firm. Powerful desktop computers, called **workstations,** with graphic, analytic, document management, and communications capabilities can pool together information from diverse perspectives and sources both inside and outside the firm. In the engineering field, knowledge work systems might use such tools to run thousands of calculations before designers are satisfied that a specific part is safe. Designers and drafting experts, such as Gillette's designers, might want to use workstations with 3-D graphics software to visualize a model of a product more fully. (See the Window on Organizations in Chapter 1.) Lawyers, in turn,

Workstations: Powerful desktop computers that combine high-quality graphics, analytical capabilities, and document management. Generally used in engineering and design applications.

WINDOW ON

TECHNOLOGY

Conquering the Paper Mountain

The United Services Automobile Association, with 13,600 employees, provides a broad range of investment, insurance, retirement, purchasing, and travel products to 2 million military officers and their families. Based in San Antonio, Texas, USAA is the largest direct writer of property and casualty insurance in the United States. Selling directly to members via mail or telephone, it is the largest mail-order firm in the United States as well. USAA receives over 100,000 letters and mails over 250,000 items daily.

USAA has developed the largest imaging system in the world, storing 1.5 billion pages. All incoming mail received each day by the policy department is scanned and stored on optical disk. The original documents are thrown away.

Six of USAA's major regional offices across the country are hooked up to its imaging network, illustrated in Figure 2.6. The network consists of image scanners, optical storage units, an IBM model 4381 small mainframe computer, and a local network to link service representatives' workstations and the scanner workstations located in the firm's mailroom. Mail clerks feed documents into a scanner, which digitizes them and transmits the data into USAA's Management Folder Software for storage on optical disk. Service representatives can retrieve a client's file on-line and view documents from IBM personal computers on their desktops. About 2000 people use the network.

Users believe that the imaging system reduces the amount of time their work would take with a paper-based system by one-third, saving paper and storage costs. Before this system was introduced, 200 clerks had to search for files in a 39,000-square-foot warehouse, a process that might take one day or up to two weeks if the files were lying on a policy reviewer's desk. Customer service has been improved because electronic documents can be accessed more rapidly. Three-week-old files can be accessed in less than one second; six-month-old letters, in 15 to 20 seconds; mail up to two years old, in less than two minutes.

Sources: "USAA: Insuring Progress," *InformationWEEK,* May 25, 1992; Lasher, Ives, and Jarvenpaa, December 1991; and Kathy Chin Leong, "IBM Exposes Image Network," *Computerworld,* May 30, 1988.

To Think About: What kinds of management, organization, and technology problems can be solved by using digital image processing?

Figure 2.6
United States Automobile Association's (USAA) imaging network. Scanners enter mail received by USAA's policy department into the imaging system, which stores and distributes the digitally processed image of the document electronically. Service representatives have immediate on-line access to clients' data.

may want to scan thousands of legal findings on their desktop before recommending a strategy. More details on these powerful desktop tools can be found in Chapter 10.

The role of knowledge work and office automation systems in the firm cannot be overestimated. As the economy shifts from relying on manufactured goods to producing services, knowledge, and information, the productivity of individual firms and the entire economy will increasingly depend on knowledge-level systems. This is one reason knowledge-level systems have been the fastest-growing applications over the last decade and are likely to grow in the future. Knowledge-level systems also have become tied in more closely with the other systems in the firm.

MANAGEMENT
INFORMATION SYSTEMS

Management information systems (MIS): Computer systems at the management level of an organization that serve the functions of planning, controlling, and decision making by providing routine summary and exception reports.

Management information systems (MIS) serve the management level of the organization, providing managers with reports and, in some cases, with on-line access to the organization's current performance and historical records. Typically, they are oriented almost exclusively to internal, not environmental or external, events. MIS primarily serve the functions of planning, controlling, and decision making at the management level. Generally, they are dependent on underlying transaction processing systems for their data.

MIS summarize and report on the basic operations of the company. The basic transaction data from TPS are compressed and are usually presented in long reports that are produced on a regular schedule. Figure 2.7 shows how a typical MIS transforms transaction-level data from inventory, production, and accounting into MIS files that are used to provide managers with reports. Figure 2.8 shows a sample report from this system.

MIS usually serve managers interested in weekly, monthly, and yearly results—not day-to-day activities. MIS address structured questions that are known well in advance. These systems are generally not flexible and have little analytical capability. For instance, one cannot instruct an MIS to "take the monthly sales figures by zip code and correlate with the Bureau of the Census estimates of income by zip code." First, a typical MIS contains only corporate internal data, not external data like the U.S. Census figures. Second, most MIS use simple routines such as summaries and comparisons, as opposed to sophisticated mathematical models or statistical techniques. Third, data on sales by zip code would not be available on a typical MIS unless a user had informed the designer several years earlier that this arrangement of data might be useful.

Figure 2.7

How management information systems obtain their data from the organization's TPS. In the system illustrated by this diagram, three TPS supply summarized transaction data at the end of the time period to the MIS reporting system. Managers gain access to the organizational data through the MIS, which provides them with the appropriate reports.

Consolidated Consumer Products Corporation
Sales by Product and Sales Region: 1995

PRODUCT CODE	PRODUCT DESCRIPTION	SALES REGION	ACTUAL SALES	PLANNED	ACTUAL VS. PLANNED
4469	Carpet Cleaner	Northeast	4,066,700	4,800,000	0.85
		South	3,778,112	3,750,000	1.01
		Midwest	4,867,001	4,600,000	1.06
		West	4,003,440	4,400,000	0.91
		TOTAL	16,715,253	17,550,000	0.95
5674	Room Freshener	Northeast	3,676,700	3,900,000	0.94
		South	5,608,112	4,700,000	1.19
		Midwest	4,711,001	4,200,000	1.12
		West	4,563,440	4,900,000	0.93
		TOTAL	18,559,253	17,700,000	1.05

Figure 2.8
A sample report that might be produced by the MIS system in Figure 2.7.

Table 2.2 describes the characteristics of typical management information systems.

Newer MIS are more flexible and may include software that lets managers structure their own reports and combine data from separate files and TPS. For instance, suppose a director of sales wanted to know if prices charged to major customers this year are keeping pace with cost increases. An MIS could tell the sales director if the customer bought as much this year as last year and could compare the profit margin between this year and last. Many older MIS do not have these features.

The Window on Management describes an MIS used by the Travelers Insurance Company to monitor its claims review procedures and to identify duplicate medical charges.

Some researchers use the term MIS to include all of the information systems that support the functional areas of the organization (Davis, 1985). However, in this book we prefer to use *computer-based information systems (CBIS)* as the umbrella term for all information systems and to consider management information systems as those that are specifically dedicated to management-level functions.

Table 2.2 CHARACTERISTICS OF MANAGEMENT INFORMATION SYSTEMS

1. MIS support structured and semistructured decisions at the operational and management control levels. However, they are also useful for planning purposes of senior management staff.

2. MIS are generally reporting and control oriented. They are designed to report on existing operations and therefore to help provide day-to-day control of operations.

3. MIS rely on existing corporate data and data flows.

4. MIS have little analytical capability.

5. MIS generally aid in decision making using past and present data.

6. MIS are relatively inflexible.

7. MIS have an internal rather than an external orientation.

8. Information requirements are known and stable.

9. MIS require a lengthy analysis and design process (on the order of one to two years).

MANAGEMENT

Computers Combat High Health Care Costs

When a woman submits a bill for an X-ray to her medical insurer, the bill won't tell if she is a woman or if she was pregnant at the time. Pregnant women should not receive X-rays. The Travelers Insurance Company believes that helping to enforce proper standards of medical care treatment can also help reduce costs. So it built a Practice Review System both to scrutinize data on claims submitted by patients and to identify redundant charges.

Travelers already had a system to review claims for appropriate procedures and billing. But the claims were evaluated in a vacuum that did not consider the patient's history. In contrast, the Practice Review System compares bills against patient data acquired during the claims submission process. If a pregnant woman submits a bill for an X-ray, the system could determine that the patient was subjected to an improper procedure. Travelers could use this information to deny payment or to review the treatment practices of the physician who ordered the X-ray.

The system also helps Travelers more closely monitor how much health care providers charge. A physician who submits a bill for a hysterectomy that includes a charge for the total procedure along with charges for each step could be deliberately double billing or merely be confused about proper billing practices. The Practice Review System automatically reviews the bill and refuses payment for inappropriate charges. Travelers might even drop the physician from its provider network if the doctor continually submits bills with redundant charges or provides inappropriate treatment.

Figure 2.9 illustrates how the system works. Using standardized procedure codes and treatment protocols that were developed by Value Health Sciences, Inc. (an offshoot of the Rand Corporation in Santa Monica, California), each bill identifies the medical procedures performed. The system can show that most of the procedures in this particular bill are redundant because they are part of the total hysterectomy procedure.

Monitoring claims this way trims Travelers' claims administration time and costs, reduces inappropriate claims payments, and promotes quality among medical care providers. In addition to aiding insurance companies such as Travelers, computers can help lower treatment costs when they are used by the physicians themselves. Indiana University researchers studying physicians using computers to order drugs and tests for hospital patients found that charges to patients were 13 percent lower than when doctors used paper and pen. The computer system provided comparative costs for tests and treatments and information to help doctors discard unnecessary tests. The physicians with computers could immediately see the costs of the tests and therapies they ordered for their patients and the cost of less expensive alternatives.

Sources: Ron Winslow, "Computers Helping Doctors Match Care with Costs Can Lower Bills, Study Says," *The Wall Street Journal*, January 20, 1993; and Bruce Caldwell, "Travelers' Software Cure," *InformationWEEK*, March 2, 1992.

To Think About: Is this a typical MIS? Why or why not? What benefits would managers derive from this system?

Figure 2.9
The report in this figure illustrates how the Travelers Insurance Practice Review System works. The physician's bill contains additional charges with different procedure codes that were actually included as part of the entire procedure. The Practice Review System can identify these redundant charges and issue the correct payment for the procedure.

Physician's Bill

DATE	PROCEDURE CODE	PROCEDURE DESCRIPTION	FEE
01/12/95	58150	Total hysterectomy	1700
01/12/95	49000	Explore abdominal cavity	500
01/12/95	57410	Pelvic exam-anesthesia	200
01/12/95	58740	Lysis of adhesions	400
01/14/95	90260	Subsequent hospital visit	90
01/16/95	90260	Subsequent hospital visit	90
		TOTAL	$2,980

Insurer's Payment

DATE	PROCEDURE CODE	PROCEDURE DESCRIPTION	FEE
01/12/95	58150	Total hysterectomy	$1,700

**Decision support systems
(DSS):** Computer systems at
the management level of an
organization that combine
data and sophisticated
analytical models to support
semistructured and
unstructured decision making.

Any system that supports a decision is a **decision support system (DSS).** Like MIS, DSS serve the management level of the organization. Information systems support decisions in vastly different ways, and DSS are a class of systems that supports decisions in a unique way (at least when compared to the past). Table 2.3 shows the characteristics of contemporary decision support systems (DSS).

DSS help managers make decisions that are semistructured, unique or rapidly changing, and not easily specified in advance. In these ways, they differ from MIS and TPS systems. DSS are quick-hit, interactive, model-oriented, and action-oriented, whereas MIS systems tend to be ponderous, batch-oriented, and data-oriented (Sprague and Carlson, 1982; Keen, 1985). DSS have to be responsive enough to run several times a day in order to correspond to changing conditions. While DSS use internal information from TPS and MIS, they often bring in information from external sources, such as current stock prices or product prices of competitors.

Clearly, by design, DSS have more analytical power than other systems; they are built explicitly with a variety of models to analyze data. Second, DSS are designed so that users can work with them directly; these systems explicitly include user-friendly software. This requirement follows both from their purpose (to inform personal decision making by key actors) and from the method of design (see Chapter 11). Third, these systems are interactive; the user can change assumptions and include new data.

An interesting, small, but powerful DSS is the voyage-estimating system of a subsidiary of a large American metals company that exists primarily to carry bulk cargoes of coal, oil, ores, and finished products for its parent company. The firm owns some vessels, charters others, and bids for shipping contracts in the open market to carry general cargo. A voyage-estimating system calculates financial and technical voyage details. Financial calculations include ship/time costs (fuel, labor, capital), freight rates for various types of cargo, and port expenses. Technical details include myriad factors such as ship cargo capacity (deadweight tons, tons-per-inch immersion, etc.), speed, port distances, fuel and water consumption, and loading patterns (location of cargo for different ports).

An existing system to calculate only operating costs, freight rates, and profit was run on the company mainframe computer. The reports could not be understood by the managers because of the wealth of technical details they contained; only one person in the MIS department could run the program; and it took several weeks to make changes in assumptions (cost of fuel, speed). Moreover, the system could not answer questions such as the following: Given a customer delivery schedule and an offered freight rate, which vessel should be assigned at what rate to maximize profits? What is the optimum speed at which a particular vessel can optimize its profit and still meet its delivery schedule? What is the optimal loading pattern for a ship bound for the U.S. West Coast from Malaysia?

Senior and middle management wanted a more interactive system that they could control and run themselves, with as many changes in data and models as they needed and with little interference from information systems professionals. Management also needed information immediately to respond to bidding opportunities. Figure 2.10 illustrates the DSS built for this company. The system operates on a powerful desktop microcomputer, provides a system of menus that

Table 2.3	CHARACTERISTICS OF DECISION SUPPORT SYSTEMS

1. DSS offer users flexibility, adaptability, and a quick response.
2. DSS allow users to initiate and control the input and output.
3. DSS operate with little or no assistance from professional programmers.
4. DSS provide support for decisions and problems whose solutions cannot be specified in advance.
5. DSS use sophisticated analysis and modeling tools.

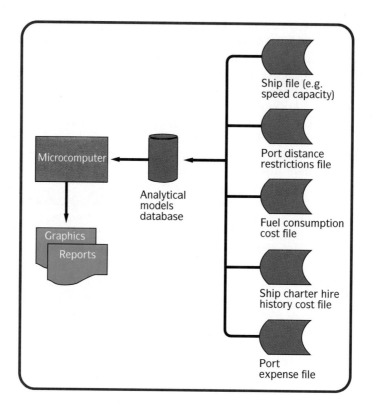

The figure labels read: Microcomputer; Analytical models database; Graphics; Reports; Ship file (e.g. speed capacity); Port distance restrictions file; Fuel consumption cost file; Ship charter hire history cost file; Port expense file.

makes it easy for users to enter data or obtain information, is totally under management control, and required about 160 person-days to build.

EXECUTIVE SUPPORT SYSTEMS

Executive support systems (ESS): Information systems at the strategic level of an organization designed to address unstructured decision making through advanced graphics and communications.

Senior managers use a category of information systems called **executive support systems (ESS)** to make decisions. ESS serve the strategic level of the organization. They address unstructured decisions and create a generalized computing and communications environment rather than providing any fixed application or specific capability. ESS are designed to incorporate data about external events, such as new tax laws or competitors, but they also draw summarized information from internal MIS and DSS. They filter, compress, and track critical data, emphasizing the reduction of time and effort required to obtain information useful to executives. Although they have limited analytical capabilities, ESS employ the most advanced graphics software and can deliver graphs and data from many sources immediately to a senior executive's office or to a boardroom.

Unlike the other types of information systems, ESS are not designed primarily to solve specific problems. Instead, ESS provide a generalized computing and telecommunications capacity that can be applied to a changing array of problems. While DSS are designed to be highly analytical, ESS tend to make less use of analytical models. Instead, they deliver information to managers on demand and on a highly interactive basis.

Questions ESS must assist in answering include the following: What business should we be in? What are the competitors doing? What new acquisitions would protect us from cyclical business swings? Which units should we sell to raise cash for acquisitions? What is the impact on earnings of proposed changes in the investment tax credit? (Rockart, 1982; Keen, 1985). Figure 2.11 illustrates a model of an ESS. It consists of workstations with menu, interactive graphics, and communications capabilities that can access historical and competitive data from internal corporate systems and external databases such as Dow Jones News/Retrieval or the Gallup Poll.

Senior executives differ in their personal styles, and all face radically changing environments and questions. Systems must be built that can adapt to these new

Executive support systems (ESS) are being used by the executives in this boardroom meeting. Video conferencing and advanced graphic software create an integrated computing and communications environment to enhance decision making.

Figure 2.11
Model of a typical executive support system. This system pools data from diverse internal and external sources and makes them available to executives in an easy-to-use form.

conditions. ESS are one response to this challenge. Because ESS are designed to be used by senior managers who often have little, if any, direct contact or experience with computer-based information systems, they incorporate easy-to-use graphic interfaces. More details on leading-edge applications of DSS and ESS can be found in Chapter 11.

Relationship of Systems to One Another: Integration

Figure 2.12 illustrates how the various types of systems in the organization are related to each other. TPS is typically a major source of data for other systems, whereas ESS is primarily a recipient of data from lower-level systems. The other types of systems exchange data as well.

But how much can or should these systems be integrated? Should organizations have a single information system that serves the entire organization and coordinates all of the special systems previously outlined? Would it not be best to have such a single, total system to ensure that information can flow where it is needed, that it is uniform, and that all new systems are coordinated?

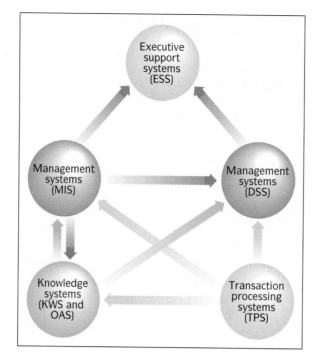

Figure 2.12
Interrelationships among systems. The various types of systems in the organization do not work independently; rather, there are interdependencies between the systems. TPS are a major producer of information that is required by the other systems which, in turn, produce information for other systems. These different types of systems are only loosely coupled in most organizations.

This total systems view, although occasionally advocated by writers in the field (along with their references to systems theory) is rapidly becoming outdated. In fact, no organization builds systems this way, and it would be foolish to try. The total systems view assumes that some specialist exists somewhere who can understand "the total information needs" of the organization (Ackoff, 1967). But the activities of a Sears, a General Motors, or even a small manufacturer are so diverse that many different specialists are needed to build different systems serving different purposes.

A more contemporary view is that systems should be integrated with one another—that is, they should provide for the systematic flow of information among different systems. This integrated approach has merits. But integration costs money, and it would be foolish to build bridges among systems simply for the sake of building bridges.

In the real world, managers provide the level of integration needed to operate the business. Connections among systems evolve over time. Most systems are built in isolation from other systems (unless some business reason suggests a different approach). Organizations do not build all systems at once; the resources required to do so would be enormous, the management problems insurmountable. With the development of new hardware and software—especially database management systems and private telecommunications systems—building bridges between new and existing systems is becoming less expensive and more reliable. See Chapter 6 for a discussion on databases and Chapter 7 for a discussion on telecommunications to further understand these developments.

Organizations pay a penalty for this evolutionary approach to systems. Systems are often not as integrated as they sometimes need to be. This situation creates bottlenecks and inefficiencies in a firm's essential business activities. Occasionally, an organization must mount a massive effort to develop new data processing and telecommunications systems that can integrate systems. General Motors (GM) purchased Electronic Data Systems (EDS), one of the United States' largest consulting firms specializing in data processing and communications services, to develop a seamless, interconnected set of systems to replace its hodgepodge of uncoordinated computer-aided design, computer-aided manufacturing, word processing, and various other systems, plus 100 telecommunications networks. GM needed to integrate its manufacturing, ordering, and delivery operations to remain globally competitive.

GM had to have more integrated systems to remain competitive. But as organizations move toward centralizing, coordinating, and controlling system evolution, they create more layers of management approval for systems and more bureaucracy in the process. Eventually, centralization reaches a saturation point, and organizations start allowing their divisions or operating units to develop systems on their own. In short, decisions to integrate systems, to centralize control, are like the tides—they ebb and flow in accordance with business conditions and values. There is no "one right level" of integration or centralization (Allen and Boynton, 1991; King, 1984).

2.3 Strategic Information Systems

Each of the major types of information systems described above is valuable for helping organizations solve an important problem. In the past few decades some of these systems have become especially critical to the firm's long-term prosperity and survival. Such systems, which are used as powerful tools for staying ahead of competitors, are called strategic information systems.

What Is a Strategic Information System?

Strategic information systems: Computer systems at any level of the organization that change the goals, operations, products, services, or environmental relationships to help the organization gain a competitive advantage.

Strategic information systems change the goals, operations, products, services, or environmental relationships of organizations to help them gain or maintain an edge over competitors. These systems may rely on new, seemingly wondrous technology, or they may use older technology in a new way to give the organization a competitive edge. The systems that have these effects may even change the business of organizations. Merrill Lynch, for instance, used information systems to change from the stock brokerage business to the financial services business. State Street Bank and Trust Co. of Boston still handles traditional banking services such as customer checking and savings accounts and loans. However, its core business is now providing data processing services for securities and mutual funds (Wilke, 1992).

In order to use information systems as competitive weapons, one must first understand where strategic opportunities for businesses are likely to be found. Two models of the firm and its environment have been used to identify areas of the business where information systems can provide advantages over competitors. These are the competitive forces model and the value chain model.

Countering Competitive Forces

Competitive forces model: Model used to describe the interaction of external threats and opportunities that affect an organization's strategy and ability to compete.

In the **competitive forces model**, which is illustrated in Figure 2.13 (Porter, 1980), a firm faces a number of external threats and opportunities: the threat of new entrants into its market; the pressure from substitute products or services; the bargaining power of buyers; the bargaining power of suppliers; and the positioning of traditional industry competitors.

Competitive advantage can be achieved by enhancing the firm's ability to deal with customers, suppliers, substitute products and services, and new entrants to its market. These in turn may change the balance of power between a firm and other competitors in the industry in the firm's favor. According to this model, businesses can use four basic competitive strategies to deal with these competitive forces: product differentiation, focused differentiation, developing tight linkages to customers and suppliers, and becoming the low-cost producer. A firm may achieve competitive advantage by pursuing one of these strategies or by

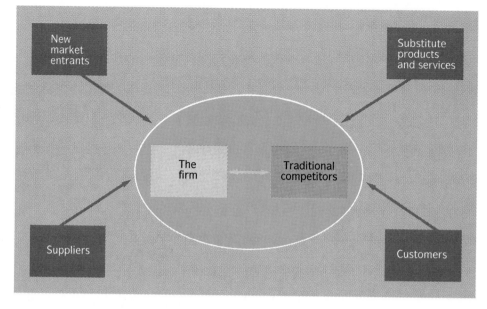

Figure 2.13
The competitive forces model. There are various forces that affect an organization's ability to compete and therefore greatly influence a firm's business strategy. There are threats from new market entrants and from substitute products and services. Customers and suppliers wield bargaining power. Traditional competitors constantly adapt their strategies to maintain their market positioning.

pursuing several strategies simultaneously. For instance, The Gillette Company described earlier is competing on quality, innovation, and cost.

PRODUCT DIFFERENTIATION

Product differentiation: Competitive strategy for creating brand loyalty by developing new and unique products and services that are not easily duplicated by competitors.

Firms can develop brand loyalty by **product differentiation**—creating unique new products and services that can easily be distinguished from those of competitors, products and services that existing competitors or potential new competitors can't immediately duplicate.

Financial institutions have led the way in using information systems to create new products and services. Citibank developed automatic teller machines (ATMs) and bank debit cards in 1977. Seeking to tap the largest retail depository market in the United States, Citibank installed its ATM machines throughout the New York metropolitan area, everywhere a depositor might find the time to use them to deposit or withdraw money. As a leader in this area, Citibank became at one time the largest bank in the United States. Citibank ATMs were so successful that Citibank's competitors, large and small, were forced to counterstrike with a technological effort of their own called the New York Cash Exchange (NYCE).

The Window on Organizations illustrates how banks such as Bank Brussels Lambert are trying to extend their competitive advantage by offering new kinds of banking services.

American Express Travel Related Services (TRS), one of the subsidiaries of the American Express Corporation, depends heavily on its digital imaging system to provide its "country club billing" service and aura of high status and quality. Many customers expect copies of their charge card transactions returned to them to substantiate tax deductions or business expenses. The huge amount of paper that must be processed to include customers' receipts with their credit card bill had become prohibitively expensive and difficult to manage. In 1984, TRS adopted a digital imaging system from Technicron Financial Services that provides reduced images of the receipts on neat laser-printed pages (Connolly and Horwitt, 1988; Markoff, 1988).

FOCUSED DIFFERENTIATION

Businesses can create new market niches by **focused differentiation**—identifying a specific target for a product or service that it can serve in a superior manner. The firm can provide a specialized product or service that serves this narrow target market better than existing competitors and that discourages potential

ORGANIZATIONS

Bank Brussels Lambert Competes with Electronic House Calls

About 70 percent of all Belgian banking transactions are conducted over computer networks. With more than $71 billion in assets, Bank Brussels Lambert, one of the largest banks in Europe, has been a leader in electronic banking services. BBL is finding new ways to extend its electronic banking services to both corporate and individual customers. Customers can now tie their personal computers into the bank's electronic network to access their accounts and to make transactions. The network handles more than 500,000 customer calls per month.

Its Home Bank service permits customers to pay bills, trade securities, and transfer funds from their home PCs. A similar service, called Office Bank, lets employees at subscribing firms do their personal banking from the desktop

systems in their offices. A growing number of customers are using the Home Bank service.

Phone Bank is the latest in the series of electronic services enabling customers to link up by phone with the Bank's vocal computer for carrying out simple banking operations such as checking account balances or transferring funds from one account to another.

Besides a network of approximately 1,000 branches, BBL also has over 200 automated Self Bank branches allowing retail customers to carry out standard banking operations.

Other services offered by this bank include Telelink, which enables businesses to make direct payments to employees and suppliers, and also to consult a number of databases; and Telefin, which al-

lows businesses to arrange financing and obtain approval on-line for their customers. About 6000 companies worldwide use the Telelink program.

To keep its electronic services running around the clock and to ensure that no transactions are lost, BBL has added extra computer hardware and software as backups against system failure.

Sources: Sally Cusack, "Belgian Bank Performs Electronic House Calls," *Computerworld*, March 30, 1992; and John J. McCormick, "Belgian Bank Expands Services," *Information WEEK*, March 23, 1992.

To Think About: How can these electronic banking services help Bank Brussels Lambert maintain a strategic advantage?

Focused differentiation:
Competitive strategy for developing new market niches where a business can compete in the target area better than its competitors.

new competitors. An information system can give companies a competitive advantage by producing data to improve their sales and marketing techniques. Such systems treat existing information as a resource that can be "mined" by the organization to increase profitability and market penetration. The sophisticated Sears system is a classic example.

Sears, Roebuck and Company continually mines its computerized data on its 40 million retail customers—the largest retail customer base in the United States—to target groups such as appliance buyers, tool buyers, gardening enthusiasts, and mothers-to-be. For instance, when a customer buys a washer-dryer from Sears, whether on credit or for cash, Sears mails a postcard advertising an annual maintenance contract. If the contract is not purchased, Sears still maintains a record of who purchased the machine, using the information the customer supplies on the written guarantee. Each year, Sears will send out an annual maintenance contract renewal form or will phone customers to keep its maintenance business humming. At the same time, Sears routinely sends out notices about special sales and products for these machines (such as soap and replacement parts). Likewise with electric hand tools. Purchasers routinely receive targeted fliers on sales and products put out by Sears.

Sears also uses its customer information database to track the purchases made by credit customers. This information is then used to target direct mail inserts that accompany the monthly credit card bill. In addition, information obtained on the initial credit application, as well as the history of credit purchases, can be used by the Sears marketing staff to target specific subgroups such as males between the ages of 40 and 50 who have a family and live in affluent zip code areas. Although Sears has closed its mail-order catalogue business, it continues to maintain its data on its 14 million catalogue customers because this infor-

Automatic Teller Machines (ATMs) give people access to their bank accounts in remote locations at any time of day. Banks who offer ATM service have a competitive advantage over banks who don't. This woman can access her money through a Bank One ATM in a convenience store.

mation is so valuable. It even started selling the catalogue mailing list to other catalogue retailers for a percentage of their catalogues' revenue.

DEVELOPING TIGHT LINKAGES TO CUSTOMERS AND SUPPLIERS

Switching costs: The expense a customer or company incurs in lost time and resources when changing from one supplier or system to a competing supplier or system.

Firms can create ties to customers and suppliers that "lock" customers into the firm's products and tie suppliers into a delivery timetable and price structure shaped by the purchasing firm. This raises **switching costs**—the cost for customers to switch to competitors' products and services—and reduces customers' bargaining power and the bargaining power of suppliers.

Baxter Healthcare International Inc. supplies nearly two-thirds of all products used by U.S. hospitals. It uses its information system to become a full-line supplier for hospitals, a one-stop source for all hospital needs. This effort requires maintaining a costly inventory of more than 120,000 items. However, it is more costly *not* to have items in stock because hospitals will switch to competitors.

Terminals tied to Baxter's own computers are installed in hospitals. When hospitals want to place an order, rather than call a salesperson or send a purchase order, they simply use a Baxter computer terminal onsite to order. The system generates shipping, billing, invoicing, and inventory information and provides customers with an estimated delivery date. With more than 80 distribution centers in the United States, Baxter can make daily deliveries of its products, often within hours of receiving an order.

This system is similar to the just-in-time delivery systems developed in Japan and now being used in the American automobile industry. In these systems, automobile manufacturers such as GM or Chrysler enter the quantity and delivery schedules of specific automobile components into their own information systems. Then these requirements are automatically captured by a supplier's order entry information system. The supplier must respond with an agreement to deliver the materials at the time specified. Thus, automobile companies can reduce the cost of inventory, the space required for warehousing components or raw materials, and construction time.

Baxter has even gone one step further. Delivery personnel no longer drop off their cartons at a loading dock to be placed in a hospital storeroom. Instead, they deliver orders directly to the hospital corridors, dropping them at nursing stations, operating rooms, and stock supply closets. This has created in effect a "stockless inventory" for the hospital, with Baxter serving as the hospitals' warehouse, substantially reducing the need for hospital storage space and personnel and lowering holding and handling costs (Caldwell, 1991). The in-hospital terminals and stockless inventory are powerful instruments for binding customers to Baxter, giving the supplier a decided competitive advantage—it would be too expensive and difficult to switch to a competitor.

Figure 2.14 compares stockless inventory with the just-in-time supply method and traditional inventory methods.

Strategic systems aimed at suppliers are designed to maximize the firm's purchasing power by having suppliers interact with its information system to satisfy the firm's precise business needs. These information systems also provide benefits for suppliers. Suppliers can continually monitor product requirements, factory scheduling, and commitments of their customers against their own schedule to ensure that enough inventory will be available.

Electronic home banking is another example of strategic information systems that "lock in" customers by making the costs of switching to a competing product prohibitive. Once customers key in all of the required digital information about their bills, department stores, checks, and so forth into a single electronic banking system, they find it very difficult to switch to another bank. The banks themselves encourage this situation by developing systems that are incompatible with each other. Once customers are locked in, banks can directly market to a captive audience a variety of banking services ranging from instant credit to stocks to cash management accounts.

INTERORGANIZATIONAL SYSTEMS AND ELECTRONIC MARKETS

Systems that link a company to its customers, distributors, or suppliers are termed **interorganizational systems** because they automate the flow of information across organizational boundaries (Barrett, 1986–1987; Johnston and

Figure 2.14
A comparison of traditional inventory and delivery practices to the *just-in-time supply method* and the *stockless inventory method*. Strategic systems for linking customers and suppliers have changed the way in which some companies handle the supply and inventory requirements of their businesses. The just-in-time supply method reduces inventory requirements of the customer while stockless inventory allows the customer to eliminate inventories entirely, resulting in a decided competitive advantage. Adapted from "Removing the Warehouse from Cost-Conscious Hospitals," *The New York Times,* March 3, 1991. Copyright © 1991 by The New York Times Company. Reprinted by permission.

1. Prevailing Delivery Practice

Inventory

Bulk storage — Delivery — Storeroom — To the ward

Most hospitals keep a large inventory of supplies that are replenished regularly by suppliers, but require a large amount of space and staff.

2. Just-In-Time Supply Method

Inventory

Bulk storage — More frequent deliveries — Storeroom — To the ward

If a hospital implements a just-in-time plan in coordination with a distributer, it can give up some of its inventory space in return for more frequent deliveries.

3. Stockless Supply Method

Inventory

Bulk storage — Daily deliveries — To the ward

A stockless supply plan shifts all inventory responsibilities to the distributor.
Deliveries are made daily, sometimes directly to departments that need supplies.

Interorganizational systems:
Information systems that automate the flow of information across organizational boundaries and link a company to its customers, distributors, or suppliers.

Electronic market: A marketplace that is created by computer and communication technologies that link many buyers and sellers via interorganizational systems.

Vitale, 1988). Such systems allow information or processing capabilities of one organization to improve the performance of another or to improve relationships among organizations. In addition to tightening linkages to customers or suppliers, interorganizational systems can lower costs and increase product differentiation.

Interorganizational systems that provide services to multiple organizations by linking together many buyers and sellers create an **electronic market.** Through computers and telecommunications, these systems function like electronic middlemen (Malone, Yates, and Benjamin, 1987). For example, Charles Schwab and Company, a discount brokerage service, sells investors software for their personal computers to obtain current price quotes for stocks, bonds, and mutual funds; to access research reports from firms such as Standard & Poor's and Dow Jones; and to execute trades themselves. Schwab customers can also place orders to trade and obtain price quotes from a touch-tone telephone.

Such information systems can dominate entire industries. For instance, computerized airline reservation systems are used by airline reservation agents and also by independent travel agents (about 80 percent of all airline tickets issued in the United States are sold by travel agents using these computerized reservation systems). Although rival systems from other airlines exist, SABRE, American Airlines' computerized reservation system, and United Airlines' Apollo system control 75 percent of the computerized reservation system market.

While these systems provide unparalleled convenience to airline travelers and travel agents, they also confer formidable market power on the two airlines. Medium-sized air carriers claimed unfair treatment by SABRE and Apollo because these reservation systems were listing American and United Airlines flights first. While legislation now prohibits airlines from employing any bias in the display of information in computerized reservation systems, this example indicates how a strategic system gives a supplier a market advantage over a distributor and a customer.

Because computerized reservation systems costs tens of millions of dollars to develop, smaller carriers have been discouraged from building their own systems. The smaller carriers have their flights listed on their bigger competitors' systems but must pay a fee to the airline owning the system every time a ticket is sold through the computerized reservation system. Thus SABRE and Apollo are also major sources of revenue for their owners.

Chapter 7 covers the technologies underlying interorganizational systems and electronic markets.

BECOMING THE LOW-COST PRODUCER

Certain strategically oriented information systems facilitate internal operations, management control, planning, and personnel. These systems are strategic if they help firms significantly lower their internal costs, allowing them to deliver products and services at a lower price than their competitors can provide. By lowering operating costs, raising profits, and making firms more efficient, such systems contribute to the survival and prosperity of the firm. The following examples describe information uses that are much more dynamic and intensive than mere management support tools.

The Wizard system developed by Avis, the car rental company, is an example of a strategic internal MIS designed to improve the firm's overall productivity. This system keeps track of the location, costs, and performance of Avis's car rental fleet. This capability, in turn, has permitted Avis to compete effectively against Hertz, National, and other car rental firms by optimizing the distribution of its car rental fleet to ensure that cars are available where there is a demand for them and that costs are kept to a minimum.

Allegheny Ludlum Corporation, a $1 billion specialty steel and metals manufacturer in Pittsburgh, Pennsylvania, has improved its fortunes steadily despite stiff foreign competition and a declining U.S. steel market. It has invested heavily in information systems aimed at coordinating personnel, manufacturing, and other sectors of the company and has one of the most sophisticated computer costing systems in the industry. The system's ability to calculate production costs per unit of time has given the company a productivity edge over competitors. Ten years ago, Allegheny had twelve competitors, but today there are only four. A network links Allegheny plants in six states. A bar-coding system gathers shop floor data that are used in other business functions such as costing, technical services, quality systems, order entry, alloy test systems, and marketing. With these systems, the company can manage internal costs and market products more effectively (Emmett, 1992).

Leveraging Technology in the Value Chain

Value chain model: Model that highlights the activities that add a margin of value to a firm's products or services, indicating where information systems can best be applied to achieve a competitive advantage.

The **value chain model** highlights specific activities in the business where competitive strategies can be best applied (Porter, 1985) and where information systems are most likely to have a strategic impact. The value chain model can supplement the competitive forces model by identifying specific, critical leverage points where a firm can use information technology most effectively to enhance its competitive position. Exactly where can it obtain the greatest benefit from strategic information systems—what specific activities can be used to create new products and services, enhance market penetration, lock in customers and suppliers, and lower operational costs? This model views the firm as a series or "chain" of basic activities that add a margin of value to a firm's products or services. These activities can be categorized as either primary activities or support activities.

Primary activities: Activities most directly related to the production and distribution of a firm's products or services.

Primary activities are most directly related to the production and distribution of the firm's products and services that create value for the customer. Primary activities include inbound logistics—including receiving and storing materials for distribution to production; operations—transforming inputs into finished products; outbound logistics—storing and distributing products; sales and marketing—including promoting and selling the firm's products; and service—including maintenance and repair of the firm's goods and services. **Support activities** make the delivery of the primary activities possible and consist of organization infrastructure (administration and management), human resources (employee recruiting, hiring, and training), technology (improving products and the production process), and procurement (purchasing input).

Support activities: Activities that make the delivery of the primary activities of a firm possible.

Value activities—those that add the most value to products and services—depend on the features of each particular firm. Businesses should develop strategic information systems for value activities that add the most value to their particular firm. Figure 2.15 illustrates the activities of the value chain, showing examples of strategic information systems that could be developed to make each of the value activities more cost effective.

For instance, a firm could save money in the inbound logistics activity by having suppliers make daily deliveries of goods to the factory, thereby lowering the costs of warehousing and inventory. A computer-aided design system similar to those used by the Bath Iron Works, Odense Shipyards, or Group Michelin S.A.—described in the Window on Organizations in Chapter 1—might support the technology activity, helping a firm to reduce costs and perhaps to design more high-quality products than the competition produces. Gillette's computer-controlled machining supports the operations activity, reducing costs and boosting quality. Such systems would be more likely to have strategic impact in a manufacturing firm, whereas an electronic scheduling and messaging system or office automation technology would more likely have strategic value in a law firm or consulting firm. In some cases many different projects, or a series of linked systems, may be required to create a strategic advantage.

Figure 2.15
Activities of the value chain. Various examples of strategic information systems for the primary and support activities of a firm that would add a margin of value to a firm's products or services.

With these examples in mind, it should be clear that information systems can transform the organization's internal operations and can alter critical balances with external environmental factors such as new products and services, customers, and suppliers. Together these internal and external strategic changes alter the firm's competitive advantage.

2.4 Implications for Managers and Organizations

Strategic information systems often change the organization as well as its products, services, and operating procedures, driving the organization into new behavior patterns. Such changes often require new managers, a new work force, and a much closer relationship with customers and suppliers. We now examine some of the implications of these changes for managers.

Strategic Alliances and Information Partnerships

Information partnership:
Cooperative alliance formed between two corporations for the purpose of sharing information to gain strategic advantage.

Companies are increasingly using information systems for strategic advantage by entering into strategic alliances with other companies where both firms cooperate by sharing resources or services. Such alliances are often **information partnerships** in which two or more firms share data for mutual advantage (Konsynski and McFarlan, 1990). They can join forces without actually merging. American Airlines has an arrangement with Citibank to award one mile in its frequent flier program for every dollar spent using Citibank credit cards. American benefits from increased customer loyalty, while Citibank gains new credit card subscribers and a highly creditworthy customer base for cross-marketing. American has also allied with MCI, awarding frequent flier miles for each dollar of long-distance billing.

Such partnerships help firms gain access to new customers, creating new opportunities for cross-selling and targeting products. They can share investments in computer hardware and software. Sometimes traditional competitors can benefit from some of these partnerships. Baxter Healthcare International offers its customers medical supplies from competitors and even office supplies through its electronic ordering channel. Companies that were traditional competitors have found such alliances to be mutually advantageous.

Managing Strategic Transitions

Strategic transitions: A movement from one level of sociotechnical system to another. Often required when adopting strategic systems that demand changes in the social and technical elements of an organization.

Adopting the kinds of systems described in this chapter generally requires changes in business goals, relationships with customers and suppliers, internal operations, and information architecture. These sociotechnical changes, affecting both social and technical elements of the organization, can be considered **strategic transitions**—a movement between levels of sociotechnical systems.

How much sociotechnical change occurs depends on the specific circumstances. Clearly, however, there is a connection between the strategy of an organization and its internal structure. As companies move to make information systems part of the overall corporate strategy, their internal structure must also change to reflect these new developments. For instance, when businesses implement state-of-the art manufacturing systems to remain competitive, they will need to redesign various organizational processes to make effective use of leading-edge manufacturing technology. Product design, sales, and finance will have to be more closely integrated with plant management.

Firms with successful strategic information systems have broken down both internal and external organizational barriers that block the sharing of data. Internally, design, sales, and manufacturing departments must work together much more closely. Federal Express's highly publicized package-tracking system shares information among operations, customer service, and accounting functions. Firestone Tire & Rubber Company made tire design information available to quality control, production, and testing groups. Externally, firms may become intimately linked with their suppliers and customers and may share each other's responsibilities. For instance, in Baxter International's stockless inventory system, Baxter has assumed responsibility for managing its customers' inventories (Johnston and Vitale, 1988).

In some cases, reshaping an organization to remain competitive may necessitate an entirely new organizational structure. General Motors, in order to produce the Saturn, a new low-cost car competitive with Japanese models, created an entirely new automotive division with a new factory, a new sales force, and

The corporate alliance between MCI and American Airlines led to this marketing campaign where flyers were awarded bonus travel miles on American for using MCI to make their phone calls.

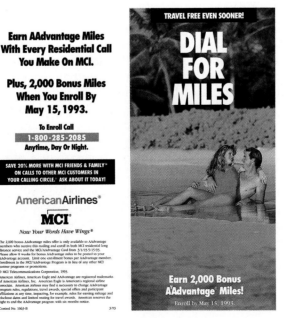

a new design team to utilize the new technologies. Not all strategic information systems require such massive change, but clearly, many do.

What Managers Can Do

Managers must determine how the organization can build information systems of strategic importance. Information systems are too important to be left entirely to a small technical group in the corporation. Senior managers must initiate the search for opportunities to develop them. Some of the important questions managers should ask themselves are as follows:

- How is the industry currently using information and communication technology? Which organizations are the industry leaders in the application of information systems technology? What does the future look like?
- Is the organization behind or ahead of the industry in its application of information systems?
- Are significant strategic opportunities to be gained by introducing information systems technology into the industry? What kinds of systems are applicable to the industry? Does it require systems to create new products and services, supplier systems, and/or sales and marketing systems?
- What is the current business strategic plan, and how does that plan mesh with the current strategy for information services?

Studies of successful strategic systems have found that they are rarely planned but instead evolve slowly over long periods of time, and they almost always originate with practical operational problems. For instance, the SABRE airline reservation system, which is often cited as a classic "strategic system," originated as a straightforward inventory control and order entry system (Copeland and McKenney, 1988; Hopper, 1990). Strategic systems, like most new products, come from closely observing real-world business situations.

| **Management Challenges** | |

1. **Integration.** On the one hand, it is necessary to design different systems for different levels and functions in the firm—TPS, MIS, DSS, OAS, KWS, and ESS. On the other hand, integrating the systems so they can freely exchange information can be technologically difficult and costly. Managers need to determine what level of systems integration is required and how much it is worth in dollars.

2. **Sustainability of competitive advantage.** The competitive advantages conferred by strategic systems do not necessarily last long enough to ensure long-term profits. Competitors can retaliate and copy strategic systems. Moreover, these systems are often expensive; costs saved by some systems are expended immediately to maintain the system. Competitive advantage isn't always sustainable. Market conditions change. The business and economic environment changes. Technology and customers' expectations change. The classic strategic information systems—American Airlines' SABRE computerized reservation system, Citibank's ATM system, and Federal Express's package tracking system, benefited by being the first in their respective industries. But then rival systems emerged. NYCE banks blunted Citibank's ATM edge. United Parcel Service, described in the opening vignette of Chapter 1, is challenging Federal Express's domination of the overnight package market, and Apollo is presenting a strong challenge to SABRE. Information systems alone cannot provide an enduring business advantage (Hopper, 1990). Systems originally intended to be strategic frequently become tools for survival, something every firm has in order to stay in business. Rather than conferring long-term competitive advantage, they become critical for a company just to keep abreast of the competition.

3. **Organizational barriers to strategic transitions.** Implementing strategic systems usually requires far-reaching sociotechnical changes. This goal is not easy to accomplish because organizational change is frequently resisted by middle and even senior managers. In fact, one of the greatest obstacles to strategic transitions may be resistance to change—both the changes that are imposed on an organization and those that employees experience as their jobs are reshaped. Even the identities of employees must change. One is no longer simply a salesperson or a member of the production department. These tasks become increasingly integrated through a single information network. To be successful, strategic transitions require changes in organizational culture (see Chapter 3).

Summary

Describe the role played by the six major types of information systems in organizations.

There are six major types of information systems in contemporary organizations: 1) transaction processing systems (TPS) at the operational level; 2) knowledge work systems (KWS) and 3) office automation systems (OAS) at the knowledge level; 4) management information systems (MIS) and 5) decision support systems (DSS) at the management level; and 6) executive support systems (ESS) at the strategic level.

The six types of systems are designed for different purposes and different audiences: Transaction processing systems (TPS) perform and record the daily routine transactions that are necessary to conduct business. They also produce information for the other systems. Many organizations today would come to a standstill if their TPS failed for a day or even a few hours. Examples are systems for order processing, airline reservations, and payroll.

Knowledge-level systems support clerical, managerial, and professional workers. They consist of office automation systems for increasing the productivity of data workers (word processing, desktop publishing, document storage, facsimile transmission, electronic mail, videoconferencing) and knowledge work systems for enhancing the productivity of knowledge workers (professional workstations, graphics, analytical models, document preparation, and communication). Knowledge work systems are increasingly tied to other systems in the firm.

Management systems (MIS and DSS) provide the management control level with reports and access to the organization's current performance and historical records. Most MIS reports condense information from TPS and are not highly analytical. Decision support systems (DSS) support management decisions when these decisions are unique, rapidly changing, and not specified easily in advance. They have more advanced analytical models than MIS and often draw on information from external as well as internal sources.

Executive support systems (ESS) support the strategic level by providing a generalized computing and communications environment to assist senior management's decision making. They have limited analytical capabilities but can draw on sophisticated graphics software and many sources of internal and external information.

Discuss the relationship between the various types of information systems.

The various types of systems in the organization exchange data with one another. TPS are a major source of data for other systems, especially MIS and DSS. ESS is primarily a recipient of data from lower-level systems.

The different systems in an organization are only loosely integrated. There is no single total system that coordinates all the systems. In most organizations the information needs of the various functional areas and organizational levels are too specialized to be served by a single system. However, integrating information from various systems is desirable and often essential for a business. Developing links among systems is costly, but so is the lack of sufficient links.

Describe the various ways that information systems can be used to create strategic advantage for firms.

Information systems can help businesses pursue the four basic competitive strategies: Information systems can be used to develop new market niches; they can lock in customers and suppliers by raising the cost of switching; they can provide unique products and services; and they can help firms provide products and services at lower cost by reducing production and distribution costs.

Describe how the competitive forces and value chain models can be used to identify opportunities for strategic information systems.

The value chain and competitive forces models can help identify areas of a business where information systems can supply a strategic advantage. The competitive forces model describes a number of external threats and opportunities faced by firms that they must counter with competitive strategies. Information systems can be developed to cope with the threat of new entrants into the market, the pressure from substitute products, the bargaining power of buyers, the bargaining power of suppliers, and the positioning of traditional industry competitors.

The value chain model highlights specific activities in the business where competitive strategies can best be applied and where information systems are most likely to have a strategic impact. This model views the firm as a series or "chain" of basic activities that add a margin of value to a firm's products or services. Information systems can have strategic impact in the activities that add the most value to the firm.

Explain why strategic information systems are difficult to build and to sustain.

Not all strategic systems make a profit; they can be expensive and risky to build. Many strategic information systems are easily copied by other firms, so that strategic advantage is not always sustainable. Implementing strategic systems often requires extensive organizational change and a transition from one sociotechnical level to another. Such changes are called strategic transitions and are often difficult and painful to achieve.

Key Terms

Batch processing
Transaction file
Master file
On-line processing
Transaction processing systems (TPS)
Knowledge work systems (KWS)
Office automation systems (OAS)
Word processing
Desktop publishing
Digital image processing
Workstations
Management information systems (MIS)
Decision support systems (DSS)

Executive support systems (ESS)
Strategic information systems
Competitive forces model
Product differentiation
Focused differentiation
Switching costs
Interorganizational systems
Electronic market
Value chain model
Primary activities
Support activities
Information partnership
Strategic transitions

Review Questions

1. What is the difference between batch and on-line processing? Diagram the difference.

2. List and briefly describe the major types of systems in organizations.

3. What are the five major types of TPS in business organizations? What functions do they perform? Give examples of each.

4. Describe the functions performed by knowledge work and office automation systems and the tools used for each.

5. What are the characteristics of MIS? How do MIS differ from TPS? From DSS?

6. What are the characteristics of DSS? How do they differ from ESS?

7. What is a strategic information system?

8. Define and compare the value chain and competitive forces models for identifying opportunities for strategic systems.

9. How can a firm use information systems to create new products and services? Give an example.

10. How can information systems help firms focus on market niche? Give an example.

11. How can a firm use an information system to "lock in" customers? Give an example.

12. How can a firm increase its overall operational productivity using information systems?

13. Define: interorganizational systems, electronic markets, and information partnerships.

14. What is a strategic transition?

15. Why are strategic information systems difficult to build?

16. How can managers find strategic applications in their firm?

Discussion Questions

1. Discuss the major factors that may prevent an organization from building a totally integrated information system that combines all six major types of systems into a single design effort.

2. Review the accounts receivable TPS described in this chapter. Explain how it could be a producer of data for other systems. Can you think of other reports that use data generated by this system?

3. Several information systems experts have claimed, "There is no such thing as a sustainable strategic advantage." Discuss.

4. How do the following kinds of systems give each company a strategic advantage? What competitive strategy does each support?

   a. Mazda Motors of America distributes software to its dealerships; the software compiles customer data on trade-ins and used car sales.

   b. Citibank has arranged with Federal Express to replace lost credit cards within 24 hours. Federal Express and Citibank computers networked together can track the creation and shipment of new cards to customers through the Federal Express hub in Memphis, Tenn.

   c. Shell Oil Corporation in Houston, Texas, introduced point-of-sale equipment for credit authorization.

   d. The Food Emporium supermarket chain is starting to use video screens attached to shopping carts. As shoppers stroll down the aisles, a sensor activates video commercials and store specials on the video screen using software attached to a computer in the store. In addition to providing information about items for sale, the video screens can give brief weather and news reports.

Group Project

In a group with three or four other classmates, research a business firm using annual reports or publications such as *Fortune* or *Business Week*. Describe some of the TPS, MIS, DSS, KWS, OAS, and ESS that might be found in the firm. Suggest appropriate strategic information systems for that particular business. Present your group's findings to the class.

CSX Information Systems Put Service on the Right Track

CSX Transportation Inc., based in Richmond, Virginia, is the leading railroad in the United States by revenue, producing gross revenue of over $4.5 billion in 1990. Like other rail freight carriers, it has been losing business for decades to the trucking and airlines industries. To cope with the intense competition and economic slowdown during the early 1990s, the firm has been using information technology to cut its work force and to operate more cost effectively. Also, it is slowly starting to pay attention to customer service. This is important because the railroads have acquired a reputation of being uncaring about customers. CSX diversified by acquiring and investing in oil and gas, real estate, and telecommunications ventures. It needed to focus more on its core transportation business.

In 1988, CSX launched a back-to-basics campaign, selling its other businesses to turn its attention to railway transport. The firm implemented computerized tracking and scheduling systems, and it looked for innovative ways to offer customers more reliable service with fewer employees. It invested in a control and communications system that would run the railroad with as little manual input as possible. The system now tracks all freight car and train movements, handles basic accounting, and provides analysis of these functions for the firm's key decision makers. A decision-support information system provides cost and revenue data on car and train inventories.

CSX introduced radio-frequency scanners to oversee the delivery of hundreds of thousands of Chrysler Corporation automobiles carried by CSX. Before this system was installed, CSX had used a three-part paper form that was placed in each automobile. Each form had to be handled manually and was eventually entered into a computer for tracking and reconciliation. Chrysler felt hampered by the paper-based system and began placing bar-code information on each vehicle.

When cars are shipped by rail, they are offloaded and stored until they are ready for final delivery to dealers by truck. With so many cars being transported, keeping track of where a particular make, model, and color is located becomes a gargantuan job. Obtaining this information quickly improves customer service and benefits both CSX and Chrysler.

CSX uses the scanners to access the bar code on each vehicle and transmits the information automatically via radio equipment to a central computer. The information automatically updates the firm's inventory and tracking system. When CSX is ready to turn the car over to the dealer, it can update the inventory and closely manage it for Chrysler.

When Chrysler is looking for a particular car to send to a dealer, CSX can locate the choice much faster. Chrysler benefits from the more accurate and timely information from the CSX system, while CSX cuts costs. Task time has been reduced 85 percent for a savings of 30 person-hours per week. With other carriers competing for the Chrysler account, CSX's investment in the scanners helped the firm preserve and even expand its relationship with its important client. The new system has dramatically shortened computer data entry time and reduced the time required to search and deliver a vehicle by 85 percent.

Other system applications include Mercury, which enables CSX and its customers to eliminate tremendous volumes of paperwork and processing by eliminating paper-based purchase orders and bills of lading. (Bills of lading are shipping instructions from the customer to the railroad.) A total of 2000 shippers use the system; therefore, eliminating the need to key in bills of lading manually produces large savings for CSX, while electronically providing shippers with the precise locations of their shipments. The system also has electronic mail, way-bill retrieval, and railcar ordering capabilities.

Major customers' demands for railcars are complex, but these requests can now be managed electronically. Shippers transmit data about their anticipated railcar needs for a two-week period electronically to CSX's computer. Since the data goes directly into CSX's scheduling system, shippers can be queued more rapidly for railcars. CSX thus has better control over its railcar inventory.

CSX believes that it recouped the $1 million required to build the Mercury system in just one year by automating bills of lading alone. Customer service benefits from faster turnaround of status requests and investigation of billing disputes. Delays or inaccuracies caused by placing shipping instructions via telephone or mail have also been eliminated. CSX estimates that it is getting a 35 percent return on its half-billion dollar investment in information technology, much of it from driving down operating costs. The number of employees has been reduced from a peak of 80,000 in the 1980s to around 38,000 today.

CSX joined forces with the AMR Corporation, which owns American Airlines, to develop a global logistics management system called Encompass. This system links a company's suppliers, customers, shippers, carriers, freight forwarders, and consignees; they can now communicate directly with one another or monitor each other's activities. For instance, by using Encompass, Procter & Gamble detected routing delays and was able to redirect inventory from European warehouses rather than tap its safety stock locations in Japan.

Sources: Julia King, "AMR and CSX Shake Hands on Logistics Deal," *Computerworld*, August 24, 1992; "CSX Switches Tracks," *InformationWEEK*, April 13, 1992; and Jon Pepper, "Getting Service on Track," *InformationWEEK*, November 11, 1991.

Case Study Questions

1. Which of the major kinds of systems are described in this case?

2. Diagram CSX's automobile delivery system with the system symbols introduced in this chapter. Then sketch a sample report that might be output by the system.

3. How much strategic advantage do these systems provide for CSX? Use the competitive forces and value chain models in your analysis.

4. What management, organization, and technology changes were required by CSX's systems?

References

Ackoff, R. L. "Management Misinformation System." *Management Science* 14, no. 4 (December 1967), pp. B140–B116.

Allen, Brandt R., and Andrew C. Boynton. "Information Architecture: In Search of Efficient Flexibility." *MIS Quarterly* 15, no. 4 (December 1991).

Bakos, J. Yannis. "A Strategic Analysis of Electronic Marketplaces." *MIS Quarterly* 15, no. 3 (September 1991).

Bakos, J. Yannis, and Michael E. Treacy. "Information Technology and Corporate Strategy: A Research Perspective." *MIS Quarterly* (June 1986).

Barrett, Stephanie S. "Strategic Alternatives and Interorganizational System Implementations: An Overview." *Journal of Management Information Systems* (Winter 1986–1987).

Barua, Anitesh, Charles H. Kriebel, and Tridas Mukhopadhyay. "An Economic Analysis of Strategic Information Technology Investments." *MIS Quarterly* 15, no. 5 (September 1991).

Beath, Cynthia Mathis, and Blake Ives. "Competitive Information Systems in Support of Pricing." *MIS Quarterly* (March 1986).

Betts, Mitch. "ATM Pioneers Reaped Market Share, Income." *Computerworld*, January 20, 1992.

Bower, Joseph L., and Thomas M. Hout. "Fast-Cycle Capability for Competitive Power." *Harvard Business Review* (November–December 1988).

Caldwell, Bruce. "A Cure for Hospital Woes." *InformationWEEK*, September 9, 1991.

Cash, J. I., and Benn R. Konsynski. "IS Redraws Competitive Boundaries." *Harvard Business Review* (March–April 1985).

Cash, James I., F. Warren McFarlan, James L. McKenney, and Lynda M. Applegate. *Corporate Information Systems Management*, 3rd ed. Homewood, IL: Irwin, 1992.

Cash, J. I., and P. L. McLeod. "Introducing IS Technology in Strategically Dependent Companies." *Journal of Management Information Systems* (Spring 1985).

Clemons, Eric K. "Evaluation of Strategic Investments in Information Technology." *Communications of the ACM* (January 1991).

Clemons, Eric K., and Michael C. Row. "McKesson Drug Co.: Case Study of a Strategic Information System." *Journal of Management Information Systems* (Summer 1988).

Clemons, Eric K., and Michael C. Row. "Sustaining IT Advantage: The Role of Structural Differences." *MIS Quarterly* 15, no. 3 (September 1991).

Connolly, James, and Elisabeth Horwitt. "American Express Sets Own Limits." *Computerworld*, December 12, 1988.

Copeland, Duncan G., and James L. McKenney. "Airline Reservations Systems: Lessons from History." *MIS Quarterly* 12, no. 3 (September 1988).

Culnan, Mary J. "Transaction Processing Applications as Organizational Message Systems: Implications for the Intelligent Organization." Working paper no. 88-10, 22nd Hawaii International Conference on Systems Sciences (January 1989).

Cushman, John H., Jr. "The High-Stakes Battle for Airline Reservations." *The New York Times*, June 18, 1989.

Davis, Gordon B., and Margrethe H. Olson. *Management Information Systems: Conceptual Foundations, Structure, and Development,* 2nd ed. New York: McGraw-Hill, 1985.

Emmett, Arielle. "Hot or Cold, Steel Maker Forges Ahead with IS." *Computerworld,* June 15, 1992.

Fedorowicz, Jane, and Benn Konsynski. "Organization Support Systems: Bridging Business and Decision Processes." *Journal of Management Information Systems* 8, no. 4 (Spring 1992).

Feeny, David F., and Blake Ives. "In Search of Sustainability: Reaping Long-Term Advantage from Investments in Information Technology." *Journal of Management Information Systems* (Summer 1990).

Gorry, G. A., and M. S. Scott-Morton. "A Framework for Management Information Systems." *Sloan Management Review* 13, no. 1 (1971).

Henderson, John C., and John J. Sifonis. "The Value of Strategic IS Planning: Understanding Consistency, Validity, and IS Markets." *MIS Quarterly* 12, no. 2 (June 1988).

Hopper, Max. "Rattling SABRE—New Ways to Compete on Information." *Harvard Business Review* (May–June 1990).

Houdeshel, George, and Hugh J. Watson. "The Management Information and Decision Support (MIDS) System at Lockheed Georgia." *MIS Quarterly* 11, no. 1 (March 1987).

Huber, George P. "Organizational Information Systems: Determinants of Their Performance and Behavior." *Management Science* 28, no. 2 (1984).

Ives, Blake, and Gerald P. Learmonth. "The Information System as a Competitive Weapon." *Communications of the ACM* (December 1984).

Ives, Blake, and Michael R. Vitale. "After the Sale: Leveraging Maintenance with Information Technology." *MIS Quarterly* (March 1986).

Janulaitis, M. Victor. "Gaining Competitive Advantage." *Infosystems* (October 1984).

Johnston, H. Russell, and Shelley R. Carrico. "Developing Capabilities to Use Information Strategically." *MIS Quarterly* 12, no. 1 (March 1988).

Johnston, H. Russell, and Paul R. Lawrence. "Beyond Vertical Integration—The Rise of the Value-Adding Partnership." *Harvard Business Review* (July–August 1988).

Johnston, H. Russell, and Michael R. Vitale. "Creating Competitive Advantage with Interorganizational Information Systems." *MIS Quarterly* 12, no. 2 (June 1988).

Keen, Peter G. W. *Competing in Time: Using Telecommunications for Competitive Advantage.* Cambridge, MA: Ballinger Publishing Company, 1986.

Keen, Peter G. W. *Shaping the Future: Business Design Through Information Technology.* Cambridge, MA: Harvard Business School Press, 1991.

Keen, Peter G. W. "A Walk Through Decision Support." *Computerworld,* January 14, 1985.

King, John. "Centralized vs. Decentralized Computing: Organizational Considerations and Management Options." *Computing Surveys* (October 1984).

Konsynski, Benn R., and F. Warren McFarlan. "Information Partnerships—Shared Data, Shared Scale." *Harvard Business Review* (September–October 1990).

Lasher, Donald R., Blake Ives, and Sirkka L. Jarvenpaa. "USAA–IBM Partnerships in Information Technology: Managing the Image Project." *MIS Quarterly* 15, no. 4 (December 1991).

Lindsey, Darryl, Paul H. Cheney, George M. Kasper, and Blake Ives. "Competitive Advantage in the Cotton Industry." *MIS Quarterly* 14, no. 4 (December 1990).

Main, Thomas J., and James E. Short. "Managing the Merger: Building Partnership Through IT Planning at the New Baxter." *MIS Quarterly* 13, no. 4 (December 1989).

Malone, Thomas W., JoAnne Yates, and Robert I. Benjamin. "Electronic Markets and Electronic Hierarchies." *Communications of the ACM* (June 1987).

Malone, Thomas W., JoAnne Yates, and Robert I. Benjamin. "The Logic of Electronic Markets." *Harvard Business Review* (May–June 1989).

Markoff, John. "American Express Goes High-Tech." *The New York Times,* July 31, 1988.

McFarlan, F. Warren. "Information Technology Changes the Way You Compete." *Harvard Business Review* (May–June 1984).

Millar, Victor E. "Decision-Oriented Information." *Datamation* (January 1984).

Miron, Michael, John Cecil, Kevin Bradcich, and Gene Hall. "The Myths and Realities of Competitive Advantage." *Datamation* (October 1, 1988).

Pastore, Richard. "Coffee, Tea and a Sales Pitch." *Computerworld,* July 3, 1989.

Porter, Michael. *Competitive Advantage.* New York: Free Press, 1985.

Porter, Michael. *Competitive Strategy.* New York: Free Press, 1980.

Porter, Michael. "How Information Can Help You Compete." *Harvard Business Review* (August–September 1985a).

Rackoff, Nick, Charles Wiseman, and Walter A. Ullrich. "Information Systems for Competitive Advantage: Implementation of a Planning Process." *MIS Quarterly* (December 1985).

Rockart, John F., and David W. DeLong. "Executive Support Systems and the Nature of Executive Work." Working paper: Management in the 1990s, Sloan School of Management, Massachusetts Institute of Technology.

Rockart, John F., and Michael E. Treacy. "The CEO Goes On-Line." *Harvard Business Review* (January–February 1982).

Scott Morton, Michael, Ed. *The Corporation in the 1990s.* New York: Oxford University Press, 1991.

Sprague, Ralph H., Jr., and Eric D. Carlson. *Building Effective Decision Support Systems.* Englewood Cliffs, NJ: Prentice-Hall, 1982.

Vitale, Michael R. "The Growing Risks of Information System Success." *MIS Quarterly* (December 1986).

Watson, Hugh D., R. Kelly Rainer, Jr., and Chang E. Koh. "Executive Information Systems: A Framework for Development and a Survey of Current Practices." *MIS Quarterly* 15, no. 1 (March 1991).

Wilke, John R. "State Street Bank Is Paved with Gold of Processing Fees." *The Wall Street Journal,* June 25, 1992.

Wiseman, Charles. *Strategic Information Systems.* Homewood, IL: Richard D. Irwin, Inc., 1988.

CHAPTER

3

Information Systems, Organizations, and Management

Schneider Responds to the New Rules of the Trucking Game

Deregulation changed the whole business environment for the trucking industry overnight. Competition between trucking firms for customers heated up. Interstate truckers no longer had to follow the rules of a regulatory bureaucracy about what kinds of freight to carry and where to take them. This same regulatory red tape had also made it difficult for customers to change carriers because only certain trucking firms could meet these regulations. Large retailers and manufacturers were also trying to slash

inventory costs and warehouses by installing just-in-time delivery systems. They wanted to use trucking firms that could transport their shipments right away.

To meet these new demands, Schneider National, North America's biggest carrier of full-truckload cargoes, used a two-pronged strategy. First, it tried to make sweeping changes in its corporate culture. CEO Don Schneider realized he had to replace his firm's regulated-utility mentality with quick reflexes

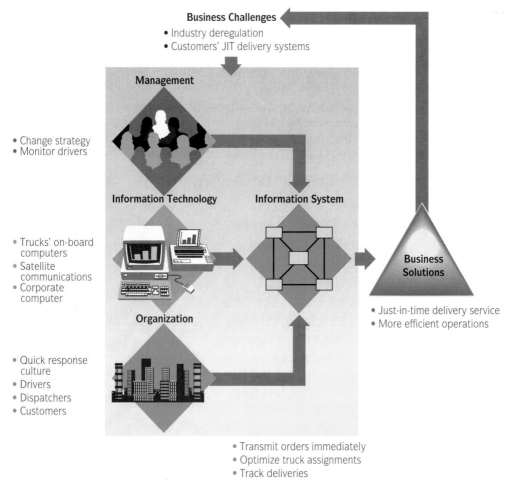

Business Challenges
- Industry deregulation
- Customers' JIT delivery systems

Management

- Change strategy
- Monitor drivers

Information Technology　　**Information System**

- Trucks' on-board computers
- Satellite communications
- Corporate computer

Organization

Business Solutions

- Just-in-time delivery service
- More efficient operations

- Quick response culture
- Drivers
- Dispatchers
- Customers

- Transmit orders immediately
- Optimize truck assignments
- Track deliveries

and an urgency to get things done. Schneider democratized the organization by calling all employees "associates" and removing status symbols like reserved parking places. He encouraged everyone, from drivers on up, to speak out on ways to improve operations. He also instituted an extra bonus paycheck based solely on performance.

Second, Schneider deployed new information systems to support these changes. In 1988, the firm equipped each truck with a computer and a rotating antenna. A satellite tracks every rig, making sure it adheres to schedule. When an order comes into headquarters, often directly via the customer's computer to Schneider's computer, dispatchers know exactly which truck in the customer's vicinity should be assigned to the job. The dispatchers send an order directly by satellite to the driver's on-board terminal, complete with directions to the destination and instructions on what gate to use and papers to collect with the merchandise. Within 15 to 30 minutes of sending an order to Schneider's computer, customers know which trucks to expect and when. The computer also monitors the trucks' speed; Schneider stipulates a 55-mile-an-hour speed limit.

Schneider is also experimenting with new shipping technologies and alliances with the railroad industry, which used to be a traditional competitor to trucking. It hopes to win business by offering intermodal transport, which moves freight by using both trucks and railroads. In some cases, it is cheaper and more efficient to ship goods this way than by using trucks alone.

Several other competitors responded to deregulation by merely lowering rates. They went bankrupt.

Sources: Marc Levinson, "Riding the Data Highway," *Newsweek,* March 21, 1994; Daniel Machalaba, "An Industry's Direction Rides on Schneider National," *The Wall Street Journal,* May 24, 1993; and Myron Magnet, "Meet the New Revolutionaries," *Fortune* (February 24, 1992).

The experience of Schneider National illustrates the interdependence of business environments, management strategy, organizational culture, and the development of information systems. Schneider National developed a new information system in response to changes in competitive pressures from its surrounding environment, but it needed to make sweeping changes to its organizational culture before it could use this system successfully. The decisions faced by Don Schneider and his managers as they designed this system are typical of those facing many senior executives. In companies both large and small, managers are asking these questions: How can we enlarge market share? Where is our industry headed? Where are we strong and where are we weak? What should our strategy be? How can we design a strategy?

In this chapter we explore the complex relationship between organizations, management, and information systems. We introduce you to the features of organizations that you will need to know about as a manager when you envision, design, build, and operate information systems. We also scrutinize the role of a manager and try to identify areas where information systems can contribute to managerial effectiveness. First we will describe the features of organizations that are related to information systems—what we call the "salient" features. Then we will examine in greater detail precisely how information systems affect organizations and how organizations affect information systems. Next we look at what managers actually do, examining the types of decisions managers make. The chapter concludes by discussing models for decision making by individuals and organizations and suggests how information systems should be built to support the decision-making process.

After completing this chapter you will be able to:

- Describe the salient characteristics of organizations.
- Describe the relationship between information systems and organizations.
- Contrast the classical and contemporary models of managerial activities and roles.
- Describe how managers make decisions in organizations
- Describe the implications of the relationship between information systems, organizations, and management decision making for the design and implementation of information systems.

3.1 Organization and Information Systems

Let us start with a simple premise based on observation and a great deal of research: Information systems and organizations have a mutual influence on each other. On the one hand, information systems must be aligned with the organization to provide information needed by important groups within the organization. At the same time, the organization must be aware of and open itself to the influences of information systems to benefit from new technologies. Information systems affect organizations, and organizations necessarily affect the design of systems.

The interaction between information technology and organizations is very complex, influenced by a great many mediating factors, including the organization's structure, standard operating procedures, politics, culture, surrounding environment, and management decisions (see Figure 3.1). Managers must be aware that information systems can markedly alter life in the organization. They cannot successfully design new systems or understand existing systems without understanding organizations. Managers decide what systems will be built, what they will do, how they will be implemented, and so forth. Sometimes, however, the outcomes are the result of pure chance and of both good and bad luck.

Figure 3.1
The two-way relationship between organizations and information technology. This complex two-way relationship is mediated by many factors not the least of which are the decisions made—or not made—by managers. Other factors mediating the relationship are the organizational culture, bureaucracy, politics, business fashion, and pure chance.

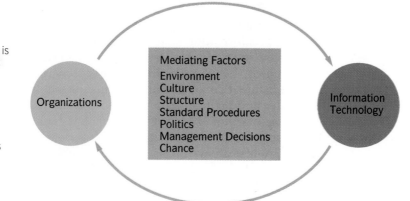

Organizations

Mediating Factors
Environment
Culture
Structure
Standard Procedures
Politics
Management Decisions
Chance

Information
Technology

In this chapter we will look closely at the impact of information systems upon the organization. This, after all, is the primary focus of managers as they decide which systems to develop or purchase and how to use them. However, we will also see the reverse—the impact of organizations upon information systems—throughout this chapter and in the rest of the text as we examine the applications and technology organizations select in order to serve the business needs of their organizations.

Because there are many types of organizations, it stands to reason that the technology of information systems will have a different impact on different types of organizations. There is no singular effect of computers; one cannot, for example, conclude that "computers flatten hierarchies" in organizations. Instead, different organizations in different circumstances experience different effects from the same technology. Before describing the impact of information systems upon organizations, we must first review the salient features of organizations.

What Is an Organization?

Organization (technical definition): A stable formal social structure that takes resources from the environment and processes them to produce outputs.

An **organization** is a stable, formal social structure that takes resources from the environment and processes them to produce outputs. This technical definition focuses on three elements of an organization. *Capital* and *labor* are primary production factors provided by the environment. The organization (the firm) transforms these inputs into products and services in a *production function*. The products and services are *consumed by environments* in return for supply inputs (see Figure 3.2). An organization is *more stable* than an informal group in terms of longevity and routineness. Organizations are *formal* legal entities, with internal rules and procedures, that must abide by laws. Organizations are also *social structures* because they are a collection of social elements, much as a machine has a structure—a particular arrangement of valves, cams, shafts, and other parts.

Figure 3.2

The technical microeconomic definition of the organization. In the microeconomic definition of organizations, capital and labor (the primary production factors provided by the environment) are transformed by the firm through the production process into products and services (outputs to the environment). The products and services are consumed by the environment which supplies additional capital and labor as inputs in the feedback loop.
(B) The microeconomic view is a technical model of the firm in which the firm combines capital and labor in a production function to produce a single product of the amount Q. The firm can freely substitute the capital for labor anywhere along the curve Q.

This definition of organizations is powerful and simple, but it is not very descriptive or even predictive of the real-world organizations that most of us belong to. A more realistic behavioral definition of an **organization** is that it is a collection of rights, privileges, obligations, and responsibilities that are delicately balanced over a period of time through conflict and conflict resolution. In this behavioral view of the firm, people who work in organizations develop customary ways of working; they gain attachments to existing relationships; and they make arrangements with subordinates and superiors about how work will be done, how much work will be done, and under what conditions. Most of these arrangements and feelings are not discussed in any formal rule book.

How do these definitions of organizations relate to information system technology? A technical view of organizations encourages us to focus upon the way inputs are combined into outputs when technology changes are introduced into the company. The firm is seen as infinitely malleable, with capital and labor substituting for one another quite easily. But the more realistic behavioral definition of an organization suggests that building new information systems or rebuilding old ones involves much more than a technical rearrangement of machines or workers—that some information systems change the organizational balance of rights, privileges, obligations, responsibilities, and feelings that has been established over a long period of time.

Technological change requires changes in who owns and controls information; who has the right to access and update that information; and who makes decisions about whom, when, and how. For instance, Schneider's new information system provided central managers with more information to monitor truck drivers' whereabouts. This more complex view forces us to look at the way work is designed and the procedures used to achieve outputs.

The technical and behavioral definitions of organizations are not contradictory. Indeed, they complement one another: The technical definition tells us how thousands of firms in competitive markets combine capital, labor, and information technology, whereas the behavioral model takes us inside the individual firm to see how that technology affects the inner workings of the organization. Section 3.2 describes how each of these definitions of organizations can help explain the relationship between information systems and organizations.

Some features of organizations are common to all organizations; others distinguish one organization from another. Let us look first at the features common to all organizations.

Why Organizations Are So Much Alike: Common Features

You might not think that Apple Computer, United Airlines, or the Aspen, Colorado, Police Department have much in common, but they do. In some respects, all modern organizations are alike because they share the characteristics that are listed in Table 3.1. A German sociologist, Max Weber, was the first to describe these "ideal-typical" characteristics of organizations in 1911. He called organizations **bureaucracies** that have certain "structural" features. According to Weber, all modern bureaucracies

- Have a clear-cut *division of labor and specialization*.
- Arrange specialists in a *hierarchy* of authority.
- Limit authority and action by abstract *rules or procedures* (standard operating procedures or SOPs).
- Create a system of *impartial and universalistic decision making*.
- Hire and promote employees on the basis of *technical qualifications and professionalism* (not personal connections).
- Are devoted to the *principle of efficiency*: maximizing output using limited inputs.

Table 3.1	STRUCTURAL CHARACTERISTICS OF ALL MODERN ORGANIZATIONS
	Clear division of labor
	Hierarchy
	Explicit rules and procedures
	Impartial judgments
	Technical qualifications for positions
	Maximum organizational efficiency

According to Weber, bureaucracies are so prevalent because they are the most efficient form of organization. They are much more stable and powerful than mercurial charismatic groups or formal aristocracies held together by the right of birth. Other scholars have supplemented Weber, identifying additional features of organizations. All organizations develop standard operating procedures, politics, and a culture.

STANDARD OPERATING PROCEDURES

Standard operating procedures (SOPs): Precise, defined rules for accomplishing tasks that have been developed to cope with expected situations.

Organizations that survive over time become very efficient, producing a limited number of products and services by following standard routines. These standard routines become codified into reasonably precise rules, procedures, and practices called **standard operating procedures (SOPs)**, which are developed to cope with virtually all expected situations. Some of these rules and procedures are written formal procedures. Most are rules of thumb to be followed in selected situations.

These standard operating procedures have a great deal to do with the efficiency that modern organizations attain. For instance, in the assembly of a car, managers and workers develop complex standard operating procedures to handle the thousands of motions in a precise fashion, permitting the finished product to roll off the line. As the Window on Organizations illustrates, any change in SOPs requires an enormous organizational effort. Indeed, the organization may need to halt the entire production process, or even create a new and expensive parallel system, which must then be tested exhaustively, before the old SOPs can be retired. Difficulty in changing standard operating procedures is one reason Detroit auto makers have been slow to adopt Japanese mass-production methods.

ORGANIZATIONAL POLITICS

People in organizations occupy different positions with different specialties, concerns, and perspectives. As a result, they naturally have divergent viewpoints about how resources, rewards, and punishments should be distributed. These differences matter to members of organizations, both managers and employees, and they result in political struggle, competition, and conflict within every organization. People use politics to gain everything worth having in a job: pay, position, job conditions, respect, prestige, and ultimately careers. Because of the stakes, players take the game very seriously. Political resistance is one of the great difficulties of bringing about change in organizations—especially the development of new information systems. Virtually all information systems that bring about significant changes in goals, procedures, productivity, and personnel are politically charged and will elicit serious political opposition.

ORGANIZATIONAL CULTURE

Organizational culture: The set of fundamental assumptions about what products the organization should produce, how and where it should produce them, and for whom they should be produced.

All organizations have bedrock, unassailable, unquestioned (by the members) assumptions that define the goals and products of the organization. **Organizational culture** is this set of fundamental assumptions, assumptions about what products the organization should produce; how it should produce them, where, and for whom. Generally, these cultural assumptions are taken totally for granted and are rarely publicly announced or spoken about. They are simply assumptions that few people, if anyone (in their right mind), would question (Schein, 1985).

ORGANIZATIONS

Learning from Japan Takes a Long Time

Hundreds of manufacturing executives and production engineers have journeyed to the Toyota Motor Corporation's Georgetown, Kentucky, plant to observe how Toyota can manufacture high-quality cars so efficiently. One reason Toyota has succeeded is by turning Henry Ford's mass-production principles on their head. Ford believed that the cheapest way to build cars was to churn out the largest number of autos by having workers repeatedly perform a simple task. By contrast, Toyota discovered that having a smaller number of workers, each capable of performing several tasks, produced cars with less inventory, less investment, and fewer mistakes. Toyota realized it must build smaller quantities of different kinds of cars to meet market requirements.

Figure 3.3 contrasts American mass production and Japanese "lean production" methods. Standard operating procedures in classic mass production try to maximize output by running machines with as few interruptions as possible. Every worker performs only one or two tasks over and over again. The goal is to keep the machines running. Standard operating procedures in a "lean production" environment require workers to minimize inventory and inventory costs while maintaining high quality standards. Workers have multiple jobs and responsibilities and are allowed to stop machines often to spot defects in each vehicle before batches are produced. Workers are encouraged to note every glitch, and, if necessary, to stop production to correct a problem.

In the Japanese auto manufacturing firms, a team of workers calculates how many seconds each task should take. Based on the speed of the assembly line, the team draws red lines to show where a car should be when work begins and where it should be when the work is completed. Workers are instructed not to start work before the car reaches the first line and to complete the job before it reaches the second line. The job is redesigned if the workers can complete the task in less time or if they cannot complete it in the time allotted.

Experts estimate that it will take years for U.S. auto makers to duplicate Toyota's efficiency. Not only must U.S. companies change the standard operating procedures on their assembly lines, but they must also find ways to involve auto workers in improving factories. This hasn't been easy because U.S. auto companies have traditionally been hierarchical and authoritarian.

Source: Doron P. Levin, "Toyota Plant in Kentucky Is Font of Ideas for U.S.," and "Detroit Is Slow to Learn from Japan," *The New York Times* (May 5, 1992).

To Think About: Why are standard operating procedures so difficult to change? What aspects of organizations must be addressed?

Everything else—technology, values, norms, public announcements, and so on—follows from these assumptions. You can see organizational culture at work by looking around your university or college. Some bedrock assumptions of university life are that professors know more than students, the reason students attend college is to learn, and classes follow a regular schedule. Organizational culture is a powerful unifying force, which restrains political conflict and promotes common understanding, agreement on procedures, and common practices. If we all share the same basic cultural assumptions, then agreement on other matters is more likely.

At the same time, organizational culture is a powerful restraint on change, especially technological change. Most organizations will do almost anything to avoid making changes in basic assumptions. At first new technologies are almost always used in ways that support existing cultures, and any technological change that threatens commonly held cultural assumptions usually meets a great deal of resistance. The Window on Organizations illustrates that one key longstanding assumption—that management should be very authoritarian and does not need to listen to the opinions of workers—is another reason why U.S. auto makers have been slow to switch to "lean production" methods.

Figure 3.3

How mass production has changed. A new leaner production system asks fewer workers to perform more tasks, thereby increasing efficiency and lowering costs. Adapted from Ty Ahmed-Taylor: "How Mass Production Has Changed," *The New York Times*, May 5, 1992. Original illustration by Al Granberg. Copyright © 1992 by The New York Times Company. Reprinted by permission.

NEW Toyota manufacturing process

DUTIES:
✓ Installing wheels and tires.
✓ Maintaining equipment
✓ Cleaning work area upon completion of other duties.
✓ Quality control.

1 If the worker spots a flaw in the production process, he pulls a cord to alert his group leader.

2 The group leader is notified when a quality control board lights up.

3 She responds in one of two ways: stopping the production line or having the flaw fixed while the car is still on the production line.

OLD Henry Ford manufacturing process

DUTIES:
✓ Installing wheels and tires.

The worker is limited to one task at a time, and does not call attention to flaws made during the production process.

Another worker checks for flaws. If a flaw is spotted, he alerts an inspector.

A repairman will fix the car before it leaves the plant but after the car goes through the entire production cycle.

Why Organizations Are So Different: Unique Features

Although all organizations do have common characteristics, no two organizations are identical. Organizations have different structures, goals, constituencies, leadership styles, tasks, and surrounding environments.

DIFFERENT ORGANIZATIONAL TYPES

One important way in which organizations differ is in their structure or shape. The differences among organizational structures are characterized in many ways. Mintzberg's classification is especially useful and simple (see Figure 3.4) for it identifies five basic kinds of organizations:

Entrepreneurial structure: Young, small firm in a fast-changing environment dominated by a single entrepreneur and managed by a single chief executive officer.

Entrepreneurial structure: Young, small, entrepreneurial firms in fast-changing environments tend to be organizations with simple structures, dominated by a single entrepreneur and managed by a single chief executive officer. Information systems typically are poorly planned and significantly behind fast-breaking production developments.

Machine bureaucracy: The large, classic bureaucracy exists in slowly changing environments, producing standardized products. It is dominated by a strategic senior management that centralizes information flow and decision authority.

Figure 3.4
Different types of organizations. Organizational types tend to be suited to specific environments: the simple entrepreneurial structure (A) and the adhocracy (E) are suited to fast changing environments. Machine (B) and divisionalized bureaucracies (D) are more suited to slowly-paced environmental changes. Professional bureaucracies (C) are suited to knowledge intensive industries where change is typically slow-paced. *Sources:* Parts A-D: Henry Mintzberg, *The Structuring of Organizations,* © 1979, pp. 311, 328, 329, 382. Reprinted by permission of Prentice-Hall, Englewood Cliffs, NJ. Part E: Courtesy of the National Film Board of Canada.

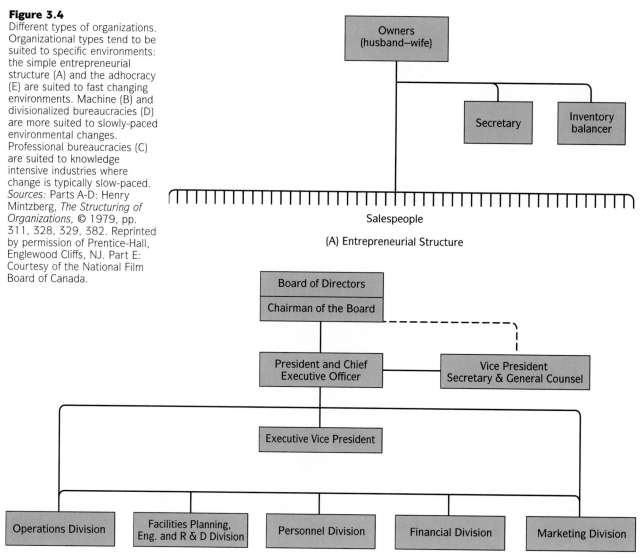

(A) Entrepreneurial Structure

(B) Machine Bureaucracy

Machine bureaucracy: Large bureaucracy organized into functional divisions that centralizes decision making, produces standard products, and exists in a slow-changing environment.

Professional bureaucracy: Knowledge-based organization such as a law firm or hospital that is dominated by department heads with weak centralized authority.

Divisionalized bureaucracy: Combination of many machine bureaucracies, each producing a different product or service, under one central headquarters.

Information systems tend to be well planned and centralized; they generally have been limited to traditional accounting, finance, simple planning, and administrative applications.

Professional bureaucracy: This structure is typical of law firms, school systems, accounting firms, hospitals, and other knowledge-based organizations that depend on the knowledge and expertise of professionals. Professional bureaucracies are dominated by department heads and have weak centralized authority. Professional members of the organization, who have considerable information and authority, create the product or service. Such organizations typically have primitive central information systems for time accounting and billing for professional services, but they often have very sophisticated knowledge work support systems for professionals. Knowledge work systems are described in greater detail in Chapter 10.

Divisionalized bureaucracy: This type of organization is the most common Fortune 500 form, a combination of many machine bureaucracies, each producing a different product or service, each operating in a different environment, all topped by a central headquarters. Information systems typically are elaborate and complex so that they can support central headquarters' financial planning and reporting requirements on one hand, and the operational requirements of

(C) Professional Bureaucracy

(D) Divisionalized Bureaucracy

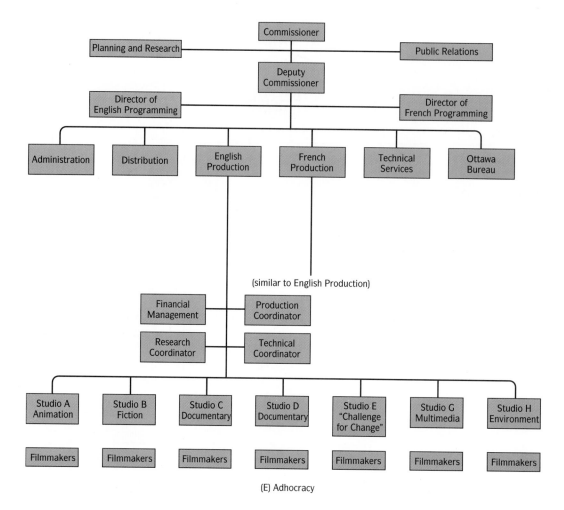

(E) Adhocracy

the divisions on the other hand. Typically there is a great deal of tension and conflict between central headquarters' IS groups and divisional IS groups.

Adhocracy: This "task force" organization is typically found in research organizations (such as the Rand Corporation), aerospace companies, medical, biomedical, electronic, and other high-tech firms that must respond to rapidly changing environments and markets or that derive revenue from government contracts. They are characterized by large groups of specialists organized into short-lived, multidisciplinary task forces focusing on new products and by weak central management that understands little of the technical work of its employees. Information systems typically are poorly developed at the central level but are often remarkably advanced within task forces, where experts build their unique systems for their narrow functions.

Adhocracy: Task force organization, such as a research organization, designed to respond to a rapidly changing environment and characterized by large groups of specialists organized into short-lived multidisciplinary task forces.

ENVIRONMENTS

Organizations have different environments, each exerting a powerful influence on the organization's structure. Generally, successful organizations in fast-changing environments are more like adhocracies—they are less hierarchical, with much authority delegated to subordinates. Organizations in stable environments tend to develop into machine bureaucracies.

Most people do not realize how fragile and short-lived formal organizations really are. Consider that less than 10 percent of Fortune 500 companies in 1918 survived more than fifty years; less than 4 percent of all federal government organizations ever created are still in existence; 50 percent of all new private organizations are out of business within five years; and bigness per se is only marginally protective against extinction and may only slow the decline (Laudon, 1989).

Working task forces use their combined skills to improve on the design and manufacturing of semiconductors at this Motorola research facility.

The main reasons for organizational failure are an inability to adapt to a rapidly changing environment and the lack of resources—particularly among young firms—to sustain even short periods of troubled times (Freeman et al., 1983). New technologies, new products, and changing public tastes and values put strains on any organization's culture, politics, operating procedures, and people. Fast-changing technologies, like information technology, pose a particular threat to organizations. At times, technological changes occur so radically as to constitute a "technological discontinuity," a sharp break in industry practice that either enhances or destroys the competence of firms in an industry (Tushman and Anderson, 1986). When technological discontinuities happen, most organizations fail to adapt, and many go out of existence, freeing up resources for new, younger organizations. For instance, Wang Laboratories, a leading manufacturer of minicomputers and word processors, was a dominant force in the computer industry during the 1970s and early 1980s. But when powerful desktop microcomputers reduced the need for minicomputers, Wang nearly went out of business. It had failed to adapt its products to the new technology.

OTHER DIFFERENCES
AMONG ORGANIZATIONS

Organizations have different shapes or structures for many other reasons also. They differ in their ultimate goals and the types of power used to achieve them. Some organizations have coercive goals (e.g., prisons); others have utilitarian goals (e.g., businesses). Still others have normative goals (universities, religious groups). Organizations also serve different groups or have different constituencies, some primarily benefiting their members, others benefiting clients, stockholders, or the public. The social roles or functions of organizations differ. Some organizations are primarily interested in politics (trying to change the distribution of benefits in society), while others play primarily economic roles (seeking to optimize the utilization of resources).

Clearly, the nature of leadership differs greatly from one organization to another, even in similar organizations that are devoted to the same goal. Some of the major leadership styles are democratic, authoritarian (even totalitarian), laissez-faire (leadership is absent), technocratic (according to technical criteria), or bureaucratic (strictly according to formal rules). These kinds of leadership can occur in any type of organization and seem to depend on chance and history.

Still another way organizations differ is by the tasks they perform and the technology they use. In some cases, organizations use routine tasks that could be programmed—that is, tasks may be reduced to formal rules that require little judgment (e.g., inventory reordering). Organizations that primarily perform routine tasks are typically like machine bureaucracies—they are hierarchical and run according to standard procedures. In other cases, organizations work with highly judgmental, nonroutine tasks (e.g., a consulting company that creates strategic plans for other companies).

As Chapters 1 and 2 make clear, all organizations have different levels, occupations, divisions, and groups. However, organizations differ in terms of what the levels are, who occupies them, and what tasks are assigned to the different levels. Moreover, each level has different concerns and a different framework of analysis. The impact of information systems will probably be different for different levels and groups within an organization. This can be seen in Figure 3.5, which describes typical organizational levels and the principal concerns at each level, providing examples of supporting information systems that are appropriate for each level.

At the individual and small-group levels of organization, information systems apply to a particular job, task, or project. At the department and division levels, information systems deal with a particular business function, product, or service. At the organization, interorganization, and organizational network levels, information systems support multiple products, services, and goals and facilitate alliances and coordination between two or more different organizations or groups of organizations.

Perhaps one of the most important and least heralded contributions of information systems is their support of a large variety of work groups that spring up in organizations and that are not even part of the formal organization chart.

Figure 3.5
Organizational levels and support systems. Systems are designed to support various levels of the organization.

Organizational Level		Activity	Example Support System
Individual	●	Job, task	Microcomputer application; personal client database; decision-support systems
Group		Project	Product scheduling; access to mainframe data; access to external data sources; dynamic information requirements; group DSS
Department		Major function	Accounts payable; warehouse; payroll; human resources; marketing; stable information requirements; MIS; major transaction systems
Division		Major product or service	Systems to support production, marketing, administration, and human resources; access to organizational financial and planning data; MIS; major transaction systems; on-line interactive systems
Organization		Multiple products, services, and goals	Integrated financial and planning systems; MIS; on-line interactive systems; ESS
Interorganization		Alliance Competition Exchange Contact	Communication systems; intelligence, observation, and monitoring systems
Organizational network		Sector of economy: related products, services; interdependencies	Informal communication systems; industry and sector-level formal reporting systems

Table 3.2 A SUMMARY OF SALIENT FEATURES OF ORGANIZATIONS

Common Features	Unique Features
Formal structure	Organizational Type
Standard Operating Procedures (SOPs)	Environments
Politics	Goals
Culture	Power
	Constituencies
	Function
	Leadership
	Tasks
	Technology
	Levels

While organization charts show the formal reporting relationships in organizations, much of the work of organizations is done by informal work groups such as task forces, interdepartmental committees, project teams, and committees. Recently developed system tools directed at support of work groups are discussed in Chapter 10.

We have developed a rather long list of salient features you should know about when considering information systems in organizations. As you can see in Table 3.2, the list of unique features of organizations is longer than the common features list. What this should suggest to you is that most organizations are quite unique. One consequence of this fact is that information systems are not completely portable from one organization to another. The impacts of systems will differ from one organization to another, and only by close analysis of a specific organization can a manager effectively design and manage information systems.

3.2 The Changing Role of Information Systems

With a solid foundation in the nature of organizations, you are now ready to look more closely at the relationship between information systems and organizations. We will begin by describing the developing role of information systems within organizations before we examine the effect information system technology has upon organizations.

The Evolution of Information Systems

Organizations have a direct impact on information technology by making decisions about how the technology will be used and what role it will play in the organization. In Chapters 1 and 2, we described the expanding role information systems have been playing within organizations. Information systems began in the 1950s as operational-level systems designed to handle elementary but vital transactions such as paying checks. By the late 1960s, management systems were being used for monitoring and controlling; and in the 1970s they were used for planning and simulations. By the 1980s, information systems had expanded into custom-built decision support systems and early strategic planning systems. In the 1990s, information systems are helping to create and disseminate knowledge and information throughout the organization through new knowledge work systems, applications providing company-wide access to data, and company-wide communications networks.

Organizations now are critically dependent upon systems and could not survive even occasional breakdowns: In most large organizations the entire cash flow is linked to information systems. System designers have begun to build redundant capabilities to account for this new situation.

Concurrent with the expanding functionality of information systems, changes occurred in the technical and organizational configuration of systems that have brought computing power and data much closer to the ultimate end users (see Figure 3.6). Isolated "electronic accounting machines" with limited functions in the 1950s gave way to large, centralized mainframe computers that served corporate headquarters and a few remote sites in the 1960s. In the 1970s, midsized minicomputers located in individual departments or divisions of the organization were networked to large centralized computers. Desktop microcomputers first were used independently and then were linked to minicomputers and large computers in the 1980s.

In the 1990s, the architecture for a fully networked organization emerged. In this new architecture, computers coordinate information flowing among desktops; between desktops, minicomputers, and mainframes; and perhaps among hundreds of smaller local networks. Information systems have become integral, one-line, interactive tools deeply involved in the minute-to-minute operations and decision making of large organizations. Chapters 4 and 7 provide detailed discussions of the technology of information systems.

The position and role of information system specialists have also evolved over time. The formal organizational unit or function that has emerged is called an **information systems department.** In the early years, the information systems group was composed mostly of **programmers,** highly trained technical specialists who wrote the software instructions for the computer. Today a growing proportion of staff members are **systems analysts,** who constitute the principal liaison between the information systems group and the rest of the organization. It is the system analyst's job to translate business problems and requirements into information requirements and systems. **Information systems managers** are leaders of teams of programmers and analysts; project managers; physical facility managers; telecommunications managers; heads of office automation groups; and, finally, managers of computer operations and data entry staff. **End users** are representatives of departments outside of the information systems group for whom applications are developed. These users are playing an increasingly large role in the design and development of information systems.

The size of the information systems department can vary greatly, depending on the role of information systems in the organization and on the organization's size. Today information systems groups often act as powerful change agents within the organization, suggesting new business strategies and new information-based products and coordinating both the development of technology and the planned changes in the organization.

Information systems department: The formal organizational unit that is responsible for the information systems function in the organization.

Programmers: Highly trained technical specialists who write computer software instructions.

Systems analysts: Specialists who translate business problems and requirements into information requirements and systems.

Information systems managers: Leaders of the various specialists in the information systems department.

End users: Representatives of departments outside the information systems group for whom information systems applications are developed.

Why Organizations Build Information Systems

The traditional answer to the question, "Why do organizations adopt information systems?" may seem very simple. Obviously, organizations adopt information systems to become more efficient, to save money, and to reduce the work force. Although this response may have been generally true in the past, it no longer comprises the only or even the primary reason for adopting systems.

Information systems have become vitally important simply to stay in business. Improvements in decision making (speed, accuracy, comprehensiveness), serving ever higher customer and client expectations, coordinating dispersed groups in an organization, complying with governmental reporting regulations, and exercising tighter control over personnel and expenditures have become important reasons for building systems (Huff and Munro, 1985).

Figure 3.6
The development of information architecture of organizations. The last five decades have seen dramatic changes in the technical and organizational configurations of systems. During the 1950s organizations were dependent on computers for a few critical functions. The 1960s witnessed the development of large centralized machines. By the late 1970s and into the 1980s information architecture became complex and information systems included telecommunications links to distribute information. During the 1990s information architecture is an enterprise wide information utility.

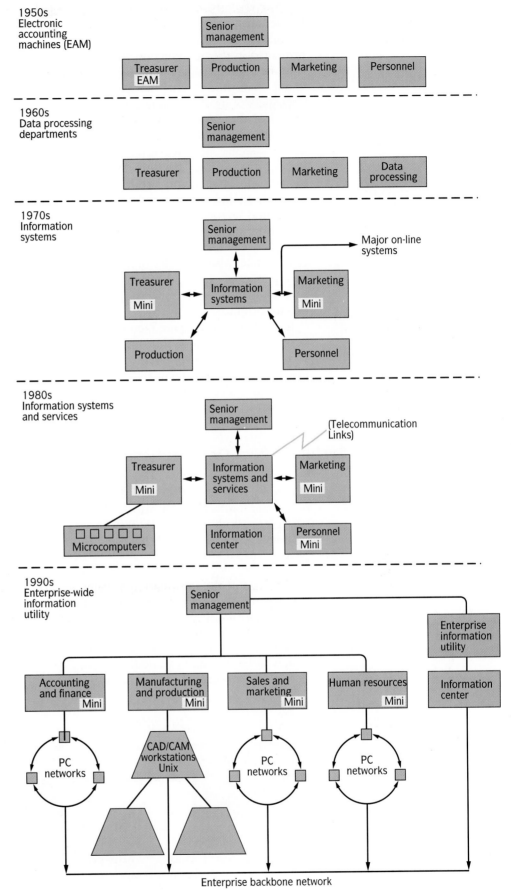

More recently, organizations have been seeking strategic advantage from information systems. We have already seen numerous examples in Chapter 2, such as Gillette, Citibank, Baxter, and Schwab, as well as the Schneider example presented in the introduction to this chapter.

Some organizations build certain systems simply because they are more innovative than others. They have values that encourage any kind of innovation, regardless of its direct economic benefit to the company. Figure 3.7 illustrates a model of the systems development process that includes many considerations other than economic. This model divides the explanations for why organizations adopt systems into two groups: *external environmental factors* and *internal institutional factors* (Laudon, 1985).

Environmental factors:
Factors external to the organization that influence the adoption and design of information systems.

Environmental factors are factors that are external to the organization that influence the adoption and design of information systems. Some external environmental factors are rising costs of labor or other resources, the competitive actions of other organizations, and changes in government regulations. In general, these can be thought of as *environmental constraints*. At the same time, the environment also provides organizations with *opportunities*: new technologies, new sources of capital, the development of new production processes, the demise of a competitor, or a new government program that increases the demand for certain products.

Institutional factors: Factors internal to the organization that influence the adoption and design of information systems.

Institutional factors are factors internal to the organization that influence the adoption and design of information systems. They include values, norms, and vital interests that govern matters of strategic importance to the organization. For instance, the top management of a corporation can decide that it needs to exercise much stronger control over the inventory process and therefore decides to develop an inventory information system. (For a similar model, see Kraemer et al., 1989.)

How Information Systems Affect Organizations

Having described the evolution of information systems and how systems may be shaped by organizations, we now shall look at the question: How do information systems affect organizations? To answer this question, we need to summarize a large body of research and theory. Some researchers base their work on economics; others take a behavioral approach.

ECONOMIC THEORIES

From an economic standpoint, information system technology can be viewed as a factor of production that can be freely substituted for capital and labor. As the cost of information systems technology falls, it is substituted for labor that historically has a rising cost. Over time, less and less capital and labor are required for a given output. Hence, information technology should result in a decline in the number of middle managers and clerical workers as information technology substitutes for their labor.

Figure 3.7
The systems development process. External environmental factors and internal institutional factors influence the types of information systems the organizations select, develop, and use.

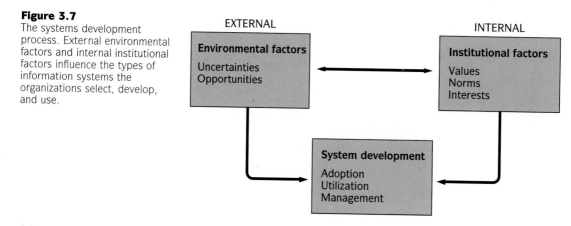

Information technology also helps firms contract in size because it can reduce transaction costs—the costs incurred by a firm when it buys on the marketplace what it does not make itself (Williamson, 1985). Traditionally, firms sought to reduce transaction costs by getting bigger: hiring more employees, vertically integrating (as General Motors did by setting up its own companies to produce its auto parts), buying their own suppliers and distributors, and taking over smaller companies. Information technology, by helping firms lower the cost of market participation (transaction costs), make it worthwhile for firms to contract with external suppliers instead of using internal sources of supply. As a result, the size of firms (measured by the number of employees) could stay constant or contract even though they increased their revenues. Finally, organizations contract in size because information technology reduces overall management costs, lowering the costs of acquiring and analyzing information required to monitor and supervise employees.

BEHAVIORAL THEORIES   While economic theories try to explain how large numbers of firms act in the marketplace, behavioral theories from sociology, psychology, and political science are more useful for describing the behavior of individual firms. Behavioral research has found that there is little evidence that information systems automatically transform organizations, although the systems may be instrumental in accomplishing this goal once senior management decides to pursue this end. Instead, researchers have observed an intricately choreographed relationship in which organizations and information technology mutually influence each other.

Behavioral researchers have theorized that information technology could change the hierarchy of decision making in organizations by lowering the costs of information acquisition and broadening the distribution of information. Information technology could bring information directly from operating units to senior managers, thereby eliminating middle managers and their clerical support workers. Information technology could permit senior managers to contact lower-level operating units directly through the use of networked telecommunications and computers, eliminating middle management intermediaries. Alternatively, information technology could distribute information directly to lower-level workers, who could then make their own decisions based on their own knowledge and information without any management intervention. Other research suggests that computerization gives more information to middle managers, empowering them to make more important decisions than in the past, thus reducing the need for large numbers of lower-level workers (Shore, 1983).

In post-industrial societies, whose primary economic outputs are services and information, authority relies more on knowledge and competence than on mere formal position. The shape of organizations should "flatten," since professional workers tend to be self-managing; and decision making should become more decentralized as knowledge and information become more widespread throughout (Drucker, 1988). Information technology should lead then to "task force" networked organizations in which groups of professionals come together—face-to-face or electronically—for short periods of time to accomplish a specific task (e.g., designing a new automobile); once the task is accomplished, the individuals join other task forces. All organizations should look more like Mintzberg's Adhocracies.

Consultants and popular business journals have suggested that organizations will also become flatter and more horizontal by reshaping themselves around business processes instead of the traditional, discrete functional departments. Figure 3.8 shows the differences between a traditional vertical organization, where groups are arranged by function, and the proposed horizontal organization, where teams are arranged by processes. For instance, instead of focusing independently on the manufacturing function in order to reduce the cost to produce each unit, management might look at the entire logistics process from receipt of raw material to receipt by the customer. Information systems can help

Figure 3.8
Some researchers and popular writers argue that information technology allows firms to reorganize themselves from vertical organizations to horizontal organizations where groups of people are arranged by processes. *Source:* John Pepper, "Horizontal Organization," *InformationWeek*, August 17, 1992. Copyright © 1992 by CMP Publications, Inc., 600 Community Drive, Manhasset, NY 11030. Reprinted from *InformationWeek* with permission.

organizations achieve great efficiencies by automating parts of these processes or by helping organizations rethink and streamline these processes. The Window on Technology describes how information technology is helping the Xerox Corporation redesign its organization.

It is not clear that all modern organizations will undergo this transformation: General Motors will have many self-managed knowledge workers in certain divisions, but it still will have a manufacturing division structured as a "machine bureaucracy," to use Mintzberg's category. In general, the shape of organizations historically changes with the business cycle and with the latest management fashions. When times are good and profits are high, firms hire large numbers of supervisory personnel; when times are tough, they let go many of these same people (Mintzberg, 1979). It is not known if the shrinkage of some firms' middle management in the early 1990s resulted from hard times or from computerization.

Another behavioral approach views information systems as the outcome of political competition between organizational subgroups for influence over the policies, procedures, and resources of the organization (Laudon, 1974; Keen, 1981; Kling, 1980; Laudon, 1986). Information systems inevitably become bound up in the politics of organizations because they influence access to a key resource—namely, information. Information systems can affect who does what to whom, when, where, and how in an organization. For instance, a major study of the efforts of the FBI to develop a national computerized criminal history system (a single national listing of the criminal histories, arrests, and convictions of over 36 million individuals in the United States) found that the state governments strongly resisted the FBI's efforts because this information would give the federal government, and the FBI in particular, the ability to monitor how states use criminal histories. This was a function that the states felt they could accomplish without federal interference. The states resisted the development of this national system quite successfully (Laudon, 1986).

Because information systems potentially change an organization's structure, culture, politics, and work, there is often considerable resistance to them when they are introduced. There are several ways to visualize organizational resistance. Leavitt (1965) used a diamond shape to illustrate the interrelated and

TECHNOLOGY

Is Xerox Becoming a Post-Industrial Organization?

Xerox Corporation virtually created the modern office. Its engineers and scientists invented the laser printer, the personal computer, and the fax machine. But it nearly went out of business because of Japanese competition and a failed initiative in the 1980s to move into financial services. Other companies, such as Apple Computer Inc., reaped the benefits from commercializing Xerox's inventions.

So Xerox decided to change its corporate identity. Instead of pushing copy machines, it decided to become a "document company" that focuses on products to help office workers create, use, and share reports, memos, and data. In 1992, Xerox designed a new horizontal organization that divides its office products business into nine new businesses aimed at markets such as small businesses and individuals, office document systems, and engineering systems. Each business does its own financial reporting and is led by a team. Xerox rearranged its manufacturing so that focused factories are dedicated to specific businesses. Most of the businesses sell

through a Customer Operations Group, which combines sales, shipping, installation, service, and billing.

To help empowered work groups and employees challenge its traditional bureaucracy, and to distribute knowledge and accountability throughout the organization, Xerox built a massive worldwide data network. The corporation began linking its worldwide computing facilities in 1984 and now has one of the world's largest corporate networks. Xerox employees can exchange information and documents anywhere in the world within minutes. The network links 43,000 desktop devices used by 65,000 of Xerox's 110,000 employees worldwide in 18 time zones.

This enterprise-wide network facilitates independent work groups. For instance, international marketing teams can easily exchange documents without being constrained by location. With just a few keystrokes, a manager can pull into his or her workstation data, which could be graphics, engineering drawings, text, or

scanned images, from Japan, Brazil, Mexico, and California. Engineers in Xerox's Palo Alto research center can work closely with marketing executives at Xerox's Connecticut corporate headquarters to bring new ideas and new products rapidly to market.

The next step is to tie Xerox's mobile employees into the corporate network through the development of "virtual offices." Xerox believes its workers of the future may not always be in buildings, and it wants to accommodate these employees.

Sources: Tim Smart, "Can Xerox Duplicate Its Glory Days?" *Business Week,* October 4, 1993; Bob Violino with Chuck Appleby, "Turning the Page at Xerox," *InformationWEEK* March 23, 1992; and Thomas A. Stewart, "The Search for the Organization of Tomorrow," *Fortune* May 18, 1992.

To Think About: What role did technology play in Xerox's reorganization? What features of Xerox's organization will change? How easy will it be to make these changes?

mutually adjusting character of technology and organization (see Figure 3.9). Here, changes in technology are absorbed, deflected, and defeated by organizational task arrangements, structures, and people. In this model, the only way to bring about change is to change the technology, tasks, structure, and people simultaneously. Other authors have spoken about the need to "unfreeze" organizations before introducing an innovation, quickly implementing it, and "refreezing" or institutionalizing the change (Kolb, 1970; Alter and Ginzberg, 1978).

Chapter 9 describes how organizational resistance causes many systems failures. Because of the difficulties of introducing new information systems, experienced systems observers approach social change through systems very cautiously.

Implications for the Design and Understanding of Information Systems

The primary significance of this section is to show you that you cannot take a narrow view of organizations and their relationship to information systems. It involves more than simply purchasing and installing technology. Organizational innovation is difficult and complex to achieve and often leads to system failure

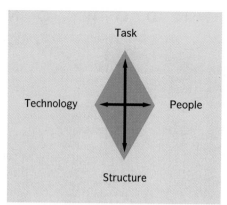

(see Chapter 9 for a description of organizational resistance in information systems projects). Experienced systems observers and managers approach systems change very cautiously. In order to reap the benefits of technology, organizational innovations—changes in the culture, values, norms, and interest-group alignments—must be managed with as much planning and effort as technology changes.

No formula takes these organizational factors into account. As a manager or designer, you should develop a checklist of factors to consider in your systems plans. In our experience, the central organizational factors in rough rank order of importance are these:

- The *environment* in which the organization must function.
- The *structure* of the organization: hierarchy, specialization, standard operating procedures.
- The *culture and politics* of the organization.
- The *type* of organization.
- The *nature and style* of leadership.
- The extent of support and understanding of *top management*.
- The *level* of organization at which the system resides.
- The principal *interest groups* affected by the system.
- The *kinds of tasks and decisions* that the information system is designed to assist.
- The *sentiments and attitudes* of workers in the organization who will be using the information systems.
- The *history of the organization:* past investments in information technology, existing skills, important programs, and human resources.

3.3 The Role of Managers in the Organization

Managers play a key role in organizations. Their responsibilities range from making decisions, to writing reports, to attending meetings, to arranging birthday parties. To determine how information systems can benefit managers, we must first examine what managers do and what information they need for decision making and their other functions. We must also understand how decisions are made and what kinds of decisions can be supported by formal information systems.

Classical Descriptions of Management

The **classical model of management**, which describes what managers do, was largely unquestioned for the more than 70 years since the 1920s. Henri Fayol and other early writers first described the five classical functions of managers as *planning, organizing, coordinating, deciding,* and *controlling.* This description of management activities dominated management thought for a long time and is still popular today.

But these terms actually describe managerial functions and are unsatisfactory as a description of what managers actually do. The terms do not address what managers do when they plan, decide things, or control the work of others. We need a more fine-grained understanding of how managers actually behave.

Behavioral Models

Contemporary behavioral scientists have discovered from observation that managers do not behave as the classical model of management led us to believe. Kotter (1982), for example, describes the morning activities of the president of an investment management firm.

7:35 A.M. Richardson arrives at work, unpacks her briefcase, gets some coffee, and begins making a list of activities for the day.

7:45 A.M. Bradshaw (a subordinate) and Richardson converse about a number of topics and exchange pictures recently taken on summer vacations.

8:00 A.M. They talk about a schedule of priorities for the day.

8:20 A.M. Wilson (a subordinate) and Richardson talk about some personnel problems, cracking jokes in the process.

8:45 A.M. Richardson's secretary arrives, and they discuss her new apartment and arrangements for a meeting later in the morning.

8:55 A.M. Richardson goes to a morning meeting run by one of her subordinates. Thirty people are there, and Richardson reads during the meeting.

11:05 A.M. Richardson and her subordinates return to the office and discuss a difficult problem. They try to define the problem and outline possible alternatives. She lets the discussion roam away from and back to the topic again and again. Finally, they agree on a next step.

In this example, it is difficult to determine which activities constitute Richardson's planning, coordinating, and decision making. **Behavioral models** state that the actual behavior of managers appears to be less systematic, more informal, less reflective, more reactive, less well organized, and much more frivolous than students of information systems and decision making generally expect it to be.

Observers find that managerial behavior actually has five attributes that differ greatly from the classical description: First, managers perform a great deal of work at an unrelenting pace—studies have found that managers engage in more than 600 different activities each day, with no break in their pace. Second, managerial activities are fragmented; most activities last for less than nine minutes; only 10 percent of the activities exceed one hour in duration. Third, managers prefer speculation, hearsay, gossip—they want current, specific, and ad hoc information (printed information often will be too old). Fourth, they prefer verbal forms of communication to written forms because verbal media provide greater flexibility, require less effort, and bring a faster response. Fifth, managers give high priority to maintaining a diverse and complex web of contacts that acts as an informal information system.

Effective managers spend a great deal of time building an interpersonal network composed of people at virtually all levels of the organization, from warehouse staff to clerical support personnel to other managers and senior management. Managers use their networks to execute personal agendas, and to accomplish their own goals (Kotter, 1982).

Managerial roles:
Expectations of the activities that managers should perform in an organization.

Interpersonal roles:
Mintzberg's classification for managerial roles where managers act as figureheads and leaders for the organization.

Informational roles:
Mintzberg's classification for managerial roles where managers act as the nerve centers of their organizations, receiving and disseminating critical information.

Decisional roles: Mintzberg's classification for managerial roles where managers initiate activities, handle disturbances, allocate resources, and negotiate conflicts.

Analyzing managers' day-to-day behavior, Mintzberg found that it could be classified into ten managerial roles. (See Table 3.3.) **Managerial roles** are expectations of the activities that managers should perform in an organization. Mintzberg found that these managerial roles fell into three categories: interpersonal, informational, and decisional.

Interpersonal roles. Managers act as figureheads for the organization when they represent their companies to the outside world and perform symbolic duties such as giving out employee awards. Managers act as leaders, attempting to motivate, counsel, and support subordinates. Managers also act as a liaison between various levels of the organization; within each of these levels, they serve as a liaison among the members of the management team. Managers provide time and favors, which they expect to be returned.

Informational roles. Managers act as the nerve centers of their organization, receiving the most concrete, up-to-date information and redistributing it to those who need to be aware of it. Managers are therefore information disseminators and spokespersons for their organization.

Decisional roles. Managers make decisions. They act as entrepreneurs by initiating new kinds of activities; they handle disturbances arising in the organization; they allocate resources to staff members who need them; and they negotiate conflicts and mediate between conflicting groups in the organization.

Implications for System Design

What are the implications for the organization's use of information systems? While managers do use formal information systems to plan, organize, and coordinate, these systems may be more limited in their impact on managers than was heretofore believed. Managers appreciate verbal, current, flexible sources of information. They will want to use information systems for such vital (to their work) tasks as interpersonal communication, setting and carrying out personal agendas, and establishing a network throughout the organization. Ad hoc (less formal) information systems that can be built quickly, use more current and up-to-date information, and can be adjusted to the unique situations of a specific group of managers will be highly valued by the modern manager.

Table 3.3   MANAGERIAL ROLES AND SUPPORTING INFORMATION SYSTEMS

Role	Behavior	Support Systems
Interpersonal Roles		
Figurehead		None exist
Leader	Interpersonal	None exist
Liaison		Electronic communication systems
Informational Roles		
Nerve center		Management information systems
Disseminator	Information	Mail, office systems
Spokesman	processing	Office and professional systems Workstations
Decisional Roles		
Entrepreneur		None exist
Disturbance handler	Decision	None exist
Resource allocator	making	DSS systems
Negotiator		None exist

Source: Authors and Mintzberg (1971).

Systems designers and builders must appreciate the importance of creating systems that can communicate with other information sources outside the organization and provide an effective means of communication among managers and employees within the organization (we discuss these kinds of systems in detail in later chapters).

Table 3.3, based upon Mintzberg's role classifications, is one look at where systems can help managers and where they cannot. The table shows that information systems do not as of yet contribute a great deal to many areas of management life. These areas will undoubtedly provide great opportunities for future systems and system designers.

3.4 Managers and Decision Making

The classical management theorists viewed decision making as the center of managerial activities. Although we now know that this is not exactly the case, decision making remains one of the more challenging roles of a manager. Information systems have helped managers communicate and distribute information; however, they have provided only limited assistance for management decision making. Because decision making is an area that system designers have sought most of all to affect (with mixed success), we now turn our attention to this issue.

The Process of Decision Making

Strategic decision making: Determining the long-term objectives, resources, and policies of an organization.

Management control: Monitoring how efficiently or effectively resources are utilized and how well operational units are performing.

Knowledge-level decision making: Evaluating new ideas for products and services and ways to communicate new knowledge and distribute information.

Operational control: Deciding how to carry out tasks specified by upper and middle management and establishing criteria for completion and resource utilization.

Unstructured decisions: Nonroutine decisions in which the decision maker must provide judgment, evaluation, and insights into the problem definition; there is no agreed-upon procedure for making such decisions.

Structured decisions: Decisions that are repetitive, routine, and have a definite procedure for handling them.

Decision making can be classified by organizational level, corresponding to the strategic, management, knowledge, and operational levels of the organization introduced in Chapter 1 (see Anthony; 1965). **Strategic decision making** determines the objectives, resources, and policies of the organization. Decision making for **management control** is principally concerned with how efficiently and effectively resources are utilized and how well operational units are performing. **Operational control** decision making determines how to carry out the specific tasks set forth by strategic and middle-management decision makers. **Knowledge-level decision making** deals with evaluating new ideas for products and services, ways to communicate new knowledge, and ways to distribute information throughout the organization.

Within each of these levels of decision making researchers classify decisions as *structured* and *unstructured*. **Unstructured decisions** are those in which the decision maker must provide judgment, evaluation, and insights into the problem definition. Each of these decisions are novel, important, and nonroutine, and there is no well-understood or agreed-upon procedure for making them (Gorry and Scott-Morton, 1971). **Structured decisions,** by contrast, are repetitive, routine, and involve a definite procedure for handling so that they do not have to be treated each time as if they were new. Some decisions are semistructured; in such cases, only part of the problem has a clear-cut answer provided by an accepted procedure.

Combining these two views of decision making produces the grid shown in Figure 3.10. In general, operational control personnel face fairly well-structured problems. In contrast, strategic planners tackle highly unstructured problems. Many of the problems encountered by knowledge workers are fairly unstructured as well. Nevertheless, each level of the organization contains both structured and unstructured problems.

In the past, most of the success in modern information systems came in dealing with structured, operational, and management control problems. But now most of the exciting applications are occurring in the management, knowledge, and strategic planning areas, where problems are either semistructured or are totally unstructured. (We discuss these applications in later chapters.)

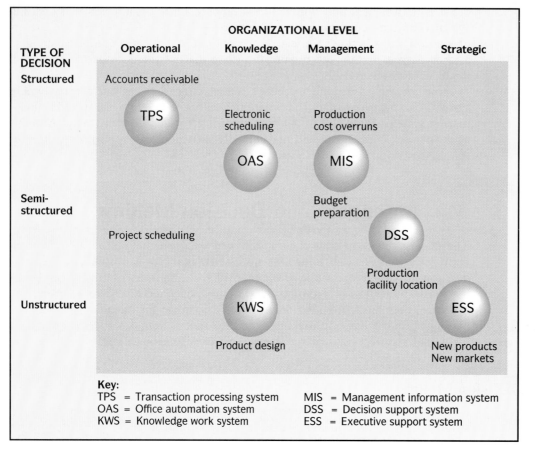

Figure 3.10
Different kinds of information systems at the various organization levels support different types of decisions. Source: Gorry and Scott-Morton (1971).

STAGES OF DECISION
MAKING

Making decisions is not a single activity that takes place all at once. The process consists of several different activities that take place at different times. Simon (1960) described four different stages in decision making: intelligence, design, choice, and implementation.

Intelligence consists of *identifying and understanding* the problems occurring in the organization—why the problem, where, and with what effects. Traditional MIS systems that deliver a wide variety of detailed information can help identify problems, especially if the systems report exceptions.

During solution **design,** the individual *designs* possible solutions to the problems. Smaller DSS systems are ideal in this stage of decision making because they operate on simple models, can be developed quickly, and can be operated with limited data.

Choice consists of *choosing* among solution alternatives. Here the decision maker might need a larger DSS system to develop more extensive data on a variety of alternatives and to use complex analytic models needed to account for all of the costs, consequences, and opportunities.

During solution **implementation,** managers can use a reporting system that delivers routine reports on the progress of a specific solution. Support systems can range from full-blown MIS systems to much smaller systems as well as project-planning software operating on microcomputers.

In general, the stages of decision making do not necessarily follow a linear path. Think again about the decision you made to attend a *specific* college. At any point in the decision-making process, you may have to loop back to a previous stage (see Figure 3.11). For instance, one can often come up with

Intelligence: The first of Simon's four stages of decision making, when the individual collects information to identify problems occurring in the organization.

Design: Simon's second stage of decision making, when the individual conceives of possible alternative solutions to a problem.

Choice: Simon's third stage of decision making, when the individual selects among the various solution alternatives.

Implementation: Simon's final stage of decision making, when the individual puts the decision into effect and reports on the progress of the solution.

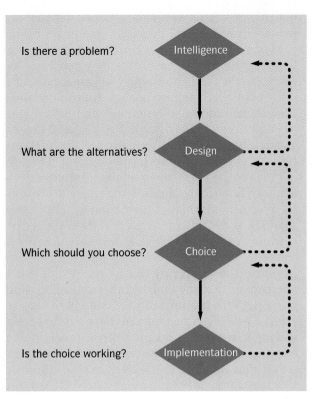

Figure 3.11
The decision-making process. Decisions are often arrived at after a series of iterations and evaluations at each stage in the process. The decision maker often must loop back through one or more of the stages before completing the process.

several designs but may not be certain about whether a specific design meets the requirements for the particular problem. This situation requires additional intelligence work. Alternatively, one can be in the process of implementing a decision, only to discover that it is not working. In such a case, one is forced to repeat the design or choice stage.

Individual Models of Decision Making

A number of models attempt to describe how people make decisions. Some of these models focus on individual decision making, whereas others focus on decision making in groups.

The basic assumption behind individual models of decision making is that human beings are in some sense rational. The **rational model** of human behavior is built on the idea that people engage in basically consistent, rational, value-maximizing calculations. Under this model, an individual identifies goals, ranks all possible alternative actions by their contribution to those goals, and chooses the alternative that contributes most to those goals. The individual can fully perceive all alternatives and consequences.

Rational model: Model of human behavior believing that people make consistent, value-maximizing calculations within certain constraints.

Criticisms of this model show that in fact people cannot specify all of the alternatives and that most individuals do not have singular goals and so are unable to rank all alternatives and consequences. Perhaps the most basic criticism is that many decisions are so complex that calculating the choice (even if done by computer) is virtually impossible (in a "simple" chess game it would take a machine 10^{95} years operating at a rate of 1 million instructions per second (MIPS) to test all moves, countermoves, and counter-countermoves from start to finish just to determine the first move!). One modification to the rational model states that instead of searching through all alternatives, people actually choose the first available alternative that moves them toward their ultimate goal (Simon, 1960). Another modification alters the rational model by suggesting that in making policy decisions, people refrain from sweeping changes and choose policies most like the previous policy (Lindblom, 1959). Finally, some scholars point out that people do not make choices, but that decision making is a continuous process in which final decisions are always being modified.

Modern psychology has further qualified the rational model by research that finds that humans differ *in how they maximize their values* and in the *frames of reference* they use to interpret information and make choices. **Cognitive style** describes underlying personality dispositions toward the treatment of information, the selection of alternatives, and the evaluation of consequences. McKenney and Keen (1974) described two decision-making cognitive styles: systematic versus intuitive types. **Systematic decision makers** approach a problem by structuring it in terms of some formal method. They evaluate and gather information in terms of their structured method. **Intuitive decision makers** approach a problem with multiple methods, using trial and error to find a solution. They tend not to structure information gathering or evaluation. Neither style is considered superior to the other. There are different ways of being rational.

More recent psychological research actually challenges the underlying assumption of rational models by showing that humans have built-in biases that can distort decision making. Worse, people can be manipulated into choosing alternatives that they might otherwise reject simply by changing the *frame of reference*. One example can be found in the research of Tversky and Kahneman (1981), who claim that humans have a deep-seated tendency to avoid risks when seeking gains but to accept risks in order to avoid losses. Putting this understanding into practice, the credit card industry lobbied retailers aggressively to ensure that any price break given to cash customers would be presented publicly as a "cash discount" rather than a "credit card surcharge." Consumers would be less willing to accept a surcharge than to forgo a discount. Other biases are listed in Table 3.4.

Cognitive style: Underlying personality disposition toward the treatment of information, selection of alternatives, and evaluation of consequences.

Systematic decision makers: Cognitive style that describes people who approach a problem by structuring it in terms of some formal method.

Intuitive decision makers: Cognitive style that describes people who approach a problem with multiple methods in an unstructured manner, using trial and error to find a solution.

Organizational Models of Decision Making

Organizational models: Models of decision making that take into account the structural and political characteristics of an organization.

Decision making is often not performed by a single individual but by entire groups or organizations. **Organizational models** of decision making take into account the structural and political characteristics of an organization. Bureaucratic, political, and even "garbage can" models have been proposed to describe how decision making takes place in organizations. We shall now consider each of these models.

Table 3.4	PSYCHOSOCIAL BIASES IN DECISION MAKING

1. People are more sensitive to negative consequences than to positive ones; for example, students generally refuse to flip a coin for $10 unless they have a chance to win $30.

2. People have no sensible model for dealing with improbable events and either ignore them or overestimate their likelihood; for example, one-in-a-million lotteries are popular, and people have an exaggerated fear of shark attacks.

3. People are more willing to accept a negative outcome if it is presented as a cost rather than a loss; for example, a man will continue playing tennis at an expensive club, despite a painful tennis elbow, by accepting the pain as a cost of the game rather than quit and accept the loss of an annual membership fee.

4. People given the same information will prefer alternatives with certain gains rather than alternatives with certain losses; people will gamble to avoid certain losses. For example, students and professional health workers were given the choice between alternative programs to fight a new disease that was expected to kill 600 people. When described in terms of lives saved, a large majority preferred a program that was certain to save 200 people over a program that had a possibility—but no certainty—of saving all 600. On the other hand, when presented in terms of lives lost, a large majority rejected a program that was guaranteed to lose 400 lives and preferred to gamble, against the odds, on a program that might save everyone but probably would lose everyone.

Source: Tversky and Kahneman, 1981.

BUREAUCRATIC MODELS

Bureaucratic models: Models of decision making where decisions are shaped by the organization's standard operating procedures (SOPs).

According to **bureaucratic models,** the most important goal of organizations is the preservation of the organization itself (e.g., the maintenance of budget, manpower, and territory). The reduction of uncertainty is another major goal. Policy tends to be incremental, only marginally different from the past, because radical policy departures involve too much uncertainty. These models depict organizations generally as not "choosing" or "deciding" in a rational sense. Rather, according to bureaucratic models, whatever organizations do is the result of standard operating procedures (SOPs) honed over years of active use.

The problems facing any large organization are too massive and too complex to be attended to by the organization as a whole. The particular actions chosen by an organization are instead an output of one or several organizational subunits (e.g., marketing, production, finance, human resources). Each of these subunits has a number of standard operating procedures—tried and proven techniques—that it invokes to solve a problem. Organizations rarely change these SOPs because they may have to change personnel and incur risks (who knows if the new techniques work better than the old ones?).

Taken together, these subunit repertoires constitute the range of short-term effective actions that leaders of organizations can take. Although senior management and leaders are hired to coordinate and lead the organization, they are effectively trapped by these parochial subunits that feed information upward and that provide standard solutions. Senior management cannot decide to act in ways that the major subunits cannot support. As a United States president discovered in a moment of national crisis, his actions were largely constrained not by his imagination but by what his pawns, bishops, and knights were trained to do (see the Window on Management).

Some organizations do, of course, change; they learn new ways of behaving, and they can be led. But all of these changes require a long time. Look around and you will find many organizations doing pretty much what they did ten, twenty, or even thirty years ago.

POLITICAL MODELS OF ORGANIZATIONAL CHOICE

Political models: Models of decision making where decisions result from competition and bargaining among the organization's interest groups and key leaders.

Power in organizations is shared; even the lowest-level workers have some power. At the top, power is concentrated in the hands of a few. For many reasons, leaders differ in their opinions about what the organization should do, and, as we made clear earlier in this chapter, these differences do matter.

Each individual in an organization, especially at the top, is a key player in the game of politics. In **political models** of decision making, what an organization does is a result of political bargains struck among key leaders and interest groups. Actions are not necessarily rational, except in a political sense. The outcome is not what any individual necessarily wanted. Instead, policy-organizational action is a compromise, a mixture of conflicting tendencies. Organizations do not come up with "solutions" that are "chosen" to solve some "problem." They come up with compromises that reflect the conflicts, the major stakeholders, the diverse interests, the unequal power, and the confusion that constitute politics.

"GARBAGE CAN" MODEL

Garbage can model: Model of decision making that states that organizations are not rational and that decisions are solutions that become attached to problems for accidental reasons.

All of the preceding models of organizational choice take as their starting point the basic notion that organizations try to adapt, and for the most part do so successfully, to changing environmental conditions. However, as we pointed out earlier in this chapter, many organizations do not survive. When severely challenged by a changing environment, organizations often prove to be nonadaptive, incapable of learning, and unchanging. A relatively new theory of decision making, called the **"garbage can" model,** takes this view. Decision making is seen as largely accidental, the product of a stream of solutions, problems, and situations that are randomly associated.

If this model is correct, it should not be surprising that the wrong solutions are applied to the wrong problems in an organization, or that, over time, a large

MANAGEMENT

Blockade by the Book

In the evening of October 23, 1962, the Executive Committee of the President (EXCOM), a high-level working group of senior advisors to President John F. Kennedy, decided to impose a naval quarantine or blockade on Cuba in order to force the Soviet Union to remove its intermediate-range ballistic missiles from the island, located 90 miles south of Miami.

The naval blockade was chosen only after the air force reported that it could not conduct what the politicians in EXCOM called a "surgical air strike" to remove the missiles. Instead, the air force recommended a massive strategic air campaign against a number of ground, air, and naval Cuban targets. This was considered extreme by EXCOM, and the only other alternative seemed to be a blockade that would give Chairman Khrush-chev plenty of time to think and several face-saving alternatives.

But EXCOM was worried that the navy might blunder when implementing the blockade and cause an incident, which in turn could lead to World War III. Secretary of Defense Robert McNamara visited the navy's Chief of Naval Operations to make the point that the blockade was not intended to shoot Russians but to send a political message.

McNamara wanted to know the following: Which ship would make the first interception? Were Russian-speaking officers on board? How would submarines be dealt with? Would Russian ships be given the opportunity to turn back? What would the navy do if Russian captains refused to answer questions about their cargo?

At that point, the Chief of Naval Operations picked up the Manual of Naval Regulations, waved it at McNamara, and said "It's all in there." McNamara responded, "I don't give a damn what John Paul Jones would have done. I want to know what you are going to do tomorrow!"

The visit ended with the navy officer inviting the Secretary of Defense to go back to his office and let the navy run the blockade.

Source: Graham T. Allison, *Essence of Decision. 1971.*

To Think About: What does this vignette tell you about decision making at a time of national crisis? Is such decision making rational?

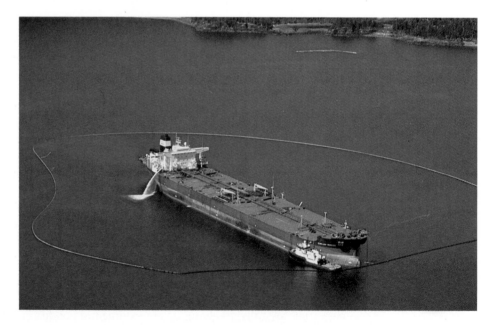

The Exxon Valdez oil tanker disaster in the Prince William sound in March 1989 is a classic example of the results of the "garbage can" model of decision making.

number of organizations make critical mistakes that lead to their demise. The Exxon Corporation's delayed response to the 1989 Alaska oil spill is an example. Within an hour after the Exxon tanker *Valdez* ran aground in Alaska's Prince William Sound on March 29, 1989, workers were preparing emergency equipment; however, the aid was not dispatched. Instead of sending out emergency crews, the Alyeska Pipeline Service Company (which was responsible for initially responding to oil spill emergencies) sent the crews home. The first full emergency crew did not arrive at the spill site until at least 14 hours after the shipwreck, by which time the oil had spread beyond effective control. Yet enough equipment and personnel had been available to respond effectively. Much of the 10 million gallons of oil fouling the Alaska shoreline in the worst tanker spill in American history could have been confined had Alyeska acted more decisively (Malcolm, 1989).

Implications for System Design

The research on decision making shows that decision making is not a simple process even in the rational individual model. Decision situations differ from one another in terms of the clarity of goals, the types of decision makers present, the amount of agreement among them, and the frames of reference brought to a decision-making situation. Information systems do not make the decision for humans but rather support the decision-making process. How this is done will depend on the types of decisions, decision makers, and frames of reference.

Research on organizational decision making should alert students of information systems to the fact that decision making in a business is a group and organizational process. Systems must be built to support group and organizational decision making. Moreover, systems must do more than merely promote decision making. They must also make individual managers better managers of existing routines, better players in the bureaucratic struggle for control of an organization's agenda, and better political players. Finally, for those who resist the "garbage can" tendencies in large organizations, systems should help bring a measure of power to those who can attach the right solution to the right problem.

As a general rule, research on decision making indicates that information systems designers should design systems that have the following characteristics:

- They are flexible and provide many options for handling data and evaluating information.
- They are capable of supporting a variety of styles, skills, and knowledge.
- They are powerful in the sense of having multiple analytical and intuitive models for the evaluation of data and the ability to keep track of many alternatives and consequences.
- They reflect understanding of group and organizational processes of decision making.
- They are sensitive to the bureaucratic and political requirements of systems.
- They reflect an honest and professional awareness of the limits of information systems.

These elements of system design form the basis for decision support systems (DSS) and group decision support systems (GDSS), discussed in Chapter 11, and for the rapid growth of knowledge-intensive systems, discussed in Chapter 10.

Management Challenges

1. **The difficulties of managing change.** Bringing about change through the development of information technology and information systems is slowed considerably by the natural inertia of organizations. Of course, organizations do change, and powerful leaders are often required to bring about these changes. Nevertheless, the process, as leaders eventually discover, is more complicated and much slower than is typically anticipated.

2. **Fitting technology to the organization (or vice versa).** On the one hand, it is important to align information technology to the business plan, to senior management's strategic business plans, and to standard operating procedures in the business. It is, after all, supposed to be the servant of the

organization. On the other hand, these business plans, senior managers, and SOPs may all be very outdated or incompatible with the envisioned technology. In such instances, managers will need to change the organization to fit the technology or to adjust both the organization and the technology to achieve an optimal "fit."

3. **Unstructured nature of important decisions.** Many important decisions, especially in the areas of strategic planning and knowledge, are not structured and require judgment and examination of many complex factors. Solutions cannot be provided by computerized information systems alone. System builders need to determine exactly what aspects, if any, of a solution can be computerized and exactly how systems can support the process of arriving at a decision.

4. **Complexity of decision making.** Individual decision making is not a simple rational process and is conditioned by decision makers' goals, psychological characteristics, and frames of reference. It is challenging to build systems that genuinely support decision making because they must provide multiple options for handling data and for evaluating information; they must support different personal styles, skills, and knowledge; and they should be easily modified as humans learn and clarify their values. Ideally, systems should not only be designed to support managers' predispositions but also to provide information supporting alternative points of view. System builders must find new ways of building systems that support decision making in an organization as a group process, conditioned by bureaucratic struggles, political infighting, and the tendency to randomly attach solutions to problems.

Summary

Describe the salient characteristics of organizations.

All modern organizations are hierarchical, specialized, and impartial. They use explicit standard operating procedures to maximize efficiency. All organizations have their own culture and politics arising from differences in interest groups. Organizations differ in goals, groups served, social roles, leadership styles, incentives, surrounding environments, and types of tasks performed. These differences create varying types of organizational structures. Mintzberg classified organizations into five structures: the simple entrepreneurial structure, machine bureaucracy, divisionalized bureaucracy, professional bureaucracy, and adhocracy.

Describe the relationship between information systems and organizations.

The impact of information systems on organizations is not unidirectional. Information systems and the organizations in which they are used interact with and influence each other. The introduction of a new information system will affect organizational structure, goals, work design, values, competition between interest groups, decision making, and day-to-day behavior. At the same time, information systems must be designed to serve the needs of important organizational groups and will be shaped by the structure, tasks, goals, culture, politics, and management of the organization. The power of information systems to transform organizations radically by flattening organizational hierarchies has not yet been demonstrated for all types of organizations.

Contrast the classical and contemporary models of managerial activities and roles.

Early classical models of management stressed the functions of planning, organizing, coordinating, deciding, and controlling. Contemporary research has examined the actual behavior of managers to show how managers get things done.

Mintzberg found that managers' real activities are highly fragmented, variegated, and brief in duration, with managers moving rapidly and intensely from one issue to another. Other behavioral research has found that managers spend considerable time pursuing personal agendas and goals and that contemporary managers shy away from making grand, sweeping policy decisions.

Describe how managers make decisions in organizations.

Decisions can be either structured, or unstructured, with structured decisions clustering at the operational level of the organization and unstructured decisions at the strategic planning level. The nature and level of decision making are important factors in building information systems for managers.

Decision making itself is a complex activity at both the individual and the organizational level. Individual models of decision making assume that human beings can accurately choose alternatives and consequences based on the priority of their objectives and goals. The rigorous rational model of individual decision making has been modified by behavioral research that suggests that rationality is limited. People select alternatives biased by their cognitive style and frame of reference. Organizational models of decision making illustrate that real decision making in organizations takes place in arenas where many psychological, political, and bureaucratic forces are at work. Thus, organizational decision making may not necessarily be rational. The design of information systems must accommodate these realities, recognizing that decision making is never a simple process.

Describe the implications of the relationship between information systems, organizations, and management decision making for the design and implementation of information systems.

Salient features of organizations that must be addressed by information systems include organizational levels, organizational structures, types of tasks and decisions, the nature of management support, and the sentiments and attitudes of workers who will be using the system. The organization's history and external environment must be considered as well.

Implementation of a new information system is often more difficult than anticipated because of organizational change requirements. Since information systems potentially change important organizational dimensions, including structure, culture, power relationships, and work activities, there is often considerable resistance to new systems.

If information systems are built properly, they can support individual and organizational decision making. Up to now, information systems have been most helpful to managers for performing informational and decisional roles; the same systems have been of very limited value for managers' interpersonal roles. Information systems that are less formal and highly flexible will be more useful than large, formal systems at higher levels of the organization.

The design of information systems must accommodate these realities. Designers must recognize that decision making is never a simple process. Information systems can best support managers and decision making if such systems are flexible, with multiple analytical and intuitive models for evaluating data and the capability of supporting a variety of styles, skills, and knowledge.

Key Terms

Organization	Information systems managers
Bureaucracy	End users
Standard operating procedures (SOPs)	Environmental factors
Organizational culture	Institutional factors
Entrepreneurial structure	Classical model of management
Machine bureaucracy	Behavioral models
Divisionalized bureaucracy	Managerial roles
Professional bureaucracy	Interpersonal roles
Adhocracy	Informational roles
Information systems department	Decisional roles
Programmers	Strategic decision making
Systems analysts	Management control

Operational control   Rational model
Knowledge-level decision making   Cognitive style
Unstructured decisions   Systematic decision makers
Structured decisions   Intuitive decision makers
Intelligence   Organizational models
Design   Bureaucratic models
Choice   Political models
Implementation   "Garbage can" model

1. What is an organization? How do organizations use information?

2. Compare the technical definition of organizations with the behavioral definition.

3. What features do all organizations have in common? In what ways can they diverge?

4. Describe the five basic kinds of organizational structures.

5. How has the role of information systems specialists in the organization changed over time?

6. Describe the two factors that explain why organizations adopt information systems.

7. Describe how information systems are believed to affect organizations from both an economic and behavioral standpoint.

8. How can information systems change organizational structure?

9. Why is there considerable organizational resistance to the introduction of information systems?

10. What are the five functions of managers described in the classical model?

11. Behavioral research has identified five characteristics of the modern manager. How do these characteristics relate to the classical model?

12. What specific managerial roles can information systems support? Where are information systems particularly strong in supporting managers, and where are they weak?

13. Define structured and unstructured decisions. Give three examples of each.

14. What are the four stages of decision making described by Simon?

15. Differentiate between individual and organizational models of decision making.

Discussion
Questions

1. You are an information systems designer assigned to build a new accounts receivable system for one of your corporation's divisions. What organizational factors should you consider?

2. It has been said that implementation of a new information system is always more difficult than anticipated. Discuss.

3. At your college or university, identify a major decision made recently by a department, an office, or a bureau. Try to apply each of the organizational models of decision making to the decision. How was information used by the various organizational participants? What are the implications for the design of information systems?

Group
Project

With a group of two or three students, examine an organization such as a local drugstore or the bookstore, cafeteria, or registrar's office in your college or university. Describe some of the features of this organization, such as its standard operating procedures, culture, structure, and interest groups. Identify an information system or series of information systems that might improve the performance of this organization, and describe the changes that the organization would have to make to use information technology successfully.

Can Sears Reinvent Itself with Information Systems Technology?

On January 25, 1993, Sears Roebuck, the nation's largest retailer, announced that it was dropping its famous "big book" catalogues, closing 113 of its stores, and eliminating 50,000 jobs. Four months earlier, Sears had announced plans to dispose of its Dean Witter securities business, Discover credit card, and Coldwell Banker real estate operations and to sell up to 20 percent of the stock in its Allstate insurance subsidiary. These moves were designed to make Sears a much smaller, leaner concern that could recapture its leadership in retailing.

During the 1980s, Sears had tried to provide middle-class consumers with almost every type of banking, investment, and real estate service in addition to selling appliances, hardware, clothes, and other goods. In recent years, Sears' financial services businesses were the healthiest parts of the company, contributing up to as much as 70 percent of its profits. What is ironic is that Sears' board of directors chose to retain its underperforming operations while it got rid of the profitable parts, and that the underperforming part represents the long-time core of the company.

The spotlight now falls on reinvigorating Sears' retail business. Will it sink or swim? Sears has steadily lost ground in retailing, moving from the number 1 position to number 3 behind discounters Wal-Mart Stores, Inc. and Kmart Corporation. Sears had been slow to remodel stores, trim costs, and keep pace with current trends in selling and merchandising. Sears could not keep up with the discounters and with specialty retailers such as Toys R Us, Home Depot, Inc., and Circuit City Stores, Inc. that focus on a wide selection of low-price merchandise in a single category. Nor could Sears compete with trend-setting department stores.

In recent years, Sears tried to catch up. It began initiatives such as the Store of the Future, brand-name merchandise, and "everyday low pricing." None of these changes revived the flagging retail business. In 1991, retail operations contributed to 38 percent of the corporate bottom line. The rest of the merchandising group's profits came from the lucrative Sears credit card. Strategies that worked well for competitors fizzled at Sears. J.C. Penney successfully refocused its business to emphasize moderately priced apparel. Everyday low pricing, the pricing strategy used by Wal-Mart and other retailers, bombed at Sears because the firm's cost structure, one of the highest in the industry, did not allow for rock-bottom prices. Everyday low pricing has become "everyday fair pricing" supplemented by frequent sales.

Sears' catalogue sales also stagnated. While the Sears "big book" catalogue, founded in 1887, had the largest revenues of any mail-order business, sales had not been profitable for twenty years. The catalogue had lost ground to specialty catalogues such as those of L.L. Bean and Lands' End.

Yet Sears is heavily computerized—it spends more on information technology and networking than other noncomputer firms in the United States except the Boeing Corporation. Why hasn't this translated into competitive advantage?

One big problem is Sears' high cost of operations. Nearly 30 percent of each dollar in sales is required to cover overhead (e.g., expenses for salaries, light bills, and advertising), compared to 15 percent for Wal-Mart and about 21 percent for Kmart. Sears now hopes to cut costs by streamlining distribution systems and by combining merchandising functions so that there are only two or three general merchandising managers instead of six. Sears also realizes that it can't compete with discounters such as Wal-Mart Corporation on price alone and hopes to build a competitive edge through superior service.

In early 1992, Sears embarked on the Store-Simplification Program, a $60 million automation project that will make Sears stores more efficient, attractive, and convenient by bringing all transactions closer to the sales floor and centralizing every store's general offices, cashiers, customer services, and credit functions. The program makes many changes in Sears' traditional retail sales efforts:

New Point-of-Sale (POS) terminals allow sales staff to issue new charge cards, accept charge card payments, issue gift certificates, and report account information to card holders. These innovations will increase savings by reducing the size of Sears' charge card group operations while making shopping more convenient for customers.

Some stores installed ATM machines to give customers cash advances against their Sears Discover credit cards.

Telephone kiosks have been installed throughout the Sears retail network. Customers can use them to inquire about service, parts, and credit; check the status of their car in the tire and auto center; or call the manager.

Customer service desks will be eliminated. Sales personnel are authorized to handle refunds and returns, eliminating the need for two separate staffs. If a customer forgets his or her charge card, he or she can obtain immediate credit by telling the cashier his or her name and address and presenting identification.

Streamlining of patterns of work in back rooms and loading docks will also trim staff and create savings. The entire simplification effort is expected to eliminate $50 million in annual back-office costs, 6900 jobs, and the customer service desks at all stores. Changes will also increase the ratio of selling space to nonselling space at Sears, so that more space can be used to generate revenues.

Sears has also been trying to reduce costs by moving its 6000 suppliers to an electronic ordering system similar to that described for Baxter Health Care (see Chapter 2). By linking its computerized ordering system directly to that of each supplier, Sears plans to eliminate paper throughout the order process and hopes to expedite the flow of goods into its stores.

Sears has stopped trying to sell everything and is focusing on selling apparel, where profits are higher, while defending its market share in hardware and appliances. The company is rearranging its merchandise displays to resemble those of more upscale department stores, building more freestanding hardware stores and moving furniture into separate emporiums.

The question is, will all these efforts make customers happier with Sears? Market research indicates that Sears continues to be the destination of choice for lawnmowers, wrenches, washing machines, and other "hard" goods. But Sears does not seem to be the place for fashionable

women's clothing, which is considered the most profitable segment of Sears' merchandising. Sears has started stocking stylish women's clothes at moderate prices, hoping to appeal to middle-income women who prize both fashion and value. Can Sears break out of its "retailing no-man's land," caught between fashionable apparel retailers and big-time discounters?

According to Edward A. Weller, a retail analyst at Montgomery Securities, Sears managers and executives have been "Sears-ized." They are so indoctrinated in tales of Sears' past glories and so entrenched in a massive bureaucracy that change takes a long time. Weller believes that Sears' biggest challenge is to transform its culture radically. Another analyst likened Sears to the civil service, in that "everything moves very slowly."

Sources: Gregory A. Patterson, " 'Face Lift' Gives Sears a Fresh Look and Better Results," *The Wall Street Journal, July 20, 1993;* Stephanie Strom, "Sears Eliminating It's Catalogues and 50,000 Jobs," *The New York Times,* January 26, 1993, "For Sears Stores, Do-or-Die Time," *The New York Times,* September 30, 1992, and "Further Prescriptions for the Convalescent Sears," *The New York Times,* October 1, 1992; Gregory A. Patterson and Francine Schwadel, "Sears Suddenly Undoes Years of Diversifying Beyond Retailing Field," *The Wall Street Journal,* September 30, 1992; Bruce Caldwell, "Sears Shops for Competitive Edge," *InformationWEEK,* January 13, 1992.

Case Study Questions

1. What management, organization, and technology factors were responsible for Sears' poor performance?

2. Do you believe that the Store-Simplification Program solves these problems? How successful do you think it will be? Why?

3. What management, organization, and technology factors were addressed by the Store-Simplification Program?

4. What theories about the relationship of information systems and organizations are illustrated by this case?

5. Put yourself in the place of a Sears merchandising executive. Plan five steps you would take in the next year to implement the new Sears strategy.

6. Visit a Sears store and observe sales patterns. What image or market message is being conveyed in the store? How is it implemented? How might it be improved? (You might make a comparison stop at Penney's or Wal-Mart or Kmart.)

References   Adams, Carl R., and Jae Hyon Song. "Integrating Decision Technologies: Implications for Management Curriculum." *MIS Quarterly* 13, no. 2 (June 1989).

Allison, Graham T. *Essence of Decision—Explaining the Cuban Missile Crisis.* Boston: Little, Brown, 1971.

Alter, Steven, and Michael Ginzberg. "Managing Uncertainty in MIS Implementation." *Sloan Management Review* 20, no. 1 (Fall 1978).

Anthony, R. N. *Control Systems: A Framework for Analysis.* Cambridge, MA: Harvard University Press, 1965.

Argyris, Chris. *Interpersonal Competence and Organizational Effectiveness.* Homewood, IL: Dorsey Press, 1962.

Barnard, Chester. *The Functions of the Executive.* Cambridge, MA: Harvard University Press, 1968.

Beer, Michael, Russell A. Eisenstat, and Bert Spector. "Why Change Programs Don't Produce Change." *Harvard Business Review* (November–December 1990).

Bell, Daniel. *The Coming of Post-Industrial Society.* New York: Basic Books, 1973.

Bikson, T. K., and J. D. Eveland. "Integrating New Tools into Information Work." The Rand Corporation, 1992. RAND/RP-106.

Blau, Peter, and W. Richard Scott. *Formal Organizations*. San Francisco: Chandler Press, 1962.

Brzezinski, Z. *Between Two Ages: America's Role in the Technetronic Era*. New York: Viking Press, 1970.

Charan, Ram. "Now Networks Reshape Organizations—For Results." *Harvard Business Review* (September–October 1991).

Cohen, Michael, James March, and Johan Olsen. "A Garbage Can Model of Organizational Choice." *Administrative Science Quarterly* 17 (1972).

DiMaggio, Paul J., and Walter W. Powell. "The Iron Cage Revisited: Institutional Isomorphism and Collective Rationality in Organizational Fields." *American Sociological Review* 48 (1983).

Drucker, Peter. "The Coming of the New Organization." *Harvard Business Review* (January–February 1988).

El Sawy, Omar A. "Implementation by Cultural Infusion: An Approach for Managing the Introduction of Information Technologies." *MIS Quarterly* (June 1985).

Etzioni, Amitai. *A Comparative Analysis of Complex Organizations*. New York: Free Press, 1975.

Fayol, Henri. *Administration industrielle et generale*. Paris: Dunods, 1950 (first published in 1916).

Freeman, John, Glenn R. Carroll, and Michael T. Hannan. "The Liability of Newness: Age Dependence in Organizational Death Rates." *American Sociological Review* 48 (1983).

George, Joey. "Organizational Decision Support Systems." *Journal of Management Information Systems* 8, no. 3 (Winter 1991–1992).

Gorry, G. Anthony, and Michael S. Scott-Morton. "A Framework for Management Information Systems." *Sloan Management Review* 13, no. 1 (Fall 1971).

Gurbaxani, V., and S. Whang. "The Impact of Information Systems on Organizations and Markets." *Communications of the ACM* 34, no. 1 (Jan. 1991).

Herzberg, Frederick. *Work and the Nature of Man*. New York: Crowell, 1966.

Huber, George P. "Cognitive Style as a Basis for MIS and DSS Designs: Much Ado About Nothing?" *Management Science* 29 (May 1983).

Huber, George P. "The Nature and Design of Post-Industrial Organizations." *Management Science* 30, no. 8 (August 1984).

Huff, Sid L., and Malcolm C. Munro. "Information Technology Assessment and Adoption: A Field Study." *Management Information Systems Quarterly* (December 1985).

Isenberg, Daniel J. "How Senior Managers Think." *Harvard Business Review* (November–December 1984).

Ives, Blake, and Margrethe H. Olson. "Manager or Technician? The Nature of the Information Systems Manager's Job." *MIS Quarterly* (December 1981).

Jaques, Elliott. "In Praise of Hierarchy." *Harvard Business Review* (January–February 1990).

Jensen, M., and W. Mekling. "Theory of the Firm: Managerial Behavior, Agency Costs, and Ownership Structure." *Journal of Financial Economics* 3 (1976).

Keen, P. G. W. "Information Systems and Organizational Change." *Communications of the ACM* 24, no. 1 (January 1981).

Keen, P. G. W., and M. S. Morton. *Decision Support Systems: An Organizational Perspective*. Reading, MA: Addison-Wesley, 1978.

Kling, Rob. "Social Analyses of Computing: Theoretical Perspectives in Recent Empirical Research." *Computing Survey* 12, no. 1 (March 1980).

Kling, Rob, and William H. Dutton. "The Computer Package: Dynamic Complexity." In *Computers and Politics,* edited by James Danziger, William Dutton, Rob Kling, and Kenneth Kraemer. New York: Columbia University Press, 1982.

Kolb, D. A., and A. L. Frohman. "An Organization Development Approach to Consulting." *Sloan Management Review* 12, no. 1 (Fall 1970).

Kotter, John T. "What Effective General Managers Really Do." *Harvard Business Review* (November–December 1982).

Kraemer, Kenneth, John King, Debora Dunkle, and Joe Lane. *Managing Information Systems.* Los Angeles: Jossey-Bass, 1989.

Laudon, Kenneth C. *Computers and Bureaucratic Reform.* New York: Wiley, 1974.

Laudon, Kenneth C. *Dossier Society: Value Choices in the Design of National Information Systems.* New York: Columbia University Press, 1986.

Laudon, Kenneth C. "Environmental and Institutional Models of Systems Development." *Communications of the ACM* 28, no. 7 (July 1985).

Laudon, Kenneth C. "A General Model of the Relationship Between Information Technology and Organizations." Center for Research on Information Systems, New York University. Working paper, National Science Foundation, 1989.

Lawrence, Paul, and Jay Lorsch. *Organization and Environment.* Cambridge, MA: Harvard University Press, 1969.

Leavitt, Harold J., and Thomas L. Whisler. "Management in the 1980s." *Harvard Business Review* (November–December 1958).

Leavitt, Harold J. "Applying Organizational Change in Industry: Structural, Technological and Humanistic Approaches." In *Handbook of Organizations,* edited by James G. March. Chicago: Rand McNally, 1965.

Leifer, Richard. "Matching Computer-Based Information Systems with Organizational Structures." *MIS Quarterly* 12, no. 1 (March 1988).

Lindblom, C. E., "The Science of Muddling Through." *Public Administration Review* 19 (1959).

Malcolm, Andrew H. "How the Oil Spilled and Spread: Delay and Confusion Off Alaska." *The New York Times,* April 16, 1989.

March, James G., and Herbert A. Simon. *Organizations.* New York: Wiley, 1958.

Markus, M. L. "Power, Politics, and MIS Implementation." *Communications of the ACM* 26, no. 6 (June 1983).

Martin, J. *The Telematic Society.* Englewood Cliffs, NJ: Prentice-Hall, 1981.

Masuda, Y. *The Information Society.* Bethesda, MD: World Future Society, 1980.

Mayo, Elton. *The Social Problems of an Industrial Civilization.* Cambridge, MA: Harvard University Press, 1945.

McKenney, James L., and Peter G. W. Keen. "How Managers' Minds Work." *Harvard Business Review* (May–June 1974).

Michels, Robert. *Political Parties.* New York: Free Press, 1962. Original publication: 1915.

Millman, Zeeva, and Jon Hartwick. "The Impact of Automated Office Systems on Middle Managers and Their Work." *MIS Quarterly* 11, no. 4 (December 1987).

Mintzberg, Henry. "Managerial Work: Analysis from Observation." *Management Science* 18 (October 1971).

Mintzberg, Henry. *The Nature of Managerial Work.* New York: Harper & Row, 1973.

Mintzberg, Henry. *The Structuring of Organizations.* Englewood Cliffs, NJ: Prentice-Hall, 1979.

Olson, Margrethe H. "The IS Manager's Job." *MIS Quarterly* (December 1981).

Parsons, Talcott. *Structure and Process in Modern Societies.* New York: Free Press, 1960.

Perrow, Charles. *Organizational Analysis.* Belmont, CA: Wadsworth, 1970.

Pindyck, Robert S., and Daniel L. Rubinfield. *Microeconomics.* New York: Macmillan, 1992.

Porat, Marc. *The Information Economy: Definition and Measurement.* Washington, D.C.: U.S. Department of Commerce, Office of Telecommunications (May 1977).

Roethlisberger, F. J., and W. J. Dickson. *Management and the Worker*. Cambridge, MA: Harvard University Press, 1947.

Schein, Edgar H. *Organizational Culture and Leadership*. San Francisco: Jossey-Bass, 1985.

Scott Morton, Michael S. *The Corporation of the 1990s*. New York: Oxford University Press, 1991.

Shore, Edwin B. "Reshaping the IS Organization." *MIS Quarterly* (December 1983).

Simon, Herbert A. "Applying Information Technology to Organization Design." *Public Administration Review* (May/June 1973).

Simon, H. A. *The New Science of Management Decision*. New York: Harper & Row, 1960.

Starbuck, William H. "Organizations as Action Generators." *American Sociological Review* 48 (1983).

Straub, Detmar, and James C. Wetherbe. "Information Technologies for the 1990s: An Organizational Impact Perspective." *Communications of the ACM* 32, no. 11 (November 1989).

Thompson, James. *Organizations in Action*. New York: McGraw-Hill 1967.

Toffler, Alvin. *Future Shock*. New York: Random House, 1970.

Turner, Jon A. "Computer Mediated Work: The Interplay Between Technology and Structured Jobs." *Communications of the ACM* 27, no. 12 (December 1984).

Tushman, Michael L., William H. Newman, and Elaine Romanelli. "Convergence and Upheaval: Managing the Unsteady Pace of Organizational Evolution." *California Management Review* 29, no. 1 (1986).

Tushman, Michael L., and Philip Anderson. "Technological Discontinuities and Organizational Environments." *Administrative Science Quarterly* 31 (September 1986).

Tversky, A., and D. Kahneman. "The Framing of Decisions and the Psychology of Choice." *Science* 211 (January 1981).

Weber, Max. *The Theory of Social and Economic Organization*. Translated by Talcott Parsons. New York: Free Press, 1947.

Williamson, Oliver E. *The Economic Institutions of Capitalism*. New York: Free Press, 1985.

Woodward, Joan. *Industrial Organization: Theory and Practice*. Oxford: Oxford University Press, 1965.

Wrapp, H. Edward. "Good Managers Don't Make Policy Decisions." *Harvard Business Review* (July–August 1984).

CHAPTER 4

Computers and Information Processing

Twin Mainframes
Keep Lufthansa Airborne

Competition is fierce in the international airline business. Increasing deregulation in Europe, rampant overcapacity, and declining premium-fare traffic have led to price wars. Although noted for its reliability and on-time flight record, Deutsche Lufthansa AG, the German airline, realized that it had to pay more attention to customer satisfaction and it had to cut costs. So Lufthansa eliminated 8400 jobs, abolished unprofitable routes, and spun off air freight, catering, and some passenger services to indepen-

dent subsidiaries. It also took special steps to keep its operations efficient and reliable.

In the late 1980s, Lufthansa found that its data from passenger reservations and check-ins, baggage handling, and flight scheduling were growing at a rate of 50 percent each year. Karlheinz Natt, Lufthansa's head of information technology, had to make sure that the firm's computer system could handle this torrent of data while maintaining and even improving upon a near-perfect reliability record of 99.9 percent.

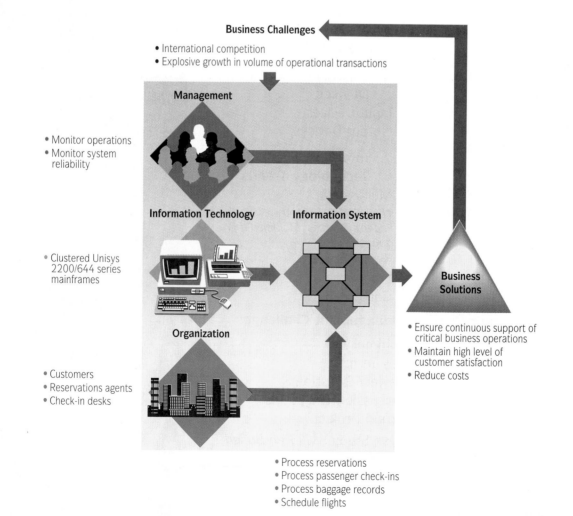

Business Challenges
- International competition
- Explosive growth in volume of operational transactions

Management
- Monitor operations
- Monitor system reliability

Information Technology
- Clustered Unisys 2200/644 series mainframes

Information System

Business Solutions
- Ensure continuous support of critical business operations
- Maintain high level of customer satisfaction
- Reduce costs

Organization
- Customers
- Reservations agents
- Check-in desks

- Process reservations
- Process passenger check-ins
- Process baggage records
- Schedule flights

Natt knew that the firm's 1100 series mainframe computers from the Unisys Corporation would soon not have enough computing capacity to deal with this problem. Moreover, a single mainframe computer alone could not process the huge volume of transactions Lufthansa anticipated. Natt decided to upgrade to more powerful mainframes and to cluster two mainframes so that both would process transactions from the same application together.

In February 1992, Lufthansa switched to two Unisys 2200/644 series mainframes. With four internal central processing units (CPUs), each of these machines has nearly twice the processing power of Lufthansa's old 1100 series mainframes. Using special software, the two machines are clustered together so that they function like a single powerful mainframe. The system is set up so that airline reservations or other transactions are processed alternately by each main processor.

Although Lufthansa had to modify some of its procedures and software to work with the new mainframe computers, the effort paid off. Natt claims the twin mainframes have saved money because they have the capacity to process all of Lufthansa's transactions without being overloaded. This decreases the chances for computer outage, which can be devastating in the airline business. If people can't make reservations or get the seats they want at the check-in desk, they will choose another carrier. Although the clustered mainframes have enough processing power to handle Lufthansa's anticipated transaction load for the next few years, Natt is already looking ahead to make sure Lufthansa's business operations wont' be limited by the machine limits of its computers.

Sources: Ferdinand Protzman, "In a New World, Lufthansa Struggles to Shed Its Old Ways," *The New York Times*, November 28, 1993; and Frederick V. Guterl, "Twin Mainframes Power Lufthansa's Reservations," *Datamation*, October 1, 1992.

By using linked mainframe computers, Lufthansa made sure it had the right amount of computing power to drive its business operations. To implement this plan, Lufthansa's management had to understand how much computer processing capacity was required by its business and the performance criteria of various types of computers. It had to know why mainframes were more appropriate for these tasks instead of minicomputers, microcomputers, or supercomputers, and it had to understand how the computer itself worked with related storage, input/output, and telecommunications technologies.

In this chapter we describe the typical hardware configuration of a computer system, explaining how a computer works and how to measure computer storage capacity and processing power. We then compare the capabilities of various types of computers and related input, output, and storage devices.

After completing this chapter you will be able to:

- Identify the hardware components in a typical computer system.
- Describe how information is represented and processed in a computer system.
- Describe the functions of the CPU and primary storage.
- Distinguish between generations of computer hardware.
- Contrast the capabilities of mainframes, minicomputers, supercomputers, microcomputers, and workstations.
- Describe the various media for storing data and programs in a computer system.
- Compare the major input and output devices.
- Describe multimedia and future information technology trends.

4.1   What Is a Computer System?

In order to understand how computers process data into information, you need to understand the components of a computer system and how computers work. No matter what their size, computers represent and process data in much the same way.

Figure 4.1
Hardware components of a computer system. A contemporary computer system can be categorized into five major components. The central processor manipulates data and controls the other parts of the computer system; secondary storage feeds data and instructions into the central processor and stores data for future use; input devices convert data and instructions for processing in the computer; output devices present data in a form that people can understand; and communications devices control the passing of information between the central processor, input and output devices, and end-users.

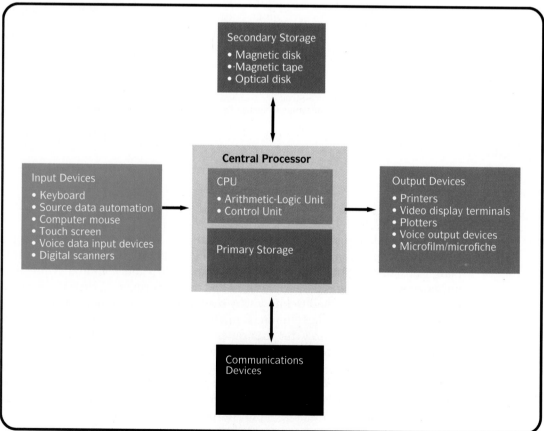

System Configuration

A contemporary computer system consists of a central processor and four other categories of hardware devices: secondary storage, input devices, output devices, and communications devices (see Figure 4.1). The central processor contains components that manipulate raw data into a more useful form and control the other parts of the computer system. Secondary storage devices (magnetic and optical disks, tape) feed data and programs into the central processor and store them for later use. Input devices, such as keyboards, digital scanners, or the computer "mouse," convert data and instructions into electronic form for input into the computer. Output devices, such as printers and video display terminals, convert electronic data produced by the computer system and display it in a form that people can understand. Communications devices help control communication between the central processor, input and output devices, and end users.

Bits and Bytes: How Computers Represent Data

Bit: A binary digit representing the smallest unit of data in a computer system. It can only have one of two states, representing 0 or 1.

Byte: A string of bits, usually eight, used to represent one number or character stored in a computer system.

In order for information to flow through a computer system and be in a form suitable for processing, all symbols, pictures, or words must be reduced to a string of binary digits. A binary digit is called a **bit** and represents either a zero or a one. In the computer, the presence of an electronic or magnetic symbol means *one* and its absence signifies *zero*. Digital computers operate directly with binary digits, either singly or strung together to form bytes. A string of eight bits is called a **byte**. Each byte can be used to represent a decimal number, a symbol, or part of a picture (see Figure 4.2).

Figure 4.3 shows how decimal numbers are represented using *true binary digits*. Each position in a decimal number has a certain value. Any number in the decimal system (base 10) can be reduced to a binary number. The binary number system (base 2) can express any number as a power of the number 2. The table at the bottom of the figure shows how the translation from binary to decimal works. By using a binary number system, a computer can express all numbers as groups of zeroes and ones. True binary cannot be used by a computer because, in addition to representing numbers, a computer must represent alphabetic characters and many other symbols used in natural language, like $ and &. This requirement led manufacturers of computer hardware to develop standard *binary codes*.

Figure 4.2
Bits and Bytes. Bits are represented by either a 0 or 1. A string of 8 bits constitutes a byte, which represents a character. The computer's representation for the word "ALICE" is a series of five bytes, where each byte represents one character (or letter) in the name.

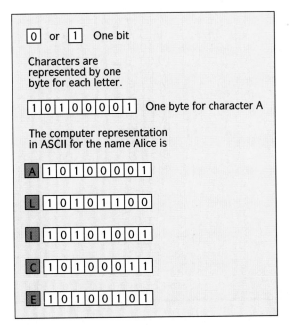

$$
\begin{aligned}
10100, \text{ which is equal to:} \quad & 0 \times 2^0 = 0 \\
& 0 \times 2^1 = 0 \\
& 0 \times 2^2 = 4 \\
& 0 \times 2^3 = 0 \\
& 0 \times 2^4 = \underline{16} \\
& 20
\end{aligned}
$$

Place	5	4	3	2	1
Power of 2	2^4	2^3	2^2	2^1	2^0
Decimal value	16	8	4	2	1

Figure 4.3
True binary digits. Each decimal number has a certain value that can be expressed as a binary number. The binary number system can express any number as a power of the number 2.

EBCDIC: Extended Binary Coded Decimal Interchange Code. Binary code representing every number, alphabetic character, or special character with 8 bits, used primarily in IBM and other mainframe computers.

There are two common codes: EBCDIC and ASCII, which are illustrated in Table 4.1. The first is the **Extended Binary Coded Decimal Interchange Code** (**EBCDIC**—pronounced ib-si-dick). This binary code, developed by IBM in the 1950s, represents every number, alphabetic character, or special character with 8 bits. EBCDIC can be used to code up to 256 different characters in one byte (2 to the eighth power equals 256).

Table 4.1   EBCDIC and ASCII Codes

Character	EBCDIC Binary	Character	ASCII-8-Binary
A	1100 0001	A	1010 0001
B	1100 0010	B	1010 0010
C	1100 0011	C	1010 0011
D	1100 0100	D	1010 0100
E	1100 0101	E	1010 0101
F	1100 0110	F	1010 0110
G	1100 0111	G	1010 0111
H	1100 1000	H	1010 1000
I	1100 1001	I	1010 1001
J	1101 0001	J	1010 1010
K	1101 0010	K	1010 1011
L	1101 0011	L	1010 1100
M	1101 0100	M	1010 1101
N	1101 0101	N	1010 1110
O	1101 0110	O	1010 1111
P	1101 0111	P	1011 0000
Q	1101 1000	Q	1011 0001
R	1101 1001	R	1011 0010
S	1110 0010	S	1011 0011
T	1110 0011	T	1011 0100
U	1110 0100	U	1011 0101
V	1110 0101	V	1011 0110
W	1110 0110	W	1011 0111
X	1110 0111	X	1011 1000
Y	1110 1000	Y	1011 1001
Z	1110 1001	Z	1011 1010
0	1111 0000	0	0101 0000
1	1111 0001	1	0101 0001
2	1111 0010	2	0101 0010
3	1111 0011	3	0101 0011
4	1111 0100	4	0101 0100
5	1111 0101	5	0101 0101
6	1111 0110	6	0101 0110
7	1111 0111	7	0101 0111
8	1111 1000	8	0101 1000
9	1111 1001	9	0101 1001

ASCII: American Standard
Code for Information
Interchange. A 7- or 8-bit
binary code used in data
transmission, microcomputers,
and some large computers.

ASCII, which stands for the **American Standard Code for Information Interchange,** was developed by the American National Standards Institute (ANSI) to provide a standard code that could be used by many different manufacturers in order to make machinery compatible. ASCII was originally designed as a 7-bit code, but most computers use 8-bit versions of ASCII. EBCDIC is used in IBM and other mainframe computers, whereas ASCII is used in data transmission, microcomputers, and some larger computers.

Parity: An extra bit built into
the EBCDIC and ASCII codes
used as a check bit to ensure
accuracy.

In actual use, EBCDIC and ASCII also contain an extra ninth **parity** or check bit. Bits can be accidentally or mistakenly changed from on to off, when data are transferred from one hardware device to another or during environmental disturbances. Parity bits are used to assist in detecting these errors. Computers are built as either *even parity* or *odd parity.* Assuming an even-parity machine, the computer expects the number of bits turned on in a byte always to be even. (If the machine were designed as an odd-parity machine, the number of bits turned on would always be odd). When the number of bits in a byte is even, the parity bit is turned off. If the number of bits in an even-parity machine in a byte is odd, the parity bit is turned on to make the total number of "on" bits even. All computer hardware contains automatic parity checking to ensure the stability of data over time.

Pixel: The smallest unit of
data for defining an image in
the computer. The computer
reduces a picture to a grid of
pixels. The term *pixel* comes
from *picture element*.

How can a computer represent a picture? The computer stores a picture by creating a grid overlay of the picture. In this grid or matrix, the computer measures the light or color in each box or cell, called a **pixel** (picture element). The computer then stores this information on each pixel. A standard high-resolution computer terminal has a 640 × 480 VGA standard grid, creating more than 300,000 pixels. Whether pictures or text are stored, it is through this process of reduction that a modern computer is able to operate in a complex environment.

Time and Size in the Computer World

Table 4.2 presents some key levels of time and size that are useful in describing the speed and capacity of modern computer systems.

Modern secondary storage devices generally operate at the speeds of **milliseconds** (thousandths of a second). For instance, a typical microcomputer could find your student record on a magnetic disk in about 15 milliseconds. It would take several seconds to find your name on a much slower tape system. (The reasons for this difference are discussed later in this chapter.) A middle-range microcomputer can execute approximately 10 million program instructions per second, or .1 **microseconds** per instruction. The central processing unit in contemporary mainframe computers can execute over 200 million instructions per second (200 MIPS). At this speed, the central processor is operating at speeds of **nanoseconds** (billionths of a second), or one instruction for every 15 nanoseconds.

Size, like speed, is an important consideration in a system. Information is stored in a computer in the form of 0s and 1s (binary digits, or bits), which are strung together to form bytes. One byte can be used to store one character, like the letter *A.* A thousand bytes (actually 1024 storage positions) are called a **kilobyte.** Small microcomputers have internal primary memories with over 600 kilobytes. A large microcomputer today can store up to 32 megabytes of information in primary memory. Each **megabyte** is approximately one million bytes. This means, theoretically, that the machine can store up to 32 million alphabetic letters or numbers. Modern secondary storage devices, such as hard disk drives in a microcomputer or disk packs in a large mainframe, store millions of bytes of information. A microcomputer may have a 240-megabyte disk, whereas a

Kilobyte: One thousand bytes
(actually 1024 storage
positions). Used as a measure
of microcomputer storage
capacity.

Megabyte: Approximately one
million bytes. Unit of
computer storage capacity.

Table 4.2 SIZE AND TIME IN THE COMPUTER WORLD

Time	Definition or Processing Speed	Application
Second	1	Time required to find a single record on a tape
Millisecond	1/1000 second	Time needed to find a single name on a disk, 1–2 milliseconds
Microsecond	1/1,000,000 second	IBM microcomputer instruction speed, .1 microseconds per instruction
Nanosecond	1/1,000,000,000 second	Mainframe instruction speed, one instruction each 15 nanoseconds
Picosecond	1/1,000,000,000,000 second	Speed of experimental devices

Size	Storage	
Byte	String of 8 bits	1 character or number
Kilobyte	1000 bytes*	Microcomputer primary memory, 640 kilobytes
Megabyte	1,000,000 bytes	Microcomputer hard disk storage 240 megabytes; mainframe primary memory 100+ megabytes
Gigabyte	1,000,000,000 bytes	External storage disk and tape
Terabyte	1,000,000,000,000 bytes	Social security programs and records

*Actually 1024 storage positions

Gigabyte: Approximately one billion bytes. Unit of computer storage capacity.

Terabyte: Approximately one trillion bytes. Unit of computer storage capacity.

large mainframe may have many disk drives, each capable of holding 8 gigabytes. A **gigabyte** is approximately one billion bytes. Some large organizations, like the Social Security Administration or the Internal Revenue Service, have a total storage capacity adding up all their disk drive capacities measured in trillions of bytes. And if all of their records were added together, including those stored on punched cards, paper records, and tapes, the total would be at the **terabyte** (thousands of billions of bytes) level of information storage.

PROBLEMS OF
COORDINATION IN
COMPUTER HARDWARE

The vast differences in the size and speed of the major elements of computer systems introduce problems of coordination. For instance, while central processing units operate at the level of microseconds, and in some cases nanoseconds, ordinary printers operate at the level of only a few hundred to a few thousand characters per second. This means that the central processing unit can process information far faster than a printer can print it out. For this reason, additional memory and storage devices must be placed between the central processing unit and the printer so that the central processing unit is not needlessly held back from processing more information as it waits for the printer to print it out.

One of the functions of communication devices and various kinds of storage areas in the system is to stage the flow of information into and out of the machine in such a way as to maximize the utilization of the central processing unit. A major development of the last thirty years in information systems has been the creation of operating systems software (see Chapter 5) and other buffering and storage devices, all of which combine to enhance the total utilization of the central processing unit.

4.2 The CPU and Primary Storage

Central processing unit (CPU): Area of the computer system that manipulates symbols, numbers, and letters and controls the other parts of the computer system.

The **central processing unit** (CPU) is part of the central processor and is the area of the computer system where the manipulation of symbols, numbers, and letters occurs. It also controls the other parts of the computer system. The CPU consists of a control unit and an arithmetic-logic unit (see Figure 4.4). Closely connected to the CPU in the central processor is **primary storage** (sometimes called primary memory or main memory), where data and program instructions are stored temporarily during processing. The characteristics of the CPU are very important in determining the speed and capabilities of a computer.

Primary Storage

Primary storage: Part of the computer that temporarily stores program instructions and data being used by the instructions for use by the CPU.

Primary storage has three functions. It stores all or part of the program that is being executed. Primary storage also stores the operating system programs that manage the operation of the computer. (These programs are discussed in Chapter 5.) Finally, the primary storage area holds data that are being used by the program. Data and programs are placed in primary storage before processing, between processing steps, and after processing has ended, prior to being returned to secondary storage or released as output.

Figure 4.4
The CPU and primary storage. The CPU retrieves data and instructions from primary storage during processing. Primary storage, often called "main memory" or "random access memory," is temporary or volatile storage. Instructions and data are lost from main memory when the computer is turned off. The instructions and data are stored in specific addresses that the CPU can access during processing.

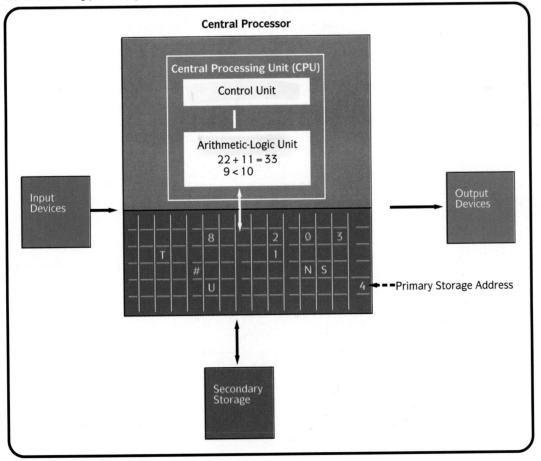

How is it possible for an electronic device like primary storage to actually store information? How is it possible to retrieve this information from a known location in memory? Figure 4.5 illustrates primary storage in an electronic digital computer. Internal primary storage is often called **RAM,** or **random access memory.** It is called RAM because it can directly access any randomly chosen location in the same amount of time. The advantage of electronic information storage is the ability to store information in a precise known location in memory and to retrieve it from that same location.

RAM: Random access memory. Primary storage of data or program instructions that can directly access any randomly chosen location in the same amount of time.

Figure 4.5 shows that primary memory is divided into memory cells. Each cell contains a set of eight binary switches or devices, each of which can store one bit of information. The set of eight bits found in each memory cell is sufficient to store one byte, using either EBCDIC or ASCII. Therefore, in each memory cell, we could store one letter, one digit, or one special symbol (such as $). Each memory cell has an individual address indicating where it is located in RAM. The computer can remember where all of the data bytes are stored simply by keeping track of their addresses. Each memory location in primary storage has a specific address—similar to a mailbox. Within this mailbox, one byte of information is stored.

Most of the information used by a computer application is stored on secondary storage devices such as disks and tapes, located outside of the primary storage area. In order for the computer to do work on information, information must be transferred into primary memory for processing. Therefore, data are continually being read into and written out of the primary storage area during the execution of a program.

Types of Semiconductor Memory

Semiconductor: An integrated circuit made by printing thousands and even millions of tiny transistors on a small silicon chip.

ROM: Read-only memory. Semiconductor memory chips that contain program instructions. These chips can only be read from; they cannot be written to.

Primary storage is actually composed of **semiconductors.** A semiconductor is an integrated circuit made by printing thousands and even millions of tiny transistors on a small silicon chip. There are several different kinds of semiconductor memory used in primary storage. RAM (random access memory), is used for short-term storage of data or program instructions. RAM is volatile: Its contents will be lost when the computer's electric supply is disrupted by a power outage or when the computer is turned off. **ROM,** or **read-only memory,** can only be read from; it cannot be written to. ROM chips come from the manufacturer with programs already "burned in" or stored. ROM is used in general-purpose computers to store important or frequently used programs (such as computing rou-

Figure 4.5
Primary storage in the computer. Primary storage can be visualized as a matrix. Each cell represents a mailbox with a unique address. In this example, mailbox [n,1] contains an 8-bit byte representing the number 0 (as coded in EBCDIC.) Each mailbox can store one byte of data or instructions.

1 byte in each mailbox

Each mailbox contains 8 switches or transistors that represent 8 bits.

tines for calculating the square roots of numbers). Other uses for ROM chips are the storage of manufacturer-specific microcodes such as the Basic Input Output System (BIOS) chip used on an IBM Personal System/2 microcomputer, which controls the handling of data within the machine.

There are two other subclasses of ROM chips: **PROM,** or **programmable read-only memory,** and **EPROM,** or **erasable programmable read-only memory.** PROM chips are used by manufacturers as control devices in their products. They can be programmed once. In this way, manufacturers avoid the expense of having a specialized chip manufactured for the control of small motors, for instance; instead, they can program into a PROM chip the specific program for their product. PROM chips, therefore, can be made universally for many manufacturers in large production runs. EPROM chips are used for device control, such as in robots, where the program may have to be changed on a routine basis. With EPROM chips, the program can be erased and reprogrammed.

PROM: Programmable read-only memory. Subclass of ROM chip used in control devices because it can be programmed once.

EPROM: Erasable programmable read-only memory. Subclass of ROM chip that can be erased and reprogrammed many times.

Arithmetic-Logic Unit

Arithmetic-logic unit (ALU): Component of the CPU that performs the principal logical and arithmetic operations of the computer.

The **arithmetic-logic unit (ALU)** performs the principal logical and arithmetic operations of the computer. The ALU need only add and subtract numbers in order to do multiplication and division, as well as addition and subtraction. Multiplication is simply rapid addition, and division is rapid subtraction. In addition to performing these arithmetic functions, an ALU must be able to determine when one quantity is greater or less than another and when two quantities are equal. The ALU can perform logical operations on the binary codes for letters as well as numbers.

Figure 4.6
The various steps in the machine cycle. The machine cycle has two main stages of operation: the instruction cycle (I-cycle) and the execution cycle (E-cycle.) There are several steps within each cycle required to process a single machine instruction in the CPU.

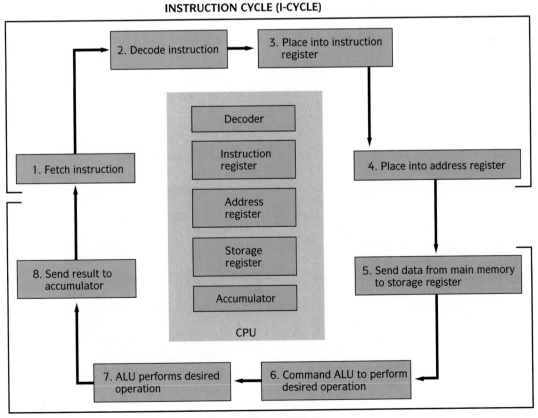

INSTRUCTION CYCLE (I-CYCLE)

- 2. Decode instruction
- 3. Place into instruction register
- Decoder
- Instruction register
- Address register
- Storage register
- Accumulator
- CPU
- 1. Fetch instruction
- 4. Place into address register
- 8. Send result to accumulator
- 5. Send data from main memory to storage register
- 7. ALU performs desired operation
- 6. Command ALU to perform desired operation

EXECUTION CYCLE (E-CYCLE)

Control Unit

Control unit: Component of the CPU that controls and coordinates the other parts of the computer system.

Machine cycle: Series of operations required to process a single machine instruction.

The **control unit** coordinates and controls the other parts of the computer system. It reads a stored program, one instruction at a time, and directs other components of the computer system to perform the tasks required by the program. The series of operations required to process a single machine instruction is called the **machine cycle.** As illustrated in Figure 4.6, the machine cycle has two parts: an instruction cycle and an execution cycle.

During the instruction cycle, the control unit retrieves one program instruction from primary storage, and decodes it. It places the part of the instruction telling the ALU what to do next in a special instruction register and places the part specifying the address of the data to be used in the operation into an address register. (A register is a special temporary storage location in the ALU or control unit that acts like a high-speed staging area for program instructions or data being transferred from primary storage to the CPU for processing.)

During the execution cycle, the control unit locates the required data in primary storage, places it in a storage register, instructs the ALU to perform the desired operation, temporarily stores the result of the operation in an accumulator, and finally places the result in primary memory. As the execution of each instruction is completed, the control unit advances to and reads the next instruction of the program.

4.3 The Evolution of Computer Hardware

Computer generations: Major transitions in computer hardware; each generation is distinguished by a different technology for the components that do the processing.

There have been four major stages, or **computer generations,** in the evolution of computer hardware, each distinguished by a different technology for the components that do the computer's processing work. Each generation has dramatically expanded computer processing power and storage capabilities while simultaneously lowering costs (see Figure 4.7). For instance, the cost of performing 100,000 calculations plunged from several dollars in the 1950s to less than

Figure 4.7
Increasing performance and falling prices of computers. MIPS: millions of instructions per second.
Adapted from "More Power for Less Money," The New York Times, *September 12, 1988.*
Copyright © 1988 by the New York Times Company. Reprinted by permission.

$0.025 in the 1980s. These generational changes in computer hardware have been accompanied by generational changes in computer software (see Chapter 5) that have made computers increasingly more powerful, inexpensive, and easy to use.

Generations of Computer Hardware

The first and second generations of computer hardware were based on vacuum tube and transistor technology, whereas the third and fourth generations were based on semiconductor technology.

FIRST GENERATION: VACUUM TUBE TECHNOLOGY, 1946–1956

The first generation of computers relied on vacuum tubes to store and process information. These tubes consumed a great deal of power, were short-lived, and generated a great deal of heat. Colossal in size, first-generation computers had extremely limited memory and processing capability and were used for very limited scientific and engineering work. The maximum main memory size was approximately 2000 bytes (2 kilobytes), with a speed of 10 kiloinstructions per second. Rotating magnetic drums were used for internal storage and punched cards for external storage. Jobs such as running programs or printing output had to be coordinated manually.

SECOND GENERATION: TRANSISTORS, 1957–1963

In the second computer generation, transistors replaced vacuum tubes as the devices for storing and processing information. Transistors were much more stable and reliable than vacuum tubes, they generated less heat, and they consumed less power. However, each transistor had to be individually made and wired into a printed circuit board, a slow, tedious process. Magnetic core memory was the primary storage technology of this period. It was composed of small magnetic doughnuts (about 1 mm. in diameter), which could be polarized in one of two directions to represent a bit of data. Wires were strung along and through these cores to both write and read data. This system had to be assembled by hand and therefore was very expensive. Second-generation computers had up to 32 kilobytes of RAM memory and speeds reaching 200,000 to 300,000 instructions per second. The enhanced processing power and memory of second-generation computers enabled them to be used more widely for scientific work and for such business tasks as automating payroll and billing.

THIRD GENERATION: INTEGRATED CIRCUITS, 1964–1979

Third-generation computers relied on integrated circuits, which were made by printing hundreds and later thousands of tiny transistors on small silicon chips. These devices were called semiconductors. Computer memories expanded to 2 megabytes of RAM memory, and speeds accelerated to 5 MIPS. This boost to processing power made it possible to develop special software called operating systems (see Chapter 5) that automated the running of programs and communications between the CPU, printers, and other devices. Third-generation computer technology introduced software that could be used by people without extensive technical training, making it possible for computers to enlarge their role in business.

FOURTH GENERATION: VERY LARGE-SCALE INTEGRATED CIRCUITS, 1980–PRESENT

The fourth generation extends from 1980 to the present. Computers in this period use very large-scale integrated circuits (VLSIC), which are packed with as many as 200,000 to over 3 million circuits per chip. Costs have fallen to the point where desktop computers are inexpensive and widely available for use in business and everyday life. The power of a computer that once took up a large room can now reside on a small desktop. Computer memory sizes have mushroomed to over one gigabyte in large commercial machines; processing speeds have exceeded 200 MIPS. In Section 4.7, we discuss the next generation of hardware trends.

VLSIC technology has fueled a growing movement toward microminiaturization—the proliferation of computers that are so small, fast, and cheap that they have become ubiquitous. For instance, many of the "intelligent" features that have made automobiles, stereos, toys, watches, cameras, and other equipment easier to use are based on microprocessors.

What Is a Microprocessor? What Is a Chip?

Microprocessor: Very large-scale integrated circuit technology that integrates the computer's memory, logic, and control on a single chip.

Word length: The number of bits that can be processed at one time by a computer. The larger the word length, the greater the speed of the computer.

eg. 32 bits & bytes/word

Megahertz: A measure of cycle speed, or the pacing of events in a computer; one megahertz equals one million cycles per second.

Data bus width: The number of bits that can be moved at one time between the CPU, primary storage, and the other devices of a computer.

Very large-scale integrated circuit technology, with hundreds of thousands (or even millions) of transistors on a single chip (see Figure 4.8), integrates the computer's memory, logic, and control on a single chip; hence the name **microprocessor,** or computer on a chip. A powerful microprocessor now widely used in personal computers is the 32-bit-66-megahertz chip such as the Intel 80486.

Some popular chips are shown in Table 4.3. Chips are measured in several ways. You will often see chips labeled as 8-bit, 16-bit, or 32-bit devices. These labels refer to the **word length,** or the number of bits that can be processed at one time by the machine. An 8-bit chip can process 8 bits or 1 byte of information in a single machine cycle. A 32-bit chip can process 32 bits or 4 bytes in a single cycle. The larger the word length, the greater the speed of the computer.

A second factor affecting chip speed is cycle speed. Every event in a computer must be sequenced so that one step logically follows another. The control unit sets a beat to the chip. This beat is established by an internal clock and is measured in **megahertz** (abbreviated MHz, which stands for millions of cycles per second). The Intel 8088 chip, for instance, originally had a clock speed of 4.47 megahertz, whereas the Intel 80486 chip has a clock speed that ranges from 25 to 66 megahertz.

A third factor affecting speed is the **data bus width.** The data bus acts as a highway between the CPU, primary storage and other devices, determining how much data can be moved at one time. The 8088 chip used in the original IBM Personal Computer, for example, had a 16-bit word length but only an 8-bit data bus width. This meant that data were processed within the CPU chip itself in 16-bit chunks, but could only be moved 8 bits at a time between the CPU,

Figure 4.8
Recent microprocessor technology. The Intel Corporation's 80486 microprocessor provides the computing power of a large mainframe of the mid-1980s. *Courtesy of Intel Corporation.*

Table 4.3 COMMON MICROPROCESSORS

Microprocessor Chip	Manufacturer	Word Length	Data Bus Width	Clock Speed (MHz)	Microcomputers Used in
8088	Intel	16	8	4.4–8	IBM PC and XT COMPAQ Portable
80286	Intel	16	16	8–28	IBM AT AT&T PC 6300 Plus
80386	Intel	32	32	16–40	IBM Personal System/2 COMPAQ 386
68020	Motorola	32	32	12.5–32	Macintosh II Macintosh SE
68030	Motorola	32	32	16–40	Macintosh IIx, IIcx
80486	Intel	32	32	25–66	Microcomputers and workstations
68040	Motorola	32	32	25	Mac Quadras
PowerPC 601	IBM, Apple, Motorola	32	64	50–100	High-end workstations and microcomputers
Pentium	Intel	32	64	60–100	High end workstations

Reduced instruction set computing (RISC): Technology used to enhance the speed of microprocessors by embedding only the most frequently used instructions on a chip.

primary storage and external devices. On the other hand, the 80486 chip, used in IBM Personal System/2 machines, and the Motorola 68030 and 68040 chips used in Macintosh microcomputers, have both a 32-bit word length and a 32-bit data bus width. Obviously, in order to get a computer to execute more instructions per second and work through programs or handle users expeditiously, it is necessary to increase the word length of the processor, the data bus width, or the cycle speed—or all three. The Window on Technology on page 120 explores another way to make microprocessors more powerful, called **reduced instruction set computing (RISC)**. RISC enhances the speed of microprocessors by embedding only the most frequently used instructions on a chip.

4.4 Mainframes, Minicomputers, Microcomputers, Workstations, and Supercomputers

Computers represent and process data the same way, but there are different classifications. We can use size and processing speed to categorize contemporary computers as mainframes, minicomputers, workstations, microcomputers, and supercomputers.

TECHNOLOGY

The Debate Over RISC

Conventional microprocessors have several hundred or more instructions hard-wired into their circuitry. These internal instructions can simplify software writing because some instructions are already embedded in the chip. On the other hand, these embedded instructions can create processing inefficiencies, taking several machine cycles to execute one instruction. For some applications, the full range of instructions is rarely used. Only 20 percent of these instructions are needed for 80 percent of the computer's tasks. If the little-used instructions are eliminated, the remaining instructions can execute much faster.

Reduced instruction set computing (RISC) chips only have the most frequently used instructions embedded in them. A RISC CPU can execute most of its instructions in one machine cycle, and sometimes multiple instructions at the same time. RISC is most appropriate for scientific and workstation computing, where there are repetitive arithmetic and logical operations on data or when there is a need for three-dimensional rendering.

Champions of RISC claim that a computer with RISC technology, less circuitry, and simpler designs can offer the performance of minicomputers costing ten times as much. Indeed, computers and workstations using RISC technology can be incredibly fast. For instance, the Digital Equipment Corporation (DEC) has developed a series of computers code-named

Alpha that are powered by one or more 64-bit RISC microprocessors with speeds ranging from 50 to 200 megahertz. At 200 megahertz, the fastest of the line has roughly the same peak performance as a small supercomputer. DEC is betting its business strategy on Alpha by developing 64-bit RISC systems ranging from palmtop computers to high-performance midrange computers and supercomputers. The company hopes these advances will keep the firm competitive in the price/performance race.

Alpha designers have worked with programmers to make switching systems to Alpha RISC computers less risky. Most of the software running on DEC's earlier line of VAX computers will not need to be rewritten to run on Alpha machines, making Alpha machines appealing for business computing as well as for scientific and engineering work. However, many firms may want to make some software changes so that their programs can take advantage of Alpha's additional computing power. DEC and commercial software firms have just started to produce software that is explicitly designed to take advantage of the features of the Alpha chip.

DEC believes that even applications that were designed for its older 32-bit computers will achieve threefold to fourfold performance gains. DEC claims Alpha should produce a 1000-fold performance improvement, to 4 billion instructions per second over the next 25 years.

IBM, Motorola, Inc., and Apple Computer Inc. have developed a PowerPC 601 RISC microprocessor, which can run both IBM and Macintosh applications very fast. Its speed is 50–100 megahertz. When used in IBM's RS/6000 workstations, it doubled performance over some previous models.

Critics believe RISC increases system costs. RISC gains in processing speed may be offset by the difficulties in dropping complex instruction-set computing. Programs written for conventional processors cannot automatically be transferred to RISC machines; new software will be required. Many RISC suppliers are starting to add more instructions to appeal to more customers, and designers of conventional microprocessors are streamlining their chips. Some analysts believe that conventional 32-bit chips will soon be able to execute any instruction in just one cycle.

Sources: "Does IS Want the Power PC?" *Datamation,* November 1, 1993; Elaine L. Appleton, "What's It All About, Alpha," *Datamation,* May 1, 1992; Hal Glatzer, "RISC Assessment," *Software Magazine,* June 1989; and John Markoff, "Computer Chip Starts Angry Debate," *The New York Times,* September 26, 1989.

To Think About: If you were an information systems manager, what criteria would you use in deciding whether to purchase a RISC computer?

Mainframes, Minis, and Micros

Mainframe: Largest category of computer, classified as having 50 megabytes to over 1 gigabyte of RAM.

Minicomputer: Middle-range computer with about 10 to 650 megabytes of RAM.

A **mainframe** is the largest computer, a powerhouse with massive memory and extremely rapid processing power. It is used for very large commercial, scientific, or military applications where a computer must handle massive amounts of data or many complicated processes. A **minicomputer** is a middle-range computer, about the size of an office desk, often used in universities, factories, or research laboratories. A **microcomputer** is one that can be placed on a desktop or carried from room to room. Microcomputers are used as personal machines as well as

Microcomputer: Desktop or portable computer with 640 kilobytes to 64 megabytes of RAM.

Workstation: Desktop computer with powerful graphics and mathematical capabilities and the ability to perform several tasks at once.

Supercomputer: Very sophisticated and powerful computer that can perform very complex computations extremely rapidly.

in business. A **workstation** also fits on a desktop but has more powerful mathematical and graphics processing capability than a microcomputer and can perform more complicated tasks at the same time than can a microcomputer. Workstations are used for scientific, engineering, and design work that requires powerful graphics or computational capabilities. A **supercomputer** is a highly sophisticated and powerful machine that is used for tasks requiring extremely rapid and complex calculations with hundreds of thousands of variable factors. Supercomputers have traditionally been used in scientific and military work, but they are starting to be used in business as well. Representative computers in each category are listed in Table 4.4.

The problem with this classification scheme is that the capacity of the machines changes so rapidly. A microcomputer today has the computing power of a mainframe from the 1980s or the minicomputer of a few years ago. This is illustrated in Figure 4.9. Powerful microcomputers have sophisticated graphics and processing capabilities similar to workstations. Microcomputers still cannot perform as many tasks at once as mainframes, minicomputers, or workstations (see the discussion of operating systems in Chapter 5); nor can they be used by as many people simultaneously as these larger machines. Still, even these distinctions will become less pronounced in the future. In another decade, desktop micros might very well have the power and processing speed of today's supercomputers.

Generally, however, mainframes can be classified as having 50 megabytes to over 1 gigabyte of RAM; minicomputers, 10 to 650 megabytes of RAM; workstations, 8 to 300 megabytes of RAM; and microcomputers, 640 kilobytes to 64 megabytes of RAM. Table 4.4 illustrates the capabilities of representative commercial computers in each of these categories today. Figure 4.10 illustrates some of the capabilities of the Sun SPARCstation, a leading-edge workstation, and of the IBM Personal System/2, a popular microcomputer.

The term *microcomputer* is sometimes used synonymously with personal computer, since micros were originally intended as primarily personal, single-user tools. However, microcomputers have become so powerful that they are no longer confined to personal information systems. Micros can operate either as individual stand-alone machines with isolated processing power or as part of a

Table 4.4   REPRESENTATIVE COMPUTERS

Type of Computer	Example	Memory (Megabytes)	Performance	Word Length (Bits)	Cost
Mainframe	IBM Enterprise System 9000	1000 (1 gigabyte)	240 MIPS	32	$55,000,000
Minicomputer	DEC VAX 7000 Model 600	64–2.35 gigabytes	124–508 transactions per second	32	$165,000–$355,000
Workstation	Sun SPARCstation 10 Model 40	32–512	50.2 SPEC int92 marks	32	$17,245 and up
Microcomputer	Compaq Prolinea Model 4633	4–32	10.8 MIPS	32	$1300–$1700
Supercomputer	Cray C90	256 megabytes–8 gigabytes	1–16 gigaflops	64	$3,000,000–$35,000,000

Note: Different computer manufacturers use different measures of computer performance. Many use MIPS, but some manufacturers prefer to measure performance in terms of transactions per second. Supercomputer performance is measured in flops (number of floating point operations per second). Workstation performance is starting to be measured by SPEC int92 marks, a benchmark for integer operations.

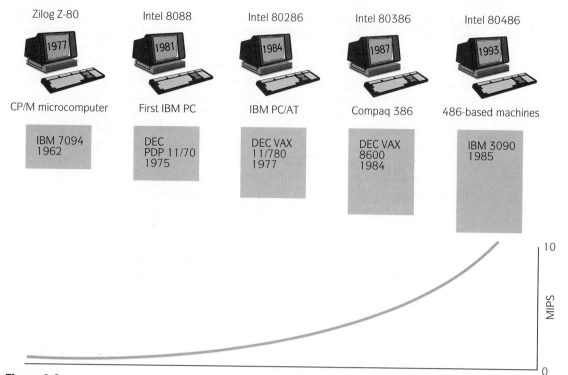

Figure 4.9
The soaring power of microcomputer technology. The power of a mainframe computer from the mid 1980s is now available for desktop computing. The illustration shows the successive generations of microcomputers, the representative microprocessor on which each is based, the comparable minicomputer or mainframe computer, and the approximate computing power of each generation.

departmental or companywide network of intelligent devices. They may be linked to other micros, telecommunications devices, workstations, or larger computers.

In either case, microcomputers are starting to do some of the work formerly performed by larger computers in business. Chapter 7 describes how microcomputers can be linked with other micros, printers, "intelligent" copy machines, and telephones to provide processing power and to coordinate the flow of work without relying on mainframes. Micros can also be linked to minicomputers and mainframes, forming companywide information networks that share hardware, software, and data resources. The use of multiple computers linked by a communication network for processing is called **distributed processing**. In contrast with **centralized processing**, in which all processing is accomplished by one large central computer, distributed processing distributes the processing work among various microcomputers, minicomputers, and mainframes linked together.

Distributed processing: The distribution of computer processing work among multiple computers linked by a communication network.

Centralized processing: Processing that is accomplished by one large central computer.

Downsizing and Cooperative Processing

In some firms, microcomputers have actually replaced mainframes and minicomputers. The process of transferring applications from large computers to smaller ones is called **downsizing**. Downsizing has many advantages. The cost per MIPS on a mainframe is almost 100 times greater than on a microcomputer; a megabyte of mainframe memory costs about 10 times more than the same amount of memory on a micro. For some applications, micros may also be easier for nontechnical specialists to use and maintain. The Window on Organizations shows how installing microcomputers can help distribute processing power to organizations with branches in many different locations, even if they are in different parts of the globe. Often microcomputers are networked so that they can share data and communicate with each other. (These issues are explored in detail in Chapter 7.)

Downsizing: The process of transferring applications from large computers to smaller ones.

Figure 4.10
A SunSPARCstation workstation and an IBM PS/2 microcomputer. The SunSPARCstation workstation (top) is used for sophisticated CAD/CAM applications. The IBM PS/2 (bottom) is a microcomputer capable of powerful applications processing. *Top: Tim Davis PhotoResearchers, Inc. Bottom: Courtesy of IBM.*

Cooperative processing: Type of processing that divides the processing work for transaction-based applications among mainframes and microcomputers.

Another computing pattern divides processing work for transaction-based applications among mainframes and microcomputers. Each type of computer is assigned the functions it performs best, and each shares processing (and perhaps data) over a communications link. For example, the microcomputer might be used for data entry and validation, whereas the mainframe would be responsible for file input and output. This division of labor is called **cooperative processing.** Micros are utilized because they can provide the same processing power much more economically than a mainframe or because they are superior at some tasks, such as providing screen presentations for the user interface. Figure 4.11 illustrates cooperative processing. Cooperative processing is not always easy to implement. It may require special communications and application software and an understanding of which functions are best handled by micros and which should reside with larger machines.

ORGANIZATIONS

Distributing Computing Power Around the Globe

The mission of U.S. Foreign Agricultural Service (FAS), an agency of the U.S. Department of Agriculture, is to boost exports of U.S. agricultural products and to track overseas sales and sales opportunities. Its 90 foreign offices around the globe send information about supply and demand via electronic messaging systems to a system in Washington, D.C. that forecasts the prices of commodities futures. Most of the overseas employees are agricultural economists.

From a computing standpoint, this represents a nightmare because FAS has to support so many different computer installations in so many different countries. The majority of FAS offices, located in U.S. embassies in other countries, have no local technical staff to support them; many are in Third World countries that are far away from

spare parts and maintenance services. How can the FAS provide computing power to these locations?

Microcomputers were the answer because they require little technical support, are easy for nontechnical specialists to install and use, and are inexpensive to purchase. The agency installed networked 33 Megahertz-Wang Laboratories 80386 personal computers in its far-flung sites, because it felt this system would provide more reliable systems under its own control and improve the sharing of data and resources among its offices.

In addition to sharing space with U.S. embassies abroad, the FAS used to share the State Department's Wang VS minicomputer. It also used old stand-alone Wang

personal computers. Now all 450 of the FAS employees overseas have new Wang PCs on their desks. Since a large proportion of its staff is composed of foreign nationals, FAS made sure that the changes in the way the system worked were minimal, so that the new hardware would not scare them off. The new PCs can send data to the United States through networks and eventually will be able to use these networks to access FAS data in Washington, D.C.

Source: Gary H. Anthes, "U.S. Agency Cultivates Pockets of Computing Around the Globe," *Computerworld*, May 25, 1992.

To Think About: Why were microcomputers an appropriate solution for the FAS?

Figure 4.11
Cooperative processing. In cooperative processing, an application is divided into tasks that run on more than one type of computer. This example shows the tasks that a microcomputer is best at performing, the tasks that a mainframe computer is best at performing, and those tasks that each type is able to perform.

Microcomputers and Workstations

Since workstations are desktop machines like microcomputers, what distinguishes a microcomputer from a workstation? Workstations have more powerful graphics and mathematical processing capabilities than microcomputers and can easily perform several tasks at the same time. They are typically used by scientists, engineers, and other knowledge workers, but are spreading to the financial industry because they have the computing power to simultaneously analyze portfolios, process securities trades, and provide financial data and news services (see Chapter 10).

Workstations are especially useful for computer-aided design (CAD) and for complex simulations and modeling. They can represent fully rendered multiple views of a physical object, such as an airplane wing, rotate the object three-dimensionally, and present design history and cost factors. Workstations can easily integrate text and graphics, displaying multiple tools, applications, and types of data simultaneously.

At present, workstations have at least 8 megabytes of RAM, 32-bit micro-processors, and the capability to perform several computing tasks at the same time (see the discussion of multitasking in Chapter 5). They come with high-resolution large-screen color monitors for detailed design work and math co-processors to speed calculations.

The distinctions between workstations and microcomputers are starting to disappear. Powerful high-end microcomputers have many of the same capabilities as low-end workstations. A low-end workstation can be purchased for around $4000–5000. As microcomputers become increasingly graphics oriented, the distinctions between the two types of computers are likely to blur further. Moreover, workstations themselves have increased in power, so that the most sophisticated workstations have some of the capabilities of earlier main-frames and supercomputers.

Supercomputers and Parallel Processing

A supercomputer is an especially sophisticated and powerful type of computer that is used primarily for extremely rapid and complex computations with hundreds or thousands of variable factors. Supercomputers have traditionally been used for classified weapons research, weather forecasting, and petroleum and engineering applications, all of which use complex mathematical models and simulations. Although extremely expensive, supercomputers are beginning to be employed in business. For instance, Northwest and other airlines use supercomputers for scheduling crews and equipment.

Supercomputers can perform complex and massive computations almost instantaneously because they can perform billions and even hundreds of billions of calculations per second—many times faster than the largest mainframes.

Figure 4.12
Sequential and parallel processing. During sequential processing, each task is assigned to one CPU that processes one instruction at a time. In parallel processing, multiple tasks are assigned to multiple processing units to expedite the result.

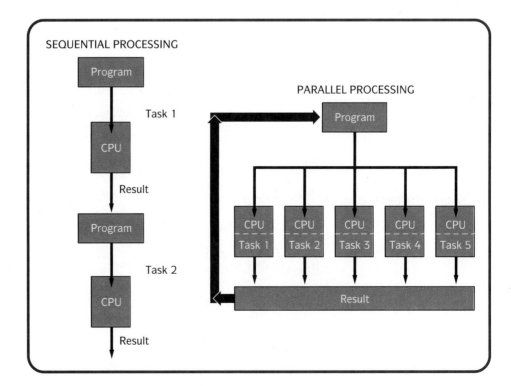

Parallel processing: Type of processing in which more than one instruction can be processed at a time by breaking down a problem into smaller parts and processing them simultaneously with multiple processors.

Supercomputers do not process one instruction at a time but instead rely on **parallel processing.** As illustrated in Figure 4.12, multiple processing units (CPUs) break down a problem into smaller parts and work on it simultaneously. Some experimental supercomputers use up to 64,000 processors. Getting a group of processors to attack the same problem at once is easier said than done. It requires rethinking of the problems and special software that can divide problems among different processors in the most efficient possible way, providing the needed data, and reassembling the many subtasks to reach an appropriate solution. Most software currently available is written for sequential processing machines.

4.5 Secondary Storage

Secondary storage: Relatively long-term, nonvolatile storage of data outside the CPU and primary storage.

Register: Temporary storage location in the ALU or control unit where small amounts of data and instructions reside for thousandths of a second just before use.

Cache: High-speed storage of frequently used instructions and data.

In addition to primary storage, where information and programs are stored for immediate processing, modern computer systems use other types of storage in order to accomplish their tasks. Information systems need to store information outside of the computer in a nonvolatile state (not requiring electrical power) and to store volumes of data too large to fit into a computer of any size today (such as a large payroll or the U.S. census). The relatively long-term storage of data outside the CPU and primary storage is called **secondary storage.**

Primary storage is where the fastest, most expensive technology is used. As shown in Table 4.5, there are actually three different kinds of primary memory: register, cache, and RAM. **Register** is the fastest and most expensive memory, where small amounts of data and instructions reside for thousandths of a second just prior to use, followed by **cache** memory (for high-speed storage of frequently used instructions and data) and RAM memory for large amounts of data. Access to information stored in primary memory is electronic and occurs almost at the speed of light. Secondary storage is nonvolatile and retains data even when the computer is turned off. There are many kinds of secondary storage; the most common are magnetic tape, magnetic disk, and optical disk. These media can transfer large bodies of data rapidly to the CPU. But since secondary storage requires mechanical movement to gain access to the data, in contrast to primary storage, it is relatively slow.

Table 4.5   DATA STORAGE DEVICES IN A MICROCOMPUTER

Type of Memory	Total Storage Capacity	Access Time
PRIMARY STORAGE		
Register	1 kilobyte	.01 microseconds
Cache	1 kilobyte	.1 microseconds
RAM	16 megabytes	.5 microseconds
SECONDARY STORAGE		
Hard disk	800 megabytes	15–20 milliseconds
High-density diskette (3.5")	2.8 megabytes	200 milliseconds
Optical disk	660 megabytes	200–500 milliseconds
Magnetic tape (¼" streaming tape backup)	40 megabytes	1–2 seconds

Magnetic Tape

Magnetic tape is an older device that is still important for secondary storage of large volumes of information. It is used primarily in mainframe batch applications and for archiving data. Generally, magnetic tape for large systems comes in 14-inch reels that are up to 3600 feet long and 0.5 inches wide. It is very similar to home cassette recording tape, but of higher quality. Figure 4.13 shows how information appears on magnetic tape using an EBCDIC coding scheme. Each byte of data utilizes one column across the width of the tape. Each column is composed of eight bits plus one check parity bit. Information can be stored on magnetic tape at different densities. Low density is 1600 bytes per inch (bpi), and densities of up to 6250 bpi are common. In addition to commercial-quality tape for large systems, microcomputers and some minicomputers use small tape cassettes, very similar to home audio cassettes, to store information.

The principal advantages of magnetic tape are that it is very inexpensive, that it is relatively stable, and that it can store very large volumes of information. It is a reliable technology because of several self-checking features (such as parity bits), and therefore is an ideal form of backup storage for other more volatile forms of memory. Moreover, magnetic tape can be used over and over again, although it does age with time and computer users must handle it carefully.

The principal disadvantages of magnetic tape are that it stores data sequentially and is relatively slow compared to the speed of other secondary storage media. In order to find an individual record stored on magnetic tape, such as a specific employment record, the tape must be read from the beginning up to the location of the desired record. This means that the CPU must read each name from the "A's" all the way to the desired name before it can locate the record. Hence, magnetic tape is not a good medium when it is necessary to find information rapidly (such as for an airline reservation system). Tape can also be damaged and is labor-intensive to mount and dismount. The environment in which it is stored must be carefully controlled. Since contemporary information systems call for immediate access to data, tape represents a fading technology, but it continues to exist in changing forms.

Figure 4.13
Magnetic tape storage. Data can be stored on nine-track magnetic tape, which is a stable and inexpensive medium. However, data are stored sequentially and therefore access and retrieval may be slow.

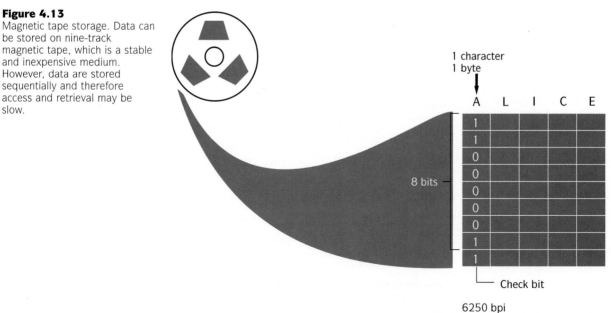

1 character
1 byte

A L I C E

8 bits

Check bit

6250 bpi

Magnetic Disk

Magnetic disk: A secondary storage medium in which data are stored by means of magnetized spots on a hard or floppy disk.

Hard disk: Magnetic disk resembling a thin steel platter with an iron oxide coating; used in large computer systems and in many microcomputers.

Cylinder: Represents circular tracks on the same vertical line within a disk pack.

Track: Concentric circle on the surface area of a disk on which data are stored as magnetized spots; each track can store thousands of bytes.

The most widely used secondary storage medium today is **magnetic disk.** There are two kinds of magnetic disks: floppy disks (used in microcomputers) and hard disks (used in commercial disk drives and microcomputers). **Hard disks** are thin steel platters with an iron oxide coating. In larger systems, multiple hard disks are mounted together on a vertical shaft. Figure 4.14 illustrates a commercial hard disk pack for a large system. It has 11 disks, each with two surfaces, top and bottom. However, although there are 11 disks, no information is recorded on the top or bottom surfaces; thus, there are only 20 recording surfaces on the disk pack. On each surface, data are stored on tracks. The disk pack is generally sealed from the environment and rotates at a speed of about 3500 rpm, creating an air-stream speed of about 50 mph at the disk surface.

Information is recorded on or read from the disk by read/write heads, which literally fly over the spinning disks. Unlike a home stereo vinyl album record player, the heads never actually touch the disk, like the needle touches the record, (which would destroy the data and cause the system to "crash,") but hover a few thousandths of an inch above it. A smoke particle or a human hair is sufficient to crash the head into the disk.

The read/write heads move horizontally (from left to right) to any of 200 positions called **cylinders.** At any one of these cylinders, the read/write heads can read or write information to any of 20 different concentric circles on the disk surface areas (called **tracks**). The cylinder represents the circular tracks on the same vertical line within the disk pack. Read/write heads are directed to a specific record using an address consisting of the cylinder number, the recording surface number, and the data record number.

The speed of access to data on a disk is a function of the rotational speed of the disk and the speed of the access arms. The read/write heads must position themselves, and the disk pack must rotate until the proper information is located. More advanced and expensive disks have access speeds of 1.5–10 milliseconds and capacities of up to 7.5 gigabytes per unit.

Each track contains several records. In general, 20,000 bytes of information can be stored on each track at densities of up to 12,000 bpi. If there are 20 such tracks and 200 cylinders in a disk pack, the total capacity of the illustrated disk pack is 80 megabytes. As noted previously, advanced commercial disks for large systems have much higher storage capacities over 1 billion bytes.

Figure 4.14
Disk pack storage. Large systems often rely on disk packs, which provide reliable storage for large amounts of data with quick access and retrieval. A typical removable disk-pack system contains 11 2-sided disks.

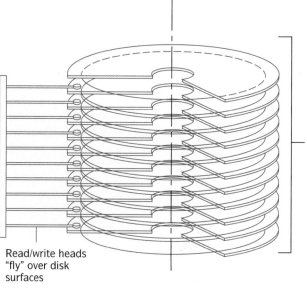

11 disks
20 recording surfaces
3500 RPMs

Read/write heads "fly" over disk surfaces

Floppy disk: Removable magnetic disk primarily used with microcomputers. The two most common standard sizes are 3.5-inch and 5.25-inch disks that are made up of polyester film with magnetic coating.

Sector: Method of storing data on a floppy disk in which the disk is divided into pie-shaped pieces or sectors. Each sector is assigned a unique number so that data can be located using the sector number.

Direct access storage device (DASD): Refers to magnetic disk technology that permits the CPU to locate a record directly, in contrast to sequential tape storage that must search the entire file.

Microcomputers also use hard disks, which can store over 500 megabytes, but 80 to 400 megabytes are the most common size. Microcomputers also use **floppy disks,** which are flat, 5.25-inch or 3.5-inch disks of polyester film with a magnetic coating. These disks have a storage capacity ranging from 360K to 2.8 megabytes and a much slower access rate than hard disks. Floppy disks and cartridges and packs of multiple disks use a **sector** method for storing data. As illustrated in Figure 4.15, the disk surface is divided into pie-shaped pieces, the actual number depending on the disk system used. (Some disks use eight sectors, others nine.) In most types of floppy disks, each sector has the same storage capacity (data are recorded more densely on the inner disk tracks). Each sector is assigned a unique number. Data can be located using an address consisting of the sector number and an individual data record number.

Magnetic disks on both large and small computers have several important advantages over magnetic tape. First, they permit direct access to individual records. Each record can be given a precise physical address in terms of cylinders and tracks, and the read/write head can be directed to go to that address and access the information in about 10 to 60 milliseconds. This means that the computer system does not have to search the entire file, as in a tape file, in order to find one person's record. This creates the possibility for on-line information systems providing an immediate response, such as an airline reservation or customer information system. Disk storage is often referred to as a **direct access storage device (DASD).**

For on-line systems requiring direct access, disk technology provides the only practical means of storage today. Records can be easily and rapidly retrieved. The cost of disks has steadily declined over the years. Moreover, as we will see in Chapter 6 in the discussion of file organization and databases, disk technology permits interrelationships among records to be built into the storage file itself. This system permits a single transaction to update or change data in a number of different files simultaneously and dramatically speeds the process of finding related records.

DASD is, however, relatively expensive compared to magnetic tape. Moreover, updating information stored on a disk destroys the old information because the old data on the disk are written over if changes are made. (In contrast, changes to data made on magnetic tape are made on a different reel of tape so that the old version of the tape can be retained and recovered.) Therefore, it becomes more difficult to back up and audit the transactions recorded on a disk. You can check this out by changing your seat selection on an airplane and then asking the clerk to tell you where you wished to sit originally. You will find that

Figure 4.15
The sector method of storing data. Each track of a disk can be divided into sectors. Disk storage location can be identified by sector and data record number.

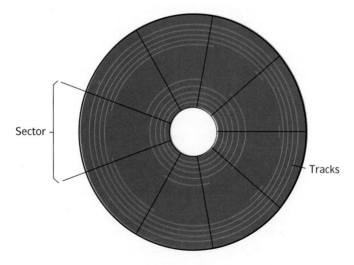

Sector

Tracks

the system has no record of your previous selection because the information has been wiped off the disk.

In addition, disks can crash. The disk drives themselves are susceptible to environmental disturbances; even smoke particles can disrupt the movement of read/write heads over the disk surface. Therefore, the environment must be relatively pure and stable. That is why disk drives are sealed in a clean room.

Optical Disks

Optical disk: Secondary storage device on which data are recorded and read by laser beams rather than by magnetic means.

Optical disks, also called compact disks or laser optical disks, store data at densities many times greater than those of magnetic disks and are available for both microcomputers and large computers. Data are recorded on optical disks when a laser device burns microscopic pits in the reflective layer of a spiral track. Binary information is encoded by the length of these pits and the space between them. Optical disks can thus store massive quantities of data, including not only text but also pictures, sound, and full-motion video, in a highly compact form. The optical disk is read by having a low-power laser beam from an optical head scan the disk.

The most common optical disk system used with microcomputers is called **CD-ROM (compact disk read-only memory).** A 4.75-inch compact disk can store up to 660 megabytes, nearly 300 times more than a high-density floppy disk. Optical disks are most appropriate for applications where enormous quantities of unchanging data must be stored compactly for easy retrieval, or for storing graphic images and sound. CD-ROM becomes an especially attractive storage medium if a minimum of 10 megabytes of data must be stored and distributed to 100 people or more. CD-ROM is also less vulnerable than floppy disks to magnetism, dirt, or rough handling.

CD-ROM: Compact disk read only memory. Read-only optical disk storage used for imaging, reference, and database applications with massive amounts of data and for multimedia.

CD-ROM is read-only storage. No new data can be written to it; it can only be read. CD-ROM has been most widely used for reference materials with massive amounts of data, such as encyclopedias, directories, or on-line databases. There are now available on CD-ROM hundreds of databases, such as marketing, legal, and demographic databases, and financial databases from Quotron, Dun & Bradstreet, and Dow Jones.

CD-ROM is also becoming popular for image processing (review the description of the United States Automobile Association's imaging system in Chapter 2). For example, the U.S. Immigration and Naturalization Service has started to distribute an alien identification card that is keyed to the cardholder's photograph, signature, and fingerprint stored on optical disk. The U.S. Department of Defense has initiated a system of networks and optical imaging to reduce the mountains of paper generated by technical design information and administrative data for weapons systems. The Ford Motor Company now sends its North American dealers CD-ROM disks with technical information for servicing Ford cars; it also sends a complete parts catalog and saves significantly by not having to mail a paper version.

WORM: Write once, read many. Optical disk system that allows users to record data only once; data cannot be erased but can be read indefinitely.

WORM (write once, read many) optical disk systems allow users to record data only once on an optical disk. Once written, the data cannot be erased, but can be read indefinitely. WORM has been used as an alternative to microfilm for archiving digitized document images. The disadvantages of CD-ROM and WORM optical disks are that their contents cannot easily be erased and written over, as can be done with magnetic disks, and that the access speed is slower than that of magnetic disks.

Magneto-optical disk: Optical disk system that is erasable. Data are recorded by a high-powered laser beam that heats tiny spots in the magnetic media.

Rewritable **magneto-optical disks,** illustrated in Figure 4.16, are starting to become cost-effective for data storage. The disk surface is coated with a magnetic material that can change magnetic polarity only when heated. To record data, a high-powered laser beam heats tiny spots in the magnetic medium that allows it to accept magnetic patterns. Data can be read by shining a lower-

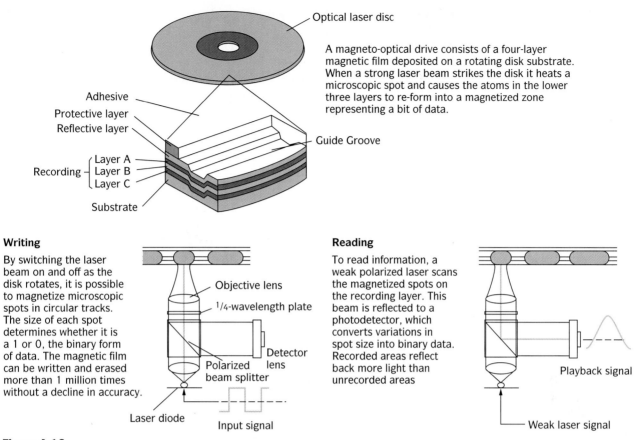

Optical laser disc

A magneto-optical drive consists of a four-layer magnetic film deposited on a rotating disk substrate. When a strong laser beam strikes the disk it heats a microscopic spot and causes the atoms in the lower three layers to re-form into a magnetized zone representing a bit of data.

Adhesive
Protective layer
Reflective layer

Guide Groove

Layer A
Recording { Layer B
Layer C

Substrate

Writing

By switching the laser beam on and off as the disk rotates, it is possible to magnetize microscopic spots in circular tracks. The size of each spot determines whether it is a 1 or 0, the binary form of data. The magnetic film can be written and erased more than 1 million times without a decline in accuracy.

Objective lens

$1/4$-wavelength plate

Detector lens

Polarized beam splitter

Laser diode

Input signal

Reading

To read information, a weak polarized laser scans the magnetized spots on the recording layer. This beam is reflected to a photodetector, which converts variations in spot size into binary data. Recorded areas reflect back more light than unrecorded areas

Playback signal

Weak laser signal

Figure 4.16
Using magneto-optical disks to record and read data. *Adapted from: Robert Pasternak, "How the Optical Disk Drive Works,"* The New York Times, *November 30, 1988. Copyright © 1988 by The New York Times Company. Reprinted by permission.*

powered laser beam at the magnetic layer and reading the reflected light. The magneto-optical disk is erasable and can be written on nearly a million times. The access speed of optical disks, while slower than that of a magnetic disk, is continuing to improve, making the optical disk a very attractive storage technology for the 1990s.

4.6 Input and Output Devices

Human beings interact with computer systems largely through input and output devices. Advances in information systems rely not only on the speed and capacity of the CPU but also on the speed, capacity, and design of the input and output devices. Input/output devices are often called peripheral devices.

Input Devices

The traditional method of data entry has been by keyboarding. Keypunching belongs to an earlier era in computing. Data entry clerks used a keypunch machine to code characters on an 80-column card, designating each character with a unique punch in a specific location on the card. An electromechanical card reader sensed the holes and solid parts of the cards. A single card could store up to 80 bytes of information (80 columns). Key-to-tape or key-to-disk machines allowed data to be keyed directly onto magnetic tape or disk for later computer processing. These methods are being replaced by more efficient and direct methods of input, although some firms still use them for their older batch applications.

Today, most data are entered directly into the computer using a data entry terminal and they are processed on-line. For instance, on-line airline reservation and customer information systems have reservation clerks or salespeople enter transactions directly while dealing with the customer, and their systems are updated immediately. In this manner, a business can eliminate a separate data entry staff and the associated costs.

THE COMPUTER MOUSE

Computer mouse: Hand-held input device whose movement on the desktop controls the position of the cursor on the computer display screen.

The "point and click" actions of the **computer mouse** have made it an increasingly popular alternative to keyboard and text-based commands. A mouse is a hand-held device that is usually connected to the computer by a cable. The computer user moves the mouse around on a desktop to control the position of the cursor on a video display screen. Once the cursor is in the desired position, the user can push a button on the mouse to select a command. The mouse can also be used to "draw" images on the screen, as well as "drag and drop" images or text around the screen.

TOUCH SCREENS

Touch screen: Input technology that permits the entering or selecting of commands and data by touching the surface of a sensitized video display monitor with a finger or pointer.

Touch screens are easy to use and are appealing to people who can't use traditional keyboards. Users can enter limited amounts of data by touching the surface of a sensitized video display monitor with a finger or a pointer. With colorful graphics, sound, and simple menus, touch screens allow the user to make selections by touching specified parts of the screen. Touch screens are proliferating in retail stores, restaurants, shopping malls, and even in some schools. For instance, music stores use Notestations, touch-screen equipped kiosks for selling sheet music. A customer can use the touch screen to scan more than 1000 titles, select a title, and listen to the first few bars of the score. A nominal payment will print the score in any key.

Touch screen technology allows users to interface with their computer systems by simply touching menu options on the sensitized video display monitor with their fingers.

Source data automation: Input technology that captures data in computer-readable form at the time and place the data are created.

Optical character recognition (OCR): Form of source data automation in which optical scanning devices read specially designed data and translate the data into digital form for the computer.

Magnetic ink character recognition (MICR): Input technology that translates characters written in magnetic ink into digital codes for processing.

Bar code: Form of OCR technology widely used in supermarkets and retail stores in which identification data are coded into a series of bars.

Pen-based input: Input devices such as tablets, notebooks, and notepads consisting of a flat-screen display tablet and a penlike stylus that digitizes handwriting.

Source data automation captures data in computer-readable form at the time and place they are created. Point-of-sale systems, optical bar-code scanners used in supermarkets, and other optical character recognition devices are examples of source data automation. **Optical character recognition (OCR)** devices translate specially designed marks, characters, and codes into digital form. One of the advantages of source data automation is that the many errors that occur when people use keyboards to enter data are almost eliminated. Bar code scanners make fewer than 1 error in 10,000 transactions, whereas skilled keypunchers make about 1 error for every 1000 keystrokes.

Moreover, source data automation permits information about events to be captured directly and immediately, with on-the-spot error correction. Businesses using these devices do not need a separate data entry staff. The principal source data automation technologies are magnetic ink character recognition, optical character recognition, pen-based input, digitizers, and voice input.

Magnetic ink character recognition (MICR) technology is used primarily in check processing for the banking industry. The bottom portion of a typical check contains characters that are preprinted using a special ink. Characters identify the bank, checking account, and check number. A MICR reader translates the characters on checks that have been cashed and sent to the bank for processing into digital form for the computer. The amount of the check, which is written in ordinary ink, must be keyed in by hand.

The most widely used optical code is the **bar code,** which is used in point-of-sale systems in supermarkets and retail stores. Bar codes are also used in hospitals, libraries, military operations, and transportation facilities. The codes can include time, date, and location data in addition to identification data; the information makes them useful for analyzing the movement of items and determining what has happened to them during production or other processes. (The discussion of the United Parcel Service in the opening to Chapter 1, and the Chapter 2 ending case on the CSX Corporation show how valuable bar codes can be for this purpose.)

Handwriting-recognition devices such as pen-based "tablets," "notebooks," or "notepads," are promising new input technologies, especially for people working in the sales or service areas or for those who have traditionally shunned computer keyboards. These **pen-based input** devices usually consist of a flat-screen display tablet and a penlike stylus.

With pen-based input, users print directly onto the tablet-sized screen. The screen is fitted with a transparent grid of fine wires that detects the presence of the special stylus, which emits a faint signal from its tip. The screen can also interpret tapping and flicking gestures made with the stylus.

Pen-based input devices transform the letters and numbers written by users on the tablet into digital form, where they can be stored or processed and analyzed. For instance, the United Parcel Service replaced its drivers' familiar clipboard with a battery-powered Delivery Information Acquisition Device (DIAD) to capture signatures (see the Chapter 1 opening vignette and photo) along with other information required for pickup and delivery. The Gillette Company supplied GridPad HD pen-based computers to its store merchandisers who are responsible for stocking stores and ensuring that Gillette products, such as Right Guard, are displayed as prominently as possible. The merchandisers had never used computers before. The merchandisers enter handwritten numbers on electronic "forms" into the notebooks and transmit the information via telephone links to Gillette. Gillette thus can receive stocking plans and information on products, pricing, and promotions immediately from the field.

This technology requires special pattern-recognition software to accept pen-based input instead of keyboard input. At present, most pen-based systems cannot recognize cursive writing. The case concluding this chapter treats this topic in more detail.

Digital scanners: Input devices that translate images such as pictures or documents into digital form for processing.

Voice input device: Technology that converts the spoken word into digital form for processing.

Digital scanners translate images such as pictures or documents into digital form and are an essential component of image processing systems such as that used by the United Services Automobile Association, described in Chapter 2.

Voice input devices convert spoken words into digital form. Voice-recognition software (see Chapter 5) compares the electrical patterns produced by the speaker's voice to a set of prerecorded patterns. If the patterns match, the input is accepted. Most voice systems still have limited "vocabularies" of several hundred to several thousand words and can accept only very simple commands. For instance, some branches of the U.S. Postal Service are using voice recognition systems to make sorting packages and envelopes more efficient. In one application, users can speak out ZIP codes instead of keying them in, so that both hands can manipulate a package.

Output Devices

Video display terminal (VDT): A screen, also referred to as a cathode ray tube (CRT). Provides a visual image of both user input and computer output.

The major data output devices are **video display terminals,** or **VDTs,** sometimes called cathode ray tube (CRT) terminals, and printers.

The CRT is probably the most popular medium for information output in modern computer systems. It works much like a television picture tube, with an electronic "gun" shooting a beam of electrons to illuminate the pixels on the screen. The more pixels per screen, the higher the resolution. CRT monitors can be classified as monochrome or color and by their display capabilities. Some display only text, whereas others display both text and graphics. Typical CRTs display 80 columns and 24 lines of text data. Display devices for graphics often utilize **bit mapping.** Bit mapping allows each pixel on the screen to be addressed and manipulated by the computer (as opposed to blocks of pixels in character addressable displays). This requires more computer memory but permits finer detail and the ability to produce any kind of image on the display screen. Special-purpose graphics terminals used in CAD/CAM and commercial art have very high resolution capabilities (1280 × 1024 pixels).

Bit mapping: The technology that allows each pixel on the screen to be addressed and manipulated by the computer.

PRINTERS

Printer: A computer output device that provides paper "hard-copy" output in the form of text or graphics.

Printers produce a printed hard copy of information output. They include impact printers (a standard typewriter or a dot matrix) and nonimpact printers (laser, inkjet, and thermal transfer printers). Most printers print one character at a time, but some commercial printers print an entire line or page at a time. Line printers capable of printing an entire line of output in a single step can print up to 3000 lines per minute. Page printers print an entire page at a time, outputting 20,000 lines per minute. Printers working with microcomputers typically provide dot matrix print at a speed of 60 to over 400 characters per second. Much slower letter-quality printers operate in the 10 to 50 character-per-second range. In general, impact printers are slower than nonimpact printers. Laser printers for microcomputers can print four to eight pages per minute. Laser printers in large computer centers can print over 100 pages per minute.

Dot matrix printer quality is generally much lower than letter quality and is used for less important documents and spreadsheets. "Intelligence," or some processing ability, is built into many newer printers and other input and output devices to take over tasks that were formerly performed by the main computer. For example, many microcomputer printers, such as the Hewlett-Packard Laserjet 4 or the Apple LaserWriter, are programmed to store graphic elements and various type fonts, which can be used selectively by different pieces of software.

OTHER DEVICES

Microfilm and microfiche have been used to compactly store output as microscopic filmed images, and they are used mainly by insurance companies or other firms that need to output and store large numbers of documents. These media are cumbersome to search through and will be replaced by optical disk technology.

High-quality graphic documents can be created using plotters with multicolored pens to draw (rather than print) computer output. Plotters are much slower than printers but are useful for outputting large-size charts, maps, or drawings.

A **voice output device** converts digital output data back into intelligible speech. Sounds are prerecorded, coded, and stored on disk, to be translated back as spoken words. For instance, when you call for information on the telephone, you may hear a computer "voice" respond with the telephone number you requested.

Voice output device: Converts digital output data into spoken words.

4.7 Information Technology Trends

Advances in materials science, manufacturing, and concepts of computing promise to maintain the historic growth pattern in hardware power. Over the last 30 years, computing costs have dropped by a factor of 10 each decade and capacity has increased by a factor of at least 100 each decade (Office of Technology Assessment, 1985). This momentum will most likely be maintained. Review Figure 4.7 again. It shows that between 1985 and 1993 the cost per MIPS on a microcomputer plummeted from about $60,000 to around $1,000. At the current rate of technological change, it should cost only $50 per microcomputer MIPS in 1995.

Today's microprocessors can put a mainframe on a desktop and eventually into a briefcase or shirt pocket. Chapter 7 shows how the traditional mainframe is being supplanted by networks of powerful desktop machines, although the mainframe will never be eliminated. The future will see even more intelligence built into everyday devices, with mainframe and perhaps even supercomputer-like computing power packed in a pocket- or notebook-sized computer. Pen, notebook, and palmtop computers will be as pervasive as handheld calculators. Computers on a chip will help guide automobiles, military weapons, robots, and everyday household devices. Computers and related information technologies will blend data, images, and sound, sending them coursing through vast networks that can process all of them with equal ease. We can see how this might be possible through the use of multimedia, superchips, and fifth-generation computers.

Multimedia

Multimedia: Technologies that facilitate the integration of two or more types of media such as text, graphics, sound, voice, full-motion video, or animation into a computer-based application.

Multimedia is defined as the technologies that facilitate the integration of two or more types of media, such as text, graphics, sound, voice, full-motion video, still video, or animation into a computer-based application. From the 1990s through the twenty-first century, multimedia will be the foundation of new consumer products and services, such as electronic books and newspapers, electronic classroom presentation technologies, full-motion video conferencing, imaging, graphics design tools, and video electronic and voice mail.

By pressing a button, a person using a computer can call up a screenful of text; another button might bring up related video images. Still another might bring up related talk or music. For instance, the New York Power Authority in White Plains, New York, has multimedia training programs that enable a sales representative to press a touch screen to see a colorful video demonstration of the software he or she is learning in a corner of the computer screen while an engineer sitting nearby can use the same multimedia training system to run through mathematical formulas with graphic animations illustrating the principles involved.

Multimedia systems combine the elements of today's personal computers (a computer, printer, keyboard, and mouse) with two new elements: audio (sound)

Figure 4.17

Multimedia applications require specially configured systems. This figure illustrates 11 components in a system used to develop a multimedia application. 1. CPU and primary storage: a minimum 80386/33 megahertz chip and 8 megabytes RAM. 2. Monitor: color monitor supporting super high resolutions from 640 × 480 to 1280 × 1024; minimum 17" screen. 3. CD-ROM: drive with 280 millisecond access time and 150 kilobits/second data transfer rate. 4. Hard disk: minimum 300 megabytes with 15 millisecond access time. 5. Stereo speakers. 6. Microphone for voice input. 7. Mouse. 8. Video input device or video board connected to a VCR or laser video disk player. 9–11. Sound card, video card, and video compression card. Adapter cards integrate sound and video into the computer and digitally compress full-motion video. *Adapted from: J. William Semich, "Multimedia Tools for Development Pros,"* Datamation, *August 15, 1992. Reprinted with permission from DATAMATION © 1992, Reed Publishing (USA) Inc.*

and video (pictures). Figure 4.17 illustrates some of the hardware components that would be required to create and run multimedia applications. Today's microcomputers can be converted to multimedia systems by purchasing special expansion boards. By the year 2000, computers will come with built-in multimedia capabilities.

The marriage of text, graphics, sound, and video data into a single application has been made possible by the advances in microprocessor and storage technologies described in this chapter. A simple multimedia system consists of a personal computer with a 32-bit microprocessor and a CD-ROM drive. A five-inch optical disk holding more than 600 megabytes of information can store an hour of music, several thousand full-color pictures, several minutes of video or animation, and millions of words. For instance, a single optical disk can store all 26 volumes of *Compton's MultiMedia Encyclopedia*. It includes 15,000 drawings, charts, photographs, and paintings, many in full color; 45 animated sequences; an hour of audio clips of famous speeches and music; and Webster's Intermediate Dictionary, plus about 9 million words.

The possibilities of this technology are endless, but the most promising business applications appear to be in training and presentations. For training, multimedia systems are appealing because they are interactive and permit two-way communication (Lambert). People can use multimedia training sessions any time of the day, at their own pace. Instructors can easily integrate words, sounds, pictures, and both live and animated video to produce lessons that capture students' imaginations. For example, students viewing "Search and Seizure," a multimedia computer lesson produced at the Harvard Law School, can press a key to stop the video of a drug arrest whenever they want to question the legality of police conduct. They can bring up case citations, constitutional texts, and judicial opinions.

The multimedia training material used by the sales people at Marion Merrell Dow Pharmaceutical allows users to display an index of a video glossary by clicking a button during the presentation of a selected topic. The last term used is highlighted. The user can view the glossary clip, return to the presentation, and be quizzed by the system. Andersen Consulting Company now delivers its business practice course on three CD-ROMs with 200 minutes of digital video and interactive training and testing techniques. By replacing classroom training, this multimedia course saves the firm $10 million per year. The Window on Management illustrates how multimedia can be used to assist Federal Express customers to send shipments using kiosks.

There will be numerous organizational applications of multimedia because multimedia is likely to be a major instrument for obtaining corporate information. When multimedia is coupled with the telecommunications technologies described in Chapter 7, desktop-to-desktop videoconferencing and file-sharing become feasible and will likely change the way people across organizations meet and interact. People will be able to capture, store, manipulate, and transmit photos and other document images and possibly full-motion video on a network as easily as they do with text. For instance, financial service firms could index a TV news report next to a related print story about a development affecting a company. Throughout this text, we will be looking at the various ways multimedia will be used in information systems.

The most difficult element to incorporate into multimedia information systems has been full-motion video because so much data must be brought under the digital control of the computer. While laser video disks and VCRs can deliver video images to microcomputers, this technology is limited to displaying images. The process of actually integrating video with other kinds of data requires special software or compression boards with dedicated video processing chips. The massive amounts of data in each video image must be digitally encoded, stored and manipulated electronically, using techniques that "compress" the digital data.

In 1992, Apple computers were the first to come equipped with software (called QuickTime [TM]) and some of the hardware to play back multimedia disks containing text, numbers, video, and sound. Microsoft Corporation has developed multimedia standards so that personal computers based on the IBM Personal System/2 model can play back and even author multimedia presentations.

A multimedia training center provides sound and images to the trainees at this facility.

MANAGEMENT

Federal Express: Multimedia in a Kiosk

Federal Express seems to have done it all. At its founding in 1973, it created a whole new industry, the overnight package delivery. After 20 years of explosive growth, the company delivers on average close to two million letters and packages overnight. Where can such an aggressive management take its company next? The answer appears to be into the world of multimedia.

Management saw several problems in their operation, despite its overwhelming success. First customers had to manually fill out dense, confusing forms to be completed prior to shipping. The shipper needed to know the zip code of the receiver and whether or not Federal Express actually delivers to that location. The whole process, beginning to end, was paper-intensive, time-consuming, and quite error-prone. Moreover, the shipper had to have access to a Fed Ex account number to be able to ship anything. Management needed to find ways to reduce the errors and paper while making their service more accessible to potential customers, including the occasional shippers who don't maintain Fed Ex accounts or have access to recipients' account numbers. Dennis Jones, Fed Ex's senior vice-president and chief information officer, took the problems, along with his idea for a solution, to IBM in the summer of 1992,

and the result was the *Fedex Online* multimedia kiosks.

The Fed Ex kiosks resemble enhanced bank automatic teller machines (ATMs). The customer steps into a self-enclosed kiosk and enters information through a video display terminal with both a touch screen and a simulated keyboard. The customer must supply the shipping address and indicate next-day or two-day delivery. The computer automatically checks the zip code for Fed Ex service. The customer can pay by entering a Fed Ex account number or by running a credit card through the magnetic card reader. The customer's credit is automatically checked, and when the process is completed, the computer prints a bar-coded shipping label. The customer attaches the label to the package and deposits it in a drop-off box to be collected later in the day. The whole process is quick, easy, and essentially error-free.

Customers can also use the kiosks to track a package, locate local Federal Express facilities, and see delivery schedules and a price list for any zip code area. They can even print out a package-tracking report should they wish, including the name of the recipient who signed for it.

The attractive multimedia kiosks use audio, still images, motion video, graphics, animation, and

text. Customers are greeted by a colorful video loop running on the monitor depicting Federal Express operations. Users touch the screen and the computer begins to lead them through the process, step by step. Animation is utilized to demonstrate to the customer how to use the credit card reader, how to affix the label to the package, and how to drop the package into the pick-up box. Audio aid is also available for customers who want it.

The kiosks were successfully tested in Memphis, Kansas City, and Minneapolis/St. Paul in 1993 and should begin appearing in other cities soon.

Sources: Anthony Ramirez, "Teller Machines Inspire a New Kiosk Business," *The New York Times*, March 31, 1993; and "Multimedia Express," IBM Multimedia Innovations, October 25, 1993.

To Think About: Why do you think the idea for the kiosk as a solution to Federal Express's problems came from management rather than from a technical staff? What are the management benefits of using kiosks? What management, organization, and technology factors did Federal Express have to address when deciding whether to use kiosks?

By the year 2000 all computers, regardless of size, will have built-in multimedia capabilities combining existing text and numbers with music, full motion and still frame video (snapshots), animation, voice messages, telephone, and fax capabilities.

Superchips

Semiconductor researchers have continued to find means of packaging circuits more densely, so that millions of transistors can be packed onto a fingernail-sized silicon wafer. The most powerful microprocessors—such as Intel's 80486 and Pentium chips; IBM, Apple, and Motorola's PowerPC; or Digital's Alpha, described in the Window on Technology—package mainframe and even supercomputerlike capabilities on a single chip.

The main way microprocessors have been made to perform faster is by shrinking the distance between transistors. This process gives the electrical current less distance to travel. Figure 4.18 shows how much progress has been made. One step in fashioning microprocessors is to etch lines in silicon wafers that form the outlines of circuits. The narrower the lines forming transistors, the larger the number of transistors that can be squeezed onto a single chip, and the faster these circuits will operate. Figure 4.18 shows that line widths have shrunk from the diameter of a hair to less than one micron and should reach one-fifth of a micron by the year 2000. The lower part of the figure shows the number of transistors on some common microprocessors and memory chips. Since the number of transistors that can fit economically onto a single silicon chip is doubling every 18 months, between 50 and 100 million transistors could conceivably be squeezed onto a single microprocessor by the year 2000. There are physical limits to this approach that may soon be reached, but researchers are experimenting with new materials to increase microprocessor speed.

Fifth-Generation Computers

Conventional computers are based on the Von Neumann architecture, which processes information serially, one instruction at a time. In the future, more computers will use parallel processing and massively parallel processing to blend

Figure 4.18
The shrinking size and growth in number of transistors. *Courtesy of Intel Corporation.*

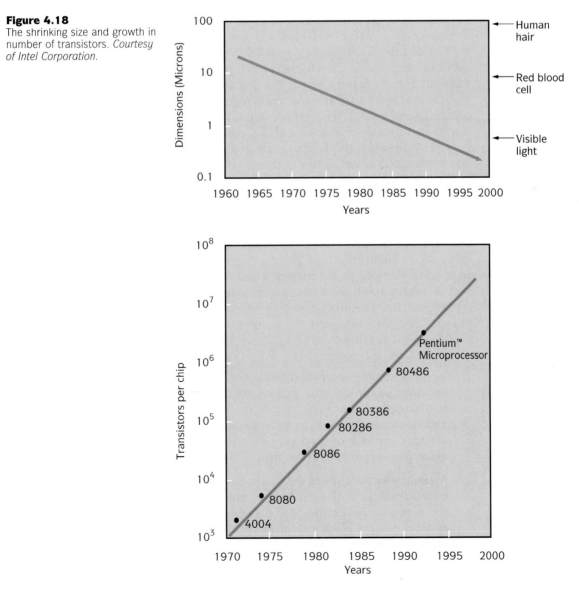

Webs of Electronic Brain Cells

COMPUTER ARCHITECTURE

Traditional computers use a single central processor to do all the computing work, one step at a time.

Parallel processing computers divide the work up among several processors operating simultaneously.

Massively parallel computers have huge networks of processors that are interwoven in complex and flexible ways.

Figure 4.19
Computer architecture. A comparison of traditional serial processing, parallel processing, and massively parallel processing. *Adapted from John Markoff, "Foray Into Mainstream for Parallel Computing," The New York Times, June 15, 1992. Copyright © 1992 by the New York Times Corporation. Reprinted by permission.*

voice, images, and massive pools of data from diverse sources, using artificial intelligence and intricate mathematical models.

Massively parallel computers, illustrated in Figure 4.19, have huge networks of processor chips interwoven in complex and flexible ways. As opposed to parallel processing, where small numbers of powerful but expensive specialized chips are linked together, massively parallel machines chain hundreds or even thousands of inexpensive, commonly used chips to attack large computing problems, attaining supercomputer speeds. For instance, Wal-Mart Stores uses a massively parallel machine to sift through an inventory and sales trend database with 1.8 trillion bytes of data. Massively parallel systems are said to have cost and speed advantages over conventional parallel computers because they can take advantage of off-the-shelf chips. They may be able to accomplish processing work for one-tenth to one-twentieth the cost of traditional mainframes or supercomputers.

Today's supercomputers can perform hundreds of billions of calculations per second. Now supercomputer makers are racing to harness tens of thousands of microprocessors and memory chips together to create super-supercomputers that can perform more than a trillion mathematical calculations each second—a teraflop. The term *teraflop* comes from the Greek *teras*, which for mathematicians means one trillion, and *flop*, an acronym for floating point operations per second. (A floating point operation is a basic computer arithmetic operation, such as addition, on numbers that include a decimal point.) In the twenty-first century, teraflop machines could support projects such as mapping the surface of planets, designing new computers, or testing the aerodynamics of supersonic airplanes, where trillions of calculations would be required.

Management Challenges

1. **Keeping abreast of technological change.** Because the technology is growing in power so rapidly and is changing basic patterns of information processing, managers must keep abreast of changes in the field. This requires time and resources. In medium to large firms, a person or small group must be assigned the task of tracking new technological developments and encouraging prototypes within the firm.

2. **Making wise purchasing decisions.** Soon after having made an investment in information technology, managers find the completed system is obsolete and too expensive given the power and lower cost of new technology. In this environment, it is very difficult to keep one's own systems up-to-date. A rather considerable amount of time must be spent anticipating and planning for technological change.

3. **Training the information systems staff and all employees.** In the transition from the mainframe computing to desktops, enormous changes in perspective and skills and attitudes are required on the part of an organization's information systems staff. Typically, they must be completely retrained every five years. All employees likewise will require extensive retraining simply to keep abreast of new ways of doing business with new information technologies.

Summary

Identify the hardware components in a typical computer system.

The modern computer system has five major categories of components: a central processor (consisting of the CPU and primary storage), input devices, output devices, secondary storage, and communications devices.

Describe how information is represented and processed in a computer system.

Digital computers store and process information in the form of binary digits called *bits*. A string of 8 bits is called a *byte*. There are several coding schemes for arranging binary digits into characters. The most common are EBCDIC and ASCII.

Describe the functions of the CPU and primary storage.

The CPU is the center of the computer, where the manipulation of symbols, numbers, and letters occurs. The CPU has two components: an arithmetic-logic unit, and a control unit. The arithmetic-logic unit performs arithmetic and logical operations on data, while the control unit controls and coordinates the other components of the computer.

The CPU is closely tied to primary memory, or primary storage, which stores data and program instructions temporarily before and after processing.

Several different kinds of semiconductor memory chips are used with primary storage: RAM (random-access memory) is used for short-term storage of data and program instructions, while ROM (read-only memory) permanently stores important program instructions. Other memory devices include PROM (programmable read-only memory) and EPROM (erasable programmable read-only memory.)

Distinguish between generations of computer hardware.

Computer technology has gone through four generations, from vacuum tubes to transistors, integrated circuits, and very-large-scale integrated circuits, each dramatically increasing computer processing power while shrinking the size of computing hardware.

Contrast the capabilities of mainframes, minicomputers, supercomputers, microcomputers, and workstations.

Depending on their size and processing power, computers are categorized as mainframes, minicomputers, workstations, supercomputers, or microcomputers. Mainframes are the largest computers, with 50 megabytes to over 1 gigabyte of RAM; minicomputers are midrange machines, with 10 to 650 megabytes of RAM; workstations are desktop machines, with powerful mathematical and graphic capabilities and 8–300 megabytes of RAM; and microcomputers are desktop or laptop machines, with 640 kilobytes to 64 megabytes of RAM.

The capabilities of microprocessors used in these computers can be gauged by their word length, data bus width, and cycle speed. Because of continuing advances in microprocessor technology, the distinctions between these various types of computers are constantly changing. Microcomputers are now powerful enough to perform much of the work that was formerly limited to mainframes and minicomputers.

Describe the various media for storing data and programs in a computer system.

The principal forms of secondary storage are tape, magnetic disk, and optical disk. Tape stores records in sequence, whereas disk permits direct access to specific records and is much faster than tape.

Compare the major input and output devices.

The principal input devices are keyboards, computer mice, touch screens, magnetic and optical character recognition, digital scanners, and voice input.

The principal output devices are printers, video display terminals, plotters, voice output devices, and microfilm and microfiche.

Describe multimedia and future information technology trends.

Multimedia integrates two or more types of media, such as text, graphics, sound, voice, full-motion video, still video, and/or animation into a computer-based application.

The future will see steady and impressive progress toward faster chips at lower cost and microprocessors with the power of today's mainframes or supercomputers. Hardware using parallel processing will be used more widely, and computers and related information technologies will be able to blend data, images, and sound.

Key Terms

Bit
Byte
EBCDIC (Extended Binary Coded Decimal Interchange Code)
ASCII (American Standard Code for Information Interchange)
Parity
Pixel
Millisecond
Microsecond
Nanosecond
Kilobyte
Megabyte
Gigabyte
Terabyte
Central processing unit (CPU)
Primary storage
RAM (random access memory)
Semiconductor
ROM (read-only memory)
PROM (programmable read-only memory)
EPROM (erasable programmable read-only memory)
Arithmetic-logic unit (ALU)
Control unit
Machine cycle
Computer generations
Microprocessor
Word length
Megahertz
Data bus width
Reduced instruction set computing (RISC)
Mainframe
Minicomputer
Microcomputer
Workstation

Supercomputer
Distributed processing
Centralized processing
Downsizing
Cooperative processing
Parallel processing
Secondary storage
Register
Cache
Magnetic tape
Magnetic disk
Hard disk
Cylinder
Track
Floppy disk
Sector
Direct access storage device (DASD)
Optical disk
CD-ROM (compact disk read only memory)
WORM (write once, read many)
Magneto-optical disk
Computer mouse
Touch screen
Source data automation
Magnetic ink character recognition (MICR)
Optical character recognition (OCR)
Bar code
Pen-based input
Digital scanners
Voice input device
Video display terminal (VDT)
Bit mapping
Printer
Voice output device
Multimedia

1. What are the components of a contemporary computer system?

2. Distinguish between a bit and a byte.

3. What are ASCII and EBCDIC, and why are they used? Why can true binary not be used in a computer as a machine language?

4. Name and define the principal measures of computer time and storage capacity.

5. What problems of coordination exist in a computing environment and why?

6. Name the major components of the CPU and the function of each.

7. Describe how information is stored in primary memory.

8. What are the four different types of semiconductor memory, and when are they used?

9. Describe the major generations of computers and the characteristics of each.

10. Name and describe the factors affecting the speed and performance of a microprocessor.

11. What are downsizing and cooperative processing?

12. What is the difference between primary and secondary storage?

13. List the most important secondary storage media. What are the strengths and limitations of each?

14. List and describe the major input devices.

15. List and describe the major output devices.

16. Distinguish between serial, parallel, and massively parallel processing.

17. What is multimedia? What technologies are involved?

1. What is the difference between a mainframe, a minicomputer, and a microcomputer? Between a mainframe and a supercomputer? Between a microcomputer and a workstation? Why are these distinctions disappearing?

2. How are the capabilities of an information system affected by its input, output, and storage devices?

3. A firm would like to introduce computers into its order entry process but feels that it should wait for a new generation of machines to be developed. After all, any machine bought now will quickly be out of date and less expensive a few years from now. Discuss.

Form a group with three or four of your classmates. Design an ideal "student desktop workstation" using the technologies described in this chapter. What input, output, and storage technologies would you select? How much processing capacity would be required? Why? What kinds of tasks could the workstation perform? How could the workstation help students learn or complete their assignments? Present your group's description to the class.

CASE STUDY

Will Pen-Based Computers Take Over?

With 2000 claims adjusters, engineers, and premium auditors, Continental Insurance of Neptune, New Jersey, wants to move its computing power out in the field with them. Notebook computers, which are used for word processing and communications, just won't do the job because a user can't work with one using just one hand and a keyboard. Furthermore, Continental Insurance's users are not stationary long enough to sit down and type. They have had to cope by leaving their computers in a hotel room and returning to do their work at the end of the day. Their work is very data intensive. For instance, a claims adjuster must investigate thefts or accidents and file numerous forms and reports with claims offices and central headquarters. Continental thinks pen-based computers might solve this problem.

Will they? Pen-based input technology promises both familiarity and ease of use. According to Tim Bajarin, an industry analyst with Creative Strategies Research International in Santa Clara, California, pen-based systems can potentially put the computer into the hands of people who have never touched the PC. White-collar executives who traditionally have shunned keyboards or field workers who need to fill out forms are the likely targets.

There are many business settings where an electronic "notepad" would be perfect. For instance, waiters could use them to take orders and get signatures for credit card receipts. Truck drivers could use notepads filled with electronic maps and forms to plan routes, keep track of deliveries, and store customers' signatures on receipts. For executives, notepads could serve as the ultimate "little black books" that store, cross-reference, and instantly retrieve names, addresses, phone numbers, and correspondence; send memos; or review and mark up documents and contracts.

Most users of pen-based systems, which are also called notepads, notebooks, or tablets, will be in mobile occupations. Users will include insurance adjusters, financial consultants, sales representatives, police, or delivery and maintenance workers. People doing this kind of work can use pen-based systems to fill out forms or to receive, edit, and retransmit faxes. Notepad computers can even be linked to other computers by telephone. The most advanced notepads will soon incorporate cellular phone circuitry so that users will be able to receive or transmit data, faxes, and phone calls just about anywhere.

Instead of a keyboard and mouse, pen-based computers use a stylus that looks and feels like a pen. People use the stylus to print directly on a tablet-sized screen. The writing is instantly captured and translated into digital form. Apple's Newton, termed a "personal digital assistant," is a widely publicized example of this technology. The Newton weighs less than one pound and is smaller than a videocassette. It has no keyboard. Instead, it recognizes handwritten notes penned on its screen with a specially designed stylus. Newton can understand printing, cursive, or a combination of the two writing styles. It acts as an electronic scheduler, calendar, and notepad. When equipped with a special insert card, Newton can serve as a pager, and when plugged into an external modem the size of a cigarette pack, it can transmit electronic mail messages or send documents to printers, fax machines, or microcomputers.

Pen input incorporates "gestures" instead of traditional commands or dragging icons. For instance, a word can be deleted by simply drawing a line through it. Users can insert a word or character by placing a caret at the desired location and tapping on the appropriate menu item. Users can move a word by circling it and drawing a line to where it belongs.

Traditional PCs require at least rudimentary keyboard skills and some training in the commands necessary to run software and keep track of stored data. The stylus com-bines the best attributes of both a mouse and a keyboard. You can use it not only to choose the software or document you want, but also to edit or enter text or numbers. Tapping with the stylus on the name of a document brings it up on the screen. Flicking the stylus at the bottom edge of the screen causes the computer to scroll through long documents. With the stylus, a user can write memos or reports. The notepad converts the hand-printed words into type, then formats the text into sentences and paragraphs as if they had been entered with a keyboard. In some pen-based models, users can draw pictures as easily as on paper, and the computer will straighten the wobbly lines and make circles perfectly round.

As simple as it sounds, the technology is still in its infancy. It cannot yet recognize all types of handwriting. At this point, many pen-based systems can primarily handle printed letters that are detached from one another, and even this ability to handle block printing has not been perfected. Users might find that some of the letters they entered were mistranslated and that considerable editing is required to get the desired result. There might not be a delete key if there is no keyboard.

Pen computer manufacturers have tried to get around these problems by stressing programs that permit a user to store his or her own written notes as a graphic image dubbed "ink" that can be called up later. But "ink" can't be easily indexed, searched, or manipulated in the way regular computer text can.

Clearly, this technology is not yet ready to support a general-purpose computer that would let users write entire business documents, enter a long series of figures, or perform other similar tasks that are still handled better by traditional pen and paper or keyboards. On the other hand, most computer tasks, such as requesting a report or a piece of data, require only a few numbers or words here or there.

To make sense of what is written on the screen, notepad computers contain special software that recognizes patterns. For some pen-based systems, users may have to "train" their machines to recognize their penmanship by repeatedly writing words and characters. This process takes about half an hour. Users of early versions of the Newton found that it took considerable practice and perseverance to get the machine to recognize their script.

Businesses have been able to make do with pen-based notepads by equipping them with special software that consists mainly of electronic forms. The pen is used primarily to check off boxes, select from lists, or highlight built-in pictures. Freehand writing in these applications is kept to a minimum and might require some "training" of the machine to recognize the user's scrawl.

Some firms have found that it isn't always easy to implement pen-based computer systems. Integrating potentially thousands of pen-based systems in the field with existing mainframes at company headquarters may prove challenging. For instance, the CSX Corporation, which has been described in the case concluding Chapter 2, developed a pen-based system that allows inspectors to draw a picture of an accident site and attach data to a report. The system transmits the information to the CSX mainframe, which issues instructions to dispatch a repair crew with accident information already in hand.

The pen-based system eliminated the need to rekey data, but it also raised worries about capturing too much data at the point of collection. The amount of information coming in from the field mushroomed with pen-based systems. Another project to arm rail car inspectors at each ramp in major depots with pen-based computers will place even more demands on the CSX mainframe. The inspectors will check off cargo content information using computerized forms. But with a thousand rail cars passing through each day, each pen-based computer is expected to transmit 2 megabytes of data to the mainframe, threatening to overwhelm its processing capacity. Still, the benefits cannot be ignored. CSX could use this system to give customers an hourly update on the location of their cargo.

Sources: Alan Deutschman, "Odd Man Out," *Fortune*, July 26, 1993; Walter S. Mossberg, "Notepad PCs Struggle with One Small Task: Deciphering Writing," The *Wall Street Journal*, July 23, 1992; Michael Fitzgerald, "Insurer Craves Pen Technology for Its Next-Generation Portable," *Computerworld*, March 2, 1992; Bob Francis, "Pen-Based Notebooks Find Their Niche," *Datamation*, October 1, 1991; and Brenton R. Schlender, "Hot New PCs that Read Your Writing," *Fortune*, February 11, 1991.

Case Study Questions

1. What are the advantages and disadvantages of pen-based computers?
2. Are pen-based computers a solution for Continental Insurance? Why or why not? What management, organization, and technology factors should be considered to make this decision?
3. Suggest some other areas of business where pen-based input would be useful.

References

Appleby, Chuck. "Taking Note of Multimedia." *InformationWEEK*, March 16, 1992.

Bell, Gordon. "The Future of High Performance Computers in Science and Engineering." *Communications of the ACM* 32, no. 9, September 1989.

Bell, Gordon. "Ultracomputers: A Teraflop Before Its Time." *Communications of the ACM* 35, no. 8, August 1992.

Datapro Information Services Group. "PowerPC: The New Generation of Computing." *Computerworld*, September 20, 1993.

Lambert, Craig. "The Electronic Tutor." *Harvard Magazine*, November–December 1990.

Markoff, John. "Foray into Mainstream for Parallel Computing." *The New York Times*, June 15, 1992.

Markoff, John. "Supercomputing's Speed Quest." *The New York Times*, May 31, 1991.

Mel, Bartlett W., Stephen M. Omohundro, Arch D. Robison, Steven S. Skiena, Kurt H. Thearling, Luke T. Young, and Stephen Wolfram. "Tablet: Personal Computer in the Year 2000." *Communications of the ACM* 31, no. 6, June 1988.

National Bureau of Standards. *Forecast of Technology Trends and Implications for Management*. Mimeo. Washington, D.C.: National Bureau of Standards, 1986.

Office of Technology Assessment. *Information Technology R & D*. Washington, D.C.: Office of Technology Assessment, U.S. Congress, 1985.

Peled, Abraham. "The Next Computer Revolution." *Scientific American* 257, no. 4, October 1987.

Press, Larry. "Compuvision or Teleputer?" *Communications of the ACM* 33, no. 3, September 1990.

Radding, Alan. "RISC Desktop Machines: PCs in Disguise?" *Computerworld*, March 23, 1992.

Reinhardt, Andy. "Pentium Changes the PC." *Byte*, July 1993.

Saffo, Paul. "Farewell PC—What's Next?" *The New York Times*, October 13, 1991.

Smarr, Larry, and Charles E. Catlett. "Metacomputing." *Communications of the ACM* 35, no. 6, June 1992.

Wetmore, Tim. "The Multimedia Challenge." *InformationWEEK*, January 13, 1992.

CHAPTER 5

Information Systems Software

Software Needed for Insight

The supermarket business is intensely competitive. Because retail supermarkets earn only between two and four cents on every pretax dollar, food retailers must sell food in large volumes as efficiently as possible, keeping their costs low and making sure that items move quickly off the shelves. Any information that gives them direction on items and quantities to stock will improve a skimpy bottom line. Can the sales data captured at their checkout counters be of use?

What can be learned about that can of soup that was just scanned at the supermarket checkout counter? The store can use the data to tally the day's sales and to identify items that need replenishing in inventory. But retailers and the firms that supply the cans of soup want to know more. They would like to use these data to determine the popularity of different varieties of soup, to predict sales preferences by regions or neighborhoods, or to measure sales volume over different seasons. But they can't make

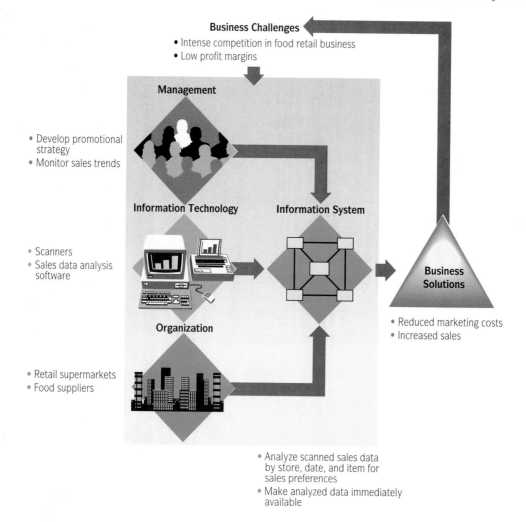

Business Challenges
- Intense competition in food retail business
- Low profit margins

Management
- Develop promotional strategy
- Monitor sales trends

Information Technology
- Scanners
- Sales data analysis software

Organization
- Retail supermarkets
- Food suppliers

Information System
- Analyze scanned sales data by store, date, and item for sales preferences
- Make analyzed data immediately available

Business Solutions
- Reduced marketing costs
- Increased sales

sense of the flood of data captured by bar-code scanners without the right software to interpret it.

Well-designed software could forecast which varieties of soup will be popular at a particular store. While sales clerks might make do by scanning one can of soup and multiplying it by the number of cans of soup purchased, the data about which kinds of soup are bought are lost.

The volumes of data traditionally compiled and sold for long-term planning by market research firms such as A.C. Nielsen, Inc. and Information Resources, Inc. (IRI) won't work. Nielsen obtained much of its information by melding consumer surveys and observations of purchases with scanned data. Both firms lacked systems that would allow clients to see on demand how all low-fat products were selling in a particular region or retail chain. Such systems would be characteristic-driven, not U.P.C. bar code driven and could cut across product categories that are now defined by bar codes. They could provide clients with data from individual stores as well as all stores, and they could provide figures daily rather than weekly. Right now it takes three or four weeks to analyze scanned data to account for inconsistencies in how different retailers use bar codes to ring up prices. This is too long to adjust product promotion plans for upcoming sales campaigns or to inform manufacturers and retailers precisely about what to keep in inventory.

One market research company, Efficient Market Services (EMS) in Deerfield, Illinois, has come up with software that would meet these needs. The EMS software consolidates sales data from the cash registers in each store, analyzes the data, and produces completed reports 12 hours after a register has closed. Food suppliers who buy the store-specific and item-specific data collected by the EMS system can use this information to make timely deliveries of their goods, to build displays, and to assess the impact of sales promotions. Nielsen and IRI are working feverishly to develop similar software. Unless they can deliver the information that their clients need, they won't be able to remain in business.

Sources: Barnaby J. Feder, "Scanning Sales with an Eye on Rival," *The New York Times,* December 2, 1993; and Bruce Caldwell, "Scanning for Insight," *InformationWEEK,* March 30, 1992.

In the last twenty-five years, public media have paid a great deal of attention to advances in computer hardware. But without the software to utilize the expanding capabilities of the hardware, the "computer revolution" would have been still-born. The retailers, suppliers, and market research firms described in the opening vignette had the data they needed and the hardware for processing these data. What prevented them from obtaining the right information to project buying trends was the lack of appropriate software.

The usefulness of computer hardware depends a great deal on available software and the ability of management to evaluate, monitor, and control the utilization of software in the organization. This chapter shows how software turns computer hardware into useful information systems, describes the major types of software, provides criteria for selecting software, and presents new approaches to software development.

After completing this chapter you will be able to:

- Describe the major types of software.
- Describe the functions of system software and compare leading microcomputer operating systems.
- Explain how software has evolved and how it will continue to develop.
- Compare strengths and limitations of the major programming languages and tools.
- Explain how to select appropriate software and programming languages.

5.1 What Is Software?

Software: The detailed instructions that control the operation of a computer system.

Software is the detailed instructions that control the operation of a computer system. Without software, computer hardware could not perform the tasks we associate with computers. The functions of software are 1) to manage the computer resources of the organization; 2) to provide tools for human beings to take advantage of these resources; and 3) to act as an intermediary between organizations and stored information.

Software Programs

Program: A series of statements or instructions to the computer.

A software **program** is a series of statements or instructions to the computer. The process of writing or coding programs is termed programming, and individuals who specialize in this task are called programmers.

Stored program concept: The idea that a program cannot be executed unless it is stored in a computer's primary storage along with required data.

The **stored program concept** means that a program must be stored in the computer's primary storage along with the required data in order to execute, or have its instructions performed by the computer. Once a program has finished executing, the computer hardware can be used for another task when a new program is loaded into memory.

Major Types of Software

System software: Generalized programs that manage the resources of the computer.

There are three major types of software: system software, application software, and end-user software. Each kind performs a different function. **System software** is a set of generalized programs that manage the resources of the computer, such as the central processing unit, communications links, and peripheral devices. Programmers who write system software are called system programmers.

Application software: Programs written for a specific business application in order to perform functions specified by end users.

Application software describes the programs that are written for or by users to apply the computer to a specific task. Software for processing an order or generating a mailing list is application software. Programmers who write application software are called application programmers.

End-user software: Software tools that permit the development of applications by end users with little or no professional programmer intervention or that enhance the productivity of professional programmers.

A special type of application software called end-user software (or fourth-generation languages) appeared in the early 1980s (see section 5.4). **End-user software** consists of software tools that permit the development of some applications directly by end users without professional programmers. Some end-user software is used to enhance the productivity of professional programmers.

The three types of software are interrelated and can be thought of as a set of nested boxes, each of which must interact closely with the other boxes surrounding it. Figure 5.1 illustrates this relationship. The system software surrounds and

Figure 5.1
The three major types of software. The relationship between the system software, application software, and end-user software can be illustrated by a series of nested boxes. System software—consisting of operating systems, language translators, and utility programs—controls access to the hardware. Application software, such as the programming languages, must work through the system software to operate. End-user software, such as the fourth-generation languages, must work through the application software and then the system software in order to operate.

controls access to the hardware. Application software must work through the system software in order to operate. Last, end-user software frequently has to work through application software and finally through system software. Each type of software must be specially designed to a specific machine in order to ensure its compatibility.

5.2 System Software

Operating system: The system software that manages and controls the activities of the computer.

System software coordinates the various parts of the computer system and mediates between applications software and computer hardware. The system software that manages and controls the activities of the computer is called the **operating system.** Other system software consists of computer language translation programs that convert programming languages into machine language and utility programs that perform common processing tasks.

Functions of the Operating System

One way to look at the operating system is as the system's chief manager. Operating system software decides which computer resources will be used, which programs will be run, and the order in which activities will take place.

An operating system performs three functions. It allocates and assigns system resources; it schedules the use of computer resources and computer jobs; and it monitors computer system activities.

ALLOCATION AND ASSIGNMENT

The operating system allocates resources to the application jobs in the execution queue. It provides locations in primary memory for data and programs and controls the input and output devices such as printers, terminals, and telecommunication links.

Thousands of pieces of work can be going on in a computer simultaneously. The operating system decides when to schedule the jobs that have been submitted and when to coordinate the scheduling in various areas of the computer so that different parts of different jobs can be worked on at the same time. For instance, while a program is executing, the operating system is scheduling the use of input and output devices. Not all jobs are performed in the order they are submitted; the operating system must schedule these jobs according to organizational priorities. On-line order processing may have priority over a job to generate mailing lists and labels.

MONITORING

The operating system monitors the activities of the computer system. It keeps track of each computer job and may also keep track of who is using the system, of what programs have been run, and of any unauthorized attempts to access the system. Information system security is discussed in detail in Chapter 13.

Obviously, the operating system of a major mainframe computer is itself a very large program. For this reason, only parts of the operating system are actually stored in the primary storage area. Most of the operating system is stored in a copy on a disk, to which primary storage has very rapid access. Whenever parts of the operating system are required by a given application, they are transferred from the disk and loaded into primary storage. The device on which a complete operating system is stored is called the **system residence device**.

System residence device: The secondary storage device on which a complete operating system is stored.

Multiprogramming, Time Sharing, Virtual Storage, and Multiprocessing

How is it possible for 1000 or more users sitting at remote terminals to use a computer information system simultaneously if, as we stated in the previous chapter, a computer can execute only one instruction from one program at a time? How can computers run thousands of programs? The answer is that the computer has a series of specialized operating system capabilities.

MULTIPROGRAMMING

Multiprogramming: A method of executing two or more programs concurrently using the same computer. The CPU only executes one program but can service the input/output needs of others at the same time.

The most important operating system capability for sharing computer resources is **multiprogramming**. Multiprogramming permits multiple programs to share a computer system's resources at any one time through concurrent use of a CPU. By concurrent use, we mean that only one program is actually using the CPU at any given moment but that the input/output needs of other programs can be serviced at the same time. Two or more programs are active at the same time, but they do not use the same computer resources simultaneously. With multiprogramming, a group of programs takes turns using the processor.

Figure 5.2 shows how three programs in a multiprogramming environment can be stored in primary storage. The first program executes until an

Figure 5.2
Single-program execution versus multiprogramming. In multiprogramming, the computer can be used much more efficiently because a number of programs can be executing concurrently. Several complete programs are loaded into memory. This memory management aspect of the operating system greatly increases throughput by better management of high-speed memory and input/output devices.

input/output event is read in the program. The operating system then directs a channel (a small processor limited to input and output functions) to read the input and move the output to an output device. The CPU moves to the second program until an input/output statement occurs. At this point, the CPU switches to the execution of the third program, and so forth, until eventually all three programs have been executed. Notice that the interruptions in processing are caused by events that take place in the programs themselves. In this manner, many different programs can be executing at the same time, although different resources within the computer are actually being utilized.

You can observe the advantages of multiprogramming by comparing multiprogramming systems to the first operating systems, which executed only one program at a time. Before multiprogramming, whenever a program read data off a tape or disk or wrote data to a printer, the entire CPU came to a stop. This was a very inefficient way to use the computer. With multiprogramming, the CPU utilization rate is much higher.

MULTITASKING

Multitasking: The multiprogramming capability of primarily single-user operating systems such as those for microcomputers.

Multitasking refers to multiprogramming on single-user operating systems such as those in microcomputers. One person can run two or more programs concurrently on a single computer. For example, a sales representative could write a letter to prospective clients with a word processing program while simultaneously using a database program to search for all sales contacts in a particular city or geographic area. Instead of terminating his or her session with the word processing program, returning to the operating system, and then initiating a session with the database program, multitasking allows the sales representative to display both programs on the computer screen and work with them at the same time.

VIRTUAL STORAGE

Virtual storage: A way of handling programs more efficiently by the computer by dividing the programs into small fixed or variable-length portions with only a small portion stored in primary memory at one time.

Virtual storage was developed after some problems of multiprogramming became apparent. Virtual storage handles programs more efficiently because the computer divides the programs into small fixed or variable-length portions, storing only a small portion of the program in primary memory at one time. First, although two or three large programs can be read into memory, a certain part of main memory generally remains underutilized because the programs add up to less than the total amount of primary storage space available. Second, given the limited size of primary memory, only a small number of programs can reside in primary storage at any given time. For example, many business programs may require up to 200K of storage, and the computer may have only 1 megabyte of primary storage. Therefore, only a few programs can reside in memory at any given time.

Only a few statements of a program actually execute at any given moment. Virtual storage takes advantage of this feature of processing. Virtual storage breaks a program into a number fixed-length portions called **pages** or into variable-length portions called segments. Each of these portions is relatively small (a page is approximately 2-4 kilobytes). The actual breakpoint between segments can be determined either by the programmer or by the operating system. This permits a very large number of programs to reside in primary memory, inasmuch as only one page or segment of each program is actually located there (see Figure 5.3).

Page: Small fixed-length section of a program, which can be easily stored in primary storage and quickly accessed from secondary storage.

All other program pages are stored on a peripheral disk unit until they are ready for execution. Virtual storage provides a number of advantages. First, primary storage is utilized more fully. Many more programs can be in primary storage because only one page of each program actually resides there. Second, programmers no longer have to worry about the size of the primary storage area. Before virtual storage, programs could obviously be no larger than the computer's main memory that stored them. With virtual storage, programs can be of

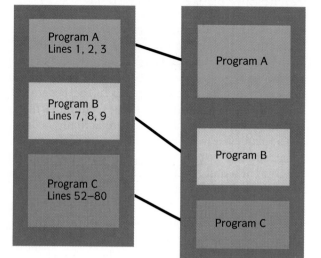

Figure 5.3
Virtual storage. Virtual storage is based on the fact that in general, only a few statements in a program can actually be utilized at any given moment. In virtual storage, programs are broken down into small sections called pages. Individual program pages are read into memory only when needed. The rest of the program is stored on disk until it is required. In this way, very large programs can be executed by small machines, or a large number of programs can be executed concurrently by a single machine.

infinite length and small machines can execute a program of any size (admittedly, small machines will take longer than big machines to execute a large program). With virtual storage, there is no limit to a program's storage requirements.

TIME SHARING

Time sharing: The sharing of computer resources by many users simultaneously by having the CPU spend a fixed amount of time on each user's program before proceeding to the next.

Time sharing is an operating system capability that allows many users to share computer processing resources simultaneously. It differs from multiprogramming in that the CPU spends a fixed amount of time on one program before moving on to another. In a time-sharing environment, thousands of users are each allocated a tiny slice of computer time (2 milliseconds). In this time slot, each user is free to perform any required operations; at the end of this period, another user is given a 2-millisecond time slice of the CPU. This arrangement permits many users to be connected to a CPU simultaneously, with each receiving only a tiny amount of CPU time. But since the CPU is operating at the nanosecond level, a CPU can accomplish a great deal of work in two milliseconds.

MULTIPROCESSING

Multiprocessing: An operating system feature for executing two or more instructions simultaneously in a single computer system by using more than one central processing unit.

Multiprocessing is an operating system capability that links together two or more CPUs to work in parallel in a single computer system. The operating system can assign multiple CPUs to execute different instructions from the same program or from different programs simultaneously, dividing the work between the CPUs. While multiprogramming uses concurrent processing with one CPU, multiprocessing uses simultaneous processing with multiple CPUs.

Language Translation and Utility Software

Source code: Program instructions written in a high-level language before translation into machine language.

Compiler: Special system software that translates a higher-level language into machine language for execution by the computer.

When computers execute programs written in languages such as COBOL, FORTRAN, or C, the computer must convert these "human readable" instructions into a form it can understand. Computers interpret binary ones and zeros, and the language translators found in system software make the conversion. System software includes special language translator programs that translate higher-level language programs written in programming languages such as BASIC, COBOL, and FORTRAN into machine language that the computer can execute. This type of system software is called a *compiler* or *interpreter*. The program in the high-level language before translation into machine language is called **source code**. A **compiler** translates source code into machine code called **object code**. Just before execution by the computer, the object code modules are joined

Object code: Program instructions that have been translated into machine language so that they can be executed by the computer.

Interpreter: A special language translator that translates each source code statement into machine code and executes it one at a time.

Utility program: System software consisting of programs for routine, repetitive tasks, which can be shared by many users.

together with other object code modules in a process called linkage editing. The resulting load module is what is actually executed by the computer. Figure 5.4 illustrates the language translation process.

Some programming languages, like BASIC, do not use a compiler but an **interpreter,** which translates each source code statement one at a time into machine code and executes it. Interpreter languages like BASIC provide immediate feedback to the programmer if a mistake is made, but they are very slow to execute because they are translated one statement at a time.

An assembler is similar to a compiler but is used to translate only assembly language (see Section 5.3) into machine code.

System software includes **utility programs** for routine, repetitive tasks, such as copying, clearing primary storage, computing a square root, or sorting. If you have worked on a computer and have performed such functions as setting up new files, deleting old files, or formatting diskettes, you have worked with utility programs. Utility programs are prewritten programs that are stored so that they can be shared by all users of a computer system and can be rapidly used in many different information system applications when requested.

Microcomputer Operating Systems

Like any other software, microcomputer software is based on specific operating systems and computer hardware. A software package written for one microcomputer operating system cannot run on another. The microcomputer operating systems themselves have distinctive features—such as whether they support multitasking or graphics work—that determine the types of applications they are suited for.

Figure 5.4
The language translation process. The source code, the program in a high-level language, is translated by the compiler into object code so that the instructions can be "understood" by the machine. These are grouped into modules. Prior to execution, the object code modules are joined together by the linkage editor to create the load module. It is the load module that is actually executed by the computer.

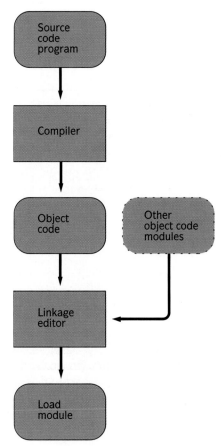

Multitasking is one of the principal strengths of operating systems such as IBM's OS/2 (Operating System/2) for the IBM Personal System/2 line of microcomputers and IBM clones or UNIX. PC-DOS and MS-DOS, the older operating system for IBM personal computers and IBM PC clones, do not allow multitasking, although the Microsoft Corporation markets Windows software to create a multitasking environment for DOS programs.

Table 5.1 compares the leading microcomputer operating systems—OS/2, UNIX, DOS, Windows NT, and the Macintosh operating system. **DOS** was the most popular operating system for 16-bit microcomputers. It is still widely used today with more powerful microcomputers based on the IBM microcomputer standard because so much available application software has been written for systems using DOS. (PC-DOS is used exclusively with IBM microcomputers. MS-DOS is used with other 16-bit microcomputers that function like the IBM microcomputer.) DOS itself does not support multitasking and limits the size of a program in memory to 640K.

OS/2 is a robust operating system that is used with 32-bit IBM Personal System/2 microcomputers and IBM clones. OS/2 can run faster than DOS (which can only address data in 16-bit chunks) because it can address data in 32-bit chunks. OS/2 is being used for more complex memory-intensive applications or those that require networking or multitasking. OS/2 supports multitasking, accommodates larger applications, allows applications to be run simultaneously, supports networked applications, and is a much more protected operating system. One application that crashes is less likely to bring the whole operating system and other applications down with it. This operating system requires powerful computer hardware—a minimum 80386 microprocessor, 4 megabytes of RAM, and 60 megabyte hard disk. OS/2 provides powerful desktop computers with mainframe operating system-like capabilities, such as multitasking and supporting multiple users in networks. The CSX Corporation described in the case concluding Chapter 2 adopted OS/2 as its corporate stan-

DOS: Operating system for 16-bit microcomputers based on the IBM Personal Computer standard.

OS/2: Powerful operating system used with the 32-bit IBM/Personal System/2 microcomputer workstations that supports multitasking, networking, and more memory-intensive applications than DOS.

Table 5.1 LEADING MICROCOMPUTER OPERATING SYSTEMS

Operating System	Features
OS/2 (Operating System/2)	Operating system for the IBM Personal System/2 line of microcomputers and IBM clones . Can take advantage of the 32-bit microprocessor. Supports multitasking and networking and can run large programs that require more than 640 K of memory.
Windows NT	32-bit operating system for microcomputers and workstations not limited to Intel microprocessors. Supports multitasking, multiprocessing and networking and can run programs that require more than 640 K of memory.
UNIX (XENIX)	Used for powerful microcomputers, workstations, and minicomputers. Supports multitasking, multi-user processing, and networking. Is portable to different models of computer hardware.
System 7	Operating system for the Macintosh computer. Supports multitasking and has powerful graphics and multimedia capabilities.
PC-DOS	Operating system for the IBM Personal Computer. Limits program use of memory to 640 K.
MS-DOS	Contains features similar to PC-DOS but is the operating system for IBM PC clones (microcomputers that function like the IBM Personal Computer).

dard because it believed OS/2 had the power to support industrial-strength applications and cooperative processing.

Windows NT is a new operating system developed by Microsoft with features that make it more appropriate for business-critical applications in networked environments than DOS or DOS with the Windows graphical user interface shell (see the following section). Windows NT uses the same graphical user interface as Windows but it has powerful multitasking and memory management capabilities. Windows NT can support existing software written for DOS and it can provide mainframe-like computing capability for new applications with massive memory and file requirements. It can address data in 32-bit chunks if required and can even support multiprocessing with multiple CPUs. Unlike OS/2, Windows NT is not tied to computer hardware based on Intel microprocessors. It can run on microcomputers and workstations using microprocessors from Mips Computer Systems Inc. or DEC's new Alpha chip (see the Window on Technology in Chapter 4). A company might choose Windows NT if it values flexibility and wants to use an operating system that can run different types of applications on a variety of computer hardware platforms using a common interface that is familiar to users. Although Windows NT can run on 80386-based microcomputers, it operates better on microcomputers or workstations with the minimum processing capacity of an 80486 microprocessor and requires 16 megabytes of RAM and a 100-megabyte hard disk.

UNIX was developed at Bell Laboratories in 1969 to help scientific researchers share data and programs while keeping other information private. It is an interactive, multi-user, multitasking operating system. Many people can use UNIX simultaneously to perform the same kind of task, or one user can run many tasks on UNIX concurrently. UNIX was developed to connect various machines together and is highly supportive of communications and networking.

UNIX was initially designed for minicomputers but now has versions for microcomputers and mainframes. UNIX can run on many different kinds of computers and can be easily customized. It can also store and manage a large number of files. At present, UNIX is primarily used for workstations, minicomputers, and inexpensive multi-user environments in small businesses, but its use in large businesses is growing because of its machine-independence. Application programs that run under UNIX can be ported from one computer to run on a different computer with little modification.

UNIX is accused of being unfriendly to users. It is powerful but very complex. It has a legion of commands, some of which are very cryptic and terse. A typing error on a command line can easily destroy important files. UNIX cannot respond well to problems caused by the overuse of system resources such as jobs or disk space. UNIX also poses some security problems, since multiple jobs and users can access the same file simultaneously. Finally, UNIX requires huge amounts of random access memory and disk capacity, limiting its usefulness for less powerful microcomputers.

System 7, the latest version of Macintosh system software, features multitasking as well as powerful graphics capabilities and a mouse-driven graphical user interface (illustrated in Figure 5.5). An extension of this operating system called QuickTime allows Macintosh users to integrate video clips, stereo sound, and animated sequences with conventional text and graphics software. (Recall the discussion of multimedia in Chapter 4.) System 7 has some features that make it attractive for global applications. For instance, it provides system-level support for Asian languages with large character sets.

Graphical User Interfaces

Whenever users interact with a computer, even a microcomputer, the interaction is controlled by an operating system. The user interface is the part of an information system that users interact with. Users communicate with an operating

Figure 5.5
System 7—Macintosh system software. System 7 supports powerful graphics capabilities as well as multitasking. Users can view multiple windows and make selections by clicking on icons in pull-down menus. *Courtesy of John Greenleigh/Apple Computer, Inc.*

Graphical user interface: The part of an operating system that users interact with that uses graphic icons and the computer mouse to issue commands and make selections.

system through the user interface of that operating system. Early microcomputer operating systems were command-driven, but the **graphical user interface,** first popularized by the Macintosh operating system, makes extensive use of icons, buttons, bars, and boxes to perform the same task. It is starting to become the dominant model for the user interface of microcomputer operating systems.

Older microcomputer operating systems, such as PC-DOS or MS-DOS, are command-driven. The user must type in commands such as DELETE C:\DATAFILE to perform tasks such as deleting a file named DATAFILE. As illustrated in Figure 5.5, the Macintosh computer uses graphical symbols called icons to depict programs, files, and activities. Commands can be activated by rolling a mouse to move a cursor about the screen and clicking a button on the mouse to make selections. A file can be deleted by dragging the file icon using the mouse to move the cursor to the "Trash" icon.

Proponents of the graphical user interface claim that graphical user interfaces save learning time because computing novices do not have to learn different arcane commands for each application. Common functions such as getting help, saving files, or printing output are performed the same way across all programs. A complex series of commands can be issued simply by linking icons. Commands are standardized from one program to the next, so that using new programs is often possible without additional training or use of reference manuals. For example, the steps involved in printing a letter created by a word processing program or a financial statement generated by a spreadsheet program should be the same. Graphical user interfaces also promote superior screen and print output communicated through graphics.

Windows: A graphical user interface shell that runs in conjunction with the DOS microcomputer operating system. Supports multitasking and some forms of networking.

Microsoft **Windows** is a highly popular graphical user interface shell that runs in conjunction with the DOS operating system. Windows supports limited multitasking and some forms of networking but shares the memory limitations of DOS. It is not considered to run very efficiently in a multitasking environment. Early versions of Windows had some problems with application crashes when multiple programs competed for the same memory space. OS/2 has its own graphical user interface called the Workplace Shell, which resembles the graphical user interface for the Macintosh computer. It provides users with a consistent graphical user interface across applications. OS/2 supports DOS applications and can run Windows and DOS applications at the same time in its own resizable windows. The chapter-ending case explores the advantages, disadvantages, and business implications of these two graphical user interfaces and their operating systems.

Selecting a Microcomputer Operating System

How should a firm go about choosing the operating system for its microcomputer-based applications? Should the decision be made only on the basis of technical merits? Should companies look at other issues such as ease of use, training, and the cost of hardware and software that use the operating system? This brief survey suggests that there are many factors to consider.

If a firm wants an operating system for its mainstream business applications, it needs an operating system that is compatible with the software required by these applications. The operating system should be easy to use and install. The user interface features of the operating system should be easy to learn. Mission-critical applications have special operating system requirements, since businesses depend on them for their continuing operation and survival. For such applications, an operating system that provides reliable support for multitasking and memory management is essential. The operating system should be able to run multiple applications quickly without having the system crash because applications are contending for the same memory space. Mission-critical applications typically have large volumes of transactions to process and require operating systems that can handle large complex software programs and massive files.

When selecting a microcomputer operating system, some key questions to ask are

- What application software runs on the operating system?
- What kind of computer hardware does the operating system run on?
- How quickly does the operating system run?
- How easy is the operating system to learn and use?
- Is the operating system designed for single users or for multiple users on networks?
- Does the operating system have strong multitasking capabilities?
- How reliable is the operating system?
- How much does it cost to install the operating system?
- What technical support and assistance is required to install and run the operating system? Where is this support available?

5.3   Application Software

Application software is primarily concerned with accomplishing the tasks of end users. Many different programming languages can be used to develop application software. Each has different strengths and drawbacks.

Generations of Programming Languages

Machine language:
Programming language consisting of the 1s and 0s of binary code.

To communicate with the first generation of computers, programmers had to write programs in **machine language**—the 0s and 1s of binary code. End users who wanted applications had to work with specialized programmers who could understand, think, and work directly in the machine language of a particular computer. Programming in 0s and 1s, reducing all statements such as add, subtract, and divide into a series of 0s and 1s, made early programming a slow, labor-intensive process.

As computer hardware improved and processing speed and memory size increased, computer languages changed from machine language to languages that were easier for humans to understand. Generations of programming languages developed to correspond with the generations of computer hardware. Figure 5.6 shows the development of programming languages over the last 50 years as the capabilities of hardware have increased.

Machine language was the first-generation programming language. The second generation of programming languages occurred in the early 1950s with the development of assembly language. Instead of using 0s and 1s, programmers could now substitute language-like acronyms and words such as *add, sub* (subtract), and *load* in programming statements. A language translator called a *compiler* converted the English-like statements into machine language.

When the third hardware generation was under way, programming languages entered their third generation as well. From the mid-1950s to the 1970s, the first higher-level languages emerged. These languages permitted mathematicians for the first time to work with computers through the use of languages such as FORTRAN (FORmula TRANslator program). Mathematicians were now able to define variables with statements such as $Z = A + B$. The software translated these definitions and mathematical statements into a series of 0s and 1s. COBOL (COmmon Business Oriented Language) permitted the use of English statements such as *print* and *sort* to be used by programmers, who did not have to think in terms of 0s and 1s.

Figure 5.6
Generations of programming languages. As the capabilities of hardware increased, programming languages developed from the first generation of machine and second generation of assembly languages of the 1950s to 1960, through the third generation high-level languages developed in the 1960s and 1970s, to the fourth-generation languages.

A. Generations

B. Specific languages

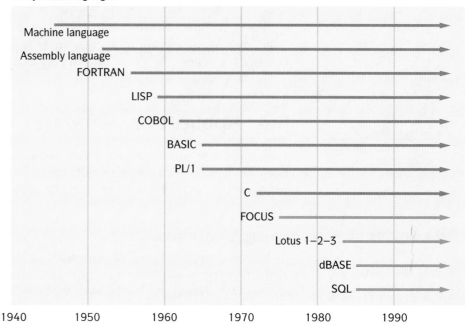

These **high-level languages** are so called because each statement in COBOL or FORTRAN generates multiple statements at the machine-language level. The use of these higher-level languages requires much faster, more efficient compilers to translate higher-level languages into machine codes.

Fourth-generation computer languages emerged in the late 1970s, and their development is still in progress. These languages dramatically reduce programming time and make software tasks so easy that nontechnical computer users can develop applications without the help of professional programmers. Fourth-generation tools also include prewritten application software packages that can be used directly by end users. Using the software package Lotus 1-2-3, for instance, users can create their own financial spreadsheets and manipulate data without programmer intervention. Such sophistication by nonspecialists using FORTRAN would have been impossible in the 1960s and 1970s.

There is, of course, a clear relationship between the increasing capacity of computer hardware and software. Each new generation of software requires more and more primary storage area, faster compilers, and larger secondary storage. Higher-level language programs require a huge amount of memory. For instance, to load the Statistical Package for the Social Sciences (SPSS), the program alone may require over 200K (200,000 bytes of primary storage). If work space is included within primary memory, up to 512K may be required.

Popular Programming Languages

Most managers need not be expert programmers, but they should understand how to evaluate software applications and to select programming languages that are appropriate for their organization's objectives. We will now briefly describe the more popular high-level and very high-level languages.

ASSEMBLY LANGUAGE

Many programmers still prefer to write programs in assembly language because this language gives them close control over the hardware and very efficient execution. Like machine language, **assembly language** (Figure 5.7) is designed for a specific machine and specific microprocessors. For instance, there is a specific assembly language associated with the Intel 80386 chip used in an IBM microcomputer. In general, there is a one-to-one correspondence between machine language and assembly language. Each operation in assembly corresponds to a machine operation. On the other hand, assembly language does make use of certain mnemonics (e.g., *load, sum*) and assigns addresses and storage locations automatically. While assembly language gives programmers great control, it is costly in terms of programmer time, is difficult to read and debug, and is difficult to learn. Assembly language is used primarily today in system software.

FORTRAN

FORTRAN (FORmula TRANslator) (Figure 5.8) was developed in 1956 to provide an easier way of writing scientific and engineering applications. FORTRAN is especially useful in processing numeric data. Many kinds of business applications can be written in FORTRAN, it is relatively easy to learn, and contemporary versions (e.g., FORTRAN 77) provide sophisticated structures for

Figure 5.7
Assembly language. This sample assembly language command adds the contents of register 3 to register 5 and stores the result in register 5.

AR 5, 3

```
READ (5,100) ID, QUANT, PRICE
TOTAL = QUANT * PRICE
```

controlling program logic. FORTRAN is not very good at providing input/output efficiency or in printing and working with lists. The syntax is very strict and keying errors are common, making the programs difficult to debug.

COBOL

COBOL (COmmon Business Oriented Language): Predominant programming language for business applications because it can process large data files with alphanumeric characters.

COBOL (COmmon Business Oriented Language) (Figure 5.9) came into use in the early 1960s. It was originally developed because the Defense Department wished to create a common administrative language for internal and external software. COBOL was designed with business administration in mind, for processing large data files with alphanumeric characters (mixed alphabetic and numeric data), and for performing repetitive tasks like payroll. Its primary data structures are records, files, tables, and lists. COBOL is easily learned by business analysts. As the most widely used programming language, it is supported by external groups, and there is an abundance of productivity aids. The weakness of COBOL is a result of its virtue. It is poor at complex mathematical calculations. There are many versions of COBOL, and not all are compatible with each other. Lengthy COBOL programs—some hundreds of thousands of lines long for major payroll programs, for example—can become so complex as to be virtually incomprehensible.

BASIC

BASIC (Beginners All-purpose Symbolic Instruction Code): General-purpose programming language used with microcomputers and for teaching programming.

BASIC (Beginners All-purpose Symbolic Instruction Code) was developed in 1964 by John Kemeny and Thomas Kurtz to teach students at Dartmouth College how to use computers. Today it is the most popular programming language on college campuses and for microcomputers. BASIC can do almost all computer processing tasks from inventory to mathematical calculations. It is easy to use, demonstrates computer capabilities well, and requires only a small interpreter. The weakness of BASIC is that it does few tasks well even though it does them all. It has no sophisticated program logic control or data structures, which makes it difficult to use in teaching good programming practices. While BASIC has only a few commands and is easily learned, subsequent versions of the language that have tried to add to the early syntax make the new versions of BASIC incompatible with the old ones. Therefore, BASIC programs often cannot be moved from one machine to another.

PL/1

PL/1 (Programming Language 1): Programming language developed by IBM in 1964 for business and scientific applications.

PL/1 (Programming Language 1) was developed by IBM in 1964. It is the most powerful general-purpose programming language because it can handle mathematical and business applications with ease, is highly efficient in input/output activities, and can handle large volumes of data.

Figure 5.9
COBOL. This sample COBOL program code is part of a routine to compute total sales figures for a particular item.

```
MULTIPLY QUANT-SOLD BY UNIT-PRICE GIVING SALES-TOTAL.
```

Unfortunately, the huge volume of COBOL and FORTRAN programs written in the private sector at great cost cannot simply be jettisoned when a newer, more powerful language comes along. There are an estimated 12 billion lines of COBOL code in production in the United States. This represents an investment of over $52 trillion. PL/1 has not succeeded largely because programmers trained in COBOL could not be convinced to learn an entirely new language; and business organizations could not be convinced to spend millions of dollars rewriting their software. PL/1 is, moreover, somewhat difficult to learn in its entirety.

PASCAL

Pascal: Programming language used on microcomputers and to teach sound programming practices in computer science courses.

Named after Blaise Pascal, the seventeenth-century mathematician and philosopher, **Pascal** was developed by the Swiss computer science professor Niklaus Wirth of Zurich in the late 1960s. Pascal programs can be compiled using minimal computer memory, so they can be used on microcomputers. With sophisticated structures to control program logic and a simple, powerful set of commands, Pascal is used primarily in computer science courses to teach sound programming practices. The language is weak at file handling and input/output and is not easy for beginners to use.

ADA

Ada: Programming language that is portable across different brands of hardware; is used for both military and nonmilitary applications.

Ada was developed in 1980 to provide the United States Defense Department with a structured programming language to serve as the standard for all of its applications. This language was initially conceived for weapons systems where software is developed on a processor and then imbedded into the weapon. It was explicitly designed so that it could be uniformly executed in diverse hardware environments. The language also promotes structured software design. U.S. government experts hope Ada will produce more cost-effective software because it facilitates more clearly structured code than COBOL.

Congress passed legislation mandating Ada for all system development work for the U.S. Department of Defense, and Ada is used in nonmilitary government applications as well. The language can also be used for general business applications since it can operate on microcomputers and is portable across different brands of computer hardware. Will Ada emerge as a software standard for the business world? Many firms do not think so, for the same reasons they did not embrace PL/1. They are not convinced that it is worth the investment and risk to abandon COBOL as the business standard.

C

C: Powerful programming language with tight control and efficiency of execution; is portable across different microprocessors and is used primarily with microcomputers.

C was developed at AT&T's Bell Labs in the early 1970s and is the language in which much of the UNIX operating system is written. C combines some of the tight control and efficiency of execution features of assembly language with machine portability. In other words, it can work on a variety of computers rather than on just one. Much commercial microcomputer software has been written in C, but C is gaining support for some minicomputer and mainframe applications. C is unlikely to dislodge COBOL for mainframe business applications, but it will be used increasingly for commercial microcomputer software and for scientific and technical applications.

LISP AND PROLOG

LISP (designating LISt Processor) and Prolog are widely used in artificial intelligence. LISP was created in the late 1950s by M.I.T. mathematician John McCarthy and is oriented toward putting symbols such as operations, variables, and data values into meaningful lists. LISP is better at manipulating symbols than at ordinary number crunching.

Prolog, introduced around 1970, is also well suited to symbol manipulation and can run on general-purpose computers, whereas LISP usually runs best on machines configured especially to run LISP programs.

5.4 New Software Tools and Approaches

Fourth-generation language: A programming language that can be employed directly by end users or less skilled programmers to develop computer applications more rapidly than conventional programming languages.

Fourth-generation languages consist of a variety of software tools that enable end users to develop software applications with minimal or no technical assistance or that enhance the productivity of professional programmers. Fourth-generation languages tend to be nonprocedural or less procedural than conventional programming languages. Procedural languages require specification of the sequence of steps, or procedures, that tell the computer what to do and how to do it. Nonprocedural languages need only to specify what has to be accomplished rather than provide details about how to carry out the task. Thus, a nonprocedural language can accomplish the same task with fewer steps and lines of program code than a procedural language.

Fourth-Generation Languages

There are seven categories of fourth-generation languages: query languages, report generators, graphics languages, application generators, application software packages, very-high-level programming languages, and microcomputer tools. Figure 5.10 illustrates the spectrum of these tools and some commercially available products in each category.

QUERY LANGUAGES

Query language: A high-level computer language used to retrieve specific information from databases or files.

Query languages are high-level languages for retrieving data stored in databases or files. They are usually interactive, on-line, and capable of supporting requests for information that are not predefined. They are often tied to database management systems (see Chapter 6) and microcomputer tools (see the following discussion). Query languages can search a database or file, using simple or complex selection criteria to display information relating to multiple records. Available query language tools have different kinds of syntax and structure, some being closer to natural language than others (Vassiliou, 1984–1985). Some support updating of data as well as retrieval. An example of a typical ad hoc query is "List all employees in the payroll department." Figure 5.11 illustrates how two different query languages, FOCUS and Query-By-Example, express this request.

REPORT GENERATORS

Report generators are facilities for creating customized reports. They extract data from files or databases and create reports in many formats. Report generators generally provide more control over the way data are formatted, orga-

Figure 5.10

Fourth-generation languages. The spectrum of major categories of "fourth-generation" languages and commercially available products in each category is illustrated. Tools range from those that are simple and designated primarily for end users to complex tools designed for information systems professionals.

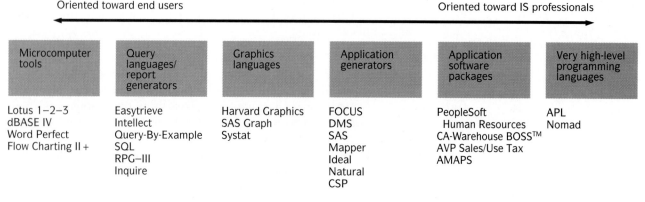

Oriented toward end users →					Oriented toward IS professionals
Microcomputer tools	Query languages/ report generators	Graphics languages	Application generators	Application software packages	Very high-level programming languages
Lotus 1–2–3	Easytrieve	Harvard Graphics	FOCUS	PeopleSoft	APL
dBASE IV	Intellect	SAS Graph	DMS	Human Resources	Nomad
Word Perfect	Query-By-Example	Systat	SAS	CA-Warehouse BOSS™	
Flow Charting II +	SQL		Mapper	AVP Sales/Use Tax	
	RPG–III		Ideal	AMAPS	
	Inquire		Natural		
			CSP		

Query: "List all employees in the Payroll department."

Using Query-By-Example:			
EMPLOYEE	EMPLOYEE #	NAME	DEPARTMENT
		P.	PAYROLL

Using FOCUS:

```
> > TABLE FILE EMPDEPT
> PRINT EMP_NAME IF DEPT EQ 'PAYROLL'
> END
```

Figure 5.11
Query languages. This figure illustrates how the simple query, "List all employees in the Payroll department," would be handled by the two different query languages: Query-By-Example and FOCUS.

Report generator: Software that creates customized reports in a wide range of formats that are not routinely produced by an information system.

nized, and displayed than query languages. The more powerful report generators can manipulate data with complex calculations and logic before they are output. Some report generators are extensions of database or query languages. The more complex and powerful report generators may not be suitable for end users without some assistance from professional information systems specialists.

GRAPHICS LANGUAGES

Graphics language: A computer language that displays data from files or databases in graphic format.

Graphics languages retrieve data from files or databases and display them in graphic format. Users can ask for data and specify how they are to be charted. Some graphics software can perform arithmetic or logical operations on data as well. SAS, Harvard Graphics, and Graph Plan are popular graphics tools.

APPLICATION GENERATORS

Application generator: Software that can generate entire information system applications; the user needs only to specify what needs to be done and the application generator creates the appropriate program code.

Application generators contain preprogrammed modules that can generate entire applications, greatly speeding development. A user can specify what needs to be done and the application generator will create the appropriate code for input, validation, updating, processing, and reporting. Most full-function application generators consist of a comprehensive, integrated set of development tools: a database management system, data dictionary, query language, screen painter, graphics generator, report generator, decision support/modeling tools, security facilities, and a high-level programming language. For unique requirements that cannot be met with generalized modules, most application generators contain *user exits* where custom-programmed routines can be inserted. Some application generators are interactive, enabling users sitting at a terminal to define inputs, files, processing, and reports by responding to questions on-line.

VERY-HIGH-LEVEL PROGRAMMING LANGUAGES

Very-high-level programming language: Programming language using fewer instructions than conventional languages. Used primarily as a professional programmer productivity tool.

Very-high-level programming languages are designed to generate program code with fewer instructions than conventional languages such as COBOL or FORTRAN. Programs and applications based on these languages can be developed in much shorter periods of time. Simple features of these languages can be employed by end users. However, these languages are designed primarily as productivity tools for professional programmers. APL and Nomad2 are examples of these languages.

APPLICATION SOFTWARE PACKAGES

A **software package** is a prewritten, precoded, commercially available set of programs that eliminates the need for individuals or organizations to write their own software programs for certain functions. There are software packages for system software, but the vast majority of package software is application software.

Software package: A prewritten, precoded, commercially available set of programs that eliminates the need to write software programs for certain functions.

Application software packages consist of prewritten application software that is marketed commercially. These packages are available for major business applications on mainframes, minicomputers, and microcomputers. They contain customization features so that they can be tailored somewhat to an organization's unique requirements. Although application packages for large complex systems must be installed by technical specialists, many application packages, especially those for microcomputers, are marketed directly to end users. Systems development based on application packages is discussed in Chapter 8.

MICROCOMPUTER TOOLS

Some of the most popular and productivity-promoting fourth-generation tools are the general-purpose application packages that have been developed for microcomputers, especially word processing, spreadsheet, data management, graphics, and desktop publishing software.

WORD PROCESSING SOFTWARE

Word processing software: Software that handles electronic storage, editing, formatting, and printing of documents.

Word processing software stores text data electronically as a computer file rather than on paper. The word processing software allows the user to make changes in the document electronically in memory. This eliminates the need to retype an entire page in order to incorporate corrections. The software has formatting options to make changes in line spacing, margins, character size, and column width. Microsoft Word and WordPerfect are popular word processing packages. Figure 5.12 illustrates a Microsoft Word screen for Windows displaying text and options such as printing, copying, searching, and deleting.

Most word processing software has advanced features that automate other writing tasks: spelling checkers, style checkers (to analyze grammar and punctuation), thesaurus programs, and mail merge programs (which link letters or other text documents with names and addresses in a mailing list).

SPREADSHEETS

Spreadsheet: Software displaying data in a grid of columns and rows, with the capability of easily recalculating numerical data.

Electronic **spreadsheet** software provides computerized versions of traditional financial modeling tools such as the accountant's columnar pad, pencil, and calculator. An electronic spreadsheet is organized into a grid of columns and rows. The power of the electronic spreadsheet is evident when one changes a value or values, because all other related values on the spreadsheet will be automatically recalculated.

Figure 5.12
Text and some of the options available in Microsoft Word for Windows. Word processors provide many easy-to-use options to create and output a text document to meet a user's specifications. *Courtesy of Microsoft.*

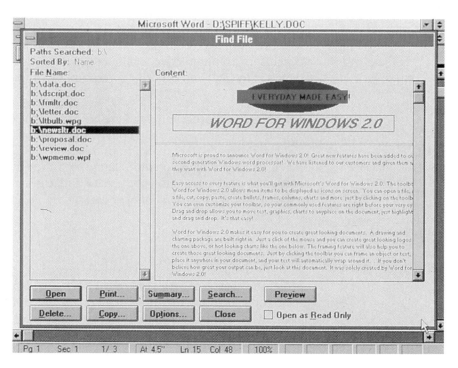

Spreadsheets are valuable for applications where numerous calculations with pieces of data must be related to each other. Spreadsheets are also useful for applications that require modeling and "what-if" analysis. After the user has constructed a set of mathematical relationships, the spreadsheet can be recalculated instantaneously using a different set of assumptions. A number of alternatives can easily be evaluated by changing one or two pieces of data without having to rekey in the rest of the worksheet. Many spreadsheet packages include graphics functions that can present data in the form of line graphs, bar graphs, or pie charts. The most popular spreadsheet packages are Lotus 1-2-3, Quattro Pro, and Microsoft Excel.

Figure 5.13 illustrates the output from a spreadsheet for a breakeven analysis and its accompanying graph.

Figure 5.13
Spreadsheet software. Spreadsheet software organizes data into columns and rows for analysis and manipulation. Contemporary spreadsheet software provides graphing abilities for clear visual representation of the data in the spreadsheets. This sample breakeven analysis is represented as numbers in a spreadsheet as well as a line graph for easy interpretation.

Total fixed cost	19,000.00
Variable cost per unit	3.00
Average sales price	17.00
Contribution margin	14.00
Breakeven point	1357

Custom Neckties Pro Forma Income Statement

Units Sold	0.00	679	1357	2036	2714
Revenue	0	11,536	23,071	34,607	46,143
Fixed Cost	19,000	19,000	19,000	19,000	19,000
Variable Cost	0	2,036	4,071	6,107	8,143
Total Cost	19,000	21,036	23,071	25,107	27,143
Profit/Loss	(19,000)	(9,500)	0	9,500	19,000

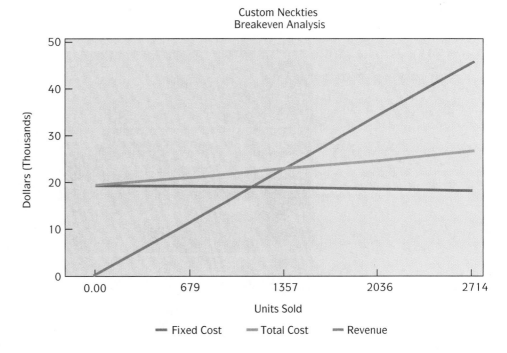

Custom Neckties
Breakeven Analysis

— Fixed Cost   — Total Cost   — Revenue

While spreadsheet programs are powerful tools for manipulating quantitative data, **data management software** is more suitable for creating and manipulating lists and for combining information from different files. Microcomputer database management packages have programming features and easy-to-learn menus that enable nonspecialists to build small information systems.

Data management software typically has facilities for creating files and databases and for storing, modifying, and manipulating data for reports and queries. A detailed treatment of data management software and database management systems can be found in Chapter 6. Popular database management software for the personal computer includes dBASE IV (R), dBASE III PLUS (R), Paradox, Rbase, and Foxbase. Figure 5.14 illustrates a screen from dBASE IV showing how the menu can be used to initiate creation of files, queries, reports, labels, forms, and applications.

INTEGRATED SOFTWARE
PACKAGES

Integrated software package:
A software package that
provides two or more
applications, such as
spreadsheets and word
processing, providing for easy
transfer of data between
them.

Integrated software packages combine the functions of the most important microcomputer software packages, such as spreadsheets, word processing, graphics, and data management. This integration provides a more general-purpose software tool and eliminates redundant data entry and data maintenance. For example, the breakeven analysis spreadsheet illustrated in Figure 5.13 could be reformatted into a polished report with word processing software without separately keying the data into both programs. Integrated packages are a compromise. While they can do many things well, they generally do not have the same power and depth as single-purpose packages.

As Chapter 8 will discuss, these advanced tools have important limitations. They are applicable only to specific areas of application development. Nevertheless, as illustrated by the Window on Management, fourth-generation tools have provided many productivity and cost-cutting benefits for businesses.

Object-Oriented Programming

A growing backlog of software projects and the need for businesses to fashion systems that are flexible and quick to build have spawned a new approach to software development with "object-oriented" programming tools. Object-oriented concepts go back to the 1970s, but it is only recently that high-capacity hardware and iconic, graphic, windowed software (see section 5.2 on graphical user interfaces) have made them a viable alternative.

Figure 5.14
Data management software. This is the main menu screen from dBASE IV, a database management software package published by Borland International Inc. All rights reserved. *Reprinted by Permission. dBASE IV and dBASE III PLUS are registered trademarks of the Borland International Inc.*

Traditional software development methods have treated data and procedures as independent components. A separate programming procedure must be written every time someone wants to take an action on a particular piece of data. The procedures act on data that the program passes to them.

WHAT MAKES
OBJECT-ORIENTED
PROGRAMMING DIFFERENT?

Object-oriented programming:
Approach to software development that combines data and procedures into a single object.

Object-oriented programming combines data and the specific procedures that operate on those data into one "object." The object combines data and program code. Instead of passing data to procedures, programs send a message for an object to perform a procedure that is already embedded into it. (Procedures are termed "methods" in object-oriented languages.) The same message may be sent to many different objects, but each will implement that message differently.

For example, an object-oriented financial application might have Customer objects sending debit and credit messages to Account objects. The Account objects in turn might maintain Cash-on-Hand, Accounts-Payable, and Accounts-Receivable objects.

An object's data are hidden from other parts of the program and can only be manipulated from inside the object. The method for manipulating the object's data can be changed internally without affecting other parts of the program. Programmers can focus on what they want an object to do, and the object decides how to do it.

Because an object's data are encapsulated from other parts of the system, each object is an independent software building block that can be used in many different systems without changing the program code. Thus, object-oriented programming is expected to reduce the time and cost of writing software by

ORGANIZATIONS

Libraries House Reusable Software

In July 1992 the U.S. Department of Defense (DOD) opened its center for Software Reuse Operations in Falls Church, Virginia. The Center provides access to the Pentagon's Defense Software Repository containing 2.2 million lines of Ada and COBOL code in 1531 reusable software modules. The software is primarily for financial and logistics applications.

DOD staff members and contractors can obtain the software using an automated catalog and retrieval system. According to Paul A. Strassman, director of the DOD's Corporate Information Management program, the DOD hopes to meet 50 percent of its needs from reusable components, which will help cut down on errors and reduce the effort required to maintain existing software. The

Corporate Information Management (CIM) program includes initiatives for software reuse, elimination of redundant systems, and reduction in the number of DOD data processing centers. Strassman expects software reuse to contribute half of CIM's $30 billion target reduction in annual software expenditures.

IBM and the Defense Advanced Research Projects Agency (Darpa) opened a similar library for reusable Ada software components in Morgantown, West Virginia, in December 1991. People can access the IBM-Darpa library, called the Asset Source for Software Engineering Technology, from a network, and they may browse through the catalog and request reusable modules and program codes. The library will transmit

programs and supporting material back to the user.

IBM and Darpa hope to create a network of such libraries. Although the current library contains only government-owned and public domain code and information, IBM is recruiting other commercial information systems vendors to list their software in the directory.

Sources: Gary H. Anthes, "Pentagon Opens Software Reuse Center," *Computerworld* (July 27, 1992); and Robert Moran, "Checking Out Software Code," *InformationWEEK* (December 9, 1991).

To Think About: How would you decide whether to utilize a reusable software library? What management, organization and technology factors would you consider?

producing reusable program code or software "chips" that can be reused in other related systems. Future software work can draw upon a library of reusable objects, and productivity gains from object-oriented technology could be magnified if objects were stored in reusable software libraries such as those described in the Window on Organizations.

OBJECT-ORIENTED PROGRAMMING CONCEPTS

Object-oriented programming is based on the concepts of **class** and **inheritance.** Program code is not written separately for every object but for classes, or general categories of similar objects. Objects belonging to a certain class have the features of that class. Classes of objects in turn can inherit all the structures and behaviors of a more general class and then add variables and behaviors unique to each object. New classes of objects are created by choosing an existing class and specifying how the new class differs from the existing class, instead of starting from scratch each time.

Class: Feature of object-oriented programming so that all objects belonging to a certain class have all of the features of that class.

Classes are organized hierarchically into superclasses and subclasses. For example, a "car" class might have a "vehicle" class for a superclass, so that it would inherit all the methods and data previously defined for "vehicle." The design of the car class would only need to describe how cars differ from vehicles. A banking application could define a Savings-Account object that is very much like a Bank-Account object with a few minor differences. Savings-Account inherits all of the Bank-Account's state and methods and then adds a few extras.

Inheritance: Feature of object-oriented programming in which a specific class of objects receives the features of a more general class.

We can see how class and inheritance work in Figure 5.15, which illustrates a tree of classes concerning employees and how they are paid. Employee is the common ancestor of the other four classes. Contractor and Paid weekly are subclasses of Employee, while Hourly and Salaried are subclasses of Paid weekly. The variables for the class are in the top half of the box, and the methods are in the bottom half. Shaded items in each box are inherited from some ancestor

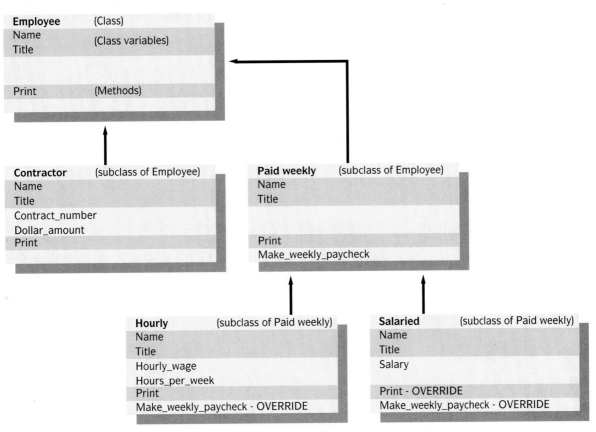

Figure 5.15
Class, subclasses, inheritance, and overriding. This figure illustrates how a message's method can come from the class itself or an ancestor class. Class variables and methods are shaded when they are inherited from above. © *Apple Computer, Inc. Used with permission.*

class. (For example, by following the tree upward, we can see that Name and Title in the Contractor, Paid weekly, Hourly, and Salaried subclasses are inherited from the Employee superclass [ancestor class].) Unshaded methods or class variables are unique to a specific class, and they override, or redefine, existing methods. When a subclass overrides an inherited method, its object still responds to the same message, but it executes its definition of the method rather than its ancestor's. Whereas Print is a method inherited from some superclass, the method Make_weekly_paycheck is specific to the Paid weekly class, and Make_weekly_paycheck-OVERRIDE is specific to the Hourly class. The Salaried class uses its own Print-OVERRIDE method.

Trends in Software Capabilities

A long-term view of software shows that the major trend is to increase the ease with which users can interact with the hardware and software. In the next few years, this trend is expected to accelerate. The Window on Technology illustrates one kind of software that is being designed to ease the interaction between humans and computers; the software presents and analyzes data geographically.

Software is becoming more interactive through the use of pointer devices such as the computer mouse, the touch screen, and the graphic pad. Voice-recognition software allows people to interact with the computer by speaking. Voice recognition software converts the spoken word into a digital form that computers can recognize. The computer responds by matching the digital translation to a vocabulary database stored in its memory, consisting of phrases, words, or phonemes (units of sound). Voice-synthesis software, on the other hand, works the

TECHNOLOGY

Mapping Solutions with Geographic Information Software

Where are our customers and competitors? How should we organize sales territories? What are the shortest routes for deliveries? Most businesses face these questions. To help answer them, for several years they have been able to call on geographic information systems (GIS) software, which visualizes and analyzes information geographically. Corporations have also used GIS to track natural resources, while governments and public interest groups have used them to track pollution and analyze crime patterns. Organizations today are finding even newer ways to use geographic information system software to tie business data to points, lines, and areas on a map, with ever more productive results.

Instead of plotting delivery routes by hand, Johanna Dairies, based in Union, New Jersey, is using digital street maps, information found in customer orders and computer-aided routing and scheduling software to define its delivery routes. By zooming in on different areas of a city, the firm can see which customers are located on each street. This process eliminates overlaps between routes and thereby reduces the distance trucks have to travel. By using GIS, Johanna Dairies was able to eliminate eight of its sixty routes in the New York area. With one route costing $100,000 per year, including driver pay, even though the firm spent $80,000 on the software and consultants, the payback started immediately.

Sears subsidiary Western Auto uses geographic software called Tactician (Tactics International, Andover, Massachusetts), combined with external demographic data, to select store locations, a common application for GIS. However, it goes much further, creating a neighborhood demographic profile to allow the new store to tailor its merchandising to the neighborhood. For example, a store in a wealthier neighborhood will emphasize accessories and polishes, while a lower-middle-class store will feature do-it-yourself auto repair products. Western Auto has found that they have now cut the breakeven time for a new store by two thirds, from 18 months down to six months.

Cigna Insurance, a giant seller of corporate health programs, uses GIS software to support its sales staff. When a potential (or current) client asked for information on the number of Cigna-affiliated doctors within a ten-mile radius of its offices, the salesperson used to present pages and pages of tabular data. Today, using software from Strategic Mapping (Santa Clara, California), that salesperson will hand the customer a map showing physician distribution. The salesperson can also incorporate data from the customer's employee database so that the client can see a comparison of health care distribution with the geographic distribution of their own employees. With analysis, the salesperson can even supply such data as the average distance from an employee residence to a health care provider.

Another insurance company, ITT Hartford, used GIS software to aid its response to Hurricane Andrew when it hit southern Florida in 1992. Its staff used software called MapInfo (Troy, NY) to track the hurricane, determine the zip codes where the most damage would be done, and then identify their policyholders in those areas. They were able quickly to project and plan for paying potential damage claims. Also they were able to dispatch insurance adjusters very rapidly to the hardest hit neighborhoods. Other insurers are using GIS to analyze such risks as proximity to earthquake faults, flood zones, and hurricane-prone areas so that they can improve their insurance underwriting.

New government and public interest group applications have also emerged. Essential Information, a nonprofit consumer watchdog organization founded by Ralph Nader, used Environmental Systems Research Institute (Redlands, California) software to analyze government home mortgage loan information in 16 cities in the United States. They were able to prove the efficacy of certain federal lending laws that were enacted to prevent redlining in the banking industry. (The Community Reinvestment Act requires a bank to lend money back to the same neighborhoods from which it receives deposits. Banks must provide a report to the Federal Financial Institution Examination Council, which breaks down deposit and loan activity at a census tract level within their market areas.) The software showed, visually and with great clarity, that banks that come under lending laws grant mortgages to minorities at a far higher rate than non-regulated mortgage companies. For example, the software showed that in 1991 in Los Angeles Sears Mortgage Corp. granted 4 percent of the loans in white neighborhoods but only 0.3 percent in minority neighborhoods, while Great Western Bank granter 4.7 percent of the loans in white neighborhoods and 16.9 percent in minority neighborhoods.

Sources: Rick Tetzeli, "Mapping for Dollars," *Fortune,* October 18, 1993; Nora Sherwood Bryan, "A Look at GIS," *Computerworld,* July 26, 1993; and David Forrest, "Seeing Data in New Ways," *Computerworld,* June 29, 1992.

To Think About: What are some other applications for geographic information software? If you were a manager, what factors would you consider to determine whether to use such software in your firm?

opposite way, converting digitized computer data back into speech. Voice-recognition and voice-synthesis systems still work with limited vocabularies. They have been used primarily for simple, routine tasks in production-line control and computer-based telemarketing but are not yet sophisticated enough for most office information systems.

5.5 How to Choose Software and Programming Languages

While managers need not become programming specialists, they should know the differences between programming languages and should be able to use clear criteria in deciding which language to use. The most important criteria will now be discussed.

Appropriateness

Some languages are general-purpose languages that can be used on a variety of problems, while others are special-purpose languages suitable for only limited tasks. Special-purpose graphics programs are excellent at creating tables but poor at routine processing of transactions. COBOL is excellent for business data processing but poor at mathematical calculations. Language selection involves identifying the use and the users.

Sophistication

High-level languages should have sophisticated control structures and data structures. Control structures shape the outcome of programs by providing clear, logical, structured programs that are easy to read and maintain. It may be impossible to create a table and then look up values in it unless the language has a table data structure capability. Languages should be selected that support many different data structures.

Organizational Considerations

In order to be effective, a language must be easily learned by the firm's programming staff, easy to maintain and change, and flexible enough so that it can

Voice recognition software converts the spoken word into digital form. This worker is using a voice recognition system to enter data into her computer system.

grow with the organization. These organizational considerations have direct long-term cost implications.

In general, sophisticated, well-structured languages are easier to learn and much easier to maintain over the long term than less sophisticated languages.

Support

It is important to purchase software that has widespread use in other organizations and is supported by many consulting firms and services. It is often less expensive to purchase software written elsewhere, or to have a service firm write it, than to develop the software internally. In these situations, it is crucial to have software that is widely used.

A different kind of support is the availability of software editing, debugging, and development aids. Because so many organizations use COBOL, there are hundreds of contemporary software development products available to assist the programming staff. The same cannot be said of Ada.

Another option is reusable software. Only a small portion of the software written is unique, novel, and specific to individual applications. Most consist of generic functions such as edit and conversion routines for Gregorian dates and edits and validation of part, employee, and account numbers. One study found that 85 percent of all programming code written in 1983 was common to many applications and theoretically could have been developed from reusable components. Firms such as the Hartford Insurance Company and GTE Data Services have been trying to support software development by creating libraries of reusable software components (refer to the Window on Organizatiions).

Efficiency

Although a less important feature than in the past, the efficiency with which a language compiles and executes remains a consideration when purchasing software. Languages with slow compilers, or interpreters like BASIC, can be expensive (in terms of programmer costs) to operate and maintain. In general, fourth-generation languages are very slow and expensive in terms of machine time. As discussed in later chapters, these languages are usually inappropriate for high-speed transaction systems, which must handle thousands of transactions per second.

Some programming languages are more efficient in the use of machine time than others. PL/1, for instance, requires a large section in memory for its compiler, whereas Pascal and BASIC have much simpler interpreters that require little primary memory. In any event, efficiency should be judged in terms of both machines and personnel. As machine costs fall, personnel costs become very important in choosing a language. As machines become less expensive per unit of memory, languages that are inefficient in machine time but very efficient in programmer time will grow in importance.

Management Challenges

1. **Increasing complexity and software errors.** While much of the software of the next decade will be rapidly generated on desktops for smaller systems and applications, a great deal of what software will be asked to do remains far-reaching and sophisticated, requiring programs that are large and complex.

   Large and complex systems tend to be error-prone, with software errors, or "bugs" that may not be revealed for years until exhaustive testing and actual use. A computerized banking system, for example, may use millions of lines of program code, written by hundreds of people, each working on small portions of the program. AT&T, for instance, found 300 errors for every 1000 lines of code in its large programs. Researchers do not know if the number of bugs grows exponentially or proportionately to the number of lines of code, nor can they tell for certain whether all segments of a complex piece of software will always work in total harmony. The process of designing and testing software that is "bug-free" is a serious quality control and management problem (see Chapter 9).

2. **The application backlog.** Advances in computer software have not kept pace with the breathtaking productivity gains in computer hardware. Developing software has become a major preoccupation for organizations. A great deal of software must be intricately crafted. Moreover, the software itself is only one component of a complete information system that must be carefully designed and coordinated with other people, as well as with organizational and hardware components. Managerial, procedural, and policy issues must be carefully researched and evaluated apart from the actual coding. The "software crisis" is actually part of a larger systems analysis, design, and implementation issue, which will be treated in detail. Despite the gains from fourth-generation languages, personal desktop software tools, and object-oriented programming, many businesses continue to face a backlog of two to three years in developing the information systems they need, or they will not be able to develop them at all.

Summary

Describe the major types of software.

The major types of software are system, application, and end-user software. Each serves a different purpose. System software manages the computer resources and mediates between application software and computer hardware. Application software is used by application programmers and some end users to develop systems and specific business applications. End-user software usually cannot be used to develop an entire system. Instead, it is used to permit untrained end users either to use a system or to build a simple application (e.g., to create a report).

Describe the functions of system software and compare leading microcomputer operating systems.

System software coordinates the various parts of the computer system and mediates between application software and computer hardware. The system software that manages and controls the activities of the computer is called the operating system. Other system software includes computer language translation programs, which convert programming languages into machine language, and utility programs, which perform common processing tasks.

The operating system acts as the chief manager of the information system, allocating, assigning, and scheduling system resources and monitoring the use of the computer. Multiprogramming, multitasking, multiprocessing, virtual storage, and time sharing enable system resources to be used more efficiently so that the computer can attack many problems at the same time.

Multiprogramming (multitasking in microcomputer environments) allows multiple programs to use the computer's resources concurrently. Multiprocessing is the use of two or more CPUs linked together working in tandem to perform a task. Time-sharing enables many users to share computer resources simultaneously by allocating each user a tiny slice of computing time. Virtual storage splits up programs into pages so that main memory can be utilized more efficiently.

In order to be executed by the computer, a software program must be translated into machine language via special language translation software—a compiler, an assembler, or an interpreter.

Microcomputer operating systems are starting to develop sophisticated capabilities such as multitasking and support for multiple users on networks. Leading microcomputer operating systems include OS/2, Windows NT, UNIX, DOS, and System 7. Microcomputer operating systems with graphical user interfaces are gaining popularity over command-driven operating systems. Windows is a popular graphical user interface shell for the DOS operating system.

Explain how software has evolved and how it will continue to develop.

Software has evolved along with hardware. The general trend is toward user-friendly high-level languages that both increase professional programmer productivity and make it possible for complete amateurs to use information systems. There have been four generations of software development: 1) machine language; 2) symbolic languages such as assembly language; 3) high-level languages such as FORTRAN and COBOL; and 4) fourth-generation languages, which are less procedural and closer to natural language than earlier generations of software. Software is starting to incorporate both sound and graphics and to support multimedia applications.

Compare strengths and limitations of the major programming languages and tools.

The most popular conventional programming languages are assembly language, FORTRAN, COBOL, BASIC, PL/1, Pascal, C, and Ada. Conventional programming languages make more efficient use of computer resources than fourth-generation languages and each is designed to solve specific types of problems.

Fourth-generation languages include query languages, report generators, graphics languages, application generators, very-high-level programming languages, application software packages, and personal computer tools. They are less procedural than conventional programming languages and enable end users to perform many software tasks that previously required technical specialists.

Object-oriented programming combines data and procedures into one "object," which can act as an independent software building block. Each object can be used in many different systems without changing program code.

Explain how to select appropriate software and programming languages.

Choosing the right software for a particular application requires some knowledge of the strengths and weaknesses of specific software products. Equally important is the support for software packages given by vendors, the ability of the organization to absorb new software, and the efficiency of the software in executing specific tasks.

Key Terms

Software
Program
Stored program concept
System software
Application software
End-user software
Operating system
System residence device
Multiprogramming
Multitasking
Virtual storage
Page
Time sharing
Multiprocessing
Source code
Compiler
Object code
Interpreter
Utility program
DOS
OS/2
Windows NT
UNIX
System 7
Graphical user interface
Windows

Machine language
High-level language
Assembly language
FORTRAN (FORmula TRANslator)
COBOL (COmmon Business Oriented
    Language)
BASIC (Beginners All-purpose Symbolic
    Instruction Code)
PL/1 (Programming Language 1)
Pascal
Ada
C
Fourth-generation language
Query language
Report generator
Graphics language
Application generator
Very-high-level programming language
Software package
Word processing software
Spreadsheet
Data management software
Integrated software package
Object-oriented programming
Class
Inheritance

1. What are the major types of software? How do they differ in terms of users and uses?
2. What is the operating system of a computer? What does it do?
3. Describe multiprogramming, time sharing, virtual storage, and multiprocessing. Why are they important for the operation of an information system?
4. Define multitasking.
5. What is the difference between an assembler, a compiler, and an interpreter?
6. Define graphical user interfaces.
7. Compare the major microcomputer operating systems.
8. What are the major generations of software, and approximately when were they developed?
9. What is a high-level language? Name three high-level languages. Describe their strengths and weaknesses.
10. Define fourth-generation languages and list the seven categories of fourth-generation tools.
11. What is the difference between fourth-generation languages and conventional programming languages?
12. What is the difference between an application generator and an application software package? Between a report generator and a query language?
13. Name and describe the most important microcomputer software tools.
14. What is object-oriented programming? How does it differ from conventional software development?
15. What are the major factors to consider when selecting software and programming languages?

1. What factors should be considered in selecting microcomputer software?
2. Your firm wishes to develop a system that will process sales orders and update inventory. The programmers in your information systems department wish to use assembly language to write the programs for this system. Is this a good idea? Discuss.
3. Several authorities have claimed that fourth-generation languages will soon replace conventional programming languages such as COBOL for implementing the vast majority of information system applications. Discuss.

OS/2 has been described as a "better Window than Windows and a better DOS than DOS." Your instructor will divide the class into two groups to debate this proposition, from both a technical and business standpoint. Use articles from computer magazines to help prepare your group's analysis.

CASE STUDY

OS/2 or Windows? Toronto Dominion Securities Inc. and Delta Airlines Select Operating Systems

Toronto Dominion Securities Inc. of Toronto Dominion Bank in Canada decided it was time for a change. Its business in government securities had been steadily growing, and its trade volume had doubled in two years. It moved to an amphitheater-like 11,000-square-foot trading floor to give its securities traders more breathing space and a bullpen-like atmosphere for developing and discussing ideas. The new trading floor also streamlined communications that are crucial to the bank's closely related businesses. The entire project cost about $20 million Canadian.

Business heads in charge of the bank's trading operations in money market, capital market, foreign exchange, and fixed income sit in the middle of the room, surrounded by their chief traders. The proximity encourages people to interact more frequently during the trading day. For instance, a trader in the Canadian–U.S. currency market can speak to the business head in charge of the Canadian and U.S. money market. Foreign exchange traders sit near the chief money market trader. If the chief money market trader says that rates are rising, the foreign exchange trader will use this information to purchase future contracts. Toronto believes that the trading room design has boosted revenues.

For the operating system for its new trading room floor, Toronto Dominion selected OS/2 Version 2.0, less than three months after this version of the operating system was formally released by IBM. There were both risks and rewards to installing this new version of the operating system so soon after its release. While there might be unforeseen bugs that often accompany new pieces of software, Toronto Dominion felt that this disadvantage was outweighed by OS/2's powerful multitasking capabilities and easier-to-use programs. The bank knew that it would not be easy to implement this new operating system and to get existing applications to run smoothly from the start. Some modifications to the data display software called TradeLook had to be coded and tested. To run an application on a new operating system, new versions of that application have to be created, tested, and retested.

OS/2 has a 32-bit operating system, which promises end users more power than 16-bit operating systems such as DOS. OS/2 also runs DOS and Windows-based programs. Toronto Dominion had other hardware and software options to choose from, such as UNIX-based workstations, but opted for OS/2 because it believed this system could best meet its needs. In the old trading room, the bank's traders used more than 100 DOS-based programs on mainframes and minicomputers to do, for instance, options analytics and trade analysis. The bank wanted to salvage its existing trading programs, allow its traders to run more than two applications at the same time, and let traders work with real-time data with the flick of a wrist. If systems did not work on the new version of OS/2, the bank planned to use an earlier version of OS/2.

The DOS-based programs required little or no modification to run on OS/2 and run smoothly, according to Andrew K. Annett, manager of the treasury systems integration, corporate, and investment banking group. With the new technology and trading room, traders can run a Lotus 1-2-3 spreadsheet and a profit-and-loss program simultaneously instead of wasting time jumping from one application to another. The bank feels that the OS/2 graphical user interface makes its systems easier to operate.

Because of OS/2 system glitches, Toronto Dominion found that the kernel—the part of the operating system that controls which applications run—was short on memory. Programmers had to scale back memory on computers that had less than 16 bytes of memory and assign lower priority to background number crunching when multiple applications were run at the same time. The result—slower processing and response time. The bank is installing new kernel software and upgrading memory to 24 megabytes.

Before finalizing its decision, Toronto Dominion talked with over 10 technology vendors about hardware and software alternatives. One was to install 30 or 40 high-end UNIX-based RISC workstations in the Toronto office, where traders make markets and take positions. But the bank's other branches focus more on sales than on trading. There, that kind of technology would not be necessary and would make integration with the rest of the bank more difficult.

Toronto Dominion has planned to link all six of its corporate investment banking centers in a computer network. Its long-term strategy calls for distributing trading inventory in real time out from its Toronto trading room to its 1000 branches and for distributing trading data to its corporate group and investment banking staff. Toronto also is thinking about providing corporate clients with the capability to execute foreign exchange transactions from their own terminals.

At about the same time Toronto Dominion selected the new version of OS/2, Delta Airlines decided to pull back from a primarily OS/2 desktop strategy to one calling for a mix of operating systems. It is replacing OS/2 with Microsoft Windows for its critical next-generation reservation system. As the most critical airline operation, the new reservation system is mainframe-based but includes intelligent front-end workstations for reservation agents. About 900 agents will use the system initially.

In December 1991 Delta had selected OS/2 for this application as well as for another important project. Delta is not abandoning OS/2 completely but has decided not to rely on OS/2 exclusively. The airline has changed its approach to avoid locking into a particular technical platform. It evaluates software for each information system application case by case and makes its selection based on cost and functionality. Delta, like all airlines, is suffering from tight finances and is likely to look for the lowest cost technology solution.

Delta's corporate culture is considered to be practical and somewhat conservative. The firm tends not to make pioneering technically aggressive or risky decisions. The firm understands that the challenge of a mixed software environment is making the software all work together. Delta is finding ways to bridge the OS/2 and Windows environments. Delta plans to continue using OS/2 for its airport traffic management system and will evaluate OS/2 for future projects.

Sources: Jenna Michaels, ''Breaking in New OS/2 Technology,'' *Wall Street Computer Review*, Vol. 9, No. 12, July 1992; and Rosemary Hamilton, ''Windows Leads Delta to Mixed Platforms,'' *Computerworld*, July 27, 1992.

Case Study Questions

1. Why is the selection of an operating system an important business decision?
2. What are the management, technology, and organization factors that should be considered when selecting an operating system?
3. If you were in charge of selecting the operating system for Toronto Dominion and Delta, which would you have chosen for each firm? Why?

References

Abdel-Hamid, Tarek K. "The Economics of Software Quality Assurance: A Simulation-Based Case Study." *MIS Quarterly* 12, no. 3 (September 1988).

Apte, Uday, Chetan S. Sankar, Meru Thakur, and Joel E. Turner. "Reusability-Based Strategy for Development of Information Systems: Implementation Experience of a Bank." *MIS Quarterly* 14, no. 4 (December 1990).

Barnett, Jim, Kevin Knight, Inderject Man, and Elaine Rich. "Knowledge and Natural Language Processing. *Communications of the ACM* 33, no. 8 (August 1990).

Bochenski, Barbara. "GUI Builders Pay Price for User Productivity." *Software Magazine,* April 1992.

Borning, Alan. "Computer System Reliability and Nuclear War." *Communications of the ACM* 30, no. 2 (February 1987).

Fallows, James. "Crash-Worthy Speedster." *The Atlantic Monthly,* February 1993.

Freedman, David H. "Programming Without Tears." *High Technology* (April 1986).

Haavind, Robert. "Software's New Object Lesson." *Technology Review,* February/March 1992.

Jalics, Paul J. "Cobol on a PC: A New Perspective on a Language and Its Performance." *Communications of the ACM* 30, no. 2 (February 1987).

Joyce, Edward J. "Reusable Software: Passage to Productivity?" *Datamation* (September 15, 1988).

Kim, Chai, and Stu Westin. "Software Maintainability: Perceptions of EDP Professionals." *MIS Quarterly* 12, no. 2 (June 1988).

Korson, Timothy D. and Vijay K. Vaishnavi. "Managing Emerging Software Technologies: A Technology Transfer Framework." *Communications of the ACM* 35 No. 9 (September 1992).

Korson, Tim and John D. McGregor. "Understanding Object-Oriented: A Unifying Paradigm." *Communications of the ACM* 33, no. 9 (September 1990).

Lauriston, Robert. "OS/2 versus Windows NT." *PC World,* February 1993.

Layer, D. Kevin and Chris Richardson. "Lisp Systems in the 1990s," *Communications of the ACM* 34 no. 9 (September 1991.)

Littlewood, Bev and Lorenzo Strigini. "The Risks of Software." *Scientific American* 267, no. 5 (November 1992).

Monarchi, David E. and Gretchen I. Puhr. "A Research Typology for Object-Oriented Analysis and Design." *Communications of the ACM* 35 no. 9 (September 1992).

Mukhopadhyay, Tridas, Stephen S. Vicinanza, and Michael J. Prietula. "Examining the Feasibility of a Case-Based Reasoning Model for Software Effort Estimation." *MIS Quarterly* 16, no. 2 (June 1992).

Nance, Barry. "Windows NT and OS/2 Compared." *Byte,* June 1992.

Nerson, Jean-Marc. "Applying Object-Oriented Analysis and Design." *Communications of the ACM* 35, no. 9 (September 1992).

Salemi, Joe. "OS/2 2.0: Does It Fulfill the Promise?" *PC Magazine* April 28, 1992.

Schonberg, Edmond, Mark Gerhardt and Charlene Hayden. "A Technical Tour of Ada." *Communications of the ACM* 35, no. 11 (November 1992).

Swanson, Kent, Dave McComb, Jill Smith, and Don McCubbrey. "The Application Software Factory: Applying Total Quality Techniques to Systems Development." *MIS Quarterly* 15, no. 4 (December 1991.)

Vassiliou, Yannis. "On the Interactive Use of Databases: Query Languages." *Journal of Management Information Systems* 1 (Winter 1984–1985).

White, George M. " Natural Language Understanding and Speech." *Communications of the ACM* 33, no. 8 (August 1990).

Wiederhold, Gio, Peter Wegner, and Stefano Ceri. "Toward Megaprogramming." *Communications of the ACM* 35, no. 11 (November 1992).

CHAPTER 6

Managing Data Resources

Organized Information Speeds Satellite Recovery

In the 1970s, the Soviet Cosmos 954 satellite crashed in a remote section of northern Canada. On impact, it released radioactive particles from its nuclear reactor. With so many nuclear-powered satellites orbiting the globe, what can be done to prevent an incident like this, or, worse, one in which the satellite hits a heavily populated area?

Scientists have been developing recovery and disposal scenarios for nuclear-powered satellites for years. In the past, these scenarios took weeks or months to develop—far too long after a crash occurred to respond effectively. The scientists prepared these simulations manually using a complex matrix, and they had to be aware of all the various options for each recovery as they made calculations.

Now scientists can generate recovery-and-disposal scenarios in minutes by using an application called Technology Hierarchy for Orbital Recovery (THOR), developed by POD Associates in Albuquerque, New Mexico. THOR uses a relational database

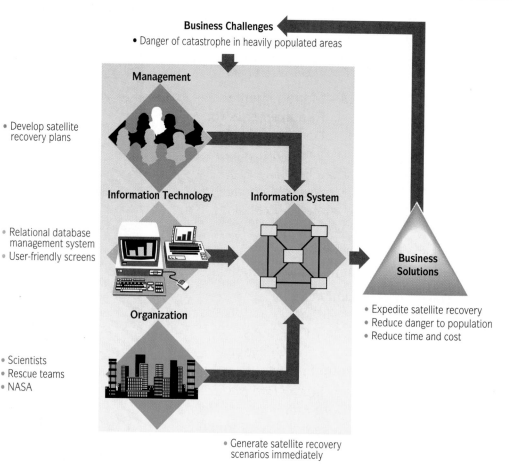

Business Challenges
• Danger of catastrophe in heavily populated areas

Management
• Develop satellite recovery plans

Information Technology
• Relational database management system
• User-friendly screens

Information System

Organization
• Scientists
• Rescue teams
• NASA

Business Solutions
• Expedite satellite recovery
• Reduce danger to population
• Reduce time and cost

• Generate satellite recovery scenarios immediately

that can store vast amounts of information collected from manufacturers and other sources on various technologies related to satellite recovery efforts. The database includes detailed data on launch sites, reactor composition, recovery vehicles, and satellite size and mass. Using menus that can be easily accessed on the computer terminal screen, scientists can input data on the type of satellite, type of reactor powering it, and whether the reactor is operational in order to design a scenario. The way the information is organized by the database software makes it easy for scientists to access and combine the information they need to generate a solution for the recovery.

THOR automatically performs the calculations the scientists need. Using the information stored in the database, scientists can present a detailed recovery scenario, including what type of recovery vehicle to use and where to launch it from. THOR is expected to save the National Aeronautic and Space Administration (NASA), the Department of Energy, and the Department of Defense a person-year's worth of work, equivalent to between $100,000 and $200,000.

Source: Christopher Lindquist, "RDBMS Helps Prevent Satellite Disaster," *Computerworld*, April 27, 1992.

The THOR satellite recovery system illustrates how much the effective use of information depends on how data are stored, organized, and accessed. Proper delivery of information not only depends on the capabilities of computer hardware and software, but also on the organization's ability to manage data as an important resource.

This chapter examines the managerial and organizational requirements as well as the technologies for managing data as a resource. First we describe the traditional file management technologies that have been used for arranging and accessing data on physical storage media and the problems they have created for organizations. Then we describe the technology of database management systems, which can overcome many of the drawbacks of traditional file management. We end the chapter with a discussion of the managerial and organizational requirements for successful implementation of database management systems.

After completing this chapter you will be able to:

- Describe traditional file organization and management techniques.
- Explain the problems of the traditional file environment.
- Describe how a database management system organizes information.

- Identify the three principal database models.
- Discuss new database trends.
- Explain the managerial and organizational requirements for creating a database environment.

6.1 Organizing Data in a Traditional File Environment

An effective information system provides users with timely, accurate, and relevant information. This information is stored in computer files. When the files are properly arranged and maintained, users can easily access and retrieve the information they need.

You can appreciate the importance of file management if you have ever written a term paper using 3 × 5 index cards. No matter how efficient your storage device (a metal box or a rubber band), if you organize the cards randomly your term paper will have little or no organization. Given enough time, you could put the cards in order, but your system would be more efficient if you set up your organizational scheme early on. If your scheme is flexible enough and well documented, you can extend it to account for any changes in your viewpoint as you write your paper.

The same need for file organization applies to firms. Well-managed, carefully arranged files make it easy to obtain data for business decisions, whereas poorly managed files lead to chaos in information processing, high costs, poor performance, and little, if any, flexibility. Despite the use of excellent hardware and software, many organizations have inefficient information systems because of poor file management.

In this section we describe the traditional methods that organizations have used to arrange data in computer files. We also discuss the problems with these methods.

File Organization Terms and Concepts

Field: A grouping of characters into a word, group of words, or complete number.

Record: A group of related fields.

File: A group of records of the same type.

Entity: A person, place, or thing about which information must be kept.

Attribute: Piece of information describing a particular entity.

A computer system organizes data in a hierarchy that starts with bits and bytes and progresses to fields, records, files, and databases (see Figure 6.1).

A bit represents the smallest unit of data a computer can handle. A group of bits, called a byte, represents a single character, which can be a letter, number, or other symbol. A grouping of characters into a word, group of words, or a complete number (such as a person's name or age), is called a **field**. A group of related fields, such as the student's name, the course taken, the date, and the grade make up a **record**; a group of records of the same type is called a **file**. For instance, all of the student records in Figure 6.1 could constitute a course file. A group of related files make up a database. The student course file illustrated in Figure 6.1 could be grouped with files on students' personal histories and financial backgrounds to create a student database.

A record describes an entity. An **entity** is a person, place, thing, or event on which we maintain information. An order is a typical entity in a sales order file, which maintains information on a firm's sales orders. Each characteristic or quality describing a particular entity is called an **attribute.** For example, order number, order date, order amount, item number, and item quantity would each be an attribute of the entity *order*. The specific values that these attributes can have can be found in the fields of the record describing the entity *order* (see Figure 6.2).

Every record in a file should contain at least one field that uniquely identifies that record so that the record can be retrieved, updated, or sorted. This identifier

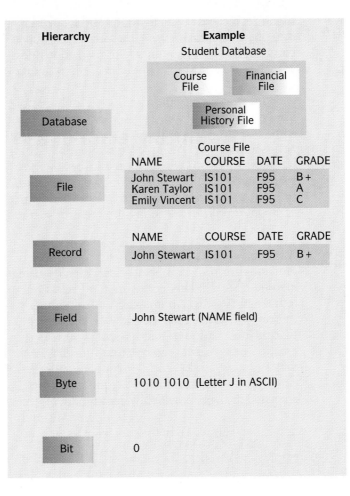

Figure 6.1
The data hierarchy. A computer system organizes data in a hierarchy that starts with the bit, which represents either a 0 or a 1. Bits can be grouped to form a byte to represent one character, number, or symbol. Bytes can be grouped to form a field, and related fields can be grouped to form a record. Related records can be collected to form a file and related files can be organized into a database.

Key field: A field in a record that uniquely identifies instances of that record so that it can be retrieved or updated.

field is called a **key field.** An example of a key field is the order number for the order record illustrated in Figure 6.2 or an employee number or social security number for a personnel record (containing employee data such as the employee's name, age, address, job title, and so forth).

Accessing Records from Computer Files

Computer systems store files on secondary storage devices. Records can be arranged in several ways on storage media, and the arrangement determines the manner in which individual records can be accessed or retrieved. One way to

Figure 6.2
Entities and attributes. This record describes the entity called ORDER and its attributes. The specific values for order number, order date, item number, item quantity, and amount for this particular order are the fields for this record. Order number is the key field because each order is assigned a unique identification number.

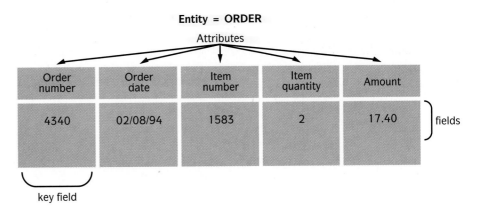

Sequential file organization: A method of storing records in which records must be retrieved in the same physical sequence in which they are stored.

Direct file organization or Random file organization: Method of storing records so that they can be accessed in any sequence without regard to their actual physical order on storage media.

organize records is sequentially. In **sequential file organization,** data records must be retrieved in the same physical sequence in which they are stored. In contrast, **direct** or **random file organization** allows users to access records in any sequence they desire, without regard to actual physical order on the storage media.

Sequential file organization is the only file organization method that can be used on magnetic tape. This file organization method is no longer popular, but some organizations still use it for batch processing applications in which they access and process each record sequentially. A typical application using sequential files is payroll, where all employees in a firm must be paid one by one and issued a check. Direct or random file organization is utilized with magnetic disk technology (although records can be stored sequentially on disk if desired). Most computer applications today utilize some method of direct file organization.

THE INDEXED SEQUENTIAL ACCESS METHOD

Indexed sequential access method (ISAM): File access method to directly access records organized sequentially using an index of key fields.

Index: A table or list that relates record keys to physical locations on direct access files.

Although records may be stored sequentially on direct access storage devices, individual records can be accessed directly using the **indexed sequential access method (ISAM).** This access method relies on an index of key fields to locate individual records. An **index** to a file is similar to the index of a book, as it lists the key field of each record and where that record is physically located in storage to expedite location of that record. Figure 6.3 shows how the index identifies the location of a specific record stored on disk. Any specific record can be located directly using its key field to find its storage address in the index. ISAM is employed in applications that require sequential processing of large numbers of records but that occasionally require direct access of individual records.

DIRECT FILE ACCESS METHOD

Direct file access method: Method of accessing records by mathematically transforming the key fields into the specific addresses for the records.

The **direct file access method** is used with direct file organization. This method employs a key field to locate the physical address of a record. However, the process is accomplished without an index. Instead, a mathematical formula called a **transform algorithm** is used to translate the key field directly into the record's physical storage location on disk. The algorithm performs some mathematical computation on the record key, and the result of that calculation is the record's physical address. This process is illustrated in Figure 6.4.

Figure 6.3

Indexed sequential access method (ISAM). ISAM allows a user to locate a record directly from a sequential file by using an index. With ISAM, records are stored on a direct access storage device (DASD) such as a disk. The index examines the unique key field of every record and finds its storage location on the disk.

File size: 1000 records

Record

| Key field 2367 | Other fields |

Transform algorithm

Divide key field by the prime number closest to maximum number of records in the file. The remainder determines the address location for the record.

$$997 \overline{)\begin{array}{r} 2 \\ 2367 \\ 1994 \\ \hline 373 \end{array}}$$

Record address = 373

Figure 6.4
The direct file access method. Records are not stored sequentially on the disk but are arranged according to the results of some mathematical computation. Here, the transform algorithm divides the value in the key field by the prime number closest to the maximum number of records in the file (in this case, the prime number is 997). The remainder designates the storage location for that particular record.

Transform algorithm:
Mathematical formula used to translate a record's key field directly into the record's physical storage location.

This access method is most appropriate for applications where individual records must be located directly and rapidly for immediate processing. Only a few records in the file need to be retrieved at one time, and the required records are found in no particular sequence. An example might be an on-line hotel reservation system.

Problems with the Traditional File Environment

According to Greek legend, Gordius, King of Phrygia, tied an intricate, complex knot in a rope, of which it was said that he who untied the knot would be master of Asia. As it turned out, Alexander the Great cut the knot and went on to become master of Asia. Many organizations have found that they tied themselves into an information-system Gordian knot of their own making. Here we describe the knot. In the following section, we show how to untie parts of the knot and cut through the rest.

Most organizations began information processing on a small scale, automating one application at a time. Systems tended to grow independently, and not according to some grand plan. Typically, each division of a multidivision company developed its own applications. Within each division, each functional area tended to develop systems in isolation from other functional areas. Accounting, finance, manufacturing, and marketing all developed their own systems and data files. Figure 6.5 illustrates the traditional approach to information processing.

Each application, of course, required its own files and its own computer program in order to operate. In general, the files used in an application were some version of the functional area master file. For instance, there was one very large master personnel file containing most of the basic information on all employees in the company, including current position and salary. However, over time, a number of smaller files extracted from the larger master file were spun off for processing efficiency as well as for specialized applications. Hence, the personnel master file spawned a payroll file, a medical insurance file, a pension file, a mailing list file, a list of employees who joined the company via

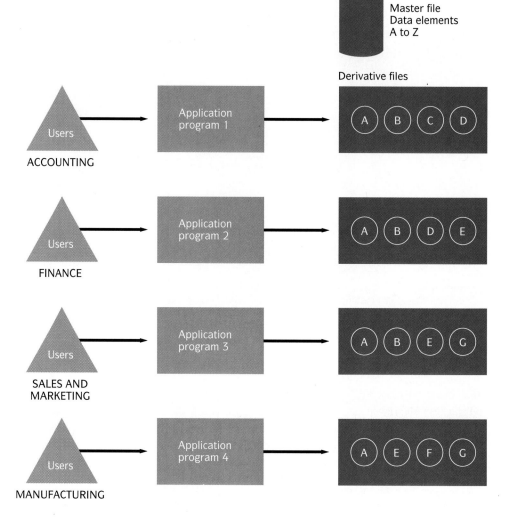

Master file
Data elements
A to Z

Derivative files

Application program 1

ACCOUNTING
Users

A B C D

Application program 2

FINANCE
Users

A B D E

Application program 3

SALES AND MARKETING
Users

A B E G

Application program 4

MANUFACTURING
Users

A E F G

Figure 6.5
Traditional file processing. The use of a traditional approach to file processing encourages each functional area in a corporation to develop specialized applications. Each application requires a unique data file that is likely to be a subset of the master file. These subsets of the master file lead to data redundancy, processing inflexibility, and wasted storage resources.

Traditional file environment: A way of collecting and maintaining data in an organization that leads to each functional area or division creating and maintaining its own data files and programs.

prior acquisitions (who were paid using a different payroll program), and so forth until tens, perhaps hundreds, of files and programs existed.

In the company as a whole, this process led to multiple master files created, maintained, and operated by separate divisions or departments. Figure 6.6 shows three separate master files: customer, personnel, and sales. Creating a simple report such as that listed in this example, sales personnel by annual sales and by principal customers, required a complex "matching" program that read each of the three files, copied pertinent records, and recombined the records into an intermediate file. This intermediate file had to be sorted in the desired sequence (sales personnel ranked by highest sales) before a final report could be printed.

Of course, every data item in the various files required a set of documents to support the file and help collect information. Often the same data item, such as product code, was collected on multiple documents by different divisions and departments. In time, the file structure of the organization became so complex that programmers developed specialties by focusing on subsets of files and programs. Eventually, the programs became totally dependent on a few programmers who understood the programs and files. If these programmers became ill or left the company, key applications failed.

There are names for this situation: the **traditional file environment;** the flat file organization (because most of the data are organized in flat files); and the data

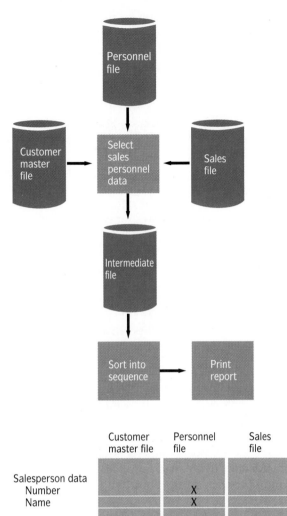

Figure 6.6
Creating a report using traditional file processing. In this example, three separate files—customer, personnel, and sales—have been created and are maintained by each respective division or department. In order to create a simple report consisting of a list of sales personnel by annual sales and principal customers, the three files had to be read, and an intermediate file had to be created. This required writing several programs. The table in the figure shows the information selected from each file.

	Customer master file	Personnel file	Sales file
Salesperson data			
Number		X	
Name		X	
Sales data			
Amount of sales			X
Customer data			
Name	X		
Address	X		

file approach (because the data and business logic are tied to specific files and related programs). By any name, the situation results in growing inefficiency and complexity.

As this process goes on for five or ten years, the firm becomes tied up in knots of its own creation. The organization is saddled with hundreds of programs and applications, with no one who knows what they do, what data they use, and who is using the data. There is no central listing of data files, data elements, or definitions of data. The organization is collecting the same information on far too many documents. The resulting problems are data redundancy, program-data dependence, inflexibility, poor data security, and inability to share data among applications.

DATA REDUNDANCY AND CONFUSION

Data redundancy: The presence of duplicate data in multiple data files.

Data redundancy is the presence of duplicate data in multiple data files. Data redundancy occurs when different divisions, functional areas, and groups in an organization independently collect the same piece of information. For instance, within the commercial loans division of a bank, the marketing and credit information functions might collect the same customer information. Because it is collected and maintained in so many different places, the same data item may have different meanings in different parts of the organization. Simple data items like the fiscal year, employee identification, and product code can take on different meanings as programmers and analysts work in isolation on different applications.

Program-data dependence: The close relationship between data stored in files and the software programs that update and maintain those files. Any change in data organization or format requires a change in all the programs associated with those files.

Program-data dependence is the tight relationship between data stored in files and the specific programs required to update and maintain those files. Every computer program has to describe the location and nature of the data with which it works. These data declarations can be longer than the substantive part of the program. In a traditional file environment, any change in data requires a change in all of the programs that access the data. Changes, for instance, in tax rates or zip code length require changes in programs. Such programming changes may cost millions of dollars to implement in each program that requires the revised data.

The development of new applications consequently takes more time and money than it would otherwise. Programmers have to write complicated programs, stripping data items from records in a variety of files to create new files. New programs require new arrangements of data. A large part of the organization's programming effort consists of updating data elements that are scattered throughout hundreds of files. In many instances, applications work with outdated data simply because of the difficulty of making updates.

LACK OF FLEXIBILITY

A traditional file system can deliver routine scheduled reports after extensive programming efforts, but it cannot deliver ad hoc reports or respond to unanticipated information requirements in a timely fashion. The information required by ad hoc requests is "somewhere in the system" but is too expensive to retrieve. Several programmers would have to work for weeks to put together the required data items in a new file. Users—in particular, senior management—begin to wonder at this point why they have computers at all.

POOR SECURITY

Because there is little control or management of data, access to and dissemination of information are virtually out of control. What limits on access exist tend to be the result of habit and tradition, as well as of the sheer difficulty of finding information.

LACK OF DATA SHARING AND AVAILABILITY

The lack of control over access to data in this confused environment does not make it easy for people to obtain information. Because pieces of information in different files and different parts of the organization cannot be related to one another, it is virtually impossible for information to be shared or accessed in a timely manner.

6.2 A Modern Database Environment

Database: Collection of data organized to service many applications at the same time by organizing data so that they appear to be in one location.

Database technology can cut through many of the problems created by traditional file organization. A more rigorous definition of a **database** is a collection of data organized to serve many applications efficiently by centralizing the data and minimizing redundant data. Rather than storing data in separate files for each application, data are stored physically to appear to users as being stored in only one location. A single database services multiple applications. For example, instead of a corporation storing employee data in separate information systems and separate files for personnel, payroll, and benefits, the corporation could create a single common Human Resources database. Figure 6.7 illustrates the database concept.

190 | Chapter 6
Managing Data Resources

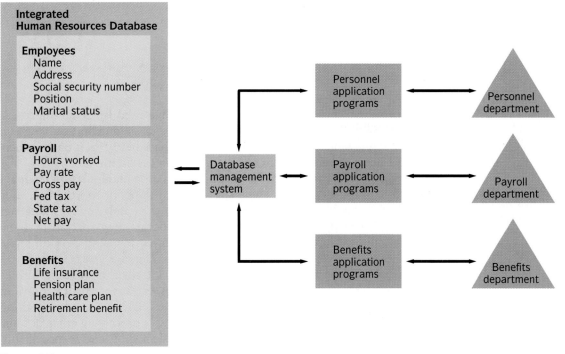

Figure 6.7
The contemporary database environment. A single Human Resources database serves multiple applications and also allows a corporation easily to draw together all of the information on various applications. The database management system acts as the interface between the application programs and the data.

Database Management Systems (DBMS)

Database management system (DBMS): Special software to create and maintain a database and enable individual business applications to extract the data they need without having to create separate files or data definitions in their computer programs.

A **database management system (DBMS)** is simply the software that permits an organization to centralize data, manage them efficiently, and provide access to the stored data by application programs. As illustrated in Figure 6.8, the DBMS acts as an interface between application programs and the physical data files. When the application program calls for a data item such as gross pay, the DBMS finds this item in the database and presents it to the application program. Using traditional data files, the programmer would have to define the data and then tell the computer where they are. A DBMS eliminates most of the data definition statements found in traditional programs.

Figure 6.8
Elements of a database management system. In an ideal database environment, application programs work through a database management system to obtain data from the database. This diagram illustrates a database management system with an active data dictionary that not only records definitions of the contents of the database but also allows changes in data size and format to be automatically utilized by the application programs.

A database management system has three components:

- A data definition language.
- A data manipulation language.
- A data dictionary.

Data definition language: The component of a database management system that defines each data element as it appears in the database.

The **data definition language** is the formal language used by programmers to specify the content and structure of the database. The data definition language defines each data element as it appears in the database before that data element is translated into the forms required by application programs.

Most DBMS have a specialized language called a **data manipulation language** that is used in conjunction with some conventional third- or fourth-generation programming languages to manipulate the data in the database. This language contains commands that permit end users and programming specialists to extract data from the database to satisfy information requests and develop applications. The most prominent data manipulation language today is **SQL**, or **Structured Query Language.** Complex programming tasks cannot be performed efficiently with typical data manipulation languages. However, most mainframe DBMS are compatible with COBOL and FORTRAN, and other third-generation programming languages, permitting greater processing efficiency and flexibility. The Window on Management on page 193 shows how special software tools and hardware are being used for highly complex queries searching massive databases that previously could not be handled either by data manipulation languages or conventional programming languages.

Data manipulation language: A language associated with a database management system that is employed by end users and programmers to manipulate data in the database.

Structured Query Language (SQL): The emerging standard data manipulation language for relational database management systems.

Data dictionary: An automated or manual tool for storing and organizing information about the data maintained in a database.

The third element of a DBMS is a **data dictionary.** This is an automated or manual file that stores definitions of data elements and data characteristics such as usage, physical representation, ownership (who in the organization is responsible for maintaining the data), authorization, and security. Many data dictionaries can produce lists and reports of data utilization, groupings, program locations, and so on. Figure 6.9 illustrates a sample data dictionary report that shows the size, format, meaning, and uses of a data element in a Human Resources database. A **data element** represents a field. Besides listing the standard name (AMT-PAY-BASE), the dictionary lists the names that reference this element in specific systems and identifies the individuals, business functions, programs, and reports that use this data element.

Data element: A field.

By creating an inventory of all the pieces of data contained in the database, the data dictionary serves as an important data management tool. For instance, business users could consult the dictionary to find out exactly what pieces of data are maintained for the sales or marketing function or even to determine all of the information maintained by the entire enterprise. The dictionary could supply business users with the name, format, and specifications required to access data for reports. Technical staff could use the dictionary to determine what data elements and files must be changed if a program is changed.

Most data dictionaries are entirely passive; they simply report. More advanced types are active; changes in the dictionary can be automatically utilized by related programs. For instance, to change zip codes from five to nine digits, one could simply enter the change in the dictionary without having to modify and recompile all user programs using zip codes.

In an ideal database environment, the data in the database are defined once and consistently and used for all applications whose data reside in the database. Application programs (which are written using a combination of the data manipulation language of the DBMS and a conventional language such as COBOL) request data elements from the database. Data elements called for by the application programs are found and delivered by the DBMS. The programmer does not have to specify in detail how or where the data are to be found.

MANAGEMENT

Sifting Through Vast Pools of Data

Traders in the financial industry are always on the lookout for information that could help them make more informed trading decisions. The problem is coming up with original pieces of information, since it is hard to make money when everyone is doing the same thing. Few traders have any time to pore over charts or sift through vast pools of financial trading data.

One possible way to find unique information is to search both current and financial market historical data for new patterns and correla-

tions. Once a trader discovers a new pattern or correlation, he or she can use that information to increase the chances of making a profitable trade. Market Information Machine (MIM), created by Logical Information Machines Inc. of Chicago, provides this capability by combining an extremely fast method of searching vast databases with a powerful desktop computer.

With MIM, traders can concoct ad hoc queries with multiple variables to determine the following:

- What happened in the bond and foreign currency markets during the three days after bond prices were up 1 percent and the German mark was up 1 percent against the dollar?
- What happened to U.S. bond prices from the first hour of trading to 1 P.M. on days that a share of IBM stock was down more than 10 points?

Extracting answers to questions like these from conventional DBMS requires complex programming. Managers using MIM can obtain answers without using a complicated programming language.

Managers in other areas could use this technology when they need to interpret vast quantities of data in order to make decisions. For instance, a sales manager using supermarket scanner data might ask MIM to show the sales of a given product in a specific region when it is on sale on Saturday between 9 A.M. and noon when the competitor is not running a coupon, and when the product is in a prime display area in supermarket aisles. Insurance firms might use the system for risk analysis.

Source: Peter H. Lewis, "A Fast Way to Discover Patterns in Vast Amounts of Data," *The New York Times*, August 30, 1992.

To Think About: What are the management benefits of systems such as the Market Information Machine?

Logical and Physical Views of Data

Logical view: Representation of data as they would appear to an application programmer or end user.

Physical view: The representation of data as they would be actually organized on physical storage media.

Perhaps the greatest difference between a DBMS and traditional file organization is that the DBMS separates the logical and physical views of the data, relieving the programmer or end user from the task of understanding where and how the data are actually stored.

The database concept distinguishes between *logical* and *physical* views of data. The **logical view** presents data as they would be perceived by end users or business specialists, whereas the **physical view** shows how data are actually organized and structured on physical storage media.

```
NAME:  AMT-PAY-BASE
FOCUS NAME:  BASEPAY
PC NAME:      SALARY

DESCRIPTION:  EMPLOYEE'S ANNUAL SALARY

SIZE:  9 BYTES
TYPE:  N          (NUMERIC)
DATE CHANGED:  01/01/85
OWNERSHIP:  COMPENSATION
UPDATE SECURITY:  SITE PERSONNEL
ACCESS SECURITY:  MANAGER, COMPENSATION PLANNING AND RESEARCH
                  MANAGER, JOB EVALUATION SYSTEMS
                  MANAGER, HUMAN RESOURCES PLANNING
                  MANAGER, SITE EQUAL OPPORTUNITY AFFAIRS
                  MANAGER, SITE BENEFITS
                  MANAGER, CLAIMS PAYING SYSTEMS
                  MANAGER, QUALIFIED PLANS
                  MANAGER, SITE EMPLOYMENT/EEO
BUSINESS FUNCTIONS USED BY:  COMPENSATION
                             HR PLANNING
                             EMPLOYMENT
                             INSURANCE
                             PENSION
                             ISP


PROGRAMS USING:  PI01000
                 PI02000
                 PI03000
                 PI04000
                 PI05000


REPORTS USING:   REPORT 124 (SALARY INCREASE TRACKING REPORT)
                 REPORT 448 (GROUP INSURANCE AUDIT REPORT)
                 REPORT 452 (SALARY REVIEW LISTING)
                 PENSION REFERENCE LISTING
```

Figure 6.9

Sample data dictionary report. The sample data dictionary report for a Human Resources database provides helpful information such as the size of the data element, which programs and reports use it, and which group in the organization is the "owner" responsible for maintaining it. The report also shows some of the other names that the organization uses for this piece of data.

Schema: The logical description of an entire database, listing all the data elements in the database and the relationships among them.

Subschema: The logical description of the part of a database required by a particular function or application program.

The logical description of the entire database, listing all of the data items and the relationship among them, is termed the **schema.** The specific set of data from the database that is required by each application program is termed the **subschema.** For example, for the human resources database illustrated in Figure 6.7, the payroll application would have a subschema consisting of employee name, address, social security number, and would specify payroll data such as pay rate and hours worked.

Suppose, for example, that a professor of information systems wanted to know at the beginning of the semester how students performed in the prerequisite computer literacy course (Computer Literacy 101) and what their current majors are. Using a database supported by the registrar, the professor would need something like the report shown in Figure 6.10.

Ideally, for such a simple report, the professor could sit at an office terminal connected to the registrar's database and write a small application program using the data manipulation language to create this report. The professor first would create the desired logical view of the data (Figure 6.10) for the application program. The DBMS would then assemble the requested data elements, which may reside in several different files and disk locations. For instance, the student major information may be located in a file called "Student," whereas the grade data may be located in a file called "Course." Wherever they are located, the DBMS would pull these pieces of information together and present them to the professor according to the logical view requested.

Student Name	ID No.	Major	Grade in Computer Literacy 101
Lind	468	Finance	A-
Pinckus	332	Marketing	B+
Williams	097	Economics	C+
Laughlin	765	Finance	A
Orlando	324	Statistics	B

Figure 6.10
The report required by the professor. The report requires data elements that may come from different files but it can easily be pulled together with a database management system if the data are organized into a database.

```
SELECT Stud_name, Stud.stud_id, Major, Grade

FROM Student, Course

WHERE Stud.stud_id = Course.stud_id

AND Course_id = "CL101"
```

Figure 6.11
The query used by the professor. This example shows how Structured Query Language (SQL) commands could be used to deliver the data required by the professor. These commands join two files, the student file (Student) and the course file (Course), and extract the specified pieces of information on each student from the combined file.

The query using the data manipulation language constructed by the professor might look something like Figure 6.11. Several DBMSs working on both mainframes and microcomputers permit this kind of interactive report creation.

In the real world, there are few registration systems that permit this kind of inquiry. Many university registration systems were created in the 1960s and are of the traditional, flat-file variety. In order to produce the report shown in Figure 6.10, a COBOL programmer would have to be hired to write several hundred lines of code. The final program would require at least three or four days of work, several test runs, debugging, and so forth. The labor costs alone would be

Sophisticated information systems are required to process the vast amount of data that is collected and organized during a typical college registration.

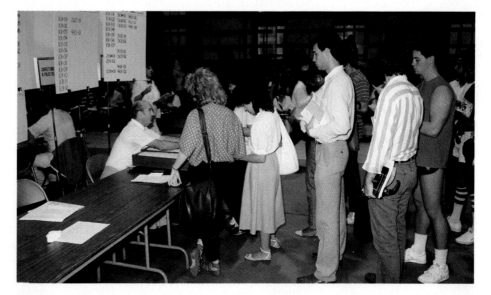

around $2,000. Several files would have to be accessed, stripped of the relevant information, and a third file would have to be created. With luck, no data inconsistencies would be found.

Imagine the cost to the university if all professors requested this or similar reports. If the university tried to meet the demand, its information processing costs would balloon rapidly. Instead, most universities simply say that the information is "in the system somewhere but is too expensive to retrieve." Only an information systems professor could understand this reply.

Advantages of Database Management Systems

The preceding discussion illustrates the advantage of a DBMS:

- Complexity of the organization's information system environment can be reduced by central management of data, access, utilization, and security.
- Data redundancy and inconsistency can be reduced by eliminating all of the isolated files in which the same data elements are repeated.
- Data confusion can be eliminated by providing central control of data creation and definitions.
- Program-data dependence can be reduced by separating the logical view of data from its physical arrangement.
- Program development and maintenance costs can be radically reduced.
- Flexibility of information systems can be greatly enhanced by permitting rapid and inexpensive ad hoc queries of very large pools of information.
- Access and availability of information can be increased.

Given all of these benefits of DBMS, one might expect all organizations to change immediately to a database form of information management. But it is not that easy, as we will see later.

6.3 Designing Databases

There are alternative ways of organizing data and representing relationships among data in a database. Conventional DBMSs use one of three principal logical database models for keeping track of entities, attributes, and relationships. The three principal logical database models are hierarchical, network, and relational. Each logical model has certain processing advantages and certain business advantages.

Hierarchical Data Model

Hierarchical data model: One type of logical database model that organizes data in a treelike structure. A record is subdivided into segments that are connected to each other in one-to-many parent–child relationships.

The earliest DBMS were hierarchical. The **hierarchical data model** presents data to users in a treelike structure. The most common hierarchical DBMS is IBM's IMS (Information Management System). Within each record, data elements are organized into pieces of records called segments. To the user, each record looks like an organization chart with one top-level segment called the *root*. An upper segment is connected logically to a lower segment in a parent–child relationship. A parent segment can have more than one child, but a child can only have one parent.

Figure 6.12 shows a hierarchical structure similar to the one used by airline reservation systems. The root segment is "Origination," which contains information about airports where flights originate. The first child is "Destination" and contains information on where flights go. The second child is "Date" (airlines generally accept reservations one year in advance). The third child is "Flight number" because on any given day there may be multiple flights to a single

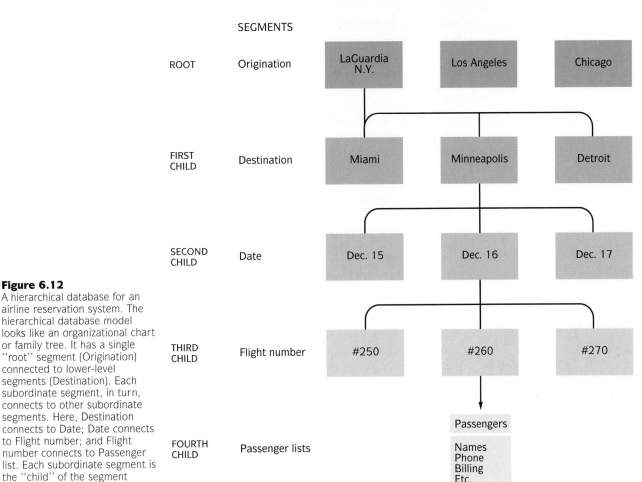

SEGMENTS

ROOT	Origination	LaGuardia N.Y.	Los Angeles	Chicago
FIRST CHILD	Destination	Miami	Minneapolis	Detroit
SECOND CHILD	Date	Dec. 15	Dec. 16	Dec. 17
THIRD CHILD	Flight number	#250	#260	#270
FOURTH CHILD	Passenger lists		Passengers Names Phone Billing Etc.	

Figure 6.12
A hierarchical database for an airline reservation system. The hierarchical database model looks like an organizational chart or family tree. It has a single "root" segment (Origination) connected to lower-level segments (Destination). Each subordinate segment, in turn, connects to other subordinate segments. Here, Destination connects to Date; Date connects to Flight number; and Flight number connects to Passenger list. Each subordinate segment is the "child" of the segment directly above it.

Pointer: A special type of data element attached to a record that shows the absolute or relative address of another record.

destination. The fourth child is "Passenger lists," which contain information on the passengers (e.g., name, local phone number, when the reservation was made, billing address, form of payment, and, in some cases, seat location).

Behind the logical view of data are a number of physical links and devices to tie the information together into a logical whole. In a hierarchical DBMS the data are physically linked to one another by a series of **pointers** that form chains of related data segments. Pointers are data elements attached to the ends of record segments on the disk directing the system to related records. In our example, if the route was LGA (New York's LaGuardia Airport), the end of the Origination segment would contain a series of pointers to all of the possible destinations. In turn, at the end of the Destination segment, there are pointers to the dates when the airline flies to that destination.

Because there are so many airports where flights originate, it would be convenient if the system could rapidly find the appropriate root segment, the origination airport. Rather than read each data segment (of which there are millions) one at a time until the right one (the root originating airport) is found, all originating airports can be stored in an index that lists the originating airports and their precise location on disk. Once this root segment is identified, pointers take over to guide the search of the database.

Network Data Model

Network data model: A logical database model that is useful for depicting many-to-many relationships.

The **network data model** is a variation of the hierarchical data model. Indeed, databases can be translated from hierarchical to network and vice versa in order to optimize processing speed and convenience. Whereas hierarchical structures depict one-to-many relationships, network structures depict data logically as many-to-many relationships.

A typical many-to-many relationship in which network DBMS excel in performance is the student–course relationship (see Figure 6.13). There are many courses in a university and many students, and students are usually enrolled in many courses.

The data in Figure 6.13 could be structured hierarchically. But this could result in considerable redundancy and a slowed response to certain types of information queries; the same student would be listed on the disk for each class he or she was taking instead of just once. Network structures reduce redundancy and, in certain situations (where many-to-many relationships are involved), respond more quickly. However, there is a price for this reduction in redundancy and increased speed: The number of pointers in network structures rapidly increases, making maintenance and operation more expensive.

Relational Data Model

Relational data model: A type of logical database model that treats data as if they were stored in two-dimensional tables. It can relate data stored in one table to data in another as long as the two tables share a common data element.

Tuple: A row or record in a relational database.

The **relational data model,** the most recent of these three database models, overcomes some of the limitations of the other two models. The relational model represents all data in the database as simple two-dimensional tables called relations. The tables appear similar to flat files, but the information in more than one file can be easily extracted and combined. Sometimes the tables are referred to as files.

Figure 6.14 shows a supplier table, a part table, and an order table. In each table, the rows are unique records and the columns are fields. Another term for a row or record in a relation is a **tuple.** Often a user needs information from a number of relations to produce a report. Here is the strength of the relational model: It can relate data in any one file or table to data in another file or table *as long as both tables share a common data element.*

To demonstrate, suppose we wanted to find in the relational database in Figure 6.14 the names and addresses of suppliers who could provide us with part number 137 or part number 152. We would need information from two tables: the supplier table and the part table. Note that these two files have a shared data element: SUPPLIER-NUMBER.

In a relational database, three basic operations are used to develop useful sets of data: select, project, and join. The *select* operation creates a subset consisting of all records in the file that meet stated criteria. "Select" creates, in other words, a subset of rows that meet certain criteria. In our example, we want to select records (rows) from the part table where the part number equals 137 or 152.

Figure 6.13

The network data model. This illustration of a network data model showing the relationship the students in a university have to the courses they take represents an example of logical many-to-many relationships. The network model reduces the redundancy of data representation through the increased use of pointers.

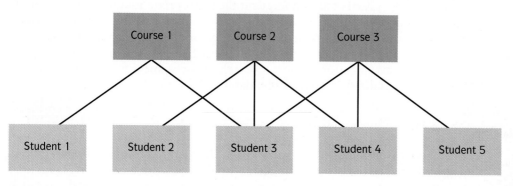

Figure 6.14
The relational data model. Each table is a *relation* and each row or record is a *tuple*. Each column corresponds to a field. These relations can easily be combined and extracted in order to access data and produce reports, provided that any two share a common data element. In this example, the ORDER file shares the data element "PART-NUMBER" with the PART file. The PART and SUPPLIER files share the data element "SUPPLIER-NUMBER."

The *join* operation combines relational tables to provide the user with more information than is available in individual tables. In our example, we want to join the now shortened part table (only parts numbered 137 or 152 will be presented) and the supplier table into a single new result table.

The *project* operation creates a subset consisting of columns in a table, permitting the user to create new tables that contain only the information required. In our example, we want to extract from the new result table only the following columns: PART-NUMBER, SUPPLIER-NUMBER, SUPPLIER-NAME, and SUPPLIER-ADDRESS.

Leading mainframe relational database management systems include IBM's DB2 and Oracle from the Oracle Corporation. FoxBase Plus from Fox Software Inc., and dBASE IV PLUS and Paradox from Borland International Inc. are examples of microcomputer relational database management systems.

Advantages and Disadvantages of the Three Database Models

The principal advantage of the hierarchical and network database models is processing efficiency. For instance, a hierarchical model is appropriate for airline reservation transaction processing systems, which must handle millions of structured routine requests each day for reservation information.

Hierarchical and network structures have several disadvantages. All of the access paths, directories, and indices must be specified in advance. Once specified, they are not easily changed without a major programming effort. Therefore, these designs have low flexibility. For instance, if you called an airline and said, "My parents gave me a ticket for a flight to an exciting resort, leaving from New York's LaGuardia Airport, but did not tell me exactly where or when. Where am I going?" you would discover that there is no way that the system can find the answer in a reasonable amount of time. This path through the data was not specified in advance. Or if the FBI called a major airline and asked about the movements in the last six months of a suspected terrorist traveling under a known assumed name, the airline could respond only after several months of programming effort (the records are kept for a period of five years on backup tapes).

Both hierarchical and network systems are programming-intensive, time-consuming, difficult to install, and difficult to remedy if design errors occur. They do not support ad hoc, English language-like inquiries for information.

The strengths of relational DBMS are great flexibility in regard to ad hoc queries, power to combine information from different sources, simplicity of design and maintenance, and the ability to add new data and records without disturbing existing programs and applications. The weakness of relational DBMS are their relatively low processing efficiency. These systems are somewhat slower because they typically require many accesses to the data stored on disk to carry out the select, join, and project commands. Selecting one part number from among millions, one record at a time, can take a long time. Of course the database can be indexed and "tuned" to speed up prespecified queries. Relational systems do not have the large number of pointers carried by hierarchical systems.

Large relational databases may be designed to have some data redundancy in order to make retrieval of data more efficient. The same data element may be stored in multiple tables. Updating redundant data elements is not automatic in many relational DBMS. For example, changing the employee status field in one table will not automatically change it in all tables. Special arrangements are required to ensure that all copies of the same data element are updated together.

Hierarchical databases remain the workhorse for intensive high-volume transaction processing. Banks, insurance companies, and other high-volume users continue to use reliable hierarchical databases such as IBM's IMS, developed in 1969. It is easier to program applications in a relational environment, but many firms do not wish to spend millions of dollars converting software from a hierarchical to a relational database management system. Many organizations have converted to DB2, IBM's relational DBMS for new applications, while retaining IMS for traditional transaction processing. For example, the United Services Automobile Association described in the Window on Technology in Chapter 2 uses DB2 only for minor programming functions. Dallas-based Texas Instruments depends on IMS for its heavy processing requirements. Texas Instruments bases its complete operations, including inventory, accounting, and manufacturing, on IMS. The firm has built up a huge library of IMS applications over twenty years, and a complete conversion to DB2 would take ten more years. As relational products acquire more muscle, firms will shift away completely from hierarchical DBMS, but this will happen over a long period of time.

Table 6.1 compares the characteristics of the different database models.

Creating a Database

In order to create a database, one must go through two design exercises, a conceptual design and a physical design. The conceptual design of a database is an abstract model of the database from a business perspective, whereas the physical design shows how the database is actually arranged on direct-access storage devices. Physical database design is performed by database specialists,

Table 6.1 COMPARISON OF DATABASE ALTERNATIVES

Type of Database	Processing Efficiency	Flexibility	End-User Friendliness	Programming Complexity
Hierarchical	High	Low	Low	High
Network	Medium–high	Low–medium	Low—moderate	High
Relational	Lower but improving	High	High	Low

whereas logical design requires a detailed description of the business informa-tion needs of actual end users of the database. Ideally, database design will be part of an overall organizational data planning effort (see Chapter 8).

The conceptual database design describes how the data elements in the data-base are to be grouped. The design process identifies relationships among data elements and the most efficient way of grouping data elements together to meet information requirements. The process also identifies redundant data elements and the groupings of data elements required for specific application programs. Groups of data are organized, refined, and streamlined until an overall logical view of the relationships among all of the data elements in the database emerges.

Database designers document the conceptual data model with an **entity-relationship diagram,** illustrated in Figure 6.15. The boxes represent entities and the diamonds represent relationships. The 1 or *M* on either side of the diamond represents the relationship among entities as either one-to-one, one-to-many, or many-to-many. Figure 6.15 shows that the entity ORDER can have only one PART and a PART can only have one SUPPLIER. Many parts can be provided by the same supplier. The attributes for each entity are listed next to the entity and the key field is underlined.

Entity-relationship diagram: Methodology for documenting databases illustrating the relationship between various entities in the database.

Figure 6.15
An Entity-Relationship diagram. This diagram shows the relationships between the entities ORDER, PART, and SUPPLIER that were used to develop the relational database illustrated in Figure 6.14.

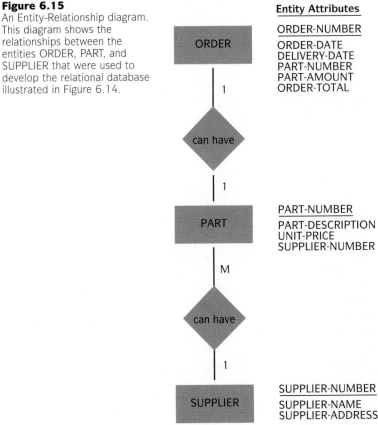

Entity Attributes

ORDER
ORDER-NUMBER
ORDER-DATE
DELIVERY-DATE
PART-NUMBER
PART-AMOUNT
ORDER-TOTAL

PART
PART-NUMBER
PART-DESCRIPTION
UNIT-PRICE
SUPPLIER-NUMBER

SUPPLIER
SUPPLIER-NUMBER
SUPPLIER-NAME
SUPPLIER-ADDRESS

6.4 Database Trends

Recent database trends include the growth of distributed databases and the emergence of object-oriented and hypermedia databases.

Distributed Processing and Distributed Databases

Distributed processing: The distribution of computer processing among multiple geographically or functionally separate locations linked by a communications network.

Distributed database: A database that is stored in more than one physical location. Parts or copies of the database are physically stored in one location and other parts or copies are stored and maintained in other locations.

Beginning in the early 1970s, information processing became more distributed with the growth of powerful telecommunications networks and the decline in computer hardware costs. Instead of relying on a single centralized mainframe computer to provide service to remote terminals, organizations began to install minicomputers and microcomputers at remote sites. These distributed processors directly serve local and regional branch offices and factories and are generally linked together in networks. The dispersion and use of computers among multiple geographically or functionally separate locations so that local computers handle local processing needs is called **distributed processing.** Chapter 7 will describe the various network arrangements for distributed processing.

It is only a short step from distributed processing to distributed databases. Although early distributed systems worked with a single centralized database, over time the smaller local systems began to store local databases as well. It soon became obvious that the central database could be entirely distributed to local processors as long as some mechanism existed to provide proper updating, integrity of data, sharing of data, and central administrative controls.

A **distributed database** is one that is stored in more than one physical location. Parts of the database are stored physically in one location and other parts are stored and maintained in other locations. There are several ways of distributing a database (see Figure 6.16). The central database (see Figure 6.16a) can be partitioned so that each remote processor has the necessary data on customers to serve its local area. Changes in local files can be justified with the central database on a batch basis, often at night. Another strategy is to duplicate the central database (see Figure 6.16b) at all remote locations (see the Window on Organizations). This strategy also requires updating of the central database on off hours.

Still another possibility—one used by very large databases like the FBI's National Crime Information Center—is to maintain only a central name index and to store complete records locally (see Figure 6.16c). A query to the central name index identifies a location where the full record can be found. Here there are no central database and no updating costs. National Westminster Bank in London uses a similar approach to maintain all of its customer account information in two massive fragmented DB2 databases. Specially developed software allows each of its 22,000 users to access the data on either database with a global catalog of where the data are stored. Another variation is an "ask-the-network" scheme (see Figure 6.16d). There is no central index of names in this design. Instead, all remote processors are polled to find a complete record. The complete record is then transferred to whatever processor requests it (Laudon, 1986).

Both distributed processing and distributed databases have benefits and drawbacks. Distributed systems reduce the vulnerability of a single, massive central site. They permit increases in systems power by purchasing smaller, less expensive minicomputers. Finally, they increase service and responsiveness to local users. Distributed systems, however, are dependent on high-quality telecommunications lines, which themselves are vulnerable. Moreover, local databases can sometimes depart from central data standards and definitions and pose security problems by widely distributing access to sensitive data. The economies of distribution can be lost when remote sites buy more computing power than they need.

Despite these drawbacks, distributed processing is growing rapidly. With the advent of microcomputers and powerful telecommunications systems, more and

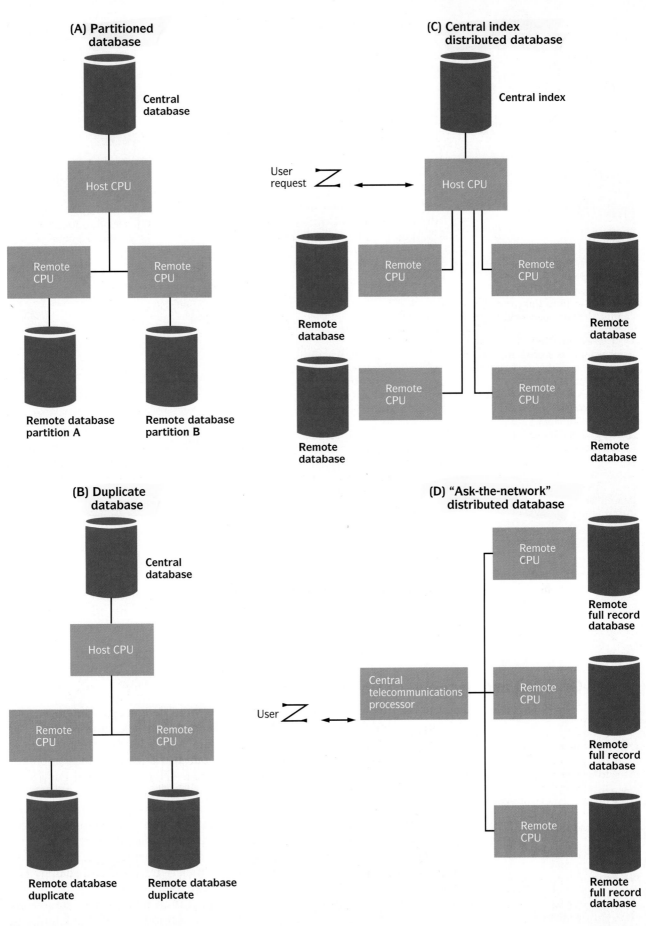

Figure 6.16

Distributed databases. There are alternative ways of distributing a database. The central database can be partitioned (A) so that each remote processor has the necessary data to serve its own local needs. The central database can also be duplicated (B) at all remote locations. In the central index distributed database (C) complete records are stored locally and can be located using a central name index. In an "ask-the-network" distributed database (D), the network polls its remote processors to locate a record and transfers the complete record to whatever processor requests it.

ORGANIZATIONS

Chase Distributes Databases for Worldwide Banking

In response to bank deregulation in the United States and the emergence of the global information economy, large U.S. banks have begun to operate nationally and internationally. The issue for $96 billion Chase Manhattan Bank NA was how to transform its organization so that it could truly serve customers internationally.

"We have multiple business units, each of which has its own customer file," says Chase's vice present of applied technology, Gene Friedman. Many customers appear many times and in multiple locations in these customer files. When a large client with international holdings asks Chase for a quick picture of its current investments, that customer does not want to wait while Chase collects data from customer files around the globe. Nor does it want an incomplete answer. Yet geographically dispersed banking units need to maintain their own data locally to better serve local clients, whether or not those clients are branches of larger, international customers. The new competitive

environment also meant that Chase needed more flexible access to the data, wherever it is stored.

Chase turned to emerging database technology for part of the answer. They had put an international network in place in 1988, well ahead of most of their competitors. In 1993, 12,000 of their 22,000 PCs worldwide were already connected to the network. Chase installed relational databases as part of the computing/communications infrastructure. The next step, according to Chief Information Officer Craig Goldman, is to import data from Chase's mainframes onto local networks serving individual locations. Goldman says they will copy data across multiple machines in offices worldwide. This will provide dispersed business units with better access to customer data stored in central database repositories. Chase will be able to replicate data in some locations once every 24 hours as replication technology has been doing for several years. However, the firm will also update

designated data continuously in true distributed database fashion. After all, Goldman observes, "If you're dealing with customer inquiries, you damn well better have the last transaction."

Friedman adds one other element to the changes the organization is undergoing: a cultural change in the way people view their work. "It's a change in the paradigm that the doers and the maintainers of this technology are used to working in," he says.

Source: Jean S. Bozman, "Chase Unifies Database View," *Computerworld*, May 24, 1993.

To Think About: Was a replicated database a good choice for Chase? Why or why not? What management, organization, and technology factors had to be addressed in creating this replicated database? Once this new technology is fully in place at Chase, what other organizational changes might it bring about?

more information services will be distributed. For large national organizations working in several regions, the question is no longer whether to distribute but how to distribute in such a way as to minimize costs and improve responsiveness without sacrificing data and system integrity.

Object-Oriented and Hypermedia Databases

Object-oriented database:
Approach to data management that stores both data and the procedures acting on the data as objects that can be automatically retrieved and shared.

Hypermedia database:
Approach to data management that organizes data as a network of nodes linked in any pattern established by the user.

Conventional database management systems were designed for homogeneous data that can be easily structured into predefined data fields and records. But many applications of the 1990s will require databases that can store and retrieve not only structured numbers and characters but also drawings, images, photographs, voice, and full-motion video (see Figure 6.17). Conventional DBMS are not well suited to handling graphics-based or multimedia applications. For instance, design data in a CAD database consist of complex relationships between many types of data. Manipulating these kinds of data in a relational system requires extensive programming to translate these complex data structures into tables and rows. An **object-oriented database,** on the other hand, stores the data and procedures as objects that can be automatically retrieved and shared. The Window on Technology describes these new capabilities.

The **hypermedia database** approach to information management transcends some of the limitations of traditional database methods by storing chunks of

TECHNOLOGY

British Telecom and Metropolitan Toronto Turn to Object-Oriented DBMS

What is an ideal database management system? According to Jay Parekh, manager of software development for British Telecom North America, Inc., it's one that can store both object-oriented and relational data and give users easy access to either data type. Parekh's company maintains the Tymnet data communications network, one of the world's largest commercial network services. About two years ago, British Telecom began building a new system to improve management of this network. The system had to graphically display each device on the network. Parekh modeled each device on the network using software objects and the C++ programming language. He chose Versant ODBMS, an object-oriented database management system from Versant Object Technology, to store these objects.

Object-oriented database management systems are especially well suited for graphics-intensive applications such as network management, telecommunications, CAD/CAM, and geographic information systems. These applications generate a great deal of graphic information that can't easily be stored as simple rows and tables in a relational DBMS. Another application for ODBMS is genetic research. Cold Spring Harbor Laboratory in Long Island City, New York, wanted to rewrite some applications that examined pictures of DNA molecules and manipulated genetic research data. A relational database wouldn't do because the laboratory wanted a database management system capable of storing images. The laboratory chose an object-oriented

database management system instread. It now has three genetic research applications based on Gemstone from the Servio Corporation in Alameda, California.

Firms interested in reusable code and decreased costs for maintaining existing software might be interested in object-oriented database management systems as well. Unlike relational or hierarchical database management systems, object-oriented DBMS store data as objects, which incorporate the processing rules needed to complete each database transaction.

A firm can't expect to replace all of its relational, hierarchical, and flat file systems with one object-oriented database management system, but it can use the ODBMS as a tool to access diverse data stores. For instance, a firm could store a complex series of commands to access data from various sources—relational databases, hierarchical databases, or flat files—as an object stored in an ODBMS to be accessed by users when needed. One click of the mouse could bring up a link to all the data stored in different types of DBMS and different machines. The ODBMS could be instructed to retrieve the data, combine them with other sources, and format them for use in a spreadsheet.

The Municipality of Metropolitan Toronto used the Gemstone ODBMS for this purpose. Since September, 1992, Toronto's information systems department has used Gemstone to bring together the city's diverse databases. Gemstone acts as an electronic index to the city's databases. For instance, if a municipal employee

needs to find out who is responsible for licensing dogs, he or she could query the system through an application running on one of several SPARCstation workstations. The request would be passed to Gemstone, which stores objects containing the code for querying the various database systems. Gemstone transmits the queries, compiles the information, and returns it to the user in a readable format.

Corporations seeking to migrate to object-oriented DBMS must recognize that their staffs have been designing relational DBMS for years, with the attitude of "If it isn't broke, why try to fix it?" Training programmers to take full advantage of object-oriented techniques requires a change in mindset. Often a firm's first few object-oriented DBMS applications tend to look more like relational applications running on an object-oriented database. Corporations that have invested ten years in relational technology might not want to switch to another technology until they have obtained a significant return on their investment.

Sources: Mike Ricciuti, "Object Databases Find Their Niche," *Datamation,* September 15, 1993; and Paul Korzeniowski, "Object-Oriented DBMSs Strive to Differentiate," *Software Magazine,* May 1992.

To Think About: Suggest some other applications for object-oriented DBMS. When adopting object-oriented DBMS, what management, organization, and technology factors would you consider?

information in the form of nodes connected by links established by the user (see Figure 6.18). The nodes can contain text, graphics, sound, full-motion video, or executable computer programs. Searching for information does not have to follow a predetermined organization scheme. Instead, one can branch instantly to related information in any kind of relationship established by the author. The relationship between records is less structured than in a traditional DBMS.

Figure 6.17
An object-oriented multimedia database. Medical data on patients in a hospital might likely be stored in a multimedia database such as this one. Doctors could access patient files including vital medical images to generate the reports and derive the information they need to deliver quality health care quickly. *Courtesy of Digital Equipment Corporation.*

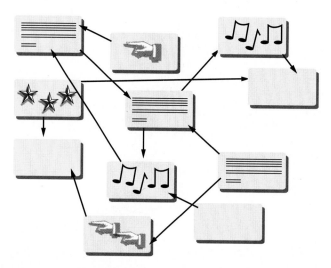

Figure 6.18
Hypermedia. In a hypermedia database, the user can choose his or her own path to move from node to node. Each node can contain text, graphics, sound, full-motion video, or executable programs.

In most systems, each node can be displayed on a screen. The screen also displays the links between the node depicted and other nodes in the database. Figure 6.19 illustrates sample nodes from Apple Corporation's HyperCard, which is based on the hypermedia concept. The node for Sugar City, Montana, is linked to a node for the state of Montana and to a node showing a map of the entire United States. The node for the state of Montana illustrated in Figure 6.19 is linked to nodes for each of the cities illustrated on the map; to a node for the map of the entire United States; and to a node to return to the Home card, the first node in the HyperCard system. HyperCard is used primarily for small, single-user applications. Massive, multi-user hypermedia databases are starting to be constructed for business and military applications (Carmel et al., 1989).

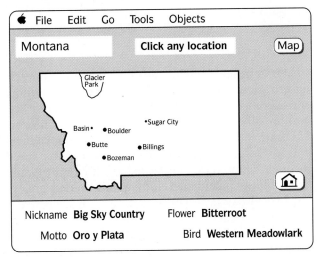

Figure 6.19

HyperCard. HyperCard programs are constructed as if they were stacks of individual cards, each of which can be linked to one or more other cards in any way the user chooses. The links do not have to follow the structured formulas of conventional databases or lists. HyperCard programs can contain digitized sound, drawings, and video images, as well as text. *Courtesy of Apple Computer, Inc.*

6.5 Management Requirements for Database Systems

Much more is required for the development of database systems than simply selecting a logical database model. Indeed, this selection may be among the last decisions. The database is an organizational discipline, a method, rather than a tool or technology. It requires organizational and conceptual change.

Without management support and understanding, database efforts fail. The critical elements in a database environment are 1) data administration, 2) data planning and modeling methodology, 3) database technology and management, and 4) users. This environment is depicted in Figure 6.20 and will now be described.

Data Administration

Database systems require that the organization recognize the strategic role of information and begin actively to manage and plan for information as a

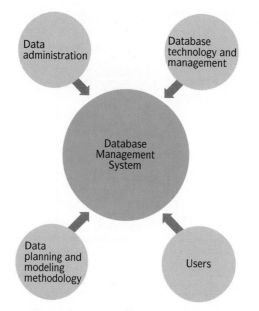

Figure 6.20
Key organizational elements in the database environment. For a database management system to flourish in any organization, data administration functions and data planning and modeling methodologies must be coordinated with database technology and management. Resources must be devoted to train end users to use databases properly.

Data administration: A special organizational function for managing the organization's data resources, concerned with data planning, information policy, maintenance of data dictionaries, and data quality standards.

corporate resource. This means that the organization must develop a **data administration** function with the power to define information requirements for the entire company and with direct access to senior management. The chief information officer (CIO) or vice president of information becomes the primary advocate in the organization for database systems.

Data administration is responsible for the specific policies and procedures through which data can be managed as an organizational resource. These responsibilities include developing information policy, planning for data, overseeing logical database design and data dictionary development, and monitoring the usage of data by information system specialists and end-user groups.

The fundamental principle of data administration is that all data are the property of the organization as a whole. Data cannot belong exclusively to any one business area or organizational unit. All data are to be made available to any group that requires them to fulfill its mission. An organization needs to formulate an **information policy** that specifies its rules for sharing, disseminating, acquiring, standardizing, classifying, and inventorying information throughout the organization. Information policy lays out specific procedures and accountabilities, specifying which organizational units share information; where information can be distributed; and who has responsibility for updating and maintaining the information.

Information policy: Formal rules governing the maintenance, distribution, and use of information in an organization.

Data Planning and Modeling Methodology

Because the organizational interests served by the DBMS are much broader than those in the traditional file environment, the organization requires enterprisewide planning for data. Enterprise analysis, which addresses the information requirements of the entire organization (as opposed to the requirements of individual applications), is needed to develop databases. The purpose of enterprise analysis is to identify the key entities, attributes, and relationships that constitute the organization's data. These techniques are described in greater detail in Chapter 8.

Database Technology and Management

Databases require new software and a new staff specially trained in DBMS techniques as well as new management structures. Most corporations develop a database design and management group within the corporate information system division that is responsible for the more technical and operational aspects of managing data. The functions it performs are called **database administration.** This group does the following:

Database administration: Refers to the more technical and operational aspects of managing data, including physical database design and maintenance.

- Defines and organizes database structure and content.
- Develops security procedures to safeguard the database.
- Develops database documentation.
- Maintains the database management software.

In close cooperation with users, the design group establishes the physical database, the logical relations among elements, and the access rules and procedures.

Users

A database serves a wider community of users than traditional systems. Relational systems with fourth-generation query languages permit employees who are not computer specialists to access large databases. In addition, users include trained computer specialists. In order to optimize access for nonspecialists, more resources must be devoted to training end users. Professional systems workers must be retrained in the DBMS language, DBMS application development procedures, and new software practices.

Management Challenges

Hierarchical database technology first became commercially available in the early 1970s. Since then, more sophisticated database models have appeared. Nevertheless, progress in creating a true database environment in organizations has been much slower than anticipated. Why? Three challenges stand out.

1. **Organizational obstacles to a database environment.** Implementing a database requires widespread organizational change in the role of information (and information managers), the allocation of power at senior levels, the ownership and sharing of information, and patterns of organizational agreement. A DBMS challenges the existing arrangements in an organization and for that reason often generates political resistance.

    In a traditional file environment, each department constructed files and programs to fulfill its specific needs. Now, with a database, files and programs must be built that take into account the full organization's interest in data. For instance, in the past the treasurer could insulate his or her data and applications from others in the organization. Some information that once "belonged" to the treasurer is now shared through the DBMS with users in other departments. Quite naturally, the treasurer may worry that other users will not treat financial data with the same care and concern as the treasurer's personnel.

2. **Cost/benefit considerations.** The costs of moving to a database environment are tangible, up front, and large in the short term (three years). Most firms buy a commercial DBMS package and related hardware. The software alone can cost one-half million dollars for a full-function package with all options. New hardware may cost an additional $1 to 2 million annually. It soon becomes apparent to senior management that a database system is a huge investment. Although the organization has spent the money on the hardware and software for a database environment, it may not reap the benefits it should because it is unwilling to make the requisite organizational changes.

    Unfortunately, the benefits of the DBMS are often intangible, backloaded, and long-term (five years). The systems that the DBMS seeks to replace generally work, although they are inefficient. Moreover, several million dollars have been spent over the years designing and maintaining existing systems. People in the organization understand the existing system after long periods of training and socialization. For all of these reasons, and despite the clear advantages of the DBMS, the short-term costs of developing a DBMS often appear to be nearly as great as the benefits. When the short-term political costs are added to the equation, it is convenient for senior management to defer the database investment. The obvious long-term benefits of the DBMS tend to be severely discounted by managers, especially those unfamiliar with (and perhaps unfriendly to) systems. Moreover, it may not be cost-effective to build organization-wide databases that integrate all of the organization's data (Goodhue et. al., September 1992).

3. **Organizational placement of the data management function.** Many organizations, seeking to avoid large commitments and organizational change, begin (and end) by buying a DBMS package and placing it in the hands of a low-level database group in the information systems department. Generally this leads to a piecemeal approach to database use; that is, small database systems will be developed for various divisions, functional areas, departments, and offices. Eventually this results in incompatible databases throughout the company and fails to address the key organizational issue: What is the role of information and who will manage it for the organization as a whole? Senior management must be persuaded to implement a data administration function and data planning methodology at the highest corporate level.

Summary

Describe traditional file organization and management techniques.

In a traditional file environment, data records are organized using either a sequential file organization or a direct or random file organization. Records in a sequential file can be accessed sequentially or they can be accessed directly if the sequential file is on disk and uses an indexed sequential access method. Records on a file with direct file organization can be accessed directly without an index.

Explain the problems of the traditional file environment.

By allowing different functional areas and groups in the organization to maintain their own files independently, the traditional file environment creates problems such as data redundancy and inconsistency, program/data dependence, inflexibility, poor security, and lack of data sharing and availability.

Describe how a database management system organizes information.

Database management systems (DBMS) are the software that permits centralization of data and data management. A DBMS includes a data definition language, a data manipulation language, and a data dictionary capability.

The most important feature of the DBMS is its ability to separate the logical and physical views of data. The user works with a logical view of data. The DBMS software translates user queries into queries that can be applied to the physical view of the data. The DBMS retrieves information so that the user does not have to be concerned with its physical location. This feature separates programs from data and from the management of data.

Identify the three principal database models.

There are three principal logical database models: hierarchical, network, and relational. Each has unique advantages and disadvantages. Hierarchical systems, which support one-to-many relationships, are low in flexibility but high in processing speed and efficiency. Network systems support many-to-many relationships. Relational systems are relatively slow but are very flexible for supporting ad hoc requests for information and for combining information from different sources. The choice depends on the business requirements.

Discuss new database trends.

It is no longer necessary for data to be centralized in a single, massive database. A complete database or portions of the database can be distributed to more than one location to increase responsiveness and reduce vulnerability and costs. There are two major types of distributed databases: replicated databases and partitioned databases.

Object-oriented databases and hypermedia databases may be alternatives to traditional database structures for certain types of applications. Both can store graphics and other types of data in addition to conventional text data to support multimedia applications. Hypermedia databases allow data to be stored in nodes linked together in any pattern established by the user.

Explain the managerial and organizational requirements for creating a database environment.

Development of a database environment requires much more than selection of technology. It requires a change in the corporation's attitude toward information. The organization must develop a data administration function and a data planning methodology. The database environment has developed more slowly than was originally anticipated. There is political resistance in organizations to many key database concepts, especially to sharing of information that has been controlled exclusively by one organizational group. There are difficult cost/benefit questions in database management. Often, to avoid raising difficult questions, database use begins and ends as a small effort isolated in the Information Systems Department.

Key Terms

Field
Record
File
Entity
Attribute
Key field
Sequential file organization
Direct or random file organization
Indexed sequential access method
 (ISAM)
Index
Direct file access method
Transform algorithm
Traditional file environment
Data redundancy
Program-data dependence
Database
Database management system (DBMS)
Data definition language
Data manipulation language

Structured Query Language (SQL)
Data dictionary
Data element
Logical view
Physical view
Schema
Subschema
Hierarchical data model
Pointer
Network data model
Relational data model
Tuple
Entity-relationship diagram
Distributed processing
Distributed database
Object-oriented database
Hypermedia database
Data administration
Information policy
Database administration

Review Questions

1. Why is file management important for overall system performance?
2. Describe how indexes and key fields enable a program to access specific records in a file.
3. Define and describe the indexed sequential access method and the direct file access method.
4. List and describe some of the problems of the traditional file environment.
5. Define a database and a database management system.
6. Name and briefly describe the three components of a DBMS.
7. What is the difference between a logical and a physical view of data?

8. List some of the benefits of a DBMS.

9. Describe the three principal logical database models and the advantages and disadvantages of each.

10. What is a distributed database, and how does it differ from distributed data processing?

11. What are object-oriented and hypermedia databases? How do they differ from a traditional database?

12. What are the four key elements of a database environment? Describe each briefly.

13. Describe and briefly comment on the major management challenges in building a database environment.

Discussion Questions

1. It has been said that you do not need database management software to have a database environment. Discuss.

2. As an information system manager, you are concerned that the percentage of your staff working on maintenance of existing programs is growing and the percentage working on new applications is declining. How could a database environment change this trend?

3. To what extent should end users be involved in the selection of a database management system and in database design?

Group Project

Form a group with half of your classmates. Consider two strategies for building a database environment. One strategy recommends that a small group be created in the information systems department to begin exploring database applications throughout the firm. The other strategy recommends the creation of a vice president of information and subsequent development of important database applications. Debate the costs and benefits of each strategy with the other group.

CASE STUDY

Can Better Data Management Help a Regional French Bank?

The Caisse Régionale de Crédit Agricole Mutuel du Lot, a regional commercial credit division of France's largest bank, runs 70 PCs, four mainframe and minicomputers, and 500 terminals. Based in Cahors, Lot, in the southwestern part of France, the operation employs 430 workers, including 40 in the data processing department.

Its parent bank, Crédit Agricole, is the seventh largest bank in the world, with assets of more than 1.4 billion francs, banking facilities in New York and Chicago, and a total of 70 million customers. Its entire workforce totals 73,700, with 530 data processing specialists. Crédit Agricole operates 91 regional banks in France, including one per French *département* such as Lot. (A *département* is similar to a state in the United States.) The bank runs more than 450 mainframe and minicomputers linking 50,000 terminals worldwide. About one-third of the French banking consumers are its clients. The bank is highly decentralized.

An extensive analysis found that Crédit Agricole du Lot needed to work with the concept of a "commercial cli-

ent." It needed a database management system that could regroup and improve access to individuals maintained in the database and that could answer many different kinds of queries that were not predefined. (Banks have traditionally maintained information based on different types of accounts—checking, savings, loans, and so forth. A client may have more than one account. If files or databases are inflexible and organized around accounts, it may be impossible to draw together all the information maintained on clients.) The bank also needed tools for targeting all of its commercial operations and for facilitating multiple access queries.

The bank had been using IBM's DL/1 (Data Language/1), an extension of IBM's hierarchical DBMS, IMS. The information the bank needed was not accessible to different applications, so bank personnel had to spend a great deal of time rekeying the same information.

Competition is very tough, and the bank wanted to boost its competitive standing through quality to improve its profitability. In particular, it wanted to produce behavior studies of different categories of clients, such as individuals, organizations, companies, and self-employed persons. The bank wanted to use the results of these studies to produce quick, targeted client profiles so it could direct its marketing campaigns toward controlling risks and credits. To do this, the bank needed to update its databases easily; to access their stored information quickly; and if required, to partition the data for particular needs.

Crédit Agricole du Lot chose CA-Datacom/DB, the relational database management system from Computer Associates International in Garden City, New York, over IBM's DB2 because it could run under the bank's existing operating system, MVS/SP. At the time of selection, DB/2 required MVS/XS or MVS/ESA, newer IBM operating systems. The hardware cost of upgrading to a new operating system would have been prohibitive. The bank could continue using its older IMS database and DL/1 and share data with the new CA-Datacom/DB database, whereas comprehensive data sharing between DB2 and DL/1 was not possible. CA-Datacom/DB has SQL capabilities.

The bank took a year longer to install the new database management system than it had originally anticipated because the vendor was late delivering the DBMS capabilities it had promised to the bank and because several minor software bugs were encountered during installation.

With the improved capabilities of the relational DBMS, Crédit Agricole du Lot also hopes to introduce more self-service features into its branches. It is installing IBM Personal System/2 microcomputer workstations and distributing portable microcomputers to its commercial staff.

Source: Mike Bucken, "Relational Gives Bank Fast Access to Queries," *Software Magazine,* March 1991.

Case Study Questions

1. Was a relational database management system the best choice for Crédit Agricole du Lot? Why or why not?

2. To what extent is selecting a database management system an important business decision?

3. What are some of the data fields that would have to be maintained in the new database?

4. What management, organization, and technology factors should be considered when selecting a database management system?

References

Butterworth, Paul, Allen Otis, and Jacob Stein. "The GemStone Object Database Management System." *Communications of the ACM* 34, no. 10 (October 1991).

Carmel, Erran, William K. McHenry, and Yeshayahu Cohen. "Building Large, Dynamic Hypertexts: How Do We Link Intelligently?" *Journal of Management Information Systems* 6, no. 2 (Fall 1989).

Date, C. J. *An Introduction to Database Systems.* 5th ed. Reading, MA: Addison-Wesley, 1990.

Date, C. J. "Twelve Rules for a Distributed Data Base." *Computerworld* (June 8, 1987).

Everest, G. C. *Database Management: Objectives, System Functions, and Administration.* New York: McGraw-Hill Book Company, 1985.

Goldstein, R. C., and J. B. McCririck. "What Do Data Administrators Really Do?" *Datamation* 26 (August 1980).

Goodhue, Dale L., Judith A. Quillard, and John F. Rockart. "Managing the Data Resource: A Contingency Perspective." *MIS Quarterly* (September 1988).

Goodhue, Dale L., Laurie J. Kirsch, Judith A. Quillard, and Michael D. Wybo. "Strategic Data Planning: Lessons from the Field." *MIS Quarterly* 16, no. 1 (March 1992).

Goodhue, Dale L., Michael D. Wybo, and Laurie J. Kirsch. "The Impact of Data Integration on the Costs and Benefits of Information Systems." *MIS Quarterly* 16, no. 3 (September 1992).

Grover, Varun, and James Teng. "How Effective Is Data Resource Management?" *Journal of Information Systems Management* (Summer 1991).

Kahn, Beverly K. "Some Realities of Data Administration." *Communications of the ACM* 26 (October 1983).

Kahn, Beverly, and Linda Garceau. "The Database Administration Function." *Journal of Management Information Systems* 1 (Spring 1985).

King, John L., and Kenneth Kraemer. "Information Resource Management Cannot Work." *Information and Management* (1988).

Kent, William. "A Simple Guide to Five Normal Forms in Relational Database Theory." *Communications of the ACM* 26, no. 2 (February 1983).

Kroenke, David. *Database Processing.* 4th ed. New York: Macmillan Publishing Company, 1992.

Laudon, Kenneth C. *Dossier Society: Value Choices in the Design of National Information Systems.* New York: Columbia University Press, 1986.

Madnick, Stuart E., and Richard Y. Wang. "Evolution towards Strategic Application of Databases through Composite Information Systems." *Journal of Management Information Systems* 5, no. 3 (Winter 1988–1989).

March, Salvatore T., and Young-Gul Kim. "Information Resource Management: A Metadata Perspective." *Journal of Management Information Systems* 5, no. 3 (Winter 1988–1989).

Martin, James. *Managing the Data-Base Environment.* Englewood Cliffs, NJ: Prentice-Hall, 1983.

Silberschatz, Avi, Michael Stonebraker, and Jeff Ullman, eds. "Database Systems: Achievements and Opportunities." *Communications of the ACM* 34, no. 10 (October 1991).

Smith, John B., and Stephen F. Weiss. "Hypertext." *Communications of the ACM* 31, no. 7 (July 1988).

CHAPTER 7

Telecommunications and the New Information Architecture

British Petroleum Innovates with Networked Computers

BP Exploration, Inc. (also known as BPX), the oil exploration arm of British Petroleum America, needed to make its operation more efficient in the face of declining oil reserves and shrinking profits in the world oil industry. One way to do this was to allow its geoscientists and engineers more immediate access to the data they needed. The company decided to give more computing power to its workers in the field by replacing its larger computers with networked microcomputers and workstations.

BPX moved technical applications, such as oilfield mapping and corrosion tracking, from its old Digital Equipment minicomputers and Cray supercomputers to microcomputers and workstations. BP can now do all of its seismic exploration—sending signals to the earth, recording them electronically, and processing them into two-dimensional cross-sections—on microcomputers or workstations. Workstations are used for geologic mapping and for simulations that previously required the massive computing power of

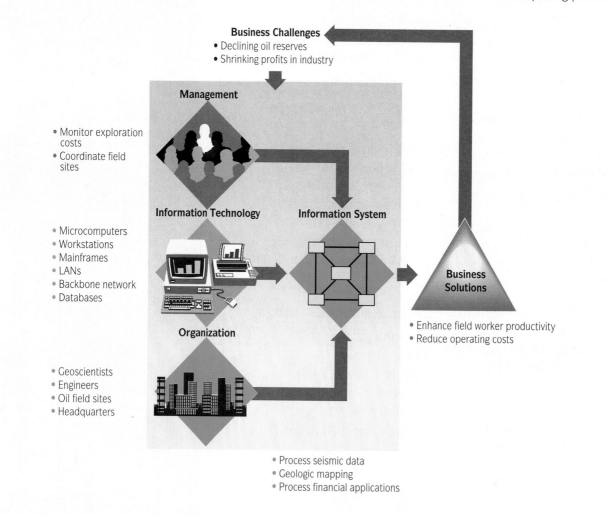

a supercomputer. Eventually, administrative and personnel functions will be moved to networks as well.

BPX installed 1200 Macintosh computers in networks that use IBM RS/6000 and Sun UNIX workstations as file servers. Many of the microcomputers are linked at BPX's headquarters building in Anchorage. All of the microcomputers have access to BP databases on the file servers. Previously, mainframes processed BPX's seismic exploration data at an annual cost of $1 million. By using the new networks, desktop microcomputers, and workstations, BPX reduced the processing cost to one-fourth of that amount. The new computing arrangement is more portable, too, since people can use some of the equipment while working at their hotels in remote locations.

Local Area Networks (LANs) also operate at BP's Prudhoe Bay Field, 800 miles north of Anchorage. These networks are tied to the Anchorage network and to other BPX facilities using the company's worldwide backbone data network, which links North America, South America, and Europe. Maps and other documents can easily be sent back and forth between departments in Anchorage and the remote field facilities.

BPX isn't abandoning its large computers entirely. IBM mainframes and DEC VAX minicomputers still run commercial financial systems. But BPX hopes to extend its desktop computing network throughout its operations worldwide.

Sources: Bruce Silver, "British Petroleum Exploration" in "Workflow: Redesigning the Enterprise," *Computerworld,* June 28, 1993; and Bob Violino, "Exploring New Fields of IT Management," *Information WEEK,* July 6, 1992.

BPX is one of many companies that has found it can benefit from recent advances in telecommunications. Many of the technical advances in computing and information systems, such as on-line processing and providing direct access to data, would be impossible without telecommunications. Telecommunications has become so essential to the conduct of business life that managers will be making telecommunications-related decisions throughout their career.

Telecommunications advances are driving some companies, like BPX, to rearrange their hardware, software, and communications capabilities into a new information architecture. Instead of relying on large mainframe computers for processing, BPX distributed computer power and information to powerful microcomputers and workstations on the desktop and tied its smaller networks into a giant companywide network. By putting more control of computer processing on the desktop and linking smaller networks into a companywide network, this new information architecture can help organizations achieve new levels of competitiveness and productivity. However, achieving these goals requires an understanding of telecommunications systems and how to make disparate hardware, software, and communications devices work together.

This chapter describes the components of telecommunications systems and shows how they can be arranged to create various types of telecommunications networks and network-based applications that can increase the efficiency and competitiveness of an organization. The key to creating networks where users can share data throughout the organization is connectivity. This chapter describes the connectivity models organizations use to link their systems and the standards that make such linkages possible. Despite the benefits of distributing computing power to the desktop and linking networks, telecommunications and the new information architecture have created new management problems. We describe those problems and their solutions so that organizations can maximize the benefits of the new architecture.

After completing this chapter you will be able to:

- Describe the components of a telecommunications network and how they work.
- Classify the various types of networks and network topologies.
- Identify telecommunications applications that can provide competitive advantages to organizations.
- Describe important standards for linking hardware, software, and networks to achieve connectivity.
- Describe problems posed by the new information architecture and recommended solutions.

7.1 The Telecommunications Revolution

Telecommunications:
Communication of information by electronic means, usually over some distance.

Telecommunications can be defined as communication of information by electronic means, usually over some distance. We are currently in the middle of a telecommunications revolution that has three components: rapid changes in the technology of communications; changes in the ownership, control, and marketing of telecommunications services; and a radically different vision of how telecommunications can be used within an organization.

For most of the last 125 years, since Alexander Bell invented the first "singing telegraph" in 1876, telecommunications was a monopoly either of the state or of a regulated private firm. In the United States, American Telephone and Telegraph (AT&T) was the largest regulated monopoly, providing virtually all telecommunications services. In Europe and in the rest of the world, there is a state post, telephone, and telegraph authority (PTT). In the United States, the monopoly ended in 1984, when the Department of Justice forced AT&T to give up its monopoly and allow competing firms to sell telecommunications services and equipment.

The end of the monopoly widened the market for new telecommunications technologies and devices, from cheaper long distance service to telephone answering equipment, cellular telephones, and private satellite communications services. These changes in the telecommunications industry were accompanied by changes in telecommunications technology. Previously, telecommunications meant voice transmission over telephone lines. Today, much telecommunications transmission is digital data transmission, using computers to transmit data from one location to another. Telephone companies have also been expanding from traditional voice communications into new information services.

Today's managers need to understand how to use telecommunications technology and how to maximize its benefits for their organization. In Chapter 2 we described how Baxter Healthcare International Inc. was able to garner nearly two-thirds of the U.S. hospital supplies business by combining a better understanding of their customers' needs with new telecommunications technology. More recently the telecommunications revolution has spawned a new vision of computing known as the *new information architecture,* which foresees great gains in competitiveness for those companies that take advantage of telecommunications technology.

In Chapter 1 we defined information architecture as the particular form that information technology takes in an organization to achieve selected goals. An organization's information architecture consists of its computer hardware and software, telecommunications links, and data files. In the new information architecture, these components are arranged to place more of the organization's computing power on the desktop and to create networks that link entire enterprises.

Features of the New Information Architecture

Figure 7.1 illustrates one example of this new architecture: the enterprise-wide network used by Brewer's Retail, Inc., based in Mississauga, Ontario, Canada, which runs a chain of over 450 beer stores throughout Ontario. The network at company headquarters consists of nine Sun SPARCserver file servers (which store data and programs), 30 SPARCstation workstations, and 110 microcomputers with 80386 microprocessors linked together. Each retail store owned by this firm has a microcomputer linked to this network. Brewer's Retail polls each retail store's microcomputer every night and uploads its sales data to one of its servers. The SPARCstation workstations are used for application development. The microcomputers at corporate headquarters use the data for accounting and other applications. All of these machines use the UNIX operating system.

Figure 7.1
The new information architecture at Brewer's Retail Inc. A network of Sun servers and development workstations work in tandem with over 100 PCs at Brewer's Retail Inc. Remote PCs, located in individual retail stores, are polled each night for data uploads. *Source: Lee Thé, "Downsize Your Database with UNIX,"* Datamation, *October 15, 1992. Reproduced with permission from DATAMATION © 1992 Reed Publishing (USA) Inc.*

How does Brewer's Retail's arrangements of machines, software, databases, and telecommunications differ from arrangements of the past? Under the old architecture, mainframes and minicomputers from the same computer manufacturer were responsible for most of the firm's information processing. Microcomputers and workstations were used independently by individual users or were linked into small localized networks. By adopting a new information architecture, Brewer's Retail now uses a mixture of various types of computer hardware that are networked together, consisting of workstations, microcomputers, minicomputers and mainframes supplied by different hardware vendors.

Under this new architecture, diverse pieces of hardware may work together on the same processing problem in what is called a **client/server model** of computing. The client/server model splits computer processing between "clients" on a network and "servers," with each function being assigned to the machine best suited to perform it. The client portion of the application typically consists of the user interface and the data input process and is used for querying a database and obtaining reports. The server part usually retrieves or processes data. The exact division of tasks varies with each application. The client/server model requires that application programs be written as two separate software components that run on different machines but that appear to operate as a single application.

With information resources much more controlled from the desktop, the system is a network; in fact, the system is composed of multiple networks: A high-capacity backbone network connects many smaller networks and devices, and the backbone may be connected to many external networks like Bitnet, Arpanet, Internet, and through the phone system to even more networks.

Client/server model: A model for computing that splits the processing between "clients" and "servers" on a network, assigning functions to the machine most able to perform the function.

Components and Functions of a Telecommunications System

The new information architecture rests on a foundation of telecommunications systems. A **telecommunications system** is a collection of compatible hardware and software arranged to communicate information from one location to another. Telecommunications systems can transmit text, graphic images, voice, or video information. A telecommunications system transmits information, establishes the interface between the sender and the receiver, routes messages along the most efficient paths, and performs elementary processing of the information to ensure that the right message gets to the right receiver. The telecommunications system controls the flow of information. Figure 7.2 illustrates the components of a typical telecommunications system. The essential components of a telecommunications system are:

Telecommunications system: Collection of compatible hardware and software arranged to communicate information from one location to another.

1. Computers to process information.
2. Terminals or any input/output devices that send or receive data.
3. Communications channels, the links by which data or voice are transmitted between sending and receiving devices in a network.
4. Communications processors, such as modems, multiplexers, and front-end processors, which provide support functions for data transmission and reception.
5. Communications software, which controls input and output activities and manages other functions of the communications network. The following sections describe how the components can be arranged into various types of networks.

TYPES OF SIGNALS: ANALOG AND DIGITAL

Information travels through a telecommunications system in the form of electromagnetic signals. Signals are represented in two ways: analog and digital. An **analog signal** is represented by a continuous waveform that passes through a

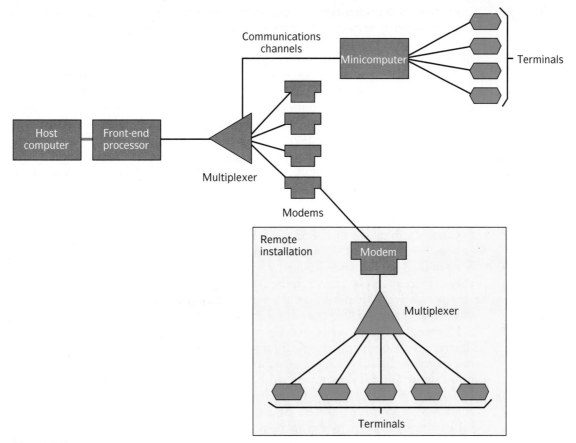

Figure 7.2
Components of a telecommunications system. This figure illustrates some of the hardware
components that would be found in a typical telecommunications system. They include computers,
terminals, communications channels, and communications processors such as modems,
multiplexers, and the front-end processor. Special communications software controls input and
output activities and manages other functions of the communications system.

Analog signal: A continuous
wave form that passes
through a communications
medium. Used for voice
communications.

Digital signal: A discrete wave
form that transmits data
coded into two discrete states
as 1-bits and 0-bits, which
are represented as on–off
electrical pulses. Used for data
communications.

Modem: Device for
translating digital signals into
analog signals and vice-versa.

communications medium. Analog signals are used to handle voice communications (such as telephone). A **digital signal** is a discrete rather than a continuous
waveform. It transmits data coded into two discrete states: 1-bits and 0-bits,
which are represented as on–off electrical pulses. Most computers communicate
with digital signals, as do many local telephone companies and some larger
networks.

If a computer sends and receives digital signals through an analog telecommunications system, such as a traditional telephone network, the digital signals
cannot be carried by the analog system until they are translated into analog
signals. The device that performs this translation is called a **modem**
(MOdulation/DEModulation). A modem not only translates the digital signals
of a computer into analog form, but also translates analog signals back into
digital form for reception by a computer (see Figure 7.3).

Figure 7.3
Functions of the modem. A modem is a device that translates digital signals from a computer into
analog form so that they can be transmitted over analog telephone lines. The modem is also used
to translate analog signals back into digital form for the receiving computer.

Channels: The links by which data or voice are transmitted between sending and receiving devices in a network.

Twisted wire: Transmission medium consisting of pairs of twisted copper wires. Used to transmit analog phone conversations but can be used for data transmission.

Coaxial cable: Transmission medium consisting of thickly insulated copper wire. Can transmit large volumes of data quickly.

Fiber optic cable: Fast, light, and durable transmission medium consisting of thin strands of clear glass fiber bound into cables. Data are transmitted as light pulses.

Microwave: High-volume, long-distance, point-to-point transmission in which high-frequency radio signals are transmitted through the atmosphere from one terrestrial transmission station to another.

Satellite: Transmission of data using orbiting satellites to serve as relay stations for transmitting microwave signals over very long distances.

Communications **channels** are the means by which data are transmitted from one device in a network to another. A channel can utilize different kinds of transmission media: twisted wire, coaxial cable, fiber optics, and wireless transmission. Each has certain advantages and limitations.

Twisted wire consists of strands of copper wire twisted in pairs and is the oldest transmission medium. Most of a building's telephone system relies on twisted wires for analog communication. Most buildings have additional cables installed for future expansion, and so there are usually a number of twisted-pair cables unused in every office of every building, which can be used for digital communications. Although it is low in cost and is already in place, twisted wire is relatively slow for transmitting data, and high-speed transmission causes interference called *crosstalk*. On the other hand, the current capacity of existing twisted-wire cables, up to 10 megabits per second, is often adequate for connecting microcomputers and other office devices.

Coaxial cable, like that used for cable television, consists of thickly insulated copper wire and can transmit a larger volume of data than twisted wire can. It is often used in place of twisted wire for important links in a telecommunications network because it is a faster, more interference-free transmission medium, with speeds of up to 200 megabits per second. However, coaxial cable is thick, hard to wire in many buildings, and cannot support analog phone conversations.

Fiber optic cable consists of thousands of strands of clear glass fiber, the thickness of a human hair, which are bound into cables. Data are transformed into pulses of light, which are sent through the fiber optic cable by a laser device at a rate of 500 kilobits to several billion bits per second. Fiber optic cable is considerably faster, lighter, and more durable than wire media and is well suited to systems requiring transfers of large volumes of data. However, it is more difficult to work with, more expensive, and harder to install. It is best used as the backbone of a network, a high-speed trunk line, and not for connecting isolated devices to that backbone.

Wireless transmission sends signals through air or space without any physical connection and can be accomplished using terrestrial microwave, satellites, cellular telephone, or infrared light rays. Terrestrial **microwave** systems transmit high-frequency radio signals through the atmosphere and are widely used for high-volume, long-distance, point-to-point communication. Because microwave signals follow a straight line and do not bend with the curvature of the earth, transmission stations must be positioned 25 to 30 miles apart, which adds to the expense of microwave. This problem can be solved by using microwave communication with satellites, a more cost-effective way to transmit large quantities of data over long distances.

Satellites are typically used for communications in large, geographically dispersed organizations that would be difficult to tie together through cabling media or terrestrial microwave. Satellites move in stationary orbits approximately 22,000 miles above the earth. Satellites can serve as relay stations for microwave signals transmitted from terrestrial stations.

Figure 7.4 illustrates the Omnitracs mobile communications system, which allows truckers and dispatchers to send electronic messages to each other by satellite. Each truck carries a terminal mounted on the dashboard and an antenna mounted on the roof. The driver enters short messages into the terminal and the antenna relays them to the satellite, which in turn bounces them to a central network computer at Qualcomm's San Diego processing center. From there the messages are transmitted by telephone or satellite to the appropriate truck dispatchers. The dispatchers can respond by sending messages back to the network computer, which passes them to the truck by satellite, where they are displayed on the truckers' terminal screens. The satellite network makes it possible for trucking firms to monitor their drivers closely and schedule routes more efficiently (see the opening vignette on Schneider National in Chapter 3).

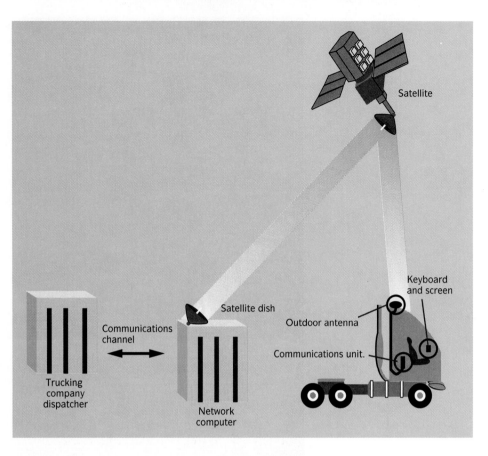

Figure 7.4:
Mobile communications systems. Satellite transmission allows geographically dispersed as well as mobile units to maintain constant communications with each other. The reliable monitoring available through satellite networks offers trucking businesses the ability to work more efficiently. *Adapted from Agis Salpukas, "Satellite System Helps Trucks Stay in Touch," The New York Times, June 5, 1991. Copyright © 1991 by The New York Times Company. Reprinted by permission.*

Other wireless transmission technologies have recently been developed and are being used in situations requiring mobile computing power. These technologies include high- or low-frequency radio or infrared light waves. In these wireless systems, a specially equipped laptop computer or terminal can transmit data coded with the recipient's unique electronic "address" to a series of local, regional, and even national switching centers, which are ultimately linked to the recipient's internal computer system.

RAM Mobile Data and Ardis are two publicly available networks that use wireless media for national two-way data transmission. Mastercard uses the RAM Mobile Data network for wireless credit-card verification terminals at county fairs or merchants' sidewalk kiosks. Otis Elevators uses the Ardis network to dispatch repair technicians around the country from a single office in Connecticut and to receive their reports.

A consortium comprising IBM and nine of the nation's largest cellular telephone companies is developing capabilities to use the country's existing analog cellular telephone network to transmit data. **Cellular telephones** (sometimes called mobile telephones) work by using radio waves to communicate with radio antennas placed within adjacent geographic areas called *cells*. As a cellular signal travels from one cell into another, a computer that monitors signals from the cells switches the conversation to a radio channel assigned to the next cell.

Cellular telephone: Device that transmits voice or data, using radio waves to communicate with radio antennas placed within adjacent geographic areas called cells.

CHARACTERISTICS OF COMMUNICATIONS CHANNELS

The characteristics of the communications channel help determine the efficiency and capabilities of a telecommunications system. These characteristics include the speed of transmission, the direction in which signals may travel, and the mode of transmission.

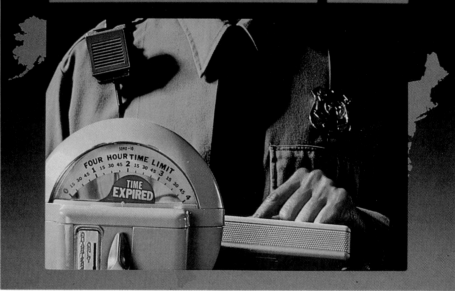

This schematic diagram (*top*) shows the network overview of the ARDIS wireless transmission system. This traffic officer (*bottom*) is using the ARDIS AGS&R communications network to record violations and enforce traffic laws.

Baud: A change in signal from positive to negative or vice-versa that is used as a measure of transmission speed.

Bandwidth: The capacity of a communications channel as measured by the difference between the highest and lowest frequencies that can be transmitted by that channel.

Transmission speed—the total amount of information that can be transmitted through any telecommunications channel—is measured in bits per second (BPS). Sometimes this is referred to as the *baud rate*. A **baud** is a binary event representing a signal change from positive to negative or vice versa. Since one signal change, or cycle, is required to transmit one or several bits per second, the transmission capacity of each type of telecommunications medium is a function of its frequency—the number of cycles per second that can be sent through that medium measured in *hertz*. The range of frequencies that can be accommodated on a particular telecommunications channel is called its **bandwidth.** The bandwidth is the difference between the highest and lowest frequencies that can be accommodated on a single channel. The greater the range of frequencies, the greater the bandwidth and the greater the channel's telecommunications transmission capacity. Table 7.1 compares the transmission speed and relative costs of the major types of transmissions media.

Table 7.1   TYPICAL SPEEDS AND COST OF TELECOMMUNICATIONS TRANSMISSION MEDIA

Medium	Speed	Cost
Twisted wire	300 BPS–10 MBPS	Low
Microwave	256 KBPS–100 MBPS	
Satellite	256 KBPS–100 MBPS	
Coaxial cable	56 KBPS–200 MBPS	
Fiber optic cable	500 KBPS–10 GBPS	High

BPS = bits per second
KBPS = kilobits per second
MBPS = megabits per second
GBPS = gigabits per second

Transmission modes are conventions for transmitting signals. These conventions are necessary for devices to communicate when a character begins or ends. **Asynchronous transmission** (often referred to as start–stop transmission) transmits one character at a time over a line, each character framed by control bits—a start bit, one or two stop bits, and a parity bit. Asynchronous transmission is used for low-speed transmission. **Synchronous transmission** transmits groups of characters simultaneously, with the beginning and ending of a block of characters determined by the timing circuitry of the sending and receiving devices. Synchronous transmission is used for transmitting large volumes of data at high speeds.

Transmission direction—the direction of data flow over a telecommunications network—must also be considered. In simplex transmission, data can only travel in one direction at all times. In half-duplex transmission, data can flow two ways but can travel in only one direction at a time. In full-duplex transmission, data can be sent in both directions simultaneously.

Asynchronous transmission: Low-speed transmission of data one character at a time.

Synchronous transmission: High-speed simultaneous transmission of large blocks of data.

COMMUNICATIONS PROCESSORS

Front-end processor: Small computer managing communications for the host computer in a network.

Concentrator: Telecommunications computer that collects and temporarily stores messages from terminals for batch transmission to the host computer.

Controller: Specialized computer that supervises communications traffic between the CPU and the peripheral devices in a telecommunications system.

Multiplexer: Device that enables a single communications channel to carry data transmissions from multiple sources simultaneously.

Communications processors, such as front-end processors, concentrators, controllers, multiplexers, and modems, support data transmission and reception in a telecommunications network.

The **front-end processor** is a small computer dedicated to communications management and is attached to the main, or host computer in a network. The front-end processor performs special processing related to communications such as error control, formatting, editing, controlling, routing, and speed and signal conversion. It takes some of the load off the host computer. The front-end processor is largely responsible for collecting and processing input and output data to and from terminals and grouping characters into complete messages for submission to the CPU of the host computer.

A **concentrator** is a programmable telecommunications computer that collects and temporarily stores messages from terminals until enough messages are ready to be sent economically. The concentrator then "bursts" signals to the host computer.

A **controller,** which is often a specialized minicomputer, supervises communications traffic between the CPU and peripheral devices such as terminals and printers. The controller manages messages from these devices and communicates them to the CPU. It also routes output from the CPU to the appropriate peripheral device.

A **multiplexer** is a device that enables a single communications channel to carry data transmissions from multiple sources simultaneously. The multiplexer divides the communications channel so that it can be shared by multiple transmission devices. The multiplexer may divide a high-speed channel into multiple channels of slower speed or may assign each transmission source a very small slice of time for using the high-speed channel.

Special **telecommunications software** is required to control and support the activities of a telecommunications network. This software resides in the host computer, front-end processor, and other processors in the network. The principal functions of telecommunications software are network control, access control, transmission control, error detection/correction, and security.

Network control software routes messages, polls network terminals, determines transmission priorities, maintains a log of network activity, and checks for errors. Access control software establishes connections between terminals and computers in the network, establishing transmission speed, mode, and direction. Transmission control software enables computers and terminals to send and receive data, programs, commands, and messages. Error-control software detects and corrects errors, then retransmits the corrected data. Security-control software monitors utilization, log-ons, passwords, and various authorization procedures to prevent unauthorized access to a network. More detail on security software can be found in Chapter 13.

A telecommunications network typically contains diverse hardware and software components that need to work together to transmit information. Different components in a network can communicate by adhering to a common set of rules that enables them to "talk" to each other. The set of rules and procedures governing transmission between two points in a network is called a **protocol**. Each device in a network must be able to interpret the other device's protocol. Although the need for standard protocols has been widely recognized, different vendors have developed their own systems. We explore the question of standards in greater detail later in this chapter.

Telecommunications software:
Special software for controlling and supporting the activities of a telecommunications network.

Protocol: Set of rules and procedures that govern transmission between the components in a network.

7.2 Types of Telecommunications Networks

A number of different ways exist to organize telecommunications components to form a network and hence provide multiple ways of classifying networks. Networks can be classified by their shape or **network topology**. Networks can also be classified by their geographic scope and the type of services provided. This section will describe the various ways of looking at networks.

Network topology: The shape or configuration of a network.

Network Topologies

One way of describing networks is by their shape, or topology. As illustrated in Figures 7.5–7.7, the three most common topologies are the star, bus, and ring.

THE STAR NETWORK

Star network: Network topology in which all computers and other devices are connected to a central host computer. All communications between network devices must pass through the host computer.

The **star network** (see Figure 7.5) consists of a central host computer connected to a number of smaller computers or terminals. This topology is useful for applications where some processing must be centralized and some can be performed locally. One problem with the star network is its vulnerability. All communication between points in the network must pass through the central computer. Because the central computer is the traffic controller for the other computers and terminals in the network, communication in the network will come to a standstill if the host computer stops functioning.

THE BUS NETWORK

Bus network: Network topology linking a number of computers by a single circuit with all messages broadcast to the entire network.

The **bus network** (see Figure 7.6) links a number of computers by a single circuit made of twisted wire, coaxial cable, or fiber optic cable. All of the signals are broadcast in both directions to the entire network, with special software to identify which components receive each message. There is no central host computer to control the network. (The main computer shown here is just another component connected to the circuit.) Messages can travel in both directions

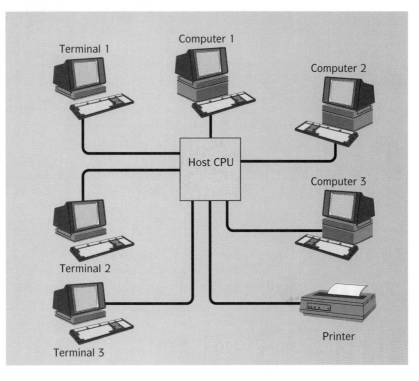

Figure 7.5
A star network topology. In a star network configuration a central host computer acts as a traffic controller for all the other components of the network. All communication between the smaller computers, terminals, and printers must first pass through the central computer.

Figure 7.6
A bus network topology. This topology allows for all messages to be broadcast to the entire network through a single circuit. There is no central host. Messages can travel in both directions along the cable. The main computer shown here is just another component connected to the circuit.

along the cable. If one of the computers in the network fails, none of the other components in the network is affected. This topology is commonly used for local area networks (LANs), discussed in the following section.

THE RING NETWORK

Ring network: Network topology in which all computers are linked by a closed loop in a manner that passes data in one direction from one computer to another.

Like the bus network, the **ring network** (see Figure 7.7) does not rely on a central host computer and will not necessarily break down if one of the component computers malfunctions. Each computer in the network can communicate directly with any other computer, and each processes its own applications independently. However, in ring topology, the connecting wire, cable, or optical fiber forms a closed loop. Data are passed along the ring from one computer to another and always flow in one direction.

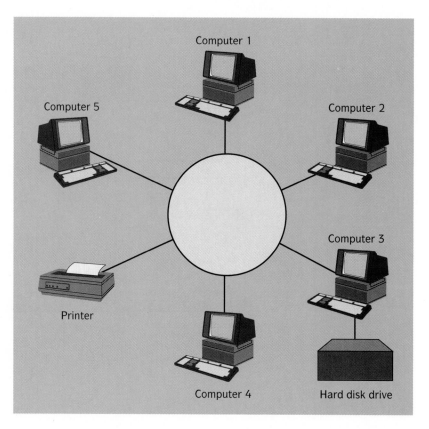

Figure 7.7
A ring network topology. In a ring network configuration, messages are transmitted from computer to computer, flowing in a single direction through a closed loop. Each computer operates independently so that if one fails, the communication through the network is not interrupted.

In the figure: Computer 1, Computer 5, Computer 2, Computer 3, Printer, Computer 4, Hard disk drive

Private Branch Exchanges and Local Area Networks (LANs)

Networks may be classified by geographic scope into local networks and wide-area networks. Local networks consist of private branch exchanges and local area networks. Local networks link local resources such as computers and terminals in the same department or building of a firm.

PRIVATE BRANCH EXCHANGES

Private branch exchange (PBX): Central switching system that handles a firm's voice and digital communications.

A **private branch exchange (PBX)** is a special-purpose computer designed for handling and switching office telephone calls at a company site. While the first PBXs performed limited switching functions, today's PBXs can carry both voice and data to create local networks. They can now store, transfer, hold, and redial telephone calls. PBXs can also be used to switch digital information among computers and office devices. For instance, you can write a letter on a microcomputer in your office, send it to the printer, then dial up the local copying machine and have multiple copies of your letter created. All of this activity is possible with a digital PBX connecting "smart" machines in the advanced office (see Figure 7.8).

The advantage of digital PBXs over other local networking options is that they utilize existing telephone lines and do not require special wiring. A phone jack can be found almost anywhere in the office building. PBXs are also supported by commercial vendors such as the local telephone company, so that the organization does not need special expertise to manage them. The primary disadvantage of PBXs is that they are limited to telephone lines and so cannot easily handle very large volumes of data.

LOCAL AREA NETWORKS

In contrast to PBXs, **local area networks (LANs)** require their own communications channels. As the term indicates, local area networks are limited in geographic scope to a radius of from several hundred to 2000 feet, although they

Figure 7.8
A PBX system. A PBX can switch digital information among telephones and among computers, copiers, printers, FAX machines, and other devices to create a local network based on ordinary telephone wiring.

Local area network (LAN):
Telecommunications network that requires its own dedicated channels and that encompasses a limited distance, usually one building or several buildings in close proximity.

can often encompass a larger geographic area by being connected to other local area networks. They have a high bandwidth, resulting in much higher transmission capacities than PBXs, reaching rates of over 100 megabits per second. They are recommended for applications requiring high volumes of data and high transmission speeds. For instance, because a picture consumes so many bits of information, an organization might require a LAN for video transmissions and graphics. LANs are typically used to connect devices in one or several buildings in close proximity.

LANs are totally controlled, maintained, and operated by end users. This produces the advantage of allowing user control, but it also means that the user must know a great deal about telecommunications applications and networking.

LANs allow organizations to share expensive hardware and software. For instance, several microcomputers can share a single printer by being tied together in a LAN. LANs can promote productivity because users are no longer dependent upon a centralized computer system (which can fail) or upon the availability of a single peripheral device such as a printer. Finally, there are many new applications—such as electronic mail, graphics, video teleconferencing, and on-line applications—requiring high-capacity networks.

The most common use of LANs is for linking microcomputers within a building or office to share information and expensive peripheral devices such as laser printers. Another popular application of LANs is in factories, where they link computers and computer-controlled machines.

Figure 7.9 illustrates a LAN employed by the Milan division of Michelin Italia, the Italian branch of the Michelin Corporation. The corporation is noted for its tires and guides to hotels and restaurants. Michelin Italia Milan's staff uses the LAN primarily for electronic filing, word processing, and graphics applications. This LAN consists of one hundred microcomputer workstations, which are attached to three Compaq 386/20 file servers, each equipped with 300-megabyte hard disks. The network also contains an Epson PC and an Olivetti M290 PC for backup and an Olivetti M290 PC serving as a gateway. The entire network and important files are backed up every night.

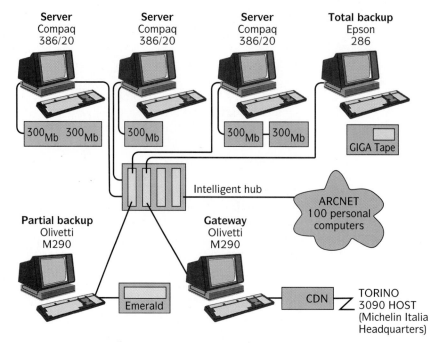

Figure 7.9
Michelin Milan's LAN. The Milan division of Michelin Italia chose ARCnet as the technology for connecting the devices in its 100-seat local area network for several reasons, including the floor plan of the Michelin building and the need for a star topology to allow upgrades to the network. *Reproduced with permission of Michelin Italy.*

File server: Computer in a network that stores various programs and data files for users of the network. Determines access and availability in the network.

Network operating system: Special software that manages the file server in a LAN and routes and manages communications on the network.

Gateway: Communications processor that connects dissimilar networks by providing the translation from one protocol to another.

Baseband: LAN channel technology that provides a single path for transmitting either text, graphics, voice, or video data at one time.

Broadband: LAN channel technology that provides several paths for transmitting text, graphics, voice, or video data so that different types of data can be transmitted simultaneously.

The **file server** acts as a librarian, storing various programs and data files for network users. The server determines who gets access to what and in what sequence. Servers may be powerful microcomputers with large hard disk capacity, workstations, minicomputers, or mainframes, although specialized computers are now available for this purpose. The server typically contains the LAN's **network operating system,** which manages the server and routes and manages communications on the network.

The network **gateway** connects the LAN to public networks, such as the telephone network, or to other corporate networks so that the LAN can exchange information with networks external to it. A gateway is generally a communications processor (hardware or software) that can connect dissimilar networks by translating from one set of protocols to another. (A *bridge* connects two networks of the same type. A *router* is used to route messages through several connected LANs or to a wide area network.)

LAN technology consists of twisted wire, coaxial, or fiber optic cable, or wireless technology that links individual computer devices, network interface cards, and software to control LAN activities. The LAN network interface card specifies the data transmission rate, the size of message units, the addressing information attached to each message, and network topology. LANs employ either a baseband or a broadband channel technology for physically connecting devices. **Baseband** products provide a single path for transmitting text, graphics, voice, or video data, and only one type of data at a time can be transmitted. **Broadband** products provide several paths so that different types of data can be transmitted simultaneously.

The primary disadvantages of LANs are that they are more expensive to install than PBXs and are more inflexible, requiring new wiring each time the LAN is moved. LANs require specially trained staff to manage and run them.

Wide Area Networks (WANs)

Wide area networks (WANs) span broad geographical distances, ranging from several miles to across entire continents. Common carriers (companies licensed by the government to provide communications services to the public, such as

Wide area network (WAN):
Telecommunications network that spans a large geographical distance. May consist of a variety of cable, satellite, and microwave technologies.

Switched lines: Telephone lines that a person can access from his or her terminal to transmit data to another computer, the call being routed or switched through paths to the designated destination.

Dedicated lines: Telephone lines that are continuously available for transmission by a lessee. Typically conditioned to transmit data at high speeds for high-volume applications.

Virtual private network: Inexpensive telecommunications over public phone lines with computers and software creating an illusion of a private network for a company.

AT&T or MCI) typically determine transmission rates or interconnections between lines, but the customer is responsible for telecommunications contents and management. It is up to the individual firm to establish the most efficient routing of messages and to handle error checking, editing, protocols, and telecommunications management.

WANs may consist of a combination of switched and dedicated lines, microwave, and satellite communications. **Switched lines** are telephone lines that a person can access from his or her terminal to transmit data to another computer, the call being routed or switched through paths to the designated destination. **Dedicated lines,** or nonswitched lines, are continuously available for transmission, and the lessee typically pays a flat rate for total access to the line. The lines can be leased or purchased from common carriers or private communications media vendors. Dedicated lines are often conditioned to transmit data at higher speeds than switched lines and are more appropriate for higher-volume transmissions. Switched lines, on the other hand, are less expensive and more appropriate for low-volume applications requiring only occasional transmission.

Figure 7.10 illustrates a wide area network that links five of Europe's national telephone companies into a pan-European network. The Global European Network (GEN) links the fiber-optic networks of five national telephone companies—Italy's Asst/Stet, the United Kingdom's British Telecom, France's Telecom, Germany's Deutsche Telekom, and Telefonica of Spain. This network provides a single point of contact for users requiring voice and data services that transcend national borders.

Individual business firms may maintain their own wide area networks. For instance, the Hewlett-Packard Corporation has a wide area network that ties together its facilities in the United States, Great Britain, France, Switzerland, Venezuela, Australia, Japan, India, Hong Kong, and Singapore. But private wide area networks are expensive to maintain. Virtual private networks are emerging as a less expensive alternative for linking widely dispersed corporate facilities. A **virtual private network** provides inexpensive telecommunications over public phone lines, with computers and software creating an illusion of a private network for a company.

Value-Added Networks (VANs)

Value-added networks are an alternative to firms designing and managing their own networks. **Value-added networks (VANs)** are private, multipath, data-only,

Figure 7.10
An example of a wide area network (WAN). Global European Network (GEN) links five European national telephone companies in a wide area network. Each country's operator acts as the go-between in linking users across borders. *Adapted from Joshua Greenbaum, "Europeans Eye Joint Fiber Net,"* InformationWEEK, *July 27, 1992. Copyright © 1992 by CMP Publications, Inc., 600 Community Drive, Manhasset, NY 11030. Reprinted from* InformationWEEK *with permission.*

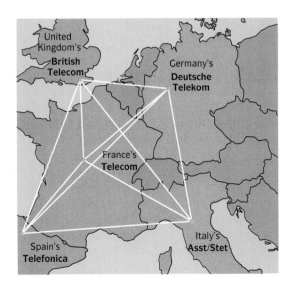

Value-added networks (VAN):
Private, multipath, data-only third party managed networks that are used by multiple organizations on a subscription basis.

third-party-managed networks that can provide economies in the cost of service and in network management because they are used by multiple organizations. That firm that sets up and manages the VAN sells subscriptions to other firms wishing to use it. Subscribers pay only for the amount of data they transmit plus a subscription fee. The network may utilize twisted-pair lines, satellite links, and other communications channels leased by the value-added carrier.

The term *value added* refers to the extra "value" added to communications channels by the telecommunications and computing services these networks provide to clients. Subscribers achieve savings because they do not have to invest in network equipment and software or perform their own error checking, editing, routing, and protocol conversion. In addition, the costs of using the network are shared among many users. The resulting costs may be lower than if the clients had leased their own lines or satellite services.

VANs are attractive for firms such as Continental Grain because they provide special services such as electronic mail and access to foreign telecommunications systems. Continental Grain switched from a private network to GE Information Services (GEIS)'s value-added network to link its 175 domestic locations with its 45 branch locations in South America, the Far East, and Europe. Continental found that switching to the value-added network reduced costs and reduced operational problems associated with networks.

The leading international value-added networks, in addition to GEIS, are Infonet, Telenet, and Tymnet. These networks provide casual or intermittent users international services on a dial-up basis and can provide a private network using dedicated circuits for customers requiring a full-time network. (Maintaining a private network may be most cost-effective for organizations with a high communications volume.)

Packet switching: Technology that breaks blocks of text into small fixed bundles of data and routes them in the most economical way through any available communications channel.

Another way value-added networks provide economies is through **packet switching**. Packet switching breaks up a lengthy block of text into small, fixed bundles of data called packets. The VAN continuously uses various communications channels to gather information and send packets. Each packet travels independently through the network (this contrasts to one firm using a leased line, for example, for one hour and then not using it for three or four hours). Packets of data originating at one source can be routed through different paths in the network, and then reassembled into the original message when they reach their destination. Thus, packet switching enables communications facilities to be utilized more fully by more users. **Frame relay** is a faster and less expensive variant of packet switching. It is a shared network service that packages data into "frames," which are similar to packets. Frame relay transmission speeds can reach 1.544 megabits per second. Frame relay, however, does not perform error correction. This is because so many of today's digital lines are cleaner than in the past and networks are more adept at correcting transmission problems. Frame relay only works successfully over reliable lines that do not require frequent retransmission because of error.

Frame relay: Shared network service technology that packages data into bundles for transmission but does not use error correction routines. Cheaper and faster than packet switching.

Asynchronous transfer mode: Networking technology that parcels information into 8-bit "cells," allowing data to be transmitted between computers of different vendors at any speed.

Most corporations today use separate networks for voice, private-line services, and data, each of which is supported by a different technology. An emerging networking technology called **asynchronous transfer mode (ATM)** may overcome some of these problems because it can seamlessly and dynamically switch voice, data, images, and video between users. ATM also promises to tie LANs and wide-area networks together more easily (LANs are generally based on lower-speed protocols, whereas WANs operate at higher speeds.) ATM technology parcels information into uniform "cells," each with 53 groups of eight bits, eliminating the need for protocol conversion. It can pass data between computers from different vendors and permits data to be transmitted at any speed the network handles. ATM currently requires fiber-optic cable, but it can attain transmission speeds over 2.5 GBPS.

7.3 How Organizations Use Telecommunications for Competitive Advantage

Citibank and Baxter International, both described in Chapter 2, were pioneers in realizing the strategic significance of telecommunications. In recent years, many other corporations have come to understand the strategic potential of networked computer systems. Telecommunications has helped eliminate barriers of geography and time, enabling organizations to accelerate the pace of production, to speed decision making, to forge new products, to move into new markets, and to create new relationships with customers. Firms that fail to consider telecommunications in their strategic plans will fall behind (Keen, 1986).

Some of the leading telecommunications applications for communication, coordination, and speeding the flow of transactions and messages throughout business firms are electronic mail, voice mail, facsimile machines (FAX), teleconferencing, videoconferencing, and electronic data interchange.

Facilitating Applications: E-Mail, Voice Mail, FAX, and Electronic Services

Electronic mail: The computer-to-computer exchange of messages.

Electronic mail, or **E-mail,** is the computer-to-computer exchange of messages. A person can use a microcomputer attached to a modem or a terminal to send notes and lengthier documents just by typing in the name of the messages's recipient. Many organizations operate their own internal electronic mail systems, but communications companies such as GTE, Telenet, MCI, and AT&T offer these services, as do on-line information services such as CompuServe and Prodigy. E-mail eliminates telephone tag and costly long-distance telephone charges, expediting communication between different parts of the organization. Nestle SA, the Swiss-based multinational food corporation, installed a new

The Prodigy Interactive Personal Service gives subscribers access to extensive information including travel, weather, education, and financial services directly from their personal computers in their homes or offices.

electronic mail system to connect its 60,000 employees in 80 countries. Nestle's European units can use the electronic mail system to share information about production schedules and inventory levels to ship excess products from one country to another.

A **voice mail** system digitizes the spoken message of the sender, transmits it over a network, and stores the message on disk for later retrieval. When the recipient is ready to listen, the messages are reconverted to audio form. Various "store and forward" capabilities notify recipients that messages are waiting. Recipients have the option of saving these messages for future use, deleting them, or routing them to other parties.

Facsimile (FAX) machines can transmit documents containing both text and graphics over ordinary telephone lines. A sending FAX machine scans and digitizes the document image. The digitized document is then transmitted over a network and reproduced in hard copy form by a receiving FAX machine. The process results in a duplicate, or facsimile, of the original.

Powerful and far-reaching digital electronic services now enable networked microcomputer and workstation users to obtain information from outside the firm instantaneously without leaving their desks. Stock prices, historical references to periodicals, industrial supplies catalogs, legal research, news articles, reference works, weather forecasts, and travel information are just some of the electronic databases that can be accessed on-line. The leading digital information services are described in Table 7.2 Many of these services offer electronic mail as well, which is the most commonly requested digital service.

Voice mail: System for digitizing a spoken message and transmitting it over a network.

Facsimile (FAX): Machine that digitizes and transmits documents with both text and graphics over telephone lines.

Teleconferencing and Videoconferencing

People can meet electronically—even though they are hundreds or thousands of miles apart—by using teleconferencing or videoconferencing. **Teleconferencing** allows a group of people to "confer" simultaneously via telephone or electronic mail group communication software (see Chapter 10). Teleconferencing that has the capability to let participants see each other over video screens is termed *video teleconferencing* or **videoconferencing**. Videoconferencing usually requires special video conference rooms and videocameras, microphones, television monitors, and a computer equipped with a codec device that converts video images and analog sound waves into digital signals and compresses them for transfer over communications channels. Another codec on the receiving end reconverts the digital signals back into analog for display on the receiving monitor. Chapter 10 will provide more detail on electronic mail and videoconferencing applications.

Teleconferencing: Ability to confer with a group of people simultaneously using the telephone or electronic mail group communication software.

Videoconferencing: Teleconferencing with the capability of participants to see each other over video screens.

Table 7.2 LEADING DIGITAL INFORMATION SERVICES

Provider	Type of Service
CompuServe	General interest/business information
Prodigy	General interest/business information
America Online	General interest/business information
Dow Jones News Retrieval	Business/financial information
Quotron	Financial information
Dialog	Business/scientific/technical information
Lexis	Legal research
Nexis	News/business information

Snapple Beverage Corporation, founded in 1972 by a handful of Brooklynites with a vision of selling all-natural fruit drinks to health food stores, came along at just the right time to capitalize on the "New Age" beverage craze. Snapple catapulted onto grocery store shelves. Although sales have doubled every year since 1988, the firm faced increased competition from partnerships among giants such as Coca-Cola Co. and Nestle, S.A. and Pepsico and Thomas J. Lipton Inc. as well as from new entrants to the beverage industry.

How could Snapple hold on to its position at the top ranks of the beverage industry? One way was to use information more intelligently and be lightning quick in its planning. To do this, Snapple had to tighten communications links with its bottlers and distributors. Snapple does not manufacture or distribute any of its products. In the past it communicated with its 24 bottlers and 300 distributors over the telephone and manually entered the information into an aging McDonnell Douglas Corporation mainframe system. This process was cumbersome and time-consuming. So Snapple moved from the mainframe to a PC-based network that provides electronic data interchange (EDI) and material requirements planning (MRP) links to its bottlers and distributors. The network uses the Novell Netware v3.11 network operating system, a mix of 150 80386 microcomputers and network super file servers. Snapple's bottlers and distributors can send information over the network daily using dial-up modems and T-1 connections.

With the EDI and MRP links, Snapple can automatically download information daily from its manufacturers and distributors, yet the bottlers and distributors can process their own information locally. The MRP system includes advanced algorithms that will help Snapple forecast demand for different soda flavors in various regions of the country. Snapple can perform various accounting functions such as accounts payable on the network using Accpac Plus for DOS accounting software from Computer Associates International.

Source: Thomas Hoffman, "Growth Spurs IS Overhaul at Snapple," *Computerworld*, September 13, 1993.

To Think About: One observer commented that Snapple's business is as much an information game as a product game. Why? Use the value chain and competitive forces models to analyze Snapple. How did telecommunications technology help Snapple enhance its competitive position?

Electronic Data Interchange

Electronic data interchange (EDI): Direct computer-to-computer exchange between two organizations of standard business transaction documents.

Electronic data interchange (EDI) is the direct computer-to-computer exchange, between two organizations, of standard business transaction documents such as invoices, bills of lading, or purchase orders. EDI saves money and time because transactions can be transmitted from one information system to another through a telecommunications network, eliminating the printing and handling of paper at one end and the inputting of data at the other. EDI may also provide strategic benefits by helping a firm "lock in" customers, making it easier for customers or distributors to order from them rather than from competitors.

The experience of Snapple Beverage in the Window on Organizations shows how EDI and other telecommunications technologies can be used to enhance a firm's strategic position.

EDI differs from electronic mail in that it transmits an actual structured transaction (with distinct fields such as the transaction date, transaction amount, sender's name, and recipient's name) as opposed to an unstructured text message such as a letter.

Figure 7.11 illustrates how EDI operates at the Cummins Engine Company. Cummins implemented EDI to automate purchasing, shipping, and payment transactions with its customers. Cummins transmits price updates and shipping notices directly to its customers' computer system. Customers in turn transmit material releases, reports on receiving discrepancies, and payment and remittance data directly to Cummins' computer system. EDI has replaced paper for these transactions.

Figure 7.11
How EDI works at Cummins Engine Company. Cummins Engine Company uses EDI to automate price, shipping, receiving, and payment transactions with its customers. Cummins' price updates and shipping notices are entered by the appropriate departments directly into the Cummins' computer system, which transmits them to its customers' computer systems. Customers' material releases, receiving reports, and payment data are also transmitted directly through the computer systems back to Cummins. *Source: Robert Knight, "EDI Hitting Stride in Data Entry," Software Magazine, February 1992.*

EDI lowers routine transaction processing costs because there is less need for data entry from hard-copy forms into computer-ready transactions. EDI reduces transcription errors and associated costs that occur when data are entered and printed out many times. However, to use EDI successfully, companies must standardize the form of the transactions they use with other firms, develop special translation software, and comply with legal requirements and restrictions.

7.4 Connectivity and Standards

Telecommunications and networks are most likely to increase productivity and competitive advantage when digitized information can move through a seamless web of electronic networks, connecting different kinds of machines, people, sensors, databases, functional divisions, departments, and work groups. Despite all of the advances in desktop processing, user-friendly software, and telecommunications technology, this goal has been difficult to realize because many different kinds of hardware, software, and communications systems still are not able to work together. They lack **connectivity**—the ability of computers and computer-based devices to communicate with one another and "share" information in a meaningful way without human intervention.

Connectivity: A measure of how well computers and computer-based devices communicate and share information with one another without human intervention.

Connectivity Problems

The following are some common examples of the absence of connectivity:

- Desktop microcomputers often cannot use data from the corporate mainframe, often cannot share information among different brands of microcomputers, and many times cannot share information meaningfully even among different pieces of software operating on the same microcomputer.
- Some corporations have multiple different E-mail systems within their own firm that cannot communicate with one another. Communication among firms is complicated by the lack of products that support E-mail standards.

- IBM, as well as other hardware vendors, sells machines and software that cannot communicate with others of the same brand because of different hardware designs and operating systems.
- Companies operating overseas have tremendous difficulty building global networks that can seamlessly tie their operations together. Different countries have different telecommunications infrastructures, many owned by national PTTs (Post, Telegraph, and Telephone monopolies) that use disparate networking standards.

There are many reasons why computers and information systems achieved such dizzying heights of incompatibility. Individual computers were designed long before computer networks were built. Before the 1980s, there were no standards for either hardware or software manufacturers; the buyers of equipment lacked market power to demand standards; and hardware and software vendors themselves encouraged product differentiation. Moreover, the process of setting standards is largely political and involves many powerful interest groups, such as private-sector industry associations of equipment, the U.S. federal government, and professional groups such as the Institute of Electrical and Electronic Engineers (IEEE), the American National Standards Institute (ANSI), the International Organization for Standardization (ISO), and the International Telephone and Telegraph Consultative Committee (CCITT).

A Garden of Buzzwords: Aspects of Connectivity

Connectivity encompasses more than just networking. There are many different qualities that an information system with connectivity will have. Let us explore some of the terms used for describing different aspects of connectivity.

Applications portability: The ability to operate the same software on different hardware platforms.

Migration: The ability to move software from one generation of hardware to another more powerful generation.

Cooperative processing: Dividing computing tasks among networked mainframes, minicomputers, microcomputers, or workstations to solve a single common problem.

Information portability: The sharing of computer files among different hardware platforms and software applications.

Interoperability: The ability of a software application to operate on two different machine platforms while maintaining the identical user interface and functionality.

Applications portability is the ability to operate the same piece of software on different types of computer hardware. Imagine, for instance, using Lotus 1-2-3 spreadsheet software on a microcomputer at work, saving the results in a file, removing the 1-2-3 program disk, taking it home, and using a Macintosh computer to complete the project.

Migration is the ability to move software from one generation of hardware to another more powerful generation. Most microcomputer software offers upward compatibility. For instance, you can run early versions of Lotus 1-2-3 on later versions of DOS (version 6.0, for example). Downward compatibility is more problematic. Much microcomputer software designed to operate under DOS 6.0 cannot operate on DOS 3.0.

Cooperative processing divides computing tasks among mainframes, minicomputers, microcomputers, or workstations to solve a single common problem. Cooperative processing is a connectivity issue because different machines must be networked and programmed so that they can work together on a single application (see Chapter 4 for a more detailed description of cooperative processing).

Information portability is the sharing of computer files among different types of computer hardware and different software applications. Currently, sharing of files is possible among applications such as word processing that can create a single file standard like ASCII text files (see the discussion of ASCII in Chapter 4). These text files can be transferred into spreadsheet or database applications, but the transfer can take place only on the same hardware platform or machine class. Because different machines and machine classes use different coding schemes (for instance, mainframes often use EBCDIC, and some smaller machines use ASCII), even information portability can be difficult.

Interoperability is the ability of a single piece of software to operate on two different kinds of computer hardware, show users an identical interface, and perform the same tasks. For instance, Microsoft Word word processing software has similar functionality and somewhat similar looks on both the Macintosh and IBM microcomputers, but different versions of the software are required to run on each type of machine.

Interoperability, as well as information and applications portability, requires open systems. **Open systems** are built upon public, nonproprietary operating systems, user interfaces, application standards, and networking protocols. In open systems, software can operate on different hardware platforms and in that sense can be "portable." It is prohibitively costly to achieve applications portability without a common shared operating system.

In the microcomputer world, most IBM-compatible microcomputers use Microsoft/IBM DOS or Microsoft Windows (an operating system shell that runs in conjunction with DOS). Their operating principles are published, and they can be used by non-IBM microcomputer makers for a minimal licensing fee. DOS has no common user interface, although the graphical user interface of Microsoft Windows is a step in this direction. By contrast, most minicomputers and mainframes have proprietary operating systems that cannot be used by different classes of machines and whose operating principles are hidden from public view and vigorously defended with high licensing fees.

Perhaps the key to truly open systems is the operating system called UNIX. UNIX originated in the research labs of AT&T in the 1970s through engineers who wanted a powerful time-sharing operating system that could operate on many different kinds of computer hardware. Since then, UNIX has come to dominate the engineering market for workstations and is starting to be used by some types of microcomputers. However, there are different versions of UNIX, and no one version has been accepted as an open systems standard.

Thus, true connectivity requires a great deal more than simply wiring together different machines or providing limited access to many different computers. Connectivity requires common operating systems, common telecommunications standards, and even common user interface standards, a similar screen look and feel across different software applications.

Open systems: Software systems that can operate on different hardware platforms because they are built on public non-proprietary operating systems, user interfaces, application standards, and networking protocols.

Standards for Achieving Connectivity

Achieving connectivity requires standards for networking, operating systems, and user interfaces. To date, there are no uniform standards that ensure that information systems can achieve the attributes of connectivity described above, but some standards do exist and others are being promoted. This section describes the most important standards that are being used today.

MODELS OF CONNECTIVITY FOR NETWORKS

Reference model: A generic framework for thinking about a problem.

Standard: Approved reference models and protocols as determined by standard-setting groups for building or developing products or services.

Because of the many interests involved in connectivity and standard setting, there are different models for achieving connectivity in telecommunications networks. A **reference model** is a generic framework for thinking about a problem. It is a logical breakdown of some activity (like communications) into a number of distinct steps or parts. Specific protocols are required in order to implement a reference model. A **protocol** is a statement that explains how a specific task, such as transferring data, will be performed. Reference models and protocols become **standards** when they are approved by important standard-setting groups or when industry builds or buys products that support the models and protocols.

Network connectivity can also be achieved without reference models or protocols by using gateways. Firms develop gateways between two disparate networks when it is impossible or too costly to integrate them by complying with reference models or standards. However, gateways are expensive to build and maintain, and they can be slow and inefficient. We now describe the most important models of network connectivity.

Open Systems Interconnect (OSI): International reference model for linking different types of computers and networks.

The **Open Systems Interconnect (OSI)** model is an international reference model developed by the International Standards Organization for linking different types of computers and networks. It is a framework for defining the functions required in a telecommunications session between two or more computers. It was designed to support global networks with large volumes of transaction processing.

OSI enables a computer connected to a network to communicate with any other computer on the same network or a different network, regardless of the manufacturer. To establish this connectivity, the OSI model divides the telecommunications process into seven layers (see Figure 7.12). Each layer in the OSI model is defined by its communications functions and deals with a specific aspect of the communications process. Each layer has one or several associated protocols. A multilayer protocol has the advantage of having each layer independent of the others so that it can be changed without affecting the other layers.

Two different computers using OSI standards would each have software and hardware that correspond to each layer of the OSI model. A message sent from one computer to the other would pass downward through all seven layers, starting with the application layer of the sending computer and passing through to the sending computer's physical layer. It would then travel over the communication channel and enter the receiving computer, rising upward through the seven layers in that machine. The process is reversed when the receiving computer responds.

Figure 7.12
The Open Systems Interconnect (OSI) reference model. The figure illustrates the seven layers defining the communication functions—for the flow of information in an OSI network.

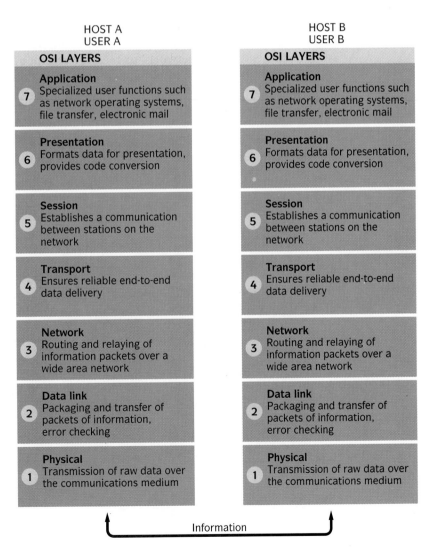

For example, if an officer at a local bank wanted information about a particular client's checking account that was stored in the bank's central host computer, he or she would enter the instructions to retrieve the client's account records into his or her terminal under control of layer 7, the application layer. The presentation layer (layer 6) would change this input data into a format for transmission. Layer 5 (the session layer) initiates the session. Layer 4 (the transport layer) checks the quality of the information traveling from user to host node. Layers 3 and 2 (the network and data link layers) transmit the data through layer 1 (the physical layer). When the message reaches the host computer, control moves up the layers back to the user, reversing the sequence.

Transmission Control Protocol/Internet Protocol (TCP/IP): U.S. Department of Defense reference model for linking different types of computers and networks.

The **Transmission Control Protocol/Internet Protocol (TCP/IP)** model is a competing reference model developed by the U.S. Department of Defense. Launched in 1972 in conjunction with network research and development done by the Defense Advanced Research Projects Agency (DARPA), its purpose was to help scientists link disparate computers. Because it is one of the oldest communications reference models, TCP/IP is still widely used, especially in the United States (Europeans tend to favor OSI). Figure 7.13 shows that TCP/IP has a five-layer reference model.

1. Physical net: Defines basic electrical transmission characteristics generated during communications.

2. Network interface: Handles addressing issues, usually in the operating system, as well as the interface between the initiating computer and the network.

3. Internet (IP): Handles system-to-system communication. This layer is a self-contained, connectionless datagram delivery process that does not depend on the network for message receipt acknowledgment. The datagram is a unit of information consisting of a header segment and text segment. The Internet Protocol receives datagrams from TCP and transmits them through the Internet.

4. Transmission Control Protocol (TCP): Performs transport. TCP supports program-to-program communication at the end-user level. The Transmission Control Protocol supports reliable transfer of information indepen-

Figure 7.13
The Transmission Control Protocol/Internet Protocol (TCP/IP) reference model. This figure illustrates the five layers of the (TCP/IP) reference model for communications as set by the U.S. Department of Defense.

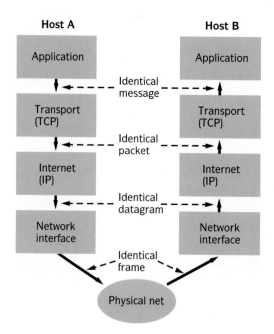

dent of the category of computer job at the higher layer (such as E-mail or log-on).

5. Application: Provides end-user functionality by translating the messages into the user/host software for screen presentation.

OTHER NETWORKING STANDARDS

Integrated Services Digital Network (ISDN):
International standard for transmitting voice, video, and data to support a wide range of service over the public telephone lines.

Standards have also been developed for transmitting digital data over public switched networks. **Integrated Services Digital Network (ISDN)** is an international digital public switched network standard for transmitting voice, video, and data over phone lines. It is an internationally endorsed plan to migrate the public telephone network to the standard use of digital technology. The CCITT (Consultative Committee on International Telephone and Telegraph), which is responsible for devising standards for ISDN implementation, defines ISDN as a network that provides end-to-end digital connectivity to support a wide range of services, including voice and nonvoice services. Users have access by a limited set of standard multipurpose customer interfaces. In the words of many industry observers, ISDN is the biggest new development in telephone communications since electronic digital switching moved into local Bell offices. In many respects, ISDN is a natural extension of digital equipment and capability from the regional Bell central office down to the desktop.

Consider the limitations of LANs and PBXs. Right now, you cannot make a telephone call on your local area network. You cannot send a FAX or video image very conveniently on your LAN. If you purchase a PBX to improve both phone service and computer connectivity in your firm, you must select and maintain equipment, and the service ends as soon as you leave the building.

Alternatively, imagine combining in one single service the following features:

- Complete voice, data, and video connection to anywhere in the world.
- Complete digital connection to any other digital device in the world, from one next door to one halfway around the world.
- Simultaneous use of voice, video, and digital devices.
- Complete freedom to move devices and people without any rewiring of buildings or special cables, and with a single physical standard.
- User-controlled definition of video, digital, and data lines. You can use a line for digital personal service this hour, reconfigure the same phone line as an incoming 800 WATS line the next hour, and in the next hour redefine the line as a video line carrying pictures of a group videoconferencing session.

Briefly, ISDN is the everything network. The goal and promise of ISDN is to provide a more functional network to transport all kinds of digital information, regardless of its source or destination. It is a vision of the public switched-phone network turning into a vast digital super expressway. ISDN offers universal data connectivity in direct digital form. Modems are not used with ISDN except when they are needed to link up with a non-ISDN user. ISDN uses standard twisted-pair copper wire to connect desktop devices to building-level concentrators. A central office switching device makes all connections to the outside world. With some simple technology changes, ordinary twisted copper telephone wire can be more fully utilized without expensive recabling.

Currently ISDN does face a number of hurdles. Standards and tariffs (charges) are still undefined; existing Basic Rate ISDN is hamstrung by its current 64 KBPS channels, which are fine for most PC applications but slow compared to 1 MBPS LANs. It is most useful in low-speed transaction-oriented networks. LANs are still more appropriate for computing-intensive applications. Progress toward an ISDN nation will be accelerated greatly by the U.S. government's Federal

The Xerox Liveboard is an electronic blackboard that incorporates computer and video technology, providing an on-line forum for interactive meetings throughout the world.

Telephone System 2000 (FTS 2000) project, described in the Window on Technology, which is heavily based upon ISDN, and efforts to expand the bandwidth of Basic Rate ISDN to 1.5 MBPS.

FIBER OPTICS
TRANSMISSION STANDARD:
FDDI

Fiber Distributed Data Interface (FDDI) is a standard for data transmission at 100 MBPS over fiber-optic cable in a ring configuration. FDDI LANs use a dual fiber optical ring configuration. Use of two rings instead of one increases reliability.

OPERATING SYSTEM
STANDARDS: THE OPEN
SYSTEMS MOVEMENT

The battle over operating system standards centers around UNIX. UNIX is the only nonproprietary operating system that can operate on all computers—from microcomputers to mainframes, and irrespective of vendor. However, the effort to make UNIX the operating system standard has encountered considerable opposition. The stakes are high. Briefly, standardized operating systems and communications links between computers would eliminate firms' dependence on one particular hardware vendor, such as IBM or DEC. Moreover, UNIX runs directly counter to the marketing plans of many large vendors. For instance, if UNIX becomes a standard, there is little need for Microsoft Corporation's Windows NT operating system or for IBM's OS/2. UNIX can deliver time-sharing, applications portability, seamless file transfer, and shared user interfaces. Because of the high stakes, vendors have split into two warring camps over the issue of what version of UNIX to support, led by IBM and DEC on one side and AT&T and Sun Corporation on the other.

Table 7.3 summarizes the standards we have described and lists other important standards for graphical user interfaces, electronic mail, packet-switching, and electronic data interchange. Any manager wishing to achieve some measure of connectivity in his or her organization should try to use them when designing networks, purchasing hardware and software, or developing information system applications.

TECHNOLOGY

FTS 2000: The New Digital Highway

The Federal Telecommunications System, used by federal employees at 1700 federal agencies, is the largest telephone system in the world. Operated by the U.S. federal government, FTS had been a relatively primitive voice-grade analog service and was fragmented, expensive, unreliable, and inefficient. So the federal government developed a powerful new telephone system called FTS 2000 (Federal Telephone System), awarding ten-year contracts to AT&T and Sprint Communications, Inc.

FTS 2000 is a new network that links 1.5 million users in 135 federal agencies in 3500 locations. The network features switched voice, data, packet-switched data, and video transmission, and dedicated high-speed, high-volume services. It can support videoconferencing, electronic mail, and

high-speed data transfer to 1.54 MBPS, and it provides emergency backup service to the public network. Initially, FTS 2000 will be able to move 70 pages of text per second from one desk to another. In essence, FTS is an ISDN standard digital network permitting each local telephone user complete access to a wide variety of services.

FTS 2000 is expected to cut the government's communications costs in half. Donald Scott, associate administrator for FTS 2000 at the General Services Agency, reported that FTS 2000 saved the federal government $500 million over three years, with prices lower than commercial rates.

FTS 2000 is the digital network for the entire U.S. government. State and local governments are expected to build similar systems in

the long run. Since almost all large businesses interact with the federal government, FTS 2000 will most likely set telecommunications standards through the next century.

Sources: Gary H. Anthes, "FTS 2000 Users Anxious to Upgrade," *Computerworld,* September 21, 1992; and United States General Accounting Office, "FTS 2000: An Overview of the Federal Government's New Telecommunications System," GAO/IMTEC-90-17FS, February 1990.

To Think About: What problems can be solved by using an ISDN standard? What would happen if the federal government did not switch to an ISDN standard? If you were a manager, what factors would you consider in deciding whether to use ISDN?

Table 7.3   Standards for Achieving Connectivity

Area	Standard or Reference Model
Networking	OSI, TCP/IP
Fiber optic transmission	FDDI
Digital public switched network transmission	ISDN
Electronic mail	X.400
Packet switching	X.25
EDI	X.12
Graphical user interface	X Windows
Operating system	UNIX

7.5 Implementing the New Information Architecture

Most knowledgeable observers now believe that it will take at least a decade to fully utilize the potential of existing desktop equipment, let alone that of equipment yet to be developed. Implementing the new information architecture has created problems as well as opportunities for organizations.

Problems Posed by the New Architecture

We have already described the connectivity problems created by incompatible network components and standards. Two additional problems stand out: ensuring network security and reliability and loss of management control over information systems.

Ensuring Network Security and Reliability: Security is of paramount importance in organizations where information systems make extensive use of networks. There are many points of access and opportunities for end users to modify data in networks. How can an organization rely on data if one cannot prove where the data came from and who modified them along the way? Downtime (periods of time in which the system is not operational) is much more frequent in networked systems than in established mainframe systems and should be considered carefully before one takes essential applications off the mainframe.

Loss of Management Control: In the 1970s, information systems were confined to a few data-processing centers in the organization. With desktop computing in the 1990s, however, the organization is composed not of 1, 2, 10, or 20 data centers, but of 1000, 5000, or 20,000 computing centers. In such an environment, it becomes difficult to ensure that any change to data or business rules is made to every application on every desktop. Furthermore, insofar as information confers power, independence, and advantage, the new information architecture has the potential to change the distribution of power, to affect the perquisites, advantages, and resources in organizations.

Some Solutions

Organizations can counteract problems created by the new information architecture by increasing end-user training, by asserting data administration disciplines, and by considering connectivity when planning their information architecture.

Education: Training to use desktop computers and networked applications is incomplete or entirely absent in many firms. Senior managers have not understood that it takes many hours for employees to learn how to use desktop applications and networks. A well-developed training program can help overcome many of the problems (Westin et. al, 1985; Bikson et al., 1985).

Data Administration Disciplines: The role of the data administration function, described in Chapter 6, becomes even more important when networks link many different applications and business areas. Organizations must systematically identify which groups are responsible for maintaining each piece of data and develop specific policies and procedures to ensure that their data are accurate and available only to authorized users.

PLANNING FOR CONNECTIVITY

Connectivity audit: A method for examining amount of connectivity an organization has by examining five areas of connectivity such as network services, user interfaces and applications.

Most organizations do not have an idea of how much connectivity they have or how much they lack. They need to perform a **connectivity audit,** which examines five areas of connectivity in an organization:

1. *Networks.* How many networks are there? For what class of machines? Who manufactures them? Where are they? How much did they cost?
2. *Network management and user support.* Who is in charge of the networks that have been identified? Are accurate records kept of utilization? What are the authorization procedures? How many staff members maintain and support each network and train its end users? How much does this cost?

Figure 7.14

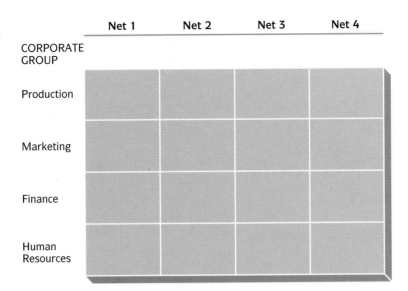

3. *Network services.* What services do the existing networks perform? For whom? How are the costs allocated?

4. *Applications.* What kinds of applications are supported by networks? How important are the applications to production and to information interchange?

5. *User interfaces.* What user interfaces are currently used? How do they connect or relate to one another? What applications run under various interfaces?

A connectivity matrix, composed of the major networks along the top axis and the major corporate user groups along the vertical axis, can help identify how networks are used and by whom (see Figure 7.14). If documented properly, the connectivity matrix should identify areas where current networks fail to provide connectivity.

The connectivity audit period is an ideal time to interview key corporate users in order to identify problem areas and potential solutions. Clearly, complete connectivity is usually not needed in most corporations (see the Window on Management). It is far more sensible to identify classes of connectivity problems and general solutions.

Management Challenges

1. **Managing LANs.** While local area networks appear to be flexible and inexpensive ways of delivering computing power to new areas of the organization, they must be carefully administered and monitored. LANs are especially vulnerable to network disruption, loss of essential data, access by unauthorized users, and infection from computer viruses (see Chapter 13). Dealing with these problems or even installing popular applications such as spreadsheets or data management software on a network requires special technical expertise, which is not normally available in end-user departments or is in very short supply.

2. **Connectivity and standards are very difficult to enforce, even when a firm's connectivity needs are well understood.** Firms are reluctant to abandon their existing, albeit incompatible, systems because these systems represent such large investments. Corporate culture and competing interest groups within the firm often resist change. Business practices tend to favor short-term efforts over the long-term planning that is essential for creating an open systems environment.

MANAGEMENT

How Noranda Moved to Companywide Standards

The last year that Noranda, the $8.5 million Canadian natural resources company, owned a mainframe computer was 1985. Its 60 operating companies now use minicomputers to handle their own processing. Noranda started distributing computing in the late 1970s with multiple minicomputers. Noranda is now implementing a client/server model of the new information architecture and it is developing a single set of companywide standards.

Noranda's management believes that establishing software and communications standards will reduce software development costs. Different business units can share common applications such as process manufacturing software for mining, pulp plants, and natural gas companies. The various business units can also share the technical skills required to develop and maintain these applications.

Only a fraction of Noranda's data flows from one operating unit to another or to corporate headquarters. However, financial data such as consolidated sales figures are sent to Noranda headquarters and are processed on Hewlett Packard computers.

Noranda's information systems group developed its own compre-

hensive set of software standards in 1990 as part of its move to UNIX open systems and client/server computing. Task forces surveyed products in various categories and selected one standard for each, based on key criteria such as usefulness and the availability of technical support around the world. Noranda selected a single relational database management system, Ingres 6.4, and Ingres application development tools, but it is allowing some business units to keep their own database software and development tools.

Noranda uses other standards such as TCP/IP for networking, the UNIX operating system, and the Open Software Foundation's OSF/Motif and Microsoft Windows for graphical user interfaces.

Noranda is using friendly persuasion to gain support for corporatewide standards among its operating units. It uses a coordinating committee called Noranda Enterprise Wide Systems (NEWS) group to gain compliance with its standards. NEWS has quarterly teleconferences, an annual on-site meeting, and monthly telephone calls. About one-third of Noranda's companies send representatives to these meetings. According

to NEWS chairman Murray Dunnigan, manager of information services at James Maclaren, Inc., a Noranda pulp and paper manufacturing unit in Masson, Quebec, NEWS gets the best people together, identifies the best practices in their companies, and the best technology. Noranda pays half the cost if an operating unit installs corporate standard software.

NEWS identified eight core applications that can be shared by many business units, but no single unit adopted more than two of them. Noranda does not maintain that it can standardize systems for the entire enterprise, but it has a model that can be applied to each operating unit.

Source: Jean S. Bozman, "Canadian Firm Uses Leverage to Enforce Enterprise-wide Standards," *Computerworld*, December 7, 1992.

To Think About: What kinds of standards are in place at Noranda? How successful has Noranda been in enforcing companywide standards? Why? How much connectivity is there at Noranda?

Summary

Describe the components of a telecommunications system and how they work.

A telecommunications system is a set of compatible devices that are used to develop a network for communication from one location to another by electronic means. The essential components of a telecommunications system are computers, terminals or other input/output devices, communications channels, communications processors (such as modems, multiplexers, controllers, concentrators and front-end processors), and telecommunications software. Different components of a telecommunications network can communicate with each other with a common set of rules termed protocols.

Data are transmitted throughout a telecommunications network using either analog signals or digital signals. A modem is a device that translates signals for transmission from analog to digital and vice versa. The principal transmission media are twisted copper telephone wire, coaxial copper cable, fiber optic cable, and wireless transmission utilizing microwave, satellite, low-frequency radio, or infrared waves.

Classify the various types of networks and network topologies.

Networks can be classified by their shape or configuration or by their geographic scope and type of services provided. Local-area networks (LANs) and private branch exchanges (PBXs) are used to link offices and buildings in close proximity. Wide-area networks (WANs) span a broad geographical distance, ranging from several miles to entire continents and are private networks that are independently managed. Value-added networks (VANs) also encompass a wide geographic area but are managed by a third party, which sells the services of the network to other companies.

The three common network topologies are the star network, the bus network, and the ring network. In a star network, all communications must pass through a central computer. The bus network links a number of devices to a single channel and broadcasts all of the signals to the entire network, with special software to identify which components receive each message. In a ring network, each computer in the network can communicate directly with any other computer, but the channel is a closed loop. Data are passed along the ring from one computer to another.

Identify telecommunications applications that can provide competitive advantages to organizations.

Using information systems for strategic advantage increasingly depends on telecommunications technology and applications such as electronic mail, voice mail, videoconferencing, FAX, and electronic data interchange (EDI). Electronic data interchange (EDI) is the direct computer-to-computer exchange between two organizations of standard business transaction documents such as invoices, bills of lading, and purchase orders.

Describe important standards used for linking hardware, software, and networks to achieve connectivity.

Connectivity is a measure of how well computers and computer-based devices can communicate with one another and "share" information in a meaningful way without human intervention. It is essential in the new information architecture where different hardware, software, and network components must work together to transfer information seamlessly from one part of the organization to another. Applications portability, open systems, migration, information portability, cooperative processing, and interoperability are all aspects of connectivity.

There are several different models for achieving connectivity in networks. Public standards like OSI and TCP/IP are recognized as important reference models for network connectivity. Each divides the communications process into layers. TCP/IP is widely used in the United States, whereas OSI is favored in Europe. ISDN is an emerging standard for digital transmission over twisted-pair telephone lines. UNIX is an operating systems standard that can be used to create open systems.

Describe problems posed by the new information architecture and recommend solutions.

Implementing the desktop revolution in a coherent way is no small task. There are problems in connecting mainframes to PCs; users can process and create their own data; much higher levels of support and training are required; and security of data weakens. Managers often face shifts in the distribution of power and a loss of control over computing. They must also rethink how information and processing power should be distributed.

Solutions include application of data administration disciplines and educating end users and technical specialists about how to use networks. While many corporations have assumed complete connectivity as a strategic goal, a more reasonable strategy would move incrementally toward greater connectivity while not giving up the vision of connectivity. The first step is to perform a connectivity audit to identify existing capabilities and future needs. From here a strategy can be developed that will lead the firm toward an amount of connectivity that is suitable for the industry and the nature of the business.

Telecommunications
Client/server model
Telecommunications system
Analog signal
Digital signal
Modem
Channels
Twisted wire
Coaxial cable
Fiber optic cable
Microwave
Satellites
Cellular telephones
Baud
Bandwidth
Asynchronous transmission
Synchronous transmission
Front-end processor
Concentrator
Controller
Multiplexer
Telecommunications software
Protocol
Network topology
Star network
Bus network
Ring network
Private branch exchange (PBX)
Local area network (LAN)
File server
Network operating system
Gateway

Baseband
Broadband
Wide area network (WAN)
Switched lines
Dedicated lines
Virtual private network
Value-added networks (VAN)
Packet switching
Frame relay
Asynchronous transfer mode (ATM)
Electronic mail (E-mail)
Voice mail
Facsimile (FAX)
Teleconferencing
Videoconferencing
Electronic data interchange (EDI)
Connectivity
Applications portability
Migration
Cooperative processing
Information portability
Interoperability
Open systems
Reference model
Standard
Open Systems Interconnect (OSI)
Transmission Control Protocol/Internet
Protocol (TCP/IP)
Integrated Services Digital Network
  (ISDN)
Connectivity audit

1. What are the characteristics of the new information architecture?

2. What is a telecommunications system?

3. Name and briefly describe each of the components of a telecommunications system.

4. Distinguish between an analog and a digital signal.

5. Name the different types of telecommunications transmission media and compare them in terms of speed and cost.

6. What is the relationship between bandwidth and the transmission capacity of a channel?

7. Name and briefly describe the three principal network topologies.

8. Distinguish between a PBX, a LAN, and a WAN.

9. Define the following:
   • Modem
   • Baud
   • File server
   • Value-added network (VAN)
   • Packet switching

10. Name and describe the telecommunications applications that can provide strategic benefits to businesses.

11. What is connectivity? Make a list and be able to discuss the meaning of the six different aspects of connectivity.

12. Compare OSI and TCP/IP. Why are they limited solutions to network connectivity problems?

13. Describe ISDN and explain why it is important.

14. Why is UNIX important to connectivity?

15. Give two examples of problems in implementing the new information architecture.

16. What are some solutions to the problems raised in the previous question?

Discussion Questions

1. Your firm has just decided to build a new headquarters building in a suburban setting. You have been assigned to work with an architect on plans for making the new building intelligent—that is, capable of supporting the computing and telecommunications needs of the business. What factors should you consider?

2. Your boss has just read in a leading business magazine that local area networks are the wave of the future. You are directed to explore how the firm can use these LANs. What words of caution and what factors should the boss consider?

3. Your employer has just announced a new strategic program to achieve complete connectivity of your firm's information systems in five years. What are some of the difficulties and potential dangers of such a policy?

Group Project

With a group of two or three of your fellow students, describe in detail the various ways that telecommunications technology can provide a firm with competitive advantage. Use the companies described in other chapters you have read so far in this book to illustrate the points you make, or select examples of other companies using telecommunications from business or computer magazines. Present your findings to the class.

CASE STUDY

Unilever Tries to Unify World Operations

The sun never sets on the worldwide holdings of Unilever, one of the world's largest multinational corporations. The sprawling conglomerate has over 350,000 employees in more than 500 companies located in 75 countries. Its holdings include T.J. Lipton, Calvin Klein Cosmetics, and Lever Brothers. Unilever's largest core business is food products. Since the 1980s, Unilever has bought more than 100 businesses and sold nearly twice as many. Nevertheless, its cost-conscious management has made sure it has a rich supply of available cash and relatively little debt.

Unilever maintains a measure of centralized control but allows decentralized operating units to meet the needs of local markets in different countries. The firm tries to "Unileverize" its managers with a common organizational culture that transcends national boundaries. Managers are trained at Unilever's international management training college near London and are assigned job positions in various countries throughout their careers.

The senior management of this London- and Rotterdam-based firm believed that with so many companies under one roof, Unilever was "drowning in technology." Unilever had many redundant systems as well as many systems that were poorly conceived and poorly implemented. Management handed Michael Johnson, Unilever's head of information technology, the responsibility of standardizing the behemoth's multitudinous hardware and software systems around an open systems architecture and bringing them together in a global network.

Unilever's old laissez-faire approach toward information systems had left it with a polyglot mix of hardware and software. Despite the official corporate policy of only using IBM, Hewlett-Packard, or DEC hardware, the firm had drastic incompatibility problems. The systems of various operating units had mushroomed out of control. To make his plan work, Johnson had to convince his three designated hardware vendors to cooperate on a cross-vendor software architecture.

According to Norman Weizer, a senior consultant with Big Six accounting firm Arthur D. Little, the challenge for global firms is to provide companywide information in a consistent, common format while allowing local units to perform effectively. Unilever wanted to pursue this goal by providing a common foundation for disparate far-flung operations without hamstringing its businesses.

Johnson moved quickly. In June 1990 he started focusing on applications portability. He told Unilever's three primary hardware suppliers—IBM, DEC, and Hewlett-Packard—that he wanted to be able to build an application and port it anywhere in the world within ten days. He especially wanted to build "competitive-edge applications" in one place, send them to other Unilever companies, and install them instantly as if the recipients had developed them themselves.

Johnson enlisted Unilever's key hardware and software vendors to agree upon an open-systems architecture for the firm that could serve as the foundation for a global network. Unilever chose the suite of standards built around the Open Software Foundation's Applications Environment Specification (AES) for systems and software throughout the corporation. AES is a massive suite of standards that includes elements of the OSF/1 operating system, the Motif graphical user interface, OSF's Distributed Computing Environment, SQL (Structured Query Language), and Posix (Posix establishes a standard interface between an applications program and an operating system rather than requiring a specific operating system).

With this base environment, Johnson added important software and database standards. Unilever chose Oracle and Sybase Inc.'s database management systems, Lotus 1-2-3 spreadsheet software, and WordPerfect word processing software. Oracle's SQL Forms and Unify Corporation's Uniface applications environments were selected as front-end software development standards.

Johnson and his team decided to use AES's distributed client/server capabilities as the foundation for Unilever's global data network. Unilever chose Sprint International to manage its pan-European data network. Eventually Unilever hopes its software tools and global network will provide the technology to manage group projects around the world.

Unilever believes its move to open systems has not stifled local technology innovation. For instance, Quest International, a Unilever food ingredients and fragrance company based in England and the Netherlands, is using AES standards to develop its critical applications. Quest is relatively small (its 1991 revenue was $842 million) and it could move quickly to new standards.

Cheeseborough-Ponds, Inc., noted for products such as Q-Tips and Vaseline, found multiple benefits in the move to open systems. It could use manufacturing applications developed by Alida Gibbs, one of Unilever's British subsidiaries, and expects to downsize each of its 74 major applications, such as payroll, benefits, and order processing, from an IBM mainframe environment onto distributed systems by 1996. The firm started using Hewlett-Packard 9000 series computers for consumer affairs processing and a corporate-wide word processing system. Cheeseborough-Ponds is linking all of its facilities using a network based on the TCP/IP reference model. The migration of applications to a distributed platform will enable users to access data 24 hours a day, a critical capability for a division of a multinational giant such as Unilever. Cheeseborough-Ponds estimates that energy reductions and quality improvements associated with the move to open systems have helped it trim annual costs by $100,000.

While Johnson has taken a strong position about standards and open systems, he does not want to disrupt the company's operations during implementation. He realizes that he will not be able to make all of Unilever's operations switch to open systems overnight. Unilever inherited hundreds of proprietary applications that Johnson wants to leave in place until his staff figures out how to make them communicate among computers. While Unilever's companywide open systems model excludes proprietary systems such as those using IBM's AS/400 minicomputer environment, it is too costly to shut down these machines right away. Johnson is letting companies with AS/400 computers delay the changeover while mandating that all new software purchased or developed for the AS/400 computers must be portable to RISC (reduced instruction set computing) machines that are compatible with AES standards.

Sources: Thomas Hoffman, "Standardization Buoys Open Systems," *Computerworld,* March 29, 1993; Joshua Greenbaum, "Unilever's Unifying Theme," *InformationWEEK,* March 2, 1992; and Floris A. Maljers, "Inside Unilever: The Evolving Transnational Company," *Harvard Business Review,* September–October 1992.

Case Study Questions

1. How serious were Unilever's connectivity problems? What management, technology, and organization factors were responsible for these problems?

2. How would you characterize Unilever's strategy for dealing with connectivity problems? Do you agree with this strategy?

3. How much connectivity should there be at a firm like Unilever? Would you recommend a five-year systems plan for Unilever to achieve a higher level of connectivity? If so, describe your plan.

References Apple Desktop Communications Solutions Reference Guide, Apple Computer, Inc., 1989. Corporate Headquarters. Rand Corporation (1985). *The New York Times* (August 3, 1988).

Benjamin, Robert I., David W. DeLong, and Michael S. Scott Morton. "The Realities of Electronic Data Interchange: How Much Competitive Advantage?" Management in the 1990s Working Paper 88:042. Sloan School of Management, MIT, 1988.

Berg, Lynn. "The SCOOP on Client/Server Costs." *Computerworld* (November 16, 1992).

Bikson, Tora K., J. D. Eveland, and Barbara A. Gutek. "Flexible Interactive Technologies for Multi-Person Tasks: Current Problems and Future Prospects." Rand Corporation (December 1988).

Bikson, Tora K., Cathleen Stasz, and Donald A. Mankin. "Computer-Mediated Work: Individual and Organizational Impact on One Corporate Headquarters." Rand Corporation (1985).

Bochenski, Barbara, "Enterprise Developers Work to Tap the Internet." *Software Magazine* (February 1992).

Borenstein, Nathaniel S. "Multimedia Electronic Mail: Will the Dream Become a Reality?" *Communications of the ACM* 34, no. 4 (April 1991).

De Pompa, Barbara. "More Power at Your Fingertips." *InformationWEEK* (December 30, 1991).

Dertouzos, Michael. "Building the Information Marketplace." *Technology Review* (January 1991).

Dion, William R. "Client/Server Computing." *Personal Workstation* (May 1990).

Donovan, John J. "Beyond Chief Information Officer to Network Manager." *Harvard Business Review* (September–October 1988).

Fisher, Sharon. "TCP/IP." *Computerworld* (October 7, 1991).

Gilder, George. "Into the Telecosm." *Harvard Business Review* (March–April 1991).

Guimaraes, Tom. "Personal Computing Trends and Problems: An Empirical Study." *MIS Quarterly* (June 1986).

Hall, Wayne A., and Robert E. McCauley. "Planning and Managing a Corporate Network Utility." *MIS Quarterly* (December 1987).

Hammer, Michael, and Glenn Mangurian. "The Changing Value of Communications Technology." *Sloan Management Review* (Winter 1987).

Hansen, James V., and Ned C. Hill. "Control and Audit of Electronic Data Interchange." *MIS Quarterly* 13, no. 4 (December 1989).

Hof, Robert D. "Computer Confusion." *Business Week* (June 10, 1991).

Huff, Sid, Malcolm C. Munro, and Barbara H. Martin. "Growth Stages of End User Computing." *Communications of the ACM* (May 1988).

Johnson, Jim. "A Survival Guide for Administrators." *Software Magazine* (December 1992).

Keen, Peter G. W. *Competing in Time.* Cambridge, MA: Ballinger Publishing Company, 1986.

Keen, Peter G. W. *Shaping the Future: Business Design Through Information Technology.* Cambridge, MA: Harvard Business School Press, 1991.

Laudon, Kenneth C. "From PCs to Managerial Workstations." In Matthias Jarke, *Managers, Micros, and Mainframes.* New York: John Wiley, 1986.

Lee, Denis M. "Usage Pattern and Sources of Assistance for Personal Computer Users." *MIS Quarterly* (December 1986).

Lee, Sunro and Richard P. Leifer. "A Framework for Linking the Structure of Information Systems with Organizational Requirements for Information Shaving." *Journal of Management Information Systems* 8, no. 4 (Spring 1992).

McNurlin, Barbara Canning. "The Rise of 'Cooperative' Systems." *EDP Analyzer* 25, no. 6 (June 1987).

"Plans and Policies for Client/Server Technology." *I/S Analyzer* 30, no. 4 (April 1992).

Pyburn, Philip J. "Managing Personal Computer Use: The Role of Corporate Management Information Systems." *Journal of Management Information Systems* (Winter 1986–87).

Railing, Larry, and Tom Housel. "A Network Infrastructure to Contain Costs and Enable Fast Response." *MIS Quarterly* 14, no. 4 (December 1990).

Rash, Wayne, Jr. "Corporate Connections." *Byte* (September 1991).

Richardson, Gary L., Brad M. Jackson, and Gary W. Dickson. "A Principles-Based Enterprise Architecture: Lessons from Texaco and Star Enterprise." *MIS Quarterly* 14, no. 4 (December 1990).

Roche, Edward M. *Telecommunications and Business Strategy.* Chicago: The Dryden Press, 1991.

Rochester, Jack B. "Networking Management: The Key to Better Customer Service." *I/S Analyzer* 27, no. 12 (December 1989).

Rowe, Stanford H. II. *Business Telecommunications.* New York: Macmillan, 1991.

Schultz, Brad. "The Evolution of ARPANET." *Datamation* (August 1, 1988).

Sinha, Alok. "Client-Server Computing." *Communications of the ACM,* 35, no. 7 (July 1992).

Smarr, Larry, and Charles E. Catlett. "Metacomputing." *Communications of the ACM* 35, no. 6 (June 1992).

Tash, Jeffrey B., and Paul Korzeniowski. "Theory Meets Reality for New Breed of APPs." *Software Magazine* (May 1992).

Torkzadeh, Gholamreza, and Weidong Xia. "Managing Telecommunications Strategy by Steering Committee." *MIS Quarterly* 16, no. 2 (June 1992).

United States General Accounting Office. "FTS 2000: An Overview of the Federal Government's New Telecommunications System." *GAO/IMTEC-90-17FS* (February 1990).

Westin, Alan F., Heather A. Schwader, Michael A. Baker, and Sheila Lehman. *The Changing Workplace.* New York: Knowledge Industries, 1985.

CHAPTER **8**

Redesigning the Organization with Information Systems

New Zealand Designs for Paperless Tax Returns

Beset by constant changes in New Zealand's tax collection management, the New Zealand Inland Revenue Department could only turn to an inflexible 20-year-old mainframe-oriented system. So in 1990 it decided to build a new $300 million information system that would automate tax filing for the country's citizens. The system's objectives were to improve efficiency, generate additional revenue, and reduce the Revenue Department's staff requirements.

The new system, dubbed Future Inland Revenue Systems and Technology (FIRST), allows taxpayers either to mail their income tax forms to a regional tax office or to transmit them electronically to the Revenue Department's computer. Tax forms that previously took three or four months to process by hand can be completed in 14 days. Such service improvements enabled the Revenue Department to cut its staff from 7000 to 5200. By 1997, the revenue de-

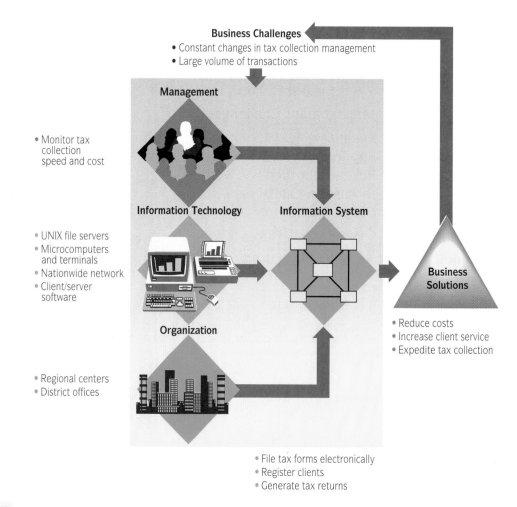

Business Challenges
- Constant changes in tax collection management
- Large volume of transactions

Management

- Monitor tax collection speed and cost

Information Technology

- UNIX file servers
- Microcomputers and terminals
- Nationwide network
- Client/server software

Information System

Business Solutions
- Reduce costs
- Increase client service
- Expedite tax collection

Organization

- Regional centers
- District offices

- File tax forms electronically
- Register clients
- Generate tax returns

partment hopes to eliminate paper tax forms, queries, and correspondence altogether.

The systems analysis process identified redundant and paper-intensive office functions. Each of the district offices of the Revenue Department was a mirror of the other. The new system design eliminated superfluous tasks. The system building team developed new client/server software programs for functions such as client registration and tax return generation. The Revenue Department decided to implement the new system slowly to leave time for user training and to minimize organizational disruptions.

After a 12-month study, the Revenue Department's Information Technology Group began building the new system. It installed a nationwide network of UNIX file servers, microcomputers, and terminals and developed client/server applications for 40 district offices and 4 regional centers. Individual transactions would be processed on microcomputers or by using terminals in the district offices, while larger applications, such as corporate management systems, remained on the agency's two mainframes.

Although the total cost of FIRST is expected to exceed $300 million, its efficiencies have already produced savings to offset more than 90 percent of this amount.

Source: John McMullen, "Taxation without Vexation," *InformationWEEK,* March 22, 1993.

New Zealand's automated tax filing system illustrates the many factors at work in the development of a new information system. Building the new system entailed analyzing the agency's problems with existing information systems, assessing people's information needs, selecting appropriate technology, and streamlining procedures and jobs. Management had to determine which system building approach to use, and then it had to monitor the system-building effort and to evaluate its benefits and costs. The new information system represented a process of organizational change.

This chapter describes how new information systems are conceived, built, and installed. It describes systems analysis and design and other core activities that must be performed to build any information system. Finally, it describes and compares the various approaches of systems building so that managers know how to choose among them.

After completing this chapter, you will be able to:

- Explain how building a new information system represents a process of organizational change.
- Identify the core activities in the systems development process.

- Distinguish between the various systems-building alternatives: the traditional systems life cycle, prototyping, application software packages, end-user development, and outsourcing.
- Understand the strengths and limitations of each approach.

8.1 Systems as Planned Organizational Change

In this text we have stressed the view of an information system as a sociotechnical entity, an arrangement of both technical and social elements. The introduction of a new information system involves much more than new hardware and software. It also includes changes in jobs, skills, management, and organization. In the sociotechnical philosophy, one cannot install new technology without considering the people who must work with it (Bostrom and Heinen, 1977). New information systems frequently mean new ways of doing business and working together. The nature of tasks, the speed with which they must be completed, the nature of supervision (its frequency and intensity), and who has what information about whom will all be decided in the process of building an information system. This is especially true in contemporary systems, which deeply affect many parts of the organization. When we design a new information system, we are redesigning the organization.

It stands to reason that deciding what new systems to build should be an essential component of the organizational planning process. Organizations need to develop an information systems plan that supports their overall business plan. Once an overall strategic business plan exists, an **information systems plan** can be developed within its context. Such a plan will serve as a road map indicating the direction of systems development, the rationale, the current situation, the management strategy, the implementation plan, and the budget (see Table 8.1).

The plan contains a statement of corporate goals and specifies how information technology supports the attainment of those goals. It shows how general goals will be achieved by specific systems projects, and it lays out specific target dates and milestones that can be used later to measure and judge the progress of the plan in terms of how many objectives were actually attained in the time frame specified in the plan.

An important part of the information systems plan is the management strategy for moving from the current situation to the future. Generally, this will indicate the key decisions made by managers concerning hardware acquisition, telecommunications, centralization/decentralization of authority, data, and hardware. Organizational changes are also usually described, including management and employee training requirements; recruiting efforts; and changes in authority, structure, or management practice.

Information systems plan: A road map indicating the direction of systems development, the rationale, the current situation, the management strategy, the implementation plan, and the budget.

Establishing Organizational Information Requirements

In order to develop an effective information systems plan, the organization must have a clear understanding of both its long- and short-term information requirements. Two principal methodologies for establishing the essential information requirements of the organization as a whole are enterprise analysis and critical success factors.

ENTERPRISE ANALYSIS (BUSINESS SYSTEMS PLANNING)

Enterprise analysis (also called business systems planning) argues that the information requirements of a firm can only be understood by looking at the entire organization in terms of organizational units, functions, processes, and data

Table 8.1   INFORMATION SYSTEMS PLAN

1. **Purpose of the Plan**
   Overview of plan contents
   Changes in firm's current situation
   Firm's strategic plan
   Current business organization
   Management strategy

2. **Strategic Business Plan**
   Current situation
   Current business organization
   Changing environments
   Major goals of the business plan

3. **Current Systems**
   Major systems supporting business
     functions
   Major current capabilities
     Hardware
     Software
     Database
     Telecommunications
   Difficulties meeting business
     requirements
   Anticipated future demands

4. **New Developments**
   New system projects
     Project descriptions
     Business rationale
   New capabilities required
     Hardware
     Software
     Database
     Telecommunications

5. **Management Strategy**
   Acquisition plans
   Milestones and timing
   Organizational realignment
   Internal reorganization
   Management controls
   Major training initiatives
   Personnel strategy

6. **Implementation Plan**
   Detailed implementation plan
   Anticipated difficulties in
     implementation
   Progress reports

7. **Budget Requirements**
   Requirements
   Potential savings
   Financing
   Acquisition cycle

Enterprise analysis: An analysis of organization-wide information requirements by looking at the entire organization in terms of organizational units, functions, processes, and data elements; helps identify the key entities and attributes in the organization's data.

elements. Enterprise analysis can help identify the key entities and attributes of the organization's data. This method starts with the notion that the information requirements of a firm or a division can be specified only with a thorough understanding of the entire organization. This method was developed by IBM in the 1960s explicitly for establishing the relationship among large systems development projects (Zachman, 1982).

The central method used in the enterprise analysis approach is to take a large sample of managers and ask them how they use information, where they get the information, what their environment is like, what their objectives are, how they make decisions, and what their data needs are.

The results of this large survey of managers are aggregated into subunits, functions, processes, and data matrices. Data elements are organized into *logical application groups*—groups of data elements that support related sets of organizational processes. One strength of enterprise analysis is that it gives a comprehensive view of the organization and of systems/data uses and gaps. Figure 8.1 is an output of enterprise analysis conducted by the Social Security Administration as part of a massive systems redevelopment effort. It shows what information is required to support a particular process, which processes create the data, and which use them. The shaded boxes in this figure indicate a logical application group. In this case, actuarial estimates, agency plans, and budget data are created in the planning process, suggesting that an information system should be built to support planning.

Enterprise analysis is especially suitable for start-up or massive change situations. For instance, it was one of the methods used by the Social Security Administration to bring about a long-term strategic change in its information processing activities. This organization had never before performed a

Figure 8.1 shows the process/data class matrix (Logical Application Groups / Data Classes / Processes). The matrix cells are reproduced below.

Group	Process	Actuarial estimates	Agency plans	Budget	Program regs./policy	Admin. regs./policy	Labor agreements	Data standards	Procedures	Automated systems documentation	Educational media	Public agreements	Intergovernmental agreements	Grants	External	Exchange control	Administrative accounts	Program expenditures	Audit reports	Organization/position	Employee identification	Recruitment/placement	Complaints/grievances	Training resources	Security	Equipment utilization	Space utilization	Supplies utilization	Workload schedules	Work measurement	Enumeration I.D.	Enumeration control	Earnings	Employer I.D.	Earnings control	Claims characteristics	Claims control	Decisions	Payment	Collection/waiver	Notice	Inquiries control	Quality appraisal
PLANNING	Develop agency plans	C	C	C	U	U									U																												
PLANNING	Administer agency budget	C	C	C	U	U					U	U	U			U	U	U		U	U					U	U	U		U		U			U		U					U	U
PLANNING	Formulate program policies	U	U		C				U							U		U						U												U							U
PLANNING	Formulate admin. policies		U		U	C	C		U							U				U	U			U																			
PLANNING	Formulate data policies		U	U		U		C	U	U																U	U	U	U														
PLANNING	Design work processes		U		U	U		C	C		U	U								U																U							U
GENERAL MANAGEMENT	Manage public affairs		U		U	U			U		C	C	C																														
GENERAL MANAGEMENT	Manage intrgovt. affairs	U	U		U	U			U		U		C	C	C									U	U								U	U		U		U		U			
GENERAL MANAGEMENT	Exchange data		U						U		U	U	U	U	U	C	U	U														U											
GENERAL MANAGEMENT	Maintain admin. accounts		U		U				U		U	U					C		U							U	U	U						U		U							
GENERAL MANAGEMENT	Maintain prog. accounts		U	U					U		U	U					C													U				U		U		U	U	U		U	
GENERAL MANAGEMENT	Conduct audits		U	U					U	U							U	U	C	U									U														
GENERAL MANAGEMENT	Establish organizations		U						U											C	U					U	U																U
GENERAL MANAGEMENT	Manage human resources		U			U	U		U											C	C	C	C	C																			
GENERAL MANAGEMENT	Provide security		U		U			U	U	U															C	C	C	C			U												
GENERAL MANAGEMENT	Manage equipment		U		U			U	U	U															C	C	C	C															
GENERAL MANAGEMENT	Manage facilities		U		U				U																U	U	C																
GENERAL MANAGEMENT	Manage supplies		U		U				U																C	U	U	C															
GENERAL MANAGEMENT	Manage workloads	U	U		U	U			U						U											U	U	U	C	C		U		U		U						U	U
PROGRAM ADMIN.	Issue social security nos.								U				U		U																C	C											
PROGRAM ADMIN.	Maintain earnings								U				U	U	U																U		C	C	C	U							
PROGRAM ADMIN.	Collect claims information				U	U			U						U																U	U				C	C	U	U	U			
PROGRAM ADMIN.	Determine elig/entlmt.								U																						U	U	U			U		C	U	U			
PROGRAM ADMIN.	Compute payments				U				U									U													U		U			U		U	C	C			
PROGRAM ADMIN.	Administer debt mgmt.				U				U									U																					U	C			
SUPPORT	Generate notices								U						U																U		U			U		U	U	U	C		
SUPPORT	Respond to prog. inquiries		U						U			U																			U			U	U	U		U	U	U	U	C	
SUPPORT	Provide quality assessment				U	U			U	U																					U			U		U		U				U	C

KEY
C = creators of data   U = users of data

Figure 8.1
Process/data class matrix. This chart depicts what data classes are required to support particular organizational processes and which processes are the creators and users of data.

comprehensive analysis of its information requirements. Instead, it had relied on a bottom-up method of responding to whatever users requested, as well as on by-product approaches where most emphasis was placed on simply performing elementary transaction processing. Enterprise analysis was used to develop a comprehensive view of how the Social Security Administration uses information.

The weakness of enterprise analysis is that it produces an enormous amount of data that is expensive to collect and difficult to analyze. Moreover, the questions frequently focus not on the critical objectives of management and where information is needed, but rather on what *existing* information is used. The result is a tendency to automate whatever exists. In this manner, manual systems may be automated while, in many instances, entirely new approaches to how business is conducted are needed, and these needs may not be addressed.

Critical success factors (CSFs):
A small number of easily
identifiable operational goals
shaped by the industry, the
firm, the manager, and the
broader environment that are
believed to assure the success
of an organization. Used to
determine the information
requirements of an
organization.

The strategic analysis or critical success factor approach argues that the information requirements of an organization are determined by a small number of **critical success factors (CSFs)** of managers. CSFs are operational goals. If these goals can be attained, the success of the firm or organization is assured (Rockart, 1979; Rockart and Treacy, 1982).

CSFs are shaped by the industry, the firm, the manager, and the broader environment. This broader focus, in comparison to that of previous methods, accounts for the description of this technique as "strategic." An important premise of the strategic analysis approach is that there is a small number of objectives that managers can easily identify and information systems can focus on.

The principal method used in CSF analysis is personal interviews—three or four—with a number of top managers to identify their goals and the resulting CSFs. These personal CSFs are aggregated to develop a picture of the firm's CSFs. Then systems are built to deliver information on these CSFs. (See Table 8.2 for an example of CSFs. For the method of developing CSFs in an organization, see Figure 8.2.)

One strength of the CSF method is that it produces a smaller data set to analyze than enterprise analysis. Only top managers are interviewed, and the questions focus on a small number of CSFs rather than a broad inquiry into what information is used or needed. This method can be tailored to the structure of each industry, with different competitive strategies producing different information systems. The CSF method also depends on the industry position and even the geographical location. Therefore, this method produces systems that are more custom-tailored to an organization. The CSF method is especially suitable for systems serving top management and for the development of decision support systems and executive support systems.

A major weakness of this method is that the aggregation process and the analysis of the data are art forms. There is no particularly rigorous way in which individual CSFs can be aggregated into a clear company pattern. Second, there is often confusion among interviewees (and interviewers) between *individual* and *organizational* CSFs. They are not necessarily the same. What can be critical to a manager may not be important for the organization. Moreover, this method is clearly biased toward top managers because they are the ones (generally the only ones) interviewed.

Redesigning Business Processes

New information systems can be powerful instruments for organizational change. Not only have they helped rationalize organizational procedures and work flows, but they can actually be used to reshape how the organization

Table 8.2 CRITICAL SUCCESS FACTORS AND ORGANIZATIONAL GOALS

Example	Goals	CSF

Profit concern	Earnings/share
	Return on investment
	Market share
	New product
		Automotive industry
		  Styling
		  Quality dealer system
		  Cost control
		  Energy standards

Nonprofit	Excellent health care Meeting government regulations Future health needs	Regional integration with other hospitals Efficient use of resources Improved monitoring of regulations

Source: Rockart (1979).

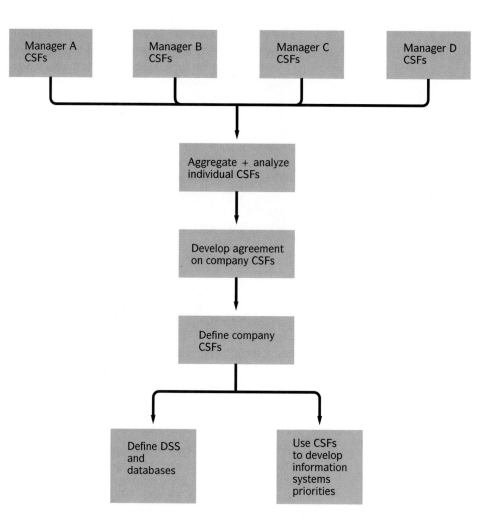

Figure 8.2
Using CSFs to develop systems.
The CSF approach relies on
interviews with key managers to
identify their CSFs. Individual
CSFs are aggregated to develop
CSFs for the entire firm. Systems
can then be built to deliver
information on these CSFs.

carries out its business or even the nature of the business itself. For instance, Baxter International's stockless inventory system described in Chapter 2 transformed Baxter into a working partner with hospitals and into a manager of its customers' supplies.

Chapter 3 described some of the ways in which information systems have helped organizations achieve great efficiencies by helping them rethink and streamline their business processes. A **business process** is a set of logically related tasks performed to achieve a defined business outcome. Some examples of business processes are developing a new product, ordering goods from a supplier, or processing and paying an insurance claim.

Business process: A set of logically related tasks performed to achieve a defined business outcome.

A new information system can radically redesign business processes to improve speed, service, and quality. If the business process is first redesigned before computing power is applied, organizations can obtain large payoffs from their investments in information technology. Business process redesign serves to reorganize work flows, combining steps to cut waste and eliminating repetitive, paper-intensive tasks (sometimes the new design eliminates jobs as well). Another term for business process redesign is *business reengineering*.

Figure 8.3 illustrates how business process redesign worked at Banc One Mortgage, an Indianapolis-based subsidiary of Banc One Corporation in Columbus, Ohio. Banc One, the twelfth largest bank in the United States, has expanded by aggressively pursuing acquisitions. In 1992, the company expected to move from handling 33,000 loans per year to 300,000 loans per year. To forestall a blizzard of paperwork, Banc One redesigned the mortgage application process so that it required fewer steps and paper forms to complete and reduced the time to process a mortgage from 17 days to only two days.

Shifting from a traditional approach helped BANC ONE Mortgage slash processing time from 17 days to two

BEFORE
Desk-to-desk approach

Paper application

Loan processing in multiple locations by specialists such as credit analysts and underwriters.

Loan servicing by specialists (insurance, escrow, etc.).

LOAN

Data entry

Closing

AFTER
Work-cell approach

Application on laptop computer

Regional production center: Teams process open applications.

Servicing: Specialists work together as a team.

LOAN

Dial-up network

Closing

LOAN

Figure 8.3
Redesigning mortgage processing at Banc One. By redesigning their mortgage processing system and the mortgage application process, Banc One will be able to handle the increased paperwork as they move from processing 33,000 loans per year to processing 300,000 loans per year. *Adapted from: Mitch Betts, "Banc One Mortgage Melts Paper Blizzard."* Computerworld, *December 14, 1992. Copyright 1992 by CW Publishing, Inc., Framingham, MA 01701. Reprinted from* Computerworld.

In the past, a mortgage applicant filled out a paper loan application. The bank entered the application transaction into its computer system. Specialists such as credit analysts and underwriters from eight different departments accessed and evaluated the application individually. If the loan application was approved, the closing was scheduled. After the closing, bank specialists dealing with insurance or funds in escrow serviced the loan. This "desk-to-desk" assembly-line approach took 17 days.

Banc One Mortgage replaced the sequential desk-to-desk approach with a speedier "work cell" or team approach. Now, loan originators in the field enter the mortgage application directly into laptop computers. Software checks the application transaction to make sure that all of the information is correct and complete. The loan originators transmit the loan applications using a dial-up network to regional production centers. Instead of working on the application individually, the credit analysts, loan underwriters, and other specialists convene electronically, working as a team to approve the mortgage. After closing, another team of specialists sets up the loan for servicing. The entire loan application process takes only two days. Loan information is also easier to access than before, when the loan application could be in eight or nine different departments. Loan originators can also dial into the bank's network to obtain information on mortgage loan costs or to check the status of a loan for the customer.

By redesigning its entire approach to mortgage processing, Banc One achieved remarkable efficiencies. Instead of automating the way it had always done mortgage processing, it completely rethought the entire mortgage application process before applying an automated system. Not all organizations have been as effective as Banc One in redesigning their business processes; organizational change cannot always be engineered to management's liking. But even if businesses cannot fully reshape their processes, new information systems provide opportunities for change.

8.2 Overview of Systems Development

Wherever their origin, new information systems are an outgrowth of a process of organizational problem solving. A new information system is built as a solution to some type of problem or set of problems the organization perceives it is facing. The problem may be one where managers and employees realize that the organization is not performing as well as expected, or it may come from the realization that the organization should take advantage of new opportunities to perform more successfully.

Review the diagrams for the vignettes at the beginning of each chapter of this text. They illustrate an information system that is a business solution to a particular set of business challenges or problems. The resulting information system is the product of a series of activities called systems development. **Systems development** refers to all the activities that go into producing an information systems solution to an organizational problem or opportunity. Systems development is a structured kind of problem solving with distinct activities. These activities consist of systems analysis, systems design, programming, testing, conversion, and production and maintenance.

Figure 8.4 illustrates the systems development process. The systems development activities depicted here usually take place in sequential order. But some of the activities may need to be repeated or some may be taking place simultaneously, depending on the approach to system building that is being employed. Note also that each activity involves interaction with the organization. Members of the organization participate in these activities, and the systems development process creates organizational changes. Chapter 9 describes the challenge of managing these organizational changes surrounding system building.

Systems development: The activities that go into producing an information systems solution to an organizational problem or opportunity.

Figure 8.4
The systems development process. Each of the core systems development activities entails interaction with the organization.

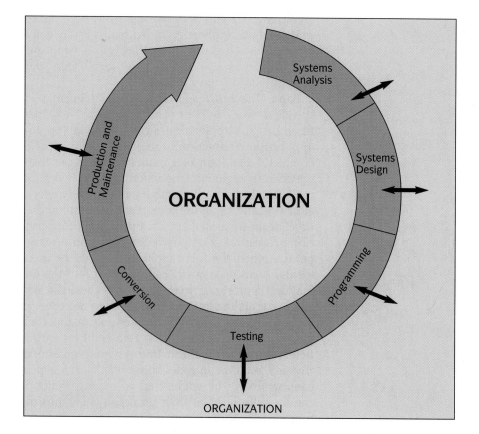

Systems Analysis

Systems analysis is the analysis of the problem that the organization will try to solve with an information system. It consists of defining the problem, identifying its causes, specifying the solution, and identifying the information requirements that must be met by a system solution.

The key to building any large information system is a thorough understanding of the existing organization and system. Thus, the systems analyst creates a road map of the existing organization and systems, identifying the primary owners and users of data in the organization. These stakeholders have a direct interest in the information affected by the new system. In addition to these organizational aspects, the analyst also briefly describes the existing hardware and software that serve the organization.

From this organizational analysis, the systems analyst details the problems of existing systems. By examining documents, work papers, and procedures; observing system operations; and interviewing key users of the systems, the analyst can identify the problem areas and objectives to be achieved by a solution. Often the solution requires building a new information system or improving an existing one.

FEASIBILITY

Feasibility study: A way to determine whether a solution is achievable, given the organization's resources and constraints.

In addition to suggesting a solution, systems analysis involves a **feasibility study** to determine whether that solution is feasible, or achievable, given the organization's resources and constraints. Three major areas of feasibility must be addressed:

Technical feasibility: Determines whether a proposed solution can be implemented with the available hardware, software, and technical resources.

Economic feasibility: Determines whether the benefits of a proposed solution outweigh the costs.

Operational feasibility: Determines whether a proposed solution is desirable within the existing managerial and organizational framework.

1. **Technical feasibility:** whether the proposed solution can be implemented with the available hardware, software, and technical resources.
2. **Economic feasibility:** whether the benefits of the proposed solution outweigh the costs.
3. **Operational feasibility:** whether the proposed solution is desirable within the existing managerial and organizational framework.

Normally the systems analysis process will identify several alternative solutions that can be pursued by the organization. The process will then assess the feasibility of each. Three basic solution alternatives exist for every systems problem:

1. To do nothing, leaving the existing situation unchanged.
2. To modify or enhance existing systems.
3. To develop a new system.

To establish economic feasibility, the analyst will have to weigh the costs and benefits of each proposed solution. Cost/benefit analysis involves adding up all the costs of a project and all of its benefits. These costs and benefits are detailed in Table 8.3. An optimal solution maximizes the amount of benefits for given costs or minimizes costs for a specified amount of benefit.

Tangible benefits: Benefits that can be quantified and assigned monetary value; they include lower operational costs and increased cash flows.

Intangible benefits: Benefits that are not easily quantified; they include more efficient customer service or enhanced decision making.

As it turns out, it is not easy to specify all of the benefits and costs precisely for many information system projects. Many benefits of sophisticated systems, such as improved decision making or higher customer satisfaction, are intangible. **Intangible benefits** such as enhanced decision-making or better customer service cannot be quantified. (In contrast, **tangible benefits,** such as reduced clerical staff or lower computer expenses, are benefits that can be quantified.) The difficulties of measuring intangible benefits may create an "application bias," because TPS that save labor produce more measurable, tangible benefits than MIS, DSS, or knowledge work systems. Yet systems that produce mainly intangible benefits may be very worthwhile and perhaps even essential to the company.

Table 8.3	Costs of Systems	Benefits of Systems

	Implementation costs
	  Computer time
	  Technical staff
	  User time
	  Cost of packages
	
	Operational costs
	  Computer time
	  Additional equipment
	  Software maintenance
	  Operating staff
	  User time
	  Supplies
	  Ongoing training costs
	  Facility costs
		Tangible
		  Cost savings
		    Increased productivity
		    Low operational costs
		    Reduced work force
		    Lower computer expenses
		    Lower outside vendor costs
		  Cost avoidance
		    Lower clerical and professional costs
		    Reduced rate of growth in expenses
		    Reduced facility costs
		Intangible
		  Improved asset utilization
		  Improved resource control
		  Improved organizational planning
		  Increased organizational flexibility
		  More timely information
		  More information
		  Increased organizational learning
		  Legal requirements attained
		  Enhanced employee goodwill
		  Increased job satisfaction
		  Improved decision making
		  Improved operations
		  Higher client satisfaction
		  Better corporate image

A written systems proposal report will describe the costs and benefits, advantages and disadvantages of each alternative. It is then up to management to determine which mix of costs, benefits, technical features, and organizational impacts represents the most desirable alternative.

ESTABLISHING INFORMATION REQUIREMENTS

Information requirements: A detailed statement of the information needs that a new system must satisfy; identifies who needs what information, and when, where, and how the information is needed.

Perhaps the most difficult task of the systems analyst is to define the specific information requirements that must be met by the system solution selected. This is the area where many large system efforts go wrong and the one that poses the greatest difficulty for the analyst. At the most basic level, the **information requirements** of a new system involve identifying who needs what information, where, when, and how. Requirements analysis carefully defines the objectives of the new or modified system and develops a detailed description of the functions that the new system must perform. Requirements must consider economic, technical, and temporal constraints, as well as the goals, procedures, and decision processes of the organization. Faulty requirements analysis is a leading cause of systems failure and high systems development costs (see Chapter 9). A system designed around the wrong set of requirements will either have to be discarded because of poor performance or will need to be heavily revised. Therefore, the importance of requirements analysis cannot be underestimated.

In many instances, building a new system creates an opportunity to redefine how the organization conducts its daily business. Some problems do not even require an information system solution, but instead need an adjustment in management, additional training, or refinement of existing organizational procedures. If the problem is information-related, systems analysis may still be required to diagnose the problem and arrive at the proper solution.

Systems Design

Systems design: Details how a system will meet the information requirements as determined by the systems analysis.

While systems analysis describes what a system should do to meet information requirements, **systems design** shows how the system will fulfill this objective. The design of an information system is the overall plan or model for that system. Like the blueprint of a building or house, it consists of all the specifications that give the system its form and structure. Information systems design is an exacting and creative task, demanding imagination, sensitivity to detail, and expert skills.

The systems designer details the system specifications that will deliver the functions identified during systems analysis. These specifications should address all of the managerial, organizational, and technological components of the system solution. Table 8.4 lists the types of specifications that would be produced during systems design.

LOGICAL AND PHYSICAL DESIGN

Logical design: Lays out the components of the information system and their relationship to each other as they would appear to users.

The design for an information system can be broken down into logical and physical design specifications. **Logical design** lays out the components of the system and their relationship to each other as they would appear to users. It shows what the system solution will do as opposed to how it is actually implemented physically. It describes inputs and outputs, processing functions to be performed, business procedures, data models, and controls. (Controls specify standards for acceptable performance and methods for measuring actual performance in relation to these standards. They are described in detail in Chapter 13.)

Table 8.4   DESIGN SPECIFICATIONS

Output
    Medium
    Content
    Timing
	Controls
	    Input controls (characters, limit, reasonableness)
	    Processing controls (consistency, record counts)
	    Output controls (totals, samples of output)
	    Procedural controls (passwords, special forms)

Input
    Origins
    Flow
    Data entry	

User interface
    Simplicity
    Efficiency
    Logic
    Feedback
    Errors
	Security
	    Access controls
	    Catastrophe plans
	    Audit trails

Database design
    Logical data relations
    Volume and speed requirements
    File organization and design
    Record specifications
	Documentation
	    Operations documentation
	    Systems documents
	    User documentation

Processing
    Computations
    Program modules
    Required reports
    Timing of outputs
	Conversion
	    Transfer files
	    Initiate new procedures
	    Select testing method
	    Cut over to new system

Manual procedures
    What activities
    Who performs them
    When
    How
    Where
	Training
	    Select training techniques
	    Develop training modules
	    Identify training facilities

	Organizational changes
	    Task redesign
	    Job design
	    Office and organization structure design
	    Reporting relationships

Physical design: The process of translating the abstract logical model into the specific technical design for the new system.

Physical design is the process of translating the abstract logical model into the specific technical design for the new system. It produces the actual specifications for hardware, software, physical databases, input/output media, manual procedures, and specific controls. Physical design provides the specifications that transform the abstract logical design plan into a functioning system of people and machines.

Like houses or buildings, information systems may have many possible designs. They may be centralized or distributed, on-line or batch, partially manual or heavily automated. Each design represents a unique blend of all of the technical and organizational factors that shape an information system. What makes one design superior to others is the ease and efficiency with which it fulfills user requirements within a specific set of technical, organizational, financial, and time constraints. Before the design of an information system is finalized, analysts will evaluate various design alternatives and select the alternative that represents the best solution for the organization.

THE ROLE OF END USERS

User information requirements drive the entire system-building effort, and so information system design demands a very high level of end user participation and control. Users must have sufficient control over the design process to ensure that the system reflects their business priorities and information needs, not the biases of the technical staff.

Working on design increases users' understanding and acceptance of the system, reducing problems caused by power transfers, intergroup conflict, and unfamiliarity with new system functions and procedures. As Chapter 9 points out, insufficient user involvement in the design effort is a major cause of system failure.

The nature and level of user participation in design vary from system to system. There is less need for user involvement in systems with simple or straightforward requirements than in those with requirements that are elaborate, complex, or vaguely defined. Less structured systems, such as decision-support applications, need more user participation to define requirements. Different levels of user involvement in design are reflected in the various alternative systems development approaches discussed later in this chapter.

Completing the Systems Development Process

The remaining steps in the systems development process translate the solution specifications established during systems analysis and design into a fully operational information system. These concluding steps consist of programming, testing, conversion, and production and maintenance.

PROGRAMMING

Programming: The process of translating the system specifications prepared during the design stage into program code.

The process of translating design specifications into software for the computer constitutes a smaller portion of the systems development cycle than design and perhaps the testing activities. But it is here, in providing the actual instructions for the machine, that the heart of the system takes shape. During **programming,** system specifications that were prepared during the design stage are translated into program code. On the basis of detailed design documents for files, transaction and report layouts, and other design details, specifications for each program in the system are prepared.

TESTING

Testing: The exhaustive and thorough process that determines whether the system produces the desired results under known conditions.

Exhaustive and thorough **testing** must be conducted to ascertain whether the system produces the right results. Testing answers the question, "Will the system produce the desired results under known conditions?"

The amount of time needed to answer this question has been traditionally underrated in systems project planning (see Chapter 9). As much as 50 percent of the entire software development budget can be expended in testing. Testing is also time-consuming: Test data must be carefully prepared, results reviewed, and corrections made in the system. In some instances, parts of the system may have to be redesigned. Yet the risks of glossing over this step are enormous.

Testing an information system can be broken down into three types of activities:

Unit testing, or program testing, consists of testing each program separately in the system. While it is widely believed that the purpose of such testing is to guarantee that programs are error free, this goal is realistically impossible (see the discussion of bugs and defects in Chapter 9). Testing should be viewed instead as a means of locating errors in programs, focusing on finding all the ways to make a program fail. Once pinpointed, problems can be corrected.

System testing tests the functioning of the information system as a whole. It tries to determine if discrete modules will function together as planned and whether discrepancies exist between the way the system actually works and the way it was conceived. Among the areas examined are performance time, capacity for file storage and handling peak loads, recovery and restart capabilities, and manual procedures.

Acceptance testing results in user and management final certification that the system is ready to be used in a production setting—when all parties are satisfied that the new system meets their standards, the system is formally accepted for installation.

It is essential that all aspects of testing be carefully thought out and that they be as comprehensive as possible. To ensure this, the development team works with users to devise a systematic test plan. The **test plan** includes all of the preparations for the series of tests previously described.

Users play a critical role in the testing process. They understand the full range of data and processing conditions that might occur within their system. Moreover, programmers tend to be aware only of the conditions treated in their programs; the test data they devise are usually too limited. Therefore, input from other team members and users will help ensure that the range of conditions included in the test data is complete. Users can identify frequent and less common transactions, unusual conditions to anticipate, and most of the common types of errors that might occur when the system is in use. User input is also decisive in verifying the manual procedures for the system.

CONVERSION

Conversion is the process of changing from the old system to the new system. It answers the question, "Will the new system work under real conditions?" Four main conversion strategies can be employed: the parallel strategy, the direct cutover strategy, the pilot study strategy, and the phased approach strategy.

In a **parallel strategy,** both the old system and its potential replacement are run together for a time until everyone is assured that the new one functions correctly. This is the safest conversion approach because, in the event of errors or processing disruptions, the old system can still be used as a backup. However, this approach is very expensive, and additional staff or resources may be required to run the extra system.

The **direct cutover** strategy replaces the old system entirely with the new system on an appointed day. At first glance, this strategy seems less costly than parallel conversion strategy. However, it is a very risky approach that can potentially be more costly than parallel activities. If serious problems with the new system are found, there is no other system to fall back on. Dislocations, disruptions, and the cost of corrections may be enormous.

The **pilot study** strategy introduces the new system to only a limited area of the organization, such as a single department or operating unit. When this pilot version is complete and working smoothly, it is installed throughout the rest of the organization, either simultaneously or in stages.

Unit testing: The process of testing each program separately in the system. Sometimes called program testing.

System testing: Tests the functioning of the information system as a whole in order to determine if discrete modules will function together as planned.

Acceptance testing: Provides the final certification that the system is ready to be used in a production setting.

Test plan: Prepared by the development team in conjunction with the users; it includes all of the preparations for the series of tests to be performed on the system.

Conversion: The process of changing from the old system to the new system.

Parallel strategy: Conservative conversion approach where both the old system and its replacement are run together until everyone is assured that the new one functions correctly.

Direct cutover: A risky conversion approach where the new system completely replaces the old one on an appointed day.

Pilot study: A strategy to introduce the new system to a limited area of the organization until it is proven to be fully functional.

Phased approach: Introduces the new system in stages either by functions or by organizational units.

Conversion plan: Provides a schedule of all activities required to install a new system.

Documentation: Descriptions of how an information system works from either a technical or end-user standpoint.

The **phased approach** strategy introduces the new system in stages, either by functions or by organizational units. If, for example, the system is introduced by functions, a new payroll system might begin with hourly workers who are paid weekly, followed six months later by adding salaried employees who are paid monthly to the system. If the system is introduced by organizational units, corporate headquarters might be converted first, followed by outlying operating units four months later.

A formal **conversion plan** provides a schedule of all the activities required to install the new system. The most time-consuming activity is usually the conversion of data. Data from the old system must be transferred to the new system, either manually or through special conversion software programs (see the Window on Organizations). The converted data then must be carefully verified for accuracy and completeness.

Moving from an old system to a new one requires that end users be trained to use the new system. Detailed **documentation** showing how the system works from both a technical and end-user standpoint is finalized during conversion time for use in training and everyday operations. Lack of proper training and documentation contributes to system failure (see Chapter 9), so this portion of the systems development process is very important.

W I N D O W   O N
ORGANIZATIONS
Conversion: Harder Than You Think!

When two companies join, what does it take for them to live happily ever after? Some say the real marriage takes place in their information systems. The merged company Outokumpu American Brass Inc. of Buffalo, New York, recently found this out. When American Brass was purchased by Outokumpu Oy of Finland, it had to split into two corporations, one based in Buffalo, and one in Kenosha, Wisconsin. Furthermore, it had to convert to the human resources system specified by its parent company.

American Brass's existing human resources system, based on a software package from Software 2000 Inc. of Hyannis, Massachusetts, simply wasn't designed to handle this problem. Most human resources software packages do not use standardized codes in the systems they sell. To convert to another human resources system, information systems specialists have to use a mixture of in-house and vendor-written conversion programs. The MIS department of

American Brass wrote its own conversion software. Other companies shared this experience.

Multifoods Corporation, a century-old food distributor operating in the United States, Canada, and Venezuela, had to add new groups of employees through mergers to its Cyborg Solution Series Human Resources payroll system so many times that its information systems staff wrote their own COBOL conversion programs and modified them as needed. The staff developed a series of programs to convert general ledger, state and local tax, exemption, deduction, health care, and salary data from other human resources systems such as those run by Automatic Data Processing (ADP), Control Data Corporation (CDC), and some home-grown systems. But data for job descriptions and benefits plan enrollments all had to be keyed in manually.

Codes mean different things in different organizations. System builders have to analyze these dif-

ferences and find a way to have them mean the same thing to everybody or no one will understand what the data mean. What one system terms *salary,* others call *pay rate, pay per period,* or *annual salary divided out.* No wonder a sizable chunk of companies merely fixes the problem the "old way" by rekeying in all of the data. Without standards on field length, data names, and descriptions, there will be no easy way to perform conversions (see Chapter 6).

Source: Bill Sharp, "Managing a Merger: HR Systems Migration," *Datamation,* February 15, 1993.

To Think About: Is conversion merely a technology issue? How helpful is conversion software? It has been said that the significance of conversion in systems development has been underestimated. Do you agree? If you were in charge of a systems development project, how would you plan for the conversion stage?

Table 8.5 SYSTEMS DEVELOPMENT

Core Activity	Description
Systems analysis	Identify problem(s) Specify solution Establish information requirements
Systems design	Create logical design specifications Create physical design specifications Manage technical realization of system
Programming	Translate design specifications into program code
Testing	Unit test Systems test Acceptance test
Conversion	Plan conversion Prepare documentation Train users and technical staff
Production and Maintenance	Operate the system Evaluate the system Modify the system

PRODUCTION AND MAINTENANCE

Production: The stage after the new system is installed and the conversion is complete; during this time the system is reviewed by users and technical specialists to determine how well it has met its original goals.

Maintenance: Changes in hardware, software, documentation, or procedures to a production system to correct errors, meet new requirements, or improve processing efficiency.

After the new system is installed and conversion is complete, the system is said to be in **production.** During this stage, the system will be reviewed by both users and technical specialists to determine how well it has met its original objectives and to decide whether any revisions or modifications are in order. Changes in hardware, software, documentation, or procedures to a production system to correct errors, meet new requirements, or improve processing efficiency are termed **maintenance.**

Studies of maintenance have examined the amount of time required for various maintenance tasks (Lientz and Swanson, 1980). Approximately 20 percent of the time is devoted to debugging or correcting emergency production problems; another 20 percent is concerned with changes in data, files, reports, hardware, or system software. But 60 percent of all maintenance work consists of making user enhancements, improving documentation, and recoding system components for greater processing efficiency. The amount of work in the third category of maintenance problems could be reduced significantly through better system analysis and design practices. Table 8.5 summarizes the systems development activities.

8.3 Alternative Systems-Building Methods

The systems development process can be carried out in a number of different ways. The remainder of this chapter describes the major alternative approaches that are used for building systems: the traditional systems life cycle, prototyping, use of purchased application software packages, end-user development, and outsourcing.

The Traditional Systems Life Cycle

The **systems life cycle** is the oldest method for building information systems and is still used today for medium or large complex systems projects. This methodology assumes that an information system has a life cycle similar to that of any living organism, with a beginning, middle, and end. The life cycle is a very

Systems life cycle: Traditional methodology for developing an information system that partitions the systems development process into six formal stages that must be completed sequentially with a very formal division of labor between end-users and information systems specialists.

formal and sequential approach to building information systems that partitions the process into six distinct stages: project definition, systems study, design, programming, installation, and post-implementation. Figure 8.5 illustrates these stages. Each stage consists of the basic activities described above that must be performed before the next stage can begin.

The life cycle methodology also has a very formal division of labor between end users and information systems specialists. Technical specialists such as systems analysts and programmers are responsible for much of the systems analysis, design, and implementation work; end users are limited to providing information requirements and reviewing the work of the technical staff. Formal sign-offs or agreements between end users and technical specialists are required as each stage is completed. Figure 8.5 also shows the product or output of each stage of the life cycle that is the basis for such sign-offs. We now describe the stages of the life cycle in detail.

STAGES OF THE SYSTEMS LIFE CYCLE

The **project definition** stage focuses on preliminary problem analysis aspects of systems analysis. It tries to answer the questions, "Why do we need a new system project?" and "What do we want to accomplish?" This stage determines whether the organization has a problem and whether that problem can be solved by

Figure 8.5

The life cycle methodology for systems development. The life cycle methodology divides systems development into 6 formal stages with specifics for milestones and end products at each stage. A typical medium-sized development project requires 2 years to complete and delivers a system with an expected life span of 3 to 8 years.

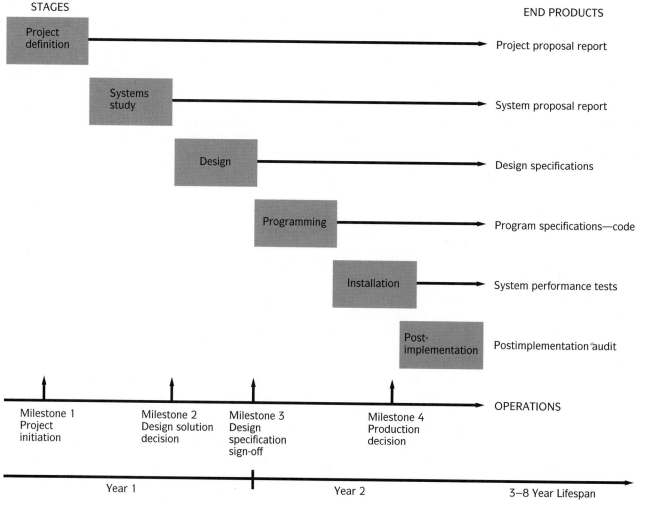

Project definition: Stage in the systems life cycle that determines whether or not the organization has a problem and whether or not the problem can be solved by launching a system project.

Systems study: Stage in the systems life cycle that analyzes the problems of existing systems, defines the objectives to be attained by a solution, and evaluates various solution alternatives.

building a new information system or by modifying an existing one. If a system project is called for, the proposal developed during this stage identifies its general objectives, specifies the scope of the project, and develops a project plan that can be shown to management.

The **systems study** stage corresponds to the systems analysis activities described earlier in this chapter and produces a report that includes the following:

- A detailed analysis of the problems of existing systems (manual or automated).
- Identification of objectives to be attained by a solution to these problems.
- Alternative solutions.
- A feasibility study of each solution alternative.
- New information system requirements.
- A project plan describing in detail the remaining life cycle activities and the tasks for each phase.

Design: Stage in the systems life cycle that produces the logical and physical design specifications for the systems solution.

Programming stage: Stage in the systems life cycle that translates the design specifications produced during the design stage into software program code.

The **design** stage produces the logical and physical design specification alternatives for the solution. Because the life cycle method emphasizes formal specifications, many of the design and documentation tools described in Chapter 9, such as data flow diagrams or program structure charts, are likely to be utilized.

The **programming stage** translates the design specifications produced during the design stage into software program code. Systems analysts work with programmers to prepare specifications for each program in the system and to prepare test plans for the various modules. These program specifications describe what each program will do, the type of programming language to be used, inputs and outputs, processing logic, processing schedules, and control statements such as those for sequencing input data. Programmers write customized program code typically using a conventional third-generation programming language such as COBOL or FORTRAN or a high-productivity fourth-generation language. Since large systems have many programs with hundreds of thousands of lines of program code, entire teams of programmers may be required.

Installation: Systems life cycle stage consisting of testing, training, and conversion; the final steps required to put a system into operation.

The **installation** stage consists of the final steps for putting the system into operation—acceptance testing, training, and conversion. The software is tested to make sure it performs properly from both a technical and a functional business standpoint. Business and technical specialists are trained to use the new system. A formal conversion strategy is selected and a plan developed that provides a detailed schedule of all of the activities required to install the new system. Using that plan, the old system is converted to the new one.

Post implementation: The final stage of the systems life cycle in which the system is used and evaluated while in production and is modified to make improvements or meet new requirements.

The **post-implementation** stage consists primarily of the maintenance activities previously described. It also includes a formal post-implementation audit conducted by users and technical specialists that determines how well the new system has met its original objectives and whether any revisions or modifications are required. Over time, the system may require so much maintenance to remain efficient and meet user objectives that it will come to the end of its useful lifespan. Once the system's life cycle comes to an end, a completely new system is called for and the cycle may begin again.

LIMITATIONS OF THE LIFE CYCLE APPROACH

The systems life cycle is still used for building large transaction processing systems (TPS) and management information systems (MIS) where requirements are highly structured and well defined. It will also remain appropriate for complex technical systems such as space launches, air traffic control, and refinery operations. Such applications need a rigorous and formal requirements analysis, predefined specifications, and tight controls over the systems building process. However, the systems life cycle methodology is costly, time-consuming, and inflexible. Volumes of new documents must be generated and steps repeated if requirements and specifications have to be revised. The methodology encourages freezing of system specifications early in the development process. It is not well suited for most of the small desktop systems that will predominate during the 1990s and the twenty-first century, which tend to be less structured and more individualized. These problems can be solved by the alternative strategies for building systems that are described in the remainder of this chapter.

Prototyping

Prototyping: Process of building an experimental system quickly and inexpensively for demonstration and evaluation so that users can better determine information requirements.

Prototype: Preliminary working version of an information system for demonstration and evaluation purposes.

Iterative: Process of repeating the steps to build a system over and over again.

Prototyping is less formal than the life cycle method. Instead of generating volumes of detailed specifications and sign-off documents, prototyping rapidly generates an experimental working model of a system for end users to evaluate. By interacting with the prototype, users can develop a clear idea of their information requirements. The prototype endorsed by the users can be used as a template to create the final system.

The **prototype** is a working version of an information system or part of the system that is meant to be only a preliminary model. Once operational, the prototype will be further refined until it conforms precisely to users' requirements. For many applications, a prototype will be extended and enhanced over and over again before a final design is accepted. Once the design has been finalized, the prototype can be converted to a polished production system.

The process of building a preliminary design, trying it out, refining it, and trying again has been called an **iterative** process of systems development because the steps required to build a system can be repeated over and over again. Although the traditional life cycle approach involves some measure of reworking and refinement, prototyping is more explicitly iterative and actively promotes system design changes. It has been said that prototyping replaces unplanned rework with planned iteration, with each version more accurately reflecting users' requirements.

Since most users cannot describe their requirements fully on paper, prototyping allows them to work with a system in order to determine exactly what they need. The methodology anticipates that they will change their minds; these changes can be incorporated easily and inexpensively during an early stage of development.

Figure 8.6 shows a four-step model of the prototyping process. The steps consist of the following:

Step 1. *Identify the user's basic requirements.* The system designer (usually an information systems specialist) works with the user only long enough to capture enough of his or her basic information needs to develop the initial prototype.

Step 2. *Develop an initial prototype.* The system designer creates a working prototype quickly, most likely using the fourth-generation software tools described in Chapter 5 that speed application development. (Some features of computer-aided software engineering [CASE] tools, described in Chapter 9, can also be used for prototyping.) The prototype may only perform the most important functions of the proposed system, or it may consist of the entire system with a restricted file.

Step 3. *Use the prototype.* The user is encouraged to work with the system in order to determine how well the prototype meets his or her needs and to make suggestions for improving the prototype.

Step 4. *Revise and enhance the prototype.* The system builder notes all changes requested by the user and refines the prototype accordingly. After the prototype has been revised, the cycle returns to step 3. Steps 3 and 4 are repeated until the user is satisfied.

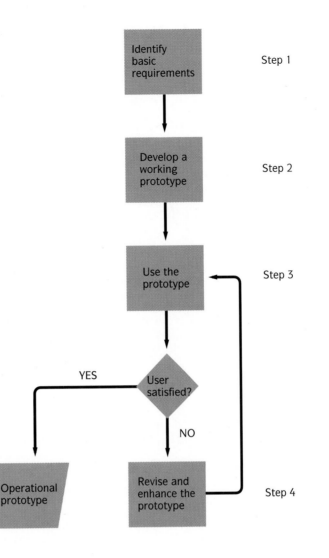

Figure 8.6
The prototyping process. The process of developing a prototype can be broken down into 4 steps. Because a prototype can be developed quickly and inexpensively, the developers can go through several iterations, repeating steps 3 and 4, in order to refine and enhance the prototype before arriving at the final operational one.

When no more iterations are required, the approved prototype furnishes the final specifications for the application. Sometimes the prototype itself is adopted as the production version of the system. Prototyping is more rapid, iterative, and informal than the systems life cycle method has proven to be.

ADVANTAGES AND DISADVANTAGES OF PROTOTYPING

Prototyping is most useful when some uncertainty exists about requirements or design solutions. For example, a major securities firm requests consolidated information to analyze the performance of its account executives. But what should the measures of performance be? Can the information be extracted from the personnel system alone, or must data from client billings be incorporated as well? What items should be compared on reports? Will intermediate processing based on some form of statistical analysis be involved? Managers may not be able to foresee how the system will work.

End-user interface: The part of an information system through which the end user interacts with the system, such as on-line screens and commands.

Prototyping is especially valuable for the design of the **end-user interface** of an information system (the part of the system that end users interact with, such as on-line display, data-entry screens and reports [see the Window on Technology]). The prototype enables users to react immediately to the parts of the system they will be dealing with. Figure 8.7 illustrates the prototyping process for an on-line calendar for retail securities brokers. The first version of the screen was built according to user-supplied specifications for a calendar to track appointments and activities. But when users actually worked with the calendar screen, they suggested adding labels for month and year and a box to indicate whether the

TECHNOLOGY

Prototyping Graphical User Interfaces: New Tools to the Rescue

UNIX is a very flexible, powerful, and portable operating system, but it can present a forbidding or ugly interface to end users. Users of UNIX applications want graphical user interfaces (GUIs) that are attractive and easy to use like Microsoft Windows or the Macintosh graphical user interface. But generating these interfaces for the users is not easy because of the inordinate amount of time required to code a graphical user interface from scratch.

Now special GUI-building tools can help out. While the tools do not generate the entire interface, they can save about 80 percent of the work time, freeing programmers to spend more time on the underlying components of the applications and to take advantage of UNIX's strengths. Two types of tools are especially helpful: interface development tools and user interface management systems.

Interface development tools, such as Builder Xcessory from Integrated Computer Solutions (ICS) in Cambridge, Massachusetts, or UIM/X from Visual Edge Software Ltd. in St. Laurent, Quebec, handle the prototyping of user interfaces and generate program code for the part of the interface

that the user would see. To use these tools, information systems specialists must be skilled in the C programming language. Most interface development tools adhere to established GUI standards, supplementing the GUI toolkit for Motif, the GUI standard used with UNIX. This feature appealed to the foreign exchange department of the Chemical Bank in New York City. The department used ICS's Builder Xcessory when it developed a trading system for Motif. Chemical Bank needed a tool for developing an interface that was both easy to use and that used the standard set of Motif graphic elements for windows, scrollbars, pop-up windows, and so forth.

User interface management systems, such as X.desktop from IXI Corporation of San Ramon, California, or Looking Glass Professional from Visix Software Inc. of Reston, Virginia, are less powerful than interface development tools but are easier to use. Most allow developers to generate user interface prototypes quickly using a mouse and a series of pull-down menus. However, few can generate complete applications by themselves. They automate generation of interface code. The remaining code must be written in C

or a fourth-generation language. So interface management systems are often used to develop prototypes for the user interface before the underlying program logic is created. Since the GUI can be developed separately from the application, the tool can be used concurrently to construct more than one GUI for the same application. For instance, one GUI might be developed for novices and another for more sophisticated professionals. Some interface management systems use proprietary toolkits that may lead to compatibility problems with future versions of Motif. In the future, these products could be producing nonstandard interfaces.

Source: Bob Francis, "GUI Builders Take on UNIX," *Datamation,* July 1, 1992.

To Think About: What would be the impact on the systems development process if tools like these were unavailable? What are the advantages and disadvantages of each of these tools? What management, organization, and technology factors would you consider in deciding whether to use one of these tools?

---

appointment had been met or an activity completed. The brokers also found that they wanted to access information that was maintained in the system about clients with whom they had appointments. The system designer added a link enabling brokers to move directly from the calendar screen to the client's records.

Prototyping has been widely hailed as a panacea for the problems inherent in the traditional systems development process. It encourages early and intense end-user involvement in the design effort and throughout the systems development life cycle (Cerveny et al., 1986). Prototyping is more likely to produce systems that fulfill user requirements. For instance, when the Du Pont Company used prototyping to build its systems, it produced more than 400 new programs with no failures (Arthur, 1992). Prototyping promises to eliminate excess development costs and design flaws. User satisfaction and morale are usually heightened because users are presented with a preliminary working system in a very short period of time.

Hello Rob! Here is your calendar of appointments and activities for today

S	M	T	W	T	F	S
30	31	1	2	3	4	5
6	7	8	9	10	11	12
13	14	15	16	17	18	19
20	21	22	23	24	25	26
27	28	29	30	31	1	2
3	4	5	6	7	8	9

Friday   18

Time	Activity	Tag
6:00am		
7:00am		
8:00am		
9:00am		
10:00am		
11:00am		
12:00pm		
1:00pm		

[OK] [Month] [Next] [Previous] ⬇ ⬆ [To Do]

(A)

Hello Susan! Here is your calendar of appointments and activities for today

S	M	T	W	T	F	S
30	31	1	2	3	4	5
6	7	8	9	10	11	12
13	14	15	16	17	18	19
20	21	22	23	24	25	26
27	28	29	30	31	1	2
3	4	5	6	7	8	9

Thursday 17 August, 1995

Done	Time	Activity	Tag	
☐ .	6:00am			(link)
☐ .	7:00am			(link)
☒ .	8:00am	Portfolio review breakfast	Roberts	(link)
☐ .	9:00am			(link)
☐ .	10:00am			(link)
☒ .	11:00am	Sales call	Fiori	(link)
☐ .	12:00pm			(link)
☐ .	1:00pm			(link)

[OK] [Month] [Next] [Previous] ⬇ ⬆ [To Do]

(B)

Figure 8.7
Prototyping a portfolio management application. This figure illustrates the process of prototyping one screen for the Financial Manager, a client and portfolio management application for securities brokers. Figure 8.7A shows an early version of the on-line appointment screen. Based on the special needs of a client, Figure 8.7B has several enhancements: a "done" indicator to show whether the task has been completed, a "link" to reference information maintained by the system on the client with whom the broker has an appointment, and a more detailed date information line.

Prototyping is best suited for smaller applications—large systems would have to be subdivided so that prototypes can be built one part at a time, which may not be possible without a thorough requirements analysis using the conventional approach (Alavi, 1984).

Rapid prototyping can gloss over essential steps in systems development. The appeal of an easily and rapidly developed prototype may encourage the development team to move too quickly toward a working model without capturing even a basic set of requirements.

The final steps to convert the prototype into a polished production system may not be carried out. Once finished, if the prototype works reasonably well, management may not see the need for reprogramming, redesign or full testing, resulting in hastily constructed systems that may be difficult to maintain and support. Since prototypes are not carefully constructed, their technical performance may be very inefficient. They may not easily accommodate large quantities of data or a large number of users in a production environment. Prototyped systems also still need to be fully documented and tested, but often these steps, too, are shortchanged. Because prototypes are constructed so effortlessly, managers may assume that testing can be handled by users on their own; any oversights in testing can be corrected later. Because the system is so easily changed, documentation may not be kept up to date.

Developing Systems with Application Software Packages

Application software package:
Set of prewritten, precoded application software programs that are commercially available for sale or lease.

Another alternative strategy is to develop an information system by purchasing an application software package. As introduced in Chapter 5, an **application software package** is a set of prewritten, precoded application software programs that is commercially available for sale or lease. Application software packages may range from a simple task (e.g., printing address labels from a database on a microcomputer) to over 400 program modules with 500,000 lines of code for a complex mainframe payroll system. Packages have flourished because so many applications are common to all business organizations. For such universal functions with standard accounting practices, a generalized system will fulfill the requirements of many organizations. Table 8.6 provides a list of common examples of commercially available application packages.

Table 8.6 EXAMPLES OF APPLICATIONS FOR WHICH APPLICATION PACKAGES ARE AVAILABLE

Accounts payable	Installment loans
Accounts receivable	Inventory control
Architectural design	Job accounting
Banking systems	Job costing
Bond and stock management	
Check processing	Library systems
Computer-aided design	Life insurance
Construction costing	Mailing labels
Data management systems	Mathematical/statistical modeling
Document imaging	Order entry
Electrical engineering	Payroll
Education	Performance measurement
E-mail	Process control
Financial control	Real estate management
Forecasting and modeling	Route scheduling
Forms design	Sales and distribution
General ledger	Savings systems
Graphics	Stock management
Government purchasing	Tax accounting
Health care	Utilities control
Health insurance	Word processing
Hotel management	Work scheduling
Human resources	

When an appropriate software package is available, it is not necessary for a company to write its own programs. A prewritten, predesigned, pretested software package can fulfill the requirements and can be substituted instead. It reduces the amount of design, testing, installation, and maintenance work as well. Since the package vendor has already done so much of the work, the time frame and costs for developing a new system can be considerably reduced. Using packaged software also frees up a firm's own internal information systems staff for other tasks or allows the firm to develop a system when its staff lacks the requisite technical expertise.

ADVANTAGES OF PACKAGES

Using other development strategies, design activities may easily consume 50 percent or more of the development effort. However, with packages, design specifications, file structure, processing relationships, transactions, and reports have already been worked out by the package vendor so that most of the design work has been accomplished. Software package programs are extensively pretested before they are marketed so that purchaser testing can be accomplished in a relatively shorter period. Vendors provide much of the ongoing maintenance and support for the system and supply enhancements that keep the system in line with technological developments. They also assume the responsibility for making changes to keep the system in compliance with changing government regulations.

Since maintenance costs can consume 50 to 80 percent of information systems budgets, the package solution is one way to cut these costs and free up internal staff for other applications. The package vendor maintains a permanent support staff with expert knowledge of the specific application package. The vendor also keeps the system and user documentation for the system up to date.

DISADVANTAGES OF PACKAGES

Package disadvantages can be considerable, even overwhelming, with a complex system. Commercial software has not yet achieved the level of sophistication and technical quality needed to produce multipurpose packages that can do everything well that users want in a specific application. To maximize market appeal, packages are geared to the most common requirements of all organizations.

What happens to the unique organizational requirements that the package does not address? To varying degrees, package software developers anticipate this problem by providing features for customization that do not alter the basic software. **Customization** features allow a software package to be modified to meet some of an organization's unique requirements without destroying the

Customization: The modification of a software package to meet an organization's unique requirements without destroying the integrity of the package software.

This screen shows a customized application for a client using the CA-Clipper software package from Computer Associates. The package is creating an interactive database from the scanned files of a technical book.

integrity of the package software. For instance, some packages may allocate parts of their files or databases to maintain an organization's own unique pieces of data; others may have a modular design that allows clients to select only the software functions they need from an array of options. Another approach to unique needs is to add front- or back-end programs that run before or after the package and do not interfere with the package software. However, these front or back ends may be far more extensive than the package software itself. Ultimately, required customizing modification and additional programming may become so expensive and time-consuming that they eliminate many advantages of the package. Figure 8.8 shows how package costs rise with the degree of customization in relation to total implementation costs.

The initial purchase price of the package can be deceptive because of these hidden implementation costs. An internal study by one company of the cost and time required to install six major application packages (including manufacturing resources planning, the general ledger, accounts receivable, and fixed assets) showed that total implementation costs ranged from 1.5 to 11 times the purchase price of the package. The ratio was highest for packages with many interfaces to other systems. The same study showed that management and support costs for the first year following installation averaged twice the original package purchase price.

SELECTING SOFTWARE PACKAGES

Application software packages must be thoroughly evaluated before they can be used as the foundation of a new information system. The most important evaluation criteria are the functions provided by the package, flexibility, user-friendliness, technical requirements, installation and maintenance effort, documentation, vendor quality, and cost. The package evaluation process is often based on a **Request for Proposal (RFP)**, which is a detailed list of questions submitted to vendors of packaged software. The RFP is likely to include questions such as the following:

Functions Included: How many of the functional requirements will the package meet?

Flexibility: How easy is the package to modify? What customization features are included (optional modules, user data areas)?

Request for Proposal (RFP): Detailed list of questions submitted to vendors of packaged software or other computer services to determine if the vendor's product can meet the organization's specific requirements.

Figure 8.8
The effects of customizing a package on total implementation costs. Installing a package always requires some modifications. But as the modifications rise, so does the cost of implementing the package. Sometimes the savings promised by the package are whittled away by excessive changes. As the number of lines of code changed approaches 5 percent of the total lines in the package, the costs of implementation rise fivefold.

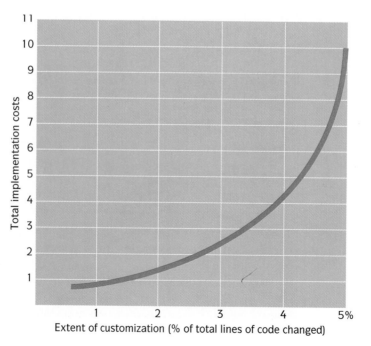

User Friendliness: How easy is the package to use and control from a non-technical standpoint? How much training is required to understand the package system?

Technical Requirements: What model computer can the package run on? What are the package's operating system, disk storage, and tape drive requirements? What kind of database/file structure does the package use?

Installation and Maintenance: How difficult would it be to convert from the current system to the package system? What is the minimum internal staff necessary for ongoing maintenance and support (applications programmers, analysts, database specialists)?

Documentation: What kind of user and system documentation does the vendor provide with the package? Is it complete, easy to understand and use?

Vendor Quality: Is the vendor experienced in this application area? Does the vendor have a strong sales and financial record? What kinds of support facilities does the vendor provide? Does the vendor have an active user group?

Cost: What is the purchase or lease price of the basic software? What does the purchase price include (add-on modules; on-line, retrieval, or screen generator facilities; consulting time; training; installation support)? Is there a yearly maintenance fee? What are the annual operating costs for the estimated volume of processing expected from the package?

When a system is developed using an application software package, systems analysis will include a package evaluation effort. Design activities will focus on matching requirements to package features. Instead of tailoring the system design specifications directly to user requirements, the design effort will consist of trying to mold user requirements to conform to the features of the package.

When a software package solution is selected, the organization no longer has total control over the system design process. Even with the most flexible and easily customized package, there are limits to the amount of tailoring allowed. Firms that are experienced in using packaged software for major business applications have noted that even the best packages cannot be expected to meet more than 70 percent of most organizations' requirements. But what about the remaining 30 percent? They will have to go unmet by the package or be satisfied by other means. If the package cannot adapt to the organization, the organization will have to adapt to the package and change its procedures.

End-User Development

End-user development: The development of information systems by end users with little or no formal assistance from technical specialists.

In many organizations, end users are developing a growing percentage of information systems with little or no formal assistance from technical specialists. This phenomenon, called **end-user development,** has been made possible by the special fourth-generation software tools introduced in Chapter 5. With fourth-generation languages, graphics languages, and microcomputer tools, end users can often access data, create reports, and develop entire information systems on their own, with little or no professional systems analyst or programmer support. Many of these end-user-developed systems can be created much more rapidly than with the traditional systems life cycle. Figure 8.9 illustrates the concept of end-user development in comparison to Traditional Systems (Life-cycle) Development.

END-USER COMPUTING
TOOLS: STRENGTHS AND
LIMITATIONS

Many organizations have reported appreciable gains in application development productivity by using fourth-generation tools. Productivity enhancements based on conventional programming languages, such as structured programming (see Chapter 9), have only resulted in a maximum productivity improvement of 25 percent (Jones, 1979). In contrast, some studies of organizations developing applications with fourth-generation tools have reported productivity gains of 300 to 500 percent (Green, 1984–85; Harel, 1985). Fourth-generation tools

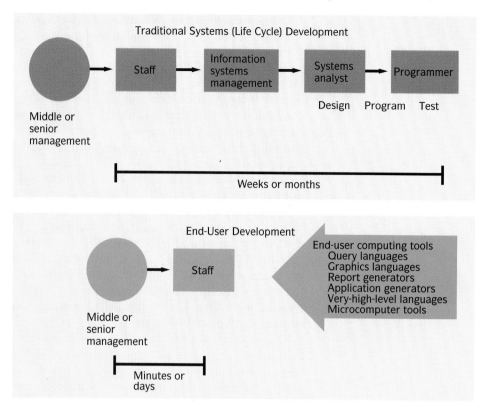

Figure 8.9
End-user versus systems life cycle development. End users can access computerized information directly or develop information systems with minimal or no formal technical assistance. On the whole, end-user developed systems can be completed more rapidly than those developed through the conventional systems life cycle. *Source: Adapted from James Martin,* Applications Development Without Programmers, © *1982, p. 119. Adapted by permission of Prentice-Hall, Englewood Cliffs, NJ.*

also have new capabilities, such as graphics, spreadsheets, modeling, and ad hoc information retrieval, that meet important business needs.

Unfortunately, fourth-generation tools still cannot replace conventional tools for some business applications because their capabilities remain limited. Fourth-generation processing is relatively inefficient, processing individual transactions too slowly and at too high a cost to make these systems suitable for large transaction processing systems. For instance, the New Jersey State Division of Motor Vehicles had a backlog of 1.4 million vehicle registration and ownership records that could not be processed quickly because the department had built its new vehicle registration system using Ideal, a fourth-generation tool. Part of the system had to be reprogrammed in COBOL to accommodate the high transaction volume.

Most fourth-generation tools are nonprocedural and cannot easily handle applications with extensive procedural logic and updating requirements, such as systems used for optimal production scheduling, or tracking daily trades of stocks, bonds, and other securities. Procedural logic must be used to specify processing functions, utility functions, error-handling conditions, specialized interfaces, and highly customized reporting. Finally, fourth-generation tools make their greatest contribution to programming and detail design and have little impact on other system-building activities. Productivity in systems analysis, procedural changes, conversion, and other aspects of design are largely independent of the choice of programming tool.

MANAGEMENT BENEFITS AND PROBLEMS

Without question, end-user development provides many benefits to organizations. These include the following:

• *Improved requirements determination* as users specify their own business needs.

- *Increased user involvement and satisfaction.* As users develop their systems themselves and control the systems development process, they are more likely to use the systems.
- *Reduced application backlog* when users are no longer totally reliant upon overburdened professional information systems specialists.

At the same time, independent end-user development has created problems for organizations because the systems created this way are outside the traditional mechanisms for information system management and control. Most organizations have not yet developed strategies to ensure that end-user-developed applications meet organizational objectives or meet quality assurance standards appropriate to their function. When systems are created rapidly, without a formal development methodology, testing and documentation may be inadequate. Completeness and validity controls may be lacking for data input and updating. Audit trails, operating controls, project controls, and standards for stable interfaces among subsystems may be missing (Chapter 13 provides more detail on these controls).

Control over data can be lost in systems that are outside the traditional information systems department. When users create their own applications and files, it will become increasingly difficult to determine where data are located and to ensure that the same piece of information (such as product number or annual earnings) is used consistently throughout the organization (more details on the problem of uncontrolled data can be found in Chapters 6 and 7).

POLICIES AND PROCEDURES TO MANAGE END-USER COMPUTING

Information center: A special facility within an organization that provides training and support for end-user computing.

How can organizations maximize the benefits of end-user applications development while keeping it under management control? We now describe several strategies.

One way both to facilitate and to manage end-user application development is to set up an information center. The **information center** is a special facility that provides training and support for end-user computing. Information centers feature hardware, software, and technical specialists that supply end users with tools, training, and expert advice so that they can create information system applications on their own. Information center consultants are available to

Employees of this corporation are taking a computer class in their corporation-sponsored information center.

instruct users and to assist in the development of more complex applications. Information center staff members combine expert knowledge of the hardware, software, and databases for end-user applications with strong interpersonal communications skills. They function primarily as teachers and consultants to users, but they may also take part in the analysis, design, and programming of more complex applications. Typical services provided by information center staff include the following:

- Evaluating new hardware and software.
- Consulting on appropriate tools and methodologies for developing applications.
- Training in high-level languages and development tools.
- Generation and modification of prototypes.
- Assistance in debugging programs.
- Assistance in accessing data.
- Assistance with applications, queries, and reports requiring high-level programming languages.
- Providing liaison with other information-processing groups (such as database specialists) that support information center resources.

Information centers provide many management benefits. They can help end users find tools and applications that will make them more productive. They prevent the creation of redundant applications. They promote data sharing and minimize integrity problems (see Chapter 6). They ensure that the applications developed by end users meet audit, data quality, and security standards.

Another important benefit of information centers is that they can help establish and enforce corporate standards for hardware and software so that end users do not introduce disparate and incompatible technologies into the firm (Fuller and Swanson, 1992; see Chapter 7). The information center will only assist users with hardware and software that have been approved by management.

In addition to using information centers, managers can pursue other strategies to ensure that end-user computing serves larger organizational goals (see Alavi, Nelson, and Weiss, 1987–88; Rockart and Flannery, 1983). Management should control the development of end-user applications by incorporating them into its strategic systems plans. The methodologies for establishing organization-wide information requirements that were described earlier in this chapter can help identify end-user applications with organization-wide benefits. Management should also develop controls on critical end-user development, such as insisting on cost justification of end-user information system projects and establishing hardware, software, and quality standards for user-developed applications.

Outsourcing Information Systems

Outsourcing: The practice of contracting computer center operations, telecommunications networks, or applications development to external vendors.

If a firm does not want to use its own internal resources to build and operate information systems, it can hire an external organization that specializes in providing these services to do the work. The process of turning over an organization's computer center operations, telecommunications networks, or applications development to external vendors of these services is called **outsourcing**. In firms where the cost of information systems function has risen rapidly, managers are also turning to outsourcing to control these costs.

ADVANTAGES AND DISADVANTAGES OF OUTSOURCING

Outsourcing is becoming popular because some organizations perceive it as being more cost-effective than it would be to maintain their own computer center and information systems staff. The provider of outsourcing services can benefit from economies of scale (the same knowledge, skills, and capacity can be shared with many different customers) and is likely to charge competitive prices for information systems services. Outsourcing allows a company with fluctuating needs for computer processing to pay for only what it uses rather than to build its own computer center to stand underutilized when there is no peak load. Some firms outsource because their internal information systems staff cannot keep pace with technological change or because they want to free up scarce and costly talent for activities with higher payback.

But not all organizations benefit from outsourcing, and the disadvantages of outsourcing can create serious problems for organizations if they are not well understood and managed. When a firm farms out the responsibility for developing and operating its information systems, it can lose control over its information systems function. Outsourcing can place the vendor in an advantageous position where the client has to accept whatever the vendor does and whatever fees the vendors charge. This dependency could eventually result in higher costs or loss of control over technological direction. Trade secrets or proprietary information may leak out to competitors because a firm's information systems are being run or developed by outsiders. This could be especially harmful if a firm allows an outsourcer to develop or to operate applications that give it some type of competitive advantage.

WHEN TO USE OUTSOURCING
If systems development and operations functions are well managed and productive, there may not be much immediate benefit that can be provided by an external vendor. However, there are a number of circumstances under which outsourcing makes a great deal of sense:

- *When there is limited opportunity for the firm to distinguish itself competitively through a particular information systems application or series of applications.* Figure 8.10 illustrates a matrix that could help firms determine appropriate applications for outsourcing. Applications such as payroll or cafeteria accounting, for which the firm obtains little competitive advantage from excellence, are strong candidates for outsourcing. On the other hand, applications such as airline reservations or plant scheduling could provide a firm with a distinct advantage over competitors. The firm

Figure 8.10
Rewards and penalties of outsourcing. This reward/penalty matrix shows that those applications with low reward for excellence and low penalty for problems are good candidates for outsourcing. *Source: Paul Clermont, "Outsourcing Without Guilt,"* Computerworld, *(September 9, 1991). Copyright 1991 by CW Publishing, Inc., Framingham, MA 01701. Reprinted from* Computerworld.

In Calgary, the heart of Canada's oil country, six major oil and gas companies decided to form a consortium to establish a common production accounting center. The center would provide both oil field accounting services and the information systems processing for these services. A team of outside contractors, consisting of a provider of computer services and an accounting firm, would manage the center.

The members of the consortium— Mobil Oil Canada; Esso Resources; Gulf Canada Resources, Ltd.; Pan-Canadian Petroleum, Ltd.; Petro-Canada; and Shell Canada Ltd.— originally banded together in early 1991 to persuade a vendor to make enhancements to the software they were all using. They then found that they could work together to solve other common problems too. These oil companies were duplicating many efforts. Oil wells are owned by numerous partners, each of whom is required to perform the same kind of accounting for functions such as royalty payments. The oil companies found that a combined information systems processing and accounting center run by an external consultant could meet up to 75 percent of each company's production accounting requirements and provide 10 percent of each company's total information sys-

tems operations if it was used as a common shared resource.

Consortium members contributed $1 to $2 million and a staff of 50 to develop a coordinated suite of 20 different accounting applications that they can share. They are examining IBM and Electronic Data Services (EDS) Corporations as potential contractors.

Consortium members believe that this outsourcing arrangement will cut information systems processing costs and trim payrolls by thousands of jobs. It will also open up a new source of revenue because the combined information-processing and accounting center can offer its services to other companies in the region.

The Canadian oil company consortium's plans illustrate how information systems outsourcing is being combined with business functions. Management is realizing that if information systems can be outsourced, other organizational functions can be taken over by outsiders as well.

The closest comparison to the Canadian consortium is the combined data-processing and accounting center operated by Andersen Consulting in Aberdeen, Scotland, for British Petroleum Exploration's North Sea oil fields. The outsourcing contract trans-

ferred 250 former members of British Petroleum's accounting and information systems staff to Andersen.

Andersen Consulting provides its customers with high-level strategic planning as well as application management, systems development, and other products and services. It helps the organization place its information systems strategy in the context of how to remain competitive, examining whether the customer should be in certain businesses or not and evaluating user departments, policies, and procedures to determine if the company is organized properly.

Sources: Bruce Caldwell, "Slick Moves in the Back Office," *InformationWEEK,* January 27, 1992; and Dennis Livingston, "Outsourcing: Look Beyond the Price Tag," *Datamation,* November 15, 1992.

To Think About: Do you think that outsourcing was the right decision for this Canadian consortium? Why or why not? What organizational changes can be set about by outsourcing? If you were a manager, what management, technology, and organization factors would you use to decide on whether to outsource your business functions along with your information systems functions?

could lose profits, customers, or market share if such systems have problems. Applications where the rewards for excellence and the penalties for failure are high should probably be developed and operated internally.

- *When the predictability of uninterrupted information systems service is not very important.* For instance, airline reservations or catalog shopping systems are too "critical" to be trusted outside. If these systems failed to operate for a few days or even a few hours, they could close down the business (see Chapter 2). On the other hand, a system to process employee insurance claims could be more easily outsourced because uninterrupted processing of claims is not critical to the survival of the firm.

- *When the firm's existing information system capabilities are limited, ineffective, or technically inferior.* Some organizations use outsourcers as an easy way to revamp their information systems technology. For instance, they might use an outsourcer to help them make the transition from traditional mainframe-based computing to a distributed client/server computing environment.

Setting technology strategy is one area that companies should not abdicate to outsourcers. The strategic task is best kept in-house.

The Window on Management shows that sometimes it makes sense for firms to outsource not only specific information system applications but also the entire business functional area supported by those applications.

Table 8.7 compares the advantages and disadvantages of each of the systems-building alternatives described in this chapter.

Table 8.7 COMPARISON OF SYSTEMS DEVELOPMENT APPROACHES

Approach	Features	Advantages	Disadvantages
Systems life cycle	Sequential step-by-step formal process Written specifications and approvals Limited role of users	Necessary for large complex systems and projects	Slow and expensive Discourages changes Massive paperwork to manage
Prototyping	Requirements specified dynamically with experimental system Rapid, informal and iterative process Users continually interact with the prototype	Rapid and inexpensive Useful when requirements uncertain or when end-user interface is important Promotes user participation	Inappropriate for large complex systems Can gloss over important steps in analysis, documentation, and testing
Application software package	Commercial software reduces need for internally developed software programs	Design, programming, installation, and maintenance work reduced Can save time and cost when developing common business applications Reduces need for internal information systems resources	May not meet organization's unique requirements May not perform many business functions well Extensive customization raises development costs
End-user development	Systems created by end users using fourth-generation software tools Rapid and informal Minimal role of information systems specialists	Users control systems building Saves development time and cost Reduces application backlog	Can lead to proliferation of uncontrolled information systems Systems do not always meet quality assurance standards
Outsourcing	Systems built and sometimes operated by external vendor	Can reduce or control costs Can produce systems when internal resources not available or technically deficient	Loss of control over the information systems function Dependence on the technical direction and prosperity of external vendors

1. **Major risks and uncertainties in systems development.** Information systems development has major risks and uncertainties that make it difficult for the systems to achieve their goals. Sometimes the cost of achieving them is too high. One problem is the difficulty of establishing information requirements, both for individual end users and for the organization as a whole. The requirements may be too complex or subject to change. Another problem is that the time and cost factors to develop an information system are very difficult to analyze, especially in large projects. Chapter 9 describes some ways of dealing with these risks and uncertainties, but the issues remain major management challenges.

2. **Determining the right systems development strategy to use.** Sometimes organizations encounter problems that cannot be addressed by any of the systems development strategies described in this chapter. For instance, a large, complex system may have some unstructured features. The ultimate configuration of the system cannot be decided beforehand because information requirements or the appropriate technology are uncertain. Alternatively, a proposed system calls for major organizational as well as technical changes. In such instances, a firm may need to pursue a strategy of phased commitment in which systems projects are broken down into smaller portions and developed piece-by-piece in phases, or a firm may need to postpone the project altogether.

3. **Controlling information systems development outside the information systems department.** There may not be a way to establish standards and controls for end-user development that are appropriate. Standards and controls that are too restrictive may not only generate user resistance but may also stifle end-user innovation. If controls are too weak, the firm may encounter serious problems with data integrity and connectivity. It is not always possible to find the right balance.

Summary

Explain how building a new information system represents a process of organizational change.

Building a new information system is a form of planned organizational change that involves many different people in the organization. Because information systems are sociotechnical entities, a change in information systems involves changes in work, management, and the organization. Information systems can bring about powerful organizational changes if they are used to redesign business processes.

Organizations should develop an information systems plan that describes how information technology supports the attainment of their goals. The plan indicates the direction of systems development, the rationale, implementation strategy, and budget. Enterprise analysis and critical success factors (CSFs) can be used to elicit organization-wide information requirements that must be addressed by the plan.

Identify the core activities in the systems development process.

The core activities in systems development are systems analysis, systems design, programming, testing, conversion, and production and maintenance. Systems analysis is the study and analysis of problems of existing systems and the identification of requirements for their solution. Systems design provides the specifications for an information system solution, showing how its technical and organizational components fit together.

Distinguish between the various systems-building alternatives: the traditional systems life cycle, prototyping, application software packages, end-user development, and outsourcing.

The traditional systems life cycle—the oldest method for building systems—breaks the development of an information system into six formal stages: project definition, systems study, design, programming, installation, and post-implementation. The stages must proceed sequentially, have defined outputs, and require formal approval before the next stage can commence.

Prototyping consists of building an experimental system rapidly and inexpensively for end users to interact with and evaluate. The prototype is refined and enhanced until users are satisfied that it captures all of their requirements and can be used as a template to create the final system.

Developing an information system using an application software package eliminates the need for internally developed software programs when developing an information system. Using a software package cuts down on the amount of design, testing, installation, and maintenance work required to build a system.

End-user development is the development of information systems by end users, either alone or with minimal assistance from information systems specialists. End-user-developed systems can be created rapidly and informally using fourth-generation software tools.

Outsourcing consists of using an external vendor to build (or operate) a firm's information systems. The system may be custom-built or may use a software package. In either case, the work is done by the vendor rather than by the organization's internal information systems staff.

Understand the strengths and limitations of each approach.

The traditional system life cycle is still useful for large projects that need formal specifications and tight management control over each stage of system building. However, the traditional method is very rigid and costly for developing a system and is not well suited for unstructured, decision-oriented applications where requirements cannot be immediately visualized.

Prototyping encourages end-user involvement in systems development and iteration of design until specifications are captured accurately. The rapid creation of prototypes can result in systems that have not been completely tested or documented or that are technically inadequate for a production environment.

Application software packages are helpful if a firm does not have the internal information systems staff or financial resources to custom-develop a system. To meet an organization's unique requirements, packages may require extensive modifications that can substantially raise development costs. A package may not be a feasible solution if implementation necessitates extensive customization and changes in the organization's procedures.

The primary benefits of end-user development are improved requirements determination, reduced application backlog, and increased end-user participation in and control of the systems development process. However, end-user development, in conjunction with distributed processing, has introduced new organizational risks by propagating information systems and data resources that do not necessarily meet quality assurance standards and that are not easily controlled by traditional means.

Outsourcing can save application development costs or allow firms to develop applications without an internal information systems staff, but it can also make firms lose control over their information systems and make them too dependent on external vendors.

Key Terms		
Information systems plan	Technical feasibility
Enterprise analysis	Economic feasibility
Critical success factors (CSFs)	Operational feasibility
Business process	Intangible benefits
Systems development	Tangible benefits
Systems analysis	Information requirements
Feasibility study	Systems design

Logical design
Physical design
Programming
Testing
Unit testing
System testing
Acceptance testing
Test plan
Conversion
Parallel strategy
Direct cutover
Pilot study
Phased approach
Conversion plan
Documentation
Production
Maintenance

Systems life cycle
Project definition
Systems study
Design
Programming stage
Installation
Post-implementation
Prototyping
Prototype
Iterative
End-user interface
Application software package
Customization
Request for Proposal (RFP)
End-user development
Information center
Outsourcing

Review Questions

1. What are the major categories of an information systems plan?

2. How can enterprise analysis and critical success factors be used to establish organization-wide information system requirements?

3. What is business process redesign? How is it related to systems development?

4. What is the difference between systems analysis and systems design?

5. What are information requirements? Why are they difficult to determine correctly?

6. Why is the testing stage of systems development so important? Name and describe the three stages of testing for an information system.

7. What is conversion? Why is it important to have a detailed conversion plan?

8. What role do programming, production, and maintenance play in systems development?

9. What is the traditional systems life cycle? What are its characteristics?

10. What are the advantages and disadvantages of building an information system using the traditional systems life cycle?

11. What is prototyping? What are the stages in the prototyping process?

12. List and describe the advantages and disadvantages of prototyping.

13. What are the principal advantages and disadvantages of using application software packages to develop an information system?

14. What is package customization? Under what circumstances can it become a problem when implementing an application software package?

15. What are the advantages and disadvantages of end-user development? What kinds of problems is it suited for?

16. What is an information center? How can information centers solve some of the management problems created by end-user development?

17. What is outsourcing? Under what circumstances should it be used for building information systems?

18. What are the advantages and disadvantages of outsourcing?

Discussion Questions

1. It has been said that information systems design cannot be directed by technical specialists alone. Discuss.

2. Information systems often have to be redesigned after testing. Discuss.

3. Some have said that the best way to avoid using professional programmers is to install an application software package. Discuss.

With a group of your classmates, obtain product information or attend a demonstration for a microcomputer application software package such as DacEasy Accounting/Payroll, Quicken, Managing Your Money, or Microsoft Profit for Windows. Write an analysis of the strengths and limitations of the package you select. Present your findings to the class.

CASE STUDY

Curing Chaos

Methodist Hospital is a large teaching hospital in Indianapolis, Indiana. In 1990, it had about 43,000 patient admissions, served 250,000 outpatients, and handled 80,000 emergency room visits. During the 1970s, Methodist Hospital purchased a mainframe-based turnkey billing and patient records system from TDS Healthcare Systems Corporation of Atlanta. A turnkey system is delivered to a customer as a complete hardware and software configuration. The client simply has to "turn the key" to begin the system. Since then, the hospital's information systems department has spent most of their time maintaining the old system and working on a five- to seven-year application backlog. User departments such as the hospital laboratory and emergency room became frustrated because their computing needs could not be satisfied. So they bought their own systems, none of which communicated with the others.

When Walter Zerrenner took over as Methodist Hospital's chief information officer in 1989, he found three strategic information systems plans sitting on a shelf. There was never any time to implement them. The plans were developed without any user input, so no one outside the information systems department was committed to them.

Zerrenner brought in a team from Andersen Consulting in Chicago to assess the state of the hospital's information systems department as well as user attitudes toward the department. The assessment turned up three incompatible wide area networks, more than 20 incompatible local area networks, and more than 100 different information systems throughout the hospital.

Information systems in different departments in Methodist Hospital used different identification codes for the same patients. Patients had to register separately in each department, often answering the same questions over and over again. The TDS patient management system showed that lab tests were scheduled but did not display the results. The results of the tests were stored on a separate departmental system in the lab. The only place to find complete information on a patient was in a paper file.

The TDS system could only be accessed from terminals located within the hospital. Physicians complained that they could not use microcomputers in their offices or in clinics to dial into the TDS system for patient information. The TDS system only kept information on patients who were formally admitted to the hospital. Even that information was only available on line for five days after a patient's discharge. If a discharged patient had unforeseen complications, his or her medical records could only be found in manual paper files. Additionally, the TDS system did not handle outpatients or people who merely came in for tests. Yet many users liked the way the TDS system worked. Dr. Chris Steffy, a resident in internal medicine, believed it was more efficient and rich in functions than other systems he had used.

Zerrenner formed a 25-member information systems planning committee with representatives from all of the hospital's major departments, including a contingent of physicians and nurses. Zerrenner and the planning committee identified three options for an improved patient information system: 1) scrap the existing systems; 2) try to make all of the existing systems communicate with each other; and 3) establish a centralized database for the data collected by individual departments.

The first solution meant walking away from the hospital's enormous investment in existing systems, which did work well for individual departments. The second solution appeared to be a logistical nightmare because the information systems department would have had to create a separate interface for every departmental system. Physicians would have had to sit at terminals and sign on and off each individual system. The third solution seemed the only reasonable choice. The database could obtain information from each departmental system and make it commonly available.

Zerrenner built a working model of the new system, called the Information Exchange Platform (IXP), for users to evaluate. People were encouraged to sit down at a workstation, sign on with a password, and use a mouse to move around sample windows, viewing patient data, graphing the results, or sending the data via E-mail to another physician for consultation. The system uses the Sybase relational database management system running on an IBM RS/6000 file server. From the prototype, the development team created a pilot system. The pilot features a patient care application that provides physicians with patient information generated by hospital procedures and an application that allows a person to access the laboratory computer system, the radiology computer system, and the physician office system on IXP microcomputer workstations.

The Information Exchange Platform was never designed to capture all of the data from individual departments. A second committee, a broad-based information systems steering committee formed by Zerrenner, is determining what information is needed by multiple departments. The project has adopted an 80/20 rule, focusing on the most important information that is used 80 percent of the time. Most of that information consists of lab, radiology, patient demographics, and electrocardiogram interpretations.

Sources: Scott D. Palmer, "A Plan That Cured Chaos," *Datamation,* January 1, 1993; and E. W. Martin, "Methodist Hospital of Indiana, Inc.," in Martin, De Hayes, Hoffer, and Perkins, *Managing Information Technology* (New York: Macmillan Publishing, 1994).

Case Study Questions

1. Prepare a report analyzing the problems with Methodist Hospital's systems. Describe the problems and their causes. What management, organization, and technology factors were responsible?

2. If you were the systems analyst for this project, list five questions you would ask during interviews to elicit the information needed for your systems analysis report.

3. Do you agree that the Information Exchange Platform was the best solution for Methodist Hospital? Why or why not? What would you recommend? Why?

4. Evaluate the approach to systems building that was used for the IXP project.

5. Describe the role of end users and technical specialists in analyzing the problem and in developing the solution.

6. What conversion strategy would you use when the Information Exchange Platform is completed?

7. Why could it be said that the Information Exchange Platform is only one part of the solution for Methodist Hospital?

References

Ahituv, Niv, and Seev Neumann. "A Flexible Approach to Information System Development." *MIS Quarterly* (June 1984).

Alavi, Maryam. "An Assessment of the Prototyping Approach to Information System Development." *Communications of the ACM 27* (June 1984).

Alavi, Maryam, R. Ryan Nelson, and Ira R. Weiss. "Strategies for End-User Computing: An Integrative Framework." *Journal of Management Information Systems* 4, no. 3 (Winter 1987–88).

Alter, Steven, and Michael Ginzberg. "Managing Uncertainty in MIS Implementation." *Sloan Management Review* 20 (Fall 1978).

Anderson, Evan A. "Choice Models for the Evaluation and Selection of Software Packages." *Journal of Management Information Systems* 6, no. 4 (Spring 1990).

Arthur, Lowell Jay. "Quick and Dirty." *Computerworld* (December 14, 1992).

Bacon, C. James. "The Uses of Decision Criteria in Selecting Information Systems/Technology Investments." *MIS Quarterly* 16, no. 3 (September 1992).

Bostrum, R. P., and J. S. Heinen. "MIS Problems and Failures: A Socio-Technical Perspective; Part I: The Causes." *MIS Quarterly* 1 (September 1977); "Part II: The Application of Socio-Technical Theory." *MIS Quarterly* 1 (December 1977).

Bullen, Christine, and John F. Rockart. "A Primer on Critical Success Factors." Cambridge, MA: Center for Information Systems Research, Sloan School of Management, 1981.

Buss, Martin D. J. "How to Rank Computer Projects." *Harvard Business Review* (January 1983).

Caldwell, Bruce. "Blue Cross, in Intensive Care, Beeps EDS." *InformationWEEK* (January 27, 1992).

Carr, Houston H. "Information Centers: The IBM Model vs. Practice." *MIS Quarterly* (September 1987).

Cerveny, Robert P., Edward J. Garrity, and G. Lawrence Sanders. "A Problem-Solving Perspective on Systems Development." *Journal of Management Information Systems* 6, no. 4 (Spring 1990).

Cerveny, Robert P., Edward J. Garrity, and G. Lawrence Sanders. "The Application of Prototyping to Systems Development: A Rationale and Model." *Journal of Management Information Systems* 3 (Fall 1986).

Christoff, Kurt A. "Building a Fourth Generation Environment." *Datamation* (September 1985).

Clermont, Paul. "Outsourcing Without Guilt." *Computerworld* (September 9, 1991).

Cotterman, William W., and Kuldeep Kumar. "User Cube: A Taxonomy of End Users." *Communications of the ACM* 32, no. 11 (November 1989).

Davenport, Thomas H., and James E. Short. "The New Industrial Engineering: Information Technology and Business Process Redesign." *Sloan Management Review* 31, no. 4 (Summer 1990).

Davis, Gordon B. "Determining Management Information Needs: A Comparison of Methods." *MIS Quarterly* 1 (June 1977).

Davis, Gordon B. "Information Analysis for Information System Development." *Systems Analysis and Design: A Foundation for the 1980's*. Ed. W. W. Cotterman, J. D. Cougar, N. L. Enger, and F. Harold. New York: Wiley, 1981.

Davis, Gordon B. "Strategies for Information Requirements Determination." *IBM Systems Journal* 1 (1982).

Davis, Gordon B, and Margrethe H. Olson. "Support Systems for Knowledge Work." In *Management Information Systems*, 2nd ed. New York: McGraw-Hill, 1985.

Davis, Sid A., and Robert P. Bostrum. "Training End Users: An Experimental Investigation of the Role of the Computer Interface and Training Methods." *MIS Quarterly* 17, no. 1 (March 1993).

Doll, William J. "Avenues for Top Management Involvement in Successful MIS Development." *MIS Quarterly* (March 1985).

Dos Santos, Brian. "Justifying Investments in New Information Technologies." *Journal of Management Information Systems* 7, no. 4 (Spring 1991).

Ein-Dor, Philip, and Eli Segev. "Strategic Planning for Management Information Systems." *Management Science* 24, no. 15 (1978).

El Sawy, Omar, and Burt Nanus. "Toward the Design of Robust Information Systems." *Journal of Management Information Systems* 5, no. 4 (Spring 1989).

Emery, James C. "Cost/Benefit Analysis of Information Systems." Chicago: Society for Management Information Systems Workshop Report No. 1, 1971.

Flatten, Per O., Donald J. McCubbrey, P. Declan O'Riordan, and Keith Burgess. *Foundations of Business Systems*, 2nd ed. Fort Worth, TX: The Dryden Press, 1992.

Franz, Charles, and Daniel Robey. "An Investigation of User-Led System Design: Rational and Political Perspectives." *Communications of the ACM* 27 (December 1984).

Fuller, Mary K., and E. Burton Swanson. "Information Centers as Organizational Innovation." *Journal of Management Information Systems* 9, no. 1 (Summer 1992).

Gerlach, James H., and Feng-Yang Kuo. "Understanding Human-Computer Interaction for Information Systems Design." *MIS Quarterly* 15, no. 4 (December 1991).

Ginzberg, Michael J. "Improving MIS Project Selection." *Omega, Internal Journal of Management Science* 6, no. 1 (1979).

Ginzberg, Michael J. "The Impact of Organizational Characteristics on MIS Design and Implementation." Working paper CRIS 10, GBA 80-110. New York University Center for Research on Information Systems, Computer Applications and Information Systems Area, 1980.

Goodhue, Dale L., Laurie J. Kirsch, Judith A. Quillard, and Michael D. Wybo. "Strategic Data Planning: Lessons from the Field." *MIS Quarterly* 16, no. 1 (March 1992).

Gould, John D., and Clayton Lewis. "Designing for Usability: Key Principles and What Designers Think." *Communications of the ACM* 28 (March 1985).

Grant, F. J. "The Downside of 4GLs." *Datamation* (July 1985).

Green, Jesse. "Productivity in the Fourth Generation." *Journal of Management Information Systems* 1 (Winter 1984–1985).

Grudnitski, Gary. "Eliciting Decision Makers' Information Requirements." *Journal of Management Information Systems* (Summer 1984).

Hammer, Michael. "Reengineering Work: Don't Automate, Obliterate." *Harvard Business Review* (July–August 1990).

Harel, Elie C., and Ephraim R. McLean. "The Effects of Using a Nonprocedural Computer Language on Programmer Productivity." *MIS Quarterly* (June 1985).

Harrison, Allison W., and R. Kelly Rainer, Jr. "The Influence of Individual Differences on Skill in End-User Computing." *Journal of Management Information Systems* 9, no. 1 (Summer 1992).

Huff, Sid L., Malcolm C. Munro, and Barbara H. Martin. "Growth Stages of End User Computing." *Communications of the ACM* 31, no. 5 (May 1988).

Janson, Marius, and L. Douglas Smith. "Prototyping for Systems Development: A Critical Appraisal." *MIS Quarterly* 9 (December 1985).

Jenkins, A. Milton. "Prototyping: A Methodology for the Design and Development of Application Systems." *Spectrum* 2 (April 1985).

Johnson, Richard T. "The Infocenter Experience." *Datamation* (January 1984).

Jones, T. C. "The Limits of Programming Productivity." Guide and Share Application Development Symposium, Proceedings. New York: Share 1979.

Kendall, Kenneth E., and Julie E. Kendall. *Systems Analysis and Design.* Englewood Cliffs, NJ: Prentice-Hall, 1991.

Kim, Chai, and Stu Westin. "Software Maintainability: Perceptions of EDP Professionals." *MIS Quarterly* (June 1988).

King, William R. "Alternative Designs in Information System Development." *MIS Quarterly* (December 1982).

Konsynski, Benn R. "Advances in Information System Design." *Journal of Management Information Systems* 1 (Winter 1984–1985).

Kozar, Kenneth A., and John M. Mahlum. "A User-Generated Information System: An Innovative Development Approach." *MIS Quarterly* (June 1987).

Kraushaar, James M., and Larry E. Shirland. "A Prototyping Method for Applications Development by End Users and Information Systems Specialists." *MIS Quarterly* (September 1985).

Laudon, Kenneth C. "CIOs Beware: Very Large Scale Systems." New York: Center for Research on Information Systems, New York University Stern School of Business, working paper, 1989.

Lientz, Bennett P., and E. Burton Swanson. *Software Maintenance Management.* Reading, MA: Addison-Wesley, 1980.

Livingston, Dennis. "Outsourcing: Look Beyond the Price Tag." *Datamation* (November 15, 1992).

Loh, Lawrence, and N. Venkatraman. "Determinants of Information Technology Outsourcing." *Journal of Management Information Systems* 9, no. 1 (Summer 1992).

Loh, Lawrence, and N. Venkatraman. "Diffusion of Information Technology Outsourcing: Influence Sources and the Kodak Effect." *Information Systems Research* 3, no. 4 (December 1992).

Lucas, Henry C., Jr. *Toward Creative Systems Design.* New York: Columbia University Press, 1974.

Lucas, Henry C., Eric J. Walton, and Michael J. Ginzberg. "Implementing Packaged Software." *MIS Quarterly* (December 1988).

Matlin, Gerald. "What Is the Value of Investment in Information Systems?" *MIS Quarterly* 13, no. 3 (September 1989).

Martin, James. *Application Development Without Programmers.* Englewood Cliffs, NJ: Prentice-Hall, 1982.

Martin, J., and C. McClure. "Buying Software Off the Rack." *Harvard Business Review* (November–December 1983).

Mason, R. E. A., and T. T. Carey. "Prototyping Interactive Information Systems." *Communications of the ACM* 26 (May 1983).

Matos, Victor M., and Paul J. Jalics. "An Experimental Analysis of the Performance of Fourth-Generation Tools on PCs." *Communications of the ACM* 32, no. 11 (November 1989).

McFarlan, F. Warren. "Portfolio Approach to Information Systems." *Harvard Business Review* (September–October 1981).

McMullen, John. "Developing a Role for End Users." *InformationWEEK* (June 15, 1992).

Nolan, Richard L. "Managing Information Systems by Committee." *Harvard Business Review* (July–August 1982).

Parker, M. M. "Enterprise Information Analysis: Cost-Benefit Analysis and the Data-Managed System." *IBM Systems Journal* 21 (1982), pp. 108–123.

Rivard, Suzanne, and Sid L. Huff. "Factors of Success for End-User Computing." *Communications of the ACM* 31, no. 5 (May 1988).

Roche, Edward M. *Managing Information Technology in Multinational Corporations.* New York: Macmillan Publishing Company, 1992.

Rockart, John F. "Chief Executives Define Their Own Data Needs." *Harvard Business Review* (March–April 1979).

Rockart, John F., and Lauren S. Flannery. "The Management of End-User Computing." *Communications of the ACM* 26, no. 10 (October 1983).

Rockart, John F., and Michael E. Treacy. "The CEO Goes on Line." *Harvard Business Review* (January–February 1982).

Rowe, Lawrence A. "Tools for Developing OLTP Applications." *Datamation* (August 1985).

Schatz, Willie. "Bailoutsourcing." *Computerworld* (January 25, 1993).

Shank, Michael E., Andrew C. Boynton, and Robert W. Zmud. "Critical Success Factor Analysis as a Methodology for MIS Planning." *MIS Quarterly* (June 1985).

Timmreck, Eric M. "Performance Measurement: Vendor Specifications and Benchmarks." In *The Information Systems Handbook,* ed. F. Warren McFarlan and Richard C. Nolan. Homewood, IL: Dow-Jones-Richard D. Irwin, 1975.

Trauth, Eileen M., and Elliot Cole. "The Organizational Interface: A Method for Supporting End Users of Packaged Software." *MIS Quarterly* 16, no. 1 (March 1992).

Australian Bank Combats Runaway Systems

Westpac Banking Corporation, the banking giant of Sydney, Australia, had high hopes for its proposed new Core System 90. Core System 90 (CS90) was supposed to create a showcase of decentralized data systems that would allow bank branch managers to create new financial products rapidly, using expert systems and easy-to-use software for designing new applications. Ultimately CS90 was supposed to redefine the role of information technology at the bank by shrinking its cumbersome information sys-

tems department and creating a more streamlined, customer-responsive organization.

These hopes were dashed. More than three years after Westpac started to develop CS90, it admitted that the project was out of control. Westpac had spent nearly $150 million on the new system but had virtually nothing to show for the effort. The system's scheduled 1993 completion date was a pipe dream. Westpac decided to cut its losses by dropping IBM as the lead software developer for the

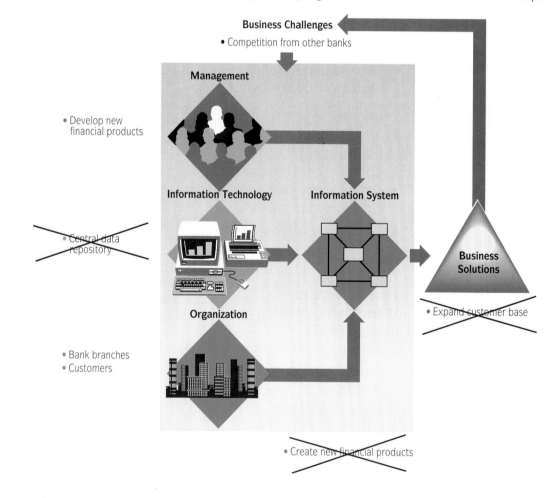

project and hiring Andersen Consulting to recommend steps to save the effort.

According to industry consultants familiar with both Westpac and IBM, CS90 was doomed to fail because it combined an ambitious business agenda with technology that didn't exist. IBM could not deliver the critical technologies it had promised for creating a central data repository that could be used throughout application development.

This system boondoggle came at exactly the wrong time for Westpac. Although the bank had $84.7 billion in assets, its loan portfolio and asset management programs were performing poorly. But Westpac is not alone. CS90 is but one of a long list of over-budget and behind-schedule computer projects. A similar fate befell Banc One and Norwest Bank in the United States when they began in 1986 to create a customer service system to tie together all of a bank's key applications along with a deposit accounting system and a loan system. Seven years and $125 million later, the system was still unfinished. The portion of the system dealing with checking, savings, and accounting for certificates of deposit was riddled with errors and did not run fast enough. A recent Peat Marwick survey showed that about 35 percent of all major information systems projects are "runaways" like the projects of these banks. Millions of dollars have been spent over budget, and projects are months or even years behind schedule.

Sources: Doug Bartholomew, "Strategic Bungling," *InformationWEEK,* October 4, 1993; and Mark Mehler, "Reining in Runaway Systems," *InformationWEEK,* December 16, 1991.

In nearly every organization, information systems take much more time and money to implement than originally anticipated, or the completed system does not work properly. Because so many information systems are trouble-ridden, designers, builders, and users of information systems should understand why they succeed or fail. Problems with information system technology such as those seen at Westpac, Banc One, and Norwest Bank are only one reason why information systems succeed or fail. Managerial and organizational factors also play a powerful role in system outcome because implementing an information system is a process of organizational change.

We have tried to explore various facets of successful information systems throughout this text, but the issues of information system quality and success are the special focus of this chapter. After first examining information system quality and the features of successful systems, we outline the problems peculiar to information systems. We then describe traditional and new methodologies and tools for improving software quality and overall system effectiveness. Finally, we explore the managerial and organizational factors that affect system outcome by looking at the process of implementation.

After completing this chapter you will be able to:

- Identify successful information systems.
- Identify major problem areas in information systems and causes of information system failure.
- Describe both traditional and new tools and methodologies for promoting software quality.
- Describe the relationship between the implementation process and system outcome.
- Describe appropriate strategies to manage the implementation process.

9.1 What Are Successful Information Systems?

What makes a successful information system? This is not always an easy question to answer because not everyone may agree about the value or effectiveness of a particular information system. But if we had to generalize, a successful system will be accurate, reliable, will work as intended, and will be widely used. The cost to develop the system will fall within the financial and budgetary limits established by the organization. The system will be of high quality.

A quality system will do the following:

- Achieve the business goals articulated by the user department.
- Operate at an acceptable cost, commensurate with the value produced for the firm.
- Meet carefully defined performance standards (such as response time and system availability).
- Produce accurate, reliable output.
- Be easy to learn and use.
- Be flexible.

Total quality management (TQM): A concept that makes quality control a responsibility to be shared by all people in an organization.

Successful information systems help promote overall quality throughout the organization, contributing to total quality management. **Total quality management (TQM)** is a concept popularized by the Japanese that makes quality a responsibility shared by all people in an organization, with the achievement of quality control as an end in itself. Everyone is expected to contribute to the overall improvement of quality—the engineer who avoids design errors, the production worker who spots defects, the sales representative who presents the product properly, and the secretary who avoids typing mistakes. Total quality management encompasses all of the functions of the organization.

Total quality management was popularized by the Japanese, who gave the responsibility for quality consistency to the workers who actually make the product or service, as opposed to a quality control department. Japanese management adopted the goal of zero defects, focusing on improving their product or service prior to delivery rather than correcting them after delivery. Studies have repeatedly shown that the earlier in the business cycle a problem is detected, the less it costs for the company to eliminate it. Thus the Japanese quality approach brought not only a shift in focus to the workers and an increased respect for product and service quality, but also lowered costs.

How Information Systems Contribute to Total Quality Management

Information systems can contribute to overall quality because the systems are deeply involved with the daily work of other departments throughout the organization. For example, IS analysts usually have taken a leading role in designing such varied departmental systems as payrolls, patent research, and chemical process control. IS professionals then maintain their knowledge of these departments through both their ongoing support of these systems and their participation in departmental information planning. In addition, often, only IS personnel know where certain data originate, how other departments use and store them, and which other functions would benefit from having access to them. With this broad understanding of the functional integration of the corporation, IS personnel can be valuable members of any quality project team.

The staff in good information systems departments has skills that are critical to the success of a quality program. Good information systems analysts are trained and experienced in analyzing and redesigning business processes. That, after all, is their job. The information systems staff is a source of ideas on the application of technology to quality issues and are often the people who make that technology available to the quality project. For example, Goodmark Foods, Inc., the leading U.S. producer of snack meats, received support from its information systems group to apply statistical analysis software to their manufacturing so workers could see when and by how much each piece of snack meat deviates from the specified weight (Mandell, 1992).

Much of information systems work is very technical. Consequently, information systems professionals can too easily look to technology as the answer to all quality problems. While technology has much to contribute, quality usually means focusing on business issues. Technology, after all, is only a tool or set of tools that, if used correctly, supports the business goals of the department or company. The Window on Organizations is an example of a successful IS quality program that was possible only because of a focus on business goals and organizational needs.

This quality assurance technician at the General Tire and Rubber Company in Charlotte, NC, is gathering real-time data on materials for manufacturing and production processing.

ORGANIZATIONS

Information Systems Help Nashua Meet Quality Goals

Even within information systems departments, quality may not be an issue of technology. Tim Gallagher, MIS director of Nashua Corporation, a $590 million manufacturer of office supplies and computer products in Nashua, New Hampshire, focused on organizational change to improve the quality of his department and of the whole corporation.

In the late 1970s, when William Conway, CEO of Nashua Corporation, brought in quality guru W. Edwards Deming to help his company improve the quality of its processes and customer service, the information systems department did not even participate in the program. Deming worked with Nashua Corporation for ten years before Gallagher joined the program. Why was there a turnaround? The answer is that Nashua faced a serious problem, and Gallagher saw the solution.

Nashua is a diverse company with nine fairly independent divisions. Like so many other companies, computer support developed at the center in the 1970s. In 1987, Gallagher realized that this centralized information systems function was a serious barrier to quality relations with customers. According to Gallagher, "It used to take us two days to process a telephone order." When a customer called in an order, the divisional order clerk had to dial into a central computer system to do a

credit check on the customer—customer and credit information were centralized. Next, the clerk would log on to a local computer to obtain pricing information, then on to a centralized computer for inventory data. Other steps followed, normally consuming two days. Such customer service had become unacceptable by the late 1980s.

The solution? Gallagher launched a five-year strategic plan to decentralize much of the information systems function. Decentralization not only addressed the customer service issue, but it also fit in with the company's overall philosophy of flattening the organization and pushing decision making down into the divisions. At each plant, small teams of users and information systems professionals were established and given real decision-making power. Each division developed its own systems, resulting in Nashua going from one computer center to nine. Nashua is working on replacing its centralized IBM 4381 (small mainframe) with smaller divisional computers ranging from DEC VAX clusters, to an IBM System/6000, four IBM System/400s and a Wang VS8360. Company-wide, the information systems staff size remained constant, but the IS organization was flattened from five levels to three.

The result on sales servicing has been dramatic. Clerks can now quote prices and produce orders

in a matter of minutes. Gallagher points out that the MIS budget has nearly doubled for the company, with the extra money being spent to equip the divisional computer centers. He believes Nashua has better systems in place at the functional level, and that the company is handling the unique requirements of each division. Nashua didn't get the best cost; instead, it got the best fit.

Quality improvement at Nashua did require new technology to allow the needed changes to occur. However, even though the change originated with the head of a technology department (information systems), the key was not technology. It was organizational change, made possible by the decentralization of the IS function. The result was a dramatic improvement in customer service throughout the whole company.

Source: Catherine Marenghi, "Nashua Keeps Quality Flame Burning in Customer Service," *Computerworld,* January 6, 1992.

To Think About: How did technology promote quality at the Nashua Corporation? Could technology alone have solved Nashua's quality problems? To make the quality improvements described here, what management, organization, and technology issues had to be addressed?

Problems with Information Systems

System failure: An information system that either does not perform as expected, is not operational at a specified time, or cannot be used in the way it was intended.

Unfortunately, as many as 75 percent of all completed large information systems are operating failures that cannot help the organization meet its quality goals. Although these systems are in production, they take so much extra time and money to implement or are so functionally deficient that businesses can't reap the expected benefits. Studies of federal government system projects have found that a large number were poorly designed, full of inaccurate or incomplete data, delivered but not used, delivered late and over budget, reworked, or abandoned (Anthes, 1992).

Many information **system failures** are not necessarily falling apart, but they clearly are either not used in the way that they were intended, or they are not used at all. Users have to develop parallel manual procedures to make these systems work properly. These failures can be traced to four basic information system problems: design, data, cost, and operations.

DESIGN

The actual design of the system fails to capture essential business requirements. Information may not be provided by the system quickly enough or in a usable format. It may even supply the wrong pieces of data. Some systems go unused because they were designed with a poor **user interface** (the part of the system that end users interact with). For example, an input form or on-line data entry screen may be so poorly arranged that no one wants to submit data. Or the procedures to request on-line information retrieval may be unintelligible. For instance, managers in a prominent commercial bank with branches throughout the United States and Europe find its batch loan account system printed reports contain pages filled with zeros, making it practically impossible to assess the status of a client's loan. The amount of the loan, the outstanding balance, and the repayment schedule must be tracked manually.

User interface: The part of the information system through which the end user interacts with the system; type of hardware and the series of on-screen commands and responses required for a user to work with the system.

DATA

The data in the system have a high level of inaccuracy, or incompleteness, or they may not be broken out properly for business purposes. For example, the employee benefits department of a multiunit manufacturing concern continues to maintain all pension calculations, preretirement estimates, and benefits analysis for the company's 20,000 employees manually, despite the presence of an automated, on-line system. Users complain that the data in the system are unreliable because they do not capture the prior benefits plan data for employees from acquisitions and because payroll earnings figures are out of date.

COST

Some systems that operate quite smoothly cost so much to implement or operate that they cannot be justified by the demonstrated business value of the information they provide. The experience of Westpac Banking Corporation in the opening vignette is typical.

OPERATIONS

Information is not provided in a timely and efficient manner because the computer operations that handle information processing may break down. For instance, the batch accounts receivable system of a medium-sized consumer products manufacturer has been aborting several times a month, while major month-end runs have been close to three weeks behind schedule. Because of excessive reruns, schedule delays, and time devoted to fixing antiquated programs, the information systems staff has had no time to work out long-term solutions. An on-line system may be operationally inadequate because the response time is too long.

These problems can be caused by technical, managerial, and organizational factors. In this section we concentrate on the technical factors, specifically those impairing software quality. In section 9.3 we examine the managerial and organizational factors behind these system problems.

The Need for Software Quality Assurance

System problems often reflect software that is of low quality. An undiscovered error in a company's credit software or process control software can result in millions of dollars of losses. Several years ago, a hidden software problem in AT&T's long distance system brought down that system, bringing the New York-based financial exchanges to a halt and interfering with billions of dollars of business around the country for a number of hours. Modern passenger and commercial vehicles are increasingly dependent upon computer programs for critical functions. A hidden software defect in a braking system could result in the loss of lives. A failure in an air traffic control system at a critical moment can hinder the controller from preventing the collision of two passenger planes, resulting in hundreds of deaths.

BUGS AND DEFECTS

Bugs: Program code defects or errors.

A major problem with software is the presence of hidden **bugs,** or program code defects. Studies have shown that it is virtually impossible to eliminate all bugs from large programs. The main source of bugs is the complexity of decision-making code. Even a relatively small program of several hundred lines will contain tens of decisions leading to hundreds or even thousands of different paths. Important programs within most corporations are usually much larger, containing tens of thousands or even millions of lines of code, each with many times the choices and paths of the smaller programs. Such complexity is difficult to document and design—designers document some reactions wrongly or fail to consider some possibilities.

Zero defects, a goal of the total quality management movement, cannot be achieved in larger programs. Complete testing is simply not possible. Fully testing programs that contain thousands of choices and millions of paths would require thousands of years. We cannot eliminate all bugs, nor can we even know with any certainty the seriousness of the bugs that do remain. Even when bugs are found, they are difficult to remove. In many cases, the effort to fix a bug will introduce an entirely new bug or series of bugs. Studies by the Predictably Dependable Computing Systems research project have shown that once a bug has been "repaired," there is only a 50–50 chance that the program will function without failure even as long as it did before the attempt to fix the bug (Little-wood and Strigini, 1992).

INABILITY TO MEET USER NEEDS

Developing software that actually meets user needs can be difficult in a process where the end user commits to the product before that product has been built. In effect, the final system is "purchased" in advance, bought "sight unseen." Defining user needs and judging the quality of the completed system have proven to be major challenges. Most systems development projects begin by defining user information requirements and specifications in the form of systems analysis and design documents.

One problem is that meeting specifications does not necessarily guarantee quality. The completed system may in fact meet the specifications but not satisfy the user's needs. This occurs because of inaccurate, incomplete, or improperly detailed specifications; functions omitted from the specifications; or changing user needs during the development period. Often quality is not quantified in the specifications so that judgments about system quality become subjective. This type of situation can easily deteriorate into finger pointing between IS and the user community, each attacking the other while not addressing system quality.

Specifications often fail to consider the system from the perspective of the users. While designers will concentrate on functionality, they frequently overlook ease of learning and use, unquestioned accuracy and reliability, or speed of response. All of these factors are important to the user of the system and so to the success of the system.

System response time is a common example of a detailed specification that is omitted or inadequately defined. A customer service representative, the end user in a customer service function, may need a query response time of no more than five seconds, but the specifications may contain no reference to response time. If at delivery the response time were ten seconds, the system would meet specifications but would not meet user needs. Perhaps a five-second response time was specified and was achieved during testing with one or two simultaneous users. Would the system satisfy this specification if response time deteriorates to 20 seconds when 100 users are on the system simultaneously? If the system does respond within five seconds 80 percent of the time when 100 people are on the system, has the system met its specifications when it fails to meet that specification the other 20 percent of the time? Can a system be expected to meet such a requirement 100 percent of the time? The lack of agreed-upon, measurable standards in specifications leads to dissatisfied users and systems that do not meet user needs.

THE MAINTENANCE NIGHTMARE

Computer software can create information system problems because it has traditionally been so difficult to maintain. Maintenance, the process of modifying a system in production use, is the most expensive phase of the systems development process. (See the discussion on maintenance in Chapter 8.) Table 9.1 indicates the size of the maintenance problem. In one-fifth of information systems departments, 85 percent of personnel hours are allocated to maintenance, leaving little time for new systems development. In most shops, nearly half of professional personnel time is spent in the maintenance of existing systems.

Why are maintenance costs so high? One major reason is organizational change. The firm may experience large internal changes in structure or leadership, or change may come from its surrounding environment. These changes affect information requirements. An equally common cause of long-term maintenance problems is faulty systems analysis and design, especially information requirements analysis. Some studies of large transaction processing systems by TRW, Inc., have found that a majority of system errors—64 percent—result from early analysis errors (Mazzucchelli, 1985).

If errors are detected early, during analysis and design, the cost to the systems development effort is small. But if they are not discovered until after programming, testing, or conversion has been completed, the costs can soar astronomically. A minor logic error, for example, that might take one hour to correct during the analysis and design stage could take 10, 40, and 90 times as long to correct during programming, conversion, and post-implementation, respectively (see Figure 9.1).

To be able to handle maintenance quickly and inexpensively, a software system must be flexible. A flexible system can more quickly and easily be repaired when problems occur. Such a system can also be modified as business requirements change over the years. For example, a sales system must be able to accommodate new products, new sales staff, and even new offices with few or no problems. Inflexibility is an all too common problem, partially because many designers do not consider the need for change as they design new systems.

Table 9.1 THE MAINTENANCE PROBLEM

Annual personnel hours	
Maintain and enhance current systems	48.0%
Develop new systems	46.1%
Other	5.9%
20% of the survey allocated 85% of its efforts to maintenance and enhancements	
Frequency of activity	
Errors—emergency	17.4%
Change—data, inputs, files, hardware	18.2%
Improve—user enhancements, efficiency, documentation, etc.	60.3%
Other	4.1%

Sources: Bennett P. Lientz and E. Burton Swanson, *Software Maintenance Management.* © 1980 Addison-Wesley Publishing Company. Reprinted by permission.

Figure 9.1

The cost of errors over the systems development cycle. The most common, most severe, and most expensive system errors develop in the early design stages. They involve faulty requirements analysis. Errors in program logic or syntax are much less common, less severe, and less costly to repair than design errors. (*Source: Alberts, 1976.*)

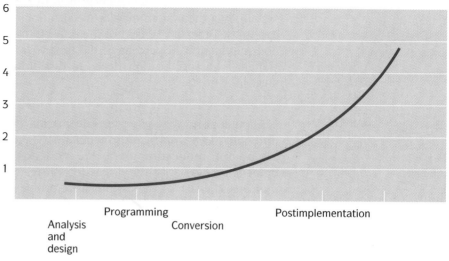

Estimate of the relative cost of repairing errors based on consultant reports and the popular trade literature

However, even if they do design a flexible system, flexibility can seem to be expensive and time-consuming. Its benefits are not always understood or appreciated by the users. Target dates and cost limitations often force developers to sacrifice flexibility in order to complete a project as promised. Unfortunately, the corporation may pay a much heavier price at a later time.

9.2 Solutions to Software Quality Problems

Information systems are complex, and solutions to information system problems are equally complex. This section focuses on technical solutions for problems concerning software quality. The following section describes managerial and organizational solutions to information system problems.

Solutions to software quality problems include using an appropriate systems development methodology, proper resource allocation during systems development, the use of metrics, attention to testing, and the use of quality tools.

Quality Tools and Methodologies

Development methodology: A collection of methods, one or more for every activity within every phase of a development project.

A **development methodology** is actually a collection of methods, one or more for every activity within every phase of a development project. The user of a methodology seldom uses every method within it during a given project because most projects do not require every possible activity. Numerous useful development methodologies exist, some suited to specific technologies, others reflecting differing development philosophies. Information systems departments, in conjunction with management of other departments, select the methodology they believe best fits the needs of their company. Larger corporations, employing multiple technologies, may select multiple methodologies to be used with differing technologies. However, the key to quality development is to select an appropriate methodology and then enforce its use. Some methodologies stress flowcharts and diagrams, others the use of verbal descriptions. The methodology must require systems requirement and specification documents that are complete, detailed and accurate, and documented in a format the user community can understand before approving it. Specifications must also include agreed-upon measures of system quality so that the system can be evaluated objectively while it is being developed and once it is completed. We cannot overemphasize that quality specifications—clear, precise representations of user needs—are critical to the development of a quality system.

RESOURCE ALLOCATION DURING SYSTEMS DEVELOPMENT

Resource allocation: Determination of how costs, time, and personnel are assigned to different activities of a systems development project.

Views on **resource allocation** during systems development have changed significantly over the years. Resource allocation determines the way the costs, time, and personnel are assigned to different phases of the project. In earlier times, developers focused on programming, with only about 1 percent of the time and costs of a project being devoted to systems analysis (determining specifications). As information systems professionals have moved closer to a business or user perspective on quality, they have come to understand the central role of specifications. Consequently, project resources are being shifted to earlier in the project cycle. More time is being spent in specifications and systems analysis, decreasing the proportion of programming time and reducing the need for so much maintenance time (see Figure 9.2). Current literature suggests that about one-quarter of a project's time and cost should be expended in specifications and analysis, with perhaps 50 percent of its resources being allocated to design and programming. Installation and post-implementation ideally should require only one-quarter of the project's resources.

SOFTWARE METRICS

Software metrics: Objective assessments of the software used in a system in the form of quantified measurements.

Software metrics can play a vital role in increasing the quality of a project. **Software metrics** are objective assessments of the system in the form of quantified measurements. Ongoing use of metrics allows the IS department and the user jointly to measure the performance of the system and identify problems as they occur. Examples of software metrics include the number of transactions that can be processed in a specified unit of time, on-line response time, the number of payroll checks printed per hour, and the number of known bugs per hundred lines of code. Unfortunately, most manifestations of quality are not so easy to define in metric terms. In those cases developers must find indirect measurements. For example, an objective measurement of a system's ease of use might be the number of calls for help the IS staff receives per month from system users.

Figure 9.2
Ideal and actual software development costs. Ideally, relatively balanced amounts of time are allowed for analysis, design, programming, and installation. About 8% of costs are allocated ideally to analysis and design, 60% to programming and installation, and 32% to long-term maintenance. Actually, however, the early stages of analysis and design receive far less resources than is desirable. Programming and installation (including all important testing) also receive less time and fewer resources than is desirable, reflecting pressure to deliver a workable system as soon as possible. As a result, systems maintenance is far more expensive than is desirable—about 50% of the total software costs over the expected life span of the system. (*Source: Alberts, 1976*).

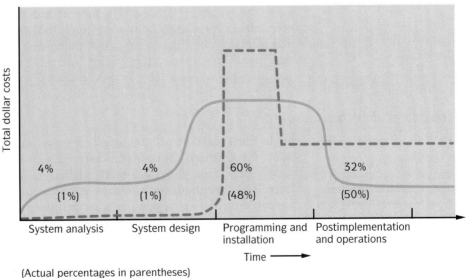

For metrics to be successful, they must be carefully designed, formal, and objective. They must measure significant aspects of the system. One warning, however: Software metrics will only be effective in judging the quality of the system if the users agree to the measurements in advance. In addition, metrics are of no value unless they are used consistently. Few IS departments make wide use of formal, objective metrics today even though studies show they can significantly improve quality.

TESTING

Early, regular, and thorough testing will contribute significantly to system quality. In general, software testing is often misunderstood. Many view testing as a way to prove the correctness of work they have done. In fact, we know that all sizable software is riddled with errors, and we must test to uncover these errors. Any other motivation will result in a less than thorough testing process.

Testing begins at the design phase. Because no coding yet exists, the test normally used is a **walkthrough**—a review of a specification or design document by a small group of people carefully selected based on the skills needed for the particular objectives being tested. Once coding begins, coding walkthroughs also can be used to review program code. However, code must be tested by computer runs. When errors are discovered, the source is found and eliminated through a process called **debugging.**

Chapter 8 described the various stages of testing required to put an information system in operation—program testing, system testing, and acceptance testing. Testing will be successful only if planned properly. Early in the project, before any testing begins, a test plan must be prepared. The plan must include test cases so that the developers can be certain that they have tested an appropriate range of valid and invalid input. Invalid input must be tested to be certain the system handles errors appropriately. Tests must also be tailored to the technology being tested.

Walkthrough: A review of a specification or design document by a small group of people carefully selected based on the skills needed for the particular objectives being tested.

Debugging: The process of discovering and eliminating the errors and defects—the bugs—in program code.

QUALITY TOOLS

Finally, system quality can be significantly enhanced by the use of quality tools. Today, many tools have been developed to address every aspect of the systems development process. Information systems professionals are using project management software to manage their projects. Products exist to document specifications and system design in text and graphic forms. Programming tools include data dictionaries, libraries to manage program modules, and tools that actually produce program code (see Chapters 5, 6, and 8). Many types of tools exist to aid in the debugging process. The most recent set of tools automates much of the preparation for comprehensive testing. Tool technology is still relatively new, and in many cases the value is still unproved. Nonetheless, tools are having a significant impact on system quality and on development costs. We will discuss various types of tools later in this section.

Structured Methodologies

Spaghetti code: Unstructured, confusing program code with tangled logic that metaphorically resembles a pot of cooked spaghetti.

Structured: Refers to the fact that techniques are instructions that are carefully drawn up, often step-by-step, with each step building upon a previous one.

In the early days of programming, few methodologies existed. User specifications were gathered in informal conversations that were written up in hard-to-follow narratives. Programs were written in complex and confusing code, referred to as **spaghetti code** because it was so undecipherable that the logic flow appeared to be as entangled as a cooked pot of spaghetti. Systems were inflexible, maintenance all but impossible.

In reaction to these early problems, new methodologies emerged in the 1970s. These methodologies incorporated a range of methods or techniques that usually are described by the terms *structured* and *top-down*. **Structured** refers to the fact that the techniques are step-by-step, with each step building upon the previous one. **Top-down** refers to an approach that progresses from the highest, most abstract level to the lowest level of detail—from the general to the specific. For example, the highest level of a top-down depiction of a human resources system

Top-down: An approach that progresses from the highest most abstract level to the lowest level of detail.

would show the main human resources functions, such as personnel, benefits, employment, and Equal Economic Opportunity (EEO). Each of these would then be exploded or decomposed down to the next layer. Benefits, for example, might include pension, employee savings, health care, and insurance. Each of these paths are broken down, layer by layer, until the material at the lowest level is easily grasped and documented. Top-down is used for analysis, design, and programming.

The traditional structured methodologies are process-oriented rather than data-oriented. While data descriptions are part of the methods, the process-oriented methodologies focus on how the data are transformed rather than on the data themselves. These methodologies are largely linear—each phase must be completed before the next one can begin. Top-down, structured methodologies have been used to develop large numbers of systems for more than two decades, so that a great many existing systems have been developed in this way. Despite growing interest in other methodologies, they remain the dominant methodological approach today.

STRUCTURED ANALYSIS

Structured analysis: Method for defining system inputs, processes, and outputs and for partitioning systems into subsystems or modules that show a logical graphic model of information flow.

Structured analysis is a widely used top-down method for defining system inputs, processes, and outputs. It offers a logical graphic model of information flow, partitioning a system into modules that show manageable levels of detail. It rigorously specifies the processes or transformations that occur within each module and the interfaces that exist between them. Its primary tool is the **data flow diagram (DFD),** a graphic representation of a system's component processes and the interfaces (flow of data) between them.

Figure 9.3 shows a simple data flow diagram for a mail-in university course registration system. The rounded boxes represent processes, which portray the transformation of data. The square represents an external entity, which is an originator or receiver of information located outside the boundaries of the

Figure 9.3
Data flow diagram for mail-in university registration system. The system has three processes: Verify availability (1.0), Enroll student (2.0), and Confirm registration (3.0). The name and content of each of the data flows appear adjacent to each arrow. There is one external entity in this system, the student. There are two data stores: the student master file and the course file.

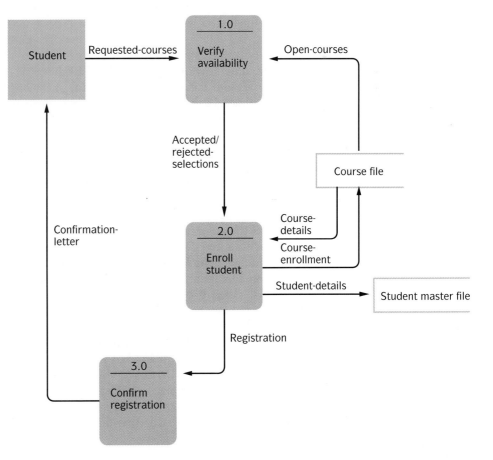

system being modeled. The open rectangles represent data stores, which are either manual or automated inventories of data. The arrows represent data flows, which show the movement between processes, external entities, and data stores. They always contain packets of data, with the name or content of each data flow listed beside the arrow.

This data flow diagram shows that students submit registration forms with their name, identification number, and the numbers of the courses they wish to take. In process 1.0, the system verifies that each course selected is still open by referencing the university's course file. The file distinguishes courses that are still open from those that have been canceled or filled. Process 1.0 then determines which of the student's selections can be accepted or rejected. Process 2.0 enrolls the student in the courses for which he or she has been accepted. It updates the university's course file with the student's name and identification number and recalculates the class size. If maximum enrollment has been reached, the course number is flagged as closed. Process 2.0 also updates the university's student master file with information about new students or changes in address. Process 3.0 then sends each student applicant a confirmation-of-registration letter listing the courses for which he or she is registered and noting the course selections that could not be fulfilled.

The diagrams can be used to depict higher-level processes as well as lower-level details. Through leveled data flow diagrams, a complex process can be broken down into successive levels of detail. An entire system can be divided into subsystems with a high-level data flow diagram. Each subsystem, in turn, can be divided into additional subsystems with second-level data flow diagrams, and the lower-level subsystems can be broken down again until the lowest level of detail has been reached.

Other tools for structured analysis include a data dictionary, which contains information about individual pieces of data and data groupings within a system. The data dictionary was discussed in Chapter 6. It defines the contents of data flows and data stores so that system builders understand exactly what pieces of data they contain. **Process specifications** describe the transformations occurring within the lowest level of the data flow diagrams. They express the logic for each process.

The output of structured analysis is a structured specification document that includes data flow diagrams for system functions, data dictionary descriptions of data flows and data stores, process specifications, and input and output documents, plus security, control, conversion, and performance requirements.

STRUCTURED DESIGN

Structured design encompasses a set of design rules and techniques that promotes program clarity and simplicity, thereby reducing the time and effort required for coding, debugging, and maintenance. The main principle of structured design is that a system should be designed from the top down in hierarchical fashion and refined to greater levels of detail. The design should first consider the main function of a program or system, then break this function into subfunctions and decompose each subfunction until the lowest level of detail has been reached. The lowest level modules describe the actual processing that will occur. In this manner, all high-level logic and the design model are developed before detailed program code is written. If structured analysis has been performed, the structured specification document can serve as input to the design process. Our earlier human resources top-down description is also a good overview example of structured design.

As the design is formulated, it is documented in a structure chart. The **structure chart** is a top-down chart, showing each level of design, its relationship to other levels, and its place in the overall design structure. Figure 9.4 shows a structure chart that can be used for a payroll system. If a design has too many levels to fit onto one structure chart, it can be broken down further on more detailed structure charts.

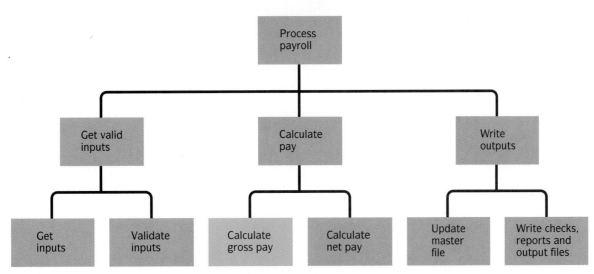

Figure 9.4
High-level structure chart for a payroll system. This structure chart shows the highest or most abstract level of design for a payroll system, providing an overview of the entire system.

STRUCTURED PROGRAMMING

Structured programming: Discipline for organizing and coding programs that simplifies the control paths so that the programs can be easily understood and modified. Uses the basic control structures and modules that have only one entry point and one exit point.

Module: A logical unit of a program that performs one or a small number of functions.

Structured programming extends the principles governing structured design to the writing of programs. It also is based upon the principle of modularization, which follows from top-down analysis and design.

Structured programming is a method of organizing and coding programs that simplifies control paths so that the programs can be easily understood and modified. Structured programming reduces the complexity created when program instructions jump forward and backward to other parts of the program, obscuring the logic and flow of the program.

Each of the boxes in the structure chart represents a component **module.** It constitutes a logical unit that performs one or a small number of functions. Ideally, modules should be independent of each other and should have only one entry to and exit from their parent modules. They should share data with as few other modules as possible. Each module should be kept to a manageable size. An individual should be able to read and understand the program code for the module and easily keep track of its functions.

Proponents of structured programming have shown that any program can be written using the three basic control constructs, or instruction patterns: 1) simple sequence, 2) selection, and 3) iteration. These control constructs are illustrated in Figure 9.5.

The *sequence construct* executes statements in the order in which they appear, with control passing unconditionally from one statement to the next. The program will execute statement A and then statement B.

The *selection construct* tests a condition and executes one of the two alternative instructions based on the results of the test. Condition R is tested. If R is true, statement C is executed. If R is false, statement D is executed. Control then passes to the next statement.

The *iteration construct* repeats a segment of code as long as a conditional test remains true. Condition S is tested. If S is true, statement E is executed and control returns to the test of S. If S is false, E is skipped and control passes to the next statement.

FLOWCHARTS

System flowchart: Graphic design tool that depicts the physical media and sequence of processing steps used in an entire information system.

Flowcharting is an old design tool that is still in use. **System flowcharts** detail the flow of data throughout an entire information system. Program flowcharts describe the processes taking place within an individual program in the system and the sequence in which they must be executed. Flowcharting is no longer recommended for program design because it does not provide top-down modular

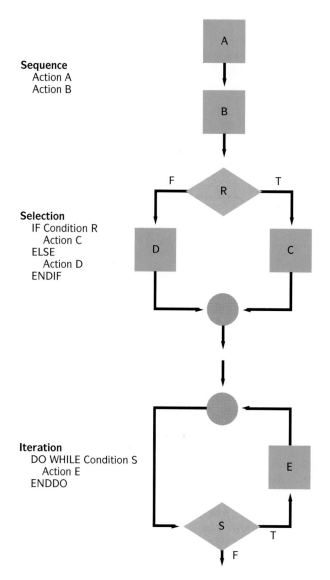

Sequence
    Action A
    Action B

Selection
    IF Condition R
        Action C
    ELSE
        Action D
    ENDIF

Iteration
    DO WHILE Condition S
        Action E
    ENDDO

Figure 9.5
Basic control constructs. The three basic control constructs used in structured programming are Sequence, Selection, and Iteration.

structure as effectively as other techniques. However, system flowcharts may still be used to document physical design specifications because they can show all inputs, major files, processing, and outputs for a system and they can document manual procedures.

Figure 9.6 illustrates a high-level system flowchart of a payroll system. The most important symbols used in this flowchart have already been described in Chapter 2 (see Figure 2.1). Flow lines show the sequence of steps and the direction of information flow. Arrows are employed to show direction if it is not apparent in the diagram. The system flowchart shows the flow of information and work in the system, the sequence of processing steps, and the physical media on which data are input, output, and stored.

LIMITATIONS OF
TRADITIONAL METHODS

The traditional structured approach has served the information systems professionals and their user communities well. Nonetheless, it has shortcomings. The process is considered, slow, inflexible, and time-consuming.

Completion of structured analysis is required before design can begin, and programming must await the completed deliverables from design. As a result, most critics consider structured methodologies to be slow and unresponsive to the fast-changing business world of the 1990s. The slowness translates into

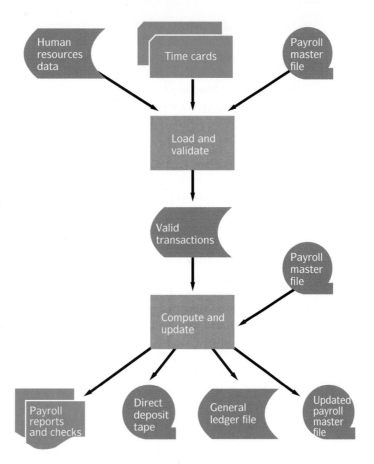

Figure 9.6
System flowchart for a payroll system. This is a high-level system flowchart for a batch payroll system. Only the most important processes and files are illustrated. Data are input from two sources: timecards and payroll-related data (such as salary increases) passed from the human resources system. The data are first edited and validated against the existing payroll master file before the payroll master is updated. The update process produces an updated payroll master file, various payroll reports (such as the payroll register and hours register), checks, a direct deposit tape, and a file of payment data that must be passed to the organization's general ledger system. The direct deposit tape is sent to the automated clearing house that serves the banks offering direct deposit services to employees.

increased cost at a time when cost cutting is very much in the spotlight. Because a large system development project will last one to two years, specifications drawn up at the beginning are bound to change as business needs change. However, a change in specifications requires that first the analysis documents and then the design documents must be modified before the programs can be changed to reflect the new requirement. Structured methodologies are function-oriented, focusing on the processes that transform the data. The storage of the data is described as an appendage to those processes. Yet business management has come to understand that the most valuable portion of information systems is the data, that most information systems must be data-oriented. Systems that focus on data can be smaller and far more flexible, making them easier to modify and more responsive to changing business needs.

In addition to the traditional methodologies and tools, system builders are turning to object-oriented development, computer-aided software engineering (CASE), and software re-engineering to help cope with information system quality problems.

Object-Oriented Software Development

Object-oriented software development: Approach to software development that de-emphasizes procedures and shifts the focus from modeling business processes and data to combining data and procedures that create objects.

In Chapter 5 we explained that object-oriented programming combines data and the specific procedures that operate on those data into one "object." Object-oriented programming is part of a larger approach to systems development called object-oriented software development. **Object-oriented software development** differs from traditional methodologies in that it shifts the focus from separately modeling business processes and data to combining data and procedures into unified objects. A system is viewed as a collection of objects and relationships among objects. The objects are defined, programmed, documented, and saved to be used as building blocks for future applications.

The objects model the way users actually work. For example, accounts receivable personnel tend to think at the level of customers, credit limits, and invoices—the same level at which objects are built. Object-oriented analysis (OOA) and object-oriented design (OOD) are based upon these objects and so more closely model the real world than previous methods.

BENEFITS OF AN
OBJECT-ORIENTED
APPROACH

Because objects are easily reusable, object-oriented software development directly addresses the issue of reusability and is expected to reduce the time and cost of writing software. Of course, no organization will see savings from reusability until it builds up a library of objects to draw upon. Object-oriented software development experience is still very limited, so it is too early to evaluate the approach. Nonetheless, early studies have been promising. Experience has shown that programming productivity gains of better than 10:1 are possible. Electronic Data Systems Corp. (EDS) studied the benefits by building a maintenance management system twice, once using structured techniques and once using object-oriented programming. EDS equalized the skill level of the two project teams and had them work from the same specifications. They found a productivity improvement of 14:1 using object-oriented programming (IDC White Paper, 1992). Maintenance costs are also lowered by reducing multiple maintenance changes. For example, when the U.S. postal system changed the zip code from five to nine digits, each traditional program within a company had to be changed. If a company's programs were object-oriented, the programmer would only have had to modify the code within the object, and the change would be reflected in all the programs using that object.

Object-oriented software development is leading to other changes in methods. Once a library of objects exists, design and programming often can begin without waiting for analysis documents. In theory, design and programming will both begin as soon as requirements are completed through the use of iterations of rapid prototyping. Object-oriented methods should increase the involvement of users both because they may find objects easier to understand and more natural to work with than traditional structured tools and because iterative prototyping places them at the center of design and even of programming.

OBSTACLES TO USING
OBJECT-ORIENTED
TECHNIQUES

Although the demand for training in object-oriented techniques and programming tools is exploding, object-oriented software development is still in its infancy and is too unproved for most companies to adopt it. No agreed-upon object-oriented development methodology yet exists, although several have been proposed. Moreover, many companies are hesitant to try it because it requires extensive staff training and a major methodological reorientation. Management is also aware that a complete switch to object-oriented development will take a long time. Most companies have a major investment in existing, structured systems that would have to be maintained until the time came that they needed replacement. Until then, the IS departments would have to retain expertise in both structured and object-oriented methods.

Computer-Aided Software Engineering (CASE)

Computer-aided software engineering (CASE): The automation of step-by-step methodologies for software and systems development to reduce the amount of repetitive work the developer needs to do.

Computer-aided software engineering (CASE)—sometimes called computer-aided systems engineering—is the automation of step-by-step methodologies for software and systems development to reduce the amount of repetitive work the developer needs to do. Its adoption can free the developer for more creative problem-solving tasks. CASE tools also facilitate creation of clear documentation and the coordination of team development efforts. Team members can share their work more easily by accessing each other's files to review or modify what has been done. Systems developed with CASE have been found to be more reliable and require repairs less often (Dekleva, 1992). Many CASE tools are microcomputer-based, with powerful graphical capabilities.

CASE tools provide automated graphics facilities for producing charts and diagrams, screen and report generators, data dictionaries, extensive reporting facilities, analysis and checking tools, code generators, and documentation generators. Most CASE tools are based on one or more of the popular structured methodologies. Some are starting to support object-oriented development. In general, CASE tools try to increase productivity and quality by doing the following:

- Enforce a standard development methodology and design discipline.
- Improve communication between users and technical specialists.
- Organize and correlate design components and provide rapid access to them via a design repository.
- Automate tedious and error-prone portions of analysis and design.
- Automate testing and control rollout.

Key elements of CASE are described in Table 9.2.

EXAMPLES OF CASE TOOLS   CASE tools have been classified in terms of whether they support activities at the front end or the back end of the systems development process. Front-end CASE tools focus on capturing analysis and design information in the early stages of systems development, whereas back-end CASE tools address coding, testing, and maintenance activities. Back-end tools help convert specifications automatically into program code. CASE products such as Andersen Consulting's Foundation and KnowledgeWare's Application Development Workbench represent more fully integrated tools that are starting to support the entire systems development process, including project management and automatic generation of program code.

Analysts use CASE tools to help capture requirements and specifications by storing the information in a CASE database, where it can be easily retrieved and

---

Table 9.2   KEY ELEMENTS OF CASE

Diagramming tools: Graphics tools for drawing symbols for data flow diagrams, structure charts, entity-relationship diagrams, or other types of diagrams associated with a particular methodology.

Syntax verifier: Verifies the accuracy and completeness of information entered into a system in conformance with the rules of a particular structured methodology.

Prototyping tools: Screen, report, and menu generators allow the analyst to paint desired screen and report layouts or menu paths through a system without complex formatting specifications or programming.

Information repository: A central information database which serves as a mechanism for storing all types of software assets—screen and report layouts, diagrams, data definitions, program code, project schedules, and other documentation. The repository coordinates, integrates, and standardizes the different pieces of information so they can be easily accessed, shared by analysts, and reused in future software work.

Code generators: These can generate modules of executable code from higher-level specifications. Some CASE tools use icons to indicate various program functions and translate these symbols into programs.

Development methodology: Some CASE products contain checklists or narratives detailing an entire development methodology that helps monitor and control the entire systems development project.

Project management tools: Some CASE tools integrate their components with popular stand-alone tools for project scheduling and resource estimation, while others incorporate project management software into the CASE tool kit.

The Construction Workstation GUI supports the development and generation of cooperative and client/server applications with such GUI elements as windows, dialogs, graphics, hot spots, and on-line help text.

revised. The CASE tools facilitate up-front design and analysis work, so that there are fewer errors to correct later on. CASE text and graphics editors help the analyst create technically correct diagrams, process descriptions, and data dictionary entries. The Window on Management illustrates how one company used a CASE tool primarily for planning, analysis, and design work.

CASE tools automatically tie data elements to the processes where they are used. If a data flow diagram is changed from one process to another, the elements in the data dictionary would be altered automatically to reflect the change in the diagram. CASE tools also contain features for validating design diagrams and specifications. Some tool kits contain prototyping features such as screen and report painters, which allow analysts to draw screen or report formats for users to review. CASE tools thus support iterative design by automating revisions and changes and providing prototyping facilities.

A central element in the CASE tool kit is the information repository, which stores all the information defined by the analysts during the project. The repository includes data flow diagrams, structure charts, entity-relationship diagrams (see Figure 9.7), data definitions, process specifications, screen and report formats, notes and comments, and test results. The CASE database can be shared by members of a project team and contains features to restrict changes to only specified analysts. (See Chapter 6 for a discussion of entity-relationship diagrams.)

THE CHALLENGE OF USING CASE

To be used effectively, CASE tools require more organizational discipline than the manual approach. Every member of a development project must adhere to a common set of naming conventions, standards, and development methodology. Without this discipline, analysts and designers will simply attempt to incorporate the CASE tool into the old, inadequate development processes. The best CASE tools enforce common methods and standards, which may discourage their use in situations where organizational discipline is lacking.

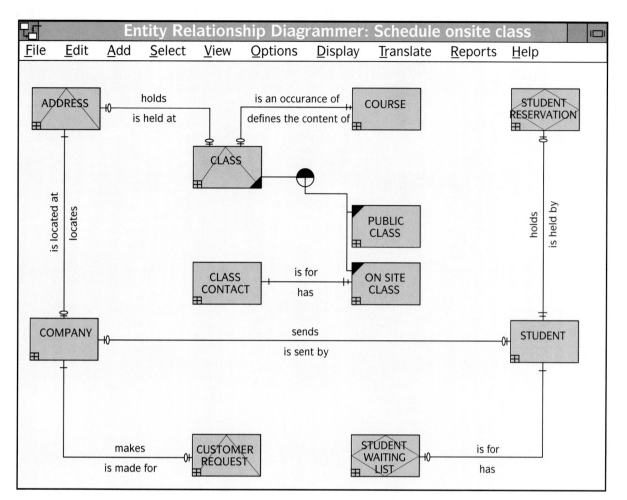

Figure 9.7
The entity-relationship diagrammer in KnowledgeWare's Application Development Workbench helps systems designers build a logical data model by documenting the types of entities found in an organization and how they relate. This CASE tool can display an entity-relationship diagram for the entire entity model or for a context-sensitive view. This figure, for example, displays only the entities and relationships relevant to the process of scheduling a class. *Diagram provided courtesy of KnowledgeWare Inc., Atlanta GA.*

CASE is not a magic cure-all. It does not enable systems to be designed automatically or ensure that business requirements are met. Systems designers still have to understand what a firm's business needs are and how the business works. Systems analysis and design are still dependent upon the analytical skills of the analyst/designer. If a firm lacks a methodology, CASE tools may be used to automate disparate, and often incompatible, practices rather than integrating or standardizing a firm's systems development approach. Table 9.3 describes the strengths and limitations of CASE tools.

Software Re-engineering

Software re-engineering:
Methodology that addresses the problem of aging software by salvaging and upgrading it so that the users can avoid a long and expensive replacement project.

Software re-engineering is a methodology that addresses the problem of aging software. A great deal of the software that organizations use was written without the benefit of a methodology such as structured analysis, design, and programming. Such software is difficult to maintain or update. Often, however, the software would serve the organization well enough to continue to be used, if only it could be more easily maintained. The purpose of re-engineering is to salvage such software by upgrading it so that users can avoid a long and expensive replacement

MANAGEMENT

Looking to the Future with CASE

Good management has the ability to anticipate the need for change and to take action before serious problems develop. Such management became evident at Washington, D.C.'s National Association of Securities Dealers, Inc. (NASD) when in 1991 it launched a project to install new software development methods and techniques. NASD is the parent of NASDAQ, the over-the-counter stock quotation system that has evolved into the second largest stock market in the United States and third largest in the world. Quality systems are the life blood of NASDAQ—its basic product is instantaneous, reliable, accurate stock market information, delivered through computer systems.

In the midst of a long period of expanding success, Bill Synnott, the director of information technology at NASD, came to the conclusion that change was needed. "Our technologies were not supporting our ability to meet our business needs," he said. NASD had to come up with an approach to get its technologies in line with these needs. NASD originally planned a bottom-up project, expecting to use reverse engineering tools to give them a structured picture of what their current systems do. Unfortunately, a large portion of its systems was written in assembly language, and no appropriate re-engineering tools existed for these languages. Therefore, they shifted

to a top-down, data-driven approach. Synnott wanted a disciplined approach, which meant using a methodology that could be enforced by a CASE tool. They chose the CASE tool IE:Expert from Information Engineering.

NASD set general project targets of a 20 percent reduction in information systems operating costs. It also aimed to produce new applications in 20 percent less time. It also wanted to reduce response time (the heart of their product). Synnott set a general goal of helping NASD to "keep our competitive edge."

NASD first used IE:Expert to build a high-level strategic model, followed by a tactical model and then more specific operational models. They plan to map current systems to the operational models. This mapping will allow them to evaluate the health of their existing systems and to make appropriate changes. However, the project encompasses more than software. IS is reviewing hardware also and has issued requests for proposals (RFPs). The staff has even found another use for IE:Expert, evaluation of third-party software being considered for purchase. For example, before purchasing a new human resources information system, they used IE:Expert to build a model of the proposed system. They are evaluating packages against that model.

IS management has been far-sighted in another critical area, personnel. They recognized early that technical staff will likely be nervous about a switch to a top-down approach. Synnott says the traditional programmers are distrustful. They don't see how you can build a substantial portion of the system from a model. One approach they have followed is helping their staff connect the changes within IS to their own careers. Pam Sweet, an assistant director of IS, put it this way: "Most of the people who are becoming involved see this as a great opportunity to broaden their scope as DP professionals." NASD hopes to have its first pilot application in production before the end of 1993.

Source: John Desmond, "Mapping the Ideal, Comparing to Real," *Software Magazine,* January 1992.

To Think About: 1. What are the management benefits of using CASE? How does CASE promote quality?
2. As the head of IS for NASD, why might you want to launch a project to map systems from the top down, even though the systems you have in production seem to be working very well? How would you sell your project to the corporate management of NASD?

Reverse engineering: The process of taking existing programs, file and database descriptions and converting them into corresponding design-level components that can then be used to create new applications.

project. In essence, developers use re-engineering to extract design and programming intelligence from existing systems, thereby creating new systems without starting from scratch. Re-engineering involves three steps: reverse engineering, revision of design and program specifications, and forward engineering.

Reverse engineering entails extracting the underlying business specifications from existing systems. Older, nonstructured systems do not have adequate documentation of the business process, the system design, or the programs. Reverse engineering tools read and analyze the program's existing code, file, and database descriptions and produce structured documentation of the system. The output will show design-level components, such as entities, attributes, and processes. With structured documentation to work from, the project team can then revise the design and specifications to meet current business requirements. In the

Table 9.3   WHAT CASE TOOLS CAN AND CANNOT DO

CASE Tools Can:

1. Automate many manual tasks of systems development.
2. Promote standardization based on a single methodology.
3. Promote greater consistency and coordination during a development project.
4. Generate a large portion of the documentation for a system, such as data flow diagrams, data models, structure charts, or other specifications.

CASE Tools Cannot:

1. Automatically provide a functional, relevant system. It is just as easy to produce a bad system as to produce a good system using CASE tools.
2. Interface easily with databases and fourth-generation languages.
3. Automatically force analysts to use a prescribed methodology or create a methodology when one does not exist.
4. Radically transform the systems analysis and design process.

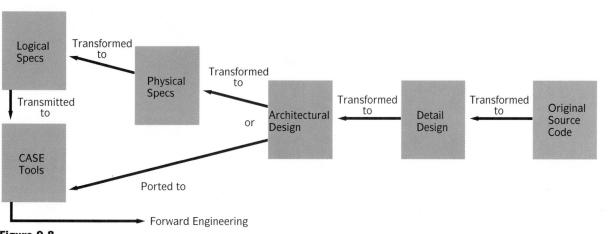

Figure 9.8
Steps in the re-engineering process. The primary function of reverse engineering is to capture the functional capabilities—the process logic—of the existing system in a simplified form that can be revised and updated for the basis of the new replacement system. *Source: Thomas J. McCabe and Eldonna S. Williamson, "Tips on Reengineering Redundant Software,"* Datamation, *April 15, 1992. Reproduced with permission from DATAMATION© 1992, Reed Publishing (USA) Inc.*

Forward engineering: The final step in re-engineering when the revised specifications are used to generate new, structured program code for a structured and maintainable system.

final step, **forward engineering,** the revised specifications are used to generate new, structured code for a structured and now maintainable system. In Figure 9.8, you can follow the reengineering process. Note that CASE tools can be used in the forward engineering step.

9.3 Managing System Implementation

In addition to technical factors associated with software quality, information system problems can be caused by the manner in which the organizational change surrounding a new information system is managed. As many MIS researchers have pointed out, the introduction or alteration of an information system has a powerful behavioral and organizational impact. It transforms the way various individuals and groups perform and interact. Changes in the way information is defined, accessed, and used to manage the resources of the organization often lead to new distributions of authority and power (Lucas, 1975). This internal organizational change breeds resistance and opposition and can

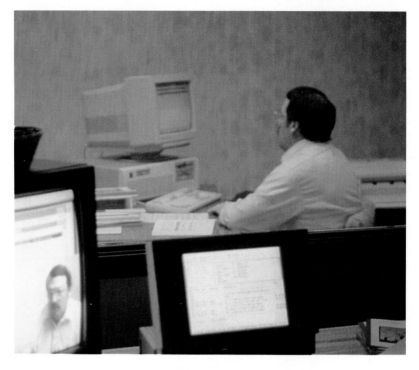

Usability labs can help technical specialists understand the needs of end users. Here, programmers observe users trying out software in special rooms with one-way mirrors and video cameras.

lead to the demise of an otherwise good system. An important characteristic of most information systems is that individuals are asked or required to change their behavior in order to make the system function.

Several studies have found that in organizations with similar environments and institutional features, the same innovation will be successful in some organizations but fail in others. Why? One approach to explaining the differences focuses on different patterns of implementation.

Causes of Implementation Success and Failure

Implementation: All of the organizational activities working toward the adoption, management, and routinization of an innovation.

In the context of change management, **implementation** refers to all of the organizational activities working toward the adoption, management, and routinization of an innovation such as a new information system. Managerial and organizational factors, such as the role of users and management in the implementation process, the manner in which the project handles complexity and risk, and the quality of management of implementation projects have a profound effect on system outcome.

SYSTEMS DEVELOPMENT AS CHANGE AGENT

Change agent: In the context of implementation, the individual acting as the catalyst during the change process to ensure successful organizational adaptation to a new system or innovation.

In the context of implementation, the systems analyst is a **change agent.** The analyst not only develops technical solutions but redefines the configurations, interactions, job activities, and power relationships of various organizational groups. The analyst is the catalyst for the entire change process and is responsible for ensuring that the changes created by a new system are accepted by all parties involved. The change agent communicates with users, mediates between competing interest groups, and ensures that the organizational adjustment to such changes is complete.

USER INVOLVEMENT AND INFLUENCE

Heavy user involvement in the design and operation of information systems afford users and management more opportunities to mold the system according to their priorities and business requirements. In addition, they are more likely to react positively to the completed system because they have been active participants in the change process.

Communication problems between end users and designers are a major reason why user requirements are not properly incorporated into information systems and why users are driven out of the implementation process. Users and information system specialists tend to have different backgrounds, interests, and priorities, and often pursue different goals. This is referred to as the **user–designer communications gap.** These differences are manifested in divergent organizational loyalties, approaches to problem solving, and vocabularies. Information system specialists, for example, often have a highly technical or machine orientation to problem solving. They look for elegant and sophisticated technical solutions in which hardware and software efficiency is optimized at the expense of ease of use or organizational effectiveness. Users, on the other hand, prefer systems that are oriented to solving business problems or facilitating organizational tasks. Often the orientations of both groups are so at odds that they appear to speak in different tongues. These differences are illustrated in Table 9.4, which depicts the typical concerns of end users and technical specialists (information system designers) regarding the development of a new information system.

User-designer communications gap: The differences in backgrounds, interests, and priorities that impede communication and problem-solving among end users and information systems specialists.

MANAGEMENT SUPPORT

If an information systems project has the backing and approval of management at various levels, it is more likely to be perceived positively by both users and the technical information services staff. Both groups will feel that their participation in the development process will receive higher-level attention, priority, and reward. Management backing also ensures that a systems project will receive sufficient funding and resources to be successful. Furthermore, all of the changes in work habits and procedures and any organizational realignments associated with a new system depend on management backing to be enforced effectively.

LEVEL OF COMPLEXITY AND RISK

Systems differ dramatically in their size, scope, level of complexity, and organizational and technical components. Some systems development projects, such as the Confirm project described in the Window on Technology, are more likely to fail because they carry a much higher level of risk than others. Researchers have identified three key dimensions that influence the level of project risk: project size, project structure, and experience with technology (McFarlan, 1981).

Project Size. The larger the project—as indicated by the dollars spent, the size of the implementation staff, the time allocated to implementation, and the number of organizational units affected—the greater the risk.

Project Structure. Projects that are more highly structured run a much lower risk than those whose requirements are relatively undefined, fluid, and constantly changing; when requirements are clear and straightforward, outputs and processes can be easily defined. Users in highly structured projects tend to know

Table 9.4   THE USER–DESIGNER COMMUNICATIONS GAP

User Concerns	Designer Concerns
Will the system deliver the information I need for my work?	How much disk storage space will the master file consume?
How quickly can I access the data?	How many lines of program code will it take to perform this function?
How easily can I retrieve the data?	How can we cut down on CPU time when we run the system?
How much clerical support will I need to enter data into the system?	What is the most efficient way of storing this piece of data?
How will the operation of the system fit into my daily business schedule?	What database management system should we use?

TECHNOLOGY

Do Mega-Projects Have Mega-Problems?

In March 1988, the Hilton Hotels Corporation; Marriott Corporation; Budget Rent-A-Car Corporation; and AMR, the parent company of American Airlines, joined forces to develop Confirm, the first system to fully integrate hotel, rental car, and airline reservations. The system was supposed to be completed in June 1992 at a cost of $125 million. Five hundred technical personnel worked on the project. But after more than three years of work, it was delayed another 18 months. The International Reservations and Information Consortium (Intrico) overseeing the project discovered major problems when the system was tested on site by the Hilton Hotels Corporation. Hilton users found that the system's user interface, mainframe transaction processing, and mainframe database did not adequately communicate with each other.

Confirm runs on two IBM 3090 mainframes. One houses the central reservations system, which runs under Transaction Processing Facility (a special operating system environment for processing heavy volumes of transactions). The other mainframe houses a DB2 relational database in an MVS (an IBM mainframe operating system) environment. The database contains decision support information such as customer histories and pricing data. The system requires application-to-application bridging between the two CPUs for some sixty applications. When processing the internal transactions, the operating systems and application software on both computers must be closely coordinated.

Intrico used Information Engineering Facility (IEF), Texas Instrument's CASE product, to automatically generate the software code that ran on the MVS operating system. However, IEF could not generate the right code to make the software that allows the two machines to communicate with the outside world work properly. This software front end, called Transaction Management Function, served as a gateway to the various airline, hotel, and rental car airport reservation systems and would direct incoming data from each center to the appropriate mainframe. The software running on the mainframe using Transaction Processing Facility was written in the C programming language.

When it came time to connect the two separately developed system modules, Intrico found that they did not communicate very well. The program sending information from one processor could not coordinate with the program receiving information in the other processor. In the event of a system crash, Confirm's DB2 database could be recovered only in pieces, not in its entirety. The problems were not insurmountable, but they would require another two years to fix. In September 1992, AMR sued the other three Confirm partners for breach of contract. Marriott countersued two days later.

Sources: Mark Halper, "Travel Firms Rush to Avert System Cutoff," *Computerworld*, April 5, 1993; John P. McPartlin, "The Collapse of Confirm," *InformationWEEK*, October 19, 1992; and Clinton Wilder, "Travel System Delayed till 93," *Computerworld*, May 11, 1992.

To Think About: Evaluate the level of complexity and risk in this project. What management, organization, and technology issues had to be addressed by the Confirm system? What problems did the project encounter? Why do you think the project had these problems? How might they have been avoided?

---

exactly what they want and what the system should do; there is a much lower possibility of their changing their minds.

Experience with Technology. The project risk will rise if the project team and the information system staff are unfamiliar with the hardware, system software, application software, or database management system proposed for the project.

These dimensions of project risk will be present in different combinations for each implementation effort. Table 9.5 shows that eight different combinations are possible, each with a different degree of risk. The higher the level of risk, the more likely it is that the implementation effort will fail.

MANAGEMENT OF THE IMPLEMENTATION PROCESS

The conflicts and uncertainties inherent in any implementation effort will be magnified when an implementation project is poorly managed and organized. Under poor management, basic elements of success may be omitted. Training to ensure that end users are comfortable with the new system and fully understand its potential uses is often sacrificed, in part because the budget is strained toward the end of a project. A systems development project without proper management

Table 9.5 DIMENSIONS OF PROJECT RISK

Project Structure	Project Technology Level	Project Size	Degree of Risk
High	Low	Large	Low
High	Low	Small	Very low
High	High	Large	Medium
High	High	Small	Medium-low
Low	Low	Large	Low
Low	Low	Small	Very low
Low	High	Large	Very high
Low	High	Small	High

will most likely suffer vast cost overruns, major time slippages, and technical performances that fall significantly below the estimated level.

How badly are projects managed? On average, private-sector projects are underestimated by one-half in terms of budget and time required to deliver the complete system promised in the system plan. A very large number of projects are delivered with missing functionality (promised for delivery in later versions). Government projects suffer about the same failure level, perhaps worse (Laudon, 1989; Helms and Weiss, 1986).

Improving Implementation Management

Not all aspects of the implementation process can be easily controlled or planned (Alter and Ginzberg, 1978). However, the chances for system success can be increased by anticipating potential implementation problems and applying appropriate corrective strategies. Strategies have also been devised for ensuring that users play an appropriate role throughout the implementation period and for managing the organizational change process. Various project management, requirements gathering, and planning methodologies have been developed for specific categories of problems.

INCREASING USER INVOLVEMENT

External integration tools: Project management technique that links the work of the implementation team to that of users at all organizational levels.

The level of user involvement should vary, depending upon both the development methodology being used and the risk level of the project (see "Controlling Risk Factors" below). Tools to involve users, **external integration tools,** include the following ways to link the work of the implementation team to users at all organizational levels:

- Users can be selected as project leaders or as the second-in-command on a project team.
- User steering committees can be created to evaluate the system's design and overall project management.
- Users can become active members of the project team.
- The project can require formal user review and approval of specifications.
- Minutes of all key design meetings can be distributed widely among users.
- Users can prepare the status reports for higher management.
- Users can be put in charge of training and installation.
- Users can be responsible for change control, putting a brake on all nonessential changes to the system once final design specifications have been completed.

OVERCOMING USER RESISTANCE

Systems development is not an entirely rational process. Users leading design activities have used their position to further private interests and to gain power rather than to promote organizational objectives (Franz and Robey, 1984). Moreover, participation in implementation activities may not be enough to overcome the problem of user resistance. The implementation process demands organizational change. Such change may be resisted because different users may be affected by the system in different ways. While some users may welcome a new system because it brings changes they perceive as beneficial to them, others may resist these changes because they believe the shifts are detrimental to their interests (Joshi, 1991).

Counterimplementation: A deliberate strategy to thwart the implementation of an information system or an innovation in an organization.

If the use of a system is voluntary, users may choose to avoid it; if use is mandatory, resistance will take the form of increased error rates, disruptions, turnover, and even sabotage. Therefore, the implementation strategy must not only encourage user participation and involvement; it must also address the issue of counterimplementation (Keen, 1981). **Counterimplementation** is a deliberate strategy to thwart the implementation of an information system or an innovation in an organization.

Strategies to overcome user resistance include user participation (to elicit commitment as well as to improve design), user education (training), management coercion (edicts, policies), and user incentives. User resistance can be addressed through changes to the new system, such as improved human factors (user/system interface) and package modification to conform to organizational procedures. Finally, users will be more cooperative if organizational problems are solved prior to introducing the new system.

MANAGING TECHNICAL COMPLEXITY

Internal integration tools: Project management technique that ensures that the implementation team operates as a cohesive unit.

Projects with *high levels of technology* benefit from **internal integration tools.** The success of such projects depends on how well their technical complexity can be managed. Project leaders need both heavy technical and administrative experience. They must be able to anticipate problems and develop smooth working relationships among a predominantly technical team.

- Team members should be highly experienced.
- The team should be under the leadership of a manager with a strong technical and project management background.
- Team meetings should take place frequently, with routine distribution of meeting minutes concerning key design decisions.
- The team should hold regular technical status reviews.
- A high percentage of the team should have a history of good working relationships with each other.
- Team members should participate in setting goals and establishing target dates.
- Essential technical skills or expertise not available internally should be secured from outside the organization.

FORMAL PLANNING AND CONTROL TOOLS

Formal planning tools: Project management technique that structures and sequences tasks; budgeting time, money, and technical resources required to complete the tasks.

Formal control tools: Project management technique that helps monitor the progress towards completion of a task and fulfillment of goals.

Projects will benefit from appropriate use of **formal planning tools** and **formal control tools.** With project management techniques such as PERT (Program Evaluation and Review Technique) or Gantt charts, a detailed plan can be developed. (PERT lists the specific activities that make up a project, their duration, and the activities that must be completed before a specific activity can start. A Gantt chart such as that illustrated in Figure 9.9 visually represents the sequence and timing of different tasks in a development project, as well as their resource requirements.) Tasks can be defined and resources budgeted. These project management techniques can help managers identify bottlenecks and determine the impact problems will have on project completion times. Depending upon the development methodology used and the size and risk of the project, the following project management techniques can be adopted:

HRIS COMBINED PLAN-HR

Gantt chart timeline columns: 1994 (Oct, Nov, Dec) · 1995 (Jan, Feb, Mar, Apr, May, Jun, Jul, Aug, Sep, Oct, Nov, Dec) · 1996 (Jan, Feb, Mar, Apr)

Task	Da	Who
DATA ADMINISTRATION SECURITY		
QMF security review/setup	20	EF TP
Security orientation	2	EF JV
QMF security maintenance	35	TP GL
Data entry sec. profiles	4	EF TP
Data entry sec views est.	12	EF TP
Data entry security profiles	65	EF TP
DATA DICTIONARY		
Orientation sessions	1	EF
Data dictionary design	32	EF WV
DD prod, coordn-query	20	GL
DD prod. coord-live	40	EF GL
Data dictionary cleanup	35	EF GL
Data dictionary maint.	35	EF GL
PROCEDURES REVISION DESIGN PREP		
Work flows (old)	10	PK JL
Payroll data flows	31	JL PK
HRIS P/R model	11	PK JL
P/R interface orient. mtg.	6	PK JL
P/R interface coordn. I	15	PK
P/R interface coordn.	8	PK
Benefits interfaces (old)	5	JL
Ben. interfaces new flow	8	JL
Ben. communication strategy	3	PK JL
New work flow model	15	PK JL
Posn. data entry flows	14	WV JL

RESOURCE SUMMARY

Name		Who	Oct 94	Nov	Dec	Jan 95	Feb	Mar	Apr	May	Jun	Jul	Aug	Sep	Oct	Nov	Dec	Jan 96	Feb	Mar	Apr
Edith Farrell	5.0	EF	2	21	24	24	23	22	22	27	34	34	29	26	28	19	14	4	3		
Woody Holand	5.0	WH	5	17	20	19	12	10	14	10	2										
Charles Pierce	5.0	CP		5	11	20	13	9	10	7	6	8	4	4	4	4					
Ted Leurs	5.0	TL		12	17	17	19	17	14	12	15	16	2	1	1	1					9
Toni Cox	5.0	TC	1	11	10	11	11	12	19	19	21	21	21	17	17	12	9	3	2		
Patricia Clark	5.0	PC	7	23	30	34	27	25	15	24	25	16	11	13	17	10	3				
Jane Lawton	5.0	JL	1	9	16	21	19	21	21	20	17	15	14	12	14	8	5				
David Holloway	5.0	DH	4	4	5	5	5	2	7	5	4	16	2								6
Diane O'Neill	5.0	DO	6	14	17	16	13	11	9	4											
Joan Albert	5.0	JA	5	6			7	6	2	1				5	5	1					
Marie Marcus	5.0	MM	15	7	2	1	1														
Don Stevens	5.0	DS	4	4	5	4	5	1													
Casual	5.0	CASL		3	4	3				4	7	9	5	3	2						
Kathy Manley	5.0	KM			1	5	16	20	19	22	19	20	18	20	11	2					
Anna Borden	5.0	AB					9	10	16	15	11	12	19	10	7	1					
Gail Loring	5.0	GL		3	6	5	9	10	17	18	17	10	13	10	10	7	17	14	13	3	1
UNASSIGNED	0.0	X										9			236	225	230	216	178	9	7
Co-op	5.0	CO		6	4					2	3	4	4	2	4	16					
casual	5.0	CAUL									3	3	3								
TOTAL DAYS			49	147	176	196	194	174	193	195	190	181	140	125	358	288	284	237	196	12	23

Figure 9.9

Formal planning and control tools help to manage information systems projects successfully. The Gantt chart in this figure was produced by a commercially available project management software package. It shows the task, person-days, and initials of each responsible person, as well as the start and finish dates for each task. The resource summary provides a good manager with the total person-days for each month and for each person working on the project to successfully manage the project. The project described here is a data administration project.

- Milestone phases can be selected.
- Specifications can be developed from the feasibility study.
- Specification standards can be established.
- Processes for project approval can be developed.

Standard control techniques can be used to chart project progress against budgets and target dates, so that deviations can be spotted and the implementation team can make adjustments to meet their original schedule.

- Disciplines can be maintained to control or freeze the design.
- Periodic formal status reports against the plan will show the extent of progress.
- Deviations from the plan can be spotted.

Controlling Risk Factors

Implementation can be further improved by adjusting the project management strategy to the level of risk inherent in each project. In order to control the risk, projects with relatively *little structure* may involve users fully at all stages, whereas more formal projects may need to adjust user involvement according to the project phase. There may be situations in which user participation is not appropriate. For example, some users may react negatively to a new design even though its overall benefits outweigh its drawbacks. Some individuals may stand to lose power as a result of design decisions (Robey and Markus, 1984). In this instance, participation in design may actually exacerbate resentment and resistance.

Projects using complex new technology are riskier and require more emphasis upon internal integration tools. Large projects can reduce risk by an increased use of formal planning and control tools.

Designing for the Organization

The entire systems development process can be viewed as planned organizational change, since the purpose of a new system is to improve the organization's performance. The development process must explicitly address the ways in which the organization will change when the new system is installed. In addition to procedural changes, transformations in job functions, organizational structure, power relationships, and behavior will all have to be carefully planned. For example, Figure 9.10 illustrates the organizational dimensions that would need to be addressed for planning and implementing office automation systems.

Although systems analysis and design activities are supposed to include an organizational impact analysis, this area has traditionally been neglected. An **organizational impact analysis** explains how a proposed system will affect organizational structure, attitudes, decision making, and operations. To integrate information systems successfully with the organization, thorough and fully documented organizational impact assessments must be given more attention in the development effort.

Organizational impact analysis: Study of the way a proposed system will affect organizational structure, attitudes, decision making, and operations.

ALLOWING FOR THE HUMAN FACTOR

The quality of information systems should be evaluated in terms of user criteria rather than just the technical criteria of the information systems staff. For example, a project objective might be that data entry clerks be able to learn the procedures and codes for four new on-line data entry screens in a half-day training session.

Areas where users interface with the system should be carefully designed, with sensitivity to ergonomic issues. **Ergonomics** refers to the interaction of people and machines in the work environment. It considers the design of jobs, health issues, and the end-user interface of information systems. The impact of the application system on the work environment and job dimensions must be carefully assessed. One noteworthy study of 620 Social Security Administration claims representatives showed that the representatives with on-line access to claims data experienced greater stress than those with serial access to the data via teletype. Even though the on-line interface was more rapid and direct than teletype, it created much more frustration. Claims representatives with on-line access could interface with a larger number of clients per day, which changed the dimensions of their jobs. The restructuring of work—involving tasks, quality of working life, and performance—had a more profound impact than the nature of the technology itself (Turner, 1984).

Ergonomics: The interaction of people and machines in the work environment, including the design of jobs, health issues, and the end-user interface of information systems.

Management and organizational researchers have suggested a *sociotechnical* approach to information system design and organizational change. **Sociotechnical design** aims to produce information systems that blend technical efficiency with sensitivity to organizational and human needs, leading to high job satisfaction (Mumford and Weir, 1979).

Sociotechnical design: Design to produce information systems that blend technical efficiency with sensitivity to organizational and human needs.

Figure 9.10
Key human organizational factors for office automation planning and implementation. For successful implementation, the planner must consider ergonomics, training, employee communications, employee participation, and legal/regulatory factors. *Reprinted with permission of G. K. Hall & Co., an imprint of Macmillan Publishing Company, from* The Changing Workplace *by Alan F. Westin et al. Copyright © 1985 by G. K. Hall & Co.*

The sociotechnical design process emphasizes participation by the individuals most affected by the new system. The design plan establishes human objectives for the system that lead to increased job satisfaction. Designers set forth separate sets of technical and social design solutions. The social design plans explore different work group structures, allocation of tasks, and the design of individual jobs. The design solution that best fulfills both technical and social objectives is selected for the final design.

Management Challenges

1. **Applying quality assurance standards in large system projects.** We have explained why the goal of zero defects in large, complex pieces of software is impossible to achieve. If the seriousness of remaining bugs cannot be ascertained, what constitutes an acceptable if not perfect performance? And even if meticulous design and exhaustive testing could eliminate all defects, software projects have time and budget constraints that often prevent management from devoting as much time to thorough testing as it should. Under these circumstances it will be difficult for managers either to define a standard for software quality or to enforce it.

2. **Dealing with the complexity of large-scale systems projects.** Large-scale systems that affect large numbers of organizational units and staff members and that have extensive information requirements are difficult to oversee, coordinate, and plan for. Implementing such systems, which have multi-year

development periods, is especially problem-ridden because the systems are so complex.

3. **Estimating the time and cost to implement a successful large information system.** There are few reliable techniques for estimating the time and cost to develop medium- to large-scale information systems. Few projects take into account the long-term maintenance costs of systems. Guidelines presented in this chapter are helpful but cannot guarantee that a large information system project can be precisely planned and given a projected budget.

Summary

Identify successful information systems.

Successful information systems are accurate, reliable, will work as intended, and will be widely used. The systems will achieve the organization's business goals, operate at acceptable cost, meet defined performance standards, and be flexible and easy to learn and use. Successful information systems are of high quality and help promote overall quality throughout the organization.

Identify major problem areas in information systems and causes of information system failure.

A high percentage of systems are considered failures because they are not used in the way they were intended. Some are not used at all. System failure is evidenced by problems with design, data, operations, or costs. The sources of system success or failure are both technical and organizational. From a technical standpoint, the major source of information system failure is inattention to software quality and overall system quality. From an organizational and behavioral standpoint, the major causes of information system failure are 1) insufficient or improper user participation in the systems development process, 2) lack of management support, 3) poor management of the implementation process, and 4) high levels of complexity and risk in systems development projects.

Describe both traditional and new tools and methodologies for promoting software quality.

Information systems quality problems can be minimized by using traditional and new systems development methodologies, software metrics, quality tools, thorough testing procedures, and by reallocating resources to put more emphasis on the early stages of the systems development cycle.

Structured analysis highlights the flow of data and the processes through which data are transformed. Its principal tool is the data flow diagram. Structured design and programming are software design disciplines that produce reliable, well-documented software with a simple, clear structure that is easy for others to understand and maintain. System flowcharts are useful for documenting the physical aspects of system design.

Computer-aided software engineering (CASE) automates methodologies for systems development. It promotes standards and improves coordination and consistency during systems development. CASE tools help system builders build a better model of a system and facilitate revision of design specifications to correct errors. Object-oriented software development is expected to reduce the time and cost of writing software and of making maintenance changes because it models a system as a series of reusable objects that combines both data and procedures. Software reengineering helps system builders reconfigure aging software to conform to structured design principles, making it easier to maintain.

Describe the relationship between the implementation process and system outcome.

Implementation is the entire process of organizational change surrounding the introduction of a new information system. One can better understand system success and failure by examining different patterns of implementation. Especially important is the relationship between participants in the implementation process, notably the interactions between system designers and users. Conflicts between the technical orientation of system designers and the business orientation of end users must be resolved. The success of organizational change can be determined by how well information systems specialists, end users, and decision makers deal with key issues at various stages during implementation.

Describe appropriate strategies to manage the implementation process.

Management support and control of the implementation process are essential, as are mechanisms for dealing with the level of risk in each new systems project. Some companies experience organizational resistance to change. Project risk factors can be brought under some control by a contingency approach to project management. The level of risk in a systems development project is determined by three key dimensions: 1) project size, 2) project structure, and 3) experience with technology. The risk level of each project will determine the appropriate mix of external integration tools, internal integration tools, formal planning tools, and formal control tools to be applied.

Appropriate strategies can be applied to ensure the correct level of user participation in the system development process and to minimize user resistance. Information system design and the entire implementation process should be managed as planned organizational change. Sociotechnical design emphasizes the participation of the individuals most affected by a new system and aims for an optimal blend of social and technical design solutions.

Key Terms

Total quality management (TQM)
System failure
User interface
Bugs
Development methodology
Resource allocation
Software metrics
Walkthrough
Debugging
Spaghetti code
Structured
Top-down
Structured analysis
Data flow diagram (DFD)
Process specifications
Structured design
Structure chart
Structured programming
Module

System flowchart
Object-oriented software development
Computer-aided software engineering (CASE)
Software re-engineering
Reverse engineering
Forward engineering
Implementation
Change agent
User–designer communications gap
External integration tools
Counterimplementation
Internal integration tools
Formal planning tools
Formal control tools
Organizational impact analysis
Ergonomics
Sociotechnical design

Review Questions

1. List at least four ways to tell a quality system.

2. What is total quality management? How can information systems contribute to it?

3. Describe the four main types of problems that can be found in failing information systems.

4. Describe two software quality problems.

5. Name and describe four solutions to software quality problems.

6. What is structured analysis? What is the role of data flow diagrams in structured analysis?

7. What are the principles of structured design? How can it promote software quality?

8. What is the relationship of structured programming to structured design?

9. Describe the use of system flowcharts.

10. What is the difference between object-oriented software development and traditional structured methodologies?

11. What is CASE? How can it promote quality in information systems?

12. What are software re-engineering and reverse engineering? How can they promote quality in information systems?

13. What is implementation? How is it related to information system success or failure?

14. What are the major causes of implementation success or failure?

15. What is the user–designer communications gap? What kinds of implementation problems can it create?

16. What project management techniques can be used to control project risk and user resistance?

Discussion
Questions

1. How can information system quality benefit from using some of the system-building approaches described in Chapter 8 (systems life cycle, prototyping, software packages, fourth-generation development, outsourcing)? What quality problems are created by each of these approaches?

2. A prominent MIS researcher has observed that "The reason most information systems have failed is that we have ignored organizational behavior problems in the design and operation of computer-based information systems" (Lucas, 1974). Discuss.

Group
Project

Form a group with two or three other students. Write a description of the implementation problems you might expect to encounter for one of the information systems described in the Window on boxes or chapter-ending cases in this text. Write an analysis of the steps you would take to solve or prevent these problems. Present your findings to the class.

CASE STUDY

A Swiss–Swedish Software Developer Becomes an Early CASE User

In 1988, ABB Network Control faced a serious product management problem that was not only costly but that also threatened to undermine the quality of their products. ABB, jointly owned by Asea of Sweden and Brown Boveri of Switzerland, is a giant European business that is headquartered in Zurich. Its Network Control division provides systems to power industry customers all over the world (the division's principal offices are in Sweden, Germany, and the United States). With systems that monitor the electrical networks run by utility companies, ABB is an international leader in its field. ABB's customers vary in size from large utilities supplying whole countries with power to small plants serving only isolated communities. The company develops its systems on Digital Equipment Corp. (DEC) VAX minicomputers and targets the code for either DEC VAXes or DEC's UNIX-based machines.

ABB's business approach is first to develop a generic software package and then to customize that package for each of its hundreds of customers. The generic version of each of their systems (products) contains hundreds of program modules. After producing customized copies of a generic system for each of its customers, ABB must manage tens of thousands of program modules for just that one product, an immense and costly job. When they develop an upgrade to the generic software, it must be applied to each of the customized versions. When a customer finds a software problem that turns out to be part of the generic system, all versions must be fixed. If the problem is part of a customization, ABB must not only fix it for that customer but also determine whether that particular customization is part of any other customers' systems, and if so, fix their systems also. Management logistics for all of this have been a nightmare.

Fixes and upgrades have always meant a great deal of repetitive coding to keep all versions up to date. In time, ABB's 300 software engineers began to find that they were spending too much time coding. They also realized that often they did not know which modules had actually been delivered to which customers. ABB rejected a possible partial solution of keeping a full copy of each system delivered to a customer. Making and storing so many copies was more than the company could handle. They realized they had to find a new answer.

The solution they adopted relied upon a CASE tool, CDD/Repository from Digital Equipment Corp. of Maynard, Massachusetts. The first repository tool ABB installed was the change control system. Change control protects files and keeps records of all changes to each file. A robust change control system will enforce security so that only individuals with proper authorization will be able to access and change files. It will automatically archive older versions of a file when changes are made, preserving as many back versions as desired, thus creating a history of changes for use if needed. A change control system will record the date and time of all changes and the name of the individual making the changes. It will even prevent two people from trying to make changes to the same software simultaneously. These change control features help ABB to manage many versions of a module and manage all the modules of a specific product.

CDD/Repository has object-oriented features that help ABB to keep track of data used to customize different customer systems. "It allows us to track the status and dependencies of our source modules, and of the tools and methods attached to different modules," says Stig Eklund, manager of quality and methods at ABB's Vasteras, Sweden, offices. "We can now tell much more easily which programs or modules are going to be affected by any planned change to the code."

One serious problem Eklund has noted is that performance-response time can be 20 or 30 seconds each time someone starts up a new function. In a system of this size, slow response time can be expensive and frustrating. Eklund has discussed this problem with DEC. They responded that their engineers are giving this problem a high priority and promise steady improvement.

One reason DEC's CASE tool was selected is that ABB develops its products on DEC VAXes and sells them for use on VAXes or DEC UNIX systems. CDD/Repository is a strategic product for DEC because it is central to Network Application Support (NAS), DEC's overall software strategy. One aim of NAS is to address the problem of getting various software tools to work together, a major industry problem. DEC promises to deliver links to other CASE tools, such as Foundation from Arthur Andersen Consulting and IEF from Texas Instruments. DEC's relationship with these and other independent software vendors remains unclear, however, because DEC is also a competitor of theirs.

DEC claims it has sold about 10,000 licenses for CDD/Repository, although industry watchers believe very few purchasers are actually using it fully. ABB was one of the first to use the product, having become a field test site for DEC. As of this writing, the repository has not been installed in either Germany or the United States because DEC has not yet released the distributed features of the product. Now that the change control system is in use, ABB is awaiting the release of other repository tools they plan to install—they expect to begin with a configuration management system. After some experience with DEC's repository, ABB believes the product has given them much greater facility to reuse code and to keep track of modifications.

Source: George Black, "Early User Building Repository Repertoire," *Software Magazine,* July 1992.

Case Study Questions

1. As manager of IS for ABB Network Control, would you have recommended the use of CDD/Repository? Why? Develop the pros and cons of the issue.

2. What problems do you think this tool will solve for ABB? What problems will it not address? Will it create any new problems for them?

3. *Vaporware* is the term the information systems industry uses for software promised but not yet available. How much of ABB's commitment to the DEC repository was based on promises and vaporware? What are the risks of ABB's commitment under these circumstances? In your answer, address the question of the significance of this product to ABB Network Control's future. Is it a risk you believe ABB should have taken? Why?

4. Still in your role as manager of ABB Network Control's IS, under what circumstances would you be willing to purchase a product while it was still being tested? How would you present this issue to your management? Why do you think ABB was willing to go this route?

5. Assume the product had been tested to DEC's satisfaction and had been released for public sale. Would you be willing to be one of the first major users of the system? Why? What are the risks? What are some of the ways you might reduce the risk?

6. ABB Network Control uses DEC hardware and software for its product development and targets their products for use on DEC equipment. What are the problems that this approach to development and marketing creates for ABB? For its customers?

References

Abdel-Hamid, Tarek K. "The Economics of Software Quality Assurance: A Simulation-Based Case Study." *MIS Quarterly* (September 1988).

Alberts, David S. "The Economics of Software Quality Assurance." Washington, D.C.: National Computer Conference, 1976 Proceedings.

Alter, Steven, and Michael Ginzberg. "Managing Uncertainty in MIS Implementation." *Sloan Management Review* vol. 20 (Fall 1978).

Anthes, Gary H. "Why Uncle Sam Can't Compute." *Computerworld* (May 18, 1992).

Banker, Rajiv D., Robert J. Kaufmann, and Rachna Kumar. "An Empirical Test of Object-Based Output Measurement Metrics in a Computer-Aided Software Engineering (CASE) Environment." *Journal of Management Information Systems* 8, no. 3 (Winter 1991–92).

Banker, Rajiv D., and Chris F. Kemerer. "Performance Evaluation Metrics in Information Systems Development: A Principal-Agent Model." *Information Systems Research* 3, no. 4 (December 1992).

Barki, Henri, and Jon Hartwick. "Rethinking the Concept of User Involvement." *MIS Quarterly* 13, no. 1 (March 1989).

Baroudi, Jack, Margrethe H. Olsen, and Blake Ives. "An Empirical Study of the Impact of User Involvement on System Usage and Information Satisfaction." *Communications of the ACM* 29, no. 3 (March 1986).

Baroudi, Jack, and Wanda Orlikowski. "A Short Form Measure of User Information Satisfaction: A Psychometric Evaluation and Notes on Use." *Journal of Management Information Systems* 4, no. 4 (Spring 1988).

Batiste, John L. "The Application Profile." *MIS Quarterly* (September 1986).

Best, James D. "The MIS Executive as Change Agent." *Journal of Information Systems Management* (Fall 1985).

Bikson, Tora K., Cathleen Stasz, and D. A. Mankin. "Computer Mediated Work. Individual and Organizational Impact in One Corporate Headquarters." Santa Monica, CA: Rand Corporation, 1985.

Boehm, Barry W. "Understanding and Controlling Software Costs." *IEEE Transactions on Software Engineering* 14, no. 10 (October 1988).

Booch, Grady. *Object Oriented Design with Applications.* Redwood City, California: Benjamin Cummings, 1991.

Bouldin, Barbara M. "What Are You Measuring? Why Are You Measuring It?" *Software Magazine* (August 1989).

Brooks, Frederick P. "The Mythical Man-Month." *Datamation* (December 1974).

Coad, Peter, with Edward Yourdon. *Object-Oriented Analysis.* Englewood Cliffs, NJ: Prentice-Hall, 1989.

Cooper, Randolph B., and Robert W. Zmud. "Information Technology Implementation Research: A Technological Diffusion Approach." *Management Science* 36, no. 2 (February 1990).

Corbato, Fernando J. "On Building Systems That Will Fail." *Communications of the ACM* Vol. 34, No. 9 (September 1991).

Cronan, Timothy Paul, and David E. Douglas. "End-user Training and Computing Effectiveness in Public Agencies: An Empirical Study." *Journal of Management Information Systems* 6, no. 4 (Spring 1990).

Davis, Fred R. "Perceived Usefulness, Ease of Use, and User Acceptance of Information Technology." *MIS Quarterly* 13, no. 3 (September 1989).

Davis, Gordon B., and Margrethe H. Olson. "Developing and Implementing Application Systems." *Management Information Systems,* 2nd ed. New York: McGraw-Hill, 1985.

Dekleva, Sasa M. "The Influence of Information Systems Development Approach on Maintenance." *MIS Quarterly* 16, no. 3 (September 1992).

DeLone, William H, and Ephrain R. McLean. "Information System Success: The Quest for the Dependent Variable." *Information Systems Research* 3, no. 1 (March 1992).

Delong, William H. "Determinants of Success for Computer Usage in Small Business." *MIS Quarterly* (March 1988).

DeMarco, Tom. *Structured Analysis and System Specification.* New York: Yourdon Press, 1978.

Dijkstra, E. "Structured Programming," in *Classics in Software Engineering,* ed. Edward Nash Yourdon. New York: Yourdon Press, 1979.

Doll, William J. "Avenues for Top Management Involvement in Successful MIS Development." *MIS Quarterly* (March 1985).

Ein-Dor, Philip, and Eli Segev. "Organizational Context and the Success of Management Information Systems." *Management Science* 24 (June 1978).

Flatten, Per O., Donald J. McCubbrey, P. Declan O'Riordan, and Keith Burgess. *Foundations of Business Systems,* 2nd ed. Fort Worth, TX: The Dryden Press, 1992.

Franz, Charles, and Daniel Robey. "An Investigation of User-Led System Design: Rational and Political Perspectives." *Communications of the ACM* 27 (December 1984).

Gane, Chris, and Trish Sarson. *Structured Systems Analysis: Tools and Techniques.* Englewood Cliffs, NJ: Prentice-Hall, 1979.

Ginzberg, M. J. "The Impact of Organizational Characteristics on MIS Design and Implementation." Working paper CRIS 10, GBA 80–110. New York University Center for Research on Information Systems, Area Computer Applications and Information Systems Area, 1980.

Ginzberg, Michael J. "Early Diagnosis of MIS Implementation Failure: Promising Results and Unanswered Questions." *Management Science* 27 (April 1981).

Gould, John D., and Clayton Lewis. "Designing for Usability: Key Principles and What Designers Think." *Communications of the ACM* 28 (March 1985).

Gullo, Karen. "Stopping Runaways in Their Tracks." *InformationWEEK* (November 13, 1989).

Helms, Glenn L., and Ira R. Weiss. "The Cost of Internally Developed Applications: Analysis of Problems and Cost Control Methods." *Journal of Management Information Systems* (Fall 1986).

Henderson-Sellers, Brian, and Julian M. Edwards. "The Object-Oriented Systems Life Cycle." *Communications of the ACM* 33, no. 9 (September 1990).

Hirscheim, R. A. "User Experience with and Assessment of Participative Systems Design." *MIS Quarterly* (December 1985).

International Data Corporation. "Object Technology: A Key Software Technology for the '90s." *Computerworld* (May 11, 1992.)

Ives, Blake, Margrethe H. Olson, and Jack J. Baroudi. "The Measurement of User Information Satisfaction." *Communications of the ACM* 26 (October 1983).

Joshi, Kailash. "A Model of Users' Perspective on Change: The Case of Information Systems Technology Implementation." *MIS Quarterly* 15, no. 2 (June 1991).

Keen, Peter W. "Information Systems and Organizational Change." *Communications of the ACM* 24 (January 1981).

Keyes, Jessica. "New Metrics Needed for New Generation." *Software Magazine* (May 1992).

Kolb, D. A., and A. L. Frohman. "An Organization Development Approach to Consulting." *Sloan Management Review* 12 (Fall 1970).

Korson, Tim, and McGregor, John D. "Understanding Object Oriented: A Unifying Paradigm." *Communications of the ACM* 33, no. 9 (September 1990).

LaPlante, Alice. "For IS, Quality is 'Job None,' " *Computerworld* (January 6, 1992).

Laudon, Kenneth C. "CIOs Beware: Very Large Scale Systems," Center for Research on Information Systems, New York University Stern School of Business, working paper, 1989.

Lederer, Albert L., Rajesh Mirani, Boon Siong Neo, Carol Pollard, Jayesh Prasad, and K. Ramamurthy. "Information System Cost Estimating: A Management Perspective." *MIS Quarterly* 14, no. 2 (June 1990).

Lederer, Albert, and Jayesh Prasad. "Nine Management Guidelines for Better Cost Estimating." *Communications of the ACM* 35, no. 2 (February 1992).

Lientz, Bennett P., and E. Burton Swanson. *Software Maintenance Management.* Reading, MA: Addison-Wesley, 1980.

Littlewood, Bev, and Lorenzo Strigini. "The Risks of Software." *Scientific American* (November 1992).

Lucas, Henry C., Jr. *Implementation: The Key to Successful Information Systems.* New York: Columbia University Press, 1981.

Lucas, Henry C., Jr. *Toward Creative Systems Design.* New York: Columbia University Press, 1974.

Lucas, Henry C., Jr. *Why Information Systems Fail.* New York: Columbia University Press, 1975.

Maletz, Mark C. "KBS Circles: A Technology Transfer Initiative that Leverages Xerox's Leadership through Quality Program." *MIS Quarterly* 14, no. 3 (September 1990).

Mandell, Mel. "Statistical Software Rings in Quality." *Computerworld* (January 6, 1992).

Markus, M. L. "Power, Politics and MIS Implementation." *Communications of the ACM* 26 (June 1983).

Martin, James, and Carma McClure. *Structured Techniques: The Basis of CASE.* Englewood Cliffs, NJ: Prentice-Hall, 1988.

Mazzucchelli, Louis. "Structured Analysis Can Streamline Software Design." *Computerworld* (December 9, 1985).

McFarlan, F. Warren. "Portfolio Approach to Information Systems." *Harvard Business Review* (September–October 1981).

McIntyre, Scott C., and Higgins, Lexis F. "Object-Oriented Analysis and Design: Methodology and Application." *Journal of Management Information Systems* 5, no. 1 (Summer 1988).

McPartlin, John P. "Uncle Sam Calls in the Reserves." *InformationWEEK* (April 27, 1992).

Moore, Gary C., and Izak Benbasat. "Development of an Instrument to Measure the Perceptions of Adopting an Information Technology Innovation." *Information Systems Research* 2, no. 3 (September 1991).

Moran, Robert. "The Case Against CASE." *InformationWEEK* (February 17, 1992).

Mumford, Enid, and Mary Weir. *Computer Systems in Work Design: The ETHICS Method.* New York: Wiley, 1979.

Norman, Ronald J., and Jay F. Nunamaker, Jr. "CASE Productivity Perceptions of Software Engineering Professionals." *Communications of the ACM* 32, no. 9 (September 1989).

Putnam, L. H., and A. Fitzsimmons. "Estimating Software Costs." *Datamation* (September 1979, October 1979, and November 1979).

Radding, Alan. "Quality is Job #1." *Datamation* (October 1, 1992).

Raymond, Louis. "Organizational Context and Information System Success: A Contingency Approach." *Journal of Management Information Systems* 6, no. 4 (Spring 1990).

Rettig, Marc. "Software Teams." *Communications of the ACM* 33, no. 10 (October 1990).

Robey, Daniel, and M. Lynne Markus. "Rituals in Information System Design." *MIS Quarterly* (March 1984).

Singleton, John P., Ephraim R. McLean, and Edward N. Altman. "Measuring Information Systems Performance." *MIS Quarterly* 12, no. 2 (June 1988).

Swanson, E. Burton. *Information System Implementation.* Homewood, IL: Richard D. Irwin Inc., 1988.

Swanson, Kent, Dave McComb, Jill Smith, and Don McCubbrey. "The Application Software Factory: Applying Total Quality Techniques to Systems Development." *MIS Quarterly,* 15, no. 4 (December 1991).

Tait, Peter, and Iris Vessey. "The Effect of User Involvement on System Success: A Contingency Approach." *MIS Quarterly* 12, no. 1 (March 1988).

Tornatsky, Louis G., J. D. Eveland, M. G. Boylan, W. A. Hetzner, E. C. Johnson, D. Roitman, and J. Schneider. *The Process of Technological Innovation: Reviewing the Literature.* Washington, DC: National Science Foundation, 1983.

Turner, Jon A. "Computer Mediated Work: The Interplay Between Technology and Structured Jobs." *Communications of the ACM* 27 (December 1984).

United States General Services Administration. "An Evaluation of the Grand Design Approach to Developing Computer-Based Application Systems." Washington, DC: General Services Administration, September 1988.

Westcott, Russ. "Client Satisfaction: The Yardstick for Measuring MIS Success." *Journal of Information Systems Management* (Fall 1985).

Westin, Alan F., Heather A. Schweder, Michael A. Baker, and Sheila Lehman. *The Changing Workplace.* White Plains, NY, and London: Knowledge Industry Publications, Inc., 1985.

White, Kathy Brittain, and Richard Leifer. "Information Systems Development Success: Perspectives from Project Team Participants." *MIS Quarterly* (September 1986).

Yin, Robert K. "Life Histories of Innovations: How New Practices Become Routinized." *Public Administration Review* (January/February 1981).

Yourdon, Edward, and L. L. Constantine, *Structured Design.* New York: Yourdon Press, 1978.

CHAPTER

10

Knowledge and Information Work Systems

The Virtual Research Institute

Unlike many leading medical schools, Harvard Medical School does not have its own teaching hospital. Instead, it uses a series of affiliated institutions in the greater Boston area, staffed by more than 10,000 physicians and medical workers. Among all of these institutions is a huge pool of expertise and knowledge that faculty and researchers and the medical school want to tap. But until recently, the setup was so huge and dispersed geographically that the vast expertise that was available was practically unreachable and unlocatable.

Jim Fitchett, the chief information officer at Harvard Medical School, decided to change this situation. He implemented the Longwood Medical Area Network (LMA Net), which now ties Harvard Medical School and eight affiliated institutions together into a virtual research institute. He linked ten additional institutions with an electronic mail system and

Business Challenges
• Research work geographically dispersed

Management
• Coordinate research
• Coordinate and monitor programs

Information Technology
• LAN
• E-mail
• Shared databases
• ISDN
• Worldwide networks

Information System

Organization
• Harvard Medical School
• Affiliated institutions
• Researchers

Business Solutions
• Expedite research
• Create joint programs
• Obtain revenue

• Share research information
• Share funding information
• Locate colleagues doing research
• Provide research information to pharmaceutical firms

shared databases. This network supports wide-scale information sharing and also gives users access to the Internet (a worldwide collection of networks linking academic researchers) and to a growing list of libraries and databases.

The network makes collaboration instantaneous. For instance, Dr. Lawrence C. Madoff, a bacterial vaccine researcher at Brigham and Women's Hospital, uses the network to access genetic database servers at Massachusetts General Hospital and to locate colleagues doing similar research. He plans to use the Internet to participate in a national multi-center study on Group B streptococcus. LMA Net also permitted the medical school to create joint programs in neonatology, nuclear medicine, and alcohol and substance abuse disciplines. Fitchett cabled the medical school campus with fiber optics and installed an Integrated Services Digital Network (ISDN).

SIMON, a medical research community database introduced in the fall of 1992, allows researchers to obtain information more rapidly and serves as a matchmaker between research projects and sources of funding. The database contains information about the research interests of all of the medical school professors and their willingness to use students to do research in labs. When Harvard Medical School receives notices of funding opportunities, it uses SI-MON to track down who is doing the kind of research that the sources are willing to fund. When SIMON was tapped during a recent funding cycle for pediatric AIDS, it turned up 14 potential candidates for funding. Four applied for grants. In addition to furthering research, SIMON can help speed up medical advances by making research information immediately available to companies interested in developing new drugs and products.

While they are erudite in other areas, many physicians and medical researchers are reluctant to use computers. According to Audrey Bernfield, Harvard Medical School's director of enrichment programs, people feel that since they can pick up their telephones and call colleagues to ask who is doing cellular biology research, they do not need computers and databases.

Fitchett found that the truly pressing need of these professionals is communication. Information is the lifeblood of medical research, especially information about what research is being conducted where and by whom and about possible sources of funding. When Fitchett installed Lotus Development Corporation's CC: Mail electronic mail system, researchers found that queries that might have gone unanswered for days were being answered in four hours. People who had questions in the middle of the night could get answers. E-mail vastly expanded the span of control researchers had over their work.

Source: Nell Margolis, "Strong Medicine," *Computerworld,* March 8, 1993.

Collaborating and communicating with other experts and sharing ideas and information are essential requirements not only for academic institutions such as Harvard Medical School, but for businesses today as well. Advanced industrial societies have shifted from manufacturing to an information economy in which the basis of wealth is the production of information and knowledge. The shift calls for new kinds of information systems to help organizations create, coordinate and distribute information to achieve their goals. Such systems are called information and knowledge work systems, and they are the focus of this chapter.

This chapter describes the emergence of information and knowledge work and the unique information requirements of information and knowledge workers. Because offices play such a pivotal role in contemporary organizations, information systems designed to support major office activities and to promote collaborative work have become increasingly critical. We describe the major types of information systems used for disseminating and coordinating the flow of information in the organization and for supporting the activities of highly skilled knowledge workers and professionals.

After completing this chapter you will be able to:

- Define information work and the information economy.
- Describe the roles of knowledge workers and data workers in the organization.
- Describe the roles and principal activities of the office in contemporary business.
- Explain the contributions of the principal types of office automation technologies.
- Understand unique requirements of knowledge work systems.
- Describe the major types of knowledge work systems.

10.1 Knowledge and Information Work

Chapter 1 introduced the emergence of information economy as one of the key challenges of information systems today. The shift to an economy where the major source of wealth and prosperity is the production and distribution of information and knowledge has profound implications for the kinds of information systems found in contemporary organizations and the way they are used.

Transformation of the Economy

Since the turn of the century, the United States, Canada, and Western Europe have been moving toward a service and information economy and away from an agricultural and manufacturing economy. Figure 1.1 in Chapter 1 shows that the percentage of people who work in offices using information to produce economic value has been rising and the percentage of workers who work with their hands in factories or on farms has been declining. (In the United States, the percentage of jobs in manufacturing has fallen from 27 percent in 1920 to 17 percent today and is expected to be 12 percent by 2005.) Among white-collar workers, the fastest growing occupations have been clerical, professional and technical workers, and managers and administrators (see Figure 10.1).

Four factors are involved in this shift. First, there has been a worldwide shift in the production of manufactured goods in which third-world and developing societies have become centers of manufacturing. At the same time, the so-called advanced societies have shifted toward services. Textile products and steel ingots are more economically produced in Asian countries, while North American and European countries are the primary sources for bioengineering services and products or computer software.

Knowledge- and information-intense products: Products that require a great deal of learning and knowledge to produce.

Second, there has been a rapid growth in knowledge and information-intense products and services. **Knowledge- and information-intense products** are products that require a great deal of learning and knowledge to produce. Intensifi-

Figure 10.1
Changes in the nature of work during the 20th century. Both the number and proportion of white-collar jobs in the U. S. labor force have grown considerably over the last 90 years, with the fastest growth occurring among clerical, professional and technical, and managerial and administrative occupations. *Adapted from "The Mechanization of Office Work" by Vincent Guiliano,* Scientific American, *September 1982. Copyright © 1982, by Scientific American, Inc. All rights reserved.*

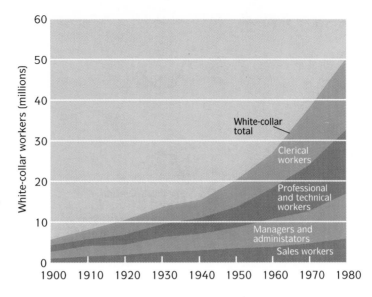

cation of knowledge utilization in the production of traditional products has increased as well. This trend is readily seen throughout the automobile industry where both design and production now rely heavily upon knowledge-intensive information technology. Over the past decade, the automobile producers have sharply increased their hiring of computer specialists, engineers, and designers while reducing the number of blue-collar production workers. Entire new information services have sprung up, such as CompuServe, Prodigy, Dow Jones News Service, and Lexis. These fields are now employing millions of people.

Third, there has been a substitution of knowledge and information workers for manual production workers within the goods sectors. Machine tool operators, for instance, have often been replaced by technicians who monitor computer-controlled machine tools. Fourth, new kinds of knowledge- and information-intense organizations have emerged that are devoted entirely to the production, processing, and distribution of information. For instance, environmental engineering firms, which specialize in preparing environmental impact statements for municipalities and private contractors, simply did not exist prior to the 1960s. These new kinds of organizations also employ millions of people.

With these changes, there were conservatively 63 million information workers in the U.S. economy (around 52 percent of the labor force) by 1980. As early as 1976, the value of information-sector products and services had already exceeded that of the manufacturing or goods sector (see Figure 10.2). By 1990, the information sector (including services) accounted for $3 out of every $4 of GNP in the United States. The shift toward information work and workers has had profound implications for the kinds of information technologies and systems found at the heart of business enterprises. Because so much of the U.S. and other advanced economies depends on knowledge and information work, any overall advance in productivity and wealth critically depends on increasing the productivity of knowledge and information workers.

What Is Knowledge and Information Work?

To describe how information systems can increase the productivity of information and knowledge workers, we need to understand what kinds of jobs these workers perform. First, we have to establish some basic definitions. Table 10.1 gives some examples of information, service, and goods industries.

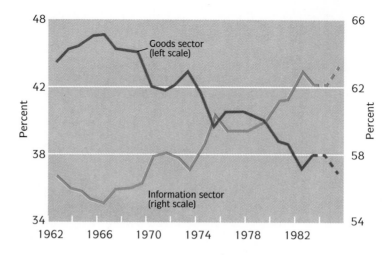

Figure 10.2:
Emergence of the information economy. The value of the information sector in the U.S. economy began to exceed the value of the manufacturing or goods sector by 1976 and has continued to surpass it into the 1990s. *Reprinted by permission of the publisher from "Technology and the Service Sector." by Stephen S. Roach,* Technological Forecasting and Social Change, *Vol. 34, No. 4, December 1988. Copyright 1988 by Elsevier Science Publishing Co., Inc.*

Table 10.1 EXAMPLES OF INFORMATION, GOODS, AND SERVICE INDUSTRIES

Information	Goods	Service
Telephone	Agriculture	Hotels
Trade	Logging	Business service
Finance	Chemicals	Auto repair
Insurance	Steel	Medical service
Education	Farm machines	Amusements

Sources: Wolff and Baumol, 1987; U.S. Census 1980.

DISTINGUISHING KNOWLEDGE AND DATA WORKERS

Information workers: People in the labor force who primarily create, work with, or disseminate information.

Information work: Work that primarily consists of creating or processing information.

Knowledge workers: People such as engineers, scientists, or architects who design products or services or create new knowledge for the organization.

Data workers: People such as secretaries or bookkeepers who primarily process and disseminate the organization's paperwork.

The U.S Department of Labor defines as **information workers** all those people in the labor force who primarily create, work with, or disseminate information. **Information work** is work that consists primarily of creating or processing information. There are two commonly accepted types of information workers: **knowledge workers** (those who primarily create new information and knowledge) and **data workers** (who primarily use, process, or disseminate information). Thus, knowledge work refers to work that primarily creates new information or knowledge. Data work is work that involves the use, manipulation, or dissemination of information.

In contrast, service workers are those people who primarily deliver a service, and goods workers are those who primarily work with physical objects or transform physical materials. Examples of each of these four kinds of workers are given in Table 10.2.

These distinctions are not always easy to apply, and some occupations like managers both create new information and distribute data. Scholars handle this ambiguity by classifying half the managers as knowledge workers and half as data workers.

Knowledge and data workers can be distinguished by the amount of formal education required for them to be qualified to work in the field. Knowledge workers—like engineers, judges, scientists, writers, and architects—all must exercise independent judgment and creativity based on their mastery of a large body of specialized knowledge. Therefore, they usually must obtain an advanced degree and/or a professional certification before beginning their work careers. Data workers, such as sales personnel, accountants, real estate agents, and secretaries, on the other hand, primarily process information and do not create it. Typically, this type of work does not require advanced educational degrees, although some college or even an undergraduate degree is often required.

Table 10.2   EXAMPLES OF OCCUPATIONS FOR KNOWLEDGE, DATA, SERVICE, AND GOODS WORKERS

Knowledge	Data	Service	Goods
Architect	Salesperson	Waiter	Teamster
Engineer	Accountant	Sanitary engineer	Welder
Judge	Lawyer	Cook	Machine operator
Scientist	Pharmacist	Nurse	Lumberman
Reporter	R.R. conductor	Hairdresser	Fisherman
Researcher	Foreman	Child care worker	Farmer
Writer	Draftsman	Gardener	Construction worker
Actuary	Real estate salesperson	Cleaner	Miner
Programmer	Secretary	Barber	Glazier
Manager*	Manager	Clergy*	Factory operative

Source: Wolff and Baumol, 1987; Porat, 1977.

*Many occupations—like managers and clergy—cannot be easily classified. Managers, for instance, sometimes create new knowledge and information when they write reports and hence often act like knowledge workers. At other times, they read and disseminate reports like data workers. Scholars handle this situation by classifying half of the managers as knowledge workers and half as data workers. A similar situation exists with clergy: They both provide a service and disseminate information. In the future we will need better data on specific occupations.

Not surprisingly, these two groups of workers tend to have different information systems needs. While data and knowledge workers both use office automation systems, data workers rely upon them as their primary or only system. However, to do their work, knowledge workers often require specific knowledge work systems based on powerful professional workstations and highly specialized software.

Information Work and Productivity

Over the past several years business has become intensely aware of competition from other industrialized economies. The United States has led the world in productivity throughout most of the twentieth century. While the United States still maintains its productivity lead, the size of that lead is shrinking as the growth of U.S. productivity declines relative to that of Germany, Japan, and many other industrialized countries.

As we have indicated, knowledge- and information-intense industries have become the fastest growing industries in the United States, while the fastest growing segment of the American labor force is the information workers. The country has also experienced a dramatic shift in capital investment patterns in recent years—in the early 1980s, for the first time, capital investment per information worker began to surpass capital investment per factory worker. In 1989, over 70 percent of all capital investment was in the area of information technology, with most of that 70 percent going directly into offices.

Thus, clearly if the United States is to increase its international competitiveness, American business must address the issue of the productivity of its information workers. The extent to which computers have enhanced the productivity of information workers is the subject of considerable debate. Some studies show that investment in information technology has not led to any appreciable growth in productivity among office workers. While productivity did rise, Morgan Stanley senior economist Stephen Roach estimates that the average white-collar productivity gain from 1980 to 1990 has only been 0.28 percent annually (Roach, 1988). Service sector productivity grew nearly 3% annually in 1991–92 but it is still too early to tell whether these gains are short-term or whether they represent an end to the stagnation of the past decade (Roach, 1993).

On the other hand, productivity changes among information workers are difficult to measure because of the problems of identifying suitable units of output for information work (Panko, 1991). How does one measure the output of a law office? Should one measure productivity by examining the number of forms completed per employee (a measure of physical unit productivity), or by examining the amount of revenue produced per employee (a measure of financial unit productivity) in an information- and knowledge-intense industry?

10.2 Information Work and Office Automation

Information work is concentrated in offices, and office automation systems have been developed to facilitate the processing, distribution, and coordination of information in the firm. Here we describe the role of offices in contemporary organizations and show how this role can be supported by various types of office automation technologies.

Three Roles of the Office Within the Organization

No longer a mundane clerical typing pool or simply a "bureaucratic nightmare," by the 1980s, scholars and computer vendors alike came to see the office as one of the most important work sites for professional knowledge and data workers. Offices today involve an incredibly diverse array of professional, managerial, sales, and clerical employees. Offices are groups composed of people who work together toward shared goals. In this sense, office work is complex and cooperative, and yet highly individualistic. It represents not a factory of collaborating workers so much as an orchestra of highly trained individuals. Offices perform three critical organizational roles (see Figure 10.3):

- They coordinate and manage the work of local professional and information workers within the organization.

Figure 10.3
The three major roles of offices. Offices perform three major roles. [1] They coordinate the work of local professionals and information workers. [2] They couple the organization to the external environment. [3] They coordinate work in the organization across levels and functions.

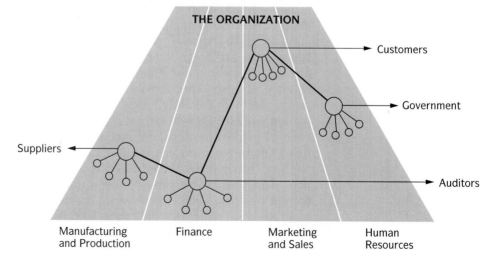

- They link the work being performed across all levels and functions throughout the organization.
- They couple the organization to the external environment, including to its clients and suppliers; when you call an organization, you call an office.

Major Office Activities

Office activities: The principal activities performed at offices; these include managing documents, scheduling and communicating with people, managing data, and managing projects.

To fulfill the roles that we have described, offices usually perform the five major **office activities** listed in Table 10.3: managing documents, scheduling individuals and groups, communicating with individuals and groups, managing data on individuals and groups, and managing projects. Table 10.3 also contains the authors' estimate, on average, of percentage of effort (capital investment and time) the office invests in each activity. For example, we estimate that document management characteristically consumes about 40 percent of the total office effort in time expended and capital investment. Information technology that has been developed to support each of these activities is listed in the far right column of the table. Some of these technologies, such as groupware, actually support more than one of these activities.

Office Activities and Technologies

Office automation systems (OAS): Computer systems, such as word processing, voice-mail systems, and video conferencing systems, that are designed to increase the productivity of information workers in the office.

Office automation systems (OAS) can be defined as any application of information technology that intends to increase productivity of information workers in the office. Fifteen years ago, office automation meant only the creation, processing, and management of documents. Today, although professional knowledge and information work remains highly document-centered, office work requires a great deal more from its office automation systems. Digital image processing—word and document—is also at the core of today's systems, as are high-speed digital communications services. Because office work involves many people jointly engaged in projects, contemporary office automation systems have powerful project management tools and group assistance tools like networked digital calendars. An ideal contemporary office automation system would involve a seamless network of digital machines linking professional, clerical, and managerial work groups and running a variety of types of software (see, again, Table 10.3).

While the first wave of office automation systems established technologies designed to support such obvious office clerical activities as word processing and simple task coordination, in the 1990s new office applications are based on emerging technologies: document management technologies, technologies for collaborative work, desktop data management technologies, and project management technologies (see Table 10.4).

MANAGING DOCUMENTS

Technologies that are used to create, process, and manage documents are known as document management technologies. These technologies include word processing, desktop publishing, document imaging, and workflow management.

WORD PROCESSING AND DESKTOP PUBLISHING

Word processing: Office automation technology that facilitates the creation of documents through computerized text editing, formatting, storing, and printing.

Word processing technology is used to create, format, edit, store, manage, and print documents. Word processing is the most widely used technology in today's offices. Its popularity is a result of the dramatic increase in productivity it has brought to all information workers—clerks, managers, and knowledge workers alike. Because the text is stored electronically rather than on paper, changes and corrections can be made in a moment without requiring the user to retype the document. The software allows an almost unlimited combination of formatting options—top, bottom, and side margins; line spacing; tabs; columns; font (character) selections and character (point) sizes; and even such formatting features as automated footnoting.

Table 10.3 OFFICE AUTOMATION: ROLES, ACTIVITIES, AND SYSTEMS IN THE MODERN OFFICE

General Roles of Offices	Activities in an Office	Percentage of Effort	Information Technology Assistance
1. Coordination and management of people and work	1. Managing documents Creating, storing/retrieving, and communicating image (analog) and digital documents	40%	Document management Word processing hardware and software Desktop publishing Digital image processing
2. Linking organizational units and projects	2. Scheduling individuals and groups Creating, managing, and communicating documents, plans, and calendars	10%	Digital calendars Electronic calendars and schedules Electronic mail Groupware
3. Coupling the organization to outside groups and people	3. Communicating with individuals and groups Initiating, receiving, and managing voice and digital communications with diverse groups and individuals	30%	Communications PBX and digital phone equipment Voice mail Groupware
	4. Managing data on individuals and groups Entering and managing data to track external customers, clients, and vendors and internal individuals and groups	10%	Data management Desktop database for client/customer tracking, project tracking, and calendar information (personal information manager)
	5. Managing projects Planning, initiating, evaluating, monitoring projects Resource allocation Personnel decisions	10%	Project management Desktop project management tools CPM and PERT methods

Source: © 1995 Azimuth Corporation

Table 10.4 EMERGING OFFICE TECHNOLOGIES OF THE 1990S

Office Activity	Emerging Technology
Managing documents	Document imaging/workflow management
Collaborative work	Groupware, E-mail, electronic calendars
Managing information	Desktop data management (personal information managers)
Managing projects	Desktop project managers

Frequently, word processing software packages include such advanced features as a dictionary for spell checking, a thesaurus, a style checker (which analyzes both grammar and punctuation), and mail merge facilities (typically used to link documents to separately stored mailing list names and addresses). Word processors often allow the user to insert graphic images into the document. In addition, these packages permit the user to produce hard copy easily on demand on most popular printers.

Desktop publishing:
Technology that produces professional-quality documents combining output from word processors with design, graphics, and special layout features.

Desktop publishing technology goes a step beyond word processing, allowing the user to produce professional publishing-quality output often using documents created with word processing software and even by entering text directly into the DTP package. A skilled user of a desktop publisher can produce brochures, newsletters, and reports that approach the quality of a professional typesetter and graphics designer. Desktop publishing packages, such as PageMaker by Aldus, surpass the options available in word processing software; these packages offer enhanced text handling and page layout capabilities. They allow the user to resize, rotate, and modify graphics images. This technology also includes a computer language, often Adobe System's Postscript, to define the page, type fonts, and graphics for high-quality laser printers and other output devices. Desktop publishing truly lives up to its name by bringing professional publishing to the desktop computer.

DOCUMENT IMAGING AND WORKFLOW SYSTEMS

While word processing and desktop publishing address the creation and presentation of documents, they only exacerbate the existing paper avalanche problem. Hundreds of billions of pieces of paper are produced by businesses each year. The U.S. banking industry handled 50 billion checks in 1990 at an average per-check handling cost of five cents, or a total handling cost of $2.5 billion. Ultramar Oil, a Long Beach, California, oil refinery, maintains about 20,000 material safety data sheets in huge notebooks; if an emergency chemical spill occurs, employees must manually search these notebooks for the appropriate sheet or sheets that contain the life-saving and damage control information they urgently need.

The issue concerns far more than sheer quantity, however. Workflow problems arising from paper handling are enormous. For instance, a large American health insurance company processes more than 80,000 claims per day; the mail room staff sorts the claims by type and category, and in the process 8 percent (about 6,500) are lost or missorted, costing the company an extra $4 million per year. According to International Data Corporation (IDC 1990), an insurance application submitted on paper would typically require about eleven clerical and six professional steps and could take 33 days (see Figure 10.4). Customer calls often require the customer service staff to locate paper documents and then call the customer back; a major New York bank estimated that if it eliminated the return calls, it could save millions of dollars every year just in the phone bill (not to mention staff time costs and customer relations problems).

Chapter 2 introduced the concept of digital image processing, whereby documents and images are converted into digitized form so that they can be stored

Document imaging systems:
Systems that employ digital image processing to store, retrieve, and manipulate a digitized image of a document, allowing the document itself to be discarded.

and accessed by the computer. **Document imaging systems** are systems that employ digital image processing to store, retrieve, and manipulate a digitized image of a document, allowing the document itself to be discarded. The system must contain a scanner that converts the document image into a bit-mapped image, storing that image as a graphic. This technology is different from optical character recognition (OCR) which "reads" a printed optical character, identifies the character by determining its pattern, and then stores it in the computer in its digital form. With OCR, a document is character-based and can be edited like any document created in a word processor. However, with imaging systems, a picture of the document is stored. With imaging systems, the document will originally be stored on a magnetic disk, where it can be retrieved instantly. When it ceases to be active, it will be transferred to an optical disk, where it will be stored for as many months or years as is needed. Optical disks, kept on-line in a **jukebox** (a device for storing and retrieving many optical disks) require up to a minute to retrieve the document automatically. A typical large jukebox will store over 10,000,000 pages (an 8 1/2″ by 11″ document usually requires about 50 kilobytes of storage after data compression).

Jukebox: A device for storing and retrieving many optical disks.

Index server: In imaging systems, a device that stores the indexes that allow a user to identify and retrieve a specific document.

An imaging system also requires an **index server** to contain the indexes that will allow users to identify and retrieve the document when needed. Once the document has been scanned, index data are entered so that the document can be retrieved in a variety of ways, depending upon the application. For example, the index may contain the document scan date, the customer name and number, the document type, and some subject information. Finally, the system must include retrieval equipment, primarily workstations capable of handling graphics, although printers are usually included.

To achieve the large productivity gains promised by imaging technology, organizations must redesign their workflow. In the past, the existence of only one copy of the document largely shaped workflow. Work had to be performed serially; two people could not work on the same document at the same time. Documents needed to be protected so they would not be lost or destroyed. Documents containing confidential data had to be locked up. Significant staff time had to be devoted to filing and retrieving documents. Critical analytical work could not be done because files could not be found—either because they were out (in use) or because they were not filed according to the kind of data the individual needs to analyze (an insurance company cannot study breast cancer claim costs if the documents are filed by the name of the insured rather than by the type of illness).

Workflow management: The process of streamlining business procedures so that documents can be moved easily and efficiently from one location to another.

Once a document has been stored electronically, workflow management can change the traditional methods of working with documents. **Workflow management** is the process of streamlining business procedures so that documents can be moved more easily and efficiently from one location to another. Imaging technology automates processes such as routing documents to different locations, securing approvals, scheduling, and generating reports. Document integrity—protection against loss, destruction, or prying eyes—can be handled through data backup, and through terminal and/or login ID security, just as with other computer data. Two or more people can work simultaneously on the same document, allowing a much quicker completion date. Work need not ever be delayed because a file is "out" or a document is "in transit." And with a properly designed indexing system, users will be able to retrieve files in many different ways, based upon the content of the document. Figure 10.4 illustrates the efficiency and productivity gains that could result from using imaging and workflow automation in the insurance underwriting application.

Let us look at an actual success story. Iowa's Central Life Assurance Co. (CLA) in Des Moines turned to imaging in an attempt to achieve a paperless workflow. CLA handles more than $18 billion in individual life insurance (operating in 44 states) and was being overwhelmed by paper. Its problems were typical: misfilings, lost documents, outdated documents mixed in with current documents, expensive floor space given over to armies of file cabinets. The

Paper system insurance application

11 clerical steps + 6 professional steps = 33 Days

Imaging system insurance application

3 clerical steps + 4 professional steps = 5 Days

Figure 10.4
Insurance underwriting application enhanced by imaging and workflow automation. The improved efficiency and reduced workflow justify the expense of an image management system. The application requiring 33 days in a paper system would take only 5 days with image management and workflow redesign, resulting in tremendous savings to the insurance company. *Source: "Image Management Systems," IDC White Paper,* Computerworld, *September 24, 1990. Copyright 1990 by CW Publishing, Inc., Framingham, MA 01701. Reprinted from* Computerworld.

company decided to try imaging technology, starting with policy applications only. It purchased Metaview, a desktop system from Metafile Information Systems, Inc. (see Figure 10.5). The images are stored magnetically for the period when the document is active, after which they are copied to a 12-inch optical disk in a Sony Corp. 50-disk jukebox. Daily, the mail room scans approximately 700 pages of applications as they are received. The mail room staff then enters the index data, checks the image for quality, and electronically routes the document to the appropriate work queue. CLA's staff uses about 60 80386 IBM PS/2s to access the applications through a fiber-optic Netframe NF 400 network. The electronic file will be updated as processing continues. Ultimately, each application file will contain all required information—application, financial reports, medical information, even photographs. Once the file is complete, the underwriters review the application and approve or deny it (Daly, 1992).

Imaging systems, combined with workflow management, can bring many benefits to an organization:

- *Cost savings, as we have documented, can be significant.* According to the International Data Corporation, such corporations as American Express, Citicorp, and Federal Express believe they are realizing annual savings of 20 percent.
- *Paper reduction is clear.* Most people will be working from electronic copies, not paper copies.
- *Linked closely to paper reduction is floor space.* One major U.S. law firm estimates that turning to document imaging freed up 80 percent of its office space.
- *Time saving is another benefit.* The same law firm claims a 50 percent reduction in time spent filing, copying, storing, and retrieving documents. This benefit can be very significant for organizations that currently archive paper documents and then require two or more days to locate these documents.
- *Work management is enhanced.* One bank mortgage department has automated the work queues so that no mortgage operator has more than five mortgages in his or her queue at a time.
- *Customer service can be dramatically improved.* Customer service staff can answer questions instantly. Customers are not placed on hold while the staff member searches for the file. Customers do not have to be called

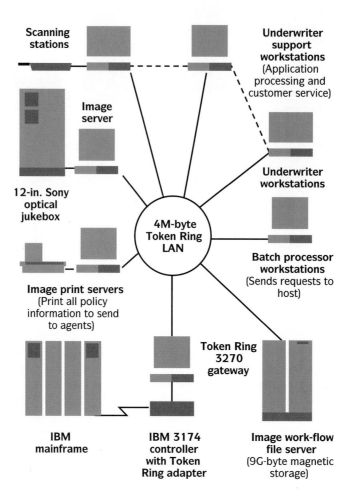

Figure 10.5
Central Life Assurance's document imaging system. A token ring LAN provides the network support to link the data entry, underwriting and policy preparation for document management at the Central Life Assurance Company. *Source: James Daly, "Insurer sees Future in Imaging Strategy,"* Computerworld, *January 6, 1992, p. 41. Copyright 1992 by CW Publishing, Inc., Framingham, MA 01701. Reprinted from* Computerworld.

back because the file is not available. Customer satisfaction can be enhanced by a company's ability to complete its work more quickly; for example, a company can respond to a medical claim in days instead of weeks.

Image technology is also a source of genuine competitive advantage. American Express card holders know that their monthly bill contains an image of each transaction because of the company's commitment to image technology (see Chapter 2). By using imaging in creative ways, American Express claims to have reduced its billing costs by 25 percent while offering its customers a new and important service at least two years before its competition.

However, installing new, far-reaching technology is usually expensive and risky. Imaging technology is no exception:

- *Imaging can be very expensive.* The average significant imaging project starts out in the $1 million to $2 million range. To succeed, the project must commence after careful planning, including a thorough up-front feasibility study.

- *Hardware and software compatibility is a major stumbling block.* While every vendor professes to have open systems, many imaging systems have connectivity problems. Even if a firm purchases a complete system from one vendor so that all parts work well together, the system may not work with the firm's existing technology. It is not uncommon for a purchaser to discover that its new imaging system is not compatible with the network already in use throughout the company. To avoid this problem, the purchaser should demand on-site testing of all components before signing an agreement with the vendor.

- *Power demands for an imaging system can be very large.* The firm should include power usage costs and any upgrading costs in its plan and estimates.
- *Major benefits will not accrue if the imaging system is installed only to increase automation of the current workflow.* Organizations must use the opportunity to make workflow changes that will provide the large productivity gains this technology promises.
- *Major workflow changes can result in organizational disruption and worker distress.* Because jobs and patterns of work are affected by imaging technology and workflow redesign, organizations should plan carefully to include a great deal of training in their imaging projects.

Reports of major productivity gains have come from both businesses and the government. However, such gains will come only if the application is chosen carefully.

Groupware: New Technology for Collaborative Work

Groupware: Software that recognizes the significance of groups in offices by providing functions and services that support the collaborative activities of work groups.

Almost all office automation software has been designed for the individual who is working alone. Yet our definition of an office (earlier in this chapter) states that offices are work groups composed of people who work together toward shared goals. **Groupware** is a new kind of software that recognizes the significance of groups in offices by providing functions and services that support the collaborative activities of work groups. The goal of groupware is to improve the effectiveness of the work group by providing electronic links between its members.

What happens in groups? Members of the group perform the following activities:

- Schedule meetings.
- Hold meetings.
- Communicate with each other.
- Collaborate to develop ideas.
- Share the preparation of documents.
- Share knowledge.
- Share information on the work each member is doing.

Groupware is a growing field of software meant to support all of these activities. No precise definition of groupware has emerged, but terms like *cooperative* and *collaborative* are commonly used when discussing it. Groupware usually includes such functions as information sharing, electronic meetings, scheduling, and E-mail. This technology requires the use of a network to connect the members of the group as they work on their own desktop computers, often in widely scattered locations. The groupware definition of groups is fluid, allowing users to define the work groups, with multiple group definitions allowed. For example, a manager may define a group of only those people who work for him. A group may be established for all employees dealing with a specific customer. A companywide group may be established. Of course, an individual will belong to as many of those groups as is appropriate.

Electronic calendaring: Software that tracks appointments and schedules in an office.

Electronic calendaring is a broadly accepted technology. Although its software has been typically used to keep track of appointments for individuals, groupware calendaring software adds a focus on group schedules, allowing individuals to view the calendars of other members of their own group. One popular function is the ability of the software automatically to search the calendars of members of the group for an acceptable meeting time and then to schedule that meeting for each individual in the group.

Electronic mail (E-mail):
Software that allows the electronic exchange of messages between users in remote locations.

Electronic mail (E-mail) is software that allows the electronic exchange of messages (see the discussion in chapter 7). Electronic mail can enhance productivity by speeding up information flow and lessening the need for placing telephone calls or paper-based messaging systems. E-mail thus reduces group coordination costs. It also creates new patterns of social interaction so that people can share new data and ideas (Sproull and Kiesler, 1991). Some E-mail systems are limited to message exchanges between users of a single computer. More commonly, however, E-mail systems also pass messages from computer to computer, sometimes within the same location, sometimes halfway round the world. Many UNIX systems accomplish this by a dial-up telephone link. However, in recent years E-mail has come more and more to reside on networks. Because groupware, by definition, must connect workers on separate computers, groupware software often includes an E-mail function, even though many purchasers of groupware already have one or more E-mail systems installed. For E-mail to be fully effective within an organization that uses multiple E-mail systems, that organization must make those systems "talk" to each other so that an individual on one system can communicate with someone on a different E-mail system.

Electronic meeting software:
Software designed to enhance the productivity of face-to-face meetings or of meetings among participants in scattered locations.

Electronic meeting software packages are designed to increase the productivity of a face-to-face group meeting or to make possible a meeting of participants in scattered locations. Some such software will do both, and some electronic meeting software utilizes videoconferencing (see the chapter-ending case study). We discuss the way in which this software enhances the decision-support function in Chapter 11.

We will discuss the remainder of the workgroup functions together, as they all involve shared messages and documents. Groupware enhances collaboration by allowing the exchange of ideas (in the form of electronic messages) on a given topic. All the messages on that topic will be saved in a group, stamped with the date, time, and author. Any group member can review the ideas of others at any time and add ideas of his or her own. Similarly, individuals can post a document for other members of the group to comment upon and/or edit. Members of a group can post requests for help from the group, and any member of the group can respond and can view the responses of other members of the group. Finally, if a group so chooses, the members of that group can store their work notes on the groupware so that all others in the group can see what progress is being made, what problems occur, what activities are planned.

LOTUS NOTES

Groupware products such as Higgins, The Coordinator, and Microsoft's Windows for Workgroups are all commercially available, but the leading groupware software is Lotus Notes from Lotus Software, in Cambridge, Massachusetts. To illustrate the power and value of groupware, we will describe the functions contained in Lotus Notes and also discuss several of its actual applications.

Lotus Notes is essentially a way to share a database over a network to create information-sharing applications. The databases are collections of documents stored in a group and can contain free-form text, graphics, file attachments, and—with additional software and hardware—sound, image, and video data.

A technological overview should help us to understand its capabilities. Lotus Notes can operate on IBM-compatible microcomputer workstations running OS/2 or Windows, Macintosh computers, or workstations running UNIX. The data are stored in a distributed database, with servers at key locations wherever needed. Lotus Notes runs on both LANs and WANs, using several popular network operating systems, such as Novell, Banyan and IBM. The user interface is Windows-like and icon-based.

Compound document:
Electronic document that consists of differing types of information acquired from separate sources such as graphics, database, spreadsheet, and text-based programs.

The software supports **compound documents,** which are documents that consist of differing types of information from separate sources; for example, a single document combining graphics, spreadsheet data, and character-based text is a compound document. Figure 10.6 illustrates a compound document displayed

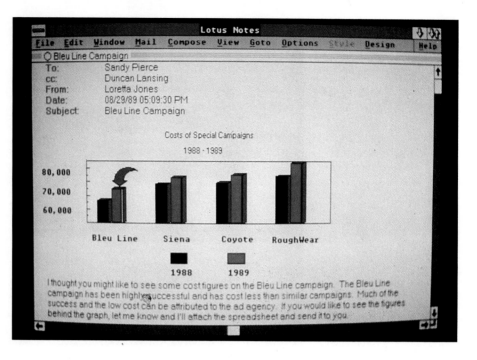

Figure 10.6
Compound document on Lotus Notes. Lotus Notes groupware provides an organization-wide forum to discuss issues and brainstorm solutions. In this example, the author is discussing the cost of a special campaign using a compound document that incorporates spreadsheet charts and a report. *Courtesy of Lotus Development Corporation.*

through Lotus Notes. In Notes the whole document—graphics, spreadsheet data and text—is stored as a single record, whereas with normal office software the various elements are stored as separate files that are combined at print time. Lotus Notes is compatible with a wide range of popular desktop word processors, spreadsheets, and graphics packages.

In Notes, each application is a separate database. The system is delivered with predefined, template applications that can be used as is or modified. The user can also create customized applications from scratch. To enter data into a database, one uses a Form (Lotus Notes comes with predefined forms, but the users can easily create their own). Each Notes database logs all pertinent communications among members of a workgroup so that the notes can be kept for future reference and shared. Members of the team can access each member's contribution and comment on it, or they can use Notes to distribute reference information to other team members. Figure 10.7 and Figure 10.6 show how Notes was used to distribute information and to pool ideas in a sales discussion database. Members of the entire organization involved in sales and marketing could access documents, comment on them, or add new information. Figure 10.7 shows a sales activity report that includes related business and customer issues.

Manufacturers Hanover Trust (MHT), one of the ten largest banks in the United States, turned to Notes originally to improve the effectiveness of its sales operation. MHT found itself with vast quantities of data that were neither well integrated nor easily accessible. Using Lotus Notes, the account officers and corporate trust sales staff now can maintain their records in a way that is organized and widely accessible. They set up a company profiles database that centralizes client and prospect information. The communications profiles database is used to keep track of day-to-day communications between the MHT staff and its customers. As MIS Vice President Rich Luciano put it, "Selling involves knowing as much about your customer as you can." Account officers can bring up a one-page summary of information on the customer, view contacts for a specific product, or examine all contacts for the past six months. MHT's staff is now able to be far more knowledgeable as it deals with customers—from knowing the nickname of the client or contact to knowing which banks that customer uses in Norway. Before Notes, sharing of information was time-consuming and was not successful if one did not know whom to ask, or if that person was on

Figure 10.7
Lotus Notes sales activity report. Activities, events, and issues can be readily discussed and shared with the various team members. *Courtesy of Lotus Development Corporation.*

vacation. Of course, in the past when a staff member left MHT, he or she took valuable information. Now all of that information is stored on Notes and is easily retrieved when needed, using a range of flexible views. The applications also help managers track staff activities, analyze the effectiveness of their time use, and plan future work (Lotus Notes Application Profile).

Groupware has not been well accepted wherever it has been installed. The Window on Organizations provides insight into the serious controversies that groupware has engendered in a number of companies.

Groupware alone is not able to promote information-sharing if team members do not feel it is in their interest to share, especially in organizations that encourage competition among employees. For instance, a sales representative might hesitate to share prospect information in a common database if it helps another person win the customer. One study of a consulting firm found that junior staff members did not want to use Notes to share valuable information because the firm had an up-or-out promotion policy and junior staff were expected to bill directly all of their time. Time spent communicating with other workers could not be billed to clients. Staff were evaluated in terms of both the quality of their work and the number of hours billed. Yet such information-intensive organizations stood to benefit substantially if people shared their expertise (Orlikowski, 1992; Press, 1992b; "Lotus Notes," 1992).

Nonetheless, it seems clear from our examples (and many others) that the use of this technology can enhance the work of a group if the applications are properly designed to fit the organization's needs and work practices. Groupware today may be compared to the situation surrounding spreadsheets ten years ago—its use is new and we can only dimly see its long-range value.

Managing Information: Desktop Databases

Desktop microcomputers provide many office workers with the opportunity to develop their own individual client tracking systems, customer lists, and supplier and vendor databases. However, most office workers do not create these databases on their own because microcomputer database languages are still too difficult for nonprogrammers to use. Instead, a new kind of software that is customized for specific data management needs of salespersons, managers, real

ORGANIZATIONS

The Groupware Controversy

Groupware focuses on technology needed to support small groups as they work together. As a result, it incorporates a broad range of office functions—the creation, editing, storage, and management of documents, electronic mail, calendaring, and even electronic videoconferencing. Individual employees, who have been accustomed to working independently, are now experiencing both the benefits and the problems of working more closely as a team. The shift in work methods, made possible by groupware, has engendered a surprising amount of contention.

Many find that groupware brings productivity gains by shortening meeting times or reducing the frequency of meetings. For example, Fred Bonner, director of computer systems for the Discovery Channel, believes that meeting room vacancies have risen by 40 percent since his company has begun using groupware. Similarly, Barry Barron, who is manager of information systems for the Port of Oakland (California), attributes the reduction in numbers of meetings at his firm to the ability of groupware to keep each department informed about other departments' activities. Groupware can make design and sales teams more efficient by promoting information sharing.

Some of the controversy arises from the functions and controls built into the software. For example, Action Technologies, Inc.'s Coordinator Workgroup Productivity System includes "voucher routing" in its groupware. To circulate a memo electronically, the software requires that the memo be classified prior to being sent. The user classifies the memo (request, consultation, order, etc.) and establishes action deadlines. The software updates the schedules of both the recipients and their groups, which includes the recipients' managers. The recipient need not have been consulted about these deadlines.

Some groupware software can record when an employee fails to meet a commitment, such as finishing a report on time, and then publicize this failure to hundreds of colleagues.

Ray Howell, who is assistant vice-president for information management in NCR's commercial insurance division, believes that many employees "might be afraid of a product that automatically schedules people, puts priorities on things, and possibly sends messages to management when they fail." He says that employees "might feel Big Brother is watching."

Christine Bullen (who studied groupware at MIT's Sloan School of Management), has found that some features in groupware software have aroused a great deal of hostility. She has heard groupware labeled as "a power tool for authoritarians," and has heard the system called "fascist existentialism." She reports that many users seek out ways to short-circuit some of the objectionable functions, particularly the requirement that a memo be classified in advance.

Group editing of documents has also generated controversy. Using Instant Update from On Technology, Inc., in Cambridge, Massachusetts, an author can use the network to make a document available to a selected list of employees for updating. Matthew Ghourdjian, IS director of Hennigan & Mercer (a Los Angeles law firm) finds that this function allows his firm to create needed legal documents rapidly. However, Greg O'Hara, a system supervisor at Wright-Patterson Air Force Base, believes that software that allows someone other than the author to update a document threatens the integrity of that document. Moreover, groupware often does not manage document update timing adequately. If two people are simultaneously editing the same document, the changes made and saved by the first person might be wiped out when the second person saves later changes.

Groupware E-mail raises additional problems. Employees comfortable with their E-mail systems may actively resist joining group discussions. The privacy of traditional E-mail systems has a different "look and feel" from the much more public space of workgroup computing.

In most large organizations, E-mail was installed by local business units, resulting in numerous, noncompatible systems being installed. A typical example is US West Communications of Denver, which has about 38,000 employees in 15 states running 14 different E-mail systems—DEC's All-In-1, IBM's PROFS, Wang's WangOffice, and a number of UNIX-based local area network systems. Most of these systems do not "talk" with each other, effectively preventing most employees from communicating through E-mail. Groupware does not solve this problem. Rather, it can only contribute to the confusion and further restrict communications by bringing in yet another E-mail system. Obviously, what many corporations need is either standardization on a single corporatewide E-mail system, or at least a limited, approved list of systems that can communicate with each other.

Sources: John R. Wilke, "Computer Links Erode Hierarchical Nature of Workplace Culture," *The Wall Street Journal*, December 9, 1993; Emma Zevik, "Getting a Grip on Groupware," *Computerworld*, March 30, 1992; John J. Xenakis, "Documents by Committee," *InformationWEEK*, December 9, 1991; and "Shared Interests," *InformationWEEK*, December 30, 1991.

To Think About: Assume your manager has asked you to make a recommendation as to whether or not your work group should install groupware. From what you know about groupware, would you recommend this technology? Why or why not? What management, organization, and technology factors would you consider in making your recommendation? What steps would you take to reduce the problems and maximize the value of the software?

Personal information manager: Packaged database tool designed to support specific office data management tasks for an information worker.

estate agents, stockbrokers, and the like is now beginning to appear. This new software is often called **personal information managers;** it consists of packaged database tools designed to support specific office data management tasks.

One example of a personal information manager is The Financial Manager (Azimuth Corporation), designed to serve the desktop information needs of account executives and portfolio managers in the financial services industry. Financial managers typically have from 500 to 1000 clients; each client has one or more accounts or portfolios of investments. Financial managers also have a full calendar of events, activities, and planned actions. In addition, each manager has several routine projects; these include sending letters to clients, telephoning clients, and prospecting for business. The Financial Manager keeps track of a manager's clients, portfolios, calendars, appointments, and projects.

Managing Projects: Desktop Project Managers

Project management software: Software that facilitates the development, scheduling, and management of a project by breaking the complex project into simpler subtasks, each with its own completion time and resource requirements.

Offices are the organization's control points that coordinate the flow of resources to projects and evaluate results. **Project management software** breaks a complex project down into simpler subtasks, each with its own completion time and resource requirements. Once a user knows what is needed by each subtask, delivery schedules can be written and resources allocated. Two traditional project management techniques (see Chapter 9) are CPM (Critical Path Method) and PERT (Program Evaluation and Review Technique).

Contemporary project managers in the 1990s have begun to use graphical user interfaces, permitting managers to operate the programs with a mouse. Project managers also have access to high-quality presentation graphics, permitting photographic slide and overhead transparency output. Whereas project management software initially focused on a single user, contemporary packages can be accessed by many members of a work group.

10.3 Knowledge Work Systems

Because knowledge work and data work are both information work, both use many of the same information systems (particularly office automation systems). However, knowledge work is also specialized; thus it requires specialized information systems. This section describes the features of knowledge work that can be supported by specific knowledge work systems.

The Role of Knowledge Work in the Organization

The Bureau of Labor Statistics defines knowledge work as having four characteristics. This definition has generally been accepted by sociologists and economists as well. First, knowledge work is supported by a codified body of knowledge that is generally and widely accepted as valid. The body of knowledge is usually found in books stored in a library. Second, this body of knowledge must be capable of being taught at universities. It differs from a skill that can only be learned through experience and apprenticeship. Third, practitioners of the body of knowledge normally must prove their mastery of that knowledge by being certified, usually either by the state or by a university. Fourth, the profession must maintain standards of admission for the practitioner through regulation by independent professional organizations. The professional bodies must also maintain professional and educational standards and guidelines and a statement of ethics. Thus the knowledge worker must have more than technique and skill. These characteristics are summarized in Table 10.5.

Table 10.5 CHARACTERISTICS OF KNOWLEDGE WORK

1. Based on codified body of knowledge
2. Body of knowledge taught at schools or universities
3. Practitioners usually require certification by the state or school
4. Practitioners regulated by independent professional organizations

Knowledge- and information-intense products and services have been expanding rapidly. Knowledge work remains critical to the development of new products in more traditional industries, including pharmaceuticals, electronics, and automobiles. It has also become central to a range of newer services such as environmental analysis and financial and investment advice. To understand knowledge work systems thoroughly, we first must explore the ways knowledge workers contribute to business firms.

Three roles stand out. Perhaps the most distinctive role of knowledge workers is to interpret the ever expanding external knowledge bases for the organization. A central purpose for hiring knowledge workers is to keep the firm abreast of developments in science, technology, the arts, and social thought. Developments in these areas often contain business opportunities or risks. As more and more value in the economy depends on knowledge and information products, the only way a firm can keep up is to invest heavily in knowledge workers. Indeed, the fastest-growing industries are those that produce information- and knowledge-intensive products.

A second role that knowledge workers are uniquely qualified to perform is as internal consultants to their firms. They can advise managers about changes in technology and science, and can bring formal models to bear on problems. They can also write reports, and provide professional expertise. While most corporations hire external consultants from time to time to supplement their work, it is the internal knowledge worker who is the main source of consulting information.

Third, knowledge workers are organizational change agents. Based on external developments in science and the arts, they are expected to evaluate and initiate change projects and to promote them.

Knowledge workers exhibit two other relevant characteristics that are unique among information workers. Their knowledge base and their understanding of what to do with that knowledge prevent them from being subjected to the same kind of supervision and authority that other information workers will be subjected to. They often know more than their boss. Therefore, they are usually autonomous. In addition, knowledge workers often are physically segregated into research areas.

Knowledge work systems (KWS): Information systems that aid knowledge workers in the creation and integration of new knowledge in the organization.

These unique roles and conditions of knowledge workers produce special requirements for the information systems they use and provide the rationale for the development of those systems. **Knowledge work systems** are specifically designed to promote the creation of new knowledge and ensure that new knowledge and technical expertise are properly integrated into the business.

Requirements of Knowledge Work Systems

Knowledge workers are focused on the expanding knowledge base external to their work group and to the organization that employs them. They need easy access to electronically stored external knowledge bases. The knowledge they must access might be in journal articles stored in libraries or in collections of scientific research or legal findings. They usually need mail links to other professionals working in universities or in other businesses. They also often need mail links to other knowledge workers working within their own organization,

MANAGEMENT

A Network for Knowledge Workers

Because modern economies have become information economies, access to knowledge is critical to the success of many companies. Yet new knowledge is expanding so swiftly that keeping up is an immense task that requires management's attention. The Internet system may help with this problem. Established in the 1970s by the U.S. Pentagon to allow academic and corporate researchers and government officials to share data using E-mail and remote computers, the Internet has become the world's largest network, with about 2,000,000 computers and 15 million users in 60 countries.

The Internet, in fact, is a network of networks—over 21,000 at last count. Member networks share software standards so that messages flow without technical restrictions. The most popular Internet function is E-mail. Many users prefer it to other public networks and even to their own corporate systems. Its E-mail is very fast, delivering in seconds or minutes a message that might take hours or days with other networks. At the same time, the technology it uses keeps the cost relatively low. Another advantage is that its E-mail system allows messages to include fax, video, and desktop print files. Cygnus Support Inc., a Mountain View, California, software company, uses the Internet E-mail to maintain contact with its Cambridge, Massachusetts, office, while SRI International, a Menlo Park, California, consulting firm, uses it to link to its London office. Salespeople all over the world find it easy to keep in contact with customers and with their offices using the Internet and laptop computers. Tom Stone, a senior editor at Addison-Wesley in Reading, Massachusetts, claims that correspon-

dence with an author that used to take a week can now be completed in a day. He now handles proposal submissions through the Internet and even allows text submission via the Internet so that he can copyedit without ever handling paper. Newspapers such as *The New York Times* and *The Economist* use the network to gather information on their readers' interests, using the E-mail system's facility to define large mailing lists. Many businesses try to be on selected mailing lists so that they can more easily keep abreast of developments in their industries. These mailing lists cover many topics worldwide, including, for example, an oil and gas industry list.

With blinding speed, the Internet can link a lone researcher sitting at a computer screen to mountains of data otherwise too expensive to tap; to large electronic meetings, work sessions, and bulletin boards; and to numerous electronic journals.

Several hundred library catalogues are on-line through the Internet, including those of such giants as the Library of Congress, the University of California, and Harvard University. General Motors claims that Internet library research is vital to its product development. In addition, users are able to search over 400 databases containing information such as the Central Intelligence Agency's world almanac, the latest satellite weather photos (updated hourly), science fiction reviews, and a molecular biology library. The network is also the source of a great deal of high-quality, free software. General Electric research physicist Dick St. Peters says his group has used "hundreds or thousands" of software packages off the network. In return his group has

made available to medical research and development sites a package it has written for medical imaging; they even use the Internet to "remotely log in and help" the users of this program if the users report having problems.

Problems with the Internet include its current lack of tight security and the overwhelming amount of information available on it. So many people are putting so much material on the network that fears are mounting about data overload and psychological burnout. (Some Internet users report receiving 500 messages a day.) Human editors and software to filter data and to pinpoint desired information are emerging Internet aids. The question facing corporate management is, "Do we make use of this network and if so, how?"

Sources: U.S. Department of Commerce; Internet Society, Reston, VA; John S. Quarterman, "What Can Businesses Get Out of Internet," *Computerworld*, February 22, 1993; John Markoff, "A Web of Networks, an Abundance of Services," *The New York Times*, February 28, 1993; and Gary H. Anthes, "Internet Tapped for Global Virtual Publishing Enterprise," *Computerworld*, March 23, 1992.

To Think About: As a member of the management team of a high-tech company, what advantages would the Internet offer you? What problems do you see with relying upon the Internet for E-mail, for research, and for a source of software? Do you think you would support or oppose using the Internet and why? What other elements would be needed in a cost-effective policy to support knowledge worker access to public information worldwide?

whether at another site within the country or abroad. Consequently, one characteristic of knowledge work systems is that they incorporate more links to external data and information than is customary with other corporate systems. The Window on Management shows the management benefits of using a network such as the Internet to provide knowledge workers with these external data.

A second characteristic of knowledge work systems is the software they require. Typically their software contains far more powerful graphic, analytic, document management, and communications capabilities than other corporate systems.

Third, knowledge work systems require considerably more computing power than is true for other information work. Engineers may need to run thousands of complex calculations to determine the strength and safety of a specific part they are designing. Lawyers may need to scan through thousands of documents and legal findings before recommending a strategy. Graphics applications are particularly greedy for computing power. To understand the greater power needs of graphics, remember that a one-page document stored in character format (an ordinary word processing document) requires perhaps 8K of disk space to store, while that document stored in a bit-mapped graphic format requires about 50K, a ratio of approximately 6:1. The computer requires a commensurate increase in power to manipulate the larger, bit-mapped file rather than the smaller character-based file. Graphic simulations have become common and even necessary to much of the work of knowledge workers, from architects to pharmaceutical research chemists. Designers and draftsmen, using computer-aided design (CAD) systems to design such products as automobile bodies, need three-dimensional graphics software to visualize and model the product on screen before producing a physical model. Even more intensive simulations, called virtual reality, can be so large as to require very large and fast supercomputers.

A user-friendly interface is very important to a knowledge worker's system. User friendly interfaces save a lot of time by allowing the user to perform the needed tasks and get to the required information without having to spend a lot of time learning how to use the computer. While saving time is important to any worker, it is more important for knowledge workers than for most other employees because a knowledge worker's time is so costly—wasting a knowledge worker's time is simply too expensive.

Finally, knowledge work systems usually require the use of workstations. As described in Chapter 4, a **workstation** is a desktop computer that is far more powerful than a conventional microcomputer. The workstation has powerful graphics, analytic, document management, and communications capabilities and the ability to perform several complicated tasks at one time. Knowledge workstations are often designed and optimized for the specific tasks to be performed so that a design engineer will require a different workstation than a lawyer. Figure 10.8 summarizes these requirements of knowledge work systems.

Workstation: Desktop computer with powerful graphics, mathematical processing, and communications capabilities as well as the ability to perform several complicated tasks at one time. Often used in scientific or design work.

Figure 10.8
Requirements of knowledge work systems. Knowledge work systems require strong links to external knowledge bases in addition to specialized hardware and software.

Examples of Knowledge Work Systems

Knowledge work systems will vary greatly, depending upon the profession and the specific application being supported. Design engineers need graphics with enough power to handle three-dimensional computer-aided design (CAD) systems. On the other hand, financial analysts are more interested in having access to a myriad of external databases and in optical disk technology so that they can access massive amounts of financial data very quickly. In this text we cannot describe all the knowledge work systems or even all of the many types of knowledge work systems. What we have done, instead, is to select three very different types of such systems as examples that will help you to understand the breadth and power of knowledge work systems. We now examine a conventional computer-aided design system, "virtual reality" systems for simulation and modeling, and a financial workstation.

COMPUTER-AIDED DESIGN: DEVELOPING A NEW PRODUCT

Computer-aided design (CAD): Information system that automates the creation and revision of designs using sophisticated graphics software.

Tires have been much the same for 100 years. They consist of rubber and composition using air pressure as a spring. Alan R. Burns, a mining engineer from Perth, Australia, had an innovative idea, and using computer-aided design software (CAD), he turned that idea into reality. Using computers and sophisticated graphics software, **computer-aided design (CAD)** automates the creation and revision of designs. Mr. Burns knew that off-road vehicle tires take a terrible beating because of the many hazards they are subjected to. The result is frequent tire replacement and repeated costly job downtime. His idea was a modular tire made of independent tread segments that could be replaced individually. The segments are not pneumatic and so are not subject to punctures. If one segment needs to be replaced, the job can be quickly done by the operator, who does not need to remove the wheel from the vehicle. The segments are bolted around the circumference of a steel wheel hub.

With the assistance of computer-aided design, Alan R. Burns was able to design and develop, and Airboss is able to manufacture and market, this revolutionary segmented tire. The tires are ideally suited for heavy equipment applications such as these earth movers because of their superior handling traction and maneuverability.

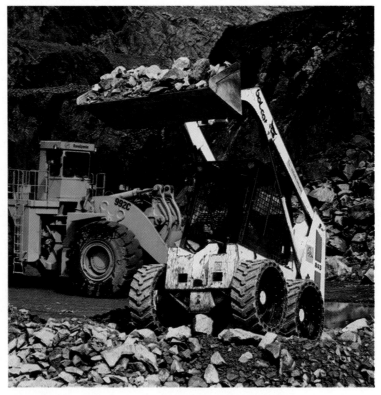

To turn his idea into an actual usable and saleable tire, Burns turned to computer modeling. But before he could begin the actual design, he needed to understand market requirements. He decided to start his venture by focusing on one market segment, and for market reasons he settled on tires for loaders used in such sectors as construction, mining, and waste dumps. Usage parameters like speed, load, temperature, and surface characteristics were turned into targets for traction, wear life, and ride performance. He then used a CAD workstation to develop a visual representation of the segment, and he modified thickness, tread shape, and other factors until an acceptable design was achieved. He also entered the usage parameter data into the software, as well as characteristics of the rubber compound being used. Utilizing CAD software, he was able to simulate operational characteristics for each visual model and to calculate the tire's stresses and strains under specified loading and usage conditions. The results were evaluated in terms of user-perceived qualities of traction, wear, and ride.

Once Burns approved a design, the same software used the same model data to design the mold tooling for the manufacture of the tire segment. The program could perform flow analysis and also could locate potential problems such as uneven cooling or shrinkage. The output of this phase became the instructions for the milling machines that cut the actual shape into tool steel. Airboss, the Australian company Burns founded to manufacture his invention, is already an apparent success (Shapiro, 1993).

The benefits of CAD systems are clear. The designer is able to produce a more sophisticated and functional design than he or she could possibly have done manually. The design is done right before production begins, significantly reducing both design time and expensive engineering changes once production has begun. Equally large savings come during the modeling function. Using a more traditional design methodology, each new design modification requires a mold to be made and a prototype to be physically tested. That process has to be repeated many times over, which is a very expensive and time-consuming process. Using a CAD workstation, the designer only needs to make a prototype toward the end of the design process. The ability of the CAD software to design the tooling and the manufacturing process also saves a great deal of time and money while producing a manufacturing process with far fewer problems.

CAD workstations are starting to be used in many areas. For example, the development of new automobiles, from idea to the first delivery, traditionally required about five years. Using CAD software, Japanese auto makers have taken about a year out of that cycle, and American manufacturers are now rapidly moving to achieve similar results. Faster development not only lowers the cost significantly, but also allows the producer to respond more quickly to changing market demands.

The new Hong Kong airport is being designed with CAD software. The Window on Technology describes this project, illustrating the wide range of specialized CAD systems that exist.

VIRTUAL REALITY: IMMERSION IN FANTASY

Virtual reality systems: Interactive graphics software and hardware that create computer-generated simulations that provide sensations that emulate real-world activities.

Virtual reality systems have visualization, rendering, and simulation capabilities that go far beyond those of conventional CAD systems. They use interactive graphics software to create computer-generated simulations that are so close to reality that users believe they are participating in a "real" world situation. Virtual reality is such a new technology that few commercial applications have been developed. While its approach may appear to be fantasy to many, its benefits may turn out to be very real.

Virtual reality is interactive in such a way that the user actually feels immersed in the "world" the computer creates. Imagine, for example, a computer version of an architectural design for a house. The house will be built for you, but for now it is still only a design in a computer. Now imagine that with the aid of the computer, you walk through that house, checking out its features and making

TECHNOLOGY

Flying High with CAD

Hong Kong's Kai Tak airport is the fifth busiest international airport in the world, and it will have reached its absolute capacity in 1994. It cannot be enlarged because it sits in the middle of densely populated Kowloon, the section of Hong Kong on the Kowloon Peninsula. A new airport will be built at a cost of $16 billion on land that will be reclaimed on a nearby island. It is being designed to meet predicted traffic through the year 2040. The airport will be connected to Hong Kong by a 1500-yard bridge, the second largest suspension bridge in the world. It will include both a highway and a rail link. Finally, a complete town for 20,000 employees will be built, including housing, shopping and commercial centers, recreation facilities, and sewage and refuse systems.

The design of the airport is a massive undertaking involving a number of design firms and an astonishing array of computer-aided design (CAD) software packages and other sophisticated technology. It also involves sophisticated, creative ways to link the designers and their designs.

A consortium called Greiner-Maunsell created the basic design. The runway design had to take into account local topology, the urban surroundings, prevalent wind patterns, and criteria from the International Civil Aviation Authority. The designers had to assume the airport would be able to accommodate 900-passenger jets that are now only on the drawing boards. CAD software from Intergraph Corp. integrates "protec-tion surfaces" into the design–complex 3-D pictures of heights and patterns that airplanes will be able to fly. All the data had to be related to the basic Hong Kong survey grid maps so that the output could be used by other disciplines designing more detailed plans of portions of the airport. The final master plan was produced using a CAD package called AutoCAD, which allows a user to overlay the basic plan without having to combine plans.

The Mott Consortium, comprising three companies, is using a CAD network to design the ¾-mile long, 60-dock terminal building. The client, Hong Kong's Provisional Airport Authority, requires that all 10,000 design and construction drawings be produced using CAD software. To integrate all the work, Mott networked 11 Intergraph workstations and about 21 486-PCs. The network allows any designer to easily call up his or her own work at any workstation or PC. The software being used includes Intergraph's Microstation for consistent interfacing, and its Modelview for visualization and perspective. CADDET from Mott MacDonald offers concrete detailing and analysis. To visualize the terminal from the view of the passenger by simulating walkthroughs, they are using Intergraph's Design Review. This software is also useful for obtaining client approval on details. The roof design is being done by Ove Arup & Partners, who are using a structural analysis package, Oasys, on a PC-LAN. Numerous other packages are being used for design of terminal details.

Other facets of the project, including land reclamation, the bridge, the highway, the railway systems, and an analysis of the town and its infrastructure, are being designed by other companies. All are using a wide array of specialized CAD programs. Each team is very dependent upon the output of work by other teams. To integrate the work, the Mott Consortium uses an optical jukebox holding 54 read-only optical disks of 650M each. Finished drawings are archived to the optical disks, where they are immediately available to all via a network. Each drawing has a version number so that it can be updated later if needed. When updates do occur that might affect the work of other teams, earlier versions of the same document are marked with a warning.

The airport project is the largest such project in the history of Hong Kong. It is difficult to imagine how this project could take place without the technology the designers have available.

Source: Ross Milburn, "Flying High," *Computer Graphics World,* February 1993.

To Think About: Do you think this project could be attempted without CAD technology? Why or why not? How would the lack of CAD technology affect the cost and timing of such a project? What benefits to the clients might have caused them to require the designers to produce all documents on CAD software?

changes on the spot until you are satisfied with the design. Perhaps the door to the bathroom opens the wrong way, or the living room is too narrow and its north window is not high enough for its width, or the light switch in the front hall is on the wrong side, or you want the linen closet in the kitchen instead of in the hallway. Once construction began, these changes would be very expensive. Even worse, you might not even realize you wanted these changes until after the house is complete and you move in. At the design stage, however, such changes are quick and inexpensive to make. This is the very real fantasy world of virtual reality—software of this type actually exists and is being used today.

How does it work? The virtual world is an implicit world, one that exists only in the computer. To enter that world, the user dons special clothing, headgear, and equipment, depending upon the application. The clothing contains sensors that record the user's movements and immediately transmit that information back to the computer. For instance, to walk through the house, you will need garb that monitors the movement of your feet, hands, and head. You will also need goggles that contain video screens and sometimes audio attachments and feeling gloves so that you can be immersed in the computer feedback. As you walk straight ahead through the house, the images in front of you come closer. If you turn to the right (or turn your head to the right), the image will shift to your left. If you open the door, you will see the door opening and the next room will appear through the doorway. Walk through that doorway and look around, and you will find you are in the next room. Turn around and you can see the previous room through the doorway (unless you already closed the door behind you).

As you might imagine, this is new and very expensive technology. However, some commercial applications have been developed and are in use. For instance, virtual reality applications are starting to be developed for the financial industry (see Figure 10.9).

Matsushita Electric Works in Japan has put virtual reality to work in its department stores; it has developed an application very similar to the house example we used above. The stores sell kitchen appliances and cabinets. To promote these products, Matsushita has created an application it calls Virtual Kitchen. The prospective buyers bring their kitchen layouts to the department store, where trained staff enters a copy of the design into the computer. The customers then don the appropriate equipment and suddenly find themselves in their own kitchen. Now they can try out the appliances in various sizes, colors, and locations. They can test new cabinets, opening and closing the cabinet doors and drawers. They can place their existing table and chairs into the picture so the scene will be very realistic. They can walk around and discover the feel and ambiance of the new kitchen. With this technology, the customer is able to buy with a great deal more confidence. Matsushita is able to make many more on-the-spot sales.

Other architectural applications have been developed. Hewlett-Packard is designing a new European office using virtual reality equipment from VPL Research of Redwood City, California. The city of Berlin, Germany, is using the

Figure 10.9
Virtual reality for Wall Street traders. This data distribution and display system uses virtual reality technology to let traders grasp otherwise unmanageable amounts of complex information. Individual instruments are presented as three-dimensional objects. *Courtesy of Maxus Systems International.*

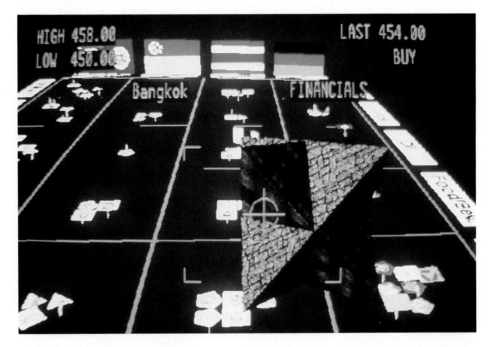

same equipment to design a new subway system to link the formerly separated East and West sections of the city. The University of North Carolina at Chapel Hill has its own virtual reality system, which it is using to design its new computer sciences building, Sitterson Hall (Newquist, March 30, 1992).

At General Electric's Research and Development Center in Schenectady, New York, GE scientists are working with a group of surgeons from Boston's Brigham and Women's Hospital to develop a virtual reality system to be used in surgery. One of their stated goals is to be able to superimpose a 3-D image of the patient onto the patient and then to operate on the image and the patient at the same time. Further in the future, they want to be able to create an image of the patient and then "walk through" that image, moving between various organs. They hope they will then be able to perform surgery on the image, surgery with such precision that no damage to surrounding tissue will occur. The surgeon's actions on the large virtual image would be duplicated by computer-controlled instruments on the patient.

While these are futuristic hopes, the GE research team is making progress. Currently, for example, they are able to use a magnetic resonance imaging machine (MRI) to make two-dimensional slice pictures of a volunteer's brain. Using virtual reality goggles, and with those MRI images as input, they are able to view the virtual brain with superb three-dimensional reality. They not only are able to rotate the brain, but are also able to peel off layers of the image to reveal the parts below. They have used these images to put a special cap on a volunteer, project the image of his own brain on that cap, and then sketch onto the cap the surgical pathway through the brain's furrows to a spot where they might need to perform surgery. While the process of operating on the image itself is still a long way away, the team does hope that within the next several years they will be able to create a "virtual" image that surgeons can have beside the operating table so that they can consult it during the operation (Naj, March 3, 1993).

INVESTMENT WORKSTATIONS: LEVERAGING KNOWLEDGE WORKERS IN THE FINANCIAL INDUSTRY

The key assets of knowledge workers are their knowledge and their time. While some knowledge workers use workstations that are on the cutting edge of technologies, others use more established technologies to leverage those two key assets. New York-based Chancellor Capital Management, Inc., developed its own investment workstations to help it manage $25 billion in assets for 300 clients. The workstations integrate the wide range of data required by portfolio managers from the firm's investment management systems and its portfolio accounting systems and make them available with the touch of a button. By providing one-stop information faster and with fewer errors, the workstations streamline Chancellor's entire investment process, from stock selection to updating accounting records.

The financial workstations eliminate much of the drudgery that goes with computers to give their traders and asset managers more time to concentrate on making decisions and developing strategies. They provide a more open, flexible system environment, one that could be tailored to an individual's needs while also being able to integrate new software when needed.

Previously Chancellor's data were stored separately in its accounting, trading, research and analytical systems. That not only meant a loss of data integrity, but also an increase in the difficulty the professional staff had in locating and accessing data. The professional staff had to use separate systems to access data on differing areas of investment.

Chancellor installed a new user interface so that users have one very friendly screen with a number of windows on it. Different users have different windows, depending upon their own needs. The user can move from one window to another with ease, noting a market trend in one window, checking a second window to determine the state of his or her assets, then to a third window to check analysts' reports on stocks he or she is interested in, and finally moving to a fourth window to execute the trades he or she has decided upon. In the past, each of these moves would have required the user to log off one system and on to another, a process that is not only time-wasting but frustrating as well. These windows represent a tremendous enhancement in speed and efficiency.

Integrating the software used in the front office and the back office enabled trading within the firm to become paperless. Chancellor also added electronic mail to its workstation network. Then the firm began to add electronic interfaces to its brokers so that even the orders to the brokers and the trade-execution confirmations became electronic (Michaels, February 1993).

Management Challenges

1. **Increased demands for employee learning and change.** Because the knowledge base and the technologies used in information and knowledge work change rapidly, people are under a great deal of pressure to continue learning and training to maintain their jobs and may need to learn new and different jobs in a short time. Organizations must identify and recruit employees who have the capacity and desire to learn, and they must devote more resources to training. If retraining fails, they may need to retire older workers earlier than in the past. This may both raise costs and create an ethical dilemma for the firm (see Chapter 15).

2. **Integration of knowledge work into the organization.** It is difficult to integrate knowledge workers into a traditional, hierarchical organization. Knowledge workers tend to be very self-directed and autonomous and are somewhat set off from the rest of the organization. They cannot be told what to do. Changes in authority structure and work arrangements are necessary if companies are to utilize their talents without alienating them.

3. **Designing information systems that truly enhance the productivity of knowledge workers.** Information systems that truly enhance the productivity of knowledge workers may be difficult to build because the manner in which information technology can enhance higher-level tasks such as those performed by managers and professionals (i.e., scientists or engineers) is not always clearly understood (Sheng et al., 1989/90). High-level knowledge workers may resist the introduction of any new technology, or they may resist knowledge work systems because such systems diminish personal control and creativity. For instance, some architects may resist using computer-aided architectural rendering systems because they fear the computer-generated representations of buildings cannot convey the individual artistry and imagination of hand-drawn renderings.

Summary

Define information work and the information economy.

Advanced economies in the United States, Canada, and Western Europe have been transformed from industrial economies where most wealth came from manufacturing to information economies where most wealth originates in information and knowledge production. Today, the majority of workers perform information work. Information work is work that consists primarily of creating or processing information.

Describe the roles of knowledge workers and data workers in the organization.

There are two kinds of information workers. Knowledge workers are employees such as engineers, architects, scientists, or attorneys, whose primary job is to create new information for the organization. Knowledge workers interpret the external knowledge base for the organization, advise management, and act as change agents to bring new knowledge into the firm. Data workers are employees such as secretaries, accountants, or salespersons, whose primary job is to process, use, or disseminate information for the organization. Managers perform both knowledge and data work.

Describe the roles and principal activities of the office in contemporary business.

Offices coordinate information work in the organization, link the work of diverse groups in the organization, and couple the organization to its external environment. Offices and office work are therefore central to the success of any contemporary organization. The major office activities are document management, communications, scheduling, data management, and project management.

Explain the contributions of the principal types of office automation technologies.

Word processing, desktop publishing, and digital imaging systems support the document management activities of the office. Electronic mail systems and groupware support its communications activities. Electronic calendar and groupware systems support scheduling activities. Desktop data management systems and customized personal information managers support data management activities. Project management systems break down complex projects into simpler subtasks, producing delivery schedules, allocating resources, and supporting the project management activities of the office.

Understand unique requirements of knowledge work systems.

Knowledge work systems require easy access to an external knowledge base; powerful computer hardware that can support software with intensive graphics, analysis, document management, and communications capabilities; and a friendly user interface. Knowledge work systems often run on workstations.

Describe the major types of knowledge work systems.

Knowledge work systems must be customized for the particular type of knowledge work being performed. Computer-aided design systems and virtual reality systems that create interactive simulations that behave like the real world require graphics and powerful modeling capabilities. Knowledge work systems for financial professionals provide access to external databases and the ability to access massive amounts of financial data very quickly.

Key Terms

Knowledge- and information-intense products	Workflow management
Information workers	Groupware
Information work	Electronic calendaring
Knowledge workers	Electronic mail (E-mail)
Data workers	Electronic meeting software
Office activities	Compound document
Office automation systems (OAS)	Personal information manager
Word processing	Project management software
Desktop publishing	Knowledge work systems (KWS)
Document imaging systems	Workstation
Jukebox	Computer-aided design (CAD)
Index server	Virtual reality systems

Review Questions

1. What are the characteristics of an information economy?

2. Describe the differences between information workers, knowledge workers, data workers, and service workers.

3. What is the relationship between information work and productivity in contemporary organizations?

4. Describe the roles of the office in organizations.

5. What are the five major activities that take place in offices?

6. What is office automation? How has it changed over time?

7. What are the principal types of information systems technology that support the roles and activities of the office? Relate each technology to the role(s) they support.

8. List and describe the uses for document imaging systems in the modern office.

9. What is groupware? How does it support information work? Describe its capabilities.

10. What are the four distinguishing characteristics of knowledge work?

11. What role do knowledge workers play in the organization?

12. What are the generic requirements of knowledge work systems? Why?

13. What is CAD? Describe its role and significance in business today.

14. What is virtual reality? How does it differ from CAD?

Discussion Questions

1. Knowledge workers tend to be treated differently than other workers within businesses today. Define the nontechnical problems these differences might create within the organization. Do you think the problems are significant? Discuss how you would deal with these problems.

2. Perhaps the largest challenge corporate management faces today is finding ways to keep up with the explosion of new information. In what ways is this critical to the future of a knowledge-intensive high-tech company? What long-range strategies do you think such companies need to institute to meet this challenge? Discuss them, their cost, their potential effectiveness.

Group Project

With three or four of your classmates, investigate a high-tech business nearby and observe the role played by knowledge workers in this business. Describe the kinds of knowledge work systems that would be valuable for that business. Define the hardware, software, data, and procedural components for each system, and design a knowledge workstation for one of these systems. Your workstation description could consist of a written report, a diagram, or both. Present your findings to the class. Alternatively, your group could select a professional occupation such as a scientist, engineer, architect, or attorney, and design a professional workstation for that occupation.

CASE STUDY

Multimedia Collaboration: A Pandora's Box?

Pandora, in Greek mythology, was created by Zeus (the principal god and ruler of all gods and humans) and was endowed with great curiosity. She was also given a box but was warned not to open it. Her curiosity won out: She opened the box and all the troubles and diseases of the world escaped before she could close it.

Olivetti Research Laboratory chose the name Pandora for its research project on multimedia systems. The research is being done at Olivetti's research lab in Cambridge, England. The team works in a science fiction environment where their office doors unlock and open as they approach, their workstation turns on, and the work they left yesterday appears almost magically on their screens.

When they check their E-mail, they see video messages left by their coworkers. A staff member can scan the other members' offices through his or her workstation to see if they are in and busy. If he or she wishes (and the others are amenable), he or she can, with no effort, start a video conference with several other staff members, again through his or her (and their) workstation. If, while he or she is in someone else's office and receives a call, it is automatically forwarded to the office being visited without the visitor having taken any action.

The magic of the doors, the automatic turning on of the computer, and the automatic phone forwarding is done through a system called Active Badge, a small badge all team members wear that emits the wearer's infrared identification every 15 seconds. Monitors throughout the site pick up the signal and relay it via a low-cost network to location servers. The servers translate the signals into position information that can keep track of who and where the wearer is and trigger action wherever appropri-

ate, such as unlocking and opening a door. Location information can be exchanged with other geographic sites using private WANs or public networks like the Internet.

The multimedia communications portion of Pandora–video messages and video conferencing–however, is the heart of

Bell Labs' Rapport system lets co-workers jointly edit computer files as they discuss them. Participants may communicate through voice and data only, as they are doing in the illustration, or add full-motion video.

With NTT's TeamWorkStation, users can transfer work from their individual screen (left) to a "shared workspace" (right) for collaboration. Tiny cameras mounted on the black boom and on the lamp send images of the user's face and desktop to the shared screen.

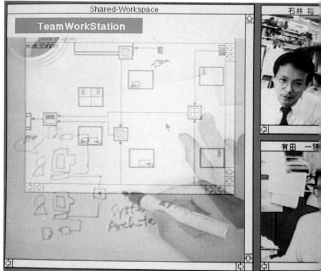

NTT's TeamWorkStation system can superimpose the image of a hand pointing and making corrections onto that of a document lying on a co-worker's desktop.

the system. The technology is relatively simple, consisting of networked, UNIX-based workstations each with a video camera, microphone, and loudspeaker attached, plus a special interface to the network to handle the audio and video. The system includes cut-and-paste facilities for editing videos and for creating text-video composite recordings. The cameras are on, pointed toward the face of the staff member when he or she is at his computer; anyone can simply scan the other offices to see who is there and if they are working. An individual can leave another a video mail message with great ease because the function is built into the system. Video conferencing is equally easy. To set the conference up, the initiator merely invites the others to join. The participants see a series of windows on their computer screens during the conference, a window showing the face of each participant plus one or more windows of documents or whatever the individuals want to share. Obviously, those in the Olivetti Research Center could just walk down the hall (and often do), but in the real world the people we want to talk with often work in different buildings, different cities, even different countries, so electronic communications is clearly here to stay, The question the researchers ask is how to make those communications more human, more flexible, and ultimately more effective.

Answering that question raises other questions on how people actually work. How lifelike does a system have to be? How important is it that we recreate the conditions of the intimate office and the face-to-face meeting? Social scientists do not agree on answers, and the differences have spawned a number of very different multimedia communications research projects.

Rapport, a project of AT&T Bell Laboratories in Holmdel, New Jersey, focuses on a uniform interface for E-mail, voice, video and computer communications. The head of the Rapport project, Sudhir Ahuja, describes that interface as a "virtual meeting room" that users "enter" on their screens. To set up a meeting, an individual calls others through the system and asks them to join in. As with Pandora, each participant sees the faces of other participants plus any document being worked on. Each can watch as one of the participants makes changes to the document (one person at a time). The cursor arrow displays the name of the person who has control of changes at that moment. Individuals can switch freely from one conference to another. A virtual meeting can remain around for days, awaiting the next activity by the participants. One interesting aspect of the Rapport approach is that Ahuja does not believe that eye contact is all that important. "Even in a regular meeting," he says, "you don't look at the person all the time–you look at the blackboard, you write, you look for information. You make eye contact occasionally, just to test whether the person is paying attention."

The Human Interface Laboratories of Japan's NTT emphasizes the hand and natural marks on paper. Each workstation uses a Macintosh computer with two screens (one for the individual and one for the shared work), a speaker phone, and two video cameras (one for the face and one mounted to show the desktop and the user's hand gestures). An individual can draw a diagram, by hand, on the document being discussed and all others will see it, including the writing hand. Hiroshi Ishii, the project designer, believes that this is a more natural method of collaboration.

Multimedia is still a technology of the future. One immediate problem is the enormous bandwidth required to carry video messages; this makes the technology very expensive. A conference between two people requires four channels (assuming one camera at each desk)–one for sound and one for video in each direction. Add others and bandwidth requirements climb geometrically– 12 channels for three participants, 24 channels for four, and so on. At this time, the expense is prohibitive, given current bandwidth costs. It is expected that technology will overcome this question in time. A second matter is the issue of how we work, how necessary the technology is, and will it improve our productivity and our creativity? If so, which are the useful approaches, and which are dead ends? The third and largest question returns us to Pandora's box– the "dark side" of the technology. How will staff members feel about having a camera pointed at them all day long? Is this technology an invasion of privacy? Will management use this facility to monitor and even "spy upon" their workers? Can these problems be handled by giving each employee a lens cap and the right to cover the lens whenever he or she wishes?

Sources: Dick Pountain, "Track People with Active Badges," *Byte,* December 1993; David Brittan, "The Promise of Multimedia Communications," *Technology Review,* May/June 1992; Andy Hopper, "The Walk-and-Wear Office," *Computerworld,* April 20, 1992.

Case Study Questions

1. How important are the traditional ad hoc office collaborations and working groups for productivity?

2. What management, organization, and technology challenges need to be overcome to install multimedia communication systems successfully?

3. What are the benefits of multimedia collaboration? Do you think the multimedia technology described in this article will contribute to improved productivity? What features and functions do you think are critical for this technology to succeed?

4. What ethical questions are raised by the Pandora project?

5. Why do you think that the Pandora project does or does not deserve the name it was given? What personnel concerns would you have if you were the head of a department and were ordered to install one of these multimedia systems? What restrictions might you require? How would you prepare your staff for the installation?

References Amaravadi, Chandra S., Olivia R. Liu Sheng, Joey F. George, and Jay F. Nunamaker, Jr. "AEI: A Knowledge-Based Approach to Integrated Office Systems." *Journal of Management Information Systems* 9, no. 1 (Summer 1992).

Applegate, Linda. "Technology Support for Cooperative Work: A Framework for Studying Introduction and Assimilation in Organizations." *Journal of Organizational Computing* 1, no. 1 (January–March 1991).

Bair, James H. "A Layered Model of Organizations: Communication Processes and Performance." *Journal of Organizational Computing* 1, no. 2 (April–June 1991).

Bermant, Charles. "Notes Records 'Fables.' " *Computerworld* (April 6, 1992).

Berst, Jesse. "Deciphering Lotus' Notes." *Computerworld* (May 18, 1992).

Bikson, Tora K., J. D. Eveland, and Barbara A. Gutek. "Flexible Interactive Technologies for Multi-Person Tasks: Current Problems and Future Prospects." Rand Corporation (December 1988).

Busch, Elizabeth, Matti Hamalainen, Clyde W. Holsapple, Yongmoo Suh, and Andrew B. Whinston. "Issues and Obstacles in the Development of Team Support Systems." *Journal of Organizational Computing* 1, no. 2 (April–June 1991).

Daly, James. "Insurer Sees Future in Imaging Strategy." *Computerworld* (January 6, 1992).

Edelstein, Herbert A. "Imaging Shifts Emphasis to Workflow Management." *Software Magazine* (November 1991).

Giuliao, Vincent E. "The Mechanization of Office Work." *Scientific American* (September 1982).

Horton, Marjorie, Priscilla Rogers, Laurel Austin, and Michael McCormick. "Exploring the Impact of Face-to-Face Collaborative Technology on Group Writing." *Journal of Management Information Systems* 8, no. 3 (Winter 1991–1992).

International Data Corporation White Paper. "Image Management Systems." *Computerworld*, September 20, 1990.

International Data Corporation White Paper. "Workgroup Technology: Tying Technology to Business Objectives."

Johansen, Robert. "Groupware: Future Directions and Wild Cards." *Journal of Organizational Computing* 1, no. 2 (April–June 1991).

Kling, Rob, and Charles Dunlop. "Controversies about Computerization and the Character of White Collar Worklife." *The Information Society* 9, no. 1 (January–March 1993).

Korzeniowski, Paul. "Building New APPS on E-mail." *Software Magazine* (March 1992).

Kusekoski, Gene. "Corporate Videotex: A Strategic Business Information System." *MIS Quarterly* 13, no. 4 (December 1989).

LaPlante, Alice. "Group(ware) Therapy." *Computerworld* (July 27, 1992).

Lee, Soonchul. "The Impact of Office Information Systems on Power and Influence." *Journal of Management Information Systems* 8, no. 2 (Fall 1991).

Liker, Jeffrey K., Mitchell Fleischer, Mitsuo Nagamachi, and Michael S. Zonnevylle. "Designers & Their Machines: CAD Use and Support in the U.S. and Japan." *Communications of the ACM* 35, no. 2 (February 1992).

Lotus Development Corporation. "Lotus Notes Application Profile" (1991).

Mann, Marina M., Richard L. Rudman, Thomas A. Jenckes, and Barbara C. McNurlin. "EPRINET: Leveraging Knowledge in the Electronic Industry." *MIS Quarterly* 15, no. 3 (September 1991).

Margolis, Nell. "Imaging: It's a Jungle in There." *Computerworld* (July 6, 1992).

Michaels, Jenna. "Managing Technology." *Wall Street & Technology* (February 1993).

Naj, Amal Kumar. " 'Virtual Reality' Isn't a Fantasy for Surgeons." *The Wall Street Journal* (March 3, 1993).

Nash, Jim. "Imaging Heals Hospital's Sick File System." *Computerworld* (March 2, 1992).

Newquist, Harvey P. "Virtual Reality's Commercial Reality." *Computerworld* (March 30, 1992).

Olson, Gary M. and Judith S. "User-Centered Design of Collaboration Technology." *Journal of Organizational Computing* 1, no. 1 (January–March 1991).

Orlikowski, Wanda J. "Learning from Notes: Organizational Issues in Groupware Implementation." Sloan Working Paper no. 3428, Cambridge, MA: Sloan School of Management, Massachusetts Institute of Technology.

Panko, Raymond R. "Is Office Productivity Stagnant?" *MIS Quarterly* 15, no. 2 (June 1991).

Porat, Marc. *The Information Economy: Definition and Measurement.* Washington, D.C.: U.S. Department of Commerce, Office of Telecommunications (May 1977).

Press, Lawrence. "Systems for Finding People." *Journal of Organizational Computing* 2, no. 3 and 4 (1992a).

Press, Lawrence. "Lotus Notes (Groupware) in Context." *Journal of Organizational Computing* 2, no. 3 and 4 (1992b).

Ramanathan, Srinivas, P. Venkat Rangan, and Harrick M. Vin. "Designing Communication Architectures for Inter-Organizational Multimedia Collaboration." *Journal of Organizational Computing* 2, no. 3 and 4 (1992).

Roach, Stephen S. "Industrialization of the Information Economy." New York: Morgan Stanley and Co., 1984.

Roach, Stephen S. "Making Technology Work." New York: Morgan Stanley and Co., 1993.

Roach, Stephen S. "Services Under Siege–The Restructuring Imperative." *Harvard Business Review* (September–October 1991).

Roach, Stephen S. "Technology and the Service Sector." *Technological Forecasting and Social Change* 34, no. 4 (December 1988).

Ruhleder, Karen, and John Leslie King. "Computer Support for Work Across Space, Time, and Social Worlds." *Journal of Organizational Computing* 1, no. 4 (1991).

Schatz, Bruce R. "Building an Electronic Community System." *Journal of Management Information Systems* 8, no. 3 (Winter 1991–1992).

Shapiro, Joshua. "From the Rugged Outback, a Quick-Fix Modular Tire." *The New York Times* (February 28, 1993).

Sheng, Olivia R. Liu, Luvai F. Motiwalla, Jay F. Nunamaker, Jr., and Douglas R. Vogel. "A Framework to Support Managerial Activities Using Office Information Systems." *Journal of Management Information Systems* 6, no. 3 (Winter 1989/90).

Smarr, Larry, and Charles E. Catlett. "Metacomputing." *Communications of the ACM* 35, no. 6 (June 1992).

Sproull, Lee, and Sara Kiesler. "A Two-Level Perspective on Electronic Mail in Organizations." *Journal of Organizational Computing* 1, no. 2 (April–June 1991).

Sproull, Lee, and Sara Kiesler. *Connections: New Ways of Working in the Networked Organization.* Cambridge, MA: MIT Press, 1992.

Starbuck, William H. "Learning by Knowledge-Intensive Firms." *Journal of Management Studies* 29, no. 6 (November 1992).

Sterling, Theodor D., and James J. Weinkam. "Sharing Scientific Data." *Communications of the ACM* 33, no. 8 (August 1990).

Westin, Alan F., Heather A. Schwader, Michael A. Baker, and Sheila Lehman. *The Changing Workplace.* New York: Knowledge Industries, 1985.

Wolff, Edward N., and William J. Baumol. "Sources of Postwar Growth of Information Activity in the U.S." C.V. Starr Center for Applied Economics, New York University, no. 87-14 (June 1987).

Enhancing Management Decision Making

The Ideal Investment Portfolio: What Does the System Say?

Redstone Advisors is a $550-million money management firm specializing in taxable and tax-exempt fixed income investments. It must track and analyze complex financial instruments under rapidly changing market conditions. Redstone has monthly policy meetings to determine how its investment portfolios will be constructed. The meetings establish general guidelines for the portfolios, such as the percentage of cash, the weight of each sector, and the average duration of the portfolios (that is, the average number of years for the underlying bonds to reach maturity). The firm then makes trades to bring its portfolios into line with the established guidelines.

To help its traders make buy-and-sell decisions, Redstone uses a LAN-based portfolio management system called PORTIA supplied by Thomson Financial Services in Boston and London. PORTIA is a real-time system with DOS, Windows, and Sun UNIX versions. It performs all of the portfolio management and accounting functions required by money management firms who deal with stocks, bonds, money market securities, options, and futures. Redstone analysts enter proposed trades into PORTIA. The system has a "what-if" capability; when they enter the proposed trades PORTIA tells them what the portfolio will look like. The traders can keep experimenting with different trades until the simulated portfolio matches the investment guidelines. They can even examine the portfolio from many angles using multiple currencies—their system's base currency, the currency of a particular security, or a cur-

rency for the selected portfolio. The system allows users to examine the impact of various currencies on investment performance. With this information, they then make the trades. Once the actual trades have been entered into PORTIA, the change is instantly reflected in a portfolio's cash balances and holdings. According to Marc Vincent, Redstone's management director, the ability to perform what-if analysis and to know exact portfolio holdings and cash balances improves productivity and decision making.

Sources: Sheila O'Henry, "The Portfolio Management and Accounting Supermarket," *Wall Street and Technology,* 11, No. 5, November 1993; and "Fixed Income Money Manager Boosts Efficiency with Flexible, Comprehensive System," *Wall Street and Technology* 10, no. 9, April 1993.

With the ability to perform complex calculations and to create "what-if" scenarios, Redstone's portfolio management system is a classic example of a decision-support system. Decision-support systems (DSS) provide powerful analytic capabilities for supporting managers during the process of arriving at a decision.

Most of the information systems described throughout this text help people make decisions in one way or another, but DSS are part of a special category of information systems that are explicitly designed to enhance managerial decision making. Other systems in this category are group decision-support systems (GDSS), which support decision making in groups, and executive support systems (ESS), which provide information for making strategic-level decisions. This chapter describes the characteristics of each of these types of information systems and shows how each actually enhances the managerial decision-making process.

After completing this chapter, you will be able to:

- Define a decision-support system (DSS) and a group decision-support system (GDSS).

- Describe the components of decision-support systems and group decision-support systems.
- Explain how decision-support systems and group decision-support systems can enhance decision making.
- Describe the capabilities of executive support systems (ESS).
- Describe the benefits of executive support systems.

11.1 Decision-Support Systems (DSS)

In the 1970s, a number of companies began developing information systems that were quite different from traditional MIS systems. These new systems were smaller (in terms of labor and cost). They were interactive (unusual at the time), and were designed to help end users utilize data and models to discuss and decide (not solve) semistructured and unstructured problems (Henderson and Schilling, 1985). By the late 1980s, these early efforts to assist individual decision making were extended to groups and entire organizations.

What Are Decision-Support Systems (DSS)?

Decision support-systems (DSS): Computer systems at the management level of an organization that combine data and sophisticated analytical models to support semistructured and unstructured decision making.

These systems are called decision-support systems (DSS). As we noted in Chapter 2, **decision-support systems (DSS)** assist management decision making by combining data, sophisticated analytical models, and user-friendly software into a single powerful system that can support semistructured or unstructured decision making. The DSS is under user control from early inception to final implementation and daily use. Figure 11.1 is a schematic diagram of a DSS.

In Figure 11.1, the relationships between DSS and the organization's existing TPS, KWS, and MIS are left deliberately vague. In some cases, DSS are linked closely to existing corporate information flows (see Chapter 2). Often, however, DSS are isolated from major organizational information systems. DSS tend to be stand-alone systems, developed by end-user divisions or groups not under central IS control, although it is obviously better if they are integrated into organizational systems when this is a functional requirement (Hogue, 1985).

DSS AS A PHILOSOPHY

DSS are designed to deliver capabilities, not simply to respond to information needs (Keen and Morton, 1982; Sprague and Carlson, 1982). DSS are more targeted than MIS systems. MIS systems provide managers with routine flows of data and assist in the general control of the organization. In contrast, DSS are tightly focused on a specific decision or classes of decisions such as routing, queueing, evaluating, and so forth. Table 11.1 summarizes the differences between MIS and DSS. In philosophy, DSS promises end-user control of data, tools, and sessions. MIS is still largely dominated by professionals: Users receive information from a professional staff of analysts, designers, and programmers. In terms of objectives, MIS focuses on structured information flows to middle managers. DSS is aimed at top managers and middle managers, with emphasis on change, flexibility, and a quick response; with DSS there is less of an effort to link users to structured information flows and a correspondingly greater emphasis on models, assumptions, and display graphics. Both DSS and MIS rely on professional analysis and design. However, whereas MIS usually follows a traditional systems development methodology, freezing information requirements before design and throughout the life cycle, DSS systems are consciously iterative, are never frozen, and in a sense are never finished.

Figure 11.1
Overview of a decision support system (DSS). The DSS is often isolated from the corporation's transaction processing systems (TPS), knowledge work systems (KWS), and management information systems (MIS). The main components of the DSS are the model base, the DSS database, and the DSS software system.

Table 11.1 DIFFERENCE BETWEEN DSS AND MIS

Dimension	DSS	MIS
Philosophy	Provide integrated tools, data, models, and language to users	Provide structured information to end users
Systems analysis	Establish what tools are used in the decision process	Identify information requirements
Design	Iterative process	Deliver system based on frozen requirements

Figure 11.2 shows how a DSS would support stock investment decisions. In this figure, a DSS is portrayed as a set of capabilities that would be useful in a number of decision processes used in making investment decisions. Making such decisions requires reviewing portfolios, individual company research data, and stock data (the databases).

Four core DSS capabilities are portrayed in Figure 11.2, and all DSS can be characterized in this manner (Sprague and Carlson, 1982):

Representations: In DSS, conceptualization of information in the form of graphs, charts, lists, reports, and symbols to control operations.

Operations: In DSS, logical and mathematical manipulations of data.

Memory aids: In DSS, capabilities to update and refresh memory, including databases, views of data, work spaces, and libraries.

Control aids: Capabilities that allow the user to control the activities and functions of the DSS.

- **Representations:** Conceptualizations of information used in making decisions, such as graphs, charts, lists, reports, and symbols to control operations.
- **Operations:** Logical and mathematical manipulations of data, such as gathering information, generating lists, preparing reports, assigning risks and values, generating statistics, and simulating alternatives.
- **Memory aids:** Databases, views of data, work spaces, libraries, links among work spaces and libraries, and other capabilities to refresh and update memory.
- **Control aids:** Capabilities that allow the user to control the activities of the DSS. They include a software language permitting user control of representations, operations, and memory, which features menus, function keys, conventions, training, "help" commands, and tutorials.

In essence, a DSS is a decision-making scratch pad, backed up by databases, that decision makers can use to support many decision-making processes. This approach to DSS as a set of core capabilities goes to the heart of the DSS philosophy and provides a benchmark against which we can compare and critique any DSS in the marketplace.

CHARACTERISTICS OF DSS: WHAT IT MEANS TO SUPPORT DECISIONS

With this understanding of the components and philosophy of DSS, it is possible to discuss more precisely what is meant by decision support. (Here it may be helpful to review Chapter 3, which discusses management decision making from several perspectives.) Chapter 3 introduces the distinction between structured, semistructured, and unstructured decisions. Structured problems are repetitive and routine, for which known algorithms provide solutions. Unstructured problems are novel and nonroutine, for which there are no algorithms for solution. One can discuss, decide, and ruminate about unstructured problems, but they

Figure 11.2
DSS approach to investment decisions. In a DSS approach to systems, the emphasis is on providing capabilities to answer questions and reach decisions. The four core capabilities are representations, operations, memory aids, and control aids. *Source: Adapted from Sprague, R. H., and E. D Carlson.* Building Effective Decision Support Systems. *Englewood Cliffs, NJ: Prentice-Hall, 1982.*

are not solved in the sense that one finds an answer to an equation (Henderson and Schilling, 1985). Semistructured problems fall between structured and unstructured problems. DSS are designed to support semistructured and unstructured problem analysis.

A well-designed DSS can be used at many levels of the organization. Senior management can use a financial DSS to forecast the availability of corporate funds for investment by division. Middle managers within divisions can use these estimates and the same system and data to make decisions about allocating division funds to projects. Capital project managers within divisions, in turn, can use this system to begin their projects, reporting to the system (and ultimately to senior managers) on a regular basis about how much money has been spent.

As noted in Chapter 3, it is a mistake to think that decisions are only made by individuals in large organizations. In fact, most decisions are made collectively. Chapter 3 describes the rational, bureaucratic, political, and "garbage-can" models of organizational decision making. Frequently, decisions must be coordinated with several groups before being finalized. In large organizations, decision making is inherently a group process, and DSS can be designed to facilitate group decision making. The next section of this chapter deals with this issue.

Finally, DSS should provide session control for end users. That is, end users should be able to find relevant data, choose and operate relevant models, and control operations without professional intervention. Professionals are, of course, needed to build the databases, model bases, and control language. Experts should be available for consultation, training, advice, and support, but sessions should be end-user driven.

Examples of DSS Applications

There are many ways in which DSS can be used to support decision making. Table 11.2 lists examples of DSS in well-known American organizations. To illustrate the range of capabilities of DSS, we will now describe some recent DSS applications.

THE ADVANCED PLANNING SYSTEM—A MANUFACTURING DSS

To support most kinds of manufacturing, companies use a type of software known as Manufacturing Resources Planning (MRPII). The typical MRPII system includes such applications as master production scheduling, purchasing, material requirements planning, and even general ledger. Many thousands of these packages have been installed around the world. While they are useful as far

Table 11.2 EXAMPLES OF DSS SYSTEMS

American Airlines	Price and route selection
Champlin Petroleum	Corporate planning and forecasting
Equico Capital Corporation	Investment evaluation
Frito-Lay, Inc.	Price, advertising, and promotion section
General Dynamics	Price evaluation
Juniper Lumber	Production optimization
Kmart	Price evaluation
National Gypsum	Corporate planning and forecasting
Southern Railway	Train dispatching and routing
Texas Oil and Gas Corporation	Evaluation of potential drilling sites
United Airlines	Flight scheduling
U.S. Department of Defense	Defense contract analysis

as they go, these packages usually run on a mainframe so that they can process massive amounts of data. As a result, they are too large and slow to be used for "what-if" simulations and too procedural to be modified into decision-support software. A Canadian company, Carp Systems International of Kanata, Ontario, sells the Advanced Planning System (APS) to give the user DSS functionality using the data from existing MRPII systems.

APS allows a range of "what-if" processing by pulling the relevant data from the manufacturing software and performing calculations based upon user-defined variables. After Hurricane Andrew hit south Florida in 1992, Trane's Unitary Productions division in Fort Smith, Arkansas, was asked to quickly ship 114 five-ton air-conditioning systems to small businesses in the affected area. Using APS, within minutes Trane's could determine not only how long it would take to build the units but also how the added production would affect their existing customer commitments. They found that they were able to fit the added production in without disrupting existing orders. They delivered the units weeks before their competition.

Another user of APS, Compaq Computer of Houston, Texas, received an order for 10,000 of one of its personal computer models in 1990, just as it was phasing the model out. Cal Monteith, Compaq's manager of master scheduling and production control, knew the firm lacked the parts. He had the task of determining both part availability and plant capacity for the added production. The Carp software allowed him quickly to break the units down to their component parts right down to the piece level. It told him precisely how many of which parts he needed and when he would need them. Armed with this information, Compaq was able to send off orders immediately for the right parts. In the end, Compaq manufactured and sold 30,000 more PC units on time, adding $6 million to the bottom line in net revenues.

Pitney Bowes, the $3.3 billion business equipment manufacturer, uses the software to simulate supply changes. Pitney Bowes carries enough manufacturing inventory to satisfy demand for 30 days. Using APS, the firm asked to see the impact if it would reduce the inventory to 15 days. APS responded with an answer within five minutes, including an estimate of what Pitney Bowes would save. Similarly, Sikorsky Aircraft of Stratford, Connecticut, claims that over a three-year period, the company has been able to use this software to help halve their inventory even while they doubled their sales.

APS is a complex piece of software costing from $150,000 to $1 million and requiring intensive computing power. It runs on an IBM RS/6000 workstation. As with any other software, users caution that APS (and similar packages) are only as good as the data. If the data are out of date or wrong, APS only allows the user to do wrong things more quickly (Rifkin, 1992).

ATLAS CRIME ANALYSIS—MAPPING CRIMINAL ACTIVITY

In the early 1970s, IBM developed an interactive system called Geodata Analysis and Display System (GADS) to enable noncomputer people to access, display, and analyze data that have geographic content and meaning. Users can load different maps, data, and analysis routines to solve many different problems. Seventeen specific applications were developed from GADS in the areas of police, school, urban planning, fire, even bus route planning. Police used the software in a number of ways, including to help a city allocate its police to the beat patrols. GADS cost several hundred thousand dollars less than solutions developed by manual methods, and yet it provided a solution that was acceptable to the police officers.

More recently, the San Bernardino, California, Sheriff's Department has begun using a newly developed DSS to aid in a range of police-related tasks. The software package, Atlas Crime Analysis, was developed by Strategic Mapping, Inc. of Santa Clara, California. The San Bernardino Sheriff's Department stores its crime data on a Digital Equipment Corporation VAX minicomputer. Atlas

Crime Analysis downloads the needed crime data from the VAX onto Intel 486-based microcomputers at 15 police stations. The software on the microcomputers matches the crime data with computerized street maps to produce the information needed, based upon the request. The software is considered very user friendly, as it relies on menus and plain English. For example, to show all burglaries on a map being displayed, the user simply selects "Burglaries" from a menu.

The county covers 20,000 square miles, a large area to map manually. The Sheriff's Department uses the Atlas software to determine the best places to patrol by having it generate maps showing criminal activity in a specific area. Alternatively, it displays geographic patterns for only certain types of crimes, such as armed robbery (see Figure 11.3 for a sample output). The county has used the software to support a court case by showing that a series of rapes occurred on the suspect's route between home and work. The Sheriff's Department has used it to plot crimes in a specific area before and after a recent parolee moved into the neighborhood. It has even used it to track a spree of shootings from an automobile. One planned use, once the software is enhanced, is to have the system automatically generate alert reports when certain crime thresholds are reached. For example, if a neighborhood normally has four to five crimes per month, the user may want a report automatically generated if the number of crimes in a month exceeds six in that neighborhood.

THE EGYPTIAN CABINET DSS

The Egyptian Cabinet is composed of the Prime Minister, 32 other ministers, and four ministerial-level committees with their staffs. Decision making here is, by its very nature, strategic because it involves questions of survival: balance of payments, deficit management, public-sector performance, economic growth, and national defense.

Decision making at these high levels of governments, or corporations, is often portrayed as a rational decision process. But in fact, decision making involves managing issues that are forced on decision makers with varying and shifting priorities. Issues circulate continuously; they enter and exit through participants and are resolved in the sense that they dissolve or go away or are overtaken by

Figure 11.3
The Atlas Crime Analysis system. Atlas Crime Analysis plots crime locations on computerized street maps to help police track crime sprees, analyze crime patterns, and compile evidence to bring suspects to court. *Courtesy of Strategic Mapping, Inc.*

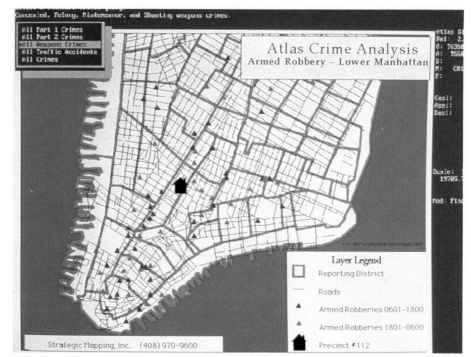

other issues. The issues are themselves complex, poorly defined, interdependent, and related to many features of society. Information is voluminous but unreliable and qualitative.

In 1985, the Egyptian Cabinet developed a three-person Information and Decision Support Center (IDSC) to assist its own decision-making process (Figure 11.4). Today, 150 people work full time providing DSS services to the cabinet on critical issues. The IDSC system is based upon a network of 110 microcomputers connected to a mainframe. Software includes standard desktop packages such as dBASE III for database management; Lotus 1–2–3 spreadsheet software; and FOCUS, a fourth-generation language and application generator, all of which have been fully converted to Arabic form. The electronic mail system is bilingual (Arabic/English).

One of the first uses of IDSC was to develop a new tariff structure to replace an inconsistent and complex structure that was thought to be impeding economic growth. The goal of the policy set forth by the cabinet was to create a consistent, simple tariff structure; increase revenues to the treasury; and promote economic growth without harming poor citizens. A microcomputer-based DSS model was built of the proposed new tariff structure, using a prototyping methodology.

The new policy activated many opposing groups. The Ministry of Industry, hoping to increase local production of auto parts, supported new tariffs on imported auto parts. This was supported as well by the Ministry of Economy, which supported local production. But the policy was opposed by the Ministry of Finance because it would reduce customs revenue.

Figure 11.4
The cabinet decision-making process with IDSC. *Source: Figure 2. The Cabinet Decision-Making Process After IDSC (El Sherif and El Sawy. Reprinted with permission from* MIS Quarterly, *Volume 12, Number 4, December 1988).*

The DSS was walked around, back and forth, from one ministry to another, making adjustments to the proposed tariffs, playing "what-if" games to see the impact of tariff changes on revenue and local employment. After one month of intensive effort, agreement was reached on the new tariff policy. Builders of the DSS felt the system reduced conflict by clarifying the tradeoffs and potentialimpacts of tariff changes. While early estimates of higher tariffs claimed $250 million in increased revenues would result, the DSS predicted $25 million. By 1987, the actual increased revenue was $28 million (El Sherif and El Sawy, 1988).

The Egyptian Cabinet's DSS illustrates the idea that a DSS is not just an application, but a generalized capability for addressing decision makers' needs. Unlike an MIS system, DSS do not simply involve a routine, steady flow of data, but instead can be flexibly responsive to new situations by using data and analytic models (even spreadsheets) to work through the consequences of decisions and assumptions.

Components of DSS

DSS database: A collection of current or historical data from a number of applications or groups.

Review Figure 11.1 again. It shows that a decision-support system has three basic components—a database, a model base, and the DSS software system. The **DSS database** is a collection of current or historical data from a number of applications or groups, organized for easy access by a range of applications. The DSS database management system protects the integrity of the data while controlling the processing that keeps the data current; it also saves historical data. DSS do not create or update data, for that is not their purpose. Rather, they use live organizational data (from such systems as production and sales) so that individuals and groups are able to make decisions based upon actual conditions.

Most DSS do not have direct access to organizational data. Instead, DSS usually use data that have been extracted from relevant databases (internal and external) and stored specifically for use by the DSS.

Model base: A collection of mathematical and analytical models that can easily be made accessible to the DSS user.

Model: An abstract representation that illustrates the components or relationships of a phenomenon.

A **model base** is a collection of mathematical and analytical models that easily can be made accessible to the DSS user. A **model** is an abstract representation that illustrates the components or relationships of a phenomenon. A model can be a physical model (such as a model airplane), a mathematical model (such as an equation), or a verbal model (such as a description of a procedure to write up an order). Each decision support system is built for a specific set of purposes and will make different collections of models available depending upon those purposes.

Perhaps the most common models available in model bases are libraries of statistical models. The software has the ability to project future outcomes by analyzing a series of data. Statistical modeling software can be used to help establish relationships, such as relating product sales to differences in age, income or other factors between communities.

Forecasting models are often used to forecast sales. The user of this type of model might supply a range of historical data to project future conditions and the sales that might result from those conditions. The decision maker could then vary those future conditions (entering, for example, a rise in raw materials costs or the entry of a new, low-priced competitor in the market) to determine how these new conditions might affect sales. Companies often use this software to attempt to predict the actions of competitors. Model libraries exist for specific functions, such as financial and risk analysis models.

Sensitivity analysis: Models that ask "what-if" questions repeatedly to determine the impact of changes in one or more factors on outcomes.

Among the most widely used models are **sensitivity analysis** models, which ask "what-if" questions repeatedly to determine the impact of changes in one or more factors on outcomes. "What-if" analysis—working forward from known or assumed conditions—allows the user to vary certain values to test results in order to better predict outcomes if changes occur in those values. What happens if we raise the price by 5 percent or increase the advertising budget by $100,000? What happens if we keep the price and advertising budget the same? Desktop spreadsheet software, such as Lotus 1–2–3 or Microsoft Excel, is often used for this purpose. Backward sensitivity analysis software (such as the Backsolver in Lotus 1–2–3) is used for goal seeking: If I want to sell one million product units next year, how much must I reduce the price of the product?

DSS software system: DSS component that permits easy interaction between the users of the system and the DSS database and model base.

The third component of DSS is the **DSS software system.** The DSS software system permits easy interaction between users of the system and the DSS database and model base. The DSS software system manages the creation, storage, and retrieval of models in the model base and integrates them with the data in the DSS database. The DSS software system also provides a graphical, easy-to-use, flexible user interface that supports the dialogue between the user and the DSS. DSS users are usually corporate executives or managers, persons with well-developed working styles and individual preferences. Often they have little or no computer experience and no patience for learning to use a complex tool, so the interface must be relatively intuitive. In addition, what works for one may not work for another. Many executives, offered only one way of working (a way not to their liking) will simply not use the system. In order to mimic a typical way of working, a good user interface should allow the manager to move back and forth between activities at will.

Building DSS

Building a DSS is different from building a TPS or MIS system. DSS generally use smaller amounts of data, do not need on-line transaction data, involve a smaller number of important users, and tend to employ more sophisticated analytic models than other systems. Because DSS are customized to specific users and specific classes of decisions, they require much greater user participation to develop. In addition, they must be flexible and must evolve as the sophistication of users grows.

FACTORS IN DSS SUCCESS AND FAILURE

As experience with DSS has grown, a number of factors have been identified as important to their success and failure. The success factors are not very different from those of MIS and other systems. These factors are described in detail in Chapter 9.

A study of 34 DSS found that DSS orientation toward top management (assistance with making important decisions) and return on investment are the most important factors in the approval process for DSS (Meador and Keen, 1984; King, 1983). This is an important finding because it highlights what organizations are looking for when they develop DSS. Organizations need support for upper management decision making, which requires custom-built, flexible, and easy-to-use systems that address important organizational problems.

11.2 Group Decision-Support Systems (GDSS)

The early work in DSS focused largely on supporting individual decision making. However, because so much work is accomplished in groups within organizations, during the late 1980s system developers and scholars began to focus on how computers can support group and organizational decision making. This work followed even earlier efforts to develop electronic aids to community and societal decision making in the 1970s, based largely on mainframes (see Laudon, 1977). As a result of the focus on computer support of group decision making, a new category of systems developed, known as group decision-support systems (GDSS).

What Is a GDSS?

Group decision-support system (GDSS): An interactive computer-based system to facilitate the solution to unstructured problems by a set of decision makers working together as a group.

A **group decision-support system (GDSS)** is an interactive computer-based system to facilitate the solution of unstructured problems by a set of decision makers working together as a group (DeSanctis and Gallupe, 1987). GDSS were developed in response to growing concern over the quality and effectiveness of meetings. The underlying problems in group decision making have been the explosion of decision-maker meetings, the growing length of those meetings, and the increased number of attendees. Estimates on the amount of a manager's time spent in meetings range from 35 to 70 percent.

Meeting facilitators, organizational development professionals, and information systems scholars have been focusing on this issue and have identified a number of discrete meeting elements that need to be addressed (Grobowski et al., 1990; Kraemer and King, 1988; Nunamaker et al., 1991). Among these elements are the following:

1. *Improved preplanning* to make meetings more effective and efficient.
2. *Increased participation* so that all attendees will be able to contribute fully even if the number of attendees is large. Free riding (attending the meeting but not contributing) must also be addressed.
3. *Open, collaborative meeting atmosphere* in which attendees from various organizational levels feel able to contribute freely. The lower-level attendees must be able to participate without fear of being judged by their management; higher-status participants must be able to participate without having their presence or ideas dominate the meeting and result in unwanted conformity.
4. *Criticism-free idea generation,* enabling attendees to contribute without undue fear of feeling personally criticized.
5. *Evaluation objectivity,* creating an atmosphere where an idea will be evaluated on its merits rather than on the basis of the source of the idea.
6. *Idea organization and evaluation,* which require keeping the focus on the meeting objectives, finding efficient ways to organize the many ideas that can be generated in a brainstorming session and evaluating those ideas not only on their merits but also within appropriate time constraints.
7. *Setting priorities and making decisions,* which require finding ways to encompass the thinking of all the attendees in making these judgments.
8. *Documentation of meetings* so that attendees will have as complete and organized a record of the meeting as may be needed to continue the work of the project.
9. *Access to external information,* which will allow significant, factual disagreements to be settled in a timely fashion, thus enabling the meeting to continue and be productive.
10. *Preservation of "organizational memory"* so that those who do not attend the meeting can also work on the project. Often a project will include teams at different locations who will need to understand the content of a meeting at only one of the affected sites.

One response to the problems of group decision making has been the adoption of new methods of organizing and running meetings. Techniques such as facilitated meetings, brainstorming, and criticism-free idea generation have become popular and are now accepted as standard. Another response has been the application of technology to the problems resulting in the emergence of group decision-support systems.

ORGANIZATIONS

The Hohenheim CATeam Room

How does the physical environment of a group decision-support system meeting room affect the work of a GDSS-supported group? How do ergonomics affect the decision-making process? These are some of the questions that were explored by information systems researchers at the University of Hohenheim, in Stuttgart, Germany. Their methodology? Do the research and design their own GDSS room—the Computer Aided Team Room, known as the CATeam Room.

The information systems specialists worked with interior and furniture design architects from the State Academy of the Arts in Stuttgart. Realizing that people's sense of privacy and their social interactions can be affected by their level of physical comfort and the design of their meeting environment, the team looked into alternative designs for meeting rooms. In their quest for a meeting room design that would enhance group work, the team consulted specialists in psychology and ergonomics and visited GDSS research laboratories in the United States.

One of the principal questions addressed by the project was the relationship of seating arrangements in the GDSS meeting room to meeting interactions. The team started with a set of basic rules that demanded a maximum of 12 participants in a meeting (a limitation set because of the small size of the room they had available). The table they endorsed at the end included built-in computer equipment that could automatically be

stored inside the table at the push of a button so that the room could be used for traditional non-GDSS meetings. The table also is modular, allowing flexibility. For example, the room could be rearranged into a U-shape for a teaching situation. The team also wanted seating arrangements that would create a friendly teamwork atmosphere. While their principles did not include a specification for participant equality, that proved, in the end, to be the deciding factor for the table set-up. This issue is particularly important because meeting attendees often come from a range of different organizational levels, creating an initial atmosphere of inequality.

The final decision for table shape called for a round table called a Roundabout (see Figure 11.5). With a round table, everyone is equal, and the arrangement is democratic. Face-to-face contact is equally possible with anyone at the table. A GDSS requires a computer projection screen so that all can view the common screens together (as well as independently on their own PCs). To support the Roundabout solution, the CATeam project decided to use two common screens opposite each other. That way everyone would be able to view a screen easily and comfortably without attendees having to turn around or otherwise disturb the symmetry of the arrangement.

The placement of the computer equipment within the table also contributed to an environment of equality. When in use, the computer screen is placed slightly be-

low table level (Figure 11.5). The team saw two advantages to this arrangement. First, no computer equipment would interfere with the attendees' eye-to-eye contact with other attendees. Second, an attendee's monitor can only be viewed by the closest neighbor, if at all. They believe that privacy, and therefore anonymity, are protected.

The Roundabout design was selected for display by the jury of the 1989 "Anno 2000 Office Design Competition" in Milan.

Sources: Henrik Lewe and Helmut Krcmar, "The Design Process for a Computer-Supported Cooperative Work Research Laboratory: TheHohenheim CATeam Room," *Journal of Management Information Systems*, Winter 1991–92; HelmutKrcmar, Henrik Lewe, and Gerhard Schwabe: *Empirical CATeam Research of Meetings.* Working Paper no. 38 of the Information Systems Department, University of Hohenheim, Germany, 1993.

To Think About:
1. This chapter listed ten specific meeting elements that need to be addressed to improve decision-making meetings. Which of these elements are addressed by the CATeam ergonomic design, and in what ways might the design improve meetings?
2. Do you believe that the physical placement of the computer is adequate for guaranteeing the privacy of an attendee's work? Can you think of ways that privacy could be further protected?

Characteristics of GDSS

How can information technology help groups to arrive at decisions? Scholars have identified at least three basic elements of GDSS: hardware, software, and people. *Hardware* refers first to the conference facility itself, including the room, the tables and chairs. Such a facility must be physically laid out in a manner that supports group collaboration. It must also include some electronic hardware, such as electronic display boards, as well as audiovisual and computer equipment. The Window on Organizations examines one important aspect to the physical setup—the ergonomics of the meeting room design.

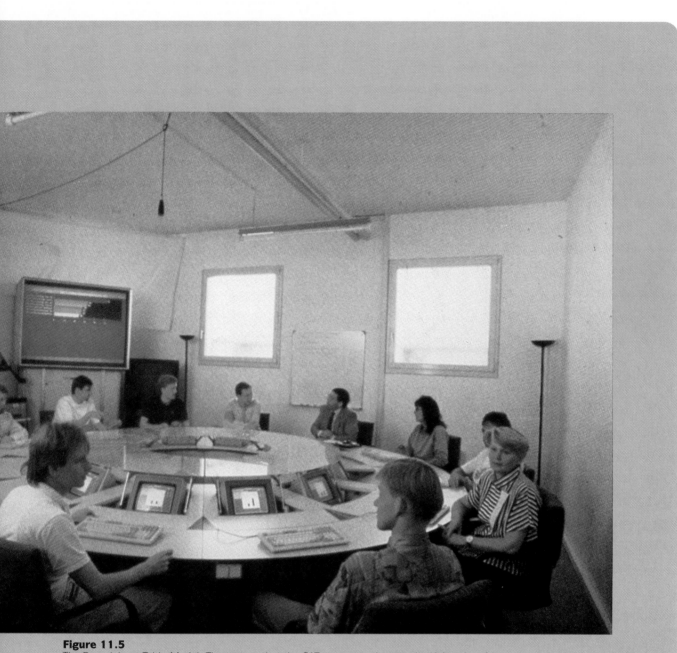

Figure 11.5
The Roundabout Table Model. The system that the CATeam researchers at the University of Hohenheim settled upon as the final design for a GDSS room table was the Roundabout table. With this design, everybody is equal, and face-to-face contact is equally possible with all participants at the table. *Courtesy of Dollinger & Partner.*

A wide range of *software tools*, including tools for organizing ideas, gathering information, ranking and setting priorities, and other aspects of collaborative work, is now being used to support decision-making meetings. We describe these tools below. *People* refers not only to the participants, but also to a trained facilitator and often to a staff that supports the hardware and software. Together these elements have led to the creation of a range of different kinds of GDSS, from simple electronic boardrooms to elaborate collaboration laboratories. See Figure 11.6 for an illustration of an actual GDSS collaborative meeting room. In a collaboration laboratory, individuals work on their own desktop

Figure 11.6
Illustration of PLEXSYS decision room. The large group room was opened in 1987, with twenty-four IBM PS/2 workstations. A gallery holds eighteen observers. The room has thirty-eight audio pick-up microphones and six video cameras with stereo audio. Two large-screen electronic displays and projectors permit playing of videotapes, discs, 35 MM slides, and computer graphics presentations. *Source: Figure 2b. Decision Room for Larger Groups (Dennis, George, Jessup, Nunamaker, and Vogel. Reprinted with permission from the* MIS Quarterly, *Volume 12, Number 4, December 1988).*

microcomputers. Their input is integrated on a file server and is viewable on a common screen at the front of the room; in most systems the integrated input is also viewable on the individual participant's screen.

One can appreciate the potential value of GDSS by examining their software tools. We describe the functions of several types of tools central to a full-blown collaboration laboratory. We then give an overview of a GDSS meeting so that you can understand its potential to support collaborative meetings. Finally, we examine how GDSS affect the problems we have described and their power to enhance group decision making.

GDSS Software Tools

Some of the features of the groupware tools for collaborative work described in Chapter 10 can be used to support group decision making. But GDSS are considered more explicitly decision-oriented and task-oriented than groupware, as they focus on helping a group solve a problem or reach a decision (Dennis et al., 1988). Groupware is considered more communication-oriented. Specific GDSS software tools include the following:

- *Electronic questionnaires* aid the organizers in pre-meeting planning by identifying issues of concern and by helping to insure that key planning information is not overlooked.
- *Electronic brainstorming tools* allow individuals simultaneously and anonymously to contribute ideas on the topics of the meeting.
- *Idea organizers* facilitate the organized integration and synthesis of ideas generated during brainstorming.
- *Questionnaire tools* support the facilitators and group leaders as they gather information before and during the process of setting priorities.
- *Tools for voting or setting priorities* make available a range of methods from simple voting, to ranking in order, to a range of weighted techniques for setting priorities or voting.
- *Stakeholder identification and analysis tools* use structured approaches to evaluate the impact of an emerging proposal upon the organization and to identify stakeholders and evaluate the potential impact of those stakeholders upon the proposed project.
- *Policy formation tools* provide structured support for developing agreement on the wording of policy statements.
- *Group dictionaries* document group agreement on definitions of words and terms central to the project.

Additional tools are available, such as group outlining and writing tools, software that stores and reads project files, and software that allows the attendees to view internal operational data stored by the organization's production computer systems.

OVERVIEW OF A GDSS MEETING

Electronic meeting system (EMS): Collaborative GDSS that uses information technology to make group meetings more productive by facilitating communication as well as decision making. Supports meetings at the same place and time or in different places and times.

An **electronic meeting system (EMS)** is a type of collaborative GDSS that uses information technology to make group meetings more productive by facilitating communication as well as decision making. It supports any activity where people come together, whether at the same place at the same time or in different places at different times (Dennis et al., 1988; Nunamaker et al., 1990/1991). IBM has a number of EMS installed at various sites, one of which is pictured in Figure 11.7. Each attendee has a workstation. The workstations are networked and are connected to the facilitator's console, which serves as both the facilitator's workstation and control panel and the meeting's file server. All data that the attendees forward from their workstations to the group are collected and saved on the file server. The facilitator is able to project computer images onto the projection screen at the front center of the room. The facilitator also has an overhead projector available. Whiteboards are visible on either side of the projection screen. Many electronic meeting rooms are arranged in a semicircle and are tiered in legislative style to accommodate a larger number of attendees.

The facilitator controls the use of tools during the meeting, often selecting from a large tool box that is part of the organization's GDSS. Tool selection is part of the pre-meeting planning process. Which tools are selected depends upon the subject matter, the goals of the meeting, and the facilitation methodology the facilitator will use.

Each attendee has full control over his or her own microcomputer. An attendee is able to view the agenda (and other planning documents), look at the integrated screen (or screens as the session moves on), use ordinary desktop microcomputer tools (such as a word processor or a spreadsheet), tap into production data that have been made available, or work on the screen associated with the current meeting step and tool (such as a brainstorming screen). However, no one can view anyone else's screens, so that an individual's work is confidential until he or she releases it to the file server for integration with the

Figure 11.7
The Collaborative Meeting Room at the University of Arizona.
Stacy Patel/J. F. Nunamaker/ Eller Graduate School of Management/ University of Arizona, Tucson.

work of others. All input to the file server is anonymous—at each step everyone's input to the file server (brainstorming ideas, idea evaluation and criticism, comments, voting, etc.) can be seen by all attendees on the integrated screens, but no information is available to identify the source of specific inputs. Attendees enter their data simultaneously rather than in round-robin fashion, as is done in meetings that have little or no electronic systems support.

Figure 11.8 shows the sequence of activities at a typical EMS meeting. For each activity it also indicates the type of tools used and the output of those tools. During the meeting all input to the integrated screens is saved on the file server. As a result, when the meeting is completed, a full record of the meeting (both raw material and resultant output) is available to the attendees and can be made available to anyone else with a need for access.

How GDSS Can Enhance Group Decision Making

GDSS are still relatively new, so firm conclusions are not yet possible. Nonetheless, scholars and business specialists have studied these systems, and the systems are now being used more widely, so that we are able at least to understand their potential benefits and even evaluate some of the tools. We look again at how GDSS affect the ten group meeting issues raised earlier.

1. *Improved pre-planning.* Electronic questionnaires, supplemented by word processors, outlining software, and other desktop PC software, can structure planning, thereby improving it. The availability of the planning information at the actual meeting also can serve to enhance the quality of the meeting. Experts seem to feel that these tools add significance and emphasis to meeting pre-planning.

2. *Increased participation.* Studies show that in traditional decision-making meetings without GDSS support the optimal meeting size is three to five attendees. Beyond that size, the meeting process begins to break down. Using GDSS software, studies show the meeting size can increase while productivity also increases. One reason for this is that attendees contribute simultaneously rather than one at a time, and can thus make more efficient use of the meeting time.

Figure 11.8
Group system tools. The sequence of activities and collaborative support tools used in an electronic meeting system (EMS) facilitates communication among attendees and generates a full record of the meeting. *Adapted from "Electronic Meeting Systems to Support Group Work," by Nunamaker, Dennis, Valacich, Vogel, and George, printed in* Communications of the ACM, *July 1991.*

Free riding is apparently decreased too, perhaps because the one or two individuals who are not working will stand out when everyone else in the room is busy at workstations. Interviews of GDSS meeting attendees indicate that the quality of participation is higher than in traditional meetings.

3. *Open, collaborative meeting atmosphere.* GDSS contribute to a more collaborative atmosphere in several ways. First, anonymity of input is essentially guaranteed. An individual need not be afraid of being judged by his or her boss for contributing a possibly off-beat idea. Anonymity also reduces or eliminates the deadening effect that often occurs when high-status individuals contribute. Even the numbing pressures of social cues are reduced or eliminated. Attendees find that GDSS meetings are often more open and freewheeling.

4. *Criticism-free idea generation.* Anonymity ensures that attendees can contribute without fear of personally being criticized or of having their ideas rejected because of the identity of the contributor. Several studies show that interactive GDSS meetings generate more ideas and more satisfaction with those ideas than verbally interactive meetings (Nunamaker et al., 1991).

5. *Evaluation objectivity.* Anonymity prevents criticism of the source of the ideas, thus supporting an atmosphere in which attendees focus on evaluating the ideas themselves. The same anonymity allows participants to detach themselves from their own ideas and so are able to view them from a critical perspective. Evidence suggests that evaluation in an anonymous atmosphere increases the free flow of critical feedback and even stimulates the generation of new ideas during the evaluation process.

6. *Idea organization and evaluation.* GDSS software tools used for this purpose are structured and are based on methodology. They usually allow individuals each to organize and then submit their results to the group (still anonymously). The group then iteratively modifies and develops the organized ideas until a document is completed. Attendees have generally viewed this approach as productive.

7. *Setting priorities and making decisions.* Anonymity helps lower-level participants have their positions taken into consideration along with the higher-level attendees.

8. *Documentation of meetings.* Evidence at IBM indicates that post-meeting use of the data is crucial. Attendees use the data to continue their dialogues after the meetings, to discuss the ideas with those who did not attend, and even to

make presentations (Grobowski et al., 1990). Some tools even enable the user to zoom in to more detail on specific information.

9. *Access to external information.* Often a great deal of meeting time is devoted to factual disagreements. More experience with GDSS will indicate whether or not GDSS technology reduces this problem.

10. *Preservation of "organizational memory."* Specific tools have been developed to facilitate access to the data generated during a GDSS meeting, allowing nonattendees to locate needed information after the meeting. The documentation of a meeting by one group at one site has also successfully been used as input to another meeting on the same project at another site.

Experience to date suggests that GDSS meetings can be more productive, make more efficient use of time, and produce the desired results in fewer meetings. One problem with understanding the value of GDSS is their complexity. A GDSS can be configured in an almost infinite variety of ways. In addition, the effectiveness of the tools will partially depend upon the effectiveness of the facilitator, the quality of the planning, the cooperation of the attendees, and the appropriateness of tools for different types of meetings. These systems are also rather expensive, so that much of the usage to date has been by corporations holding meetings at university GDSS research facilities. Because of their high price, GDSS integration into daily corporate life must await further evidence of their effectiveness.

Researchers have noted that the design of an electronic meeting system is only one of a number of contingencies that affect the outcome of group meetings. Other factors, including the nature of the group, the task, and the context, also affect the process of group meetings and meeting outcomes (Dennis et al., 1988; Nunamaker et al., 1991).

11.3 Executive Support Systems (ESS)

Executive support systems (ESS): Information systems at the strategic level of an organization designed to address unstructured decision making through advanced graphics and communications.

We have described how DSS and GDSS help managers make unstructured and semistructured decisions. **Executive support systems (ESS)** also help managers with unstructured decisions, focusing on the information needs of senior management. Combining data from both internal and external sources, ESS create a generalized computing and communications environment that can be applied to a changing array of problems. ESS help senior executives spot problems, identify opportunities, and forecast trends.

The Role of ESS

Briefing books: On-line data in the form of fixed-format reports for executives.

Drill down: The ability to move from summary data down to lower and lower levels of detail.

Prior to ESS, it was common for executives to receive numerous fixed-format reports, often hundreds of pages every month (or even every week). The first systems developed specifically for executives in the early 1980s were mainframe systems designed to replace that paper, delivering the same data to the executive in days rather than in weeks. Executives had access to the same data, only it was on-line in the form of reports. Such systems were known as senior management **briefing books.** Using a briefing book, executives usually could **drill down** (move from a piece of summary data down to lower and lower levels of detail). Briefing books did not spread widely through the executive suites. The data that could be provided by briefing books were limited and the briefing books were too inflexible.

By the late 1980s, ways were found to bring together data from throughout the organization and allow the manager to select, access, and tailor them easily as needed. Today, an ESS is apt to include a range of easy-to-use desktop analytical tools. Use of the systems has migrated down several organizational levels so that the executive and his or her subordinates are able to look at the same data in the same way.

Today's systems try to avoid the problem of data overload so common in paper reports because the data can be filtered or viewed in graphic format (if the user so chooses). Systems have maintained the ability to drill down (even starting from a graph). However, with access to so much critical data, designers must be certain that any ESS protects against altered data finding their way back to the originating system.

One limitation in ESS is that they use data from systems designed for very different purposes. Often data that are critical to the executive are simply not there. For example, sales data coming from an order entry transaction processing system are not linked to marketing information, a linkage the executive would find useful. External data are now much more available in many ESS systems. Executives need a wide range of external data, from current stock market news to competitor information, industry trends, and even projected legislative action. Through their ESS, many managers have access to news services, financial market databases, economic information, and whatever other public data they may require.

ESS today include tools for modeling and analysis. For example, many ESS use Lotus 1-2-3, Excel, or other spreadsheets as the heart of their analytical tool base (see the Window on Technology). With only a minimum of experience, most managers find they can use these common software packages to create graphic comparisons of data by time, region, product, price range, and so on. Costlier systems include more sophisticated specialty analytical software.

ESS are increasingly being used by employees several levels below the senior executives. This has solved the problem of members of executives' staffs working from different data than the executive, and this is one of the reasons use of these systems is spreading. Middle management will use the same data in a somewhat different manner, focusing on their own area of responsibility and emphasizing plan-versus-actual analysis (variances between forecasts and actual results).

Developing ESS

ESS are executive systems, and executives create special development problems (we introduced this topic in section 11.1). Because executives' needs change so rapidly, most executive support systems are developed through prototyping. A major difficulty for developers is that high-level executives expect success the first time. Developers must be certain that the system will work before they demonstrate it to the user. In addition, the initial system prototype must be one that the executive can learn very rapidly. Finally, if the executive finds that the ESS offers no added value, he or she will reject it.

One area that merits special attention is the determination of executive information requirements. ESS need to have some facility for environmental scanning. A key information requirement of managers at the strategic level is the capability to detect signals of problems in the organizational environment that indicate strategic threats and opportunities (Walls et al., 1992). The ESS needs to be designed so that both external and internal sources of information can be used for environmental scanning purposes. The Critical Success Factor methodology for determining information requirements (see Chapter 8) is recommended for this purpose.

Because ESS could potentially give top executives the capability of examining other managers' work without their knowledge, there may be some resistance to ESS at lower levels of the organization. Implementation of ESS should be carefully managed to neutralize such opposition (see Chapter 9).

Cost justification presents a different type of problem with ESS. Since much of an executive's work is unstructured, how does one quantify benefits for a system that primarily supports such unstructured work? An ESS is often justified in advance by the intuitive feeling that it will pay for itself (Watson et al., 1991). If ESS benefits can ever be quantified, it is only after the system is operational.

TECHNOLOGY

Spreadsheets Team Up with ESS

Executive support systems are usually high-priced custom programs running on mainframes that simplify and present complex data for top management. So what are ESS doing with spreadsheets? The answer is, providing new views of data that were not available before and providing a relatively easy way to collect the data that executives want to use.

Early ESS plucked data from mainframe financial systems and simplified them, graphically illustrating key performance indicators and highlighting variances between forecasts and actual results. An ESS might provide an overview of a company's financial and business condition, using performance indicators such as the firm's profit margin or the average number of minutes customers wait on the telephone for customer service. The system might use arrows near the numbers to indicate whether the performance measures are improving, staying the same, or declining, and it might color-code the numbers to indicate whether the situation has reached a state of alarm.

But today's ESS can do much more. They have capabilities to let executives examine areas that warrant further attention, or go through the process of drilling down. For instance, a manager might drill down to find sales and operating expense amounts separately and drill even further to see the dollar figures for individual sales regions. The level of detail conceivably could unfold all the way down to individual invoices and inventory items.

Contemporary ESS can attach snapshots of spreadsheets to various reports; they can compile disparate data and let users work through multiple levels of detail to find the information; or they can use spreadsheets as a front end to examine vast quantities of business data. In many instances, systems allowing high-level executives access to spreadsheets let them see the underlying formulas and the assumptions that were used to calculate the numbers. For instance, they could see that a

forecast was based on a 6 percent interest rate and either say "I believe that" or not. Senior executives can see information that they were not seeing in hard copy reports.

The Bertelsmann Music Group (BMG) uses spreadsheets to make it easier to collect its ESS data. BMG is a very large German record and publishing group, owning such well-known companies as RCA and Arista records and Bantam, Doubleday, and Dell books. To give the top managers in Germany and the United States daily sales data, local managers enter the data onto 78 copies of their One-up spreadsheet program running on desktop computers in 39 countries. BMG uses General Electric's electronic mailbox service daily to collect the scattered spreadsheet data onto an IBM mainframe sitting in Indianapolis, Indiana. The data are then downloaded into Commander EIS, where executives at 20 sites can use the system to spot emerging trends and to analyze actual and historical data compared to plans and forecasts.

An executive who wants to get a high-level picture of business activities may need data from a number of disparate spreadsheets, a daunting task if done manually. Boston Edison Co., a Massachusetts-based electric utility, addresses this problem using Clipper, a database package from Computer Associates. Clipper includes a module that allows the creators of their 1–2–3 spreadsheets to upload the spreadsheets into Clipper for storage. Users of the Boston Edison Co.'s ESS can then retrieve them with just a click on an icon, using their ESS menu.

The Boston Edison approach has a major problem, however—the spreadsheets are static, and data cannot be further massaged. Material Service Corp., a division of General Dynamics is addressing that deficiency through a product called DrillDown from Specialized Systems & Software. According to Iris Sherman, Material Service's manager of personal information systems, DrillDown can group and

total records (rolling up, the opposite of drilling down). For example, if their company stores sales invoices on 1–2–3, DrillDown will create aggregate sales figures that can then be given to management. Executives can then use DrillDown to look at the totals or to drill down to the details as they wish. For example, they might look at sales by region, by product within that region, and even by salesperson. DrillDown includes one very handy feature: As executives search through the data, DrillDown will create a template of the search that can be saved to enable the same drilling in the future even without training in the product.

As their analytic and graphic power has grown, spreadsheets have become the presentation tool of choice for many. Using Microsoft Windows, data stored in dedicated databases can now easily be loaded into a spreadsheet (through Microsoft's Dynamic Data Exchange). As a result, some corporations are now using spreadsheets as front ends to their ESS. Not surprisingly, one of these companies is Lotus Development Corp. Their spreadsheet of choice? Their own 1–2–3! Lotus's homegrown ESS, the Lotus Information System (LIS) is used by about 100 executives, including Chairman Jim Manzi. Key data are stored in SQL Server, a database manager. Users access the system through a graphical, icon-based dialogue. The data can be analyzed using the full power of 1–2–3. In addition, LIS provides 17 predeveloped views, from sales figures to daily stock prices.

Sources: Michael Vizard, "Recording Company Stays on Top of Its Numbers with EIS," *Computerworld*, July 5, 1993; and Don Steinberg, "EIS Meets 1–2–3," *Lotus*, September 1992.

To Think About: From management, organization, and technology standpoints, what are the advantages of off-the-shelf spreadsheet software like Lotus 1–2–3 in developing an ESS? What are the disadvantages of using such software?

MANAGEMENT

Fidelity Brings Financial Data to Executives' Fingertips

Privately held Fidelity Investments, Inc. of Boston manages more than $200 billion through its famous array of Fidelity Funds. In 1990, Fidelity commissioned Coopers & Lybrand to conduct a 12-week efficiency study. The study concluded that management could not obtain important day-to-day operational information as easily as it needed to do so. Control of the data was too centralized.

One sign of this problem was management's weekly 45-page report on Fidelity's financial health. The report had three problems: The data came only weekly; management could not easily analyze the data because they were paper-bound; and the preparation of the report required 10 employees to spend several days a week gathering the data from diverse business units.

To eliminate the extra footwork, Fidelity replaced the 45-page financial health report with an ESS called the Financial and Management Information System (FAMIS). FAMIS is a client/server-based sys-

tem that uses Microsoft's Excel for Windows spreadsheet as a front end to bring relevant data to financial executives with a few keystrokes. The system collects the data from Fidelity's various business units and stores it in a Sybase database. Users click on a Windows icon that brings up the data in an Excel spreadsheet format. Users can manipulate the data using any of the many Excel spreadsheet analytical and graphics tools. They can also extract the data for use with a Windows-based modeling tool. Instead of pasting together a report from diverse spreadsheets and databases, analysts and managers can access the data on-line, saving the weekly report preparation time of ten employees. Windows ad hoc query and reporting capabilities have also been added. Users can extract data and store the data on LANs for sharing with work groups. Bill Niemi, director of distributed systems development at Fidelity, believes that when fully developed, the system will eliminate the need for one or two full-time financial analysts.

FAMIS was initially rolled out to 100 users, but the goal is to have it sit on over 350 desks, mostly those of chief financial officers and financial analysts. Fidelity would like FAMIS to provide financial managers with the ability to extract such data as the number of new accounts sold for the Magellan fund. In the past, it might have taken the information systems department a week to produce that data, or the data might not have been available at all. Niemi believes the system will be a long-run success because it will give the financial managers the ability to access the latest data in a timely way.

Source: Anita Amirrezvani, ''Fidelity Investments Builds EIS to Simplify Access to Financial Data,'' *Computerworld,* April 6, 1992.

To Think About: What were the management benefits of FAMIS? What management, organization, and technology factors had to be addressed in building FAMIS?

Benefits of ESS

How do executive support systems benefit managers? As we stated earlier, it is difficult at best to cost-justify an executive support system. Nonetheless, interest in these systems is growing, so it is essential to examine some of the potential benefits scholars have identified.

Much of the value of ESS is found in their flexibility. These systems put data and tools in the hands of executives without addressing specific problems or imposing solutions. Executives are free to shape the problems as they need to, using the system as an extension of their own thinking processes. These are not decision-making systems; they are tools to aid executives in making decisions.

The most visible benefit of ESS is their ability to analyze, compare, and highlight trends. The easy use of graphics allows the user to look at more data in less time with greater clarity and insight than paper-based systems can provide. In the past, executives obtained the same information by taking up days and weeks of their staffs' valuable time. By using ESS, those staffs and the executives themselves are freed up for the more creative analysis and decision making in their jobs.

Executives are using ESS to monitor performance more successfully in their own areas of responsibility. Some are also using these systems to monitor key performance indicators. The timeliness and availability of the data result in needed actions being identified and taken earlier. Problems can be handled before they become too damaging; opportunities can also be identified earlier as well.

ESS can and do change the workings of organizations. Immediate access to so much data allows executives to better monitor activities of lower units reporting to them. That very monitoring ability often allows decision making to be decentralized and to take place at lower operating levels. Executives are often willing to push decision making further down into the organization as long as they can be assured that all is going well. ESS can enable them to get that assurance. A well-designed ESS could dramatically improve management performance and increase upper management's span of control.

The Window on Management on page 393 looks at some effects of an ESS at Fidelity Investments, one of the largest investment firms in the world.

We will close our examination of ESS by looking at actual examples of ESS systems in use.

An executive can use the various graphing and financial analysis tools available through the menus of Commander EIS to create a graphic image of the overall quality measures for the corporation.

Examples of ESS

To illustrate the various ways in which ESS can enhance management decision making, we now describe two executive support systems, one for private industry and one for the public sector. These systems were developed for very different reasons and serve their organizations in different ways.

PRATT & WHITNEY

Pratt & Whitney is a multibillion-dollar corporation located in East Hartford, Connecticut, whose Commercial Engine Business (CEB) produces jet engines. The firm's executives view customer service and product performance as the heart of their business and therefore the heart of their strategic plan to expand their market share. They purchased Commander EIS, a leading ESS package from Comshare. Commander EIS features colorful presentations and a pictorial menu that can be learned intuitively, with variances and exceptions highlighted in color. Users can access data with a touch screen, mouse, or keyboard and they can zoom in for deeper levels of detail by either navigating on their own or by following predefined paths.

Implementation began with a prototype built for the president of CEB, Selwyn Berson. Commander EIS allows Berson to track key quality and reliability measures for each jet engine model by customer. The data are shown from existing production systems and provide information on reliability, spare engine and parts availability, and deliveries. Using this system, CEB is able to answer customers' questions regarding repair status and can project how long repairs will take. Berson and others are able to drill down to determine reasons for repairs on specific engines. They also are capable of drilling down to specific data on service to an individual customer. Thus, CEB executives are able to determine where quality improvements need to be made in terms of both customer service and engine quality. CEB's ESS is helping them to meet their strategic plan objectives. The system was originally used by about 25 senior executives, although Pratt & Whitney expects the number of users to grow to over 200 (I/S Analyzer, January 1992).

NEW YORK STATE OFFICE OF GENERAL SERVICES

The New York State Office of General Services (OGS) is responsible for servicing other state agencies throughout New York. Its services include (but are not limited to) design and construction, maintenance of state buildings, food and laundry services to both correctional facilities and health-related institutions, statewide vehicle management, and centralized printing. With this diversity of services, an annual budget well over $500 million, and more than 4000 employees, executive oversight was a nightmare. Until 1986, OGS automatically received annual budget increases in line with inflation rates. Budget deficits were made up through supplemental allocations by the legislature. OGS felt no pressures to improve efficiency or stay within its budget. That changed in 1986 when a new administrative head of the agency was appointed. He decided that the organization had to operate in a more efficient, effective, and responsive manner. He also wanted to avoid year-end deficits. These objectives required better management at the top.

The first module of a new OGS ESS was implemented in 1988. The system allows the executives to monitor status by program, comparing budget to actual expenditures and showing estimated expenditures through the remainder of the fiscal year. Management can drill down to see specific details in any category. The system contains only raw data, allowing the users great flexibility in aggregating and analyzing it to meet their needs. For example, users are able to view a single expense category by month across organizations, or view several months of expenses for a given unit. Because the raw data are there, the executives can drill down to the source. The system includes exception reporting so that budget problems are highlighted and detected early. Executives are also using the system to compare budgetary control by units to spot personnel performance problems.

Since the system was developed for a government agency, the cost was of more than normal concern—the system had to be built inexpensively. The system uses ordinary microcomputers networked with the agency's mainframe and off-the-shelf, standard, inexpensive software tools. The total cost was less than $100,000. The system is menu-driven and very easy to use. New users are trained through a 30-minute demonstration, and experience has shown that this is all that they need. No user manual is available.

One interesting by-product of the system has been the need to develop productivity measures. Future development will focus on the area of performance analysis, attempting to answer such questions as how many people are required to work in specific units. The ESS called for OGS to measure something that it had never measured before. The work of developing these measures should in itself contribute to the drive for more efficiency (Mohan et al., 1990). This ESS is helping the Office of General Services enhance management control.

Management Challenges

1. **Building information systems that can actually fulfill executive information requirements.** Even with the use of Critical Success Factors and other information requirements determination methods, it may still be difficult to establish information requirements for ESS and DSS serving senior management. Chapter 3 has already described why certain aspects of senior management decision making cannot be supported by information systems because the decisions are too unstructured and fluid. Even if a problem can be addressed by an information system, senior management may not understand their true information needs. For instance, senior managers may not agree on the firm's critical success factors, or the critical success factors they describe may be inappropriate or outdated if the firm is confronting a crisis requiring a major strategic change.

2. **Integrating DSS and ESS with existing systems in the business.** Even if system builders do know the information requirements for DSS or ESS, it may not be possible to fulfill them using data from the firm's existing information systems. Various MIS or TPS may define important pieces of data, such as the time period covered by fiscal year, in different ways. It may not be possible to reconcile data from incompatible internal systems for analysis by managers. A significant amount of organizational change may be required before the firm can build and install effective DSS and ESS.

Summary

Define a decision-support system (DSS) and a group decision-support system (GDSS).

A decision-support system (DSS) is an interactive system under user control that combines data, sophisticated analytical models, and user-friendly software into a single powerful system that can support semistructured or unstructured decision making. A group decision-support system (GDSS) is an interactive computer-based system to facilitate the solution of unstructured problems by a set of decision makers working together as a group rather than individually.

Describe the components of decision-support systems and group decision-support systems.

The components of a DSS are the DSS database, the model base and the DSS software system. The DSS database is a collection of current or historical data from a number of applications or groups that can be used for analysis. The model base is a collection of mathematical and analytical models that are used for analyzing the data in the database. The DSS software system allows users to interact with the DSS database and model base directly through the user interface.

Group decision-support systems (GDSS) have hardware, software, and people components. Hardware components consist of the conference room facilities, including seating arrangements and computer and other electronic hardware. Software components include tools for organizing ideas, gathering information, ranking and setting priorities, and documenting meeting sessions. People components include participants, a trained facilitator, and staff to support the hardware and software.

Explain how decision-support systems and group decision-support systems can enhance decision making.

Both DSS and GDSS support steps in the process of arriving at decisions. DSS provide results of model-based analysis that help managers design and evaluate alternatives and monitor the progress of the solution that was adopted. GDSS help decision makers meeting together to arrive at a decision more efficiently and are especially useful for increasing the productivity of meetings larger than four or five people. However, the effectiveness of GDSS is contingent upon the nature of the group, the task, and the context of the meeting.

Describe the capabilities of executive support systems (ESS).

Executive support systems (ESS) help managers with unstructured problems that occur at the strategic level of management. ESS provide data from both internal and external sources and provide a generalized computing and communications environment that can be focused and applied to a changing array of problems. ESS help senior executives spot problems, identify opportunities, and forecast trends. They can filter out extraneous details for high-level overviews or they can drill down to provide senior managers with detailed transaction data if required.

Describe the benefits of executive support systems.

ESS help senior managers analyze, compare, and highlight trends so that they more easily may monitor organizational performance or identify strategic problems and opportunities. ESS may increase the span of control of senior management and allow decision making to be decentralized and to take place at lower operating levels.

Key Terms		
Decision-support systems (DSS)		Sensitivity analysis
Representations		DSS software system
Operations		Group decision-support system (GDSS)
Memory aids		Electronic meeting system (EMS)
Control aids		Executive support systems (ESS)
DSS database		Briefing books
Model base		Drill down
Model		

Review Questions

1. What is a decision-support system (DSS)? How does it differ from a management information system (MIS)?

2. What are the four capabilities of a DSS?

3. How can DSS support unstructured or semistructured decision making?

4. What are the three basic components of a DSS? Briefly describe each.

5. In what ways is building decision-support systems different from building traditional MIS systems?

6. What is a group decision-support system (GDSS)? How does it differ from a DSS?

7. What are the three underlying problems in group decision making that have led to the development of GDSS?

8. Describe the three elements of a GDSS.

9. Name five GDSS software tools.

10. What is an electronic meeting system (EMS)?

11. For each of the three underlying problems in group decision making referred to in question 7, describe one or two ways GDSS can contribute to a solution.

12. How did technological changes in the 1980s allow more effective ESS to be developed?

13. In what ways is building executive support systems different from building traditional MIS systems?

14. What are the benefits of ESS? How do they enhance managerial decision making?

Discussion Questions

1. Some have argued that all information systems support decision making. The argument holds that conceptually, a DSS is just a good MIS. Discuss.

2. What kinds of skills must you, as an end user of systems, have in order to participate in the design and use of a DSS?

3. Identify an organization with which you are familiar. Identify specific areas where DSS could help decision making and describe the DSS you would recommend.

Group Project

With three or four of your classmates, identify several groups in your university that could benefit from a GDSS. Design a GDSS for one of those groups, describing its hardware, software, and people elements. Present your findings to the class.

CASE STUDY

Setting a Strategy for Executive Support Systems

This case is based on a real-world company with a real-world dilemma, although the names have been changed to enable the circumstances to be made public. The names and positions of the experts whose recommendations we will examine are real. These four experts bring four different perspectives to the case.

The company, Thor Industries, is a U.S.-based aerospace/defense company operating in a highly competitive and cost-conscious government market. Thor recently went through a major reorganization that has left the IS department severely overburdened. The company has a high-level ESS Planning Committee made up of the vice presidents of information systems, production, finance, engineering, and sales/marketing. That committee has just launched its first ESS project.

The ESS Planning Committee informed David Saunders, Vice President of MIS, that it wants an ESS to span several Thor operating groups, using data from a number of current mainframe, midrange, and server-based databases and applications. The purpose of the ESS is to facilitate joint development of budgets, schedules, and measures of progress and to monitor the ongoing performance of major projects. The ESS has to be easy to use. The system will be based on a network of desktop equipment and will heavily emphasize graphics.

Saunders sees the project as a real opportunity for his staff to become more closely involved with the company while they build their own skills and reputations. But he has a number of concerns. First, the project has high profile inside the company because it is beamed toward senior management—*he* must succeed. Second, the chairman of the ESS Planning Committee, Howard Leaderman, has informed Saunders that there will be a budget large enough to allow software and hardware purchases but that IS will be "evaluated on its ability to manage costs over the long term." Third, Saunders' senior staff is apprehensive because they do not know desktop technology and are concerned that they will lose their value to the company. They also fear that the project will result in their being moved into line units as ongoing support where, they believe, their careers will be damaged. Some of the lower-level staff are also concerned because their experience is primarily with technology that could now become out-of-date. Saunders does have one advantage in his staff—some of his lower-level employees have gained extensive experience at Thor over the past several years installing desktop systems. Saunders has also already prepared some of his management for the coming changes in IS technology—for example, Leaderman has just attended a client/server conference on Saunders' recommendation.

What follows are the recommendations to Saunders made by four people with real experience in planning such projects.

Phil Carpenter, Marketing Manager of Mozart Systems, proposes a strategy that preserves Thor's investment in its current systems. He recommends that the system be built on top of the existing mainframe, midrange, and server-based data, leaving that data and the systems that produce it in place. Thor should develop a graphical microcomputer-based executive information system that will act as a bridge to data stored in disparate locations. The system would provide an easy, intuitive way to view and manipulate data from multiple sources without changing the software code of the company's underlying business applications.

To do so requires a careful selection of a development tool. The tool not only must create an easy-to-use graphical interface (which many tools do), but it must also have some capabilities for accessing databases using SQL (Structured Query Language) and for linking up to mainframes and minicomputer systems (which few tools do).

Advantages of this approach are many. Investment in current systems will indeed be protected—they will not be touched. Staff fears should be allayed because the company will continue to need the same staff as before. Little additional training will be needed, so costs will be kept down. Costs will be minimized in another way also. The approach will require the purchase of only a modest amount of hardware and software and will mainly use Thor's existing stock. Development time will also be minimal, with the use of the appropriate user-friendly tool (he does not recommend a specific tool).

Saj-Nicole A. Joni, Regional Practice Manager for Microsoft Consulting, also sees leaving current production systems in place for now. She would build a client/server-based ESS on top of the existing systems. However, she raises a whole set of different issues, most of which are nontechnical.

Successful executive information systems require a strong sense of ownership and support from top management. Joni wonders if the project has the necessary charter to go forward and to make the key decisions that will affect the involved divisions. She wants to know where the clear executive project ownership is that must exist if the project is to avoid failure. Thor's executives appear enthusiastic, but the specifications for the ESS do not answer questions such as the following: What are the critical short-term business issues to be addressed by the system? What are the long-term issues? Who will use the system and how will they use it? How will this ESS actually improve the way Thor's executives manage the business?

This project will result in a major change in how critical data are used at high levels and how the data are shared. Thor's management needs to define the information that will be used, and it needs to ensure that the ESS will provide a fair and consistent view of that information across divisions. The system designers should develop a clear data model based on the executives' information needs for meeting business objectives. Joni does not believe that modifying Thor's existing applications will provide the unified information that top management needs on its desktop.

Joni wonders if the project is addressing such major information systems issues as restructuring the department, reducing headcount, or retraining workers. She believes that with such a high-visibility and high-impact project, IS should form a special project team made up of smart, eager volunteers. The team should be supplemented by outside expertise in building GUI-based ESS client/server systems.

Joni believes that client/server technology is the direction of the future. Thor does not yet have a centralized client/server infrastructure. She suggests that Thor start to construct such an infrastructure with an open architecture using appropriate standards. She recommends that the graphical user interface for the ESS be built with off-the-shelf tools to standardize application interfaces and to provide flexibility for the future.

Ronald Sella is Manager of Emerging Technology Services for Information Builders, Inc. Sella believes that the most difficult issues for Thor are the human ones—retraining Saunders' staff and redefining job descriptions. He recommends that Saunders solve his problem by purchasing a third-party, 4GL-based ESS package.

Sella sees several "human factor" advantages to using a purchased ESS package. First, the IS staff would remain in their traditional positions, thus eliminating their fears over their future. They would, however, have to provide some technical support to the project and its resulting system. Second, training is minimal and easy. The ESS software vendor will train Thor's staff to use the software and will provide technical support for that software. System development using the 4GL software will, he believes, be relatively easy; for this reason, he suggests purchasing such a package.

Sella also recommends that Saunders base the new system on client/server technology, suggesting that the database software be SQL-based and relational to facilitate multivendor cross-platform connectivity. The software used by the new ESS system must support access to a wide variety of databases so that it can access Thor's current data. Costs would be limited because Thor would have to purchase little new software or hardware and would avoid large training or reorganization costs.

Jim Powell, Distributed Information Services manager for Texas Instruments, brings a focus on changing technology to the discussion. He believes that the emergence of client/server technology has been an information systems watershed, bringing changes as significant as the development of microcomputers did in the beginning of the 1980s. Powell concludes that Thor must pursue the change to client/server technology—the risks of doing so are less than in staying with technology that is becoming outdated.

A technology transition of such fundamental importance cannot simply happen. Powell recommends that Saunders make a reformulation of Thor IS strategy his first priority. He then urges the setting of very clear architectural standards to push new development toward the emerging environment. He also warns Saunders not to "manually hard code each [client/server] application." He believes that Thor will be developing hundreds of such applications over the coming five to ten years. Such a large amount of work must be done in a standardized way, using a software development tool.

Powell raises yet another issue, one he believes Saunders has not addressed. The growth of microcomputers and now the change to client/server technology means that data will no longer be centralized. They will be "spread out across thousands of workstations and hundreds of servers." Controlling and even just keeping track of data is a massive problem that Saunders must address.

Finally, Powell believes the staff issues are also critical—but he has a very different slant. He notes that IS professionals keep close track of changes in their industry. Regardless of what they are saying, Powell asserts, Saunders' IS staff will ultimately be more troubled by working in a company where technology is falling behind than by working in one that is moving to leading-edge technology. To help the staff make the transition, he emphasizes the need for an organized training program to teach new skills. He also urges the company to map out new career paths for the staff. As he says, "It will not happen by osmosis."

Which strategy for building ESS should Saunders follow?

Source: Damian Rinaldi and John Desmond, "Preserve Investment or Move On?" *Software Magazine,* March 1992.

Case Study Questions:

1. If you were in David Saunders' position, what would you recommend? Why? Develop the pros and cons of your decision. What management, organization, and technology issues would you consider?

2. None of the four consultants lay out the risks of their recommendations. Add a paragraph to each description delineating those risks.

3. Joni raises the issue of effective executive sponsorship. Why do you think she stresses this issue? Why will this particular project need such strong, high-level leadership?

4. All the recommendations dealt with staff issues, with several of them stressing these issues above all others. From what you know, do you believe the staff problem will be as significant as they indicate? Why? How would you handle the staff issue? Why?

5. Two of the experts (Joni and Powell) urge that Saunders use this project to make a transition to client/server technology, indicating this as a fundamental shift in IS strategic direction. Assuming they are correct about the direction of technology, do you think Saunders should make this technology shift? Why? What are the risks of making that shift through the ESS high-visibility project? Would you accept Joni and Powell's client/server recommendations? Why?

References

Alavi, Maryam, and Erich A. Joachimsthaler. "Revisiting DSS Implementation Research: A Meta-Analysis of the Literature and Suggestions for Researchers." *MIS Quarterly* 16, no. 1 (March 1992).

Betts, Mitch. "Computer Maps Help Cops Catch Crooks." *Computerworld* (February 15, 1993).

Bonzcek, R. H., C. W. Holsapple, and A. B. Whinston. "Representing Modeling Knowledge with First Order Predicate Calculus." *Operations Research* 1 (1982).

Chidambaram, Laku, Robert P. Bostrom, and Bayard E. Wynne. "A Longitudinal Study of the Impact of Group Decision Support Systems on Group Development." *Journal of Management Information Systems* 7, no. 3 (Winter 1990/1991).

Dennis, Alan R., Jay F. Nunamaker, Jr., and Douglas R. Vogel. "A Comparison of Laboratory and Field Research in the Study of Electronic Meeting Systems." *Journal of Management Information Systems* 7, no. 3 (Winter 1990/1991).

Dennis, Alan R., Joey F. George, Len M. Jessup, Jay F. Nunamaker, and Douglas R. Vogel. "Information Technology to Support Electronic Meetings." *MIS Quarterly* 12, no. 4 (December 1988).

DeSanctis, Geraldine, Marshall Scott Poole, Howard Lewis, and George Desharnias. "Computing in Quality Team Meetings." *Journal of Management Information Systems* 8, no. 3 (Winter 1991–92).

DeSanctis, Geraldine and R. Brent Gallupe. "A Foundation for the Study of Group Decision Support Systems." *Management Science* 33, no. 5 (May 1987).

Easton, George K., Joey F. George, Jay F. Nunamaker, Jr., and Mark O. Pendergast. "Two Different Electronic Meeting Systems." *Journal of Management Information Systems* 7, no. 3 (Winter 1990/1991).

El Sawy, Omar. "Personal Information Systems for Strategic Scanning in Turbulent Environments." *MIS Quarterly* 9, no. 1 (March 1985).

El Sherif, Hisham, and Omar A. El Sawy. "Issue-Based Decision Support Systems for the Egyptian Cabinet." *MIS Quarterly* 12, no. 4 (December 1988).

Gallupe, R. Brent, Geraldine DeSanctis, and Gary W. Dickson. "Computer-Based Support for Group Problem-Finding: An Experimental Investigation." *MIS Quarterly* 12, no. 2 (June 1988).

Ginzberg, Michael J., W. R. Reitman, and E. A. Stohr (ed). *Decision Support Systems*. New York: North Holland Publishing Co., 1982.

Gopal, Abhijit, Robert P. Bostrum, and Wynne W. Chin. "Applying Adaptive Structuration Theory to Investigate the Process of Group Support Systems Use." *Journal of Management Information Systems* 9, no. 3 (Winter 1992–93).

Grobowski, Ron, Chris McGoff, Doug Vogel, Ben Martz, and Jay Nunamaker. "Implementing Electronic Meeting Systems at IBM: Lessons Learned and Success Factors." *MIS Quarterly* 14, no. 4 (December 1990).

Henderson, John C., and David A. Schilling. "Design and Implementation of Decision Support Systems in the Public Sector." *MIS Quarterly* (June 1985).

Hiltz, Starr Roxanne, Kenneth Johnson, and Murray Turoff. "Group Decision Support: Designated Human Leaders and Statistical Feedback." *Journal of Management Information Systems* 8, no. 2 (Fall 1991).

Ho, T. H., and K. S. Raman. "The Effect of GDSS on Small Group Meetings." *Journal of Management Information Systems* 8, no. 2 (Fall 1991).

Hogue, Jack T. "Decision Support Systems and the Traditional Computer Information System Function: An Examination of Relationships During DSS Application Development." *Journal of Management Information Systems* (Summer 1985).

Hogue, Jack T. "A Framework for the Examination of Management Involvement in Decision Support Systems." *Journal of Management Information Systems* 4, no. 1 (Summer 1987).

Houdeshel, George, and Hugh J. Watson. "The Management Information and Decision Support (MIDS) System at Lockheed, Georgia." *MIS Quarterly* 11, no. 2 (March 1987).

Jessup, Leonard M., Terry Connolly, and Jolene Galegher. "The Effects of Anonymity on GDSS Group Process with an Idea-Generating Task." *MIS Quarterly* 14, no. 3 (September 1990).

Keen, Peter G. W., and M. S. Scott Morton. *Decision Support Systems: An Organizational Perspective*. Reading, MA: Addison-Wesley, 1982.

King, John. "Successful Implementation of Large Scale Decision Support Systems: Computerized Models in U.S. Economic Policy Making." *Systems Objectives Solutions* (November 1983).

Kraemer, Kenneth L., and John Leslie King. "Computer-Based Systems for Cooperative Work and Group Decision Making." *ACM Computing Surveys* 20, no. 2 (June 1988).

Laudon, Kenneth C. *Communications Technology and Democratic Participation*. New York: Praeger, 1977.

Le Blanc, Louis A., and Kenneth A. Kozar. "An Empirical Investigation of the Relationship Between DSS Usage and System Performance." *MIS Quarterly* 14, no. 3 (September 1990).

Lewe, Henrik, and Helmut Krcmar. "A Computer-Supported Cooperative Work Research Laboratory." *Journal of Management Information Systems* 8, no. 3 (Winter 1991–92).

McLeod, Poppy Lauretta, and Jeffry R. Liker. "Electronic Meeting Systems: Evidence from a Low Structure Environment." *Information Systems Research* 3, no. 3 (September 1992).

Meador, Charles L., and Peter G. W. Keen. "Setting Priorities for DSS Development." *MIS Quarterly* (June 1984).

Mohan, Lakshmi, William K. Holstein, and Robert B. Adams. "EIS: It Can Work in the Public Sector." *MIS Quarterly* 14, no. 4 (December 1990).

Nunamaker, J. F., Alan R. Dennis, Joseph S. Valacich, Douglas R. Vogel, and Joey F. George. "Electronic Meeting Systems to Support Group Work." *Communications of the ACM* 34, no. 7 (July 1991).

Panko, Raymond R. "Managerial Communication Patterns." *Journal of Organizational Computing* 2, no. 1 (1992).

Post, Brad Quinn. "A Business Case Framework for Group Support Technology." *Journal of Management Information Systems* 9, no. 3 (Winter 1992–93).

Rifkin, Glenn. " 'What-If' Software for Manufacturers." *The New York Times* (October 18, 1992).

Rockart, John F., and David W. DeLong. "Executive Support Systems and the Nature of Work." Working Paper: Management in the 1990s, Sloan School of Management (April 1986).

Rockart, John F., and David W. DeLong, *Executive Support Systems: The Emergence of Top Management Computer Use.* Homewood, IL: Dow-Jones Irwin, 1988.

Sambamurthy, V., and Marshall Scott Poole. "The Effects of Variations in Capabilities of GDSS Designs on Management of Cognitive Conflict in Groups." *Information Systems Research* 3, no. 3 (September 1992).

Sanders, G. Lawrence, and James F. Courtney. "A Field Study of Organizational Factors Influencing DSS Success." *MIS Quarterly* (March 1985).

Silver, Mark S. "Decision Support Systems: Directed and Nondirected Change." *Information Systems Research* 1, no. 1 (March 1990).

Sprague, R. H., and E. D. Carlson. *Building Effective Decision Support Systems.* Englewood Cliffs, NJ: Prentice-Hall, 1982.

Stefik, Mark, Gregg Foster, Daniel C. Bobrow, Kenneth Kahn, Stan Lanning, and Luch Suchman. "Beyond the Chalkboard: Computer Support for Collaboration and Problem Solving in Meetings." *Communications of the ACM* (January 1987).

"The New Role for 'Executive Information Systems.' " *I/S Analyzer* (January 1992).

Turban, Efraim. *Decision Support and Expert Systems,* 2nd ed. New York: Macmillan, 1990.

Turoff, Murray. "Computer-Mediated Communication Requirements for Group Support." *Journal of Organizational Computing* 1, no. 1 (January–March 1991).

Tyran, Craig K., Alan R. Dennis, Douglas R. Vogel, and J. F. Nunamaker, Jr. "The Application of Electronic Meeting Technology to Support Senior Management." *MIS Quarterly,* 16, no. 3 (September 1992).

Vogel, Douglas R., Jay F. Nunamaker, William Benjamin Martz, Jr., Ronald Grobowski, and Christopher McGoff. "Electronic Meeting System Experience at IBM." *Journal of Management Information Systems* 6, no. 3 (Winter 1989/90).

Volonino, Linda, and Hugh J. Watson. "The Strategic Business Objectives Method for EIS Development." *Journal of Management Information Systems* 7, no. 3 (Winter 1990/1991).

Walls, Joseph G., George R. Widmeyer, and Omar A. El Sawy. "Building an Information System Design Theory for Vigilant EIS." *Information Systems Research* 3 no. 1 (March 1992).

Watson, Hugh J., Astrid Lipp, Pamela Z. Jackson, Abdelhafid Dahmani, and William B. Fredenberger. "Organizational Support for Decision Support Systems." *Journal of Management Information Systems* 5, no. 4 (Spring 1989).

Watson, Hugh J., R. Kelly Rainer, Jr., and Chang E. Koh. "Executive Information Systems: A Framework for Development and a Survey of Current Practices." *MIS Quarterly* 15, no. 1 (March 1991).

Watson, Richard T., Geraldine DeSanctis, and Marshall Scott Poole. "Using a GDSS to Facilitate Group Consensus: Some Intended and Unintended Consequences." *MIS Quarterly* 12, no. 3 (September 1988).

Artificial Intelligence

Singapore Money Managers Use Machines to Pick Stocks

What makes international stock markets tick? There is no exact science to provide the answer because not all factors that influence financial data are known, and their interrelationship is highly complex. Nevertheless, Singapore-based Koeneman Capital Managers is trying to come closer to the answer by using artificial intelligence software. Its goal is to uncover the economic factors that drive global stock performance in the world's 11 major equity markets and the emerging Asian markets in Hong Kong, Thailand, Indonesia, Korea, and Taiwan.

KCM manages over $400 million in total assets, half of which comes from Australian pension and other funds. The firm uses a contrarian investment strategy, trying to sell in a rising stock market and to buy when the market is falling. KCM's base in Singapore gives it both a front-row view of emerging Asian equity markets and access to advanced information system technology that can help make the strategy work.

KCM rents time on an NEC SX-1A supercomputer at Singapore Technologies, a government-affiliated technology center, to run special artificial intelligence software that builds predictive models for selecting international stocks. The software can sift through vast streams of data about economic conditions, stock prices, interest rates, and currency exchange rates to find subtle cause-and-effect patterns that would be impossible for humans to discern. KCM uses the findings to build models that predict how stocks will perform under a wide range of variable factors in each of the major equity markets. The models attempt to determine what factors drive asset returns by testing out millions of combinations. After creating and testing the models, KCM tailors them to conditions specific to each country.

The models provide information to help KCM make buy-and-sell decisions, but they do not make the decisions themselves. According to Geoffrey Wang, KCM's director of investment technology, KCM makes stock trading decisions using qualitative judgment along with the output of its quantitative tools. The models for evaluating equity performance may be totally automated, but humans are still needed to determine whether the models make financial and economic sense.

Have KCM's models paid off? In the world of finance, any information that provides a company with the slightest advantage over competitors can produce millions in extra profits. John K. Koeneman, KCM's founder, believes that the firm's use of superior information system technology has created that advantage. While most international money management firms with Far East portfolios were slaughtered by the 65 percent decline in share price in Japanese stocks, just before the beginning of the Persian Gulf War in January 1991, KCM's country valuation models had warned it to exit the Japanese market. In 1992, KCM was the top performing money management firm in the Pacific region.

Source: Ivy Schmerken, "Research Reaches New Heights," *Wall Street & Technology,* November 1992.

By using artificial intelligence techniques, Koeneman Capital Managers was able to develop sophisticated models to predict the behavior of stocks. Other artificial intelligence applications capture the knowledge of recognized experts and make that knowledge available to other workers in the organization. Organizations can benefit from a variety of software and hardware techniques for acquiring, retaining, and leveraging knowledge, provided they understand both the potential benefits and pitfalls.

This chapter explains what artificial intelligence is and what artificial intelligence systems can and cannot do. It shows how expert systems, neural networks, and other artificial intelligence techniques capture knowledge and intelligence while pointing out their limitations. The chapter then describes how these techniques can create information systems that capture knowledge and intelligence for organizations; the chapter also identifies the requirements of successful artificial intelligence applications.

After completing this chapter you will be able to:

- Define artificial intelligence.
- Describe how artificial intelligence techniques evolved.
- Define an expert system and explain how it is built.
- Define neural networks and show how they are used in business.
- Identify other intelligent techniques.

12.1 What Is Artificial Intelligence?

The effort to use computers to understand or imitate aspects of human intelligence began in the 1950s. In 1956, Marvin Minsky (now at MIT), Claude Shannon of Bell Laboratories, and other innovators in the early study of computers and intelligence met at a conference at Dartmouth College. John McCarthy, then an assistant professor of mathematics at Dartmouth, coined the term *artificial intelligence* for the theme of the conference. The conference's high point was the unveiling of what some people thought was the first expert system, Logic Theorist. The system processed nonnumerical symbols instead of crunching numbers, and it proved several theorems in the *Principia Mathematica* of Alfred North Whitehead and Bertrand Russell. No magazine would publish the proof of the theorems because the results had been produced by a machine. This was the first software to claim properties of artificial intelligence. Ever since that time, skeptics, pundits, journalists, and serious scholars have argued over what artificial intelligence means.

What Artificial Intelligence Is and Is Not

Artificial intelligence: The effort to develop computer-based systems that can behave like humans, with the ability to learn languages, accomplish physical tasks, use a perceptual apparatus, and emulate human expertise and decision making.

Artificial intelligence is commonly defined as the effort to develop computer-based systems (both hardware and software) that behave as humans. Such systems would be able to learn natural languages, accomplish coordinated physical tasks (robotics), utilize a perceptual apparatus that informs their physical behavior and language (visual and oral perception systems), and emulate human expertise and decision making (expert systems). Such systems would also exhibit logic, reasoning, intuition, and the just plain common-sense qualities that we associate with human beings. Figure 12.1 illustrates the elements of the artificial intelligence family. Another important element here is "intelligent" machines, the physical hardware that performs these tasks.

Figure 12.1
The artificial intelligence family. The field of AI currently includes many initiatives: natural language, robotics, perceptive systems, expert systems, and intelligent machines.

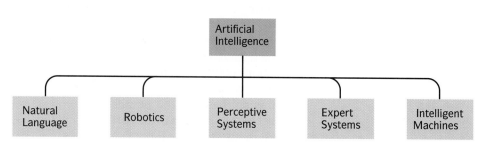

No existing system comes close to possessing any of these human qualities, but what has been developed is nevertheless of profound interest. Artificial intelligence has become, without doubt, the most controversial subject in computer science and information systems circles, as well as in the broader community of scholars and decision makers. Since the Renaissance, men and women in their physical form and mental accomplishments have been at the center of the cultural universe, the measure of all things. Now to be joined by a lowly machine, an artificial, inanimate object, represents a challenging cultural revolution that most people resist. Critics of the study of artificial intelligence argue that it is a waste of time and resources, a study dotted with significant failures and few accomplishments that succeeds only insofar as it denigrates the power and elegance of human thought processes. The most militant critics argue that artificial intelligence insults the very nature and role of human beings.

Supporters of the study of artificial intelligence point to the noble goal of using it as a way of understanding human intelligence and as a vehicle for distributing expertise. Artificial intelligence systems, if they could be developed, might lead to a quantum leap in social wealth and well-being. The new technology, supporters argue, will increase individual and social potential by distributing knowledge more widely.

In this chapter, we will try to avoid making judgments about whether artificial intelligence is a worthwhile pursuit. Instead, we will give the views of both critics and supporters, as well as some real-world examples. You can decide for yourself whether artificial intelligence is a worthwhile pursuit with potential real-world benefits.

Human and Artificial Intelligence

Before describing artificial intelligence, it is worthwhile to distinguish more fully between *artificial* and human intelligence because successful artificial intelligence systems are neither artificial nor intelligent. A thermostat and an autopilot are the best examples of systems that solve problems in a goal-oriented, machine-like, artificial way. Yet no one calls thermostats or autopilots intelligent.

This raises the question: What would a truly *artificial intelligent* system look like? Successful artificial intelligence systems are based on human expertise, knowledge, and selected reasoning patterns (syllogisms, rules of thumb, etc.). Existing artificial intelligence systems do not come up with new and novel solutions to problems. Practical artificial intelligence systems that try to reproduce the expertise of humans do not behave like human experts at all, but rather are limited to mundane (albeit important) tasks. Existing systems extend the powers of experts, but in no way substitute for them or "capture" much of their intelligence. Briefly, all systems currently available lack the common sense and generality of naturally intelligent machines like human beings.

Now let us examine *human* intelligence. As it turns out, human intelligence is vastly complex and obviously much broader than computer or information systems. Philosophers, psychologists, and other students of human cognition have all recognized that key aspects of human intelligence are beyond description and therefore are not easily imitated by a consciously designed machine—if a problem cannot be described, it cannot be programmed. Human intelligence involves a variety of capabilities, including reasoning, "intelligent" behavior, the use of metaphor and analogy, and the creation and use of concepts. We will discuss two here that are central to human intelligence but cannot be replicated on computers at this time.

A key factor that distinguishes human beings from other animals is their ability to develop associations and to use metaphors and analogies such as "like" and "as." Using metaphor and analogy, humans create new rules, apply old rules to new situations, and at times act intuitively and/or instinctively without rules.

Much of what we call "common sense" or "generality" in humans resides in the ability to create metaphor and analogy.

Human intelligence also includes a unique ability to impose a conceptual apparatus on the surrounding world. Meta-concepts, such as cause and effect and time, and concepts of a lower order, such as breakfast, dinner, and lunch, are all imposed by human beings on the world around them. Thinking in terms of these concepts and acting on them are central characteristics of intelligent human behavior.

Artificial intelligence refers to an effort to develop machines that can reason, behave intelligently, compare, and conceptualize. While this may be a noble effort, clearly none of the successful systems described in this chapter comes close to achieving this form of human intelligence. However, what has been developed through this effort is of interest and is starting to provide some benefits to organizations. Moreover, there is no evidence that systems capable of exhibiting some kinds of intelligent behavior could not be developed in the future.

The Development of Artificial Intelligence

Top-down approach: In the history of artificial intelligence, the effort to develop a logical analog to how the brain works.

The story of artificial intelligence, or AI, is really two stories.[1] One is the history of efforts to develop physical machines that mimic what people currently think is the way an animal or human physical brain works. This is called the **bottom-up approach,** the effort to build a physical analog to the human brain. A second story focuses on the effort to develop a logical analog to how the brain works, or the **top-down approach.**

THE BOTTOM-UP APPROACH

Bottom-up approach: In the history of artificial intelligence, the effort to build a physical analog to the human brain.

The beginnings of contemporary AI started in World War II with the concept of "feedback." Norbert Weiner, a scientist and mathematician at MIT in the 1940s, developed a method of radar control of antiaircraft guns for the U.S. army that required calculating the expected location of an aircraft based on new information—"feedback"—from radar. This early period of self-correcting artillery machines started the physical or bottom-up approach to artificial intelligence. Weiner went on to propose in several books that feedback could explain how humans think. He believed that the principle could be applied to make machines think like humans.

Warren McCulloch, a biologist interested in brain function, and Walter Pitts, a mathematician, used Weiner's idea of feedback to develop a theory of how brains work. In their theory, a brain was composed of millions of neuron cells, which processed binary numbers (they were either "on" or "off") that were connected into a network that took in feedback or information from the environment. Learning was simply a matter of teaching the neurons in a brain how to respond to the environment. In 1960 these ideas were taken further by Cornell scientist Frank Rosenblatt. Rosenblatt demonstrated a machine called a Perceptron, which was composed of 400 photoelectric cells that could perceive

[1]Actually, the story of AI is much deeper and more controversial than can be presented here in such a brief introduction. Involved in this larger debate are questions about the nature of human beings and knowledge, the proper relationship between responsible human beings and machines, and the difference between promise and reality. For a positive view of AI, see Edward A. Feigenbaum and Pamela McCorduck, *The Fifth Generation: Artificial Intelligence and Japan's Computer Challenge to the World,* Reading, MA.: Addison-Wesley, 1985 and Paul M. Churchland and Patricia Smith Churchland, "Could A Machine Think?" *Scientific American,* January 1990. For a counter view of AI, see Hubert L. Dreyfus and Stuart E. Dreyfus, *Mind Over Machine: The Power of Human Intuition and Expertise in the Era of the Computer,* New York: The Free Press, 1986 and John R. Searle "Is the Brain's Mind a Computer Program?" *Scientific American,* January 1990.

letters or shapes. It could recognize letters (as long as they were all the same size and type) and could be taught: Operators would increase or decrease voltages in certain areas of the machine when mistakes were made.

Interest in the bottom-up approach then lagged for years, but by the 1980s work began on word, pattern, and image recognition and on neural network machines that attempt to emulate the physical thought processes of the human brain. In section 12.3, we describe neural networks in greater detail.

THE TOP-DOWN APPROACH   One of the first top-down efforts was the Logic Theorist, introduced in 1956 at the Dartmouth Summer Research Project on Artificial Intelligence. Its developers, Herbert Simon and Alan Newell, used software that mimicked deductive logic: selecting the correct rules and postulates so as to create a coherent, logical chain of "if x then y" statements from premises to conclusion. The problem with this approach was that for even simple real-world problems, hundreds of thousands, or millions, of such rules are required.

In the 1960s, newly developed third-generation computers made it possible to consider thousands of computations per second to test out millions of rules, one at a time. But even a simple game like chess contains 10^{120} possible moves.

NorthWest Airlines Inc. uses an AI-based expert auditing system, which is responsible for ensuring that airline passenger tickets are properly priced and that the correct travel agency commission is applied.

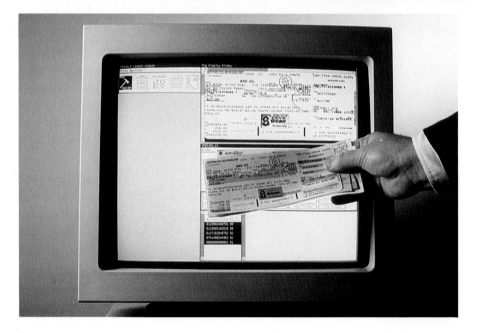

Combinatorial explosion:
In computer processing, the
overload that results when
trying to test more rules to
reach a solution than the
computer is capable of
handling.

Faster computers proved not to be a total solution. Ways had to be found to pare down the search tree in order to avoid a **combinatorial explosion**. A combinatorial explosion arises when a problem requires a computer to test more rules than it has the capacity to examine in order to reach a solution. An exhaustive search through all possibilities on a chessboard would quickly swamp all the computers known to exist in the 1980s. In order to avoid a combinatorial explosion, some rules of thumb or heuristics are needed. New search strategies and decision trees were developed to reduce the need for an exhaustive search.

From these developments emerged expert systems, which consist of a limited number of rules for a very specific and limited domain of human expertise (such as making a mortgage decision or chess). A major effort of AI systems today is to develop simple rules that can pare down the search tree and make searching efficient. In limited areas of expertise, from diagnosing a car's ignition system, to classifying biological specimens, the rules of thumb used by real-world experts can be understood, codified, and placed in a machine. In the next section we explain what expert systems are and how they work.

12.2 Knowledge-Based Expert Systems

Expert system:
Knowledge-intensive
computer program that
captures the expertise of a
human in limited domains of
knowledge.

An **expert system** is a knowledge-intensive program that solves a problem by capturing the expertise of a human in limited domains of knowledge and experience. An expert system can assist decision making by asking relevant questions and explaining the reasons for adopting certain actions.

Some of the common characteristics of expert systems are the following:

- They perform some of the problem-solving work of humans.
- They use knowledge in the form of rules or frames.
- They interact with humans.
- They can consider multiple hypotheses simultaneously.

Expert systems are different from thermostats and autopilots insofar as they attempt to base their actions on human knowledge rather than physical principles. Today, expert systems are quite narrow, shallow, and brittle. They lack the breadth of knowledge and the understanding of fundamental principles of a human expert. Expert systems today do not "think" as a human being does. A human being perceives significance, works with abstract models of causality, and can jump to conclusions. Expert systems do not resort to reasoning from first principles, do not draw analogies, and lack common sense.

Above all, expert systems are not generalized experts or problem solvers. They typically perform very limited tasks that can be performed by professionals in a few minutes or hours. Problems that cannot be solved by human experts in the same short period of time are far too difficult for an expert system. As it turns out, cloning a human expert is impossible with today's tools, although parts of human expertise can be captured by computer programs, including expert system languages.

How Expert Systems Work

Four major elements compose an expert system: the knowledge domain or base, the development team, the AI shell, and the user. Subsequently, we will describe each of these parts.

Knowledge base: Model of human knowledge that is used by expert systems.

What is human knowledge? AI developers sidestep this thorny issue by asking a slightly different question: How can human knowledge be modeled or represented in a way that a computer can deal with it? This model of human knowledge used by expert systems is called the **knowledge base.** Three ways have been devised to represent human knowledge and expertise: rules, semantic nets, and frames.

A standard structured programming construct (see Chapter 9) is the IF–THEN construct, in which a *condition* is evaluated. If the condition is true, an *action* is taken. For instance:

IF
    INCOME>$45,000 (condition)
    PRINT NAME AND ADDRESS (action)

A series of these rules can be a knowledge base. Any reader who has written computer programs knows that virtually all traditional computer programs contain IF–THEN statements. The difference between a traditional program and a **rule-based expert system** program is one of degree and magnitude. AI programs can easily have 200 to 10,000 rules, far more than traditional programs, which may have 50 to 100 IF–THEN statements. Moreover, in an AI program the rules tend to be interconnected and nested to a far larger degree than in traditional programs, as shown in Figure 12.2. The order in which the rules are searched

Rule-based expert system: An AI program that has a large number of interconnected and nested IF–THEN statements or "rules" that are the basis for the knowledge in the system.

Figure 12.2
Rules in an AI program. An expert system contains a number of rules to be followed when utilized. The rules themselves are interconnected; the number of outcomes is known in advance and is limited; there are multiple paths to the same outcome; and the system can consider multiple rules at a single time. The rules illustrated are for simple credit-granting expert systems.

depends in part on what information the system is given. Multiple paths lead to the same result, and the rules themselves can be interconnected. The system is not necessarily sequential. Hence the complexity of the rules in a rule-based expert system is considerable.

Could you represent the knowledge in the *Encyclopedia Britannica* this way? Probably not, because the **rule base** would be too large, and not all the knowledge in the encyclopedia can be represented in the form of IF–THEN rules. In general, expert systems can be efficiently used only in those situations where the domain of knowledge is highly restricted (such as in granting credit) and involves no more than a few thousand rules.

Semantic nets can be used to represent knowledge when the knowledge base is composed of easily identified chunks or objects of interrelated characteristics. Semantic nets can be much more efficient than rules. They use the property of inheritance to organize and classify objects. A condition like "IS A" ties objects together—"IS A" is a pointer to all objects of a specific class. For instance, Figure 12.3 shows a semantic net that is used to classify kinds of automobiles. All specific automobiles in the lower part of the diagram inherit characteristics of the general categories of the automobiles above them. Insurance companies can use such a semantic net to classify cars into rating classes.

Knowledge **frames** also organize knowledge into chunks, but the relationships are based on shared characteristics rather than a hierarchy. This approach is grounded in the belief that humans use "frames" or concepts to make rapid sense out of perceptions. For instance, when a person is told to "look for a tank and move when you see one," experts believe humans invoke a concept or frame of what a tank should look like. Anything that does not fit this concept of a tank is ignored. In a similar fashion, AI researchers can organize a vast array of information into frames. The computer is then instructed to search the database of frames and list connections to other frames of interest. The user can then follow the various pathways pointed to by the system.

Figure 12.4 shows a part of a knowledge base organized by frames. A "CAR" is defined by characteristics or slots in a frame as a vehicle with four wheels, a gas or diesel motor, and an action like rolling or moving. This frame could be related to just about any other object in the database that shares any of these characteristics, such as the tank frame.

Rule base: The collection of knowledge in an AI system that is represented in the form of IF–THEN rules.

Semantic nets: Expert systems that use the property of inheritance to organize and classify knowledge when the knowledge base is composed of easily identifiable chunks or objects of interrelated characteristics.

Frames: Method of organizing expert system knowledge into chunks, but the relationships are based on shared characteristics determined by the user rather than a hierarchy.

Figure 12.3
Semantic nets to model knowledge. Knowledge can be organized into semantic nets with inheritance. All lower levels inherit the characteristics of those objects above. For example, a Dodge Caravan inherits the characteristics of "family car" as well as "automobile." The link among levels is crucial; in this case, the link is "is-a." In other instances it could be "produces," "looks like," and so forth.

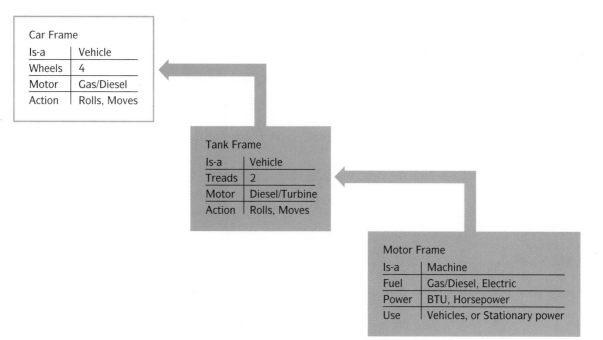

Figure 12.4
Frames to model knowledge. Knowledge and information can be organized into frames in a manner similar to semantic nets. Frames capture the relevant characteristics of the objects of interest. This approach is based on the belief that humans use "frames" or concepts to narrow the range of possibilities when scanning incoming information in order to make rapid sense out of perceptions.

THE DEVELOPMENT TEAM

Knowledge engineer: Specialist who elicits information and expertise from other professionals and translates it into a set of rules, frames, or semantic nets for an expert system.

An AI development team is composed of one or several "experts" who have a thorough command over the knowledge base and one or more **knowledge engineers** who can translate the knowledge (as described by the expert) into a set of rules, frames, or semantic nets. A knowledge engineer is similar to a traditional systems analyst, but has special expertise in eliciting information and expertise from other professionals.

THE SHELL

AI shell: The programming environment of an expert system.

Inference engine: The strategy used to search through the rule base in an expert system: can be forward or backward chaining.

Forward chaining: Strategy for searching the rule base in an expert system that begins with the information entered by the user and searches the rule base to arrive at a conclusion.

The **AI shell** is the programming environment of an expert system. AI systems can be developed in just about any programming language, such as BASIC or Pascal. In the early years of expert systems, computer scientists used specialized programming languages, such as LISP or PROLOG, that could process lists of rules efficiently. Today a growing number of expert systems use either the C language or, more commonly, AI shells, which are user-friendly development environments. AI shells can quickly generate user interface screens, capture the knowledge base, and manage the strategies for searching the rule base. The best of these AI shells generate C code, which can then be integrated into existing programs or tied into existing data streams and databases.

One of the most interesting parts of expert systems is the **inference engine.** The inference engine is simply the strategy used to search through the rule base. Two strategies are commonly used: forward chaining and backward chaining (see Figure 12.5).

In **forward chaining,** the inference engine begins with the information entered by the user and searches the rule base to arrive at a conclusion. The strategy is to "fire," or carry out, the action of the rule when a condition is true. In Figure 12.5, beginning on the left, if the user enters a client with income greater than $100,000, the engine will fire all rules in sequence from left to right. If the user then enters information indicating that the same client owns real estate, another

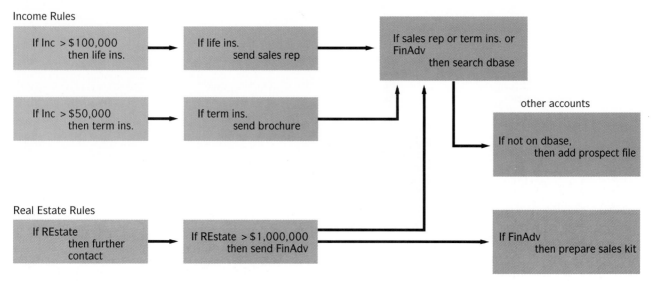

Income Rules

| If Inc > $100,000 then life ins. | → | If life ins. send sales rep | → | If sales rep or term ins. or FinAdv then search dbase |

| If Inc > $50,000 then term ins. | → | If term ins. send brochure |

other accounts

If not on dbase, then add prospect file

Real Estate Rules

| If REstate then further contact | → | If REstate > $1,000,000 then send FinAdv |

If FinAdv then prepare sales kit

Figure 12.5
Inference engines in expert systems. An inference engine works by searching through the rules and "firing" those rules that are triggered by facts gathered and entered by the user. Basically, a collection of rules is similar to a series of nested "IF" statements in a traditional software program; however, the magnitude of the statements and degree of nesting are much greater in an expert system.

pass of the rule base will occur and more rules will fire. The rule base can be searched each time the user enters new information. Processing continues until no more rules can be fired.

Backward chaining: Strategy for searching the rule base in an expert system that acts like a problem solver by beginning with a hypothesis and seeking out more information until the hypothesis is either proved or disproved.

In **backward chaining,** an expert system acts more like a problem solver who begins with a question and seeks out more information to evaluate the question. The strategy for searching the rule base starts with a hypothesis and proceeds by asking the user questions about selected facts until the hypothesis is either confirmed or disproved. In our example in Figure 12.5, ask the question, "Should we add this person to the prospect database?" Begin on the right of the diagram and work toward the left. You can see that the person should be added to the database if a sales rep is sent, term insurance is granted, or a financial advisor will be sent to visit the client.

THE USER   The role of the user is both to pose questions to the system and to enter relevant data to guide the system along. The user may employ the expert system as a source of advice or to perform tedious and routine analysis tasks.

Examples of Successful Expert Systems

There are many successful expert systems, such as Countrywide Funding's CLUES loan underwriting system, described in the Window on Management. However, there is no accepted definition of *successful*. What is successful to an academic ("It works!") may not be successful to a corporation ("It cost a million dollars!"). While some of the better-known expert systems are quite large and cost millions of dollars, others are less expensive and tackle interesting but smaller problems. Some of the most celebrated systems are not used to facilitate routine decision making. Finding out which successful systems are used on a daily basis is difficult because corporations regard this information as proprietary. Nevertheless, we can briefly describe some of the better-known commercial success stories.

Whirlpool uses the *Consumer Appliance Diagnostic System* (CADS) to help its customer service representatives handle its 3 million annual telephone inquiries. The system expedites customer service by directing customers to a single source of help without delay. Previously, customers who had a problem or

MANAGEMENT

Will You Get the Loan? Ask the System

It is axiomatic to say that we live in a world of big businesses. Yet large size creates problems that organizational management must solve if the organization is to survive and prosper. How can critical centrally determined policies be carried out at large and small sites scattered throughout the country (or world)? How can management know that the staff is working efficiently? In some growing companies, expert systems have been one of the tools used to address these problems.

Countrywide Funding Corp. in Pasadena, California, is one such company. They are loan underwriters with about 400 underwriters in 150 offices around the country. The company has seen rapid, continuing growth. In planning for that growth, Countrywide's chief underwriting officer, Ralph Mozilo, asked the key question, "How do you get consistent and high-quality [loan] decisions across the country with a work force that large?" His answer was CLUES (Countrywide's Loan Underwriting Expert System), a microcomputer-based expert system designed to make preliminary creditworthiness decisions on loan requests.

Development of CLUES began in 1991. By the fall of 1992, CLUES was being tested in six offices around the country. The system has about 400 rules. As part of the test, every loan application handled by a human underwriter

was fed to CLUES. Mozilo's standards required that to be successful the system had to agree with the underwriter in 95 percent of the cases. However, Countrywide will not rely on CLUES to reject loans because the expert system cannot be programmed to handle exceptional situations such as those involving a self-employed person or complex financial schemes. An underwriter will review all rejected loans and will make the final decision.

As a result of this system, Mozilo can be comfortable that his underwriters at offices all over the country will apply uniform standards in handling loans. Rapid expansion should not threaten his ability to maintain appropriate organizational controls. In addition, CLUES offers productivity benefits. Traditionally an underwriter could handle six or seven applications a day. Using CLUES, the same underwriter can evaluate at least sixteen per day. The productivity gain comes because CLUES can review the pile of forms filled out by each loan applicant and can issue a preliminary decision in eight seconds; the underwriter will usually need about 45 minutes to do the same work. Countrywide expected CLUES to pay back its $1.5 million development cost within the first year, in addition to winning Countrywide more business.

Mozilo indicates that the system has other benefits as well. Compa-

nies that issue loans are legally restrained by equal opportunity laws. Therefore, management needs to know that its underwriters are not racially discriminating in their lending practices. Mozilo points out that CLUES "is color blind." CLUES, he said, "is another step in making sure irrelevant factors are ignored in lending."

In the process of developing CLUES, Mozilo was surprised at what was found out about the loan decision-making process. When he and his staff sat down and wrote loans in front of the knowledge engineers, they found out that there were about 50 decision-making questions asked in making a determination about a loan. Mozilo hence discovered that his approach to loan writing was very intuitive.

Source: Jim Nash, "State of the Market, Art, Union, and Technology," *AI Expert,* January 1993.

To Think About: What are four rules that might be included in the CLUES system? Is loan underwriting an appropriate application for an expert system? Why or why not? What management, organization, and technology factors would you want to consider before implementing such a system? What are the management benefits of using such a system?

question about Whirlpool products might have to be put on hold or directed to two or three different representatives before their questions could be answered. Whirlpool developed CADS using Aion's Development System for OS/2 as its expert system shell. Two knowledge engineers worked with one programmer and three of the company's customer service experts to capture 1000 rules for 12 product lines. By 1999, Whirlpool expects to use CADS to respond to 9 million calls annually.

MSE—*Market Surveillance Expert*—is used by the American Stock Exchange to assist analysts investigating cases of insider trading. The system was built using a shell from Exsys Inc., which uses Lotus 1-2-3 spreadsheets as the knowledge base and a set of built-in rules to guide the inference engine.

TradeCenter is used by Merrill Lynch and several other Wall Street firms to act as an assistant to traders by watching price movements reported by real-time price feeds. Traders often have to keep track of a dozen different screens, with each screen divided into several different windows. There is simply too much information for any human to monitor in real time properly. TradeCenter keeps track of the information a trader wants to follow and reports price movements accordingly. The service displays, for instance, forty-day price tick charts, money-flow analysis, commodity prices, synthetic instrument and basket analysis, and a real-time ticker at the bottom of the screen showing prices on major markets.

The Securities and Exchange Commission (SEC) requires that all publicly held companies submit detailed financial statements to the SEC on a monthly and a quarterly basis. This information is of enormous utility to competitors and other persons interested in the financial health of firms. The Arthur Andersen Company developed an expert system to read corporate proxy statements with a sophistication unmatched by the average human investigator. When the system is asked to identify, for instance, companies that have taken actions in the past year to dodge a leveraged buy-out attempt, it searches for concepts rather than specific words, just as a knowledgeable investor would.

The Digital Equipment Corporation (DEC) and Carnegie-Mellon University developed XCON in the late 1970s to configure VAX computers on a daily basis. The system configures customer orders and guides the assembly of those orders at the customer site. XCON is used by major functions such as sales and marketing, manufacturing and production, and field service; it plays a strategic role at DEC.

Table 12.1 describes these and other well-known expert systems in terms of their size and programming languages. As can be seen, these systems generally

Table 12.1 SOME WELL-KNOWN EXPERT SYSTEMS

Name of System or Project	Brief System Description	Method of Verification	Number of Rules	Programming Language
Authorizer's Assistant (American Express)	Authorize credit transactions	Field test	850	ART
Hub Slaashing (American Airlines)	Recommend flight schedule changes when airports disrupted	Field test	39	C
CLUES (Countrywide Funding Corp.)	Authorize loans	Field test	400	Inference Corp. ART—IM (AI shell)
Robot (Ford Motor)	Diagnose sick robots	Field test	200	Texas Instruments Personal Consultant
Mail Prospector (R.R. Donnelly)	Test mailing lists	Field test	NA	More/2
Heuristic Dendral	Identify organic compounds by analysis of mass spectrograms	Field use	400	Interlisp
MYCIN	Diagnose certain infectious diseases and recommend appropriate drugs	Scientific (BV)	400	Interlisp
Prospector	Aid geologists in evaluating mineral sites for potential deposits	Field use	Largest knowledge base, 212 assertions and 133 inference rules	DEC 10
XCON (DEC)	Configure VAX computer systems	Field use	10,000	OPS4 (implemented in MACLISP)

NA = Not available

ORGANIZATIONS

Case-Based Reasoning Keeps Customers Happy

In today's customer service-oriented, highly competitive environment, high-tech hardware, software, and appliance manufacturers are daily flooded with customer phone calls crying for help. Keeping those customers satisfied requires many companies to spend millions of dollars annually to maintain large, technically skilled customer-support staffs. And as technology becomes more central to our lives, this problem will only swell. How can a company rein in costs while satisfying customer needs? Enter Compaq Computer.

In late 1992 Compaq Computer Corporation of Houston, Texas, did something no company had done before. They began giving away expensive artificial intelligence software to customers purchasing their Pagemarq printer. In the process, they have been able to cut their customer-support staff, saving $10 to $20 million annually.

The software, developed for Compaq by Inference Corporation, diagnoses printer problems. It uses a new AI technology known as *case-based reasoning*. The AI knowledge base is a series of several hundred actual cases of Pagemarq printer problems—war stories. Faced with a problem, the user begins by describing the problem to the case-based computer system. Then the system swiftly searches through actual cases, discarding unrelated cases, latching on to related cases. If needed during the search, the software will ask the user for more information in order further to narrow the search. In the end it will usually settle on one or more cases relevant to the problem described.

Inference Corp. originally developed the software in 1991 to aid Compaq customer-support technicians in answering customer printer problem questions. Until 1991, a customer calling about a printer producing smudged output would first reach an operator who, of course, could not analyze the problem. The operator had to listen to a description of the problem in order to determine which technician to transfer the calling customer to. The customer sat on hold while the call was transferred, and then had to describe the problem all over again while the technician tried to come up with an answer—(most frustrating.) When the new case-based software was made available to the technicians, the task of analyzing the problem and suggesting solutions was speeded up. But it still required one or more phone calls, a great deal of the customer's time and patience, and a large, expensive, Compaq customer-support staff.

Then in 1992 someone had a competitive advantage insight—give the software to customers when they purchase the printer. Now that same customer can solve her own problem quickly (smile!) while Compaq can cut its customer-support staff. For example, the woman with smudged output bypasses Compaq and instead runs the software (stored on her own computer). It searches its knowledge base, usually identifying one or more relevant cases that sug-gest solutions (in this instance perhaps a specific part needs cleaning). The software then displays detailed pictures of the printer and the relevant printer parts so the user can fix the problem herself.

One interesting question immediately arises. If Compaq has been so successful by distributing this software to unravel printer problems, why not do the same with their main product line, computers? Couldn't they save a great deal more money that way? The answer, according to Avron Barr, Inference's director of marketing, is that "Once you get into computers, then it gets a lot more complicated." Computers are more complex than printers, the potential problems a great deal more diverse. Instead of holding several hundreds of cases, such software would need to hold thousands of cases, requiring much larger storage media. Distributing such software to customers simply is simply not feasible with current technology.

Source: Sabra Chartrand, "Compaq Printer Can Tell You What's Ailing It," *The New York Times,* August 4, 1993.

To Think About: If distributing the printer AI system solved a key problem for Compaq, do you think it will create other problems? What might they be? If Compaq's use of case-based software has been so successful for them, do you think other companies will do the same? What managerial, organizational, and technological problems will they face if they try to do so?

have a minimum of several hundred rules. Note Digital Equipment Corporation's XCON, which started out with 250 rules but has expanded to about 10,000.

Case-Based Reasoning

Most expert systems work by applying a set of rules against a knowledge base, both of which are extracted from human experts. For certain problems, such as service and support for customers purchasing a computer printer, as described in the Window on Organizations, systems employing case-based reasoning can be

Case-based reasoning:
Artificial intelligence
technology that represents
knowledge as a database of
cases.

more useful. In **case-based reasoning**, past experiences of human specialists, represented as "cases," are stored in a database for later retrieval when the user encounters a new case. The system searches for similar parameters within new cases, finds the closest fit, and applies the solutions of the old case to the new case. Successful solutions are tagged to the new case, stored together in the knowledge base, and applied to the new case. Unsuccessful solutions are also appended to the new case along with an explanation of why the solutions didn't work. In contrast to rule-based expert systems, the knowledge base for the case-based reasoning system is continuously expanded and refined by users.

Building an Expert System

Building an expert system is similar to building other information systems, although building expert systems is an iterative process, with each phase possibly requiring several iterations before a full system is developed. While no agreed-upon development cycle yet exists, we describe typical steps here.

The team members must first select a problem appropriate for an expert system. Then they will develop a prototype system to test assumptions about how to encode the knowledge of experts. Next they will develop a full-scale system, focusing mainly on the addition of a very large number of rules. When the experts and the knowledge engineers are satisfied that the system is complete, it can be tested by a range of experts within the organization against the performance criteria established in earlier stages. Once tested, the system will then be integrated into the data flow and work patterns of the organization. Finally, as with other systems, the expert system must be maintained. Typically the environment in which an expert system operates is continually changing so that the expert system must also continually change. Some expert systems, especially large ones, are so complex that in a few years the maintenance costs will equal the development costs. In the case of XCON (see Table 12.1), about 30 to 50 percent of the approximately 10,000 rules are changed each year.

Problems with Expert Systems

A thorough understanding of expert systems also requires awareness of their current limitations and problems.

EXPERT SYSTEMS ARE
LIMITED TO CERTAIN
PROBLEMS

In answer to the question, "Why do some expert systems work?" critics point out that virtually all successful expert systems deal with problems of classification in which there are relatively few alternative outcomes and in which these possible outcomes are all known in advance. Contrary to early promises, expert systems do best in automating lower-level clerical functions. Even in these comparatively simple situations, however, expert systems require large, lengthy, and expensive development efforts. For these kinds of problems, hiring or training more experts may be less expensive than building an expert system.

IMPORTANT THEORETICAL
PROBLEMS EXIST

There are significant theoretical problems in knowledge representation. "IF–THEN" knowledge exists primarily in textbooks. There are no adequate representations for deep causal models or temporal trends. No expert system, for instance, can write a textbook on information systems or engage in other creative activities not explicitly foreseen by system designers. Many experts cannot express their knowledge using an "IF–THEN" format. Expert systems cannot yet replicate knowledge that is intuitive, based on analogy and on a "sense of things."

EXPERT SYSTEMS ARE NOT APPLICABLE TO MANAGERIAL PROBLEMS

The applicability of expert systems to managerial problems is currently highly limited. Managerial problems generally involve drawing facts and interpretations from divergent sources, evaluating the facts, and comparing one interpretation of the facts with another; they do not involve analysis or simple classification. Expert systems based on the prior knowledge of a few known alternatives are unsuitable to the problems managers face on a daily basis.

EXPERTISE IS COLLECTIVE

For many problems there are no single experts. Expertise may be distributed throughout an organization. Coordinating this expertise to formulate policies and actions is a key focus of management efforts. Expert systems cannot help here because they cannot synthesize knowledge from several different experts any better than ordinary systems analysis and design can.

EXPERT SYSTEMS ARE EXPENSIVE TO TEACH

The knowledge base of expert systems is fragile and brittle; it cannot learn or change over time. In fast-moving fields like medicine or the computer sciences, keeping the knowledge base up-to-date is a critical problem.

A MORE LIMITED ROLE FOR EXPERT SYSTEMS

Even the critics point out that research on artificial intelligence and expert systems is useful. It may be entirely appropriate that artificial intelligence researchers based in university laboratories continue contemplating toy problems and simplistic models of cognition to highlight certain themes and issues. Moreover, expert systems may be used as electronic checklists for lower-level employees in service bureaucracies like banking, insurance, sales, and welfare agencies. There is clearly a market for software products that includes artificial intelligence, or just smart programming. When it comes to more complex problems, however, it is a very long step from the classroom to the factory floor, battlefield, or corporate boardroom.

12.3 Other Intelligent Techniques

Clearly the pursuit of artificial intelligence will remain a persistent theme for many years. While some considerable progress will be made in expert systems, the development of parallel processing at the hardware level—the idea of breaking up a problem into many small components and then processing each component simultaneously using hundreds or even thousands of computers operating in parallel—is likely to unleash a host of new possibilities. Subsequently, we review briefly the development of other intelligent computing techniques that stand the best chance in the 1990s of developing into major fields of business applications.

Neural Networks

Neural network: Hardware or software that attempts to emulate the processing patterns of the biological brain.

There has been an exciting resurgence of interest in bottom-up approaches to artificial intelligence in which machines are designed to imitate the physical thought process of the biological brain. Figure 12.6 shows two neurons from a leech's brain. The soma, or neuron at the center, acts like a switch, stimulating other neurons and being stimulated in turn. Emanating from the neuron is an axon, which is an electrically active link to the dendrites of other neurons. Axons and dendrites are the "wires" that electrically connect neurons to one another. The junction of the two is called a synapse. This simple biological model is the metaphor for the development of neural networks. **Neural networks** consist of hardware or software that attempts to emulate the processing patterns of the biological brain.

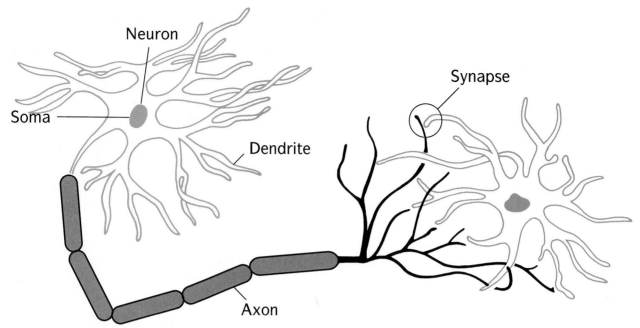

Figure 12.6
Biological neurons of a leech. Simple biological models, like the neurons of a leech, have influenced the development of artificial or computational neural networks in which the biological cells are replaced by transistors, or entire processors. *Source: Defense Advance Research Projects Agency (DARPA), 1988. Unclassified. Hereinafter "DARPA, 1988."*

The human brain has about 100 billion (10^{11}) neurons, each having about 1000 dendrites, which form 100,000 billion (10^{14}) synapses. The brain operates at about 100 hertz (each neuron can fire off a pulse 100 times per second)—very slow by computer standards where, for example, an Intel 80486 chip operates at up to 100 megahertz, or millions of cycles per second, executing one instruction at a time. But the brain's neurons operate in parallel, and the human brain can accomplish about 10^{16} or ten million billion interconnections per second. This far exceeds the capacity of any known machine, or any machine now planned or ever likely to be built with current technology.

But elementary neuron circuits can be built and studied, and far more complex networks of neurons have been simulated on computers. Figure 12.7 shows an artificial neural network with two neurons. The resistors in the circuits are variable and can be used to "teach" the network. When the network makes a mistake (i.e., chooses the wrong pathway through the network and arrives at a false conclusion), resistance can be raised on some circuits, forcing other neurons to fire. If this learning process continues for thousands of cycles, the machine "learns" the correct response.

One feature that distinguishes neural networks from digital computers is the inherent parallelism: The simple neurons or switches are highly interconnected and operate in parallel. Instead of a single personal computer executing a single instruction at a time, imagine 64,000 personal computers all connected to one another and all working simultaneously on parts of the same problem. A *neural network computer* can be defined, then, as an interconnected set of parallel switches or processors for which the network can be controlled by intervention. In neural networks the physical machine emulates a human brain and can be taught from experience.

THE DIFFERENCE BETWEEN
NEURAL NETWORKS AND
EXPERT SYSTEMS

What is different about neural networks? Whereas expert systems, like most traditional systems, seek to emulate or model a human expert's way of solving a set of problems, neural network builders claim they do not model human

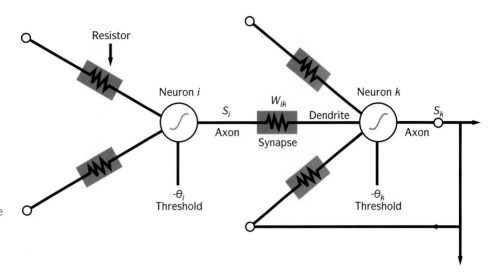

Figure 12.7
Artificial neural network with two neurons. In artificial neurons, the biological neurons become processing elements (switches), the axons and dendrites become wires, and the synapses become variable resistors that carry weighted inputs (currents) that represent data. Source: DARPA, 1988.

intelligence, do not program solutions, do not use knowledge engineers, and do not aim to solve specific problems per se. Instead of putting intelligence into programs, neural network designers seek to put the intelligence into the hardware in the form of a generalized capability to learn. The idea is to build machines that solve entire classes of problems. Furthermore, the expert system is highly specific to a given problem and cannot be easily retrained, while the neural network can be more easily modified and taught to recognize automobiles or animals or to solve other visual pattern recognition problems.

Take a simple problem like identifying a cat. An expert system approach would interview hundreds of people to understand how humans recognize cats. This would result in a large set of rules, or frames, programmed into an expert system. A television camera connected to the system would scan shapes in the environment, and the system would analyze the signals against the rule base of the system. After scanning a few thousand rules, one at a time, the system would label each perceived object as either a cat or not a cat.

In contrast, a trainable neural network would be brought to the test site, connected to the television, and started out on the process of learning. Every time a cat was not correctly perceived, the system's interconnections would be adjusted. When cats were correctly perceived, the system would be left alone and another object scanned.

Although the most powerful neural network machine today can only approximate the thinking ability of a bee or cockroach, useful neural network applications are being developed. Because of the way neural nets "learn," they can identify relationships and patterns and are appropriate for making classifications, generalizations, or decisions in cases where less than 100 percent accuracy can be tolerated.

The pattern-recognition power of neural networks is starting to be harnessed by medicine, as is illustrated by the Window on Technology. The chapter-opening vignette illustrates that neural network applications are also now being used by the financial industry to discern patterns in vast pools of data that might help investment firms predict the performance of equities, corporate bond ratings, or corporate bankruptcies. (Lin, 1993).

In another example, Mellon Bank in Pittsburgh, Pennsylvania, is using a neural network to help detect credit card fraud. The network was taught to recognize irregular patterns in charge card purchases and to evaluate potentially fraudulent transactions.

Neural nets cannot always guarantee a completely certain solution, arrive at the same solution again with the same input data, or always guarantee the "best"

TECHNOLOGY
Computers That See and Learn

By combining the ability of neural networks to *learn* with technology that allows computers to *see,* important and exciting applications involving pattern recognition are now being developed.

Pap smear tests, used to detect cervical cancer, have until recently relied solely on a visual examination of every smear to find abnormal cells. The technician uses a microscope to search each smear for the telltale abnormal cells that indicate cancer or a precancerous condition. Most smears will be negative (contain only healthy cells), indicating the absence of cancer. However, each smear might contain up to 500,000 cells, and only a tiny percentage of the cells might be abnormal, making it very difficult to locate them. Manually searching the cells is a slow, tedious, and inexact process. Estimates are that 30 to 50 percent of all positive smears (those containing abnormal cells) are falsely rated negative—that the cancerous condition is not identified and treated in 30 to 50 percent of the cases.

Neural network technology has been used to develop a system that reduces the error rate to about 3 percent. Papnet by Neuromedical Systems Inc. of Suffern, New York, examines all the cells in the smear and selects the 128 most abnormal cells for display on the monitor. However, the computer is not able to make the final decision—that takes human judgment. The technician will review the selected cells and have the software mark and record any that are deemed to be truly abnormal. Using this system, the technician requires less than one-fifth the time to examine a smear while achieving perhaps ten times the accuracy of the existing manual methods.

Papnet had to learn to distinguish between normal and abnormal cells. It was shown thousands of both normal and abnormal cells. The cells were in many different positions, even touching and overlapping, as they would be in real life. Many different color stains were used. When Papnet improperly identified a cell, the system

was corrected, and in this way it slowly *learned* to distinguish between normal and abnormal. Papnet's accuracy has been verified through studies done at Montefiore Medical Center in the Bronx, New York.

Neural networks have also been used to aid in the reading of the magnetic ink numbers at the bottom of paper checks. Conventional check readers have trouble with checks because the numbers are often blurred, off-center, or incomplete. Onyx, developed by Verifone of Redwood City, California, uses shape recognition to identify most numbers, even when the numbers have the same printing problems. This unusual product is a point-of-sale (POS) system, used to verify a check at a retail store much as the salesclerk would verify a credit card. With widespread use, the system should allow more retail outlets to accept checks without risk.

Sources: Kay Keppler, "Neural Nets Clarify Pap Smears," *AI Expert,* January 1993; Hal Glatzer, "Neural Networks Take On Real-World Problems," *Computerworld,* August 10, 1992.

To Think About: Neural networks still involve a new technology, not yet widely used or well proven. As a middle-level manager, under what conditions would you recommend this new technology? What are the risks of being the first to introduce such technology in your company? How would you handle these risks?

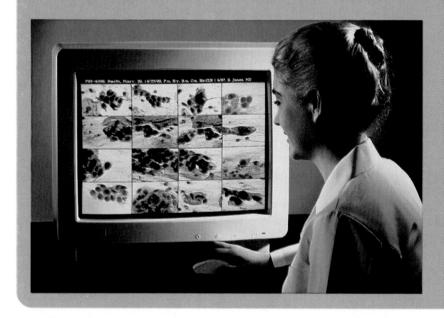

solution (Trippi and Turban, 1989–1990). Both the chapter-opening vignette and these examples suggest that in most current applications, neural networks are best used as aids to human decision makers instead of as substitutes for them.

Parallel Sensor Systems

Parallel sensor system: A machine consisting of many nodes that each act as a processor feeding information to a hierarchy of higher-level nodes.

Suppose a hospital wanted to watch and monitor all of its patients at once, or wished to closely monitor all the indicators on a single patient simultaneously to alert nurses in case something is wrong or to continually analyze the patient's health status? Could a computer, or collection of computers, keep track of all this information?[2]

One solution is to use a **parallel sensor system,** which is a machine consisting of a series of nodes. Each node functions like a processor or computer that continually receives information from lower-level sensors, evaluates the information, requests more if needed, and reports to higher-level nodes. Figure 12.8 illustrates a parallel sensor system called the Trellis machine by one of its inventors, David Gelernter, a computer scientist at Yale University. The machine depicted here is only one portion of the Trellis machine, showing how raw blood pressure is tracked. The Trellis machine uses sensors to track blood pressure and heart rate and sends this information upward through the "trellis" to processors, which evaluate the data. Each processor in the hierarchy evaluates the data and directs them upward to processors at the next level. Higher-level units may send queries downward to obtain additional information or to change the behavior of a lower-level unit based on a high-level hypothesis. Other parts of the machine monitor other indicators of health.

Fuzzy Logic

Fuzzy logic: Rule-based AI that tolerates imprecision by using nonspecific terms called membership functions to solve problems.

Traditional computer programs require precision—on/off, yes/no, right/wrong. However, we human beings do not experience the world this way. We might all agree that 120 degrees is hot, and –40 degrees is cold, but is 75 degrees hot, warm, comfortable, or cool? The answer depends on many factors—the wind, the humidity, the individual experiencing the temperature, one's clothing, one's expectations. Many of our activities are also inexact. Tractor-trailer drivers would find it nearly impossible to back their rig into a space precisely specified to less than an inch on all sides. Fuzzy logic, a relatively new, rule-based development in AI, tolerates imprecision and even uses it to solve problems we could not have solved before. **Fuzzy logic** consists of a variety of concepts and techniques for representing and inferring knowledge that is imprecise, uncertain, or unreliable. Fuzzy logic can create rules that use approximate or subjective values and incomplete or ambiguous data. By expressing logic with some carefully defined imprecision, fuzzy logic is closer to the way people actually think than traditional IF–THEN rules.

Ford Motor Co. has developed a fuzzy logic application that backs a simulated tractor-trailer into a parking space. The application uses the following three rules:

IF the truck is *near* jackknifing, THEN *reduce* the steering angle.
IF the truck is *far away* from the dock, THEN steer *toward* the dock.
IF the truck is *near* the dock, THEN point the trailer *directly at* the dock.

[2]This section benefits from an article by David Gelernter, "The Metamorphosis of Information Management," *Scientific American* (August 1989). This article outlines a number of possibilities for extending computing through parallel processing to areas heretofore impossible.

Figure 12.8
Parallel sensor machines. A Trellis machine for monitoring patients has sensors at the bottom that send information up the hierarchy to units that consider ever more complex hypotheses about the patient's status (arrows indicate connections between units). Higher-level units may send queries and comments down the trellis to elicit additional information or to change the behavior of a lower-level unit based on a high-level hypothesis. *Source: David Gelernter, "The Metamorphosis of Information Management,"* Scientific American, *August 1989. Copyright © 1989 by Scientific American, Inc. All rights reserved.*

The following set of fuzzy logic rules control interest rates; they were developed by Lofti Zadeh of the University of California at Berkeley (widely regarded as the founder of fuzzy logic programming):

Increase interest rates *slightly* IF unemployment is *low* AND inflation is *moderate*.

Increase interest rates *sharply* IF unemployment is *low* AND inflation is *moderate* BUT rising *sharply*.

Decrease interest rates *slightly* IF unemployment is *low* BUT increasing AND inflation rate is *low* and *stable*.

This logic makes sense to us as human beings, for it represents how we think as we back that truck into its berth or make economic decisions.

How does the computer make sense of this programming? The answer is relatively simple. The terms (known as *membership functions*) are imprecisely defined so that, for example, in Figure 12.9 *cool* is between 50 degrees and 70 degrees, although the temperature is most clearly cool between about 60 degrees and 67 degrees. Note that cool is overlapped by *cold* or *warm*. To control the room environment using this logic, the programmer would develop similarly imprecise definitions for humidity and other factors such as outdoor wind and temperature. The rules might include one that says *If the temperature is cool or cold and the humidity is low while the outdoor wind is high and the outdoor temperature is low, raise the heat and humidity in the room.* The computer would combine the membership function readings in a weighted manner and, using all the rules, raise and lower the temperature and humidity.

Fuzzy logic is widely used in Japan and is gaining popularity in the United States. Its popularity has occurred partially because managers find they can use it to reduce costs and shorten development time. Fuzzy logic code requires few IF–THEN rules, making it simpler than traditional code. The rules required in the trucking example above, plus its term definitions, might require hundreds of IF–THEN statements to implement in traditional logic. Rockwell International uses fuzzy logic to control motor idling because they are able to reduce system implementation time by a factor of ten. Compact code requires less computer capacity, allowing Sanyo Fisher USA to implement camcorder controls without adding expensive memory to their product.

Fuzzy logic also allows us to solve problems not previously solvable, thus improving product quality. In Japan, Sendai's subway system uses fuzzy logic controls to accelerate so smoothly that standing passengers need not hold on. Mitsubishi Heavy Industries in Tokyo has been able to reduce the power consumption of its air conditioners by 20 percent through implementing control programs in fuzzy logic. The auto-focus device in our cameras is only possible because of fuzzy logic.

Management has found fuzzy logic useful for decision making and organizational control. A Wall Street firm had a system developed that selects companies for potential acquisition, using the language stock traders understand. Recently a system has been developed to detect possible fraud in medical claims submitted by health care providers anywhere in the United States. Fuzzy logic technology is rapidly becoming a major factor in the AI field.

Figure 12.9
Implementing fuzzy logic rules in hardware. The membership functions for the input called temperature are in the logic of the thermostat to control the room temperature. Membership functions help translate linguistic expressions such as "warm" into numbers that can be manipulated by the computer. *Source: James M. Sibigtroth, "Implementing Fuzzy Expert Rules in Hardware," AI Expert, April 1992. © 1992 Miller Freeman, Inc.*

Why Business Should Be Interested in Artificial Intelligence

We must remember always that in describing these systems, we use this word *intelligence* only metaphorically. These machines are not human. There is a difference between a "model" of human knowledge and human knowledge itself. Economists who "model" the economy never claim that their models "are" the economy. It is well to remember the limitations of artificial intelligence. Given these limitations and the experimental nature and high costs of artificial intelligence systems, why should businesses be interested in them at this point? The most important reasons are the following:

- To preserve expertise that might be lost through the retirement, resignation, or death of an acknowledged expert.
- To store information in an active form—to create an organizational knowledge base—that many employees can examine, much like an electronic textbook or manual, so that others may learn rules of thumb not found in textbooks.
- To create a mechanism that is not subject to human feelings like fatigue and worry. This may be especially useful when jobs may be environmentally, physically, or mentally dangerous to humans. These systems may also be useful advisors in times of crisis.
- To eliminate routine and unsatisfying jobs that are currently held by human beings.
- To maintain the strategic position of a company in an industry. Expert systems, like other systems, can be used as a marketing device, to reduce the cost of production or to improve existing product lines.

All of these contributions of artificial intelligence have potential strategic importance. Clearly, most progress in artificial intelligence of direct relevance to general business has been made in expert systems, but neural systems are rapidly developing more powerful applications than expert systems.

<table>
<tr><td>

Management Challenges

</td><td>

1. **Creating robust expert systems.** Expert systems must be changed every time there is a change in the organizational environment. Every time there is a change in the rules used by experts, they have to be reprogrammed. It is difficult to provide expert systems with the flexibility of human experts.

2. **Creating cost-effective expert systems.** Many thousands of businesses have undertaken experimental projects in expert systems, but only a small percentage have created expert systems that are actually used on a production basis. We have already described the problems of building and maintaining expert systems and the limitations of expert system applications. In many cases, expert systems that would be genuinely useful in business settings cannot be cost-justified.

3. **Determining appropriate applications for artificial intelligence.** Finding suitable applications for artificial intelligence techniques is not so easy. Some parts of business processes are rule-based; others are based on patterns, and still others are based on exhaustive searching of manual files for the "needle in the haystack." Identifying the business process, identifying the right technique, and determining how to build the system requires a focused effort.

</td></tr>
</table>

Summary

Define artificial intelligence.

Artificial intelligence is the development of computer-based systems that behave like humans. There are five members of the artificial intelligence family tree: natural language, robotics, perceptive systems, expert systems, and "intelligent" machines. The field of artificial intelligence is controversial because of disagreements about theory, practical worth, and social consequences.

Describe how artificial intelligence techniques evolved.

Artificial intelligence has two main thrusts. The bottom-up approach attempts to mimic the physical human brain at the machine level. Norbert Weiner's "feedback" machines, Frank Rosenblatt's Perceptron, and contemporary neural network computers are based on this approach. The top-down approach attempts to represent human knowledge through logic. Newell and Simon's Logic Theorist and contemporary expert systems are the leading examples of this school of thought.

Define an expert system and explain how it is built.

Expert systems are knowledge-intensive computer programs that solve problems that heretofore required human expertise. The systems embody human knowledge using rules, frames, or concepts. Expert systems have four components: the knowledge base, the development team, the AI shell, and the user. The knowledge base can be represented using rules, semantic nets, or frames. The strategy to search through the knowledge base, called the inference engine, can use either forward or backward chaining. Development of expert systems requires the use of prototyping and special knowledge engineers to elicit knowledge from the organization's experts.

Define neural networks and show how they are used in business.

Neural networks consist of hardware and software that attempts to mimic the thought processes of the human physical brain. Neural networks are notable for their ability to "learn" without programming and to recognize patterns that cannot be easily described by humans. They are being used in science, medicine, and business primarily to discriminate patterns in massive amounts of data.

Identify other intelligent techniques.

Other examples of machine intelligence are parallel sensor machines and fuzzy logic. Fuzzy logic is a software technology that expresses logic with some carefully defined imprecision so that it is closer to the way people actually think than traditional IF–THEN rules. Fuzzy logic has been used for controlling physical devices and is starting to be used for limited decision-making applications.

Key Terms

Artificial intelligence	Knowledge engineer
Bottom-up approach	AI shell
Top-down approach	Inference engine
Combinatorial explosion	Forward chaining
Expert system	Backward chaining
Knowledge base	Case-based reasoning
Rule-based expert system	Neural network
Rule base	Parallel sensor system
Semantic nets	Fuzzy logic
Frames	

Review Questions

1. What is artificial intelligence?
2. What are the five elements of artificial intelligence research?
3. What is the difference between artificial intelligence and natural or human intelligence?
4. What are the two major lines of development in artificial intelligence research? Describe the key aspects of each.
5. State a good working definition of an expert system.
6. Describe each of the elements of an expert system.
7. What are frames and semantic nets?
8. What is meant by forward- and backward-chaining expert systems?
9. Cite three examples of successful expert systems. How many rules does each possess?
10. What is case-based reasoning?
11. What is the difference between knowledge engineering and conventional systems analysis?
12. Describe five problems and limitations of expert systems.
13. Describe a neural network. How does it work? How does it exhibit "intelligence"?
14. What kinds of tasks would a neural network be good at?
15. Define and describe parallel sensor systems and fuzzy logic.
16. State four reasons why business should be interested in artificial intelligence.

Discussion Questions

1. A famous person has declared that artificial intelligence will lead to a fundamental redistribution of knowledge because all persons will be able to have their own knowledge-based system, giving them access to knowledge that heretofore only experts have possessed. Discuss.
2. The CEO, in an effort to cut middle-management costs, has just announced a major effort to use artificial intelligence and expert systems to assist managers

and, if possible, through attrition, to reduce the total cost of management. Discuss.

3. Describe some information system applications that would benefit from using fuzzy logic.

Group
Project
With a group of your classmates, find a task in an organization (near your college or university) that requires some intelligence to perform and that might be suitable for an expert system. Describe as many of the rules required to perform this task as possible. Interview and observe the person performing this task. Consider changing the task in order to simplify the system. Report your findings to the class.

CASE STUDY

Venturing Into the Brave New World of Artificial Intelligence

Introduction of new technology is a complex issue for corporate management. Risks can be high, and costs can be great. Management must have a vision and a tolerance for those risks if it wants its company to be a leader. Management also must have effective strategies that will offer significant benefits while handling the problems and limiting the losses.

American Express originally ventured into artificial intelligence in 1984. It was one of the earliest companies to do so. The first project was an attempt to develop an expert system to aid in managing foreign exchange rates, a function that goes to the heart of their business. When the project was declared a failure and abandoned before completion, the company could easily have stopped. But they did not. Instead, they began to build a system to support the work of their credit authorizers. That project succeeded.

Today that system, titled Authorizer's Assistant, has saved American Express tens of millions of dollars by doing the work of 700 credit authorizers. The credit authorizers sit at terminals and decide whether to approve a charge. Since American Express has no credit limits on its cards, credit authorization is a crucial function to reduce the use of stolen cards and the accumulation of high charge card bills by people who cannot afford to pay. At the same time, credit authorizers do not want to deny credit to legitimate cardholders, which may result in losing business. Early tests showed that the system was accurate 95.5 percent of the time, compared to a human average of 85 percent.

Before Authorizer's Assistant, a credit authorizer would look at as many as 16 screens of data per customer, a cumbersome process that resulted in too many wrong authorization decisions. Authorizer's Assistant distills the knowledge of AmEx's best authorizers into an 850-rule expert system that assists and works with human authorizers. The system requires only two screens and recommends credit approval, disapproval, or further search.

Spurred on by this success, AmEx then went on to build Credit Assistant, which helps its staff review accounts for credit risk and for fraud. The company estimates that this system saves $1.4 million annually while ensuring consistent credit policies worldwide.

Why did these projects succeed? A number of factors are obvious. American Express grasped the potential significance of the technology to its core business, as is clear from the pivotal nature of the functions it selected to address in its first development projects. The early date of these initial projects reveals management's willingness to take a risk. Management's cancellation of the project before its completion indicates that it understood both the risk and the necessity of limiting it. Finally, management's commitment can be seen by its willingness to proceed on to other projects.

Perhaps most important, American Express management had vision. In the 1980s, most other companies were avoiding long-term spending commitments because of the emphasis the financial markets placed on short-term profit and immediate payback. At American Express, management knew how critical new technology was to the long-term health of their company. In 1984, Louis Gerstner, the CEO of American Express's Travel Related Services division, set up a corporate technology research fund, meant to give 100 percent funding to cutting-edge technology application projects. He quickly received proposals for all kinds of projects from a range of business units.

In reviewing the proposals, Gerstner quickly realized that the projects had a problem. Gerstner could be sure neither of the commitment of the proposing units nor of the long-term benefits. Gerstner realized that the source of the problem was his own offer to have American Express's corporate group fully fund the projects. The proposing units risked nothing, so they needed neither commitment nor careful evaluation of a project to make a proposal. Such projects are designed for failure. Gerstner quickly revised the offer. His fund would supply only 40 percent of the cost of a project. A further 40 percent would have to come from the proposing business unit itself, all but guaranteeing commitment and a careful evaluation of that project's long-term contribution. In addition, Gerstner was interested in benefits that could be shared by other business units as well. Therefore, he required that the final 20 percent had to come from a second business unit.

This fund spawned Authorizer's Assistant and other projects in expert systems and artificial intelligence. The careful design of the funding process gave American Express management the confidence they needed to continue funding, despite the early failure. Today, American Express has justifiably earned its reputation as a leader in the field of AI. They have also demonstrated one effective way to manage technological change for success.

Source: Harvey P. Newquist III, "AI at Amex," *AI Expert,* January 1993.

Case Study Questions

1. Can you suggest other ways in which the corporate technology fund benefited American Express? What problems do you see with that fund?

2. What do you think would have been the advantages and disadvantages to American Express if its management had waited five to seven years before attempting to develop systems using AI (as most companies did)?

3. What management, organization, and technology issues should be addressed when a firm considers a new artificial intelligence project?

References

Barker, Virginia E., and Dennis E. O'Connor. "Expert Systems for Configuration at Digital: XCON and Beyond." *Communications of the ACM* (March 1989).

Basu, Amit, and Alan R. Heyner. "Embedded Knowledge-Based Systems and Box Structure Methods." *Journal of Management Information Systems* 8 no. 4 (Spring 1992).

Blanning, Robert W., David R. King, James R. Marsden, and Ann C. Seror. "Intelligent Models of Human Organizations: The State of the Art." *Journal of Organizational Computing* 2, no. 2 (1992).

Bobrow, D. G., S. Mittal, and M. J. Stefik. "Expert Systems: Perils and Promise." *Communications of the ACM* 29 (September 1986).

Braden, Barbara, Jerome Kanter, and David Kopcso. "Developing an Expert Systems Strategy." *MIS Quarterly 13*, no 4 (December 1989).

Brody, Herb. "The Neural Computer." *Technology Review* (August/September 1990).

Byrd, Terry Anthony. "Implementation and Use of Expert Systems in Organizations: Perceptions of Knowledge Engineers." *Journal of Management Information Systems 8*, no. 4 (Spring 1992).

Carlson, David A., and Sudha Ram. "A Knowledge Representation for Modeling Organizational Productivity." *Journal of Organizational Computing 2*, no. 2 (1992).

Churchland, Paul M., and Patricia Smith Churchland. "Could a Machine Think?" *Scientific American* (January 1990).

Clifford, James, Henry C. Lucas, Jr. and Rajan Srikanth. "Integrating Mathematical and Symbolic Models Through AESOP: An Expert for Stock Options Pricing." *Information Systems Research 3*, no. 4 (December 1992).

Cox, Earl. "Applications of Fuzzy System Models." *AI Expert* (October 1992).

Cox, Earl. "Solving Problems with Fuzzy Logic." *AI Expert* (March 1992).

Creecy, Robert H., Brij M. Masand, Sephten J. Smith, and Davis L. Waltz. "Trading MIPS and Memory for Knowledge Engineering." *Communications of the ACM 35*, no. 8 (August 1992).

Dhar, Vasant. "Plausibility and Scope of Expert Systems in Management." *Journal of Management Information Systems* (Summer 1987).

Feigenbaum, Edward A. "The Art of Artificial Intelligence: Themes and Case Studies in Knowledge Engineering." *Proceedings of the IJCAI 5* (1977).

Feigenbaum, Edward A., and J. A. Feigenbaum (eds.). *Computers and Thought.* New York: McGraw-Hill, 1963.

Feigenbaum, Edward A., and Pamela McCorduck. *The Fifth Generation: Artificial Intelligence and Japan's Computer Challenge to the World*. Reading, MA: Addison-Wesley, 1985.

Gelernter, David. "The Metamorphosis of Information Management." *Scientific American* (August 1989).

Griggs, Kenneth. "Visual Aids that Model Organizations." *Journal of Organizational Computing 2*, no. 2 (1992).

Hayes-Roth, Frederick. "Knowledge-Based Expert Systems." *Spectrum IEEE* (October 1987).

Hinton, Gregory. "How Neural Networks Learn from Experience." *Scientific American* (September 1992).

Jacobs, Paul S., and Lisa F. Rau. "SCISOR: Extracting Information from On-line News." *Communications of the ACM 33*, no. 11 (November 1990).

Leonard-Barton, Dorothy, and John J. Sviokla. "Putting Expert Systems to Work." *Harvard Business Review* (March–April 1988).

Lin, Frank C., and Mei Lin. "Neural Networks in the Financial Industry." *AI Expert* (February 1993).

Marsden, James R., David E. Pingry, and Ming-Chian Ken Wang. "Intelligent Information and Organization Structures: An Integrated Design Approach." *Journal of Organizational Computing 2*, no. 2 (1992).

McCarthy, John. "Generality in Artificial Intelligence." *Communications of the ACM* (December 1987).

Meador, C. Lawrence, and Ed G. Mahler. "Choosing an Expert System Game Plan." *Datamation* (August 1, 1990).

Meyer, Marc H. and Kathleen Foley Curley. "An Applied Framework for Classifying the Complexity of Knowledge-Based Systems." *MIS Quarterly 15*, no. 4 (December 1991).

"M.1 Makes a Direct Hit." *PC Magazine* (April 16, 1985).

Michaelson, Robert, and Donald Michie. "Expert Systems in Business." *Datamation* (November 1983).

Motiwalla, Luvai, and Jay F. Nunamaker, Jr. "Mail-Man: A Knowledge-Based MAIL Assistant for Managers." *Journal of Organizational Computing 2*, no. 2 (1992).

Mykytyn, Kathleen, Peter P. Mykytyn, Jr., and Craig W. Stinkman. "Expert Systems: A Question of Liability." *MIS Quarterly 14*, no. 1 (March 1990).

Nash, Jim. "Expert Systems: A New Partnership." *AI Expert* (December 1992).

Rich, Elaine. *Artificial Intelligence*. New York: McGraw-Hill, 1983.

Searle, John R. "Is the Brain's Mind a Computer Program?" *Scientific American* (January 1990).

Self, Kevin. "Designing with Fuzzy Logic." *Spectrum IEEE* (November 1990).

Sibigtroth, James M. "Implementing Fuzzy Expert Rules in Hardware." *AI Expert* (April 1992).

Simon, H. A., and A. Newell. "Heuristic Problem Solving: The Next Advance in Operations Research." *Operations Research 6* (January–February 1958).

Stein, Eric W. "A Method to Identify Candidates for Knowledge Acquisition." *Journal of Management Information Systems 9*, no. 2 (Fall 1992).

Storey, Veda C., and Robert C. Goldstein, "Knowledge-Based Approaches to Database Design." *MIS Quarterly 17*, no. 1 (March 1993).

Stylianou, Anthony C., Gregory R. Madey, and Robert D. Smith. "Selection Criteria for Expert System Shells: A Socio-Technical Framework." *Communications of the ACM 35*, no. 10 (October 1992).

Sviokla, John J. "Expert Systems and Their Impact on the Firm: The Effects of PlanPower Use on the Information Processing Capacity of the Financial Collaborative." *Journal of Management Information Systems 6*, no. 3 (Winter 1989–90).

Sviokla, John J. "An Examination of the Impact of Expert Systems on the Firm: The Case of XCON." *MIS Quarterly 14*, no. 5 (June 1990).

Tam, Kar Yan. "Automated Construction of Knowledge-Bases from Examples." *Information Systems Research 1,* no. 2 (June 1990).

Tank, David W., and John J. Hopfield. "Collective Computation in Neuronlike Circuits." *Scientific American* (October 1987).

Trippi, Robert, and Efraim Turban. "The Impact of Parallel and Neural Computing on Managerial Decision Making." *Journal of Management Information Systems 6,* no. 3 (Winter 1989–1990).

Turban, Efraim, and Paul R. Watkins. "Integrating Expert Systems and Decision Support Systems." *MIS Quarterly* (June 1986).

Wallich, Paul. "Silicon Babies." *Scientific American* (December 1991).

Waltz, David L. "Artificial Intelligence." *Scientific American* (December 1982).

Weitzel, John R., and Kenneth R. Andrews. "A Company/University Joint Venture to Build a Knowledge-Based System." *MIS Quarterly 12,* no. 1 (March 1988).

Weitzel, John R., and Larry Kerschberg. "Developing Knowledge Based Systems: Reorganizing the System Development Life Cycle." *Communications of the ACM* (April 1989).

Weizenbaum, Joseph. *Computer Power and Human Reason—From Judgment to Calculation.* San Francisco: Freeman, 1976.

Weizenbaum, Joseph. "ELIZA—A Computer Program for the Study of Natural Language Communication Between Man and Machine." *Communications of the ACM* (January 1983).

White, George M. "Natural Language Understanding and Speech Recognition." *Communications of the ACM 33,* no. 8 (August 1990).

Zadeh, Lotfi A. "The Calculus of Fuzzy If/Then Rules." *AI Expert* (March 1992).

CHAPTER

13

Controlling Information Systems

Flood Brings Chicago's Systems to a Standstill

On April 13, 1992, a construction crew driving pilings into the Chicago River accidentally caused a leak in a network of coal delivery tunnels that had been built at the turn of the century. Within hours, more than 250 million gallons of water poured into the tunnels below Chicago's business district. The ensuing flood caused power failures and water damage that forced Chicago's businesses to a standstill.

Electrical cables supplying power to these businesses were shielded, but their electrical systems were not. Commonwealth Edison cut power to 200 buildings, and 200,000 people had to be evacuated immediately. The flood hit the headquarters of the Chicago Board of Trade (CBOT) which contains the computers that run Chicago's commodity trading systems and offices of 80 member brokerages. (The

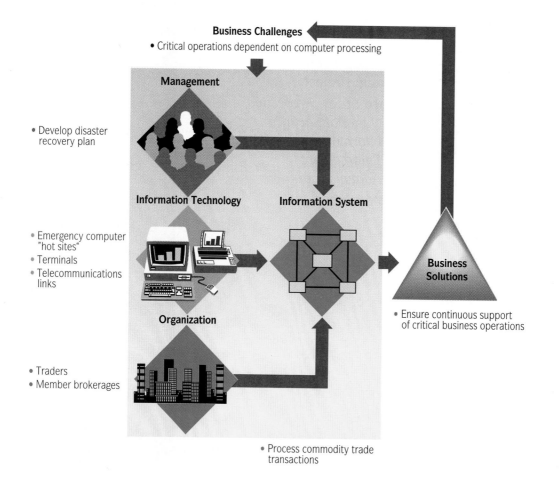

Chicago Board of Trade processes between 500,000 and 600,000 commodity futures transactions daily.) All trading stopped. Major banks, retail stores, and government centers were crippled. Billions of dollars reportedly were lost.

For most firms the problem was not flood water but power and telecommunications outages. Flood waters gushed into the sub-basement of the building occupied by Arthur Andersen, SC, a leading information systems consulting firm. The flood battered down the walls of an electrical vault, wiping out a packet-switched network that Andersen used to deliver its North American payroll. The network also carried time reports used for billing clients. A simultaneous power failure at another building brought down Andersen's mainframe.

Some firms, including the Chicago Board of Trade, had contingency plans for such disasters. Half of CBOT's 140-member staff packed backup tapes and traveled 35 miles to a Northbrook, Illinois, ''hot site'' run by Sungard Recovery Services to provide emergency computing facilities to subscribing businesses. Just six hours after the disaster, CBOT resumed processing trading transactions at its temporary computer headquarters. It arranged for brokers to use 30 terminals at the Chicago Mercantile Exchange, about five blocks away from its crippled headquarters, and terminals at 35 other firms. The terminals were linked by modem to CBOT's temporary mainframe facilities at Sungard. CBOT had daily reports required by traders flown by helicopter from the Sungard computer center to Chicago. The exchange was able to fully open trading.

Firms like CBOT that had disaster recovery plans also switched their information system operations to other computer centers. About 18 companies used the facilities of Comdisco Disaster Recovery Services. Other firms armed small groups of workers with laptop computers, cellular phones, fax, and copy machines, and had them work in local hotel rooms outside the evacuated downtown district.

Sources: ''Down and Out in Chicago,'' *InformationWEEK,* April 20, 1992; Julia King, ''Traders Wheel, Deal, Soar to Keep Chicago Commodities Exchange Humming in Flood,'' *Computerworld,* June 29, 1992; and Ellis Booker and Jim Nash, ''Great Chicago Flood of '92: IS Groups Stay High and Dry,'' *Computerworld,* April 20, 1992.

V ulnerability to floods and other natural disasters is but one of many problems that organizations relying on computer-based information systems may face. Hardware and software failures, employee errors, and use by unauthorized people may prevent information systems from running properly or running at all.

Computer systems play such a critical role in business, government, and daily life that organizations must take special steps to protect their information systems and ensure that they are accurate and reliable. The Chicago Board of Trade and other Chicago firms with disaster recovery plans took these steps; others did not. This chapter describes how information systems can be *controlled* so that they serve the purposes for which they are intended.

After completing this chapter you will be able to:

- Show why automated information systems are so vulnerable to destruction, error, and abuse.
- Describe the role of controls in safeguarding information systems.
- Distinguish between general controls and application controls.
- Describe the most important techniques for controlling information systems.
- Identify the factors that must be considered when developing the controls for information systems.
- Explain the importance of auditing information systems.

13.1 System Vulnerability and Abuse

Before computer automation, data about individuals or organizations were maintained and secured as paper records dispersed in separate business or organizational units. Information systems concentrate data in computer files that can potentially be accessed more easily by large numbers of people and by groups outside the organization. Consequently, automated data are more susceptible to destruction, fraud, error, and misuse.

When computer systems fail to run or work as required, firms that depend heavily on computers experience a serious loss of business function. Figure 13.1

Figure 13.1

Downtime's Downside. The study, commissioned by Stratus Computer Inc. and conducted by New York research firm Find/SVP, surveyed 450 IS executives at Fortune 1000 firms. It found that unplanned system downtime occurs nine times per year, on average; systems stay down an average four hours; and customer dissatisfaction and lost productivity are the two most negative effects of the crashes. *Adapted from John P. McPartlin, "The True Cost of Downtime," InformationWEEK (August 3, 1992). Reprinted by permission of InformationWeek and Stratus Computer, Inc.*

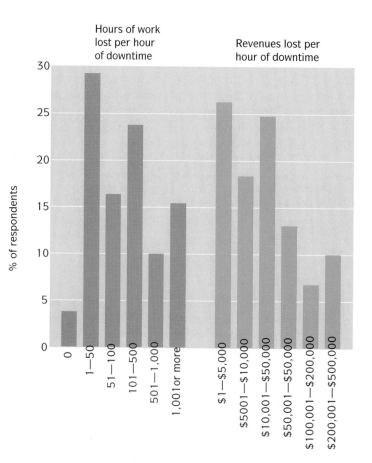

shows the results of one survey of 450 Fortune 1000 firms: Disruptions in computer service cost U.S. businesses $4 billion a year and result in at least 37 million hours of lost worker productivity. The longer computer systems are "down," the more serious the consequences for the firm. Some firms relying on computers to process their critical business transactions might experience a total loss of business function if they lose computer capability for more than a few days.

Why Systems Are Vulnerable

There are many advantages to information systems that are properly safeguarded. But when large amounts of data are stored in electronic form they are vulnerable to many more kinds of threats than when they exist in manual form. For example, an organization's entire recordkeeping system can be destroyed by a computer hardware malfunction. Table 13.1 lists the most common threats against computerized information. They can stem from technical, organizational, and environmental factors compounded by poor management decisions.

Computerized systems are especially vulnerable to such threats for the following reasons:

- A complex information system cannot be replicated manually. Most information cannot be printed or is too voluminous to be handled manually.
- There is usually no visible trace of changes in computerized systems because computer records can be read only by the computer.
- Computerized procedures appear to be invisible and are not easily understood or audited.
- The development and operation of automated systems require specialized technical expertise, which cannot be easily communicated to end users. Systems are open to abuse by highly technical staff members who are not well integrated into the organization. (Programmers and computer operators can make unauthorized changes in software while information is being processed or can use computer facilities for unauthorized purposes. Employees may make unauthorized copies of data files for illegal purposes.)
- Although the chances of disaster in automated systems are no greater than in manual systems, the effect of a disaster can be much more extensive. In some cases, all of the system's records can be destroyed and lost forever.
- On-line information systems are even more difficult to control because data files can be accessed immediately and directly through computer terminals. Legitimate users may gain easy access to computer data that were previously not available to them. They may be able to scan records or entire files that they are not authorized to view. By obtaining valid users' logons and passwords, unauthorized individuals can also gain access to such systems. The chances of unauthorized access to or manipulation of data in on-line systems are considerably higher than in the batch environment.

Table 13.1   THREATS TO COMPUTERIZED INFORMATION SYSTEMS

Hardware failure	Fire
Software failure	Electrical problems
Personnel actions	User errors
Terminal access penetration	Program changes
Theft of data, services, equipment	Telecommunications problems

New Vulnerabilities

Advances in telecommunications and computer software have magnified these vulnerabilities. Through telecommunications networks, information systems in different locations can be interconnected. The potential for unauthorized access, abuse, or fraud is not limited to a single location but can occur at any access point in the network.

Additionally, more complex and diverse hardware, software, organizational, and personnel arrangements are required for telecommunications networks, creating new areas and opportunities for penetration and manipulation. Wireless networks using radio-based technology are even more vulnerable to penetration because radio frequency bands are easy to scan. The vulnerabilities of telecommunications networks are illustrated in Figure 13.2. Developing a workable system of controls for telecommunications networks is a complex and troubling problem.

The efforts of "hackers" to penetrate computer networks have been widely publicized. A **hacker** is a person who gains unauthorized access to a computer network for profit, criminal mischief, or personal pleasure. The potential damage from intruders is frightening. In July 1992, a Federal grand jury in Manhattan indicted five computer hackers who belonged to a group called the Masters of Deception. They were charged with breaking into the information systems of three regional telephone companies, numerous credit bureaus, and BankAmerica Corporation, stealing telephone service and selling information on how to obtain credit reports.

Most recently, alarm has risen over hackers propagating **computer viruses,** rogue software programs that spread rampantly from system to system, clogging computer memory or destroying programs or data. The most notorious virus outbreak occurred in November 1988, when Robert Morris, a brilliant computer science student, introduced a program through a Cornell University terminal that spread uncontrollably throughout the Internet network, which ties

Hacker: A person who gains unauthorized access to a computer network for profit, criminal mischief, or personal pleasure.

Computer virus: Rogue software programs that are difficult to detect and spread rapidly through computer systems, destroying data or disrupting processing and memory systems.

Figure 13.2

Telecommunications network vulnerabilities. Telecommunications networks are highly vulnerable to natural failure of hardware and software and to misuse by programmers, computer operators, maintenance staff, and end users. It is possible to "tap" communications lines and illegally intercept data. High-speed transmission over twisted wire communications channels causes interference called crosstalk. Radiation can disrupt a network at various points as well.

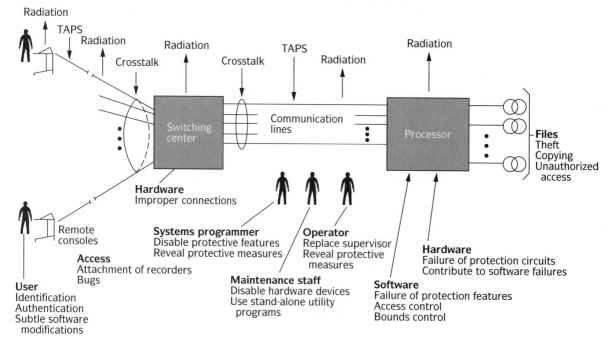

together numerous other networks, including National Science Foundation Network (NSF Net) which links universities, research labs, and other institutions. Morris intended his program to reside quietly on Internet computers, but it echoed throughout the network in minutes, tying up computer memory and storage space as it copied and recopied itself hundreds of thousands of times.

The virus was quickly detected, but hundreds of computer centers in research institutions, universities, and military bases had to shut down. Estimates of the number of systems actually infected ranged from 6,000 to 250,000. A virus that was not intended to harm caused upwards of $100 million in lost machine time, lost access, and direct labor costs for recovery and cleanup.

In addition to spreading via computer networks, viruses can invade computerized information systems from "infected" disks from an outside source or through infected machines. The potential for massive damage and loss from future computer viruses remains. Figure 13.3 illustrates four stages of viral infection, each progressively more difficult and expensive to recover from.

Fears mounted about predictions of a Michelangelo virus that was scheduled to erupt on March 6, 1992 to destroy computer data on hard disks around the globe. The virus was so-named because its creator programmed it to come alive on Michelangelo's 517th birthday. Alarmists worried that hundreds of thousands of systems could be affected. Fortunately, when the dreaded day arrived, only a few hundred systems reported damage. Organizations were able to use antivirus software and screening procedures to reduce the chances of infection. **Antivirus software** is special software designed to check computer systems and disks for the presence of various computer viruses. Often the software can eliminate the virus from the infected area.

Advances in computer software have also increased the chances of information system misuse and abuse. Using fourth-generation languages, discussed in Chapter 5, end users can now perform programming functions that were formerly reserved for technical specialists. They can produce programs that inadvertently create errors, and they can manipulate the organization's data for illegitimate purposes. Chapter 15 contains a detailed discussion of computer crime and abuse. The Window on Organizations describes one example of how easily data can be manipulated for extremely harmful purposes.

The growth of database systems, where data are shared by multiple application areas, has also created new vulnerabilities. All data are often stored in one common location, but many users may have the right to access and modify them. It may not be easy to identify who is using or possibly misusing the data in such circumstances. Since the data are typically used by more than one organizational unit, the effect of an error may reverberate throughout the organization. There may also be less chance of discovering errors, since each functional unit has less individual control over the data, and therefore has fewer grounds for knowing whether the computer is right.

Antivirus software: Software designed to detect and often eliminate computer viruses from an information system.

Concerns for System Builders and Users

The heightened vulnerability of automated data has created special concerns for the builders and users of information systems. These concerns include disaster, security, and administrative error.

DISASTER   Computer hardware, programs, data files, and other equipment can be destroyed by fires, power failures, or other disasters. Such disasters can disrupt normal operations and even bring an entire organization to a standstill. It may take many years and millions of dollars to reconstruct destroyed data files and computer programs. If an organization needs them to function on a day-to-day basis, it will no longer be able to operate. This is why Visa USA Inc., for example, employs elaborate emergency backup facilities.

Virus →

Local main memory
- Affects currently executing application
- Simple to remove
- Limited damage if contained

Fixed local storage
- May infect all stored applications
- Potential local data damage
- Requires one to five man-hours to remove
- Moderate damage if caught in time

Shared file system

—Utilities —Compilers —Editors —Tools	—Shared applications	—Communications —System files

- Widespread system infection
- May cause substantial damage
- Complex recovery

Systemwide removable media

Floppy disks	Write-once read-many disks	Removable hard disks	Tape backups
Widely dispersed Difficult to locate Easy to overlook		Archived for considerable periods May reintroduce old infection	

- Extremely difficult to recover
- Media may not be traceable
- Probability of reinfection is extremely high

Figure 13.3
How bad is it? Four stages of viral infection. The degree of damage to a computer system can be assessed by the level of penetration of the virus. At the first stage, the virus is contained in local main memory; it then moves to the second stage, residing in fixed local storage. At this point the virus is still localized and damage would be moderate if the virus were detected and eradicated at this time. Once the virus self-replicates and infects the shared file system, complex recovery is required to restore any damage and to remove the virus. The fourth stage, infection of the systemwide removable media, is extremely difficult to recover and the probability of reinfection is very high. *Source: Computer Virus Industry Association. Adapted from John D. McAfee, "Managing the Virus Threat,"* Computerworld, *February 13, 1989. Copyright 1989 by CW Publishing Inc. Framingham, MA. 01701. Reprinted from* Computerworld.

Visa USA Inc. has duplicate mainframes, duplicate network pathways, duplicate terminals, and duplicate power supplies. Visa even uses a duplicate data center in McLean, Virginia, to handle half of its transactions and to serve as an emergency backup to its primary data center in San Mateo, California.

Fault-tolerant computer systems contain extra hardware, software, and power supply components that can back the system up and keep it running to prevent system failure. Fault-tolerant computers contain extra memory chips, processors, and disk storage devices. (See the Window on Technology.) They can use special software routines or self-checking logic built into their circuitry to detect hardware failures and automatically switch to a backup device. Parts from these computers can be removed and repaired without disruption to the computer system.

Fault-tolerant computer systems: Systems that contain extra hardware, software and power supply components that can back the system up and keep it running to prevent system failure.

ORGANIZATIONS

Should the Public Have Access to the Global Positioning System?

Unauthorized and wrongful use of electronic data is a major problem for many organizations. But what happens if responsible people have legitimate differences over the appropriate use of certain sets of data and disagree on the need to keep that data secret? The question of what data an organization keeps secret and what it makes available to the public is an ongoing issue. Witness the public fury when auto manufacturers reveal previously secret test data about safety hazards on certain automobile models. Note the laws many governments have on their books regulating the use of insider information in financial trading and mandating the availability of personal credit data. However, the issue takes on special significance when critical military data are the subject of a dispute over their use and over the need to keep them secret. That is precisely the dispute that has arisen over data produced by the United States Defense Department's Global Positioning System (GPS).

The Global Positioning System is the latest development in the continuing search to be able to pinpoint exact locations on the earth, a critical need ever since human beings began sailing out of sight of land thousands of years ago. It was originally designed by the U.S. Department of Defense as part of a weapons system that could pinpoint precision attacks by missiles. The GPS uses signals sent from 24 satellites orbiting the earth to pinpoint a location anywhere on earth. Receivers take signals transmitted by the satellites and translate them using an algorithm into points of latitude and longitude. The GPS is the most accurate navigation and targeting system ever devised.

GPS satellites transmit two navigation signals. One, which is available to commercial users in shipping and aviation, has a built-in error. It can bring users to within 328 feet of a known location. The second is an unadulterated signal that can only be detected by special military receivers. It can target almost any point on earth to within

38 feet. Many who watched the news reports out of the Gulf War remember vividly the guided missiles that were able to fly through the doors of a targeted building, a precision made possible by GPS technology.

The problem is, GPS signals are broadcast all over the world, and unless scrambled in some way, they are available to be used by anyone. They provide an inexpensive way for countries and terrorist groups to launch their own accurately-targeted guided missiles. Defense experts worry that with current computer hardware and software technology, enemy nations could tap into GPS data and create a signal that is precise enough to guide their missiles to U.S. targets. For a relatively modest cost, nations can combine satellite imagery, which can be purchased from the U.S., France, and Russia, with small, high-speed computers and GPS receivers to create a constantly updated digital map with almost pinpoint accuracy. A number of countries in the world are now capable of using GPS-guided cruise missiles, including Egypt, India, Indonesia, Iran, Iraq, Israel, North Korea, Pakistan, and Taiwan. The equipment to use GPS for this purpose is commercially available and easily obtainable.

Even using the scrambled signal, a margin of error of 328 feet off target is precise enough to target certain kinds of arms, such as atomic bombs and chemical weapons. Moreover, the FAA and the Coast Guard have proven themselves more than capable of using technology to correct the precision of the data, an alternative foreign governments and terrorist groups could also easily use.

The U.S. Coast Guard is building a series of land-based radio beacons that, used in conjunction with the GPS signals, will allow a ship at sea to designate its location to within 16 feet. As a Coast Guard spokesperson said, with the ability to locate a ship so precisely, "we have taken the search out of search and rescue." The FAA and the International Air Transport Association

(which represents 95 percent of the world's airlines) also plan to increase the system's precision through signals emanating from land-based stations. Using this planned adjunct system, an airplane would be able to pinpoint its own location to within 10 feet, allowing pilots to make landings in bad weather at any of 5,000 runways in the U.S. alone. Airlines believe that using the GPS could save them hundreds of millions of dollars by enabling them to fly more efficient routes. Such improvements are eagerly sought by the flying public, the airlines, the insurance companies, and everyone else. Everyone else, that is, except the Department of Defense which owns the data. The Department of Defense wants the GPS data to be broadcast in code in order to make it impossible for anyone else to use.

Solutions to the conflict over the use of this data have been offered. One is that the system would simply be turned off at a moment of crisis. However, that solution raises several problems. If the system is turned off, not only will mischief makers in other countries be denied access to it, but the U.S. missiles and military aircraft also will not be able to use it. In addition, at the moment the system is turned off, hundreds of commercial flights that are depending upon the system could be endangered. European countries are reluctant to use a system that the United States could shut down at any time.

Sources: Daniel Pearl, "FAA Clears Civilian Airlines to Use Military Satellite Signals in Navigation," *The Wall Street Journal,* February 18, 1994 and John J. Fialka, "Airliners Can Exploit U.S. Guidance System, But So Can Enemies," *The Wall Street Journal,* August 26, 1993.

To Think About: How do you think you might solve the issue of these conflicting interests? Think of and describe other situations where data security might be or is an issue with legitimate interests on both sides.

TECHNOLOGY

Fault Tolerance Backs Up a Single European Currency

If the European Community is a unified economic area, it makes sense to have it use a single currency and a central bank. Anticipating a single European Currency Unit (ECU) and European Central Bank, European banks have selected fault-tolerant computer systems from Stratus Computer Inc. to run clearing systems for cross-border ECU transactions. Fault-tolerant computers contain one or more duplicates of every part and guarantee maximum downtime of no more than a few minutes a year.

The ECU, which derives its value from a basket of European currencies, was initially symbolic but is expected to be adopted by all members of the European Community. Banks need to ensure that payments in that currency can be cleared in the best way possible.

Any clearing system for a single European currency must be extremely efficient and reliable. Foreign exchange systems must be linked. The European Central Bank must be able to perform open market operations similar to the U.S. Federal Reserve System. In 1992, the ECU Banking Association, which represents 90 European banks, processed 40 billion ECUs a day. The clearing system cannot afford failure. There are

critical points in the day, especially toward the end of the day's trading cycle, when it needs to provide information back to other banks.

The Stratus systems, which are widely used in European trading rooms (more than 80 percent of London's stock market uses Stratus equipment), can support greatly increased transaction flows in critical on-line transaction processing environments. Stratus's fault-tolerant design is especially well-suited to financial number crunching. The machines are designed to keep working even when they break.

One director of a London investment bank observed that the Stratus hardware is very reliable, as is the vendor's customer assistance center. Stratus machines automatically interface with its customer assistance center so that there are diagnostics and alarms when things go wrong. Most of the components are backed up with duplicates. The system is modular, so that failure of one component will not spell disaster. If a unit fails, it does not take other modules down too. Faulty components are easily replaced. Built-in battery packs can support the system even during power failures. Stratus computers offer the high-risk

financial community an unmatched level of reliability.

Securities dealers use Stratus systems to alert the marketplace to prices and to process buy and sell orders. The system updates itself in real-time as trades are made, and it reports deals immediately to the London Stock Exchange. The system even calculates profit and relays details for back-office settlement in real time.

However, some dealers question Stratus's staying power as a major computer hardware vendor and the compatibility of new Stratus models with various versions of UNIX.

Source: Bob O'Connor, "Stratus Adopts European Accent," *InformationWEEK* (August 17, 1992).

To Think About: Why are fault-tolerant computers an appropriate technology for currency clearing systems? Can you suggest other applications that would benefit from fault-tolerant technology? What are the disadvantages of using the Stratus fault-tolerant computers for European currency clearing?

MANAGEMENT

Managing Network Security: The Enemy Within

Desktop data and LANs represent the weak link in many corporate security chains. As corporations move critical data from mainframes to distributed networked environments, LANs have become a major cost drain. Various estimates put losses from networked data abuse at close to $2 billion each year. The original security measures companies designed for their centralized mainframe computer systems may no longer fit. Securing networks has become a major management problem.

It is widely agreed that users, rather than new technology, pose the biggest threat to network security. Managers need to find ways to teach users sound security procedures and to ensure that users adhere to them. Most managers are more concerned about security breaches created by employees inside the firm than about penetration of networks by outsiders.

Jack Skalon, network administrator for University Hospital Consortium in Oak Brook, Illinois, combines commonsense policies with the security features built into the NetWare network operating system to monitor network users in order to keep security tight among the organization's 115 users on 10 Novell file servers. Skalon scans the network four or five times a week to make sure all software is licensed and certified virus-free. The hospital keeps the computer room locked and off-limits to all but a few selected supervisors.

United Parcel Service scans its network drives for viruses each day and ties an information system audit into an annual accounting audit at all UPS sites. The firm checks to see that its security procedures are being followed at the same time it is measuring costs.

Hypobank in New York disables access to the floppy disk drive for all microcomputers throughout the bank. If a user tries to insert a disk into the off-limits drive, a product called Watchdog Director made by Fisher International Systems Corporation in Naples, Florida, flashes a warning message and creates an audit trail to identify who has been trying to load disks.

The trick is to be effective without costly overkill. Not every site or application requires bulletproof security unless it houses mission-critical data. DHL Airways uses this enough-but-not-too-much approach to manage its LAN security. It sorts key financial data on a secure mainframe but is moving to distributed networked IBM RISC System/6000 workstations and plans to run a new accounting system on a networked IBM AS/400 minicomputer. IBM assured Michael Lanier, DHL's chief information officer, that it had security capabilities for such networks.

According to Robert Courtney, head of a LAN security consulting firm in Port Ewen, New York, the issue is accountability. If managers cannot hold people accountable for their actions, no amount of technology will help.

Sources: Joseph Maglitta and John P. Mello, Jr., "The Enemy Within," *Computerworld* (December 7, 1992), and Jon Pepper, "The Bigger the Network, the Scarier," *InformationWEEK* (September 7, 1992).

To Think About: One manager has said that information protection is technology and psychology. Do you agree? Why?

On-line transaction processing: Transaction processing mode in which transactions entered on-line are immediately processed by the computer.

Fault-tolerant technology is used by firms for critical applications with heavy on-line transaction processing requirements. In **on-line transaction processing,** transactions entered on-line are immediately processed by the computer. Multitudinous changes to databases, reporting, or requests for information occur each instant.

Rather than build their own backup facilities, many firms contract with disaster recovery firms, such as Comdisco Disaster Recovery Services in Rosemont, Illinois, and Sungard Recovery Services headquartered in Wayne, Pennsylvania. The chapter opening vignette showed how these disaster recovery firms provide "hot sites" housing spare computers at various locations around the country where subscribing firms can run their critical applications in an emergency. Disaster recovery firms also offer "cold sites," special buildings designed to house computer equipment; they do not contain computers, but they can be made operational in one week.

SECURITY

Security: Policies, procedures, and technical measures used to prevent unauthorized access, alteration, theft, or physical damage to information systems.

Security refers to the policies, procedures, and technical measures used to prevent unauthorized access or alteration, theft, and physical damage to record systems. Security can be promoted with an array of techniques and tools to safeguard computer hardware, software, communications networks, and data. We have already discussed disaster protection measures. The Window on Management shows how management policies and procedures can make networks more secure. Other tools and techniques for promoting security will be described in subsequent sections.

ERRORS Computers can also serve as instruments of error, severely disrupting or destroying an organization's recordkeeping and operations. Errors in automated systems can occur at many points in the processing cycle: through data entry, program error, computer operations, and hardware. Figure 13.4 illustrates all of the points in a typical processing cycle where errors can occur. Even minor mistakes in automated systems can have disastrous financial or operational repercussions. For instance, on February 25, 1991, during Operation Desert Storm, a Patriot missile defense system operating at Dharan, Saudi Arabia, failed

Figure 13.4
Points in the processing cycle where errors can occur. Each of the points illustrated in this figure represents a control point where special automated and/or manual procedures should be established to reduce the risk of errors during processing.

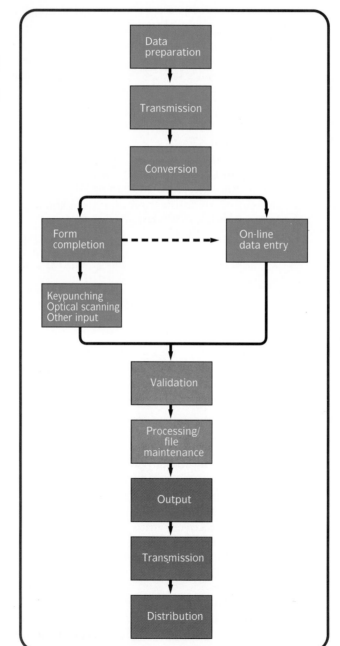

to track and intercept an incoming Scud missile launched by Iraq. The failure was traced to a software error in the system's weapons control computer. The Scud hit an Army barracks, killing 28 Americans.

13.2 Controls

To minimize errors, disaster, computer crime, and breaches of security, special policies and procedures must be incorporated into the design and implementation of information systems. The combination of manual and automated measures that safeguard information systems and ensure that they perform according to management standards is termed controls. **Controls** consist of all the methods, policies, and organizational procedures that ensure the safety of the organization's assets, the accuracy and reliability of its accounting records, and operational adherence to management standards.

> **Controls:** All of the methods, policies, and procedures that ensure protection of the organization's assets, accuracy and reliability of its records, and operational adherence to management standards.

In the past, the control of information systems was treated as an afterthought, addressed only toward the end of implementation, just before the system was installed. Today, however, organizations are so critically dependent on information systems that vulnerabilities and control issues must be identified as early as possible. The control of an information system must be an integral part of its design. Users and builders of systems must pay close attention to controls throughout the system's life span.

Computer systems are controlled by a combination of general controls and application controls.

General controls are those that control the design, security, and use of computer programs and the security of data files in general throughout the organization. On the whole, general controls apply to all computerized applications and consist of a combination of system software and manual procedures that create an overall control environment.

> **General controls:** Overall controls that establish a framework for controlling the design, security, and use of computer systems throughout an organization.

Application controls are specific controls unique to each computerized application, such as payroll, accounts receivable, and order processing. They consist of both controls applied from the user functional area of a particular system and from programmed procedures.

> **Application controls:** Specific controls unique to each computerized application.

General Controls

General controls are overall controls that ensure the effective operation of programmed procedures. They apply to all application areas. General controls include the following:

- Controls over the system implementation process.
- Software controls.
- Physical hardware controls.
- Computer operations controls.
- Data security controls.
- Administrative disciplines, standards, and procedures.

> **IMPLEMENTATION CONTROLS**
>
> **Implementation controls:** Audit of the systems development process at various points to make sure that it is properly controlled and managed.

Implementation controls audit the system development process at various points to ensure that it is properly controlled and managed. The system development audit should look for the presence of formal review points at various stages of development that enable users and management to approve or disapprove the implementation. (Examples of such review points are user and management sign-offs on the initial systems proposal, design specifications, conversion, testing, and the postimplementation audit described in Chapter 8.)

The system development audit should also examine the level of user involvement at each stage of implementation and check for the use of a formal cost/benefit methodology in establishing system feasibility. The audit should also look for the use of controls and quality assurance techniques for program development, conversion, and testing. (These issues are discussed in Chapters 8–9).

An important though frequently neglected requirement of systems building is appropriate documentation. Without good documentation that shows how a system operates from both a technical and a user standpoint, an information system may be difficult, if not impossible, to operate, maintain, or use. The system development audit should look for system, user, and operations documentation that conforms to formal standards.

SOFTWARE CONTROLS

Software controls: Controls to ensure the security and reliability of software.

Program security controls: Controls designed to prevent unauthorized changes to programs in systems that are already in production.

Controls are essential for the various categories of software used in computer systems. **Software controls** monitor the use of system software and prevent unauthorized access of software programs, system software, and computer programs.

System software controls govern the software for the operating system, which regulates and manages computer resources to facilitate execution of application programs. System software controls are also used for compilers, utility programs, reporting of operations, file setup and handling, and library recordkeeping. System software is an important control area because it performs overall control functions for the programs that directly process data and data files. **Program security controls** are designed to prevent unauthorized changes to programs in systems that are already in production.

HARDWARE CONTROLS

Hardware controls: Controls to ensure the physical security and correct performance of computer hardware.

Hardware controls ensure that computer hardware is physically secure and check for equipment malfunction. Computer hardware should be physically secured so that it can be accessed only by authorized individuals. Access to rooms where computers operate should be restricted to computer operations personnel. Computer terminals in other areas or microcomputers can be kept in locked rooms. Computer equipment should be specially protected against fires and extremes of temperature and humidity. Organizations that are critically dependent on their computers must also make provisions for emergency backup in case of power failure.

Many kinds of computer hardware also contain mechanisms that check for equipment malfunction. Parity checks detect equipment malfunctions responsible for altering bits within bytes during processing. Validity checks monitor the structure of on-off bits within bytes to make sure that it is valid for the character set of a particular computer machine. Echo checks verify that a hardware device is performance ready. Chapter 4 discusses computer hardware in detail.

COMPUTER OPERATIONS CONTROLS

Computer operations controls: Procedures to ensure that programmed procedures are consistently and correctly applied to data storage and processing.

Computer operations controls apply to the work of the computer department and help ensure that programmed procedures are consistently and correctly applied to the storage and processing of data. They include controls over the setup of computer processing jobs, operations software and computer operations, and backup and recovery procedures for processing that ends abnormally.

Instructions for running computer jobs should be fully documented, reviewed, and approved by a responsible official. Controls over operations software include manual procedures designed to both prevent and detect error. These include specified operating instructions for system software, restart and recovery procedures, procedures for the labeling and disposition of input and output magnetic tapes, and procedures for specific applications.

Human-operator errors at a computer system at the Shell Pipeline Corporation caused the firm to ship 93,000 barrels of crude oil to the wrong trader. This

NOV 06,FRI 13:41:

Sophisticated computer operations controls monitor the computer operations across the nation for this corporation.

one error cost Shell $2 million. A computer operator at Exxon Corporation headquarters inadvertently erased valuable records about the 1989 grounding of the Exxon *Valdez* and the Alaskan oil spill that were stored on magnetic tape. Such errors could have been avoided had the companies incorporated tighter operational safeguards.

System software can maintain a system log detailing all activity during processing. This log can be printed for review so that hardware malfunction, abnormal endings, and operator actions can be investigated. Specific instructions for backup and recovery can be developed so that in the event of a hardware or software failure, the recovery process for production programs, system software, and data files does not create erroneous changes in the system.

DATA SECURITY CONTROLS

Data security controls:
Controls to ensure that data files on either disk or tape are not subject to unauthorized access, change, or destruction.

Data security controls ensure that data files on either disk or tape are not subject to unauthorized access, change, or destruction. Such controls are required for data files when they are in use and when they are being held for storage. It is easier to control data files in batch systems, since access is limited to operators who run the batch jobs. However, on-line and real-time systems are vulnerable at several points. They can be accessed through terminals as well as by operators during production runs.

When data can be input on-line through a terminal, entry of unauthorized input must be prevented. For example, a credit note could be altered to match a sales invoice on file. In such situations, security can be developed on several levels:

- Terminals can be physically restricted so that they are available only to authorized individuals.
- System software can include the use of passwords assigned only to authorized individuals. No one can log on to the system without a valid password.
- Additional sets of passwords and security restrictions can be developed for specific systems and applications. For example, data security software can limit access to specific files, such as the files for the accounts receivable system. It can restrict the type of access so that only individuals authorized to update these specific files will have the ability to do so. All others will only be able to read the files or will be denied access altogether.

Systems that allow on-line inquiry and reporting must have data files secured. Figure 13.5 illustrates the security allowed for two sets of users of an on-line personnel database with sensitive information such as employees' salaries, benefits, and medical histories. One set of users consists of all employees who perform clerical functions such as inputting employee data into the system. All individuals with this type of profile can update the system but can neither read nor update sensitive fields such as salary, medical history, or earnings data. Another profile applies to a divisional manager, who cannot update the system but who can read all employee data fields for his or her division, including medical history and salary. These profiles would be established and maintained by a data security system. A multilayered data security system is essential for ensuring that this information can be accessed only by authorized persons. The data security system illustrated in Figure 13.5 provides very fine-grained security restrictions, such as allowing authorized personnel users to inquire about all employee information except in confidential fields such as salary or medical history.

Although the security risk of files maintained off-line is smaller, such data files on disk or tape can be removed for unauthorized purposes. These can be secured in lockable storage areas, with tight procedures so that they are released only for authorized processing. Usage logs and library records can be maintained for each removable storage device if it is labeled and assigned a unique identity number.

ADMINISTRATIVE CONTROLS **Administrative controls** are formalized standards, rules, procedures, and control disciplines to ensure that the organization's controls are properly executed and

Figure 13.5
Security profiles for a personnel system. These two examples represent two security profiles or data security patterns that might be found in a personnel system. Depending upon the security profile, a user would have certain restrictions on access to various systems, locations, or data in an organization.

SECURITY PROFILE 1

User: Personnel Dept. Clerk

Location: Division 1

Employee Identification
Codes with This Profile: 00753, 27834, 37665, 44116

Data Field Restrictions	Type of Access
All employee data for Division 1 only	Read and Update
• Medical history data	None
• Salary	None
• Pensionable earnings	None

SECURITY PROFILE 2

User: Divisional Personnel Manager

Location: Division 1

Employee Identification
Codes with This Profile: 27321

Data Field Restrictions	Type of Access
All employee data for Division 1 only	Read Only

enforced. The most important administrative controls are 1) segregation of functions, 2) written policies and procedures, and 3) supervision.

Segregation of functions is a fundamental principle of internal control in any organization. In essence, it means that job functions should be designed to minimize the risk of errors or fraudulent manipulation of the organization's assets. The individuals responsible for operating systems should not be the same ones who can initiate transactions that change the assets held in these systems. Responsibilities for input, processing, and output are usually divided among different people to restrict what each one can do with the system. For example, the individuals who operate the system should not have the authority to initiate payments or to sign checks. A typical arrangement is to have the organization's information systems department responsible for data and program files and end users responsible for initiating input transactions or correcting errors. Within the information systems department, the duties of programmers and analysts are segregated from those of computer equipment operators. (The organization of the information systems department is discussed in Chapter 3.)

Written policies and procedures establish formal standards for controlling information system operations. Procedures must be formalized in writing and authorized by the appropriate level of management. Accountabilities and responsibilities must be clearly specified.

Supervision of personnel involved in control procedures ensures that the controls for an information system are performing as intended. With supervision, weaknesses can be spotted, errors corrected, and deviations from standard procedures identified. Without adequate supervision, the best-designed set of controls may be bypassed, short-circuited, or neglected.

Weakness in each of these general controls can have a widespread effect on programmed procedures and data throughout the organization. Table 13.2 summarizes the effect of weaknesses in major general control areas.

Table 13.2 EFFECT OF WEAKNESS IN GENERAL CONTROLS

Weakness	Impact
Implementation controls	New systems or systems that have been modified will have errors or fail to function as required.
Software controls (program security)	Unauthorized changes can be made in processing. The organization may not be sure of which programs or systems have been changed.
Software controls (system software)	These controls may not have a direct effect on individual applications. Since other general controls depend heavily on system software, a weakness in this area impairs the other general controls.
Physical hardware controls	Hardware may have serious malfunctions or may break down altogether, introducing numerous errors or destroying computerized records.
Computer operations controls	Random errors may occur in a system. (Most processing will be correct, but occasionally it may not be.)
Data file security controls	Unauthorized changes can be made in data stored in computer systems or unauthorized individuals can access sensitive information.
Administrative controls	All of the other controls may not be properly executed or enforced.

Application Controls

Application controls are specific controls within each separate computer application, such as payroll or order processing. They include both automated and manual procedures that ensure that only authorized data are completely and accurately processed by that application. The controls for each application should take account of the whole sequence of processing, manual and computer, from the first steps taken to prepare transactions to the production and use of final output.

Not all of the application controls discussed here are used in every information system. Some systems require more of these controls than others, depending on the importance of the data and the nature of the application.

Application controls focus on the following objectives:

1. *Completeness of input and update.* All current transactions must reach the computer and be recorded on computer files.
2. *Accuracy of input and update.* Data must be accurately captured by the computer and correctly recorded on computer files.
3. *Validity.* Data must be authorized or otherwise checked with regard to the appropriateness of the transaction. (In other words, the transaction must reflect the right event in the external world. The validity of an address change, for example, refers to whether a transaction actually captured the right address for a specific individual.)
4. *Maintenance.* Data on computer files must continue to remain correct and current.

Application controls can be classified as 1) input controls, 2) processing controls, and 3) output controls.

INPUT CONTROLS

Input controls check data for accuracy and completeness when they enter the system. There are specific input controls for input authorization, data conversion, data editing, and error handling.

Input authorization. Input must be properly authorized, recorded, and monitored as source documents flow to the computer. For example, formal procedures can be set up to authorize only selected members of the sales department to prepare sales transactions for an order entry system. Sales input forms might be serially numbered, grouped into *batches,* and logged so that they can be tracked as they pass from sales units to the unit responsible for inputting them into the computer. The batches may require authorization signatures before they can be entered into the computer.

Data conversion. Input must be properly converted into computer transactions, with no errors as it is transcribed from one form to another. Transcription errors can be eliminated or reduced by keying input transactions directly into computer terminals from their source documents. (Point of sale systems can capture sales and inventory transactions directly by scanning product bar codes.)

Batch control totals can be established beforehand for transactions grouped in batches. These totals can range from a simple document count to totals for quantity fields such as total sales amount (for the batch). Computer programs count the batch totals from transactions input. Batches that do not balance are rejected.

On-line, real-time systems can also utilize control totals to reconcile with hard copy documents that feed input.

Edit checks. Various routines can be performed to edit input data for errors before they are processed. Transactions that do not meet edit criteria will be rejected. The edit routines can produce lists of errors to be corrected later. The most important types of edit techniques are summarized in Table 13.3.

An advantage of on-line, real-time systems is that editing can be performed up front. As each transaction is input and entered it can be edited, and the terminal

Input controls: Procedures to check data for accuracy and completeness when they enter the system, including input authorization, batch control totals, and edits.

Input authorization: Proper authorization, recording, and monitoring of source documents as they enter the computer system.

Data conversion: Process of properly transcribing data from one form into another form for computer transactions.

Batch control totals: A type of input control that requires counting transactions or any quantity field in a batch of transactions prior to processing for comparison and reconciliation after processing.

Edit checks: Routines performed to verify input data and correct errors prior to processing.

Table 13.3 IMPORTANT EDIT TECHNIQUES

Edit Technique	Description	Example
Reasonableness check	To be accepted, data must fall within certain limits set in advance, or they will be rejected.	If an order transaction is for 20,000 units and the largest order on record was 50 units, the transaction will be rejected.
Format checks	Characteristics of the contents (letter/digit), length, and sign of individual data fields are checked by the system.	A nine-position Social Security number should not contain any alphabetic characters.
Existence checks	The computer compares input reference data to tables or master files to make sure that valid codes are being used.	An employee can have a Fair Labor Standards Act code of only 1, 2, 3, 4, or 5. All other values for this field will be rejected.
Dependency checks	The computer checks whether a *logical* relationship is maintained between data for the *same* transaction. When it is not, the transaction is rejected.	A car loan initiation transaction should show a logical relationship between the size of the loan, the number of loan repayments, and the size of each installment.
Check digit	An extra reference number called a *check digit* follows an identification code and bears a mathematical relationship to the other digits. This extra digit is input with the data, recomputed by the computer, and the result compared with the one input.	See the check digit in Figure 13.6 for a product code using the Modulus 11 check digit system.

operator can be notified immediately if an error is found. Alternatively, the operator may fail to correct the error on purpose or by accident. The system can be designed to reject additional input until the error is corrected or to print a hard-copy error list that can be reviewed by others.

PROCESSING CONTROLS

Processing controls: Routines for establishing that data are complete and accurate during processing.

Run control totals: Procedures for controlling completeness of computer updating by generating control totals that reconcile totals before and after processing.

Computer matching: Processing control that matches input data to information held on master files.

Processing controls establish that data are complete and accurate during updating. The major processing controls are run control totals, computer matching, and programmed edit checks.

Run control totals reconcile the input control totals with the totals of items that have updated the file. Updating can be controlled by generating control totals during processing. The totals, such as total transactions processed or totals for critical quantities, can be compared manually or by computer. Discrepancies are noted for investigation.

Computer matching matches the input data with information held on master or suspense files, with unmatched items noted for investigation. Most matching occurs during input, but under some circumstances it may be required to ensure completeness of updating. For example, a matching program might match employee time cards with a payroll master file and report missing or duplicate time cards.

Edit checks verify reasonableness or consistency of data. Most edit checking occurs at the time data are input. However, certain applications require some

Product Code:	2	9	7	4	3
Weight:	6	5	4	3	2
Multiply each product code number by weight:	12	45	28	12	6

Sum results: $12 + 45 + 28 + 12 + 6 = 103$

Divide the sum by modulus: $103/11 = 9$ with remainder of 4

Subtract remainder from modulus number to obtain check digit: $11 - 4 = 7$

Add check digit to original product code to obtain new code: 297437

Figure 13.6
Check digit for a product code. This is a product code with the last position as a check digit, as developed by the Modulus 11 check digit system, the most common check digit method. The check digit is 7 and is derived by the steps listed in this figure. Errors in the transcription or transposition of this product code can be detected by a computer program that replicates the same procedure for deriving the check digit. If a data-entry person mistakenly keys in the product number as 29753, the program will read the first five digits and carry out the Modulus 11 process. It will derive a check digit of 4. When this is compared to the original check digit on the last position of the product code, the program will find that the check digits do not match and that an error has occurred.

type of reasonableness or dependency check during updating as well. For example, consistency checks might be utilized by a utility company to compare a customer's electric bill with previous bills. If the bill was 500 percent higher this month compared to last month, the bill would not be processed until the meter was rechecked.

OUTPUT CONTROLS

Output controls: Ensure that the results of computer processing are accurate, complete, and properly distributed.

Output controls ensure that the results of computer processing are accurate, complete, and properly distributed. Typical output controls include the following:

- Balancing output totals with input and processing totals.
- Reviews of the computer processing logs to determine that all of the correct computer jobs executed properly for processing.
- Audits of output reports to make sure that totals, formats, and critical details are correct and reconcilable with input.
- Formal procedures and documentation specifying authorized recipients of output reports, checks, or other critical documents.

Developing a Control Structure: Costs and Benefits

Information systems can make exhaustive use of all of the control mechanisms previously discussed. But they may be so expensive to build and so complicated to use that the system is economically or operationally unfeasible. Some cost/benefit analysis must be performed to determine which control mechanisms provide the most effective safeguards without sacrificing operational efficiency or cost.

One of the criteria that determine how much control is built into a system is the *importance of its data*. Major financial and accounting systems, for example, such as a payroll system or one that tracks purchases and sales on the stock exchange, must have higher standards of controls than a system to inventory employee training and skills or a "tickler" system to track dental patients and remind them that their six-month checkup is due.

Standing data, the data that are permanent and that affect transactions flowing into and out of a system (e.g., codes for existing products or cost centers) require closer monitoring than individual transactions. A single error in transaction data will affect only that transaction, while a standing data error may affect many or all transactions each time the file is processed.

The cost effectiveness of controls will also be influenced by the efficiency, complexity, and expense of each control technique. For example, complete one-for-one checking may be time-consuming and operationally impossible for a system that processes hundreds of thousands of utilities payments daily. But it might be possible to use this technique to verify only critical data such as dollar amounts and account numbers, while ignoring names and addresses.

A third consideration is the *level of risk* if a specific activity or process is not properly controlled. System builders can undertake a **risk assessment,** determining the likely frequency of a problem and the potential damage if it were to occur. For example, if an event is likely to occur no more than once a year, with a maximum of a $1000 loss to the organization, it would not be feasible to spend $20,000 on the design and maintenance of a control to protect against that event. However, if that same event could occur at least once a day, with a potential loss of over $300,000 a year, $100,000 spent on a control might be entirely appropriate.

Table 13.4 illustrates sample results of a risk assessment for an on-line order processing system that processes 30,000 orders per day. The probability of a power failure occurring in a one-year period is 30 percent. Loss of order transactions while power is down could range from $5000 to $200,000 for each occurrence, depending on how long processing was halted. The probability of embezzlement occurring over a yearly period is about 5 percent, with potential losses ranging from $1000 to $50,000 for each occurrence. User errors have a 98 percent chance of occurring over a yearly period, with losses ranging from $200 to $40,000 for each occurrence. The average loss for each event can be weighted by multiplying it by the probability of its occurrence annually to determine the expected annual loss. Once the risks have been assessed, system builders can concentrate on the control points with the greatest vulnerability and potential loss. In this case, controls should focus on ways to minimize the risk of power failures and user errors.

In some situations, organizations may not know the precise probability of threats occurring to their information systems, and they may not be able to quantify the impact of events that disrupt their information systems. In these

Table 13.4   ON-LINE ORDER PROCESSING RISK ASSESSMENT.

Exposure	Prob. of Occurr. (%)	Loss Range/ Average ($)	Expected Annual Loss ($)
Power failure	30	5000–200,000 (102,500)	30,750
Embezzlement	5	1000–50,000 (25,500)	1,275
User error	98	200–40,000 (20,100)	19,698

This chart shows the results of a risk assessment of three selected areas of an on-line order processing system. The likelihood of each exposure occurring over a 1-year period is expressed as a percentage. The next column shows the highest and lowest possible loss that could be expected each time the exposure occurred and an "average" loss calculated by adding the highest and lowest figures together and dividing by 2. The expected annual loss for each exposure can be determined by multiplying the "average" loss by its probability of occurrence.

instances, management may choose to describe risks and their likely impact in a qualitative manner (Rainer, Snyder, and Carr, 1991).

To decide which controls to use, information system builders must examine various control techniques in relation to each other and to their relative cost effectiveness. A control weakness at one point may be offset by a strong control at another. It may not be cost effective to build tight controls at every point in the processing cycle if the areas of greatest risk are secure or if compensating controls exist elsewhere. The combination of all of the controls developed for a particular application will determine its overall control structure.

13.3 Auditing Information Systems

Once controls have been established for an information system, how do we know that they are effective? To answer this question, organizations must conduct comprehensive and systematic *audits*. Large organizations have their own internal auditing group that is charged with this responsibility.

The Role of Auditing in the Control Process

MIS audit: Identifies all the controls that govern individual information systems and assesses their effectiveness.

An **MIS audit** identifies all of the controls that govern individual information systems and assesses their effectiveness. To accomplish this, the auditor must acquire a thorough understanding of operations, physical facilities, telecommunications, control systems, data security objectives, organizational structure, personnel, manual procedures, and individual applications.

The auditor should collect and analyze all of the material about a specific information system, such as user and system documentation, sample inputs and outputs, and relevant documentation about integrity controls. The auditor usually interviews key individuals who use and operate the system concerning their activities and procedures. Application controls, overall integrity controls, and control disciplines are examined. The auditor should trace the flow of sample transactions through the system and perform tests, using, if appropriate, automated audit software.

The audit lists and ranks all control weaknesses and estimates the probability of their occurrence. It then assesses the financial and organizational impact of each threat. Figure 13.7 is a sample auditor's listing of control weaknesses for a loan system. It includes a section for notifying management of such weaknesses and for management's response. Management is expected to devise a plan for countering significant weaknesses in controls.

Data Quality Audits

Data quality audit: Survey of files and samples of files for accuracy and completeness of data in an information system.

An important aspect of information system auditing is an analysis of data quality. **Data quality audits** are accomplished by the following methods:

- Surveying end users for their perceptions of data quality.
- Surveying entire data files.
- Surveying samples from data files.

Unless regular data quality audits are undertaken, organizations have no way of knowing to what extent their information systems contain inaccurate, incomplete, or ambiguous information. Some organizations, such as the Social Security Administration, have established data quality audit procedures. These procedures control payment and process quality by auditing a 20,000-case sample of beneficiary records each month. The FBI, on the other hand, did not conduct a

| Function: Personal Loans _____ | | Prepared by: ____ J. Ericson _____ | | Received by: _____ T. Barrow _____ | |
| Location: Peoria, Ill. _____ | | Preparation date: __ June 16, 1995 _____ | | Review date: _____ June 28, 1995 ____ | |

Nature of Weakness and Impact	Chance for Substantial Error		Effect on Audit Procedures	Notification to Management	
	Yes/ No	Justification	Required Amendment	Date of Report	Mangement Response
Loan repayment records are not reconciled to borrower's records during processing.	Yes	Without a detection control, errors in individual client balances may remain undetected.	Confirm a sample of loans.	5/10/95	Interest Rate Compare Report provides this control.
There are no regular audits of computer-generated data (interest charges).	Yes	Without a regular audit or reasonableness check, widespread miscalculations could result before errors are detected.		5/10/95	Periodic audits of loans will be instituted.
Programs can be put into production libraries to meet target deadlines without final approval from the Standards and Controls group.	No	All programs require management authorization. The Standards and Controls group controls access to all production systems, and assigns such cases to a temporary production status.			

Figure 13.7
Sample auditor's list of control weaknesses. This chart is a sample page from a list of control weaknesses that an auditor might find in a loan system in a local commercial bank. This form helps auditors record and evaluate control weaknesses and shows the result of discussing those weaknesses with management, as well as any corrective actions taken by management.

comprehensive audit of its record systems until 1984. With few data quality controls, the FBI criminal record systems were found to have serious problems.

A recent study of the FBI's computerized criminal record systems found a total of 54.1 percent of the records in the National Crime Information Center System to be inaccurate, ambiguous, or incomplete, and 74.3 percent of the records in the FBI's semi-automated Identification Division system exhibited significant quality problems. A summary analysis of the FBI's automated Wanted-Persons File also found that 11.2 percent of the warrants were invalid. A study by the FBI itself found that 6 percent of the warrants in state files were invalid and that 12,000 invalid warrants are sent out nationally each day.

The low levels of data quality in these systems have disturbing implications.

- More than 14,000 persons are at risk of being falsely detained and perhaps arrested because of invalid warrants.

- In addition to their use in law enforcement, computerized criminal history records are increasingly being used to screen employees in both the public and private sectors. This is the fastest growing use of these records in some states. Many of these records are incomplete and show arrests but no court disposition; that is, they show charges without proof of conviction or guilt. Many individuals may be denied employment unjustifiably because these records overstate their criminality.

- These criminal record systems are not limited to violent felons. They contain the records of 36 million people, about one-third of the labor force. Inaccurate and potentially damaging information is being maintained on many law-abiding citizens.

The level of data quality in these systems threatens citizens' constitutional right to due process and impairs the efficiency and effectiveness of any law enforcement programs in which these records are used (Laudon, 1986a).

Data that are inaccurate, untimely, or inconsistent with other sources of information can also create serious operational and financial problems for businesses. When bad data go unnoticed, they can lead to bad decisions, product recalls, and even financial losses. For instance, Geer DuBois, a New York advertising agency, lost a $25 million a year account after the agency's billing system failed to credit the client for a six-figure payment. Even though Geer DuBois repaid the client with interest, the client decided to use another advertising firm. First Financial Management Corporation of Atlanta had to restate its earnings for the first nine months of the year because a subsidiary had lost track of some records after changing its accounting system (Wilson, 1992).

Management Challenges

1. **Controlling large distributed multi-user networks.** No system is totally secure, but large distributed multi-user networks are especially difficult to secure. Security becomes more problematic when networks are no longer confined to individual departments or groups or to centralized mainframe systems. It is very difficult to assert companywide control over networks using numerous hardware, software, and communications components when thousands of workers can access networks from many remote locations.

2. **Subjectivity of risk analysis.** Risk analysis depends on assumptions. For instance, the flawed Patriot missile system described earlier in this chapter was originally designed to work under a much less stringent environment than that in which it was actually used during Operation Desert Storm. Subsequent analyses of its effectiveness were downgraded from 95 percent to 13 percent (Neumann, 1993). Since risks are only potential events, not certainties, they are often either overestimated or underestimated. Measures to avoid risk can also be used to stifle innovation or change.

3. **Designing systems that are neither overcontrolled nor undercontrolled.** The biggest threat to information systems is posed by authorized users, not outside intruders. Most security breaches and damage to information systems come from organizational insiders. If there are too many passwords and authorizations required to access an information system, the system will go unused. Controls that are effective but that do not prevent authorized individuals from using a system are difficult to design.

Summary

Show why automated information systems are so vulnerable to destruction, error, and abuse.

Organizations have become so dependent on computerized information systems that they must take special measures to ensure that these systems are properly controlled. With data easily concentrated into electronic form and many procedures invisible through automation, systems are vulnerable to destruction, misuse, error, fraud, and hardware or software failures. The effect of disaster in a computerized system can be greater than in manual systems because all of the records for a particular function or organization can be destroyed or lost. On-line systems and those utilizing telecommunications are especially vulnerable because data and files can be immediately and directly accessed through computer terminals or at many points in the telecommunications network. Computer "viruses" can spread rampantly from system to system, clogging computer memory or destroying programs and data.

Describe the role of controls in safeguarding information systems.

Controls consist of all the methods, policies, and organizational procedures that ensure the safety of the organization's assets, the accuracy and reliability of its accounting records, and adherence to management standards. For computerized information systems, controls consist of both manual and programmed procedures. Controls that safeguard information system security are especially important in today's on-line networked environment.

Distinguish between general controls and application controls.

There are two main categories of controls: general controls and application controls. General controls control the overall design, security, and use of computer programs and files for the organization as a whole. They include physical hardware controls; system software controls; data file security controls; computer operations controls; controls over the system implementation process; and administrative disciplines.

Application controls are controls unique to specific computerized applications. They focus on the completeness and accuracy of input, updating and maintenance, and the validity of the information in the system. Application controls consist of input controls, processing controls and output controls.

Describe the most important techniques for controlling information systems.

Some of the principal application control techniques are programmed routines to edit data before they are input or updated; run control totals; and reconcile input source documents with output reports.

Identify the factors that must be considered when developing the controls for information systems.

To determine what controls are required, designers and users of systems must identify all of the control points and control weaknesses and perform risk assessment. They must also perform a cost/benefit analysis of controls and design controls that can effectively safeguard systems without making them unusable.

Explain the importance of auditing information systems.

Comprehensive and systematic MIS auditing can help organizations to determine the effectiveness of the controls in their information systems. Regular data quality audits should be conducted to help organizations ensure a high level of completeness and accuracy of the data stored in their systems.

Key Terms

Hacker	Administrative controls
Computer virus	Segregation of functions
Antivirus software	Input controls
Fault-tolerant computer systems	Input authorization
On-line transaction processing	Data conversion
Security	Batch control totals
Controls	Edit checks
General controls	Processing controls
Application controls	Run control totals
Implementation controls	Computer matching
Software controls	Output controls
Program security controls	Standing data
Hardware controls	Risk assessment
Computer operations controls	MIS audit
Data security controls	Data quality audit

Review Questions

1. Why are computer systems more vulnerable than manual systems to destruction, fraud, error, and misuse? Name some of the key areas where systems are most vulnerable.

2. Name some features of on-line information systems that make them difficult to control.

3. What are fault-tolerant computer systems? When should they be used?

4. What are controls? What distinguishes controls in computerized systems from controls in manual systems?

5. What is the difference between general controls and application controls?

6. Name and describe the principal general controls for computerized systems.

7. Describe how each of the following serve as application controls: batching, edits, computer matching, run control totals.

8. What kinds of edit techniques can be built into computer programs?

9. How does MIS auditing enhance the control process?

10. What is the function of risk assessment?

11. Why are data quality audits essential?

12. What is security? List and describe controls that promote security for computer hardware, computer networks, computer software, and computerized data.

Discussion
Questions
1. It has been said that controls and security should be one of the first areas to be addressed by information system designers. Discuss.

2. The Young Professional Quarterly magazine publishing company receives thousands of subscription orders by mail each day. A document is created for each order. The order documents are batched in groups of thirty to fifty, and a header form is completed showing the total number of documents per batch. The documents are then keyed and verified by separate data entry clerks and processed each night. An edit/validation program rechecks the number of units in each batch. It prints valid and invalid batch reports and posts valid batches to a valid transaction file. The valid transaction file is fed to a series of programs that update Young Professional Quarterly's inventory, produce sales invoices, and feed the accounts receivable system. The Valid Batch Report is reconciled to the totals on the batch headers. Batches listed in the Invalid Batch Report are reviewed, corrected, and resubmitted.

   List and discuss the control weaknesses in this system and their impact. What corrective measures would you suggest?

3. Suppose you were asked to help design the controls for an information system. What pieces of information would you need?

4. Many organizations, such as Visa USA, cited earlier in this chapter, take elaborate precautions for backing up their computer systems. Why is this essential? What considerations must be addressed by a backup plan?

Group
Project
Form a group with two or three other students. Write a description of the general and application controls that might be used for one of the systems described in the Window on boxes or chapter-ending cases in this text (the Stride Rite system in Chapter 1, the Travellers claims review and CSX systems in Chapter 2, or the Credit Agricole system in Chapter 6 could be analyzed). Present your findings to the class.

CASE STUDY

Protecting National Security Information at the Drug Enforcement Administration

The Drug Enforcement Administration was established in 1973 under the Department of Justice to enforce laws and regulations relating to the use and distribution of legal and illegal drugs. The agency consists of 7000 agents and other employees with domestic and foreign offices located worldwide. DEA uses information systems to process highly sensitive information or national security information collected from a variety of sources. Such information includes detailed data on known or suspected drug violators and informants and data on domestic and international drug operations.

The DEA maintains some of this data on paper and some in computerized form. It is putting less emphasis on improving arrest and seizure statistics and more on systematically analyzing drug trafficking organizations to pinpoint efforts more effectively. It replaced outdated equipment in its 19 divisions with 2000 high-speed Unisys workstations, linking all its divisions to a central database.

Executive Order 12356, dated April 2, 1982, requires federal agencies to establish controls to ensure that classified information is protected and guarded from unauthorized access. Justice Department policy requires its component agencies, including DEA, to ensure that adequate security safeguards are in place for its computer systems and to identify those systems that process classified data.

In February 1991, DEA informed the Justice Department that it had an inventory of computers that process classified information. The inventory was based on a survey conducted by the Office of Security Programs. The General Accounting Office found that this inventory did not include computers that DEA headquarters and its Division B use to process classified data because headquarters offices were never surveyed and Division B did not respond to requests for this information. DEA's Division A did not report any classified computer systems either in response to the Office of Security Programs survey. The GAO also found Division A personnel using computers to process classified information.

In accordance with federal guidelines, Justice Department policy requires that computer systems processing classified information be approved by the Department Security Officer and have the necessary security safeguards in place, including security safeguards for protecting classified data transmitted on networks. GAO observed many instances where DEA headquarters and division personnel were using DEA's Office Automation system routinely to process classified data. This system had not been approved for processing national security information and DEA had not completed a risk analysis of the system.

DEA began installing the Office Automation system in 1987. DEA's Office Automation workstations were operated in open, unshielded work areas and used fixed-disk storage devices. Federal guidelines discourage the use of this equipment because information may be inadvertently stored on the computer's fixed disk and be vulnerable to retrieval by unauthorized persons. The guidelines recommend computer equipment with removable storage media only for processing classified information in open areas. (The U.S. Attorney's Office in Lexington, Kentucky, made headlines when it sold surplus Department of Justice computer equipment containing sensitive grand jury material and information on confidential informants in 1991.)

The equipment was not TEMPEST-protected. TEMPEST is a technology that shields computer equipment to keep electromagnetic emissions from being intercepted and deciphered by eavesdroppers. The workstations were connected by data communications lines that were not encrypted. The Office Automation network allowed individuals working on workstations in one office to access data stored in workstations located elsewhere and used by others. Any DEA employee could use the system to obtain classified data stored in another employee's workstation without that employee's knowledge. Employees of the original equipment vendor had access to Office Automation workstations because the vendor-issued system passwords had never been changed.

The GAO studied DEA's procedures for controlling access to areas where computer equipment is used. Table 13.5 summarizes the results of GAO's analysis of physical security at DEA.

Another problem was found at headquarters and the two division offices. There, contract cleaning and maintenance personnel (who do not have national security clearances) were allowed to work unescorted in areas where computers process national security information. Janitorial staff were permitted to work alone in these areas before and after regular business hours. Computers in each of these offices were often left signed on and unattended. Electric card-key devices on doors to areas that contain national security information are turned off during normal working hours. The doors are left open. Division security staff were

Table 13.5 PHYSICAL SECURITY WEAKNESSES AT DEA HEADQUARTERS AND DIVISIONS

	DEA Headquarters	Division A	Division B
Inadequately controlled access to sensitive areas	X	X	X
Individuals without national security clearances working unescorted in sensitive areas	X	X	X
Unattended computers left signed on[a]	X	X	X
Computer-generated materials left unattended and unsecured		X	X
Documents left unattended and unsecured	X	X	X
Safes left open and unattended	X	X	

[a]A computer operational state allowing a user to access data files and retrieve information.

not reviewing card-key access logs to see who was entering these areas after normal working hours. The GAO found that one card-key that was reported lost was still active. Individual card-keys with the same access codes had been issued to groups of individuals, including non-DEA employees. DEA employees did not wear security badges.

The GAO found that Division B had not changed the locks to its division offices since their installation in 1985. DEA and task force employees reported 17 instances in which their keys were either lost or stolen, including master keys to all areas where computers process national security information and where employees regularly collect, analyze, and store this information. An employee reported the loss of office keys on a key chain marked with the initials DEA. The Division Security Office informed GAO that the locks were being rekeyed and that Division B is being relocated to a new space that has a card-key system.

At both DEA divisions the GAO found that floppy diskettes labeled as containing classified information were routinely left unattended in open and unprotected mail trays. Anyone could access these trays. The GAO observed several instances at DEA headquarters where documents labeled as classified were left unsecured in areas where cleaning personnel were working. In one, documents marked classified were left out on a desk next to a window on the first floor. After notifying a DEA employee that the documents were classified, GAO investigators returned five minutes later and found that the documents were still unattended. In another instance, GAO investigators found a classified document lying unattended in the machine tray of a facsimile machine located in an open mail room where non-DEA personnel work regularly. GAO investigators found many instances at DEA headquarters and division offices where documents labeled classified were left unattended in open cubicles and unlocked offices. They observed open and unattended safes that DEA personnel said contained national security information.

Examining another major DEA field location, a Department of Justice review team found that 1) DEA personnel were processing and storing national security information on unapproved and unprotected computer equipment; 2) communications lines connecting remote workstations were not safeguarded to meet national security requirements; 3) individuals with access to sensitive areas did not have proper security clearances; and 4) access to the Sensitive Compartmented Information Facility that houses highly classified information was not properly controlled.

DEA officials said they knew of no instance where classified information was compromised.

Sources: United States General Accounting Office, "Computer Security: DEA Is Not Adequately Protecting National Security Information," GAO/IMTEC-92-31 (February 1992), and Jason Forsythe, "New Weapons in Drug Wars," *InformationWEEK* (July 16, 1990).

Case Study Questions

1. Write an analysis of the control weaknesses in DEA systems.

2. What are the possible consequences of these control weaknesses?

3. What management, organization and technology factors were responsible for these weaknesses?

4. What recommendations would you make to correct these weaknesses?

References

Borning, Alan. "Computer System Reliability and Nuclear War." *Communications of the ACM* 30, no. 2 (February 1987).

Boockholdt, J. L. "Implementing Security and Integrity in Micro-Mainframe Networks." *MIS Quarterly* 13, no. 2 (June 1989).

Buss, Martin D. J., and Lynn M. Salerno. "Common Sense and Computer Security." *Harvard Business Review* (March–April 1984).

Charette, Ron. "Inside RISKS: Risks with Risk Analysis." *Communications of the ACM* 34, no. 5 (June 1991).

Chaum, David. "Security Without Identification: Transaction Systems to Make Big Brother Obsolete." *Communications of the ACM* 28 (October 1985).

Halper, Stanley D., Glenn C. Davis, Jarlath P. O'Neill-Dunne, and Pamela R. Pfau. *Handbook of EDP Auditing.* Boston: Warren, Gorham and Lamont, 1985.

Hoffman, Lance. *Rogue Programs.* New York: Van Nostrand Reinhold, 1990.

"Information Security and Privacy." *EDP Analyzer* (February 1986).

Kahane, Yehuda, Seev Neumann, and Charles S. Tapiero. "Computer Backup Pools, Disaster Recovery, and Default Risk." *Communications of the ACM* 31, no. 1 (January 1988).

King, Julia. "It's C.Y.A. Time." *Computerworld* (March 30, 1992).

Laudon, Kenneth C. "Data Quality and Due Process in Large Interorganizational Record Systems." *Communications of the ACM* 29 (January 1986a).

Laudon, Kenneth C. *Dossier Society: Value Choices in the Design of National Information Systems*. New York: Columbia University Press, 1986b.

Littlewood, Bev and Lorenzo Strigini. "The Risks of Software." *Scientific American*, 267, no. 5 (November 1992).

Loch, Karen D., Houston H. Carr, and Merrill E. Warkentin. "Threats to Information Systems: Today's Reality, Yesterday's Understanding." *MIS Quarterly* 16, no. 2 (June 1992).

Maglitta, Joe, and John P. Mello, Jr. "The Enemy Within." *Computerworld* (December 7, 1992).

Neumann, Peter G. "Risks Considered Global(ly)." *Communications of the ACM* 35, no. 1 (January 1993).

Perrow, Charles. *Normal Accidents*. New York: Basic Books, 1984.

Rainer, Rex Kelley, Jr., Charles A. Snyder, and Houston H. Carr. "Risk Analysis for Information Technology." *Journal of Management Information Systems* 8, no. 1 (Summer 1991).

Post, Gerald V., and J. David Diltz. "A Stochastic Dominance Approach to Risk Analysis of Computer Systems." *MIS Quarterly* (December 1986).

Straub, Detmar W. "Controlling Computer Abuse: An Empirical Study of Effective Security Countermeasures." Curtis L. Carlson School of Management, University of Minnesota (July 20, 1987).

Tate, Paul. "Risk! The Third Factor." *Datamation* (April 15, 1988).

Thyfault, Mary E., and Stephanie Stahl. "Weak Links." *InformationWEEK* (August 10, 1992).

United States General Accounting Office. "Computer Security: DEA Is Not Adequately Protecting National Security Information." *GAO/IMTEC-92-31* (February 1992).

United States General Accounting Office. "Computer Security: Virus Highlights Need for Improved Internet Management." *GAO/IMTEC-89-57* (June 1989).

United States General Accounting Office. "Patriot Missile Defense: Software Problem Led to System Failure at Dharan, Saudi Arabia." *GAO/IMTEC-92-26* (February 1992).

Weber, Ron. *EDP Auditing: Conceptual Foundations and Practice*. 2nd ed. New York: McGraw-Hill, 1988.

Wilson, Linda. "Devil In Your Data," *InformationWEEK* (August 31, 1992).

DuPont's New Chemistry for International Business

In 1903, E. I. DuPont de Nemours & Co., shook up the business world when it launched an innovative approach to centralized management. Now, in order to remain globally competitive, it is shaking up its organizational chemistry again.

DuPont is a $40 billion conglomerate with five principal business segments producing chemicals, fibers, gasoline, polymers, and specialties such as agricultural and electronics products. More than 40 percent of DuPont's sales come from the oil company, Conoco. DuPont is under serious challenge from competitors overseas. For instance, former buyers of DuPont nylon in China are now likely to produce the nylon themselves. DuPont is responding by shedding businesses and products that are either unprofitable or that do not fit well with its strategic mix. It is also restructuring its organization, moving toward a nonhierarchical team-based management

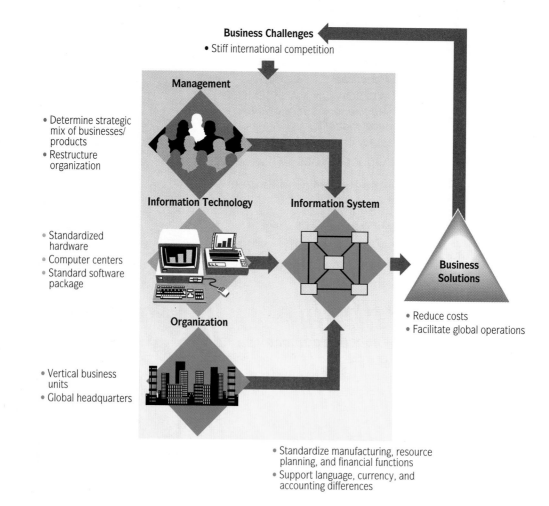

style that it believes is more appropriate for a far-flung global company.

Part of this restructuring consists of converting DuPont's global information systems to a set of common standards, hardware and software platforms, and vendors. DuPont cut down on redundant systems, seeing no competitive advantage in having separate information systems for entering an order, managing inventory, or paying a bill in each of its vertical business units. It reduced the number of computer centers housing Digital Equipment Corporation VAX minicomputers from 150 to 75. These computer centers help control plant production and operate distribution centers. DuPont also cut its hardware vendors from 100 to a dozen, making DEC, IBM, and Apple Computer Corporation its primary suppliers.

DuPont installed an application software package from SAP America, the U.S. unit of SAP A.G., the German software firm, to provide standard software for manufacturing resource planning and financial applications that could be used by its various business units. The software can accommodate differences in language, currency, and accounting practices. DuPont believes that all of these measures not only reduce costs but support its global operations.

Source: Chuck Appleby, "The Teflon Company," *InformationWEEK* (December 21, 1992).

D uPont is one of many business firms that are moving toward global forms of organization that transcend national boundaries. But DuPont could not make this move unless it restructured itself and reorganized its information systems. DuPont switched to a less centralized organizational structure, consolidated its computer centers, streamlined its computer hardware, and standardized some of its information systems so that the same system could be used by disparate business units in different countries.

The changes DuPont made are some of the changes in international information infrastructures—the basic systems needed to coordinate worldwide trade and other activities—that organizations need to consider if they want to operate across the globe. Information technology is both a powerful driver of the movement toward international business, and a powerful servant. This chapter explores how to organize, manage, and control the development of international information systems.

After completing this chapter you will be able to:

* Identify the major factors behind the growing internationalization of business.

- Choose among several global strategies for developing business.
- Understand how information systems support different global strategies.
- Manage the development of international systems.
- Understand the main technical alternatives in developing global systems.

14.1 The Growth of International Information Systems

We have already described two powerful worldwide changes driven by advances in information technology that have transformed the business environment and posed new challenges for management. One is the transformation of industrial economies and societies into knowledge- and information-based economies. The other is the emergence of a global economy and global world order.

The precise outlines of the new global world order are unclear but the general dimensions and features are unmistakable. The goal from the American point of view is to become the world's leading supplier of sophisticated products, high valued-added services, and new useful knowledge, designs, and ideas. In this pursuit, the United States is in direct competition with Western Europe and Japan, to be joined by China, and a resurgent middle Europe in the middle of the twenty-first century. The new world order will sweep away national corporations, national industries, and national economies controlled by domestic politicians. Many of the Fortune 500, the 500 largest U.S. corporations, will disappear in the next 50 years, mirroring past behavior of large firms since 1900. Except for a few nimble survivors, most of these dinosaurs will be replaced by fast-moving networked corporations that transcend national boundaries. It is vital that you as future managers understand the forces moving us toward this new world order, and learn how to control this new empire.

In 1970 only 5 percent of the manufactured goods sold in the United States were imported and 30 percent of the labor force worked in manufacturing. Today, about 21 percent of the manufactured goods sold in the country are imported and only about 17 percent of the labor force works in manufacturing.[1] A similar story can be told about Europe and Japan: The growth of international trade has radically altered domestic economies around the globe. About $1 trillion worth of goods, services, and financial instruments—one fifth of the annual U.S. Gross National Product—changes hands each day in global trade.

Consider the notebook computer as an example. The CPU is likely to have been designed and built in the United States; the DRAM (or dynamic random access memory, which makes up the majority of primary storage in a computer) was designed in the United States but built in Malaysia; the screen was designed and assembled in Japan using American patents; the keyboard is from Taiwan; and finally assembly was in Japan where the case was also made. Management of the project was located in Silicon Valley along with marketing, sales, and finance that coordinated all the myriad activities from financing and production to shipping and sales efforts. None of this would be possible without powerful international information and telecommunication systems, an international information systems infrastructure.

For today's manager this means that in order to compete effectively you will need a global perspective on business and the support systems needed to conduct business on an international scale.

---

[1] See *Statistical Abstract of the United States*, Tables No. 1409 and 1301.

Developing the International Information Systems Infrastructure

International information systems infrastructure: The basic information systems required by organizations to coordinate worldwide trade and other activities.

This chapter describes how to go about building an international information systems infrastructure suitable for your international strategy. An infrastructure is the constellation of facilities and services, such as highways or telecommunications networks, required for organizations to function and prosper. An **international information systems infrastructure** consists of the basic information systems required by organizations to coordinate worldwide trade and other activities. As we noted in Chapter 1, a firm will not be able to achieve its goals and strategies without appropriate information systems. Figure 14.1 illustrates the reasoning we will follow throughout the chapter, and depicts the major dimensions of an international information systems infrastructure.

Business driver: A force in the environment to which businesses must respond and that influences the direction of business.

The basic strategy to follow when building an international system is first to understand the global environment in which your firm is operating. This means understanding the overall market forces or *business drivers* that are pushing your industry toward a global competition. A **business driver** is a force in the environment to which businesses must respond and that influences the direction of the business. Likewise, examine carefully the inhibitors or negative factors that create *management challenges*—factors that could scuttle the development of a global business. Once you have examined the global environment, you will need to consider a *corporate strategy for competing in that environment*. How will your firm respond? You could ignore the global market and focus on domestic competition only, sell to the globe from a domestic base, or organize production and distribution around the globe. There are many in-between choices.

Figure 14.1
International information systems infrastructure. The major dimensions for developing an international information systems infrastructure are the global environment, the corporate global strategies, the structure of the organization, the management and business procedures, and the technology platform.

Global Environment:
Business Drivers & Challenges

Corporate Global Strategies

Organization Structure

Management & Business Procedures

Technology Platform

International Information Systems Infrastructure

Once you have developed a strategy, it is time to consider *how to structure your organization* so it can pursue the strategy. How will you accomplish a division of labor across a global environment? Where will production, administration, accounting, marketing and human resource functions be located? Who will handle the systems function?

Once you have designed an international organization, you will have to consider the management issues in implementing your strategy and making the organization design come alive. Key here will be the design of business procedures. How can you discover and manage user requirements? How can you induce change in local units to conform to international requirements? How can you re-engineer on a global scale, and how can you coordinate systems development?

The last issue to consider is the technology platform. Although changing technology is a key driving factor leading toward global markets, you need to have a corporate strategy and structure before you can rationally choose the right technology.

Once you have completed this process of reasoning you will be well on your way toward an appropriate international information infrastructure capable of achieving your corporate goals. Let us begin by looking at the overall global environment.

The Global Environment: Business Drivers and Challenges

Table 14.1 illustrates the business drivers in the global environment that are leading all industries toward global markets and competition.

The global business drivers can be divided into two groups: general cultural factors and specific business factors. There are five easily recognized general cultural factors driving internationalization since World War II. Information, communication, and transportation technologies have created a *global village* in which communication (by telephone, television, radio, or computer network) around the globe is no more difficult and not much more expensive than communication down the block. Moving goods and services to and from geographically dispersed locations has fallen dramatically in cost.

Global culture: The development of common expectations, shared artifacts, and social norms among different cultures and peoples.

The development of global communications has created a global village in a second sense: there is now a **global culture** created by television and other globally shared media like movies which permits different cultures and peoples to develop common expectations about right and wrong, desirable and undesirable, heroic and cowardly. A shared culture, with shared cultural artifacts like news programs and movies, permits the emergence of shared *societal norms*

Table 14.1 THE GLOBAL BUSINESS DRIVERS

General Cultural Factors:

Global communication and transportation technologies
Development of "global culture"
Emergence of global social norms
Political stability
Global knowledge base

Specific Business Factors:

Global markets
Global production and operations
Global coordination
Global economies of scale

The universally recognizable McDonald's menu offers Russian diners a full selection of burgers, fries, and drinks. McDonald's patrons in Japan will find the same choices available to them in Japanese. The golden arches translate across all languages and cultures.

concerning proper attire, proper consumption, good and bad government. These cultural and societal sentiments are bolstered by a prolonged period of *political stability* on a global scale not seen in the modern age. The collapse of the Eastern bloc has speeded up enormously the growth of a world culture, increased support for capitalism and business, and reduced the level of cultural conflict considerably.

A last factor to consider is the growth of a *global knowledge base.* At the end of World War II, knowledge, education, science, and industrial skills were highly concentrated in North America, Europe, and Japan, with the rest of the world euphemistically called the "Third World." This is no longer true. Latin America, China, Southern Asia, and Eastern Europe have developed powerful educational, industrial, and scientific centers, resulting in a much more democratically and widely dispersed knowledge base.

These general cultural factors leading toward internationalization result in four specific global business factors that affect most industries. The growth of powerful communications technologies and the emergence of world cultures creates the condition for *global markets*—global consumers interested in consuming similar products that are "culturally" approved. Coca-Cola, American tennis shoes (made in Korea but designed in Los Angeles), and Dallas (a TV show) can now all be sold in Latin America, Africa, and Asia.

Responding to this demand, *global production and operation* has emerged with precise on-line coordination between far-flung production facilities and central headquarters thousands of miles away. At Sealand Transportation, a major global shipping company based in Newark, New Jersey, shipping managers in Newark can watch the loading of ships in Rotterdam on-line, check trim and ballast, and trace packages to specific ship locations as the activity proceeds. This is all possible through an international satellite link.

The new global markets and pressure toward global production and operation have called forth whole new capabilities for *global coordination* of all factors of production. Not just production, but also accounting, marketing and sales, human resources, and systems development (all the major business functions) can now be coordinated on a global scale. Frito Lay, for instance, can develop a marketing sales force automation system in the United States, and once provided, may try the same techniques and technologies in Spain. Micro marketing—marketing to very small geographic and social units—no longer means marketing to neighborhoods in the United States, but to neighborhoods throughout the world! In our notebook computer example above, design has become internationalized and coordinated through shared culture (defining what is good design) and dense communications networks. These new levels of global coordination permit for the first time in history the location of business activity according to comparative advantage. Design should be located where it is best accomplished, as should marketing, production, and finance.

Finally, global markets, production, and administration create the conditions for powerful, *sustained global economies of scale.* Production driven by worldwide global demand can be concentrated where it can be best accomplished, fixed resources can be allocated over larger production runs, and production runs in larger plants can be scheduled more efficiently and precisely estimated. Lower cost factors of production can be exploited wherever they emerge. The result is a powerful strategic advantage to firms that can organize globally.

These general and specific business drivers have greatly enlarged world trade and commerce. Figure 14.2A shows that world trade is growing faster than the world gross domestic product (GDP). Figure 14.2B shows that in the United States, world trade is growing faster than the economy as a whole.

Not all industries are similarly affected by these trends. Clearly, manufacturing has been much more affected than services that still tend to be domestic—and highly inefficient. However, the localism of services is breaking down in telecommunications, entertainment, transportation, financial services, and general business services, including law. Clearly those firms within an industry who can understand the internationalization of their industry and respond appropriately will reap enormous gains in productivity and stability.

BUSINESS CHALLENGES

While the possibilities of globalization for business success are enormous, it would be a mistake to think the path toward a truly global economy is free of fundamental obstacles, or that your company can simply coast to international glory. Far from it. Fundamental forces are operating to inhibit a global economy and to disrupt international business. Table 14.2 lists the most common and powerful challenges to the development of global systems.

Figure 14.2a
The growth of world trade compared to the growth of the world gross domestic product (GDP) (1950–1990). As can be seen from this graph, world trade is growing faster than world gross domestic product (GDP.) *Source: U.S. Department of State, Bureau of Intelligence and Research, Report No. IRR 220, 1991.*

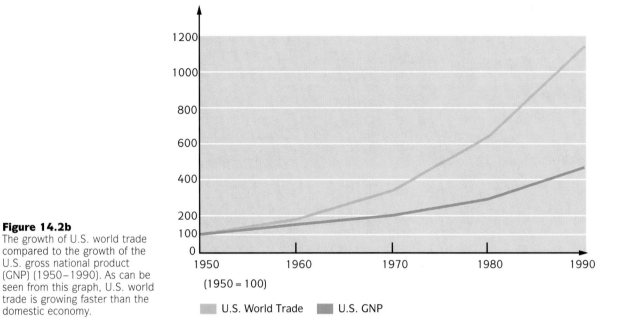

Figure 14.2b
The growth of U.S. world trade compared to the growth of the U.S. gross national product (GNP) (1950–1990). As can be seen from this graph, U.S. world trade is growing faster than the domestic economy.

Table 14.2 CHALLENGES TO GLOBAL BUSINESS SYSTEMS

General

Cultural particularism: Regionalism, nationalism.

Social expectations: "Brand name" expectations; work hours

Political laws: Transborder data and privacy laws.

Specific

Standards: Different EDI, E-Mail, telecommunications standards

Reliability: Phone networks not reliable

Speed: Data transfer speeds differ, slower than U.S.

Personnel: Shortages of skilled consultants

Particularism: Making judgments and taking actions on the basis of narrow or personal characteristics.

At a cultural level, **particularism**, making judgments and taking action on the basis of narrow or personal characteristics, in all its forms (religious, nationalistic, ethnic, regionalism, geopolitical position) rejects the very concept of a shared global culture, and rejects the penetration of domestic markets by "foreign" goods and services. Differences among cultures produce differences in social expectations, politics, and ultimately legal rules. In certain countries, like the United States, consumers expect "domestic" name brand products to be built domestically, and are disappointed to learn that much of what they thought of as domestically produced is in fact foreign made.

Different cultures produce different political regimes. Among the many different countries of the world there are different laws governing the movement of information, information privacy of citizens, origins of software and hardware in systems, and radio and satellite telecommunications. Even the hours of business, and the terms of business trade vary greatly across political cultures. These different legal regimes complicate global business and must be taken into account when building global systems.

Transborder data flow: The movement of information across international boundaries in any form.

For instance, European countries have very strict laws concerning transborder data flow and privacy. **Transborder data flow** is defined as the movement of information across international boundaries in any form. Some European countries prohibit the processing of financial information outside their boundaries or the movement of employee information to foreign countries. The European

WINDOW ON

ORGANIZATIONS

Snarled by Accounting Rules

Suppose you are the chief financial officer of a global consumer products company with 25 national subsidiaries. Each prepares its own financial statements. How do you get consistent data to figure out how the entire organization is performing? It's not easy, and might be virtually impossible.

Accounting practices diverge sharply from one country to another. Although the European Community and European Free Trade Association are creating a vast "single market" spanning 19 countries, there is no agreement on a single set of accounting standards. Accountants have radically different ideas of the proper way to value assets and total up profits and losses, reflecting their national laws and traditions.

For instance, German companies generally do not recognize profit from a project until it is completed and they have been paid. British firms, in contrast, start posting a profit before completion when they are reasonably certain they will get the money. Many companies on the European continent do not report per-share earnings, which is considered vital among

U.S. and British firms. Complicating matters further, European companies have myriad ways of defining net profit, shareholders' equity, and extraordinary items.

Each country's accounting practices are intertwined with its legal system, tax code, and business philosophy. Britain, the United States and the Netherlands share a primarily Anglo-Saxon business tradition that separates tax calculations from reports to shareholders and which uses more flexible accounting rules. Accountants focus on presenting a "true and fair view" of the company as opposed to adhering to rigid rules with the objective of showing shareholders how fast profit is growing. The accounting goals of most continental countries, on the other hand, emphasize compliance with strict rules and holding down tax liabilities. These countries are less interested in impressing investors. Many Germans are even appalled by the lack of precise rules in Anglo-Saxon accounting. Since Anglo-Saxon and German accounting do not even share the same basic goals, it is hard to imagine a single accounting system that could serve both sides.

These diverging accounting practices inhibit cross-border business in a number of ways. Investors may be deterred from buying shares abroad because they cannot understand foreign accounting statements even when the language is translated. Investment analysts generally cannot make meaningful comparisons such as which European country has the cheapest food company shares. Companies have trouble identifying healthy companies for cross-border acquisitions or cooperation. Multinational firms must present the same accounting reports in different formats.

Source: Bob Hagerty, "Differing Accounting Rules Snarl Europe," *The Wall Street Journal* (September 14, 1992).

To Think About: Why are changes in SOPs an enormous organizational effort? How easily could information systems deal with the problems described here? If you were a manager of a multinational firm, how easy would it be to create a management reporting system? Why?

Commission (the highest planning body for the integration of Europe) is considering a Digital Services Data Protection Directive that would restrict the flow of information to countries (like the United States) that do not meet strict European information laws on personal information. That means, for instance, that a French marketing manager may not be able to use his or her credit card in New York because the credit information cannot be forwarded to the United States given its privacy laws. In response, most multinational firms develop information systems within each European country to avoid the cost and uncertainty of moving information across national boundaries.

Cultural and political differences profoundly affect organizations' standard operating procedures. A host of specific barriers arise from the general cultural differences, everything from different reliability of phone networks to the shortage of skilled consultants (see Steinbart and Nath, 1992). The Window on Organizations illustrates how such differences have shaped accounting procedures in various countries, seriously complicating the process of international management.

Language remains a significant barrier. Although English has become a kind of standard business language, this is truer at higher levels of companies and not throughout the middle and lower ranks. Software may have to be built with local language interfaces before a new information system can be successfully implemented.

Currency fluctuations can play havoc with planning models and projections. Although a great deal of progress has been made in developing a common currency for the European Economic Community, occasionally this regime breaks down, evidenced by the British pound fluctuation in 1992 and 1993, or the American dollar fluctuating from 1990 to 1994 against the Japanese yen and stronger European currencies. In the absence of world currency, or a world bank, currency fluctuations remain a major source of business uncertainty.

These inhibiting factors must be taken into account when you are designing and building an international infrastructure for your business.

State of the Art

Where do firms now have international applications and where do they plan expansion in the future? Figure 14.3 indicates the state of the art in terms of current applications and likely future growth areas of international systems infrastructure.

One might think, given the opportunities for achieving competitive advantages outlined above, and the interest in future applications, that most international companies have rationally developed marvelous international systems architectures. Nothing could be further from the truth. Most companies have inherited patchwork international systems from the distant past, often based on concepts of information processing developed in the 1960s—batch-oriented reporting from independent foreign divisions to corporate headquarters, with little on-line control and communication. At some point, corporations in this situation will face powerful competitive challenges in the market place from firms who have rationally designed truly international systems. Still other companies have recently built technology platforms for an international infrastructure, but have nowhere to go with it because they lack global strategy. For instance, one survey of 100 global firms found that 52 percent never or rarely considered information systems when devising global strategies (Cox, 1991).

Figure 14.3

Frequency and type of business entities supported by global systems and databases. Most current IT applications are relatively simple office systems involving budgeting, communications, and general ledger financial coordination. Most corporations have local human resource and equipment/facilities systems. In the future, global firms plan to expand product support, customer service, and supplier systems to global stature. *Source: Adapted from Blake Ives and Sirkka Jarvenpaa, "Wiring the Stateless Corporation: Empowering the Drivers and Overcoming the Barriers," SIM Network, September/October 1991, p. 4C. Reprinted courtesy of Society for Information Management.*

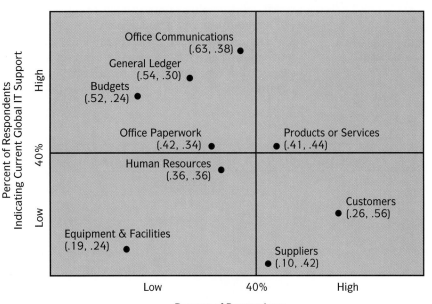

As it turns out, there are significant difficulties in building appropriate international infrastructures. The difficulties involve planning a system appropriate to the firm's global strategy, structuring the organization of systems and business units, solving implementation issues, and choosing the right technical platform. Let us examine these problems in greater detail.

14.2 Organizing International Information Systems

There are three organizational issues facing corporations seeking a global position: choosing a strategy, organizing the business, and organizing the systems management area. The first two are closely connected, so we will discuss them together.

Global Strategies and Business Organization

There are four main global strategies that form the basis for global firms' organizational structure. These four strategies are domestic exporter, multinational, franchiser, and transnational. Each of these strategies is associated with a specific business organizational structure (see Table 14.3). For simplicity, we describe three kinds of organizational structure or governance: centralized (in the home country), decentralized (dispersed to local foreign units), and coordinated (all units participate as equals). There are other types of governance patterns observed in specific companies (e.g., authoritarian dominance by one unit, a confederacy of equals, a federal structure balancing power among strategic units, and so forth; see Keen, 1991).

Domestic exporter: Global strategy characterized by heavy centralization of corporate activities in the home country of origin.

The **domestic exporter** strategy is characterized by heavy centralization of corporate activities in the home country of origin. Nearly all international companies begin this way, and some move on to other forms. Production, finance/accounting, sales/marketing, human resources, and strategic management are set up to optimize resources in the home country. International sales are sometimes dispersed using agency agreements or subsidiaries, but even here foreign marketing is totally reliant on the domestic home base for marketing themes and strategies. Caterpillar Corporation and other heavy capital equipment manufacturers fall into this category of firm.

Multinational: Global strategy that concentrates financial management and control out of a central home base while decentralizing production, sales, and marketing operations to units in other countries.

The **multinational** strategy often concentrates financial management and control out of a central home base while decentralizing production, sales, and marketing operations to units in other countries. The products and services on sale in different countries are adapted to suit local market conditions. The organization becomes a far-flung confederation of production and marketing

Table 14.3   GLOBAL BUSINESS STRATEGY AND STRUCTURE

BUSINESS FUNCTION	Strategy			
	Domestic Exporter	Multinational	Franchiser	Transnational
Production	Centralized	Dispersed	Coordinated	Coordinated
Finance/Accounting	Centralized	Centralized	Centralized	Coordinated
Sales/Marketing	Mixed	Dispersed	Coordinated	Coordinated
Human Resources	Centralized	Centralized	Coordinated	Coordinated
Strategic Management	Centralized	Centralized	Centralized	Coordinated

Franchiser: Firm where the product is created, designed, financed, and initially produced in the home country, but must rely heavily on foreign personnel for further production, marketing, and human resources.

facilities in different countries. Many financial service firms, along with a host of manufacturers like General Motors, Chrysler, and Intel fit this pattern.

Franchisers are an interesting mix of old and new. On the one hand the product is created, designed, financed and initially produced in the home country, but for product-specific reasons must rely heavily on foreign personnel for further production, marketing, and human resources. Food franchisers like McDonald's, Mrs. Fields' Cookies, and Kentucky Fried Chicken fit this pattern. McDonald's created a new form of fast-food chain in the United States, and continues to rely largely on the United States for inspiration of new products, strategic management, and financing. Nevertheless, because the product must be produced locally—it is perishable—extensive coordination and dispersal of production, local marketing, and local recruitment of personnel are required. Generally, foreign franchisees are clones of the mother country units, yet fully coordinated worldwide production that could optimize factors of production is not possible. For instance, potatoes and beef can generally not be bought where they are cheapest on world markets but must be produced reasonably close to the area of consumption.

Transnational: Truly globally managed firms which have no national headquarters; value-added activities are managed from a global perspective without reference to national borders, optimizing sources of supply and demand and taking advantage of any local competitive advantage.

Transnational firms are the stateless, truly globally managed firms which may represent a larger part of international business in the future. Transnational firms have no single national headquarters but instead have many regional headquarters and perhaps a world headquarters. In a **transnational** strategy, nearly all of the value-adding activities are managed from a global perspective, without reference to national borders, optimizing sources of supply and demand wherever they appear, and taking advantage of any local comparative advantages. Transnational firms take the globe as their management frame of reference, not the home country. The governance of these firms has been likened to a federal structure in which there is a strong central management core of decision making, but considerable dispersal of power and financial muscle throughout the global divisions. Few companies have actually attained transnational status but Citicorp, Sony, Ford, and others are attempting this transition.

Information technology and improvements in global telecommunications are giving international firms more flexibility to shape their global strategies. Protectionism and a need to serve local markets encourage companies to disperse production facilities and at least become multinational. At the same time, the drive to achieve economies of scale and take advantage of short-term local advantages forces transnationals toward a global management perspective and a concentration of power and authority. Hence, there are forces of decentralization and dispersal, as well as forces of centralization and global coordination. (Ives and Jarvenpaa, 1991).

Global Systems to Fit the Strategy

The configuration, management, and development of systems tend to follow the global strategy chosen (Roche, 1992; Ives and Jarvenpaa, 1991). Figure 14.4 depicts one view of typical arrangements, recognizing that some firms' systems may not fit the pattern precisely. By "systems" we mean the full range of activities involved in building information systems: conception and alignment with the strategic business plan, systems development, and ongoing operation. For the sake of simplicity, we consider four types of systems configuration. *Centralized systems* are those where systems development and operation occurs totally at the domestic home base. *Duplicated systems* are those where development occurs totally at the home base, but operations are handed over to autonomous units in foreign locations. *Decentralized systems* are those where each foreign unit designs its own, totally unique solutions and systems. Last, *networked* systems are those in which system development and operations occur in an integrated and coordinated fashion across all units. As can be seen in Figure 14.4, domestic exporters tend to have highly centralized systems in which a

SYSTEM CONFIGURATION	STRATEGY			
	Domestic Exporter	Multinational	Franchiser	Transnational
Centralized	X			
Duplicated			X	
Decentralized	x	X	x	
Networked		x		X

Figure 14.4
Global strategy and systems configurations. The large Xs show the dominant pattern, and the small xs show the emerging patterns. For instance, domestic exporters rely predominantly on centralized systems but there is continual pressure and some development of decentralized systems in local marketing regions.

single domestic systems development staff develops worldwide applications. Multinationals offer a direct and striking contrast: Here foreign units often devise their own systems solutions based on local needs with few if any applications in common with headquarters (the exception being financial reporting and some telecommunications applications). Franchisers have the simplest systems structure: like the products they sell, franchisers develop a single system usually at the home base and then replicate it around the world. Each unit—no matter where it is located—has the same identical applications. Last, the most ambitious form of system development is found in the transnational: Networked systems are those in which there is a solid, singular global environment for developing and operating systems. This usually presupposes a powerful telecommunications backbone, a culture of shared applications development, and a shared management culture that crosses cultural barriers. The networked systems structure is most visible in financial services where the homogeneity of the product, money, and money instruments, seems to overcome cultural barriers.

Reorganizing the Business

How should a firm organize itself for doing business on an international scale? Developing a global company and an information systems support structure requires following these principles:

1. Organize value-adding activities along lines of comparative advantage. For instance, marketing/sales functions should be located where they can best be performed, for least cost and maximum impact; likewise with production, finance, human resources, and information systems.

2. Develop and operate systems units at each level of corporate activity—national, regional, and international. In order to serve local needs, there should be *host country systems units* of some magnitude. *Regional systems* units should handle telecommunications and systems development across national boundaries that take place within major geographic regions (European, Asian, American). *Transnational systems units* should be established to create the linkages across major regional areas and coordinate the development and operation of international telecommunications and systems development (Roche, 1992).

3. Establish at world headquarters a single office responsible for development of international systems, a global Chief Information Officer (CIO) position.

Many successful companies have devised organizational systems structures along these principles. The success of these companies relies not just on proper organization. A key ingredient is a management team that can understand the risks and benefits of international systems, and that can devise strategies for overcoming the risks. We turn to these management topics next.

14.3 Managing Global Systems

The survey of 100 large global corporations referenced earlier in which 52% never or rarely considered information systems when developing global strategies also found that CIOs believed the development and implementation of international systems were their most difficult problems. Table 14.4 lists what these CIOs believed were the principal management problems posed by developing international systems. The percentage of respondents indicates the percentage of survey respondents who believed each issue created a serious difficulty for the firm.

It is interesting to note that these problems are the chief difficulties managers experience in developing ordinary domestic systems as well! But these are enormously complicated in the international environment.

A Typical Scenario: Disorganization on a Global Scale

Let us look at a common scenario. A traditional multinational consumer goods company based in the United States and operating in Europe would like to expand into Asian markets and knows that it must develop a transnational strategy and a supportive information systems structure. Like most multinationals it has dispersed production and marketing to regional and national centers while maintaining a world headquarters and strategic management in the United States. Historically, it has allowed each of the subsidiary foreign divisions to develop its own system. The only centrally coordinated system is financial controls and reporting. The central systems group in the United States focuses only on domestic functions and production. The result is a hodgepodge of hardware, software, and telecommunications. The mail systems between Europe and the United States are incompatible. Each production facility uses a different manufacturing resources planning system (or different version with local variations), and different marketing, sales, and human resource systems. The technology platforms are wildly different: Europe is using mostly UNIX-based file servers and PC clones on desktops. Communications between different sites are poor

Table 14.4 MANAGEMENT ISSUES IN DEVELOPING INTERNATIONAL SYSTEMS

	Percentage of Respondents
Agreeing on common user requirements	88%
Inducing procedural business changes	79%
Coordinating applications development	77%
Coordinating software releases	69%
Encouraging local users to take on ownership	58%

Source: Adapted from Butler Cox, *Globalization: The IT Challenge.* Amdahl Executive Institute (Sunnyvale, California, 1991).

given the high cost and low quality of European intercountry communications. The U.S. group is moving from an IBM mainframe environment centralized at headquarters to a highly distributed network architecture based on a national value-added network, with local sites developing their own local area networks. The central systems group at headquarters was recently dispersed to the U.S. local sites in the hope of serving local needs better and reducing costs.

What do you recommend to the senior management leaders of this company who now want to pursue a transnational strategy and develop an information systems infrastructure to support a highly coordinated global systems environment? Consider the problems you face by re-examining Table 14.4. The foreign divisions will resist efforts to agree on common user requirements—they have never thought about much other than their own units' needs. The systems groups in American local sites, which have been recently enlarged and told to focus on local needs, will not easily accept guidance from anyone recommending a transnational strategy. It will be difficult to convince local managers anywhere in the world that they should change their business procedures to align with other units in the world, especially if this might interfere with their local performance. After all, local managers are rewarded in this company for meeting local objectives of their division or plant. Finally, it will be difficult to coordinate development of projects around the world in the absence of a powerful telecommunications network, and difficult to encourage local users to take on ownership in the systems developed. What should you recommend given these typical obstacles?

Strategy: Divide, Conquer, Appease

Core systems: Systems that support functions that are absolutely critical to the organization.

Figure 14.5 lays out the main dimensions of a solution. First, consider that not all systems need to be coordinated on a transnational basis—only some "core" systems are truly worth sharing from a cost and feasibility point of view. **Core systems** are systems that support functions that are absolutely critical to the organization. Other systems should only be partially coordinated because they share key elements, but they do not have to be totally common across national boundaries. For such systems, a good deal of local variation is possible and desirable. A last group of systems are peripheral and truly provincial, and are needed to suit local requirements only.

DEFINE CORE BUSINESS PROCESSES

Business processes: Sets of logically related tasks performed to achieve a defined business outcome; each business process typically involves many functional areas working together.

How do you identify "core systems?" The first strategic step is to define a short list of truly critical core business processes. Business processes have been defined before in Chapter 8, which you should review. Briefly, **business processes** are sets of logically related tasks performed to achieve a defined business outcome, such as shipping out correct orders to customers or delivering innovative products to the market. Each business process typically involves many functional areas working together, effectively communicating and coordinating.

The way to identify these core business processes is to conduct a workflow analysis. How are customer orders taken, what happens to them once they are taken, who fills the orders, and how are they shipped to the customer? What about suppliers? Do they have access to manufacturing resource planning systems so supply is automatic? You should be able to identify and set priorities in a short list of ten business processes that are absolutely critical for the firm.

Next, can you identify centers of excellence for these processes? Is the customer order fulfillment superior in the United States, manufacturing process control superior in Germany, and human resources superior in Asia? You should be able to identify some areas of the company, for some lines of business, where a unit stands out in the performance of one or more business functions.

When you understand the business processes of a firm, you can rank order them. You can then decide which processes should be core applications, centrally coordinated, designed, and implemented around the globe, and which should be

Figure 14.5
Agency and other coordination costs increase as the firm moves from local option systems toward regional and global systems. However, transaction costs of participating in global markets probably decrease as firms develop global systems. A sensible strategy is to reduce agency costs by developing only a few "core" global systems which are vital for global operations, leaving other systems in the hands of regional and local units. *Adapted from Edward M. Roche,* Managing Information Technology in Multinational Corporations. *New York: Macmillan, 1992.*

Global Core Business Processes

Global Core Systems

Regional Coordinated Systems

Local Option Systems

Regional Business Processes

Local Business Processes

Geographic Business Scope

Business Systems Scope

regional and local. At the same time, by identifying the critical business processes, the really important ones, you have gone a long way to defining a vision of the future that you should be working towards.

IDENTIFY CORE SYSTEMS TO COORDINATE CENTRALLY

By identifying the critical core business processes, you begin to see opportunities for transnational systems. The second strategic step is to conquer the core systems and define these systems as truly transnational. The financial and political costs of defining and implementing transnational systems are extremely high. Therefore, keep the list to an absolute minimum, letting experience be the guide, and erring on the side of minimalism. If building a transnational system appears too daunting, it may be useful to identify the data elements required for global decision-making and build bridges between different systems to deliver this firm-wide data (Roche, 1992). By dividing off a small group of systems as absolutely critical, you divide opposition to a transnational strategy. At the same time, you can appease those who oppose the central worldwide coordination implied by transnational systems by permitting peripheral systems development to go on unabated, with the exception of some technical platform requirements.

CHOOSE AN APPROACH: INCREMENTAL, GRAND DESIGN, EVOLUTIONARY

A third strategic step is to choose an approach. Avoid piecemeal approaches. These will surely fail for lack of visibility, opposition from all who stand to lose from transnational development, and lack of power to convince senior management that the transnational systems are worth it. Likewise, avoid *grand design* approaches that try to do everything at once. These also tend to fail because they fail to focus resources. Nothing gets done properly, and opposition to organizational change is needlessly strengthened because the effort requires huge resources. An alternative approach is to evolve transnational applications from existing applications with a precise and clear vision of the transnational capabilities the organization should have in five years.

MAKE THE BENEFITS CLEAR   What is in it for the company? One of the worst situations to avoid is to build global systems for the sake of building global systems. From the beginning, it is crucial that senior management at headquarters and foreign division managers clearly understand the benefits that will come to the company as well as to individual units. While each system offers unique benefits to a particular budget, the overall contribution of global systems lies in four areas.

Global systems—truly integrated, distributed, and transnational systems—contribute to superior management and coordination. A simple price tag cannot be put on the value of this contribution, and the benefit will not show up in any capital budgeting model. It is the ability to switch suppliers on a moment's notice from one region to another in a crisis, the ability to move production in response to natural disasters, and the ability to use excess capacity in one region to meet raging demand in another.

A second major contribution is vast improvement in production, operation, and supply and distribution. Imagine a global value chain, with global suppliers and a global distribution network. For the first time, senior managers can locate value-adding activities in regions where they are most economically performed.

Third, global systems mean global customers and global marketing. Fixed costs around the world can now be amortized over a much larger customer base. This will unleash new economies of scale at production facilities.

Last, global systems mean the ability to optimize the use of corporate funds over a much larger capital base. This means, for instance, that capital in a surplus region can be moved efficiently to expand production of capital-starved regions; that cash can be managed more effectively within the company and put to use more effectively.

These strategies will not by themselves create global systems. You will have to implement what you strategize and this is a whole new challenge.

Implementation Tactics: Cooptation

Cooptation: Bringing the opposition into the process of designing and implementing the solution without giving up control over the direction and nature of the change.

The overall tactic for dealing with resistant local units in a transnational company is cooptation. **Cooptation** is defined as bringing the opposition into the process of designing and implementing the solution without giving up control over the direction and nature of the change. As much as possible, raw power should be avoided. Minimally, however, local units must agree on a short list of transnational systems and raw power may be required to solidify the idea that transnational systems of some sort are truly required.

How should cooptation proceed? Several alternatives are possible. One alternative is to permit each country unit the opportunity to develop one transnational application first in its home territory, and then throughout the world. In this manner, each major country systems group is given a piece of the action in developing a transnational system, and local units feel a sense of ownership in the transnational effort. On the down side, this assumes the ability to develop high quality systems is widely distributed, and that, say, the German team, can successfully implement systems in France and Italy. This will not always be the case. Also, the transnational effort will have low visibility.

A second tactic is to develop new transnational centers of excellence, or a single center of excellence. There may be several centers around the globe that focus on specific business processes. These centers draw heavily from local national units, are based on multinational teams, and must report to worldwide management—their first line of responsibility is to the core applications. Centers of excellence perform the initial identification and specification of the business process, define the information requirements, perform the business and systems analysis, and accomplish all design and testing. Implementation, however, and pilot testing, occur in World Pilot Regions where new applications are installed and tested first. Later, they are rolled out to other parts of the globe. This phased roll-out strategy is precisely how national applications are successfully developed.

Wrapping Up: The Management Solution

We can now reconsider how to handle the most vexing problems facing managers developing the transnational information system infrastructures that were described in Table 14.4.

Legitimacy: The extent to which one's authority is accepted on grounds of competence, vision, or other qualities.

- *Agreeing on common user requirements:* Establishing a short list of the core business processes and core support systems will begin a process of rational comparison across the many divisions of the company, develop a common language for discussing the business, and naturally lead to an understanding of common elements (as well as the unique qualities that must remain local).

- *Inducing procedural business changes:* Your success as a change agent will depend on your legitimacy, your actual raw power, and your ability to involve users in the change design process. **Legitimacy** is defined as the extent to which your authority is accepted on grounds of competence, vision, or other qualities. The selection of a viable change strategy, which we have defined as evolutionary but with a vision, should assist you in convincing others that change is feasible and desirable. Involving people in change, convincing them that change is in the best interests of the company and their local units is a key tactic.

- *Coordinating applications development:* Choice of change strategy is critical for this problem. At the global level there is simply far too much complexity to attempt a grand design strategy of change. It is far easier to coordinate change by making small incremental steps toward a larger vision. Imagine a five-year plan of action rather than a two-year plan of action, and reduce the set of transnational systems to a bare minimum in order to reduce coordination costs.

- *Coordinating software releases:* Firms can institute procedures to ensure that all operating units convert to new software updates at the same time so that everyone's software is compatible.

- *Encouraging local users to take on ownership:* The key to this problem is to involve users in the creation of the design without giving up control over the development of the project to parochial interests. Recruiting a wide range of local individuals to transnational centers of excellence helps send the message that all significant groups are involved in the design and will have an influence.

Even with the proper organizational structure and appropriate management choices, it is still possible to stumble over technological issues. Choices of technology, platforms, networks, hardware, and software are the final elements in building transnational information system infrastructures.

14.4 Technology Issues and Opportunities

Information technology is itself a powerful business driver encouraging the development of global systems, but it creates significant challenges for managers. Global systems presuppose that business firms develop a solid technical foundation and are willing to continually up-grade facilities.

The Main Technical Issues

Hardware, software, and telecommunications pose special technical challenges in an international setting. The major hardware challenge is finding some way to standardize the firm's computer hardware platform when there is so much variation from operating unit to operating unit and from country to country. Managers will need to think carefully about where to locate the firm's computer centers and about how to select hardware suppliers. The major global software challenge is finding applications that are user friendly and that truly enhance the productivity of international work teams. The major telecommunications challenge is making data flow seamlessly across networks shaped by disparate national standards. Overcoming these challenges requires systems integration and connectivity on a global basis.

HARDWARE AND SYSTEMS INTEGRATION

The development of transnational information system infrastructures based on the concept of "core" systems raises questions about how the new core systems will fit in with the existing suite of applications developed around the globe by different divisions, different people, and for different kinds of computing hardware. The goal is to develop global, distributed, and integrated systems. Briefly, these are the same problems faced by any large domestic systems development effort. However, the problems are more complex because of the international environment. For instance, in the United States, IBM hardware and IBM operating systems have played the predominant role in building core systems for large organizations, whereas in Europe UNIX has been much more commonly used for large systems. How can the two be integrated in a common transnational system?

There are two choices to solve integration problems: Remain with a proprietary architecture (generally IBM), or move new core systems to an open architecture. Generally, an open architecture means a UNIX foundation, a client/server architecture, and reliance on PC DOS/Windows machines or UNIX machines on the desktop.

The correct choice will often depend on the history of the company's systems, and the extent of commitment to proprietary systems. For instance, finance and insurance firms typically relied almost exclusively on IBM proprietary equipment and architectures in the 1980s and it would be extremely difficult and cost-ineffective to abandon that equipment and software. Newer firms and manufacturing firms generally find it much easier to adopt open UNIX systems for international systems. As we pointed out in previous chapters, open UNIX-based systems are far more cost-effective in the long run, provide more power at a cheaper price, and preserve options for future expansion.

Once a hardware platform is chosen, the question of standards has to be addressed. Just because all sites use the same hardware does not guarantee common, integrated systems. Some central authority in the firm has to establish data, as well as other technical standards, for sites to comply with. For instance, technical accounting terms must be standardized (e.g., the beginning and end of the fiscal year—review the Window on Organizations), as well as the acceptable interfaces between systems, communications speeds and architectures, and network software.

CONNECTIVITY

The heart of the international systems problem is telecommunications—linking together the systems and people of a global firm into a single integrated network just like the phone system but capable of voice, data, and image transmissions. The Window on Technology explains why an integrated global network is extremely difficult to create.

Firms have two basic options for providing international connectivity: Build their own international private network, or rely on a network service based on the public switched networks throughout the world.

W I N D O W   O N

TECHNOLOGY

Global Networks: A Colossal Headache

If you are a multinational corporation looking to meld your organization into a global entity unfettered by geographic boundaries and time zones, what you want is a global network that seamlessly provides the data to tie your operations together. The problem is, you won't be able to find it.

Many countries cannot even fulfill basic business telecommunications needs such as obtaining reliable circuits, coordinating among different carriers and the regional telecommunications authority, obtaining bills in a common currency standard, and obtaining standard agreements for the level of telecommunications service provided. Many firms find themselves grappling with inconsistent telecommunications service, unreliable costs, and tariff and regulatory problems. Figure 14.6 illustrates the range of these problems.

Europe, for instance, is a hodge-podge of disparate national technical standards and service levels. The problem is especially critical for banks or airlines which must move massive volumes of data around the world. Although most circuits leased by multinational corporations are fault-free more than 99.8 percent of the time, line quality and service vary widely from the north to the south of Europe. Network service is much more unreliable in southern Europe.

European firms realized some time ago the need for developing connectivity standards. The European Economic Community has endorsed EDIfact as the European electronic data interchange (EDI) standard, but the existing European standards for networking and EDI are very industry-specific and country-specific. Most Euro-

pean banks use the SWIFT (Society for Worldwide Interbank Financial Telecommunications) protocol for international funds transfer, while automobile companies and food producers often use industry-specific or country-specific versions of standard protocols for EDI. Complicating matters further, the United States standard for EDI is ANSI (American National Standards Institute) X.12. Although the Open Standards Interconnect (OSI) reference model for linking networks is more popular in Europe than it is in the United States, it is not universally accepted. Various industry groups have standardized on other networking architectures, such as Transmission Control Protocol/Internet Protocol (TCP/IP); IBM's proprietary Systems Network Architecture (SNA); and Digital Equipment's proprietary network architecture, Decnet. Even standards such as ISDN (Integrated Services Digital Network) vary from country to country.

Sources: Stephanie Stahl, "Global Networks: The Headache Continues," *InformationWEEK* (October 12, 1992); Richard L. Hudson, "Multinational Companies in Europe Demand Improvement in Phone Lines," *The Wall Street Journal* (August 3, 1992); and Elisabeth Horwitt, "Systems without Borders," *Computerworld* (August 12, 1991).

To Think About: What are the managerial, organizational, and technological implications of these international connectivity problems? If you were the head of information systems for a multinational company, how would you deal with these problems?

A Sorry Sojourn
Problems users have encountered in building global networks

- Backup circuit cost
- No end-to-end management
- Delivery lead times
- Tariffs
- Inconsistent service
- No diverse routing
- Fault reporting
- Cost monitoring
- Inconsistent standards
- Lack of qualified staff
- Equipment approval
- Circuit quality
- Resale restrictions

Difficulty   Extreme difficulty

Percentage cited   0   10   20

Figure 14.6
Problems users have encountered in building global networks. *Adapted from Stephanie Stahl, "Global Networks: The Headache Continues,"* InformationWEEK *(October 12, 1992). Copyright © 1992 by CMP Publications, Inc., 600 Community Drive, Manhasset, NY 11030. Reprinted from InformationWEEK with permission.*

MANAGEMENT

Multinationals Tackle Software Incompatibility

If you are the Chief Information Officer (CIO) of a global chemical company with 300 plants in 43 divisions and 30 national subsidiaries, how do you get consistent data to run your worldwide organization? Chances are, you can't.

Multinationals are likely to have at least five or six different hardware platforms—some IBM, some Digital Equipment, some Hewlett-Packard, some Fujitsu, some Siemens Nixdorf. Each division is likely to have its own systems, shaped by national characteristics. Language differences, such as writing from right to left, also get in the way, as do national disparities in accounting and taxation methods. Painless global software compatibility is virtually impossible.

One solution is to standardize on application software packages. Courtaulds Plc., a London-based conglomerate that makes everything from tea bags to synthetic fiber clothing and bottle tops, has to manage more than 100 business units in 37 countries around the world. Each of these units developed software programs that are woefully incompatible with each other. Bill Stubbins, a group information technology executive in Courtauld's London home office, decided to look for a common enterprisewide software package for manufacturing resource planning that could be used throughout the company and all of its units.

According to Stubbins, it did not make sense to have each division and business unit shop for themselves. He believed that if Courtauld's corporate information systems group did a thorough analysis of commercially available software packages, all of its businesses would benefit. The corporate information systems department wanted individual MIS departments to focus on applying software packages to their businesses rather than creating the software themselves.

Assisted by the Manchester, England, branch of Andersen Consulting, Stubbins and his staff polled 12 vice presidents of manufacturing at 12 major business units, six in the United Kingdom, five in the United States, and one in Germany. They started with a list of 52 manufacturing resource planning software packages and eventually pared it down to five. Stubbins finally chose two, MFG Probe, a software package from QAD, a software vendor near Ventura, California, and Gemms, a fourth-generation relational database product from Datalogix. The two packages have eighteen modules between them, covering everything from sales order processing, inventory control, quality management, manufacturing scheduling, purchase ledgers, and distribution requirements planning.

Stubbins believes that standardizing on a package reduces the risk of implementation failure. The more effort the information systems department puts into the same system, the more it can reassure users that it can do it right. Another advantage is cost leveraging. The central information systems department can purchase software at a discount because it purchases packages as a group rather than for each individual unit.

A major hurdle is convincing Courtauld's business units that they won't have to change their business strategies to use the software packages. Eleven business units have installed the package. Stubbins claimed he would be pleased if 85 percent of the business units sign up for one of the two standard packages.

Dell Computer Corporation of Austin, Texas, with 20 international business units and 1,777 of its 6,100 employees working outside the United States, found its international business was growing faster than its domestic side. Dell is developing consistent and focused strategies for its European business and requires a unified sales and marketing function shared by its major subsidiaries in these countries. The new strategy, for instance, might outline an innovative way of marketing account development mailings. Without standardized systems, Dell would not be able to install the account mailing upgrades, and a standard system that was truly integrated could pass the strategy along from the marketing and operations group to the subsidiaries on-line.

One possibility is for the firm to put together its own private network based on leased lines from each country's PTT (Post, Telegraph, and Telephone authorities). Each country, however, has different restrictions on data exchange, technical standards, and acceptable vendors of equipment. These problems magnify in certain parts of the world. In Europe and the United States, reliance on PTTs makes more sense while these public networks expand services to compete with private providers.

The second major alternative to building one's own network is to use one of several expanding network services. With deregulation of telecommunications around the globe, private providers have sprung up to service business customers' data needs, along with some voice and image communications.

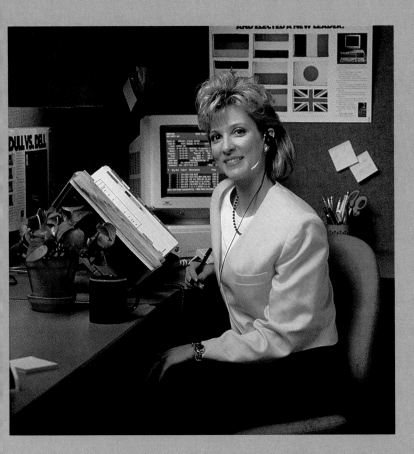

standardized sales system will actually benefit them and not just accumulate data at some central office is critical.

A significant advantage of standardization is reduced training costs. The cost of training people to use a new system and then paying them to operate it can easily exceed hardware and software expenditures. When people change jobs or divisions within a company, standardized software offers large productivity savings.

The biggest managerial hurdle is getting a buy-in from managers overseas. Otherwise, managers may resist the new software or may not implement the software the way it was intended. Experts also advise allocating twice as much time for setting up global software systems as for domestic systems and making sure that the package is well-supported by the vendor abroad

Sources: Johanna Ambrosio, "Global Software?" *Computerworld,* August 2, 1993 and Jason Forsythe, "The Global Data Dilemma," *InformationWEEK,* April 27, 1992.

Dell is exploring the use of a standardized sales and marketing software package.

Standardizing sales procedures across national boundaries can present challenges. In the United Kingdom, sales accounts are traditionally assigned at the company level, with one sales representative handling an entire company. But in the United States, accounts are allocated on a location-by-location basis. A global sales and marketing system has to be flexible enough to accommodate these different national sales structures. Convincing sales representatives that a new

To Think About: What are the management benefits of using a standard software package in a multinational corporation? What problems can software packages solve for multinational corporations? What problems do they create?

Although common in the United States, IVANs (International Value-Added Network Services) are expanding in both Europe and Asia. These private firms offer value-added telecommunications capacity usually rented from local PTTs or international satellite authorities, and then resell it to corporate users. IVANs add value by providing protocol conversion, operating mailboxes and mail systems, and offering integrated billing that permits a firm to track its data communication costs. Currently these systems are limited to data transmissions, but in the future they will expand to voice and image.

SOFTWARE   Compatible hardware and communications provide a platform but not the total solution. Also critical to global core infrastructure is software (see the Window

作表
作表機能では、数値を入力するだけでなく、式を入力してデータを計算することもできます。

文字装飾
文字の字体や大きさを自由に変更できます。また、文字を反転したり下線をつけて強調し、文章にメリハリがつけられます。

スマートアイコン
主要なコマンドをボタン化したのが、スマートアイコンです。アイコンをクリックするだけで、簡単にコマンドを実行できます。

図形部品
あらかじめプログラムに収められている図形部品は、全部で、124種類。図形部品だけでなく絵を描いて貼り込むことや、他のアプリケーションの図形ファイルを呼び出すことも可能です。

ツール
文章中の文字を指定して、自動的に目次や索引を作成する機能や変更を加えた箇所を一目で探せる修正記録など便利なツールも豊富にとりそろえています。

グラフ作成
グラフの種類は12種類。文書作成中にグラフのデータを入力しグラフが作成できます。また、クリップボード経由でまたは他のアプリケーションファイルから、データを読み込みグラフ化することも可能です。

スタイルシート
ビジネスで頻繁に使われる定型文書のひな型（スタイルシート）を用意しました。必要な文字を入力してスタイルを選ぶだけで美しい文書ができあがります。

The AmiPro GUI is easily recognizable to users of this Lotus Development Corporation word processor with SmartIcons and pull down menus. All text screens and menu options in the user interface have been translated into Japanese to accommodate end users in Eastern Asia.

on Management). The development of core systems poses unique challenges for software: How will the old systems interface with the new? Entirely new interfaces must be built and tested if old systems are kept in local areas (which is common). These interfaces can be costly and messy to build. If new software must be created, another challenge is to build software that can be realistically used by multiple business units from different countries when these business units are accustomed to their unique procedures and definitions of data.

Aside from integrating the new with the old systems, there are problems of human interface design and functionality of systems. For instance, in order to be truly useful for enhancing productivity of a global workforce, software interfaces must be easily understood and mastered quickly. Graphical user interfaces are ideal for this but presuppose a common language—often English. When international systems involve knowledge workers only, English may be the assumed international standard. But as international systems penetrate deeper into management and clerical groups, a common language may not be assumed and human interfaces must be built to accommodate different languages and even conventions.

What are the most important software applications? While most interntional systems focus on basic transaction and MIS systems, there is an increasing emphasis on international collaborative work groups. *EDI—* electronic data interchange—is a common global transaction processing application used by manufacturing and distribution firms to connect units of the same company, as well as customers and suppliers on a global basis. *Groupware systems* like electronic mail, videoconferencing, Lotus Notes, and other products supporting shared data files, notes, and electronic mail are much more important to knowledge- and data-based firms like advertising firms, research-based firms in medicine and engineering, and graphics and publishing firms (see Chapter 10).

New Technical Opportunities

There are four major technical advances that should fall in price and gain in power over the next few years that have importance to global networking and systems. After many years of stagnant development, PTTs in Europe and local Bell operating companies in the United States are finally moving ISDN (Integrated Services Digital Network) into the marketplace. Chapter 7 has described the benefits of using ISDN as an international standard for transmitting voice, images, and data over the public telephone network. ISDN will make networking services of all kinds as readily available as a phone jack in the wall. International ISDN services are just now becoming available as the United States and other countries extend their geographic coverage.

Virtual private networks: The ability to custom-configure a network using a portion of the public switched network to create the illusion of a private network for a company.

Virtual private networks (see Chapter 7) add features to the basic public telephone system that are usually only available to private networks. The basic idea of these services is that the local phone company provides each corporate user the ability to custom configure a network and use whatever portion of the public switched net is needed to do the job while charging only for services used. In a sense, the phone company becomes a digital network company, providing many features of a private network for firms operating internationally. This is an improvement over leasing entire lines, or capabilities as in a VAN when you may not need them.

Finally, a variety of satellite systems are being developed that will revolutionize communications because they bypass existing ground-based systems. Motorola in partnership with others, for instance, is developing a worldwide 40-satellite system that will permit hand-held mobile units carried by sales personnel to communicate with headquarters via voice or computer anywhere in the world at any time. Thus, a sales person in China could send an order confirmation request to the home office in London effortlessly and expect a reply instantly. The evolution of digital cellular phone technology will greatly increase the number of cellular communications units and cellular networks, which in turn may use Motorola's systems to connect subscribers into a new worldwide network. Much of the 1990s will be spent building these kinds of communicate and compute anytime, anywhere networks.

Management Challenges

1. **The social and political role of "stateless" firms.** It is one thing to talk about a stateless transnational firm, but the people who work in these firms do have states, cultures, and loyalties; the operating divisions of these firms do in fact reside in various nation states with their own laws, politics, and cultures. It is unclear precisely how these stateless firms fit into the national cultures that they must serve. In reality, so-called stateless firms have had to be very careful to show local populations that they in fact do serve the interests of the state and broader culture.

2. **The difficulties of managing change in a multicultural firm.** While engineering change in a single corporation in a single nation can be difficult, costly, and long-term, bringing about significant change in very large scale global corporations can be daunting. Agreeing on "core business processes" in a transnational context, and then deciding on common systems either requires extraordinary insight, a lengthy process of consensus building, or the exercise of sheer power.

3. **Lines of business and global strategy.** Firms will have to decide whether some or all of their lines of business should be managed on a global basis. There are some lines of business in which local variations are slight, and the possibility exists to reap large rewards by organizing globally. Microcomputers and power tools may fit this pattern, as well as industrial raw materials. Other consumer goods may be quite different by country or region. It is likely that firms with many lines of business will have to maintain a very mixed organizational structure.

Summary

Identify the major factors behind the growing internationalization of business.

There are both general cultural factors as well as specific business factors to consider. The growth of cheap international communication and transportation has created a "global culture" with stable expectations or norms. Political stability and a growing global knowledge base that is widely shared contribute also to the global culture. These general factors create the conditions for global markets, global production, coordination, distribution, and global economies of scale.

Choose among several global strategies for developing business.

There are four basic international strategies: domestic exporter, multinational, franchiser, and transnational. The trend is toward a transnational strategy in which all factors of production are coordinated on a global scale. However, the choice of strategy is a function of the type of business and product.

Understand how information systems support different global strategies.

There is a connection between firm strategy and information system design. Transnational firms must develop networked system configurations and permit considerable decentralization of development and operations. Franchisers almost always duplicate systems across many countries and use centralized financial controls. Multinationals typically rely on decentralized independence among foreign units with some movement toward development of networks. Domestic exporters are typically centralized in domestic headquarters with some decentralized operations permitted.

Manage the development of international systems.

Implementing a global system requires an implementation strategy. Typically, global systems have evolved without conscious plan. The remedy is to define a small subset of core business processes and focus on building systems which could support these processes. Tactically, you will have to coopt widely dispersed foreign units to participate in the development and operation of these systems, being careful not to lose overall control.

Understand the main technical alternatives in developing global systems.

The main hardware and telecommunications issues are systems integration and connectivity. The choices for integration are either to go with a proprietary architecture or with an open systems technology like UNIX. Global networks are extremely difficult to build and operate. Some measure of connectivity may be achieved either by relying on local PTT authorities to provide connections, building a system oneself, or relying on private providers to supply communications capacity. The trend appears towards growing reliance on private providers, although public authorities and PTTs are moving forward rapidly with ISDN and other digital services to compete with private companies. The main software issue concerns building interfaces to existing systems and providing much-needed group support software.

Key Terms

International information systems infrastructure	Franchiser
Business driver	Transnational
Global culture	Core systems
Particularism	Business processes
Transborder data flow	Cooptation
Domestic exporter	Legitimacy
Multinational	Virtual private networks

1. What are the five major factors to consider when building an international information system infrastructure?

2. Describe the five general cultural factors leading toward growth in global business and the four specific business factors. Describe the interconnection among these factors.

3. What is meant by a global culture?

4. What are the major challenges to the development of global systems?

5. Why have firms not planned for the development of international systems?

6. Describe the four main strategies for global business and organizational structure.

7. Describe the four different system configurations that can be used to support different global strategies.

8. What are the major management issues in developing international systems?

9. What are three principles to follow when organizing the firm for global business?

10. What are three steps of a management strategy for developing and implementing global systems?

11. What is meant by cooptation, and how can it be used to build global systems?

12. Describe the main technical issues facing global systems.

13. Describe three new technologies that can help firms develop global systems.

1. As a member of your company's global information systems group that oversees development of global core systems, what criteria would you use to determine if an application should be developed as a global application or as a peripheral local application?

2. As the CEO of a domestic exporter with large production facilities in the U.S., you are considering moving toward a multinational model by creating production facilities in Europe and Asia. What strategy would you follow in building an international information infrastructure; what applications would you recommend be shared and global or common; and how would you implement the strategy?

With a group of students, identify an area of emerging information technology and explore how this technology might be useful for supporting global business strategies. For instance, you might choose an area like digital telecommunications (e.g., electronic mail, wireless communications, value added networks), or collaborative work group software, or new standards in operating systems, or EDI. It will be helpful to choose a business scenario to discuss the technology. You might choose, for instance, an automobile parts franchiser, or a clothing franchise like the Limited Express as example businesses. What applications would you make global, what core business processes would you choose, and how would the technology be helpful?

CASE STUDY

Retooling Black & Decker For Global Operations

Black & Decker had worked its way out of a market share slump and decline in the early 1980s to become the world's largest manufacturer and distributor of power tools for the do-it-yourself market in the 1990s. After losing market share for both professional and home use tools in the early 1980's, CEO Nolan Archibald, who joined

Black & Decker in 1985, instituted a "cut and build" strategy: cut expenses to the bone and plow the savings back into new products. Then, in 1989, Black & Decker acquired Emhart Corporation (a diversified company known for its home improvement products such as Kwiket locks and Price Pfister faucets, commercial/industrial products, and information systems and services.) With the acquisition, Black & Decker doubled sales from $2.2 billion to $4.8 billion in 1991. Approximately fifty percent of Black & Decker's product sales come from overseas. One way Black & Decker plans to retain its worldwide leadership is through the development of global information systems. According to CEO Archibald, IS was one area where progress was not being made toward a global operational capability. "We couldn't get information into the hands of managers to run things as well as we'd like to," explained Archibald.

Black & Decker applied the "cut and build" strategy to IS with a new twist: "push and pull." Since 1988 the company has tried to push development resources and computing power down as close to the end user as possible while at the same time pulling together computer hardware and software resources on a global basis. Here are some of their specific accomplishments:

- Linked acquired business operations via standard financial reporting systems.
- Implemented EDI and bar coding selectively at major retailers in the United States and initiated pilot projects in Europe.
- Initiated development of a strategic IS plan to support global business operations.
- Shifted some IS development to business units.
- Consolidated multiple mainframe data centers and initiated migrations from mainframes to PCs, LANs and midrange platforms, and consolidated telecommunications networks.
- Implemented a total quality process in IS.

The point of global systems, according to Black & Decker, is to "improve management of information flow on a worldwide basis, but still have the feel that things are local and are getting done on a timely basis." In Europe Black & Decker has run into difficulties trying to consolidate data centers and introduce common systems. Data definition is a real problem because Black & Decker operates in 15 European countries. In the United States it was much more centralized, but in Europe, Black & Decker, like most multinationals, was organized on a country basis with each country running its own show. This meant that there was no standard coding structure for products, customers, spare parts, invoices, or bills of lading. In short,

the entire paper processing enterprise was for local needs. Business has certain inherent inefficiencies if each country produces its own parts manuals, each with different numbers. On the other hand, a company cannot force common systems or data definitions that are contrary to local practices. You have to be flexible, allowing for different languages, accounting methods, products, and retail markets.

Black & Decker's European MIS Director started the long process toward common systems by focusing on those countries where Black & Decker has large manufacturing facilities (Italy, Germany, and the United Kingdom). From 1986 to 1989, Black & Decker standardized the manufacturing countries on IBM mainframes and adopted the same CAD/CAM software standards for engineering and design as used in the United States.

Common worldwide financial systems were developed. It used to take several weeks to roll up the year-end figures from 40 different financial reports produced by 120 Black & Decker offices around the world. The reports used to be delivered by courier, fax, and E-mail, causing cumbersome administration.

The solution was a common financial software package. Black & Decker's U.S. businesses converted to a PC-based software package. In 1993 the Micro Control system was rolled out to all offices throughout the globe. Budgets are produced on Micro Control templates and then reported automatically to corporate headquarters. Now, year-end results are available in a couple of days (not weeks). Monthly budgets can be done in days.

Even with common software, some problems remain. The most significant is data architecture, and behind this problem, the question of what's best: global or regional definitions and systems, and business. For instance, it may be best to develop regional suppliers, closer to the factories, and closer to ultimate customers. If this is true, it may be best to develop regional data definitions rather than imposing some grand worldwide standard that does not satisfy anyone in Europe, the United States or Asia. If regional is better, this means parts, customer numbers, and vendors should be defined regionally. Currently, Black & Decker is building repositories for key corporate data in both North America and Europe.

Sales support systems offer an interesting insight into these kinds of issues. Black & Decker has several experiments in the United States and Europe with EDI. In the United States there is a common set of standards for EDI, but in Europe EDI has made progress mostly in the United Kingdom and Sweden, with other countries trailing behind and with slightly different standards in each country.

Sources: Susan Caminiti, "A Star Is Born," *Fortune: The Tough New Consumer* (Autumn/Winter 1993) and Bruce Caldwell, "Black & Decker Retools," *InformationWeek* (September 23, 1991).

Case Study Questions

1. What kind of a global business strategy do you think Black & Decker is pursuing? Are they pursuing the right kind of systems appropriate for their business strategy?

2. How should Black & Decker decide on whether to develop global, regional, and local systems?

3. Is there a contradiction between "global information management" and the feeling that things are being done locally in a timely manner?

4. What should Black & Decker managers do about the different EDI standards in Europe? How can they convince retailers or vendors to adopt common standards? Which ones should they adopt—U.S. or European?

References

Cash, James I., F. Warren McFarlan, James L. McKenney, and Lynda M. Applegate. *Corporate Information Systems Management.* 3rd edition. Homewood, IL: Irwin, 1992.

Chismar, William G. and Laku Chidambaram. "Telecommunications and the Structuring of U.S. Multinational Corporations." *International Information Systems* 1, no. 4 (October 1992).

Cox, Butler. *Globalization: The IT Challenge.* Sunnyvale, CA: Amdahl Executive Institute, 1991.

Deans, Candace P. and Michael J. Kane. *International Dimensions of Information Systems.* Boston, MA: PWS-Kent, 1992.

Deans, Candace P., Kirk R. Karwan, Martin D. Goslar, David A. Ricks, and Brian Toyne. "Key International Issues in U.S.-Based Multinational Corporations." *Journal of Management Information Systems* 7, no. 4 (Spring 1991).

Dutta, Amitava. "Telecommunications Infrastructure in Developing Nations." *International Information Systems* 1, no. 3 (July 1992).

Holland, Christopher, Geoff Lockett, and Ian Blackman. "Electronic Data Interchange Implementation: A Comparison of U.S. and European Cases." *International Information Systems* 1, no. 4 (October 1992).

Ives, Blake, and Jarvenpaa, Sirkka. "Applications of Global Information Technology: Key Issues for Management." *MIS Quarterly* 15, no. 1 (March 1991).

Ives, Blake, and Jarvenpaa, Sirkka. "Global Information Technology: Some Lessons from Practice." *International Information Systems* 1, no. 3 (July 1992).

Karin, Jahangir and Benn R. Konsynski. "Globalization and Information Management Systems." *Journal of Management Information Systems* 7, no. 4 (Spring 1991).

Keen, Peter. *Shaping the Future.* Cambridge, MA: Harvard Business School Press, 1991.

King, William R., and Vikram Sethi. "An Analysis of International Information Regimes." *International Information Systems* 1, no. 1 (January 1992).

Mannheim, Marvin L. "Global Information Technology: Issues and Strategic Opportunities." *International Information Systems* 1, no. 1 (January 1992).

Nelson, R. Ryan, Ira R. Weiss, and Kazumi Yamazaki. "Information Resource Management within Multinational Corporations: A Cross-Cultural Comparison of the U.S. and Japan." *International Information Systems* 1, no. 4 (October 1992).

Neumann, Seev. "Issues and Opportunities in International Information Systems." *International Information Systems* 1, no. 4 (October 1992).

Palvia, Shailendra, Prashant Palvia, and Ronald Zigli, eds. *The Global Issues of Information Technology Management.* Harrisburg, PA: Idea Group Publishing, 1992.

Roche, Edward M. *Managing Information Technology in Multinational Corporations.* New York: Macmillan, 1992.

Steinbart, Paul John, and Ravinder Nath. "Problems and Issues in the Management of International Data Networks." *MIS Quarterly* 16, no. 1 (March 1992).

Ethical and Social Issues in Information Systems

Should Automation Stamp Out Jobs?

The United States Post Office has been under intense public pressure to provide better service while keeping its rates down. To combat a rising tide of red ink, it embarked on a six-year $3.5 billion automation project designed to save $3 billion in annual salary expenses. The Post Office started to mechanize mail handling down to the carrier level. It began using optical character recognition (OCR) technology to expedite letter sorting and handling. Envelopes with neatly typed or printed ZIP codes pass through optical character recognition equipment, which reads the ZIP codes, applies bar codes, and sorts and sends the envelopes out. In cases where OCR could not determine the ZIP code, the Post Office planned to use an imaging system to put a video image of the address on a terminal screen so that operators could key in the ZIP code for remote printing of the bar code on the envelope. The Post Office planned to have all letters and eventually other classes of parcel post bar coded by 1995.

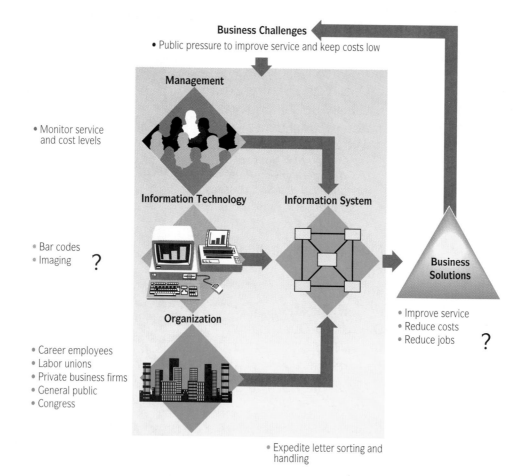

But when Postmaster General Marvin Runyon took office in May, 1992, he put the automation project on hold for a close review. Congress and organized labor were protesting the job reductions that directly resulted from the automation. The Post Office planned to eliminate 40,000 positions through early retirement.

Although less than one-third of the automated equipment has been installed, what was put in place enabled the Post Office to cut more than 39,000 jobs through attrition over three years, reducing the number of career employees to 748,961. In September 1992, Representative Frank McCloskey of Indiana reported a "feeling of gloom and hysteria" among postal employees at a House subcommittee meeting. Job cuts appeared to be accelerating. The Post Office expected to eliminate another 22,000 career employee positions by 1995.

The General Accounting Office pointed out that automation was not a magic bullet that could reverse the trend toward rising postal expenses, noting that wage and benefit increases amounted to four times the amount saved by cutting labor costs in 1991. The GAO found that the Post Office had not been able to manage the work force to realize the full potential of automation. However, business analysts have applauded the Post Office's efforts to reduce inefficiencies and to respond to customers. For instance, the bar-code technology that was installed has cut the postage bills for some of the Post Office's largest customers, such as CoreStates Financial Corporation in Philadelphia, who receive hefty discounts for doing their own bar coding.

Runyon has been in a tight spot. He made a commitment to hold postal rates steady through 1994.

Sources: Gary H. Anthes, "Postal Service Sorts Through Automation." *Computerworld,* October 4, 1993 and Paula Klein, "Stamping Out Jobs," *InformationWEEK,* September 28, 1992.

The Post Office automation plan promised savings for both private industry and the general public but it also threatened to eliminate the jobs of many valuable employees. Faced with these alternatives, what should the Post Office do? The plight of the Post Office is an example of an ethical dilemma created by information systems, one that is shared by many organizations today.

Balancing the need for efficiency with responsibility toward employees is one of many ethical and social issues faced by organizations using information systems. Others include establishing information rights, including the right to privacy; protecting intellectual property rights; establishing accountability for the consequences of information systems; setting standards to safeguard system quality that protect the safety of individuals and society; and preserving values and institutions considered essential to the quality of life in an information society. This chapter describes these issues and suggests guidelines for dealing with these questions.

After completing this chapter you will be able to:

- Understand the relationship among ethical, social, and political issues raised by information systems.
- Identify the main moral dimensions of an information society and apply them to specific situations.
- Apply an ethical analysis to difficult situations.
- Understand specific ethical principles for conduct.
- Develop corporate policies for ethical conduct.

15.1 Understanding Ethical and Social Issues Related to Systems

In Chapter 1 we identified one of the key management challenges facing you as the ethical and socially responsible use of information systems. Now it is time to put some flesh on that call.

Ethics: Principles of right and wrong that can be used by individuals acting as free moral agents to make choices to guide their behavior.

Ethics refers to the principles of right and wrong that can be used by individuals acting as free moral agents to make choices to guide their behavior. Information technology and information systems pose unique problems for both individuals and societies because they create opportunities for social change. It is sometimes possible to create social change in a "socially responsible manner," one that takes into account the delicate balances among groups arrived at in the past. With new information technology it will also be possible for you—if you cast all your ethics aside—to decentralize power in an organization, invade the privacy of your employees while you improve service to customers, reach markets served by your global competitors and cause widespread unemployment, engage in new kinds of criminal activity as your company seeks to protect itself from information disclosures, and create new kinds of products which eliminate older products and the employment of people who make those products.

Information technology is certainly not the first technology to offer these potentials for radical social change. Steam engines, electricity, internal combustion engines, telephone and radio—each in their day offered new opportunities for social change and for individual action. At the same time, these new technologies threatened existing distributions of power, money, rights, and obligations—in short, the things considered worth having. Likewise with information technology: The development of IT will produce losers and winners, will produce benefits for many, and costs for others. In this situation, what is the ethical and socially responsible course of action?

Technology does not stand "outside" of society, acting upon it. Instead, technology—its manufacturers, benefactors, users—is a social phenomenon itself subject to all the constraints of other social actors. Among these constraints is the notion of social responsibility: you can and will be held accountable for your actions.

A Model for Thinking about Ethical, Social and Political Issues

Ethical, social and political issues are of course tightly coupled together. The ethical dilemma you may face as a manager of information systems typically is reflected in social and political debate. One way to think about these relationships is given in Figure 15.1.

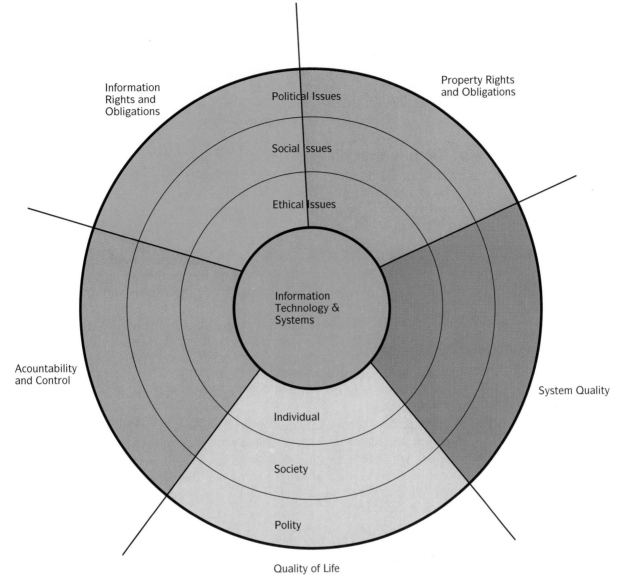

Figure 15.1
The relationship between ethical, social and political issues in an information society. The introduction of new information technology has a ripple effect, raising new ethical, social and political issues that must be dealt with on the individual, social, and political levels. These issues have five moral dimensions: information rights and obligations, property rights and obligations, system quality, quality of life, and accountability and control.

Imagine society as a more or less calm pond on a summer day, a delicate ecosystem in partial equilibrium with individuals and with social and political institutions. Individuals know how to act in this pond because social institutions (family, education, organizations) have developed well-honed rules of behavior, and these are backed up by laws developed in the political sector that prescribe behavior and promise sanctions for violations. Now toss a rock into the center of the pond. But imagine instead of a rock that the disturbing force is a powerful shock of new information technology and systems hitting a society more or less at rest. What happens? Ripples, of course.

Suddenly individual actors are confronted with new situations often not covered by the old rules. Social institutions cannot respond overnight to these ripples—it may take years to develop etiquette, expectations, "socially responsible," "politically correct" attitudes, or approved rules. Political institutions also require time before developing new laws and often require the demonstration of real harm before they act. In the meantime, you may have to act. You may be forced to act in a legal "gray area."

We can use this model as a first approximation to the dynamics which connect ethical, social, and political issues. This model is also useful for identifying the main moral dimensions of the "information society" which cut across various levels of action—individual, social, and political.

Five Moral Dimensions of the Information Age

A review of the literature on ethical, social and political issues surrounding systems identifies five moral dimensions of the information age which we introduce here and explore in greater detail in Section 15.3. The five moral dimensions are as follows:

Information rights: The rights that individuals and organizations have with respect to information that pertains to themselves.

- *Information rights and obligations:* What **information rights** do individuals and organizations possess with respect to information about themselves? What can they protect? What obligations do individuals and organizations have concerning this information?
- *Property rights:* How will traditional intellectual property rights be protected in a digital society where tracing and accounting for ownership is difficult, where ignoring such property rights is so easy?
- *Accountability and control:* Who can and will be held accountable and liable for the harm done to individual and collective information and property rights?
- *System quality:* What standards of data and system quality should we demand to protect individual rights and the safety of society?
- *Quality of life:* What values should be preserved in an information- and knowledge-based society? What institutions should we protect from violation? What cultural values and practices are supported by the new information technology?

Before going on to analyze these dimensions we should briefly review the major technology and system trends which have heightened concern about the issues above.

Key Technology Trends Which Raise Ethical Issues

In what ways have information technology and systems created the ethical issues described above? In fact, these ethical issues long preceded information technology—they are the abiding concerns of free societies everywhere. Nevertheless, information technology has heightened ethical concerns, put stress on existing social arrangements, and made existing laws obsolete or severely crippled. There are four key technological trends responsible for these ethical stresses.

The doubling of computing power every 18 months since the early 1980s has made it possible for most organizations to utilize information systems for their core production processes. As a result, our dependence on systems and our vulnerability to system errors and poor data quality have increased. Occasional system failures heighten public concern over our growing dependence on some critical systems. Social rules and laws have not yet adjusted to this dependence. Standards for ensuring the accuracy and reliability of information systems (see Chapters 9 and 13) are not universally accepted or enforced.

Advances in data storage techniques and rapidly declining storage costs have been responsible for the multiplying databases on individuals—employees,

The EMASS data tower provides state of the art mass data
storage and retrieval facilities for its clients.

customers, and potential customers—maintained by private and public organizations. These advances in data storage have made the routine violation of individual privacy both cheap and effective. For example, EMASS Storage Systems of Dallas advertises its new mass storage system as one capable of holding up to 10,000 terabytes of data in a 27 square foot space, at a media cost of $2 a gigabyte, a data transfer rate of 15 megabytes per second, and a record access time of a few seconds (*Datamation*, 1992 and 1993). This is a bit slow for on-line transaction processing, and slower than even a 600 megabyte CD-ROM with record access times of 150 milliseconds. Still, such huge terabyte size storage systems are cheap enough for regional and even local retailing firms to use in identifying customers.

Advances in data mining techniques for large data bases are a third technological trend that heightens ethical concerns. For instance, cheap parallel supercomputers are used by Hallmark Cards, Kmart, Wal-mart Stores Inc., American Express, and others to very rapidly identify buying patterns of customers and suggest appropriate responses. One retailer examined customer "buying trips" as the unit of analysis. They discovered that if someone in the Midwest buys disposable diapers at 5 P.M., the most common thing next purchased is a six-pack of beer. The retailer decided, therefore, to put beer and snacks next to the diapers rack (*The Wall Street Journal,* December 23, 1992). These data mining techniques further shrink the penumbra of privacy created by older less powerful technologies.

But the impact of widely distributed supercomputing also has equity implications for society. As with mainframes of the past, supercomputing capacity

On June 10 and June 11, 1991, Alecia Swasy, a Pittsburgh-based reporter for *The Wall Street Journal* reported in the *Journal* that, according to inside sources at the Procter & Gamble Company, a senior executive was under pressure to resign and that the company might sell several unprofitable divisions. Based in Cincinnati, Ohio, Procter & Gamble is one of the world's largest consumer products companies with such brand names as Tide detergent, Crest toothpaste, and many other products.

In response to the articles, senior executives of Procter & Gamble, and corporate security officer Jim Jessee, asked the Cincinnati police to determine if any current or former employees were leaking confidential corporate information to *The Wall Street Journal*. In response to the complaints from the company, the Hamilton County Prosecutor subpoenaed Cincinnati Bell Telephone Company to identify all 513 area code numbers that had dialed Ms. Swasy's home or office telephones in Pittsburgh during an eight-week period that started on March 1, 1991. Cincinnati Bell serves 655,297 customers in the 513 area code, which also includes localities in Kentucky and Pennsylvania. About 13 million calls are placed each month in the 513 area code.

Cincinnati Bell refused comment on what it actually turned over to the prosecutor, but said that it

routinely complies with subpoenas. A phone company spokesman said that under normal procedures the company's computers would have automatically searched its customer list and printed out the originating numbers, but not the names or addresses, of calls to Ms. Swasy's telephones.

Ohio has several statutes that prohibit the unauthorized disclosure of trade secrets or transmission of any confidential information, formulas, customer lists, or other tangible pieces of information that would be valuable to a company and its competitors.

Civil liberties experts argued that Procter & Gamble's actions, and those of the prosecutor, may have violated the privacy rights of thousands of people, not to mention their First Amendment and Fourth Amendment guarantees of freedom of speech, and protections against unreasonable search and seizure. Much depends on how the investigation was actually carried out. If Procter & Gamble turned over its records of current and former employees and the police matched their list against the records from the phone company, then the rights of uninvolved parties may not have been violated. But if police learned the names of people unaffiliated with Procter & Gamble who called the *Journal*, or if they turned over an entire list of numbers of people who called the *Journal* to Procter & Gamble, then

Fourth Amendment protections were violated.

One privacy expert argued that technological capacity has gone over the line of reasonable search and seizure when a computer system permits you to scan millions of calls made by hundreds of thousands of customers in order to identify who called a person based on the suspicion that a crime may have been committed.

Source: Randall Rothenberg, "Search for News Leak Spurs Ohio Phone Sweep," *The New York Times* (August 16, 1991).

To Think About: If instead of phone records the records involved were letters sent and received through the post office, do you think the prosecutor should have or would have been able to subpoena all mail correspondence between Swasy and citizens in the (513) area code? Why are telephone records different from mailed letters? What do you think the public reaction to Procter & Gamble's actions was? What is your reaction? Who should be held responsible for the large scale sweep of telephone calls if it is determined this action violated the First and Fourth Amendments? Procter & Gamble management, the security officer, the phone company, or the prosecutor?

will largely be dominated by elite groups in society—large business and government organizations, and the dominant professional and business classes running these institutions. In turn, these large groups may grow to become far more powerful vis-à-vis individuals and small groups than is now the case.

Last, *advances in telecommunications infrastructure* like ISDN (Integrated Services Digital Network) and proposed national telecommunications networks like the National Research Education Network (NREN)—see the Window on Technology—promise to reduce greatly the cost of moving large data sets, and open the possibility of mining large data sets remotely using smaller desktop machines. Local Bell operating companies (BOCs) have been slow to adopt ISDN for lack of regulatory incentives. But more and more regulators are moving to allow the BOCs to distribute a wide range of data services (e.g., news, sports, movies, and data along with voice, and even to own the contents of what they distribute) over the strong opposition of the Newspaper Association and the Cable Television Industry Association.

By the year 2000 it is conceivable that many homes and business offices will have communication lines with up to 100 megabits per second capacity. This capability will radically reduce the cost of mining huge terabyte size databases, permitting the invasion of privacy on a scale and precision unimaginable to us now. Even the Census Bureau would lose its shelter: With commonly available census data on blocks, along with other data, we could easily pick out information about individuals with great regularity.

The development of national digital superhighway communication networks widely available to individuals and businesses poses many ethical and social concerns. Who will account for the flow of information over these networks? Will you be able to trace information collected about you? What will these networks do to the traditional relationships between family, work, and leisure? How will traditional job designs be altered when millions of "employees" become subcontractors using mobile offices that they themselves must pay for?

In the next section we will consider some ethical principles and analytical techniques for dealing with these kinds of ethical and social concerns.

15.2 Ethics in an Information Society

Ethics is a concern of humans who have freedom of choice. Ethics is about individual choice: When faced with alternative courses of action, what is the correct moral choice? When freedom of choice is restricted or impaired for whatever reason—reasoning ability, situational factors, or forced choice—then ethical analysis is less appropriate. What are the main features of "ethical choice?"

Basic Concepts: Responsibility, Accountability, and Liability

Responsibility: Accepting the potential costs, duties, and obligations of one's decisions.

Accountability: The mechanisms for assessing responsibility for decisions made and actions taken.

Liability: The existence of laws that permit individuals to recover the damages done to them by other actors, systems, or organizations.

Ethical choices are decisions made by individuals who are responsible for the consequences of their actions. Responsibility is a feature of individuals and is a key element of ethical action. **Responsibility** means that you accept the potential costs, duties, and obligations for the decisions you make. **Accountability** is a feature of systems and social institutions: it means that mechanisms are in place to determine who took responsible action. Systems and institutions where it is impossible to find out who took what action are inherently incapable of ethical analysis or ethical action. Liability extends the concept of responsibility further to the area of laws. **Liability** is a feature of political systems in which a body of law is in place which permits individuals to recover the damages done to them by other actors, systems, or organizations. Due process is a related feature of law-governed societies: it means a process in which laws are known and understood and there is an ability to appeal to higher authorities to ensure that the laws were applied correctly.

These basic concepts form the underpinning of an ethical analysis of information systems and those who manage them. First, as we discussed in Chapter 3, information technologies are filtered through social institutions, organizations, and individuals. Systems do not have "impacts" all by themselves. Whatever information system impacts exist are a product of institutional, organizational, and individual actions and behaviors. Second, responsibility for the consequences of technology falls clearly on the institutions, organizations, and individual managers who choose to use the technology. Using information technology in a "socially responsible" manner means that you can and will be held accountable for the consequences of your actions. Third, in an ethical political society, individuals and others can recover damages done them through a set of laws characterized by due process. The example of Procter & Gamble's efforts to detect an information leak among its employees is an instructive illustration of the difficulties of applying these principles.

Ethical Analysis

When confronted with a situation that seems to present ethical issues, how should you analyze and reason about the situation? Here's a five-step process that should help:

1. *Identify and describe clearly the facts.* Find out who did what to whom, and where, when, and how. You will be surprised in many instances how wrong the initially reported facts typically are, and often you will find that simply getting the facts straight helps define the solution. It also helps to get the opposing parties involved in an ethical dilemma to agree on the facts.

2. *Define the conflict or dilemma and identify the higher order values involved.* Ethical, social and political issues always reference higher values. The parties to a dispute all claim to be pursuing higher values (e.g., freedom, privacy, protection of property, and the free enterprise system).

   Typically, an ethical issue involves a dilemma: two diametrically opposed courses of action that support worthwhile values. In the Procter & Gamble case, you have two competing and opposing values: the right of a company to protect its internal information processes, and the rights of individuals to be free from unreasonable search and seizure, as well as to speak their minds.

3. *Identify the stakeholders.* Every ethical, social, and political issue has stakeholders: players in the game who have an interest in the outcome, who have invested in the situation, and usually who have vocal opinions. Find out who these groups are and what they want. This will be useful later when designing a solution.

4. *Identify the options that you can reasonably take.* You may find that none of the options satisfy all the interests involved, but that some options do a better job than others. Sometimes arriving at a "good" or ethical solution may not always be a "balancing" of consequences to stakeholders.

5. *Identify the potential consequences of your options.* Some options may be ethically correct, but disastrous from other points of view. Other options may work in this one instance, but not be generalizable to other similar instances. Always ask yourself, "What if I choose this option consistently over time?"

Once your analysis is completed, what ethical principles or rules should you use to make a decision? What higher-order values should inform your judgement?

Candidate Ethical Principles

While you are the only one who can decide which among many ethical principles you will follow, and how you will give priority to them, it is helpful to consider some ethical principles with deep roots in many cultures that have survived throughout recorded history.

1. Do unto others as you would have them do unto you (the Golden Rule). Putting yourself into the situation of others, and thinking of yourself as the object of the decision, can help you think about "fairness" in decision making.

2. If an action is not right for everyone to take, then it is not right for anyone (**Immanuel Kant's Categorical Imperative**). Ask yourself, "If everyone did this, could the organization, or society, survive?"

3. If an action cannot be taken repeatedly, then it is not right to be taken at any time (**Descartes' rule of change**). This is the slippery-slope rule: An action may bring about a small change now that is acceptable, but if repeated would bring unacceptable changes in the long run. In the vernacular, it might be stated as "once started down a slippery path you may not be able to stop."

4. Take the action that achieves the higher or greater value (the **Utilitarian Principle**). This rule assumes you can prioritize values in a rank order, and understand the consequences of various courses of action.

5. Take the action that produces the least harm, or the least potential cost (**Risk Aversion Principle**). Some actions have extremely high failure costs of very low probability (e.g., building a nuclear generating facility in an urban area), or extremely high failure costs of moderate probability (speeding and automobile accidents). Avoid these high failure cost actions, with greater attention obviously to high failure cost potential of moderate to high probability.

6. Assume that virtually all tangible and intangible objects are owned by someone unless there is a specific declaration otherwise. (This is the ethical "no free lunch" rule.) If something created by someone else is useful to you, it has value and you should assume the creator wants compensation for his or her work.

None of these ethical rules can survive the detailed analytical mind of a contemporary philosopher or critical pundit. They have too many logical and substantive exceptions to be absolute guides to action. Nevertheless, actions that do not easily pass these rules deserve some very close attention and a great deal of caution if only because the appearance of unethical behavior may do as much harm to you and your company as actual unethical behavior.

Some Real-World Ethical Dilemmas

The recent ethical problems described below illustrate a wide range of issues. Some of these issues are obvious ethical dilemmas. Others represent some type of breach of ethics. In either instance, there are rarely any easy solutions.

Continental Can: Based in Norwalk, Connecticut, Continental Can Co. developed a human resources database with files on all of its employees. Besides the typical employee data, the system included the capability to "red flag" employees nearing retirement or approaching the age at which a pension would be vested in the individual. Throughout the 1980s, when the red flag went up, management would fire the person even after decades of loyal service. In 1991 a federal district court in Newark, New Jersey, awarded ex-employees $445 million for wrongful dismissal (McPartlin, June 22, 1992).

Software bomb at Revlon: In 1988 Revlon Inc., one of the world's largest cosmetics firms, contracted with a small software firm called Logisticon Inc. to develop inventory control software for the sum of $600,000. In October 1990, the Revlon vice president for systems development, Nathan Amitai, sought to terminate the contract, claiming the work had not been "up to expectations." At that point, Revlon owed Logisticon $180,000 but refused to pay this amount

---

Immanuel Kant's Categorial Imperative: A principle that states that if an action is not right for everyone to take it is not right for anyone.

Descartes' rule of change: A principle that states that if an action cannot be taken repeatedly, then it is not right to be taken at any time.

Utilitarian Principle: Principle that one should take the action that achieves the higher or greater value.

Risk Aversion Principle: Principle that one should take the action that produces the least harm or incurs the least cost.

Ethical no free lunch rule: Assumption that all tangible and intangible objects are owned by someone else unless there is a specific declaration otherwise and that the creator wants compensation for his work.

until work for the first phase of the project was completed. Logisticon President Donald Gallagher blamed any performance faults on bugs in Revlon's systems, and demanded payment. Revlon refused.

At 2:30 A.M. on October 16, 1990, Revlon systems personnel reported systemwide breakdowns in Logisticon software. Logisticon faxed a letter to Revlon the next day, stating, "Logisticon disabled the operation of its Dispatcher System software last night but took great care to do it in an orderly fashion and not violate or corrupt your data. If you use or attempt to use Logisticon proprietary software to restart the Dispatcher System application package, we believe there is a real possibility that you could corrupt your data, and we will not be responsible. When and if agreement is reached on outstanding payments, systems can be restored in a few hours."

During the next three days, sales from the two affected distribution facilities "were brought to a standstill," resulting in the loss of millions of dollars of orders, and temporary layoffs of hundreds of workers. The systems were restored by Logisticon by October 19. On October 22, Revlon filed suit against Logisticon, charging intentional interference with contractual relations, trespass, conversion, misappropriation of trade secrets, and breach of contract and warranty. One of Revlon's complaints was that Logisticon did not mention in the contract with Revlon that a "drop dead" or software bomb device had been implanted in the software. Had this been a part of the contract, Revlon would have acted differently (Caldwell, 1990).

Technological Threats at AT&T: In March 1992, four months before entering into contract negotiations with the Communications Workers of America (CWA) and the International Brotherhood of Electrical Workers (IBEW), AT&T announced that it was introducing technology that would replace one-third of its 18,000 long-distance operators by 1994. The unions quickly branded the announcement as an "intimidation tactic" designed to soften up the unions' demands for higher wages and better working conditions.

AT&T plans to use voice recognition software to reduce the need for human operators by allowing computers to recognize a customer's responses to a series of computerized questions. New algorithms called "word spotting" allow the computer to recognize speech that is halting, stuttering, paused, or ungrammatical.

AT&T claims the new technology will permit it to eliminate 3000 to 6000 operator jobs nationwide, and 200 to 400 management positions. It will also be able to close 31 offices in 21 states. Long-distance operators earn anywhere from $10,300 to $27,100 a year, with benefits adding another third of the cost. AT&T claims not all workers will be dismissed and that many will be retrained for other positions.

Communications Workers of America officials expressed outrage at AT&T's announcement at the time, especially the announcement that entire offices will be closed. AT&T now claims it made the announcement because of leaks from the union officials and that managers only wanted to inform workers before the news spread further (Ramirez, March 4, 1992).

E-mail privacy at EPSON: In March 1990, E-mail administrator Alana Shoars filed a suit in Los Angeles Superior Court alleging wrongful termination, defamation, and invasion of privacy by her former employer, Epson America Inc. of Torrance, California. She sought $1 million in damages. In July 1990, Shoars filed a class suit seeking $75 million for 700 Epson employees and approximately 1800 outsiders whose E-mail may have been monitored. Shoars contends that she was fired because she questioned the company's policy of monitoring and printing employees' E-mail messages. Epson claims that Shoars was fired because she opened an MCI:Mail account without permission. Many firms claim that they have every right to monitor the electronic mail of their employees because they own the facilities, intend their use to be for business purposes only, and create the facility for a business purpose (Rifkin, 1991).

In each instance, you can find competing values at work, with groups lined up on either side of a debate. A close analysis of the facts can sometimes produce compromised solutions that give each side "half a loaf." Try to apply some of the principles of ethical analysis described above to each of these cases. What is the right thing to do?

15.3 The Moral Dimensions of Information Systems

In this section, we take a closer look at the five moral dimensions of information systems first described in Figure 15.1. In each dimension we identify the ethical, social, and political levels of analysis and illustrate with real-world examples the values involved, the stakeholders, and the options chosen.

Information Rights: Privacy and Freedom in an Information Society

Privacy: The claim of individuals to be left alone, free from surveillance or interference from other individuals, organizations, or the state.

Privacy is the claim of individuals to be left alone, free from surveillance or interference from other individuals or organizations, including the state. Claims to privacy are also involved at the workplace: millions of employees are subject to electronic and other forms of hi-tech surveillance. Information technology and systems threaten individual claims to privacy by making the invasion of privacy cheap, profitable, and effective.

The claim to privacy is protected in the U.S., Canadian, and German constitutions in a variety of different ways, and in other countries through various statutes. In the United States, the claim to privacy is protected primarily by the First Amendment guarantees of freedom of speech and association, the Fourth Amendment protections against unreasonable search and seizure of one's personal documents or home, and the guarantee of due process.

Due process has become a key concept in defining privacy where absolutist claims to be left alone are not tenable. Due process requires that a set of rules or laws exist which clearly define how information about individuals will be treated, and what appeal mechanisms are available. Perhaps the best statement of the due process in record keeping is given by the Fair Information Practices doctrine developed in the early 1970s.

Fair Information Practices (FIP): A set of principles originally set forth in 1973 that governs the collection and use of information about individuals and forms the basis of most U.S. and European privacy law.

Most American and European privacy law is based on a regime called Fair Information Practices (FIP) first set forth in a report written in 1973 by a federal government advisory committee (U.S. Department of Health, Education, and Welfare, 1973). **Fair Information Practices** (FIP) is a set of principles governing the collection and use of information about individuals. The five fair information practices principles are shown in Table 15.1.

Table 15.1 FAIR INFORMATION PRACTICES PRINCIPLES

1. There should be no personal record systems whose existence is secret.
2. Individuals have rights of access, inspection, review, and amendment to systems that contain information about them.
3. There must be no use of personal information for purposes other than those for which it was gathered without prior consent.
4. Managers of systems are responsible and can be held accountable, and liable for the damage done by systems, for their reliability and security.
5. Governments have the right to intervene in the information relationships among private parties.

FIP principles are based on the notion of a "mutuality of interest" between the record holder and the individual. The individual has an interest in engaging in a transaction, and the recordkeeper—usually a business or government agency—requires information about the individual to support the transaction. Once gathered, the individual maintains an interest in the record, and the record may not be used to support other activities without the individual's consent.

Fair Information Practices form the basis of 13 federal statutes listed in Table 15.2 that set forth the conditions for handling information about individuals in such areas as credit reporting, education, financial records, newspaper records, cable communications, electronic communications, and even video rentals.

In the United States, privacy law is enforced by individuals who must sue agencies or companies in court in order to recover damages. European countries and Canada define privacy in a similar manner to that in the United States, but they have chosen to enforce their privacy laws by creating Privacy Commissions or Data Protection Agencies to pursue complaints brought by citizens.

Despite this legislation, most Americans feel there is less privacy today than ever. Public opinion polls show that when it comes to information privacy, most Americans are bewildered, fearful, confused, and increasingly distrustful about public policy in this area. According to a recent Harris poll, 76 percent of Americans believe they have lost all control over personal information, and 67 percent believe that computers must be restricted in the future to preserve privacy (Equifax, 1992). There are several causes of this erosion of public confidence: distrust of all institutions, the rapid growth of computer transactions not protected by any privacy legislation, and the loss of control over personal information which individuals, in fact, experience in a highly computerized transaction-oriented society. The development of law is clearly lagging far behind the reality of computer-based information.

ETHICAL ISSUES   The ethical privacy issue in this information age is as follows: Under what conditions should I (you) invade the privacy of others? What legitimates intruding into others' lives through unobtrusive surveillance, through market research, or by whatever means? Do we have to inform people we are eavesdropping? Do we have to inform people that we are using credit history information for employment screening purposes?

Table 15.2 FEDERAL PRIVACY LAWS IN THE U.S.

(1) General Federal Privacy Laws
Freedom of Information Act, 1968 as Amended (5 USC 552)
Privacy Act of 1974 as Amended (5 USC 552a)
Electronic Communications Privacy Act of 1986
Computer Matching and Privacy Protection Act of 1988
Computer Security Act of 1987
Federal Managers Financial Integrity Act of 1982

(2) Privacy Laws Affecting Private Institutions
Fair Credit Reporting Act, 1970
Family Educational Rights and Privacy Act of 1978
Right to Financial Privacy Act of 1978
Privacy Protection Act of 1980
Cable Communications Policy Act of 1984
Electronic Communications Privacy Act of 1986
Video Privacy Protection Act of 1988

The social issue of privacy concerns the development of "expectations of privacy" or privacy norms, as well as public attitudes. In what areas of life should we as a society encourage people to think they are "in private territory" as opposed to public view? For instance, should we as a society encourage people to develop expectations of privacy when using electronic mail, cellular telephones, bulletin boards, the postal system, the workplace, the street? Should expectations of privacy be extended to criminal conspirators?

The political issue of privacy concerns the development of statutes which govern the relations between record keepers and individuals. Should we permit the FBI to prevent the commercial development of encrypted telephone transmissions so they can eavesdrop at will? Should a law be passed to require direct marketing firms to obtain the consent of individuals before using their names in mass marketing (a consensus database). Should E-mail privacy—regardless of who owns the equipment—be protected in law? In general, large organizations of all kinds—public and private—are reluctant to give up the advantages which come from the unfettered flow of information on individuals. Civil liberties and other private groups have been the strongest voices supporting restraints on large organization information gathering activities.

Property Rights: Intellectual Property

Contemporary information systems have severely challenged existing law and social practice which protects private intellectual property. In so doing, information systems have resulted in the loss of billions of dollars in software sales due to outright theft or piracy, and retarded the growth of the software industry by reducing its profitability. At the same time, the existence of so much stolen "free" software, the ease of creating perfect copies, has greatly expanded the use of software and hardware.

Intellectual property: Intangible property created by individuals or corporations which is subject to protections under trade secret, copyright, and patent law.

Intellectual property is considered to be intangible property created by individuals or corporations and is subject to a variety of protections under three different legal traditions: trade secret, copyright, and patent law. Each provides different kinds of protections for software (Graham, 1984).

Trade secret: Any intellectual work product used for a business purpose that can be classified as belonging to that business provided it is not based on information in the public domain.

Any intellectual work product—a formula, device, pattern, or compilation of data—used for a business purpose can be classified as a **trade secret,** provided it is not based on information in the public domain. Trade secrets have their basis in state law, not federal law, and protections vary from state to state. In general, trade secret laws grant a monopoly on the ideas behind a work product, but it can be a very tenuous monopoly.

Software that contains novel or unique elements, procedures, or compilations can be included as a trade secret. Trade secret law protects the actual ideas in a work product and not just their manifestation. In order to make this claim, the creator or owner must take care to bind employees and customers with nondisclosure agreements and to prevent the secret from falling into the public domain.

The limitation of trade secret protection is that while virtually all software programs of any complexity contain unique elements of some sort, it is difficult to prevent the ideas in the work from falling into the public domain when the software is widely distributed.

Copyright: A statutory grant that protects creators of intellectual property against copying by others for any purpose for a period of 28 years.

Copyright is a statutory grant which protects creators of intellectual property against copying by others for any purpose for a period of 28 years. Since the first Federal Copyright Act of 1790, and the creation of the Copyright Office to register copyrights and enforce copyright law, Congress has extended copyright protection to books, periodicals, lectures, dramas, musical compositions, maps, drawings, artwork of any kind, and motion pictures. Since the earliest days, the

Congressional intent behind copyright laws has been to encourage creativity and authorship by ensuring that creative people receive the financial and other benefits of their work. Copyright provides a limited monopoly on the commercial use of a work, but does not protect the ideas behind a work. Most industrial nations have their own copyright laws, and there are several international conventions and bilateral agreements through which nations coordinate and enforce their laws.

In the mid 1960's the Copyright Office began registering software programs, and in 1980 Congress passed the Computer Software Copyright Act, which clearly provides protection for source and object code, for copies of the original sold in commerce, and sets forth the rights of the purchaser to use the software while the creator retains legal title.

Copyright protection is explicit and clear-cut: it protects against copying of entire programs or their parts. Damages and relief are readily obtained for infringement. The drawback to copyright protection is that the underlying ideas are not protected, only their manifestation in a work. A competitor can use your software, understand how it works, and build his or her own software that follows the same concepts without enfringing on a copyright.

"Look and feel" copyright infringement law suits are precisely about the distinction between an idea and its expression. For instance, in the early 1990s Apple Computer sued Microsoft Corporation and Hewlett-Packard Inc. for infringement of the expression of Apple's Macintosh interface. Among other claims, Apple claimed that the defendants copied the expression of overlapping windows. The defendants counterclaimed that the idea of overlapping windows can only be expressed in a single way, and therefore was not protectable under the "merger" doctrine of copyright law. When ideas and their expression merge, the expression cannot be copyrighted. In general, courts appear to be following the reasoning of a 1989 case—Brown Bag Software v. Symantec Corp.—in which the court dissected the elements of software alleged to be enfringing. The court found that neither similar concept, function, general functional features (e.g., drop-down menus) or colors are protectable by copyright law (Brown Bag v. Symantec Corp., 1992).

PATENTS

Patent: A legal document that grants the owner an exclusive monopoly on the ideas behind an invention for 17 years; designed to ensure that inventors of new machines or methods are rewarded for their labor while making widespread use of their inventions.

The first patent was granted by Congress in 1790, and the Patent Office was established in 1836. A **patent** grants the owner an exclusive monopoly on the ideas behind an invention for 17 years. The Congressional intent behind patent law was to ensure that inventors of new machines, devices, or methods receive the full financial and other rewards of their labor and yet still make widespread use of the invention possible by providing detailed diagrams for those wishing to use the idea under license from the owner of the patent. The granting of a patent is determined by the Patent Office and relies on court rulings.

The key concepts in patent law are originality, novelty, invention. The Patent Office did not accept applications for software patents routinely until a 1981 Supreme Court decision which held that computer programs could be a part of a patentable process. Since then hundreds of patents have been granted and thousands await consideration.

The strength of patent protection is that it grants a monopoly on the underlying concepts and ideas of software. The difficulty is passing stringent criteria of non-obviousness (e.g., the work must reflect some special understanding and contribution), originality, and novelty, as well as years of waiting to receive protection.

Contemporary information technologies, especially software, pose a severe challenge to existing intellectual property regimes, and therefore create significant ethical, social, and political issues. Digital media differ from books, periodicals, and other media in terms of ease of replication, ease of transmission, ease of alteration, difficulty classifying a software work as a program, book, or

The look and feel of the Microsoft Windows Program Manager's control panel is similar to the Control Panel for a Macintosh System 7. Both systems use windows, scroll bars, icons, and pull-down menus to interface with the users.

even music, compactness—making theft easy, and difficulties in establishing uniqueness. (See Samuelson, October 1991.)

ETHICAL ISSUES   The central ethical issue posed to individuals concerning copying software is, should I (you) copy for our own use a piece of software protected by trade secret, copyright, and/or patent law? In the information age, it is so easy to obtain perfect, functional copies of software, that the software companies themselves have abandoned software protection schemes to increase market penetration. Enforcement of the law is rare. However, if everyone copied software, very little new software would be produced because creators could not benefit from the results of their work.

There are several property-related social issues raised by new information technology. Most experts agree that the current intellectual property laws are breaking down in the information age. The vast majority of Americans report in surveys that they routinely violate some minor laws—everything from speeding, to taking paper clips from work, to copying software. The ease with which software can be copied contributes to making us a society of lawbreakers. In 1990, the Software Publishers Association (SPA) estimated it lost $2.4 billion or half the total of $5.7 billion in software sales. Copied software is routinely found in both personal and business settings (Markoff, July 27, 1992). These routine thefts threaten significantly to reduce the speed with which new information technologies can be and will be introduced, and thereby threaten further advances in productivity and social well-being.

The main property-related political issue concerns the creation of new property protection measures to protect investments made by creators of new software. Apple, Microsoft, and 900 other hardware and software firms formed the Software Publishers Association (SPA) to lobby for new protection laws and enforce existing laws. SPA has distributed more than 30,000 copies of SPAaudit—a software inventory management tool used by corporations to establish control over software used on individual PCs; established a toll free antipiracy hotline (1-800-388-7478) for employees to report on their corporations; completed 75 surprise audits or raids; sent 560 cease and desist letters; and filed more than 100 lawsuits since its inception (80 percent against corporations, 20 percent against bulletin board operators, training facilities, schools and universities). The SPA has developed a model Software Code of Ethics, described in the following Window on Organizations.

Allied against SPA are a host of groups and millions of individuals who resist efforts to strengthen antipiracy laws, and instead encourage situations where software can be copied. These groups believe that software should be free, that antipiracy laws cannot in any event be enforced in the digital age, or that software should be paid for on a voluntary basis (shareware software). According to these groups, the greater social benefit results from the free distribution of software and the "benefits" of software should accrue to the creators in the form of greater prestige perhaps but not in the form of profits.

Accountability, Liability and Control

Along with privacy and property laws, new information technologies are challenging existing liability law and social practices for holding individuals and institutions accountable. If a person is injured by a machine controlled in part by software, who should be held accountable and therefore held liable? Should a public bulletin board or an electronic service like Prodigy or CompuServe permit the transmission of pornographic or offensive material (as broadcasters), or should they be held harmless against any liability for what users transmit (as is true of common carriers like the telephone system)? Is Prodigy a common carrier? If you outsource your information processing, can you hold the external vendor liable for injuries done to your customers? Try some real-world examples.

In February 1992, hackers penetrated the computer network of Equifax, Inc. in Atlanta, Georgia, one of the world's largest credit reporting bureaus that sells 450 million reports annually. Consumer files, credit card numbers and other confidential information were accessed. The company is working with police and reviewing all files to catch the criminals. When finished, it will notify all affected customers. Who is liable for any damages done to individuals (King, 1992)?

On March 13, 1993, a blizzard hit the East Coast of the United States, knocking out an EDS (Electronic Data Systems Inc.) computer center in Clifton, New Jersey. The center operated 5200 ATM machines in 12 different networks across the country involving more than one million card holders. In the two weeks required to recover operations, EDS informed its customers to use alter-native ATM networks operated by other banks or computer centers, and offered to cover more than $50 million in cash withdrawals. Because the alternative networks did not have access to the actual customer account balances, EDS is at substantial risk of fraud. Cash withdrawals were limited to $100 per day per customer to reduce the exposure. Most service was restored by March 26. Al-though EDS had a disaster recovery plan, it did not have a dedicated backup facility. Who is liable for any economic harm caused individuals or businesses who could not access their full account balances in this period (Joes, 1993)?

These cases point out the difficulties faced by IS executives who ultimately are responsible for the harm done by systems developed by their staffs.

In general, insofar as computer software is part of a machine, and the machine injures someone physically or economically, the producer of the software and the operator can be held liable for damages. Insofar as the software acts more like a book, storing and displaying information, courts have been reluctant to hold authors, publishers and booksellers liable for contents (the exception being instances of fraud or defamation), and hence courts have been wary of holding software authors liable for "book-like" software.

In general it is very difficult (if not impossible) to hold software producers liable for their software products when those products are considered like books, regardless of the physical or economic harm which results. Historically, print publishers, books, or periodicals have not been held liable because of fears that liability claims would interfere with First Amendment rights guaranteeing freedom of expression.

What about "software as service"? ATM machines are a service provided to bank customers. Should this service fail, customers will be inconvenienced and perhaps harmed economically if they cannot access their funds in a timely manner. Should liability protections be extended to software publishers and operators of defective financial, accounting, simulation, financial, or marketing systems?

Software is very different from books. Software users may develop expectations of infallibility about software; software is less easily inspected than a book, and more difficult to compare to other software products for quality; and software claims actually to perform a task rather than describe a task like a book; people come to depend on services essentially based on software. Given the centrality of software to everyday life, the chances are excellent that liability law will extend its reach to include software even when it merely provides an information service.

Liability and accountability are also at the heart of debates over the responsibility and freedoms of computer bulletin boards and networks. The Window on Organizations, examining the Prodigy network, describes a recent lawsuit seeking to establish the liability of a Bulletin Board user.

There are virtually no liabilities imposed on book publishers, bookstores, or newspapers (outside of outright defamation and certain local restrictions on pornographic materials). This is because of the historic roles these media have played in the evolution of First Amendment rights. Telephone systems are regulated "common carrier" monopolies. Corporations are granted a monopoly on telephone service with no liability for content of messages transmitted. In return they must provide access to all, at reasonable rates, and achieve acceptable reliability. Broadcasters are granted monopolies by the Federal Communications Commission, which allocates frequency spectrum according to the 1934 Communications Act and subsequent amendments. In return, broadcasters are subject to a wide variety of federal and local constraints on content and facilities. Cable television systems are directly regulated by Congress, as well as by states and localities. They too are liable for content of messages and are subject to many local regulations on content and community service.

ETHICAL ISSUES The central liability-related ethical issue raised by new information technologies is whether or not individuals and organizations who create, produce, and sell systems (both hardware and software) are morally responsible for the consequences of their use. If so, under what conditions? What liabilities (and responsibilities) should the user assume, and what should the provider assume?

SOCIAL ISSUES The central liability-related social issue concerns the expectations that society should allow to develop around service-providing information systems. Should individuals (and organizations) be encouraged to develop their own backup

ORGANIZATIONS

Liability on the Prodigy Network

Medphone Corporation is a New Jersey manufacturer of transtelephonic defibrillators, devices that allow doctors to transmit computer signals remotely via a telephone system to heart patients undergoing shock therapy. The firm sued a disgruntled investor, Mr. DeNigris of Babylon, New York, for posting statements on Prodigy—the electronic information service run by IBM and Sears. The suit alleges that DeNigris violated securities laws when he posted a notice that said "The bottom line is that insiders are waiting to unload big amounts of the stock before the company collapses," and "No cash, no sales, no profits, and terrible management." Medphone claims these statements are not true and violate securities laws against stock price manipulation through spreading of false information.

DeNigris is a $47,000 a year government worker who lost $9,000 on Medphone stock. He said that if he had any idea that the Prodigy bulletin board would subject him to a libel suit and allegations of security fraud, he never would have bought a personal computer in the first place. DeNigris complained:

"If this is what a bulletin board is all about, my goodness."

Prodigy receives 60 million messages a year, and according to George Perry, Prodigy's general counsel, is in no position to do the kind of fact checking and analysis that is performed by a newspaper to protect against libel claims. However, Prodigy does monitor messages posted to bulletin boards to maintain a "family environment."

In the only other similar case to date, CompuServe was sued for posting libelous statements. In this case (Cubby v. CompuServe), the court ruled that CompuServe acted more like a bookstore and would not be held responsible for libelous messages posted to its bulletin boards. Some lawyers claim that Prodigy is liable for messages posted on its system because it failed to screen them and did not exercise due care. Other lawyers claim it is best if Prodigy—like CompuServe—does not screen any messages, thereby insulating itself from liability. Screening implies censorship and this would interfere with First Amendment rights of free speech, and perhaps increase the risk of

liability (what if a false defaming message somehow were missed by the Prodigy censor?). According to some lawyers, if bulletin boards and networks are held liable for the messages posted on their systems or sent through their systems, most providers would get out of the business.

In a chilling afternote, Prodigy has complied with subpoenas from the Medphone attorneys seeking the names of people who read DeNigris' Prodigy message, or who communicated with him over Prodigy. This means the Prodigy network records can be used to trace communication patterns among users, perhaps further chilling the atmosphere for the free exchange of ideas.

Source: Arthur S. Hayes, "Computer Message Prompts Libel Suit," *The Wall Street Journal* (March 26, 1993).

To Think About: What are the implications of a monitored computer bulletin board? Of one that has no restrictions? What measures would you take to prevent bulletin boards from being used for posting libelous statements?

devices to cover likely or easily anticipated system failures, or should organizations be held strictly liable for system services they provide? If organizations are held strictly liable, what impact will this have on the development of new system services? Can society permit networks and bulletin boards to post libelous, inaccurate, and misleading information that will harm many persons? Or should information service companies become self-regulating, self-censoring?

POLITICAL ISSUES
The leading liability-related political issue is the debate between information providers of all kinds (from software developers to network service providers) who want to be relieved of liability insofar as possible (thereby maximizing their profits), and service users—individuals, organizations, communities—who want organizations to be held responsible for providing high quality system services (thereby maximizing the quality of service). Service providers argue they will withdraw from the marketplace if they are held liable, while service users argue that only by holding providers liable can we guarantee a high level of service and compensate injured parties. Should legislation impose liability or restrict liability on service providers? This fundamental cleavage is at the heart of numerous political and judicial conflicts.

System Quality: Data Quality and System Errors

The debate over liability and accountability for unintentional consequences of system use raises a related but independent moral dimension: What is an acceptable, technologically feasible level of system quality (see Chapter 9)? At what point should system managers say, "Stop testing, we've done all we can to perfect this software. Ship it!" Obviously, individuals and organizations cannot be held responsible or liable for "acts of God" or technologically unavoidable errors. They may be held responsible for avoidable consequences, foreseeable consequences, which they have a duty to perceive and correct. And there is a gray area: some system errors are foreseeable and correctable only at very great expense, an expense so great that pursuing this level of perfection is not feasible economically—no one could afford the product. What if the product was not offered on the marketplace, would social welfare as a whole not advance and perhaps even decline? Carrying this further, just what is the responsibility of a producer of computer services—should it withdraw the product that can never be perfect, warn the user, or forget about the risk (caveat emptor—let the buyer beware)?

As we have discussed in Chapters 9 and 13, three principal sources of poor system performance are software bugs and errors, hardware or facility failures due to natural or other causes, and poor input data quality. Chapter 9 established that zero defects in software code of any complexity cannot be achieved and the seriousness of remaining bugs cannot be estimated. Hence, there is a technological barrier to perfect software and users must be aware of the potential for catastrophic failure. Nevertheless, there are industry standard test routines which if followed can produce software of acceptable but not perfect performance. For life-dependent applications additional protection is possible by independently building redundant software modules and checking their results against one another.

System hardware and facility failures are much better documented and more easily managed. Redundancy of processors in mission critical applications can reduce the probabilities of failure by known amounts; and even weather system patterns routinely used by civil engineers in designing buildings and bridges can be used as a rationale (by responsible system developers) to build emergency backup facilities for mission critical and life dependent applications.

Perhaps the single largest cause of system failure is seemingly trivial: poor input data quality. A survey of 50 large business CIOs found that half of the executives believed their corporate data were less than 95 percent accurate (Bulkeley, 1992). Some of the glitches are reported in Table 15.3.

While software bugs and facility catastrophe are likely to be widely reported in the press, by far the most common source of business system failure is data quality. A total of 70 percent of IS executives in a recent survey reported data corruption as a source of business delay, 69 percent said their corporate data accuracy was unacceptable, and 44 percent said no systems were in place to check database information quality (Wilson, 1992).

ETHICAL ISSUES

The central quality-related ethical issue raised by information systems is at what point should I (or you) release software or services for consumption by others? At what point can you conclude that your software or service achieves an economically and technologically adequate level of quality? What are you obliged to know about the quality of your software, its procedures for testing, and its operational characteristics?

SOCIAL ISSUES

The leading quality-related social issue once again deals with expectations: do we want as a society to encourage people to believe that systems are infallible, that data errors are impossible? Or do we instead want a society where people

Table 15.3 ILLUSTRATIVE REPORTED DATA QUALITY PROBLEMS

- An airline inadvertently corrupted its database of passenger reservations while installing new software and for months planes took off with half loads.

- A manufacturer attempted to reorganize its customer files by customer number only to discover the sales staff had been entering a new customer number for each sale because of special incentives for opening new accounts. One customer was entered 7000 times. The company scrapped the software project after spending $1 million.

- J. P. Morgan, a New York bank, discovered that 40 percent of the data in its credit-risk management database was incomplete, necessitating doublechecking by users.

- Several studies have established that 5–12 percent of bar code sales at retail grocery and merchandise chains are erroneous and that the ratio of overcharges to undercharges runs as high as 5:1, with 4:1 as a norm. The problem tends to be human error in keeping shelf prices accurate, and corporate policy which fails to allocate sufficient resources to price checking, auditing, and development of error-free policies. The cause of the high overcharge has not yet been determined but the pattern is disturbing, suggesting intentional behavior.

Sources: Bulkeley, op. cit., and Doug Bartholomew, "The Price is Wrong," *InformationWEEK* (September 14, 1992).

are openly skeptical and questioning of the output of machines, where people are at least informed of the risk? By heightening awareness of system failure, do we inhibit the development of all systems which in the end contribute to social well-being?

POLITICAL ISSUES   The leading quality-related political issue concerns the laws of responsibility and accountability. Should Congress establish or direct the National Institute of Science and Technology (NIST) to develop quality standards (software, hardware, data quality) and impose those standards on industry? Or should industry associations be encouraged to develop industry-wide standards of quality? Or should Congress wait for the marketplace to punish poor system quality, recognizing that in some instances this will not work (e.g., if all retail grocers maintain poor quality systems, then customers have no alternatives)?

Quality of Life: Equity, Access, Boundaries

Not all sins are crimes. The negative social costs of introducing information technologies and systems are beginning to mount as the power of the technology bounds upwards. Many of these negative social consequences are not violations of individual rights defended in the Constitution or statute, nor are they property crimes. Nevertheless, these negative consequences can be extremely harmful to individuals, societies, and political institutions. Computers and information technologies potentially can destroy valuable elements of our culture and society even while they bring us benefits. If there is a balance of good and bad consequences to the use of information systems, who do we hold responsible for the bad consequences? Below, we briefly examine just some of the negative social consequences of systems, considering individual, social, and political responses.

BALANCING POWER: One of the earliest fears of the computer age was that huge centralized main-
CENTER VS. PERIPHERY   frame computers would centralize power at corporate headquarters and in the nation's capital, resulting in a "Big Brother" society suggested in George Orwell's novel *1984*. The shift towards highly decentralized computing in the 1990s, coupled with an ideology of "empowerment" of thousands of workers, and the decentralization of decision making to lower organizational levels, have reduced

The massive crater underneath the World Trade Center was the result of the terrorist attack on Feburary 26, 1993. The blast killed 5 people, injured more than 300 people, and knocked out the communications, electrical, fire, safety and computer systems that supported the Towers.

fears of power centralization in institutions. Yet much of the "empowerment" and devolution described in popular business magazines is trivial. Lower-level employees may be empowered to make minor decisions about their work pace, and they may be able in some cases to stop the production line on observing defects, but the key policy decisions may be as centralized as in the past. Many of the participatory mechanisms dreamed up by consultants to tap into the profitable ideas of the workforce bring unclear and inequitable rewards to employees.

RAPIDITY OF CHANGE: REDUCED RESPONSE TIME TO COMPETITION

Information systems have helped to create much more efficient national and international markets. The now more efficient global marketplace has reduced the normal social buffers which permitted businesses many years to adjust to competition. "Time-based competition" has an ugly side: The business you work for may not have enough time to respond to global competitors and may be wiped out in a year, along with your job. We stand the risk of developing a "just-in-time society" with "just-in-time jobs" and "just-in-time" workplaces, families, and vacations.

MAINTAINING BOUNDARIES: FAMILY, WORK, LEISURE

Parts of this book were produced on trains, planes, as well as on family "vacations," and what otherwise might have been "family" time. The danger to ubiquitous computing, telecommuting, nomad computing, and the "do anything anywhere" computing environment is that it might actually come true. If so, the traditional boundaries that separate work from family and just plain leisure will be weakened. While authors have traditionally worked just about anywhere (typewriters have been portable for nearly a century), the advent of information systems, coupled with the growth of knowledge work occupations, means that more and more people will be working when traditionally they would have been playing or communicating with family and friends. The "work umbrella" now extends far beyond the eight-hour day.

Weakening these institutions poses clear-cut risks. Family and friends historically have provided powerful support mechanisms for individuals, and they act as balance points in a society by preserving "private life," providing a place for one to collect one's thoughts, to think in ways contrary to one's employer, and to dream.

DEPENDENCE AND VULNERABILITY

Our businesses, governments, schools and private associations like churches are incredibly dependent now on information systems and therefore highly vulnerable. With systems now as ubiquitous as the telephone system, it is startling to remember that there are no regulatory or standard setting forces in place similar to telephone, electrical, radio, television, or other public utility technologies. Information systems are unprecedented as a technology for their lack of societal oversight. The evolution of a national computer network in the 1990s in the United States will result in a highly decentralized network, so that no single node failure can affect the nation. Nevertheless, the absence of standards and the criticality of some system applications will probably call forth demands for national standards, perhaps regulatory oversight.

Consider, for instance, that on any given business day more than $1 trillion worth of electronic transactions occur in New York City, and that a recent mayoral task force discovered that 90 percent of the large businesses in the city had no disaster contingency plan (Office of the Mayor, 1991).

While distributed networks are seemingly more resistant to disaster than centralized mainframe installations, the terrorist attack on the World Trade Center—business home to more than 50,000 workers and hundreds of LANs—on February 26, 1993 demonstrated that it may be far easier to protect and backup a 20,000 square foot centralized data center than it is to achieve similar results for over one million square feet of office space.

COMPUTER CRIME AND ABUSE

Computer crime: The commission of illegal acts through the use of a computer or against a computer system.

Computer abuse: The commission of acts involving a computer that may not be illegal but are considered unethical.

Computer crime can be defined as the commission of illegal acts through the use of a computer or against a computer system. Computers or computer systems can be the object of the crime (destroying a company's computer center or a company's computer files) as well as the instrument of a crime (stealing computer lists by illegally gaining access to a computer system using a home microcomputer). Simply accessing a computer system without authorization, or intent to do harm, even by accident, is now a federal crime. **Computer abuse** is the commission of acts involving a computer which may not be illegal but are considered unethical.

No one knows the magnitude of the computer crime problem—how many systems are invaded, how many people engage in the practice, or what is the total economic damage. Many companies are reluctant to report computer crimes because they may involve employees. The most economically damaging kinds of computer crime are introducing viruses, theft of services, disruption of computer systems, and theft of telecommunications services. Computer crime has been estimated to cost over $1 billion in the United States, and an additional billion dollars if corporate and cellular phone theft is included. "Hackers" is the pejorative term for persons who use computers in illegal ways. Federal law enforcement officials have estimated that 50,000 computer users "hack" at some time or another, while others put the number at a more modest 5,000 (Sterling, 1992).

Computer viruses (see Chapter 13) have grown exponentially since 1987: More than 1,000 viruses have been documented. The average corporate loss for a bad virus outbreak is $250,000, and the probability of a large corporation experiencing a significant computer virus infection in a single year is 50 percent according to some experts. However, examination of large-scale empirical data by IBM suggests a much lower rate of infection, on the order of 38 incidents per 100,000 PC machines, largely because most PCs are stand-alone machines or are tied into local networks that inherently limit the spread of viruses (Markoff, November 1, 1992). In a population like that of the United States, with more than 50 million microcomputers, this would suggest a total of 19,000 infections annually. This is no doubt an underestimate. While many firms now use antivirus software, the sale of more than 400,000 computer networks in the United States in 1992 will surely increase the probability of infections.

Below we describe some illustrative computer crimes:

- "Hacker" Robert T. Morris, a computer science student at Cornell University, unleashed a computer virus over the Internet Network on

November 2, 1988, jamming thousands of machines in tens of networks throughout the system. He was convicted under the Computer Fraud and Abuse Act, given three years probation, a $10,000 fine, and 400 hours of community service.

- In July 1992, a Federal grand jury indicted five members of a group of hackers calling themselves MOD—Masters of Deception. Theirs was one of the largest thefts of computer information and services in history. The hackers were charged with computer tampering, computer fraud, wire fraud, illegal wiretapping, and conspiracy. The group broke into over 25 of the largest corporate computer systems in the United States, including TRW Information Services (a prominent credit reporting firm), Southwestern Bell Corporation, New York Telephone, and Pacific Bell. The group stole and resold credit reports, credit card numbers, and other personal information. Federal investigators used court-ordered wiretaps to monitor the calls of members. The firms blamed their own lax security and a philosophy of "openness" for not detecting the hackers themselves. All the hackers involved were under 22 years of age (Tabor, 1992).

- At AT&T's British headquarters in London, three technicians set up their own company in 1992, assigned it a 900 number, and then programmed AT&T computers to dial the number often. The loss amounted to just under $500,000 before the fraud was accidentally detected.

- In 1990, the Pinkerton Detective Agency discovered that employee Marita Juse had been siphoning off more than $1 million since 1988. Juse had been given a computer code to access Pinkerton bank accounts. She had discovered a second code that was required to provide payment authorization. The authorization code was given to her by her boss who told her to cancel it. Instead, she used it for two years without detection (Carley, 1992).

In general, it is employees—insiders—who have inflicted the most injurious computer crimes because they have the knowledge, access, and frequently a job-related motive to commit such crimes.

Congress responded to the threat of computer crime in 1984 with the Computer Fraud and Abuse Act (enacted in 1984 and amended in 1986). This act makes it illegal to access a computer system without authorization. Most of the states have similar laws, and nations in Europe have similar legislation. Other existing legislation covering wire tapping, fraud, conspiracy by any means, regardless of technology employed, is adequate to cover computer crimes committed so far.

EMPLOYMENT: TRICKLE-DOWN TECHNOLOGY AND RE-ENGINEERING JOB LOSS

Re-engineering work (see Chapter 8) is typically hailed in the information systems community as a major benefit of new information technology. Much less frequently noted is that redesigning business processes could potentially cause millions of middle level managers and clerical workers to lose their jobs. Worse, if re-engineering actually worked as claimed, these workers could not find similar employment in the society because of an actual decline in demand for their skills. One economist has raised the possibility that we will create a society run by a small "high tech elite of corporate professionals . . . in a nation of the permanently unemployed" (Rifkin, 1993). Some have estimated that if re-engineering were seriously undertaken by the Fortune 1000 companies, about 25 percent of the U.S. labor force could be displaced. But re-engineering is being seriously used at only 15 percent of American service and manufacturing companies, and the average reduction in employment in downsizing companies is 10 percent in a year. Several surveys have documented re-engineering failure rates at from 50 to 90 percent (Cafasso, 1993). While re-engineering projects can produce 50 percent declines in employment, this is rare and likely to happen in companies facing declining demand.

Economists are much more sanguine about the potential job losses. They believe relieving bright educated workers from re-engineered jobs will result in these workers moving to better jobs in fast-growth industries. Left out of this equation are blue-collar workers, and older, less well-educated middle managers. It is not clear that these groups are infinitely malleable or can be retrained easily for high-quality (high-paid) jobs. Fortunately, demographers point out, the economy tends to generate jobs to accommodate whatever the existing labor is. In the period from 1960 to 1990, the labor force doubled because of the entrance of women and minorities. In the period from 1990 to 2010, the labor force is expected to be stagnant or even decline in size. Re-engineering may be necessary to accommodate a no-growth labor force. Alternatively, careful planning and sensitivity to employee needs can help companies redesign work to minimize job losses.

EQUITY AND ACCESS: INCREASING RACIAL AND SOCIAL CLASS CLEAVAGES

Does everyone have an equal opportunity to participate in the digital age? Will the social, economic, and cultural gaps which exist in American and other societies be reduced by information systems technology? Or will the cleavages be increased, permitting the "better off" to become still better off? When and if computing becomes ubiquitous, does this include the poor as well as the rich?

The answers to these questions are clearly not known, the differential impact of systems technology on various groups in society is not well studied. What is known is that information and knowledge, and access to these resources through educational institutions and public libraries, are inequitably distributed. Access to computers is distributed inequitably along racial and social class lines as are many other information resources. Left uncorrected, we could end up creating a society of information haves, computer literate and skilled versus a large group of information have-nots, computer illiterate and unskilled.

Poor children attending poor school districts are less likely to use computers at school. Children from wealthy homes are five times as likely to use PCs for school work than poor children. Schools and other institutions make up for some of the social disparities in access in computing, but not all. Potentially we could create a society of information haves and information have-nots.

HEALTH RISKS: RSI, CVS, AND TECHNOSTRESS

Repetitive stress injury (RSI): Occupational disease that occurs when muscle groups are forced through the same, repetitive actions with high impact loads or thousands of repetitions with low impact loads.

Carpal tunnel syndrome (CTS): Type of RSI in which pressure on the median nerve through the wrist's bony carpal tunnel structure produces pain.

In 1980, at the beginning of the microcomputer revolution, no one thought that by 1992 business would be paying $20 billion a year to compensate and treat victims of the most important occupational disease today: **repetitive stress injury (RSI)**. RSI occurs when muscle groups are forced through the same, repetitive actions often with high impact loads (like tennis) or tens of thousands of repetitions under low impact loads (like working at a computer keyboard.)

The single largest source of RSI is computer keyboards. Forty-six million Americans use computers at work, and 185,000 cases of RSI are reported each year according to the National Center for Health Statistics. The most common kind of computer-related RSI is **carpal tunnel syndrome (CTS)** in which pressure on the median nerve through the wrist's bony structure called a "carpal tunnel" produces pain. The pressure is caused by constant repetition of keystrokes: in a single shift a word processor may perform 23,000 keystrokes. Symptoms of carpal tunnel syndrome include numbness, shooting pain, inability to grasp objects, and tingling. So far, more than 1.89 million workers have been diagnosed with carpal tunnel syndrome.

Treating RSI is expensive; on average, $29,000 per case. Affected workers generally cannot sue a company for exposing them to poorly constructed keyboards because of state workmen compensation laws that remove liability from companies and pay workers directly for lost income. However, there are more than 100 lawsuits outstanding against keyboard and computer manufacturers (Feder, 1992).

Apple Computer Corporation offers an ergonomically designed keyboard and mouse. The adjustable keyboard and desktop bus mouse can be positioned to meet the needs of any user.

Computer vision syndrome (CVS): Eye strain condition related to cathode ray tube (CRT) use, with symptoms including headaches, blurred vision, and dry, irritated eyes.

Technostress: Stress induced by computer use whose symptoms include aggravation, hostility toward humans, impatience, and enervation.

RSI is avoidable. Designing workstations for a neutral wrist position (using a wrist rest to support the wrist), proper monitor stands, and footrests all contribute to proper posture and reduced RSI. New ergonomically correct keyboards are also an option. These measures should be backed up by frequent rest breaks, rotation of employees to different jobs, and moving towards voice or scanner data entry.

RSI is not the only occupational illness caused by computers: back and neck pain, leg stress, and foot pain also result from poor ergonomic designs of workstations (see Table 15.4).

Computer vision syndrome (CVS) refers to any eye strain condition related to cathode ray tube (CRT) use. Its symptoms are headaches, blurred vision, and dry and irritated eyes. The symptoms are usually temporary (Furger, 1993).

The newest computer-related malady is **technostress,** defined as a computer-use induced stress and whose symptoms are aggravation, hostility towards humans, impatience, and enervation. According to the National Council on Compensation Insurance, occupational disease claims for stress doubled in 1980 (from 5 percent to 10 percent of claims), and in California stress claims for compensation have increased 500 percent since 1980. The California Workers

Table 15.4 COMPUTER-RELATED DISEASES

Disease/Risk	Incidence
RSI	185,000 new cases a year
Other joint diseases	Unknown
Computer Vision Syndrome	10 million cases a year
Miscarriage	Unknown. Related to manufacturing chemicals
Technostress	5–10 million cases
VDT Radiation	Unknown impacts

Compensation Institute has concluded that exposure to computer-intense environments is a major factor in stress disease (McPartlin, 1990; Brod, 1982). The problem according to experts is that humans working continuously with computers come to expect other humans and human institutions to behave like computers, providing instant response and attentiveness, with an absence of emotion. Computer-intense workers are aggravated when put on hold during a phone call, tend to yell or mutter at ATM machines that are slow, become incensed or alarmed when their PCs take a few seconds longer to perform a task, lack empathy for humans, and seek out friends who mirror the characteristics of their machines. Technostress is thought to be related to high levels of job turnover in the computer industry, high levels of early retirement from computer-intense occupations, and elevated levels of drug and alcohol abuse.

The incidence of technostress is not known but is thought to be in the millions in the United States and growing rapidly. Although frequently denied as a problem by management, computer-related jobs now top the list of stressful occupations based on health statistics in several industrialized countries. The costs worldwide of stress are put at $200 billion. In the United Kingdom, 10 percent of the gross national product is eaten up by the effects of stress, not all of it computer related (McPartlin, 1993).

To date the role of CRT radiation in occupational disease has not been proven. Video display terminals (VDTs) emit nonionizing electric and magnetic fields at low frequencies. These rays enter the body and have unknown effects on enzymes, molecules, chromosomes, and cell membranes. Early studies suggesting a link between low level EMFs (electromagnetic fields) and miscarriages have been contradicted by one later, superior study published in 1991 (Schnorr, 1991; Stevens, 1991). Longer-term studies are investigating low-level EMFs and birth defects, stress, low birth weight, and other diseases. All manufacturers have reduced CRT emissions since the early years of 1980, and European countries like Sweden have adopted very stiff radiation emission standards.

The computer has become a part of our lives—personally as well as socially, culturally, and politically. Like so many technologies that came before, information systems technology can be used to elevate the human spirit and well being. But like other technologies, it often acts as a mirror, reflecting our foibles and even exaggerating them at times. We did not analyze the ethical, social, and political issues of each social impact in this section, but they should be obvious to readers. It is unlikely the issues and our choices will become easier in the near future as information technology continues to transform our world. The development of a national electronic superhighway described in the Window on Technology suggests that all the ethical and social issues we have described will be heightened further as we move into the first digital century.

Management Actions: A Corporate Code of Ethics

Some corporations have developed far reaching corporate IS codes of ethics—Federal Express, IBM, American Express, and Merck and Co. But most firms have not developed these codes of ethics, which leaves them at the mercy of fate, and their employees in the dark about expected correct behavior. There is some dispute concerning a general code of ethics (about 40 percent of the American Fortune 500 firms have such codes) versus a specific information systems code of ethics (about 40 percent of Fortune 500 firms). As managers, you should strive to develop an IS-specific set of ethical standards for each of the five moral dimensions:

- *Information rights and obligations.* A code should cover topics like employee E-mail privacy, work place monitoring, treatment of corporate information, and policies on customer information.

The Coming of a National Digital Superhighway Raises Many Ethical and Social Issues

In 1989, Congress passed the High Performance Computing Act that provided $3 billion in seed money to spur the development of supercomputer centers in the United States and a very high capacity network called the National Research Education Network (NREN) to connect universities and research centers. The bill was spearheaded by then-Senator Albert Gore, who went on to become Vice President of the United States in 1992. Gore and President Bill Clinton began building on the High Performance Computing Act by suggesting a much larger-scale national computing network to connect individuals, businesses, libraries, research centers, and universities. According to one pundit, the proposed national computing network would be the "mother of all networks," a network of networks like the Internet. Largely fiberoptic, the network would handle data, voice, and video images at 100 megabits per second to the household, with a 3 gigabit national backbone—enough to be called the "everything network of your dreams."

Here are just some of the projected benefits: Students could do research using the National Library of Congress, or any library in the country with full text retrieval possible; medical care would improve because patient records could be transferred anywhere they were needed; remote diagnosis by faraway specialists would be possible; scientists and engineers around the world could cooperate on the design of new products; video fans could call up any movie

and view it; working at home would be common because there would be as much information at home as in the office; business would improve because the network could act as a huge order-entry system, eliminating paper waste and slow response time.

Briefly, the social impact of a national supernetwork is likely to be as great as the building of the transcontinental railway and the interstate highway system combined. The cost: hundreds of billions of dollars.

The national computing network requires rewiring America with fiberoptic cable to the household or neighborhood switch (from which ordinary twisted wire can be used to transmit into individual households); new hardware switches and/or upgrading the existing telephone system; and new software.

Who should build the network (and pay for it)? Owners of existing networks—like AT&T and other long distance companies—want the government to stay out and instead want to evolve the telephone network and existing technologies like ISDN (Integrated Services Digital Network). Critics charge the phone companies will never invest the money needed, and ISDN is too slow anyway. Moreover, if private enterprise develops the network, they might charge so much that universities, libraries, and homeowners could not afford to use it. The Clinton administration wants to make sure that everyone can use the services. Vice President Al Gore has

reiterated that schools should have the same access to the information superhighway as homes. The new services, including picture telephones, two-way television, and links to the Library of Congress archives should be available to "virtually everyone" just as basic telephone service is now. The major computer manufacturers like Apple, DEC, IBM, and others have formed a group called the Computer Systems Policy Project to lobby for a large government leadership role in building the network.

Sources: Daniel Pearl, "Gore Says Telecommunications Laws Need Easing, but 'Safety Net' to Stay," *The Wall Street Journal*, December 22, 1993 and Computer Systems Policy Project, "Perspectives on the National Information Infrastructure" (January 12, 1993).

To Think About: What impact will the proposed national computing network have on the moral dimensions described above, especially on information rights and obligations, property rights, and accountability and control?
If the network were to become as important as proponents argue, what happens if network service is disrupted, even temporarily?
Who should build the national computing network? What analogies to transcontinental railroads, interstate highways, and telephone utilities seem appropriate? Is it in the interests of U.S. citizens and taxpayers to fund this network?

- *Property rights and obligations.* A code should cover topics like software licenses, ownership of firm data and facilities, ownership of software created by employees on company hardware, and software copyrights. Specific guidelines for contractual relationships with third parties should be covered as well.
- *Accountability and control.* The code should specify a single individual responsible for all information systems, and underneath this individual

others who are responsible for individual rights, the protection of property rights, system quality, and quality of life (e.g., job design, ergonomics, employee satisfaction). Responsibilities for control of systems, audits, and management should be clearly defined. The potential liabilities of systems officers, and the corporation, should be detailed in a separate document.

- *System quality.* The code should describe the general levels of data quality and system error that can be tolerated with detailed specifications left to specific projects. The code should require that all systems attempt to estimate data quality and system error probabilities.

- *Quality of life.* The code should state that the purpose of systems is to improve the quality of life for customers and for employees by achieving high levels of product quality, customer service, and employee satisfaction and human dignity through proper ergonomics, job and work flow design, and human resource development.

Management Challenges

1. **Understanding the moral risks of new technology.** Rapid technological change means that the choices facing individuals, the balance of risk and reward, and the probabilities of apprehension for wrongful acts all change as well. In this environment it will be important for management to conduct an ethical and social impact analysis of new technologies. One might take each of the moral dimensions described in this chapter and briefly speculate on how a new technology will impact each dimension. There will be no right answers for how to behave but there should be considered management judgment on the moral risks of new technology.

2. **Establishing corporate ethics policies that include IS issues.** As managers you will be responsible for developing corporate ethics policies and for enforcing them and explaining them to employees. Historically the IS area is the last to be consulted and much more attention has been paid to financial integrity and personnel policies. But from what you now know after reading this chapter, it is clear your corporation should have an ethics policy in the IS area covering such issues as privacy, property, accountability, system quality, and quality of life. The challenge will be in educating non-IS managers to the need for these policies, as well as educating your workforce.

Summary

Understand the relationship among ethical, social, and political issues raised by information systems.

Ethical, social, and political issues are closely related in an information society. Ethical issues confront individuals who must choose a course of action, often in a situation where two or more ethical principles are in conflict (a dilemma). Social issues spring from ethical issues. Societies must develop expectations in individuals about the correct course of action, and social issues then are debates about the kinds of situations and expectations that societies should develop so that individuals behave correctly. Political issues spring from social conflict and have to do largely with laws that prescribe behavior and seek to use the law to create situations where individuals behave correctly.

Identify the main moral dimensions of an information society and apply them to specific situations.

There are five main moral dimensions that tie together ethical, social, and political issues in an information society. These moral dimensions are information rights and obligations, property rights, accountability and control, system quality, and quality of life.

Apply an ethical analysis to difficult situations.

An ethical analysis is a five-step methodology for analyzing a situation. The method involves identifying the facts, values, stakeholders, options, and consequences of actions. Once the analysis is completed, you can begin to consider what ethical principle you should apply to a situation in order to arrive at a judgment.

Understand specific ethical principles for conduct.

Six ethical principles are available to judge your own conduct (and that of others). These principles are derived independently from several cultural, religious and intellectual traditions. They are not hard and fast rules and may not apply in all situations. The principles are the Golden Rule, Immanuel Kant's Categorical Imperative, Descartes' rule of change, the Utilitarian Principle, the Risk Aversion Principle, and the ethical no free lunch rule.

Develop corporate policies for ethical conduct.

For each of the five moral dimensions, corporations should develop an ethics policy statement to assist individuals and to encourage the correct decisions. The policy areas are as follows. Individual information rights: spell out corporate privacy and due process policies. Property rights: clarify how the corporation will treat property rights of software owners. Accountability and control: clarify who is responsible and accountable for information. System quality: identify methodologies and quality standards to achieve. Quality of life: identify corporate policies on family, computer crime, decision making, vulnerability, job loss, and health risks.

Key Terms		
Ethics	Fair Information Practices
Information rights	Intellectual property
Responsibility	Trade secret
Accountability	Copyright
Liability	Patent
Immanuel Kant's Categorial Imperative	Computer crime
Descartes' rule of change	Computer abuse
Utilitarian Principle	Repetitive stress injury (RSI)
Risk Aversion Principle	Carpal tunnel syndrome (CTS)
Ethical no free lunch rule	Computer vision syndrome (CVS)
Privacy	Technostress

Review Questions

1. In what ways are ethical, social, and political issues connected? Give some examples.
2. What are the key technological trends that heighten ethical concerns?
3. What are the differences between responsibility, accountability, and liability?
4. What are the five steps in an ethical analysis?
5. Identify six ethical principles.
6. What are meant by "privacy" and "fair information practices"?
7. What are the three different regimes that protect intellectual property rights?
8. Why is it so difficult to hold software services liable for failure or injury?
9. What is the most common cause of system quality problems?
10. Name four "quality of life" impacts of computers and information systems.
11. What is technostress, and how would you measure it?
12. Name three management actions that could reduce RSI injuries.

Discussion Questions

1. Why should anyone care about unemployment caused by re-engineering? Won't these workers be rehired at some point in the future when business gets better?

2. If everyone copied software, there would be no real market for software products, and producers of software would go out of business. Is this really true? What ethical principle is being applied in this statement? Discuss.

3. Should producers of software-based services like ATMs be held liable for economic injuries suffered when their systems fail?

Group Projects

1. With three or four of your classmates, develop a corporate ethics code on privacy. Be sure to consider E-mail privacy, employee monitoring of work sites as well as hallways, entrances, and restrooms. You should also consider corporate use of information about employees concerning their off-job behavior (e.g., lifestyle, marital arrangements, and so forth). Present your ethics code to the class.

2. With three or four of your classmates, interview managers of your university information systems department concerning university ethics policies in the systems area. Does your university have an ethics policy for students and employees? What is it? You could also interview a local firm rather than university officials. Present your findings to the class.

CASE STUDY

Virgin Atlantic: Corporate Hacking by British Airways

In a tough battle for market share, anything goes, right? Maybe, until you're caught, and then you'll be sorry. That's what happened to British Airways, which up until a few years ago was a major state-owned embarrassment. Under Lord King, British Airways moved in a few years to become one of the world's most profitable airlines based largely on its transatlantic service and protection and dominance at Heathrow Airport against other competitors. Not by being nice, but by being toughminded and fiercely competitive on price and service, King was able to turn British Airways into one of Europe's premiere examples of a success story.

In 1991 an upstart company called Virgin Atlantic began offering cheaper fares between the lucrative New York and London markets. Founded by Richard Branson, a former music entrepreneur, Virgin achieved great success in the United States as the cheap, fashionable way to travel to Europe. The downside was that Virgin had smaller facilities and flew at odd hours at first. As it learned the marketplace, its staff, facilities, and schedule improved. For training, maintenance, and passenger reservations it relied on its big competitor British Airways. In this respect, Virgin Atlantic was quite different from an earlier American phenomenon called Peoples' Express which attempted to perform all its own services and had no reservation alliances.

But when Virgin Atlantic started "cherry picking" a substantial number of British Airway's best first class and repeat business customers, British Airways started to look for new ways to compete. It cancelled cooperation on maintenance and training; it approached Virgin's custom-

ers in the media directly and tried to woo them away. This was all fair competition. But then British Airways went too far and successfully devised a corporate hacking scheme to break into Virgin's reservation lists posted on British Airway's own reservation system.

Former British Airways employee Sadig Khalifa explained that he and other British Airways staff were taught how to wiretap into a segment of the British Airways Booking System computer that Virgin rented. Perusing the list of passengers, British Airways was able to identify the home telephone numbers and addresses of first-class passengers, along with the basic flight information. Passengers were then called, according to Virgin's lawyers, by British Airways staff, who enticed them to switch their bookings to British Airways. In a public flurry of comments and charges, Virgin's lawyers charged British Airways with libeling Richard Branson and Virgin Atlantic.

The case was settled out of court in January 1993 before it was even heard in court. British Airways agreed to apologize to Virgin Atlantic and Richard Branson for making false statments, pay $935,000 to Virgin and Branson, and pick up $3 million in court costs.

Observers noted that British Airways' actions were also a violation of England's Data Protection Act, which makes it a crime to interfere with electronic communications and data systems. Critics noted, however, that the kind of wiretapping involved could be accomplished easily with a few hundred dollars in equipment from Radio Shack. Virgin Atlantic had taken no measures to protect its communication link with the Booking System.

Sources: "Tactics and Dirty Tricks," *The Economist* (January 16, 1993), and Elizabeth Heichler, "Airline Hacking Case Reveals CRS' Security Shortcomings," *Computerworld* (January 18, 1993).

Case Study Questions

1. What managerial, technological, and organizational factors allowed the Virgin Airlines–British Airways case to develop?

2. Which of the six ethical principles apply here?

3. We have described five moral dimensions of the information age. Pick one of these dimensions and describe the ethical, social and political aspects of this case. In particular, what would you have done if you were Sadig Khalifa? Or Lord King?

References

Barlow, John Perry. "Electronic Frontier: Private Life in Cyberspace." *Communications of the ACM* 34, no. 8 (August 1991).

Brod, Craig. *Techno Stress—The Human Cost of the Computer Revolution.* Reading MA: Addison-Wesley, 1982.

Brown Bag Software v. Symantec Corp. 960F2D1465 (Ninth Circuit, 1992).

Bulkeley, William M. "Databases Plagued by a Reign of Error." *The Wall Street Journal* (May 26, 1992).

Cafasso, Rosemary. "Rethinking Reengineering." *Computerworld* (March 15, 1993).

Caldwell, Bruce, with John Soat. "The Hidden Persuader." *InformationWEEK* (November 19, 1990).

Carley, William M. "Rigging Computers For Fraud or Malice Is Often an Inside Job." *The Wall Street Journal* (August 27, 1992).

Computer Systems Policy Project. "Perspectives on the National Information Infrastructure." January 12, 1993.

Datamation, December 15, 1992.

Dejoie, Roy, George Fowler, and David Paradice, eds. *Ethical Issues in Information Systems.* Boston: Boyd & Fraser, 1991.

"EMASS® Is Mobil's Mass Storage Solution." *Datamation* (September 15, 1993).

Equifax Report on Consumers in the Information Age, A National Survey. Equifax Inc., 1992.

Feder, Barnaby J. "As Hand Injuries Mount, So Do the Lawsuits." *The New York Times* (June 8, 1992).

Furger, Roberta. "In Search of Relief for Tired, Aching Eyes." *PC World* (February 1993).

Graham, Robert L. "The Legal Protection of Computer Software." *Communications of the ACM* (May 1984).

Joes, Kathryn. "EDS Set to Restore Cash-Machine Network." *The New York Times* (March 26, 1993).

King, Julia. "It's CYA Time." *Computerworld* (March 30, 1992).

Kling, Rob. "When Organizations Are Perpetrators: The Conditions of Computer Abuse and Computer Crime." *Computerization & Controversy: Value Conflicts & Social Choices,* ed. Charles Dunlop and Rob Kling. New York: Academic Press, 1991.

McPartlin, John P. "A Question of Complicity." *InformationWEEK* (June 22, 1992).

McPartlin, John P. "Environmental Agency 'Held Hostage' by Outsourcer." *InformationWEEK* (March 9, 1992).

McPartlin, John P. "Ten Years of Hard Labor." *InformationWEEK* (March 29, 1993).

McPartlin, John P. "The Terrors of Technostress." *InformationWEEK* (July 30, 1990).

Markoff, John. "Computer Viruses: Just Uncommon Colds After All?" *The New York Times* (November 1, 1992).

Markoff, John. "Though Illegal, Copied Software is Now Common." *The New York Times* (July 27, 1992).

Mason, Richard O. "Four Ethical Issues in the Information Age." *MIS Quarterly* 10, no. 1 (March 1986).

Mykytyn, Kathleen, Peter P. Mykytyn, Jr., and Craig W. Slinkman, "Expert Systems: A Question of Liability." *MIS Quarterly* 14, no. 1 (March 1990).

Neumann, Peter G. "Inside RISKS: Computers, Ethics and Values." *Communications of the ACM* 34, no. 87 (July 1991).

Neumann, Peter G. "Inside RISKS: Fraud by Computer." *Communications of the ACM* 35, no. 8 (August 1992).

Office of the Mayor, New York City. "The Trillion Dollar Gamble." 1991.

Oz, Effy. "Ethical Standards for Information Systems Professionals." *MIS Quarterly* 16, no. 4 (December 1992).

Pollack, Andrew. "San Francisco Law on VDTs is Struck Down." *The New York Times* (February 14, 1992).

Ramirez, Anthony. "AT&T to Eliminate Many Operator Jobs." *The New York Times* (March 4, 1992).

Rifkin, Glenn. "The Ethics Gap." *Computerworld* (October 14, 1991).

Rifkin, Jeremy. "Watch Out for Trickle-Down Technology." *The New York Times* (February 24, 1993).

Samuelson, Pamela. "Digital Media and the Law." *Communications of the ACM* 34, no. 10 (October 1991).

Samuelson, Pamela. "Legally Speaking: First Amendment Rights for Information Providers?" *Communications of the ACM* 34, no. 6 (June 1991).

Samuelson, Pamela. "Legally Speaking: Liability for Defective Electronic Information." *Communications of the ACM* 36, no. 1 (January 1993).

Schnorr, Teresa M. "Miscarriage and VDT Exposure." *New England Journal of Medicine* (March 1991).

Sterling, Bruce. *The Hacker Crackdown: Law and Disorder on the Computer Frontier.* New York: Bantam Books, 1992.

Stevens, William K. "Major U.S. Study Finds No Miscarriage Risk from Video Terminals." *The New York Times* (March 14, 1991).

Straub, Detmar W. Jr., and Rosann Webb Collins. "Key Information Liability Issues Facing Managers: Software Piracy, Proprietary Databases, and Individual Rights to Privacy." *MIS Quarterly* 14, no. 2 (June 1990).

Straub, Detmar W. Jr., and William D. Nance. "Discovering and Disciplining Computer Abuse in Organizations: A Field Study." *MIS Quarterly* 14, no. 1 (March 1990).

"Supercomputers Manage Holiday Stock." *The Wall Street Journal* (December 23, 1992).

Tabor, Mary W., with Anthony Ramirez. "Computer Savvy, With an Attitude." *The New York Times* (July 23, 1992).

United States Department of Health, Education and Welfare. *Records, Computers and the Rights of Citizens.* Cambridge: MIT Press, 1973.

Wilson, Linda. "Devil in Your Data." *InformationWEEK* (August 31, 1992).

Wolinsky, Carol, and James Sylvester. "Privacy in the Telecommunications Age." *Communications of the ACM* 35, no. 2 (February 1992).

INTERNATIONAL CASE STUDIES

Geelong and District Water Board[1]

Joel B. Barolsky and Peter Weill, University of Melbourne (Australia)

Joe Adamski, the Geelong and District Water Board's (GDWB) Executive Manager Information Systems, clicked his mouse on the phone messages menu option. Two messages had been left. The first was from an IT manager from a large Sydney-based insurance company confirming an appointment to "visit the GDWB and to assess what the insurance company could learn from the GDWB's IT experience." The second was from the general manager of another large water board asking whether Adamski and his team could assist, on a consultancy basis, in their IT strategy formulation and implementation.

The site visit from the insurance company was the 35th such request the Board had received since the completion of the first stage of their IT infrastructure investment strategy in January 1992. These requests were a pleasant diversion but the major focus of the GDWB's IT staff was to nurture and satisfy the increasing demands from the operational areas for building applications utilizing the newly installed IT infrastructure. The Water Board also faced the problem of balancing further in-house developments with external requests for consulting and demands from the GDWB's IT staff for new challenges and additional rewards.

ORGANIZATION BACKGROUND

The GDWB was constituted as a public utility of the Australian State of Victoria in July 1984 following an amalgamation of the Geelong Waterworks and Sewerage Trust and a number of other smaller regional water boards. The Board has the responsibility for the collection and distribution of water and the treatment and disposal of wastewater within a 1,600 square mile region in the southwest part of the State. In 1991, the permanent population serviced by the Board exceeded 200,000 people, this number growing significantly in the holiday periods with an influx of tourists.

The GDWB financed all its capital expenditure and operational expenditure through revenue received from its customers and through additional loan borrowings. Any profits generated were reinvested in the organization or used to pay off long-term debt. For the financial year 1990/91 the Board invested over $35.3 million in capital works and spent over $25 million in operating expenditure. Operating profit for the year 1990–91 exceeded $62.4 million on total assets of $292.5 million.

[1]A summarized version of a case study written by Joel B. Barolsky and Peter Weill of the Graduate School of Management, University of Melbourne, Australia. It was written as the basis of discussion rather than to illustrate either effective or ineffective handling of a managerial situation. Copyright © by Joel B. Barolsky and Peter Weill. Funding for this research was provided by IBM Consulting (USA).

In 1992, the GDWB was headed by a Governing Board with a State Government-appointed chairperson and eight members, elected by the residents of the community, who each sat for a three-year term. Managerial and administrative responsibilities were delegated to the GDWB's Executive Group which consists of the CEO and Executive Managers from each of the five operating divisions, namely Information Systems, Finance, Corporate Services, Engineering Development and Engineering Operations. From 1981 to 1992, the number of GDWB employees across all divisions rose from 304 to 454.

The GDWB's head office, situated in the regional capital city of Geelong, housed most of the Board's customer service, administrative, engineering, IT and other managerial staff. Complementing these activities, the GDWB operated five regional offices and a specialized 24-hour emergency contact service.

Commenting on the Board's competitive environment at the time, the GDWB's CEO, Geoff Vines, stated, "Although the organization operated in a monopolistic situation there still were considerable pressures on us to perform efficiently. Firstly, and most importantly, our objective was to be self funding—our customers wouldn't tolerate indiscriminate rate increases as a result of our inefficiencies and we could not go cap in hand to the State Government. Secondly, the amalgamation trend of water boards was continuing and the stronger the Board was the less likely it would be a target of a takeover. And thirdly, we did in a sense compare ourselves with private sector organizations and in some ways with other water boards. We had limited resources and we have to make the most of them."

KEY PROBLEM AREAS

Relating the situation up until the mid-1980's, Vines said that the Board faced a major problem in collectively identifying its largest assets—the underground pipes, drains, pumps, sewers and other facilities. He explained that most of these facilities were installed at least two or three meters below the surface and therefore it was almost impossible to gain immediate physical access to them. The exact specifications of each particular asset could only be ascertained through a thorough analysis of the original installation documentation and other geophysical surveys and maps of the area.

The limitations on identifying these underground facilities impacted operational performance in a number of key areas:

- most of the maintenance work conducted by the Board was based on reactive responses to leaks and other faults in the systems. It was difficult to introduce a coordinated preventative maintenance program because it was not possible to accurately predict when a particular pipe or piece of equipment was nearing the end of its expected life span.

- only a limited number of hard copies of this facility information could be kept. This significantly reduced the productivity of the engineering and operations' staff, especially in remote areas where they had to request this information from the central record-keeping systems. Backlogs and inaccuracies in filing also impacted efforts to repair, upgrade or install new piping, pumps and other equipment. On numerous occasions changes would be made to one set of plans without the same changes being recorded on the other copies of the same plans. Engineers designing improvements to existing facilities were often confronted with the problem of not being sure whether they were using the most up-to-date information of the facilities currently installed in the area concerned.

- the Board could not place realistic replacement values and depreciation charges on these underground assets.

With over 100,000 rateable properties in its area of responsibility, the GDWB maintained a centralized paper filing system containing more than a billion pages of related property information. The documents, most of which were of different sizes, quality, and age, were divided into 95,000 different files and sorted chronologically within each file. Access to the documents was made difficult as larger documents were cumbersome to copy and older documents were beginning to disintegrate. Having just one physical storage area significantly increased the potential exposure to fire and other risks and limited the wider distribution and sharing of the information. In the early 1980s, it was commonplace for a customer request for a statement of encumbrances placed at one of the GDWB's regional offices to take in excess of four weeks. The delays usually centered on finding the appropriate documents at the Property Services' central files, making the necessary copies, and transferring the documents back to the regional offices.

THE INFORMATION SYSTEMS DIVISION

In 1985, PA Consulting was commissioned to conduct a comprehensive review of the Board's strategy, management, operations structures and systems. One of the recommendations made by the consultants was that the Board should institute a more systematic approach to strategic planning. A major outcome of the planning process that followed was to create a new division for computing services and to recruit a new manager for this new area who reported directly to the CEO. The EDP Division was created with the objectives of "satisfying the Board's Information System needs through the provision of integrated and secure corporate computer systems and communication networks." Vines said that the Board needed a stand-alone information services group that could be used as a resource center for all users and that could add value to the work conducted by each functional group within the Board.

In April 1987, Joe Adamski was employed to fill the new position of EDP Manager (later changed to Executive Manager Information Systems). At the time of his arrival, only a small part of the GDWB's work systems were computerized, the main components of which included:

- a 'low-end' IBM System 38, primarily to run financial and other accounting software and some word processing applications. The System ran an in-house developed rate collection system which kept basic information on ratepayers including property details and consumption records;

- 19 "dumb" terminals—none of the Board's regional offices had terminal access to the central computer systems;

- a terminal link to the local university's DEC 20 computer to support the technical and laboratory services; and

- four stand-alone PCs, running some individual word processing packages as well as spreadsheet (Lotus 1–2–3), basic CAD and data base applications.

Computer maintenance, support and development was allocated to the Finance Division and delegated to an EDP supervisor (and three staff) who reported to the Finance Manager. Adamski noted, "The computer set-up when I joined was pretty outdated and inefficient. For example, the secretarial staff at Head Office were using the System 38's word processing facility and had to collect their dot matrix printouts from the computer room situated on the ground floor of the five-story building. In the technical area, some water supply network analysis data was available through the use of the DEC 20 system; however, hard copy output had to be collected from the University which was over five kilometers away. Most of the design engineers were using old drafting tables with rulers, erasers and pencils as their only drafting tools."

Recognizing that some users required immediate solutions to problems they were facing, the Board purchased additional terminals, peripherals and stand-alone microcomputers for the various areas thought to be in greatest need. Adamski said that these additional purchases further compounded some of the Board's computer-related problems. "We had a situation where we had at least four different CAD packages in use in different departments and we couldn't transfer data between them. There was a duplication of peripheral equipment with no sharing of printers, plotters and other output devices. In addition, various managers began to complain that system expertise was too localized and that there was little compatibility between the various applications."

PLANNING THE NEW ROLE FOR IT

In July 1988, Adamski initiated a long-term computing strategy planning process with the establishment of a special planning project team with both IT and user representatives. The team embarked on a major program of interviews and discussion with all user areas within the Board. They investigated other similar public utilities across Australia to assess their IT strategies and infra-structures and made contact with various computer hardware and software vendors to determine the latest available technologies and indicative costs.

The Project Team developed a comprehensive corporate computing strategy that would provide, as Adamski put it, the "quantum leap forward in the Board's IT portfo-lio." Adamski said that central to the computing strategy that was devised was that there should be as much inte-gration and flexibility as possible in all the Board's tech-nical and administrative systems. "Linked to this strat-egy was the notion that we should strive for an "open systems" approach with all our applications. This meant that each system had to have publicly specifiable inter-faces or "hooks" so that each system could talk to each other. From the users' perspective an open systems ap-proach meant that all the different applications looked pretty much the same and it was simple and easy to cross over from one to the other. It also meant that if we weren't happy with one particular product within the portfolio or we wanted to add a new one we could do it without too much disruption to the whole system."

He continued, "A key decision was made that we should build on our existing IT investments. With this in mind we had to make sure that the new systems were able to use the data and communicate with the System 38. We wanted only one hardware platform using only one op-erating system and only one relational data base man-agement system (RDBMS). We also wanted only one ho-mogenous network that was able to cater to a number of protocols and interfaces such as the network system for the microcomputers, workstations and the Internet connection. There also had to be a high degree of com-patibility and interaction with all the data files and appli-cations that were proposed. In view of this, we chose a UNIX platform with a client/server architecture."

In addition to specifying the software components of the system, the Project Team outlined the hardware that was necessary to run the new systems and the addi-tional staff that needed to be hired. To achieve the stated computing strategies and benefits, the Team also recommended that implementation take place over three key stages, with a formal progress review insti-tuted at the end of each stage.

APPROVAL

In February 1989 the corporate computing strategy planning process was completed and Adamski pre-sented the key recommendations to the Governing Board. In his presentation, Adamski stated that the in-frastructure cost of implementing the strategy was esti-mated to be about $5 million for the entire project (ex-cluding data capture costs) and that the project would take up to the end of 1995 for full commissioning.

Vines stated, "From my perspective, the proposed IT strategy took into account the critical functions in the organization that needed to be supported, such as cus-tomer services, asset management and asset creation. These were fundamental components of the Board's corporate objectives and the computer strategy pro-vided a means to realize these objectives and provide both short- and long-term benefits. There were some immediate short-term benefits, such as securing prop-erty services data that had no backup, and productivity gains in design and electronic mail. From a long-term perspective, I believe you can never really do an accu-rate rate-of-return calculation and base your decision solely on that. If you did you probably would never make such a large capital investment in IT. We did try to cost-justify all the new systems as best we could but we stressed that implementing IT strategy should be seen as providing long-term benefits for the entire organiza-tion that were not immediately measurable and would come to fruition many years later. Until all the informa-tion was captured and loaded on the IT facilities from the manual systems, the full benefits could not be realized."

Following an extensive and rigorous tendering process, it was decided that the Board should follow a multi-vendor solution as no one vendor could provide a total solution. Sun Microsystems was selected as the major hardware vendor and was asked to act as "prime con-tractors" in implementation. As prime contractors Sun was paid one project fee and then negotiated separate contracts with all other suppliers.

IMPLEMENTATION

In April 1990, the implementation of the IT strategy commenced with the delivery of the Sun file servers and workstations and installation of a homogenous network throughout the Board. Adamski said that the implemen-tation stage went surprisingly smoothly. "We didn't fire anybody as a direct result of the new systems, but jobs were changed. There was some resistance to the new technology—most of it was born out of unfamiliarity and fear of not having the appropriate skills. Some people were very committed in doing things "their way." When some of these people started to perceive tangible pro-ductivity benefits, their perspectives started to change. We tried to counsel people as best we could and en-courage them to experiment with the new systems. Most people eventually converted but there were still some objectors."

Adamski added that while they were implementing the new systems it was important for the IS Division not to lose sight of its key objectives and role within the orga-nization. "We had to make sure that we didn't get car-ried away with the new whiz-bang technology and re-duce our support and maintenance of the older, more conventional systems. For example, the Board went onto a new tariff system and we had to make significant changes to our rating system to accommodate this. Having an application generator in place significantly improved the systems upgrade time."

In May 1992, the Board's computer facilities included 4 Sun file servers, 80 Sun workstations, 100 microcom-

SUN SPARC WORKSTATIONS

LASER PRINTERS
ELECTROSTATIC PLOTTERS
PEN PLOTTERS
ACSNET MODEM

IP

NFS

SUN SERVERS
CAD
FIS
COMMS
PC
DATABASE

EPOCH SERVER
ARCHIVE/IMAGE

WIMS

EAGLE

FIS

LANDMASTER

INGR

CADD

DRAFTMASTER

DRMS

WP OA

DTM

4D

DRMS

INGRES RDBMS AND 4GL

IP

IP

NFS

PERSONAL COMPUTERS

FIELD DATA RECORDERS

MITEK GATEWAY

IBM SYSTEM 38

FINANCIAL SYSTEMS

PRINTERS

DISPLAY

SCANNERS

DIPS

TOWER

MIPS IMAGE MANAGER

OPTICAL JUKE BOX

FIS: Facilities Information System.
CADD: Computer Aided Design and Drafting.
WIMS: Water Information Management System.
DIPS: Document Image Processing System.
DTM: Digital Terrain Modelling.

DRMS: Drawing Retrieval and Management System.
EAGLE: Engineering and Graphics Language Environment (CADCOM).
WP OA: Word Processing and Office Automation.
NFS: Network File System.
IP: Internet Protocol.

Figure 1
GDWB corporate computing system.

puters, 40 terminals, and the IBM System 38 Model 700. By this time, the IS Division had implemented the following components of the systems (see Figure 1 for a schematic of the systems):

(1) **A Document Imaging Processing System (DIPS)** used for scanning, storing and managing all documents on each property within the GDWB region which were being kept in the 95,000 separate paper files. This system was also used for the storage, backup and retrieval of 25,000 engineering plans and drawings. DIPS gave designated Head Office departments and regional offices real-time access to all property documentation and allowed them to print out scanned images when required. The system had a sophisticated indexing system that facilitated easy retrieval of stored images by users and access by other programs. Figure 2 presents a copy of a scanned property plan from DIPS.

(2) A digital mapping **Facilities Information System (FIS)** that provided for the storage, management and on-going maintenance of all graphic (map related) and nongraphic information relating to water and wastewater services, property information, property boundaries, and easements throughout the Board's region. The FIS system provided a computerized "seamless" geographic map covering the entire GDWB region. The system encompassed the storing of all maps in digital form and attaching map coordinates to each digital point. Every

point on a digital map was linked to a unique X and Y coordinate, based on the standard Australian Mapping Grid system, and had a specific address linked to it. Once each point on a map was precisely addressed and identified, specific attributes were attached to it. These attributes were then used as methods of recording information or used as indexes for access to/by other programs, for example, sewer pipe details, property details, water consumption, vertical heights above sea level, etc. The selected map area with all the related attributes and information was then displayed graphically in full color on a high resolution workstation monitor (see Figure 3).

The FIS allowed cross referencing to financial, rating and consumption data (through indexing) held on the System 38. It also enabled each underground facility to be numbered, catalogued and identified as an asset with their associated data being integrated into other asset management systems. The FIS enabled data stored on a particular map to be "layered," with water pipes at one layer, sewer pipes at another, property boundaries at a third, future plans at another, and so on. This gave users the ability to recall maps in layers and to select the level and amount of detail they required. The system was centered around a mouse-driven graphic interface where the user zoomed in and out and/or panned around particular areas—at the broadest level, showing the whole of southern Victoria, and at the most detailed, the individual plumbing and

Figure 2
Example of a building plan kept for each rateable property.

drainage plan of one particular property (through cross-referencing to the DIPS system).

(3) A Computer Aided Design and Drafting (CADD) system that provided an integrated programmable 3-D environment for a range of civil, mechanical, electrical, surveying and general engineering design and drafting applications. It offered the following features:

- Display manipulation, including multiple angle views, zooms and pans;

- Geometric analysis, including automatic calculation of areas, perimeters, moments of inertia and centroids; and

- Various customization features such as user-defined menus and prompts and a user-friendly macro language.

Figure 3
Illustration of the type of information available on the Facilities Information System.

(4) **Word Processing and Office Automation (WP/OA)** systems providing users the ability to prepare quality documentation integrating graphics, spreadsheets, mail merge and data bases, as well as other utilities such as electronic mail and phone message handling.

(5) **A Relational Database Management System and a 4th Generation Language** as a base foundation for the development of new applications. Some of the RDBMS applications included:

- A Drawing and Retrieval Management System (DRMS) to control the development, release and revision of all CADD projects and files; and
- A Water Information Management System (WIMS) used for the storage and management of hydrographic engineering and laboratory data, both current and historical.

OUTCOMES

Vines said that one of the most important strategic outcomes of the changes introduced had been the way in which decision-making at all levels with the organization had been enhanced. "This improvement is largely due to the fact that people have now got ready access to information they have never had before. This information is especially useful in enhancing our ability to forward plan. The flow and reporting of financial information has also speeded up and we now complete our final accounts up to two months earlier than we used to. In the areas that have come on-line there has been a definite improvement in productivity and in customer service. The CADD system, for example, is greatly enhancing our ability to design and plan new facilities. The turnaround time, the accuracy of the plans and the creativity of the designers have been improved dramatically. In many departments there has been a change in work practices—some of the mundane activities are handled by the computer, allowing more productive work to be carried out, like spending more time with customers. Our asset management and control also started to improve. There was greater integrity in the information kept, and having just one central shared record meant that updating with new data or changes to existing data was far more efficient."

Adamski added that the initial reaction by Board staff to the whole corporate computing strategy "ranged from scepticism to outright hostility." He continued, "By the end of 1991, I would say that there had been a general reversal in attitude. Managers started to queue outside my office asking if we could develop specific business applications for them. They had begun to appreciate what the technology could do and most often they suddenly perceived a whole range of opportunities and different ways in which they could operate. One manager asked me, for example, if we could use document imaging technology to eliminate the need for any physical paper flows within his office. Technically this was possible but it was not really cost justifiable and the corporate culture would not really have supported it. Putting together the IS Division budget is now a difficult balancing act with a whole range of options and demands from users. I now ask the users to justify the benefits to be derived from new application proposals and I help out with the cost side. Cost/benefit justification usually drives the decisions as well as the "fit" with the existing IT and other corporate objectives. What also must be considered is that these objectives are not written in stone. They are flexible and can and should adjust to changes in both the internal and external environment."

A number of GDWB staff indicated that the new systems had enhanced their ability to fulfill their work responsibilities:

- A customer service officer at one of the Board's regional offices stated that the DIPS had enabled her to respond to customer requests for encumbrance statements within a matter of minutes instead of weeks. She added that a number of customers had sent letters to their office complimenting them on the improvements in the service they received. She said that new DIPS system had "flow on" benefits that weren't fully recognized. She cited the case where local architects were able to charge their clients less because they had more ready access to information from the GDWB.

- A maintenance manager declared that the FIS system had enabled his department to predict when pipes and drains should be replaced before they actually ruptured or broke down, by examining their installation dates and the types of materials used. He said this process over time started to shift the emphasis of his department's maintenance work from being reactive to being more preventative. He added that the system also enabled him to easily identify and contact the residents that would be affected by the work that the Board was going to do in a particular area. He said that the FIS enabled him to plot out with his mouse a particular area of a map on his screen. It would then "pick up" all the relevant properties in the area and identify the names and addresses of the current ratepayers residing in those properties.

- A secretary to a senior head office manager said that despite being a little daunted at first by the new wordprocessing system, she felt the system had helped her considerably. She said that besides the obvious benefits in being able to prepare and edit documents on a WYSIWYG screen, she also had the ability of viewing as well as integrating scanned property plans, correspondence, and other documents from the DIPS System.

Adamski said that one of the flow-on benefits from the FIS system in particular was that the Board had the potential of selling the information stored on the system to authorities such as municipal councils and other public utilities such as Telecom, the State Electricity Commission and the Gas and Fuel Corporation. He added that they had also considered marketing the information to private organizations such as building managers, architects and property developers, and that the return from these sales could significantly reduce the overall costs in developing the FIS system.

THE FUTURE

Commenting on the future prospects for the Board's IS Division, Adamski said, "There are some very complex applications that we are developing but we now have the skills, the tools, and the infrastructure to develop them cost-effectively and to ensure that they deliver results. I think one of the main reasons why we are in this fortuitous position is that we chose a UNIX platform with client/server processing and a strong networking backbone. It gives us the flexibility and integration that we set out to achieve and we will need in the future to realize both our long- and short-term objectives. It's a lot easier now to cost-justify requests for new applications. The challenges ahead lie in three areas. Firstly, it's going to be difficult to consistently satisfy all our users' needs in that their expectations will be increasing all the time and they will become more demanding. We have to recognize these demands and at the same time keep investing in and maintaining our infrastructure. Secondly, we still have some way to go in developing a total corporate management information system. There are still some "islands of data" floating around and the challenge is to get it all integrated. And thirdly, as the most senior IT manager at the Board I have to make sure that we retain our key IT staff and we compensate them adequately, both monetarily and in providing them stimulating and demanding work."

Case Study Questions

1. Describe the Geelong and District Water Board and the environment in which they operate. What problems did GDWB have before 1988? What were the management, organization, and technology factors that contributed to those problems?

2. Describe the role of information systems at GDWB and the GDWB's information system portfolio before July 1988.

3. Describe and critique the process of upgrading GDWB's information systems portfolio.

4. How did GDWB justify its investments in new information system technology? What were the benefits? How were they justified? What additional information would you need to determine whether these investments were worthwhile?

5. What should Geoff Vines and Joe Adamski do next?

Vinwood Offshore Petroleum

Alan Underwood, Queensland University of Technology (Australia)

One of Australia's largest petroleum conglomerates, Vinwood Offshore Petroleum, is currently halfway through implementation of its information technology migration plan. The plan is aimed at making better use of organizational data in day-to-day operations and management decision making. The company had reviewed its information technology strategy in 1989 and began looking for new ways to use information technology to enhance its future business development.

Vinwood's plan focuses on creating a cohesive information environment, which it has named Gaze, to facilitate the sharing of communications across the geographically distant locations of its organization (Perth and Karratha in Western Australia, and Melbourne in Victoria), and the integration of the functions performed at these distant locations through a common communications platform.

Vinwood's information resources group convinced the six companies that were business partners involved in Vinwood of the logic and soundness of the proposed IS strategy. "We had a different vision for our computing resources, to help us to manage information. One thing not widely acknowledged is [that] computing is all about automating autonomous manual tasks. Information, as a resource of any organization, needs to be managed, just like every other asset. Up to now many have thought you don't need to manage that resource. Management agreed with our concept of managing the information resource base in the same manner as you manage other assets. Then you are in a position to make strategic use of information to enhance business performance based on what IS is doing and which can tell us where the business is headed."

Gaze is expected to improve Vinwood's business operations by strengthening communications, creating simpler work procedures and making better information analyses available to assist decision making. Ernie Hannan, the manager of information resources at Vinwood, described the history of the project, saying, "A few years back we reviewed our IS strategy. There were some major items in our agenda that were specific to our organization's structure which we needed to look at. We have a large office system within the organization with close to 1650 users. This is an important part of Vinwood's computing platform." He claims the IS changes that had been started are well underway, have been well received by users and will ultimately contribute to Vinwood's future business productivity.

An important component of the plan was the implementation of an integrated office system using a client/server architecture. Vinwood decided to switch to a new hardware platform based on Digital Equipment Corporation technology. Vinwood had developed under the

Data General platform for years but, in 1988–89, Data General abandoned development of its comprehensive electronic office (CEO) to start developing in UNIX. This prompted Vinwood to look at its IS strategies and future decisions.

"We decided, because of Data General's technology direction change, we would have to make a significant investment whatever we decided—either to change the platform or, if we stuck with Data General, to upgrade to their new platform so we could develop in a platform that will continue into the future," Hannan said. "We decided that from a networking point of view and where we should head in terms of systems we were much better off moving towards Digital." He added that Vinwood's "computer infrastructure was getting old and maintenance costs were high. As a result of the change we will be able to give updated tools at a lower operating cost."

Digital's integrated office system, along with the use of LANs, will provide a foundation for future Gaze components. For office automation, Vinwood decided it was better to move to Digital's All-In-One with added features and incorporating WordPerfect's word processing system. All-In-One is the simplest way for users to access the new integrated office system. For those using this method, all computing is done on the central computer. Mailing and printing documents will be faster and easier with All-In-One than with Data General's comprehensive electronic office (CEO), Hannan claimed.

Another method of accessing the integrated office system is by using TeamLink. "WordPerfect and Digital produce TeamLink, a Windows-based product that runs on a client/server architecture," says Hannan. "This is a new product, still a test version, but it has unleashed the power of the PCs and central processing. The PC (client) accesses the central computer (server) for services such as electronic mail and document filing. This takes greater advantage of the PC's power. TeamLink runs in the Windows environment. TeamLink can do a lot of processing and information on PCs. It works on the same principle as LANs."

Vinwood started implementing the office system this year. Before moving to the new integrated office system environment, pilots were run in certain departments to ensure the general migration was smooth and painless. The changes implemented to date have already achieved significant productivity gains and relieved many administration headaches.

There are six components to Gaze. Vinwood's integrated office system and All-In-One is just one of those components. The information network, another component, is completed and already implemented. It has the advantage of being upgraded easily. The network, which covers a wide range of the company's activities, has proven easy to use and presents information in a meaningful format. Vinwood's LAN, a high speed, flexible communications network for PC users, provides a range of personal productivity services through printer, application, and file services.

The application service provides access to software that is required occasionally, which means that users no longer have to do without because they cannot justify keeping their own copy. Consequently the application services provides many users with the right tools at a lower cost to Vinwood. The file server gives access to disk space on the central computer. By storing PC files on the central computer, regular backups are performed by the computer center. "You can allow other staff to access your disk space, providing a simple method for sharing PC files among members of your work group, or anyone else on the LAN."

Some applications give line managers information about their people, while others, such as performance information, are focused on small groups. Generally the information is presented in summary form though detailed information is available to the manager with graphical presentation used where possible.

Gaze is presently targeting electronic forms. Vinwood already makes use of some electronic data interchange (EDI) by transferring information to banks and other financial institutions and has started electronic purchasing with firms. With Gaze it is possible to put building blocks in place that will interact and be expandable to monitor business performance and improve productivity, communications, work procedures and work flow.

Source: Janet Rosenberg, "Woodside's IOS Leads to Productivity Advantages." *Pacific Computer Weekly,* October 2, 1992.

Case Study Questions

1. Why did Vinwood need to change its information technology platform? What management, organization, and technology issues had to be addressed before moving from Data General to Digital Equipment Corporation technology?

2. What model of information architecture is illustrated here? Were other alternatives appropriate for Vinwood? Why or why not?

3. Comment on the manager's statement ". . . computing is all about automating autonomous manual tasks" in the context of management decision-making.

4. Identify the management benefits of using proprietary packages such as All-In-One or WordPerfect for office and decision-making applications.

Ginormous Life Insurance Company

Len Fertuck, University of Toronto (Canada)

Ginormous Life is an insurance company with a long tradition. The company has four divisions. Each operates its own computers. The IS group provides analysis, design and programming services to all the divisions. The divisions are actuarial, marketing, operations, and investment, all located at the corporate headquarters building. Marketing also has field offices in twenty cities across the country.

The Actuarial Division is responsible for the design and pricing of new kinds of policies. They use purchased industry data and weekly summaries of data obtained from the Operations Division. They have their own DEC minicomputer, running the UNIX operating system, to store data files. They do most of their analysis on microcomputers and Sun workstations, either on spreadsheets or with a specialized interactive language called APL.

The Marketing Division is responsible for selling policies to new customers and for follow-up of existing customers in case they need changes to their current insurance. All sales orders are sent to the Operations Division for data entry and billing. They use purchased external data for market research and weekly copies of data from operations for follow-ups. They have their own DEC VAX minicomputer with dumb terminals for clerks to enter sales data. There are also many microcomputers used to analyze market data using statistical packages like SAS.

The Operations Division is responsible for processing all mission-critical financial transactions, including payroll. They record all new policies, send regular bills to customers, evaluate and pay all claims, and cancel lapsed policies. They have all their data and programs on a large IBM ES/9000 mainframe. The programs are often large and complex because they must service not only the fifteen products currently being sold, but also the 75 old kinds of policies that are no longer being sold, but still have existing policy holders. Clerks use dumb terminals to enter and update data. Application programs are almost always written in COBOL. Some recent applications have used a SQL relational database to store data, but most use COBOL flat files. The average age of the transaction processing programs is about ten years.

The Investment Division is responsible for investing premiums until they are needed to pay claims. Their data consists primarily of internal portfolio data and research data obtained by direct links to financial data services. They have a DEC minicomputer to store their data. The internal data are received by a weekly download of cash flows from the Operations Division. External data are obtained as needed. They use microcom-

puters to analyze data obtained from the mini or from commercial data services.

A controlling interest in Ginormous Life has recently been purchased by Financial Behemoth Corp. The management of Financial Behemoth has decided that the firm's efficiency and profitability must be improved. Their first move has been to put Dan D. Mann, a hot-shot information systems specialist from Financial Behemoth, in charge of the Information Systems Division. He has been given the objective of modernizing and streamlining the computer facilities without any increase in budget.

In the first week on the job, Dan discovered that none of the staff of 200 information systems specialists know anything about CASE tools, End-User Computing or LANs. All microcomputer applications have been purchased, so no one has experience in implementing microcomputer systems. There is no evidence of any formal Decision Support Systems or Executive Information Systems in the organization. There have been a few tentative experiments with DB2, a relational database product, purchased from IBM, their mainframe vendor. Most managers say that "they do not need all those fancy Executive Information Systems." They would be happy if Information Systems would just provide basic reports on the financial performance of each product line and customer group.

There have been some problems with these systems. Maintenance is difficult and costly because almost every change to the data structure of applications in operations requires corresponding changes to applications in the other divisions. There has been a growing demand in other divisions for faster access to operations data. For instance, the Investment Division claims that they could make more profitable investments if they had continuous access to the cash position in operations. Marketing complains that they get calls from clients about claims and cannot answer them because they do not have current access to the status of the claim. Management wants current access to a wide variety of data in summary form so they can get a better understanding of the business. The IS group says that it would be difficult to provide access to data in operations because of security considerations. It is difficult to ensure that users do not make unauthorized changes to the COBOL files.

The IS group complains that they cannot deliver all the applications the users want because they are short-staffed. They spend 90 percent of their time maintaining the existing systems, most of which are in the COBOL language. The programmers are mostly old and experienced and employee turnover is unusually low, so there is not likely to be much room for improvement by further training in programming. Morale is generally good despite the perception of overwork. Employees often remark that the company is a very pleasant and benevolent place to work. At least they did until rumors of deregulation and foreign competition started to sweep the industry.

Dan began to look for ways to solve the many problems of the Information Systems Division. He solicited proposals from various vendors and consultants in the computer industry. After a preliminary review of the proposals, Dan was left with three broad options suggested by IBM, Oracle Corp., and Systemotion, a local consulting firm. The proposals are briefly described below.

IBM proposed an integrated solution using IBM hardware and software. The main elements of their proposal are:

- *Data and applications will remain on a mainframe.* The IBM ES/9000 series of hardware running their proprietary operating system will provide mainframe services. Mainframe hardware capacity will have to be approximately doubled. AS/400 minicomputers running under the OS/400 operating system will replace DEC minicomputers. RS/6000 workstations running AIX, a flavor of the UNIX operating system, can be used for actuarial computations. All hardware will be interconnected with IBM's proprietary SNA network architecture. Microcomputers will run under the OS/2 operating system and the IBM LAN Server to support both Microsoft Windows applications and locally designed applications that communicate with mainframe databases.

- *A DB2 relational database will store all data on line.* Users will be able to access any data they need through their terminals or through microcomputers that communicate with the mainframe.

- *Legacy systems will be converted using re-engineering tools,* like Design Recovery and Maintenance Workbench from Intersolve, Inc. These will have the advantage that they will continue to use the COBOL code that the existing programmers are familiar with. New work will be done using CASE tools with code generators that produce COBOL code.

- *Proven technology.* The IBM systems are widely used by many customers and vendors. Many mission-critical application programs are available on the market that address a wide variety of business needs.

Oracle Corp. proposed that all systems be converted to use their Oracle database product and its associated screen and report generators. They said that such a conversion would have the following advantages:

- *Over 75 hardware platforms are supported.* This means that the company is no longer bound to stay with a single vendor. Oracle databases and application programs can be easily moved from one manufacturer's machine to another manufacturer's

machine by a relatively simple export and import operation as long as applications are created with Oracle tools. Thus the most economical hardware platform can be used for the application. Oracle will also access data stored in an IBM DB2 database.

- *Integrated CASE tools and application generators.* Oracle has its own CASE tool and its own form and report generators. Databases designed with the Oracle CASE tool can be automatically created in an Oracle database using CASE*Generator. SQL*Forms, one of their application generation tools, can design and generate screens for a wide variety of terminals. The same design can be implemented on dumb terminals, a Macintosh, X-Windows in UNIX, or Systems Application Architecture (SAA) in an IBM environment. Applications are created using graphic tools that eliminate the need for a language like COBOL. In fact, the programmer cannot see the underlying language that is being used for implementation. The designer works entirely with visual prototyping specifications. SQL*ReportWriter can generate reports in the same way.

- *Vertically integrated applications.* Oracle sells a number of common applications, like accounting programs, that can be used as building blocks in developing a complete system. These applications could eliminate the need to redevelop some applications.

- *Distributed network support.* A wide variety of common network protocols like SNA, DecNet, Novell, and TCP/IP are supported. Different parts of the database can be distributed to different machines on the network and accessed or updated by any application. Access can be controlled at the file, record, or field level for each user on the system. All data are stored on line for instant access. The data can be stored on one machine and the applications can be run on a different machine, including a microcomputer or workstation, to provide a client/server environment. The ability to distribute a database allows a large database on an expensive mainframe to be distributed to a number of cheaper minicomputers.

Systemotion proposed a state-of-the-art system using the Sybase Object Oriented Relational Data Base Management System (OORDBMS) with applications implemented in a Microsoft Windows environment. This proposal offers the following advantages:

- *A modern object-oriented database.* Sybase is a relatively new entrant in the database field so it is able to exploit the benefits of an object-oriented approach without having to worry about a large number of legacy applications already coded in an older non-object-oriented version. This means that it is possible to include complex validation rules in the database rather than having to code them in the application code. This reduces application testing and speeds development as well as improving data integrity.

- **Client/server systems.** Since Sybase is object-oriented, it is a natural product for a client/server environment. It becomes particularly easy to install the database on a server (commonly one or more Hewlett-Packard or DEC minicomputers) and place the applications and entry screens on microcomputers or workstations like those from Sun Microsystems. Object-oriented applications can be easily built using graphic languages like Power Builder or Visual Basic. The database can be easily extended to store graphics like photos or scanned documents. This could allow business re-engineering to reduce the paper burden that is common in insurance firms. The client applications would run on a LAN with Microsoft SQL Server, a networked relational DBMS server.
- **Open UNIX environment.** Many programs have been written for the UNIX operating system. UNIX can be run on many different hardware platforms and network communication systems. This openness will make it possible to integrate applications on a number of platforms while obtaining the cost benefits of downsizing to smaller platforms.
- **Easy integration with purchased Windows applications.** The object-oriented approach meshes well with the Windows environment that has a feature called Object Linking and Embedding (OLE), which permits direct reference from one Windows software product to another. Thus it is quite easy to write a program that obtains data from a central database and brings it into a spreadsheet, like Excel, where it can be analyzed, manipulated, or graphed. The graph, in turn, can be embedded in a word processor report. If new data are downloaded into the spreadsheet, the graph will automatically be updated whenever the report is opened in the word processor. This makes it easy to satisfy management needs for information within the word-processing or spreadsheet environment they are familiar with. It also makes it relatively easy to create customized management and executive information systems. In addition, many functions can be performed directly by purchased Windows programs to eliminate the need to design, build, and maintain many applications.

Dan is not sure which approach to take for the future of Ginormous Life. He appreciates that whichever route he follows, the technology will have an enormous impact on the kinds of applications his staff will be able to produce in the future and the way in which they will produce them. He is concerned about industry trends toward downsizing and distribution of systems. While this trend may eventually prove to be more efficient, his staff does not have much experience with the new technologies that would be required. He is uncertain about whether there will be a sufficient payoff to justify the organizational turmoil that will result from a major change in direction.

Dan must prepare a strategy for the renewal of the Information Systems Division over the next three years. As his assistant, he has asked you to address the following questions:

Case Study Questions

1. Prepare a list of factors or issues that must be considered in developing a strategy and selecting a technology platform for Ginormous.
2. Analyze how each of the three proposals performs on each factor or issue. If you find issues that a proposal fails to address, advise Dan as to the significance of the omission and how you think the proposal might be modified to address that issue.
3. Advise Dan on special criteria, if any, he might need to apply when evaluating a proposal for a company-wide information strategy coming from a technology vendor. Explain your reasoning.
4. Assuming Dan were to make his decision without seeking further information from the proposers, recommend to him which proposal he should accept and your reason for selecting that proposal.
5. Based upon your advice in the previous question, state the order in which each component of the new technology should be introduced and the reason for selecting the order.

Kone Elevators

Tapio Reponen, Turku School of Economics and Business Administration (Finland)

Elevators are products that are made according to customer specification. Each building is different, and the products have to fit the building's structure and framework. However, the elevator components can often be selected from a range of standard components either in predefined sets (pre-engineered, standard elevators) or in custom-made combinations (nonstandard elevators). The following description illustrates how information systems can support the process of elevator sales, order, and delivery at Kone Elevators, an international elevator manufacturer with headquarters in Helsinki, Finland.

"Kone Lifts, good morning. Larry Liftagain speaking. How can I help you?"

"Good morning. This is Mr. Beaver from Bayswater Builders. I would like to have a quotation for a lift for our new project, please."

The pre-engineered elevator sale is usually handled by the salesman himself, using tools, materials, and procedures provided by sales support, engineering, and manufacturing. If the salesman needs additional information or if the equipment is outside the pre-engineered range, he contacts the Engineering department for further calculations and specifications.

Larry's sales tool kit consists of his PC with its tendering system, traffic analysis and simulation programs, price and material lists, and his sales guide and technical information binders. He also needs tools to communicate with his own back-up in sales support and in engineering. This is possible either by electronic mail and messaging systems or by conventional phone and fax. Finally, he will enter the order received in the Order book and project management system, where the elevator will be managed and followed up from the specification throughout material order, installation and testing to final hand-over to the customer. After customer hand-over, the data are transferred to the maintenance and call-out system for the guarantee period and often beyond.

Tender Enquiry

"Yes, Mr. Beaver, we will be pleased to provide you with a quotation, but I'll need some information from you to specify the type of the lift. What type of building are we dealing with?"

"A small office building, with six floors."

"How many occupants will there be on each floor? Have you reserved any space for the lift shaft and the machine room? Is the machine room on top or at the bottom of the building?"

Tender Preparation

Larry has obtained all the data that he needs: the customer details, building drawings, and the specification request from the architect or consultant. He inputs these to the tendering system. The elevator type, load, travel height and number of stops provide the basic range and specification. The further items to be specified are the door type, width, height, control features, elevator car interior, signals and push buttons on car and landings. The specification is made by selecting from a predefined list of items. If the item combinations are restricted or not allowed, a message will be displayed. If the customer requests a feature that does not appear on the standard list, it can either be added as a local item, which will be purchased from a subcontractor, or the salesman can ask for a specification from the Kone factory.

Based on the items selected, the basic tender price is calculated. The price includes the value of materials, which can be partly from a Kone factory and partly from local subcontractors; the installation and labor cost; elevator service during the guarantee period; any adjustable items for market area or building customer type, possibly indexing and discounts included.

The tender documents will be produced by combining the selected values and parameters to predefined letter and text blocks in word-processing. The tender letters and technical description of the items tendered can be modified by the salesman, if required to suit this particular customer and project.

Tender Follow-up and Negotiation

"Good morning, Larry! Nice Monday, the sun is shining and the sky is blue! What's up this week?"

"Good morning, boss! I just printed out my action list for this week. The first thing I'll do is to follow up a tender I sent to Bayswater Builders last week. Then I have another three outstanding tenders which I need to track. The project we tendered in Brighton is due to be decided this week and I'm 90 percent sure we're going to get it."

When the tenders are registered in the salesman's system, the follow-up and updating of data can take place in an organized way. During the negotiations the elevator specifications often change, alternative options are submitted to the customer, the price is negotiated, and the schedules and installation programs are agreed on. All changes and modifications are done by changing parameters in the original tender. Different versions are saved and the full tender history is available for sales managers and salesmen themselves, if required.

Order Booking

"Good afternoon, Mr. Liftagain, this is Mr. Beaver from Bayswater Builders. At our meeting this morning we decided to give the lift order to Kone, for the price and specifications agreed in your revised quotation on Friday. I will send you the letter of instruction confirming this. When can you give me the detailed schedule and the final drawings?"

The order was received, but this is just the start for the next phase of the job: the implementation. The order is transferred from the tendering system to the order book, job numbers are opened, the customer details, commercial details, cost budget estimate, elevator specification, and project schedule are entered.

Interface to other systems

Information about the new order is sent automatically to the financial department, who will open job numbers in the accounting systems. The new elevators will appear in order book reports for the sales and branch managers and other authorized users.

The factory will be informed about the new order received. This can take place at order booking, or in cases where the drawings and completion of specification is handled locally by the salesman, the complete order is sent to the factory at no-return point—just in time for the manufacture.

Drawings

After the tender and specification have been agreed, the production of layout and design drawings starts. These drawings are produced either by the salesman or by the engineering department when technical expertise and advanced CAD systems are required. The salesman's drawing system can be a parameter driven PC CAD, which fills the building and elevator dimensions into predefined layout sheets. This enables the salesman to submit standard drawings to the architect and builder in a few minutes or hours, sometimes even in their office.

Installation planning and scheduling

"Hi Larry, this is Bob! Listen, I noticed on my capacity plan that you've booked a new order with Bayswater Builders—well done! When you're ready with the specs (= technical specifications), can you arrange the handover to Peter, who I've appointed as supervisor. He will also make the detailed installation plan and coordinate the deliveries from the factory, as usual. I can see in his labor plan that he has two men available in September for the installation work. The estimated hours proposed by the computer say we will take 3 weeks to complete, so we can achieve the handover to customer on 1st October, as planned."

Factory Order

When the drawings have been approved, the remaining items of the specification have been agreed on, and the car interior and landing features designed, the salesman fills in the order form and specification for the factory.

When the order form is in electronic format, the system checks whether the components, options and the combinations are allowed, the dimensions are within acceptable limits, and all mandatory items have been specified. The completed order is sent electronically to the supplying factory. The order consists of the material list, order header and customer details, contact person, delivery groups and required schedule.

The order confirmation is received, including confirmed transfer price, delivery groups and schedules.

Any items that are purchased locally from subcontractors are specified. Prices and schedules are agreed and monitored.

Site and Installation activities

"Good morning, gentlemen, welcome to our Monday site meeting. The building works are progressing on schedule and the lift installation is due to start next week. We have the Installation Supervisor Peter Jones from Kone Lifts here to agree on the next steps. Peter, can you tell us about your program?"

"Good morning, all. The lift installation is due to start next Monday and to continue for 3 weeks. I have two men working on site and I will be visiting twice a week. The materials will arrive in two shipments. The first one, consisting of the shaft and machine room equipment, will arrive next Monday. The doors, car finishes and signal equipment will arrive the following Monday. I have spoken to your transport manager and he has arranged for your truck driver to assist in moving the equipment from the lorry to the area assigned by the site manager. The installation work will progress in 11 steps—here is the step-by-step plan—starting from unloading and distributing the material, installing the machine room equipment, and ending at commissioning and testing. The time allowed for each activity, you can see in this schedule. My guys will be filling in time sheets and progress reports every week which will be used for the payroll and monitoring of site progress. . . ."

Handover

"Hello Mr. Beaver, how are you? You have a nice group of lifts in here, completed all on time, as planned. Let's take a closer look. . . . So, everything is in order, we have received your interim payments, the final invoice will be sent to you today. I would like to introduce you to out Maintenance Manager Paul Simon. He and his guys will be looking after your lifts for the next 12 months, as per our contract. If you have any further projects, please don't hesitate to contact us."

This is a typical successful elevator order-delivery process, which demonstrates all parts of the process. Selling is not always so easy and becomes more complicated and harder all the time.

KONE ELEVATORS

Kone Elevators is the third largest elevator manufacturer in the world, the market share being around 15 percent, compared to Otis Elevators' (in the U.S.) 25 percent and Shindler's (in Switzerland) 19 percent. The company employs more than 17,000 people worldwide, fewer than one in ten of whom are Finnish. The primary strategic objective, since the late 1960's, has been the creation of a multinational elevator and escalator company via the acquisition of national elevator companies in various countries.

Kone Oy was founded in 1910, and the first elevator was delivered eight years later. In 1968 Kone expanded from the Finnish domestic market into Scandinavia by acquiring the Swedish company ASEA, tripling elevator deliveries in the process. The second step in intensive acquisition took place in 1975 when Kone acquired the Westinghouse elevator and escalator business in Europe, thus doubling sales.

The 1980s saw Kone's breakthrough in North America, and in Europe expansion continued when two leading Italian elevator companies, Sabiem and Fiam, joined the organization in 1985 and 1986 respectively. During 1987, joint-venture operations for elevator production were started in Australia, India and Turkey.

On two occasions the company has absorbed nonprofitable operations as large or even larger than itself and turned them into profitable ones. Profitability has been restored through using the same business concept in all units.

Each acquisition constitutes a separate case. Kone has tried to handle them very flexibly with their own schedules, measures and models. Following acquisition the role of each new unit has been thought over, and some of its operations have been standardized with other units of the corporation. Sometimes the changes have taken several years, and there have been some cultural differences. Although Kone has a similar business concept in each unit, it's been realized in different ways in different countries. On occasions tough measures have had to be used in order to remove obstacles to company reorganization.

Kone has learned several cultural lessons. For instance, in Italy you have to agree on everything with top management. Direct contacts with different functions such as accounting failed to work, if the decisions had not been made first at the top level. Implementing new models and systems therefore took more time than expected. In Germany the thinking was quite functional; users thought that it was the task of the systems specialists from Finland to implement new systems without bothering them.

Kone is now a global company whose operations have been organized into five areas: Europe North, Central, and South, Asia-Pacific, and the Americas. Each area is headed by a full-time Area Director. The sales of new elevators and installations are organized by local companies in each country. Within each area, there is one Engineering Center for product engineering and design and tailoring to customer orders. The Engineering Center compiles and delivers market specific elevators from Kone standard components to local customers.

Component manufacturing is organized globally so that in Europe, for example, there are over ten component factories in different countries. The elevator components are transported to the Logistics Center, which is located with the Engineering Center. The Engineering and Logistics Centers are the area service centers of the elevator delivery process. On site elevator installation is carried out in each country by the local organization. A locally competitive product, an elevator that meets customer requirements, is developed in each area, but Kone's standard components are used in all areas.

- Sales and Installations, separate companies in each country.
- Engineering and logistics, one unit within each geographical area.
- Components production, a global operation.

COMPETITION IN THE ELEVATOR BUSINESS

The elevator business is a highly competitive one, with overcapacity in production. The demand for new elevators and industrial cranes is on the decline in all markets except the Far East. The downturn in the construction industry seems set to last, since in many countries there is overproduction of both office space and flats. In such a situation the competition for market shares is fierce, and there is a great deal of pressure on price levels.

The business in elevator modernization, maintenance, and repair continues to grow and form an increasingly significant proportion of the sales industry. In this line of business there is a structural, permanent-looking change happening to which companies must adapt. The focus in building new elevators must be shifted toward maintenance. In this competitive situation the maintenance of customer service is extremely important.

Kone Elevators aims at competitive success through a decentralized business concept, the aim of which is to combine economies of scale and local flexibility. The key element in Kone strategy is the global logistics system, which is based on common basic system modules that can be modified and localized to suit local users' needs. The global logistics system informs every person involved in the process of the tasks they need to perform in order to get the elevator delivered and installed on time. The system makes it possible to schedule and record major activities, such as orders to the Engineering Center, component orders released, installations programmed, elevators shipped and installations completed. Each elevator order can be tracked down on screens or reports at the main points of the process. With this system, Kone salesmen can give more reliable and quicker responses to customer requirements.

With this global mode of operation Kone has been successful in a very difficult competitive situation. A combination of good customer service and cost effectiveness has been achieved. However, the structural change in competition offers new challenges to Kone's management, in terms of how to adapt the company to the changing environment.

Director of Information Systems Markku Rajaniemi stated from his Helsinki headquarters that:

"During the 80's many medium-sized elevator companies disappeared from the market, mostly through acquisition. Small companies survived by flexibility and low cost, big companies developed their products and activities and utilized economies of scale, while mid-sized companies were caught in between and got eaten up by the big ones. Kone has also grown by acquiring typically medium-sized companies with small resources for developing activities and low economies of scale. We organized the activities so that local companies can benefit from Kone development activities and scale advantages.

Our competitiveness is very much based on our systems to manage the global logistics where orders, components and products are moving between countries. We try to combine global scale and local flexibility with our three level management (global, area, and country)."

INFORMATION TECHNOLOGY IN KONE ELEVATORS

Kone Elevators has a decentralized data processing set-up, with around 200 medium-size computers (HP9000, AS400) and with around 200 Local Area Networks (NOVEL). The main operating systems are UNIX, OS400, OSF-UX and DOS. In international data transmission different services from multiple network operators are used. The transmission protocols are TCP/IP and SNA Routers.

Kone's information technology strategy is roughly as follows:

The main corporate activities are research and testing of new technologies, updating Elevators Headquarters IT on corporate technical standards, and negotiating and managing frame agreements with corporate-wide hardware and software suppliers. Development, management and support of Kone's international telecommunications network is an important task.

Elevator Headquarters concentrates on developing and updating technical standards and the application architecture, developing the Kone Elevators application portfolio in line with business needs and priorities, and organizing support and maintenance of portfolio applications. Providing Kone units with adequate support in general and specific IT issues is also important.

Company IT activities involve defining business requirements and analyzing business benefits, procuring hard-ware and software in line with Kone's technical standards, and managing implementation projects. They also include running local computer operations and the development and maintenance of local applications and adaptations. Managing the migration of the local infrastructure towards harmonization constitutes an important task.

Kone Elevators has a common applications architecture, which maps out the main applications in a unit, describes their functionality and defines their interfaces. It also describes the underlying common data structure and how the various applications access data. The applications architecture is a vital communication vehicle in developing, implementing and maintaining systems applications.

The technical standard defines the hardware, software and telecommunications solutions applicable in the units. Deviations from these standards are allowed only after consultation with headquarters' IT function.

Altogether this is a very coordinated decentralized solution. Units have to work within a given frame, but they take care of their own operations. Within the framework there is some flexibility for individual solutions.

In the units, coordination has been experienced as mainly positive, although some complaints have been made about the fact that matters had been defined in too great detail. Personnel in the information systems function are, however, of the opinion that the input of coordination has even been limited, so that the function's resources would just suffice to provide sufficient support to the local unit.

At Kone Elevators there are around one hundred IS professionals who are mainly decentralized in different units. The objective of the IS function is to obtain software that is as complete as possible, in order for its own software production to be as limited as possible. Total IS costs are around 2 percent of sales, an average level in manufacturing.

The applications are divided into three different areas:

- Management systems, e.g. management accounting and budgeting
- Operations support, e.g. logistic systems
- Resource management, e.g. personnel administration, supplier control and customer service.

Kone has concentrated on internal systems. It has not invested much on external links. They have thought that it is enough to have information less frequently, but in a reliable and consistent form. Recently, however, there has been discussion on how to improve the quality of market information, but there are no ongoing projects.

References

Annual Report, Kone 1992.
Hurskainen Jorma, Business Process Approach to Global Logistics Case: Kone Elevators, in Joining the Global Roll, Jahnukainen and Vepsäläinen (eds), Helsinki 1992, pp. 86–102.

Rajaniemi Markku, Process Development in Perspective, ibid, pp. 132–138.
Interviews, Ulla Mäkelä and Markku Rajaniemi, Kone Elevators.

Case Study Questions

1. What kind of global strategy is Kone Elevators pursuing?

2. Evaluate Kone's information systems in light of this strategy. How well do they support it?

3. Evaluate Kone's strategy for managing its international information systems infrastructure.

4. How easy would it have been for Kone to implement the order-delivery system described at the beginning of this case on an international basis? What management, organization, and technology issues had to be addressed?

5. How strategic is the order-delivery system described here for a firm such as Kone? Why?

Festo Pneumatic

Helmut Krcmar and Bettina Schwarzer, University of Hohenheim (Germany)

Festo, a medium-sized German company headquartered in Esslingen, with 3500 employees around the world, is one of the world market leaders in the field of pneumatics and device control. The company was founded in 1925 and opened its first subsidiary, in Italy, in 1956. By now Festo has branches in 187 countries, offering full service for its products around the world (See Figure 4). Festo has four major product groups: Festo Electronic, which offers products and services for electronic device control; Festo Tooltechnic, offering electronic and air-pressure tools for crafts and industry; Festo Didactic, which provides courses for all kinds of device control; and finally Festo Pneumatic, which manufactures valves and cylinders and provides complete solutions for device control.

The major group is Festo Pneumatic, which specializes in the design and manufacturing of valves and cylinders, offering 35,000 components and 4,000 products by catalogue. It also provides custom-made solutions for device control in which cylinders are combined with other Festo components according to specific customer requirements. This combined approach of manufacturing components and offering complete solutions distinguishes Festo from most of its competitors in the pneumatic business. All products are designed and produced in Germany. Only in the case of special made-to-order cylinders does production take place in the subsidiaries to meet customer requirements. Of the products manufactured in Germany, 55% are exported.

Festo Pneumatic has 35 subsidiaries and more than 100 branch offices selling its products. In general, all pneumatic products are designed and manufactured in Germany; therefore the same product is available around the world. As parts are shipped all over the world from the German production site and warehouse, all orders have to be processed centrally. Processing a workload of about 200–300 orders with an average of 4 items per order from each of the major subsidiaries daily, Festo Pneumatic is dependent on a global computer system.

Even though Festo is a fairly small company with only 1000 employees abroad, it is highly internationalized and continuously expanding its international engagements, now turning to Eastern Europe. The subsidiaries are independent companies, but are dependent on the German headquarters because they neither design nor manufacture products. Festo Pneumatic Germany views its subsidiaries as "shops" for selling the company's products in foreign markets. Not only in the business area but also in the field of information systems Festo pursues a centralized approach. Hardware and software are selected in the corporate headquarters, which also provides systems support. The major advantage of this approach is cost savings; detailed knowledge of the sys-

tems can be centralized in one place. Any changes in the system only have to be made in one place and are then taken to all subsidiaries. This not only reduces costs but also guarantees that the system is the same everywhere.

In 1976, confronted with continuing international growth and an increasing workload, Festo Pneumatic decided to implement a common system in the headquarters and the subsidiaries to be able to handle and improve order processing, logistics, and production on an international basis. The goals pursued with the system were "high quality of customer service" and "minimized stock levels." To match the structure of their international operations Festo decided to implement one common system for all subsidiaries, as they had exactly the same information processing requirements in their data exchange with the headquarters. As there was no standardized software package available at that time, a system was developed in-house starting in 1976. Development took place in the headquarters and beginning in 1978 the system was introduced in the subsidiaries.

Due to the lack of standardized software packages at that time and the high costs of in-house development, most competitors did not have sophisticated systems in place when Festo introduced its first integrated system. At that time the rationale for systems development was not strategic advantage—the idea of strategic information systems was not yet known—but simply to make order processing on an international basis more efficient. Still, Festo realized that the new system helped them to gain competitive advantage; the time for order processing was shortened and Festo was able to respond quicker to customer requests.

Over the years the system has been continuously improved to meet changing requirements. Festo's current FIP-2 system, used for order processing, logistics, and manufacturing, was developed based on its experiences with the first system. All components of the old system that worked well are also used in the new system, with new technology replacing the components that were no longer appropriate. The FIP-2 system is based on the Cobol 85, RPG, and High Level RPG programming languages and uses TurboImage for database management.

Before systems development took place, the hardware platform was carefully chosen by experts after a one-year study of different vendors. The main criterion for hardware selection was scalability, to make sure that the same hardware could be used in subsidiaries of different sizes. Festo headquarters always used IBM computers but it selected Hewlett Packard computers for its subsidiaries. Today Festo's 24 subsidiary headquarters run the system on HP 3000 computers with the RISC-technology based operating system MPE/iX. No matter

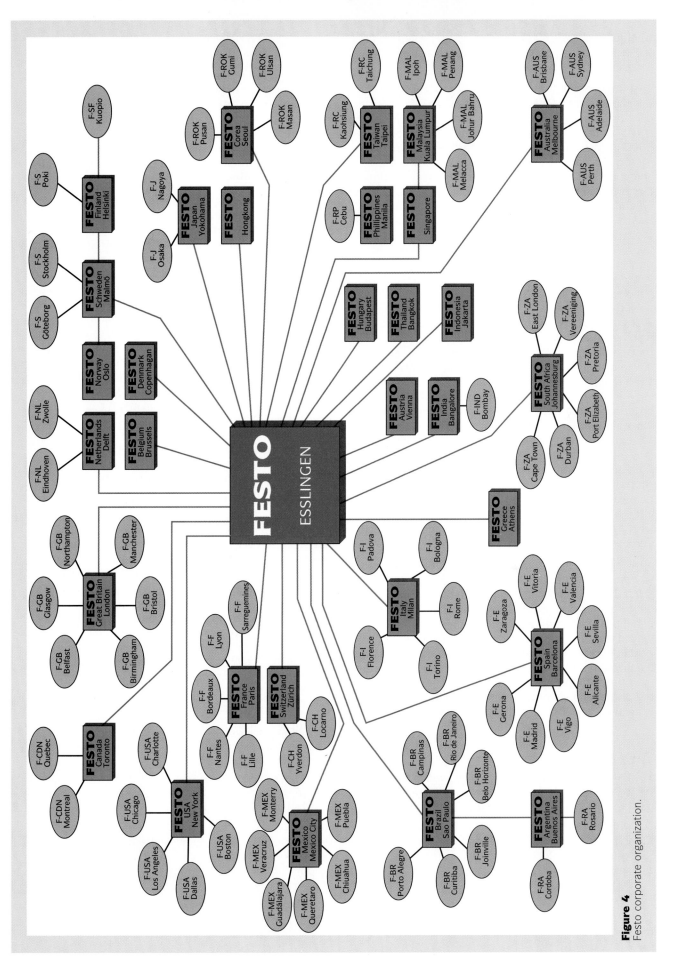

Figure 4
Festo corporate organization.

whether four or 2000 people are using the system at the same time, all users can work in the same systems environment.

Customers order in the subsidiaries' branches by either telephone or FAX (in some cases there are shops for over-the-counter sales). Festo's branch offices in various countries use microcomputers linked directly to an HP 3000 in each subsidiary's headquarters for order entry. An order is entered into the FIP-2 system on a microcomputer and then transmitted to subsidiary headquarters either immediately or once a day, depending on the type of connection between the branch office and subsidiary headquarters. There the order is checked for availability of components in the country's own warehouse. If the components are available, the order is processed in the country. Otherwise, the orders are collected and transmitted every hour or once a day (depending on the size and importance of the subsidiary) via an X.25 packet-switched network to an HP 3000 in Festo headquarters in Germany. The HP 3000 at German headquarters in turn transforms the data to make processing on an IBM 3090 mainframe possible. The IBM mainframe is linked to Festo's German branches, so German orders are entered directly into this system. The IBM combines orders from abroad with the German orders and processes them. The system checks the stocks in the German warehouse and the production schedule and returns with a confirmation of the order to the subsidiaries, stating the expected date of delivery. Data are then transmitted to an AEG 80–30 computer which is used to manage the warehouse. Festo reports no problems with these linkages on either a national or international level, although some problems may arise when transmitting data to and from technologically underdeveloped countries such as Brazil.

If the components are in stock, the AEG 80-30 in the warehouse handles the request. A warehouse note is printed, giving information on where the components are to be found in the warehouse and how many components are needed for the order. The parts are removed from the warehouse and commissioned. The worker enters the "finished" status into the system and a delivery note, the bill and a confirmation of the order are printed by the system. These papers are put into the packet and sent to the subsidiary either on the road or by air. The subsidiary either puts the components in its own warehouse or puts together the required parts for the individual orders.

Apart from the orders processed together, customer-specific orders can be transmitted to the German headquarters. In this case, all components for the order are packed together and marked in the German warehouse. They are delivered to the subsidiary together with the other parts. After checking them in the subsidiary they can be delivered directly to the customer without putting them into the warehouse.

Designing one common system for use in different countries was not as easy as it sounds and caused a number of problems. Apart from the different languages that are required, for example in printed material for the use of the customer, country-specific features have to be implemented. For example, in Italy the revenue authorities require that bills sent to the same customer have to be numbered in the correct order of issue, whereas in other countries the revenue authorities have their own numbering system and are not interested in the number on the bill. If special features are only needed in one country Festo allows the subsidiary to make the changes itself, providing support for the systems support people in the subsidiaries if needed. If several countries have the same requirements, the changes are made at headquarters and then implemented abroad. In making the changes at headquarters, so far only headquarters systems personnel has been involved. This policy is being changed in order to gain advantage of the knowledge available in the subsidiaries.

Whereas in former times, the system provided Festo with a competitive advantage as the system allowed faster processing of orders, the competitive situation has changed over the years due to the increasing availability of standard software. Today, software is readily available, and in order to be able to compete all companies use integrated systems. Festo has adapted to the new situation and is focusing on improving customer service. One potential area for benefits that has been identified is incorporating expert systems into the system. Expert systems can support the sales people in their meetings by suggesting system configurations. Thereby the ordering process can be speeded up and qualitatively improved.

Case Study Questions

1. What kind of global strategy is Festo Pneumatic pursuing?

2. Evaluate Festo's FIP-2 system in light of this strategy. How well does this system support it?

3. Evaluate Festo Pneumatic's strategy for managing its international information systems infrastructure.

4. How much competitive advantage does Festo's FIP-2 system provide?

5. What problems did Festo have implementing its order processing, logistics and production system? What management, organization, and technology issues had to be addressed?

6. Festo's order processing, logistics, and production system is custom-developed. In this particular instance, is it an advantage or disadvantage to have custom-built software?

Corning Telecommunications Division (A): The Flexible Manufacturing Systems Project

Andrew Boynton, International Institute for Management Development (Switzerland)

Driving across the Gibson Bridge toward his office in July 1990, Bob McAdoo, senior vice president and head of manufacturing for the Telecommunications division of Corning, Inc., thought about the appropriations request he would be discussing with his staff on Friday morning. The division was requesting $5 million for a new planning and scheduling system plus a reconfigured information system to cope with manufacturing changes at its Wilmington, NC, plant, where Corning made optical waveguides. Such a sum was not an incidental capital investment. Moreover, exactly what they would be getting for the money was hard to say. The budget for hardware and packaged software was dwarfed by the costs of design work and consultants. The consultants would be designing a system that had never been built before, and after problems with the last systems-development project, ATLAS, the idea of breaking new ground in software was troubling. (ATLAS, even though it was a well-understood business data system, had been two years late and millions over budget.) In addition, no one could tell McAdoo if the proposed Flexible Manufacturing System (FMS) would work once it was designed, written, and implemented. All they would say is that they "didn't think the plant could continue to work without it."

OPTICAL WAVEGUIDES

Optical waveguides are glass fibers that allow communication by light rather than electricity. One fifth thinner than a human hair, the core of these fibers can carry more than 16,000 simultaneous phone conversations (compared with 24 for copper wire). Unlike copper, optical fiber can also carry information in both directions (sending and receiving) simultaneously. Fibers can transmit light more than 100 miles without regeneration and operate 20,000 feet under water with a 40-year life. Despite their close resemblance to fishing line when coated, fibers can withstand 1 million pounds per square inch of tensile stress. Optical fiber can also carry more information much faster than copper wire. Fiber's carrying capacity of 1.8 billion bits per second could transmit the Encyclopedia Britannica and the Bible around the earth together in less than 2 seconds.

Optical fibers behave like "light pipes." Because of their differences in composition, the refractive index of the core is higher than that of the outer coat (cladding). As a result, light rays traveling through the core will be reflected back into the core if they stray from a straight line and bounce into the core/cladding interface. Conse-

quently, light stays in the core even when the fiber is bent.

The two types of fiber are multimode and single mode. Multimode is primarily used for local building-to-building and intrabuilding wiring, where its comparatively large core size contributes to reduced installation costs. Multimode is available in several glass and coating designs, which when combined with various optical performance levels, results in a wide and increasing variety of stock-keeping units (SKUs).

Single-mode fiber is used primarily by telephone companies. Initial applications were for long-distance telecommunication applications by companies like MCI, AT&T, and Sprint. New types of fiber and coatings, and declining systems costs after 1983, led to many new applications by regional telephone companies (e.g., Bell South), cable television companies, and long-distance communication companies. Given the efforts by telephone companies to emphasize product standardization and compatibility of competing vendors' products, fewer single-mode than multimode fiber SKUs existed. Single-mode fiber represented approximately 90% of the market volume.

Corning sold almost all of its fiber to optical-fiber cablers. A few cablers accounted for approximately 80% of Corning's sales, with 200 customers making up the remaining 20%. Essentially, cablers packaged the optical fiber in a variety of materials to protect it during installation and to limit the effects of its installed environments. From a materials point of view, cablers added little to the value of the fiber, and the fiber itself was a large portion of the cost of fiber cabling. Excess capacity plagued the cabling industry, and barriers to entry were low. Telephone companies' purchases comprised 70% of the optical-cable market, and these companies were adept at creating a level playing field through specification standards and purchasing strategies. Product quality and service were important to the phone companies, but these parameters were viewed largely as requirements for entry. Bidding to attract the phone companies' business was fierce. Overall, profits for optical cablers tended to be low, which was consistent with the financial performance they achieved when these same cablers had been copper-wire cablers.

As the costs of fiber optic systems declined, phone-company fiber-cable installation migrated from long-haul telecommunications trunks (e.g., MCI) through regional telecommunications (e.g., Bell South) interoffice trunks joining central-office switching systems to feeder

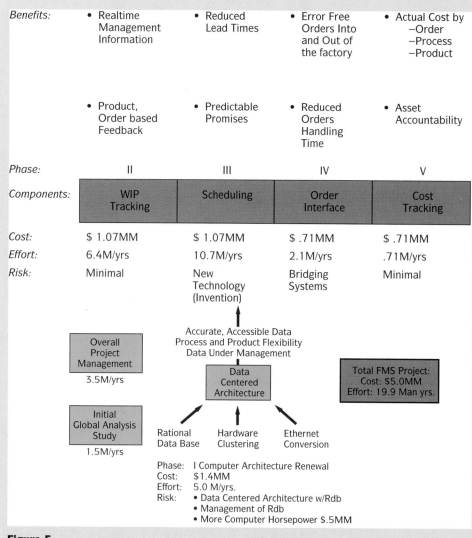

Figure 5
Corning Telecommunications Division (A): flexible manufacturing systems.

cables connecting central-office switches directly to large businesses or to residential neighborhoods (see Figure 5). Phone companies were betting that optical systems' costs would decline to the degree that they would be no different than the costs of a copper wire system for final telephone line connections to residences (distribution and drop cables). When the fiber could be installed to the home, the phone companies would be able to take advantage of fiber's unlimited capacity to provide a raft of new information services such as video entertainment on demand, home shopping, and home education. This development would allow the phone companies to become the aggressive, high-growth information firms that had been envisioned at the time of divestiture.

The cable television market also used single mode fiber, to improve picture quality and channel capacity and as a defensive posture against the phone companies, who were interested in entering the home entertainment video market. Cable TV's mass deployment of fiber has lagged the phone companies by five years, but growth since 1988 has been strong.

Beyond the phone companies and cable TV markets, another large and growing segment was premises wiring of banks, corporate offices, universities, hospitals, industrial complexes, and brokerage houses. These customers made up the market for multimode fiber. Standards had not progressed as far in this segment, and several different multimode glass and fiber designs serviced the market. Given the lack of concentrated purchasing observed in the phone company segment, the buying patterns were not as orderly. Many fiber cablers and systems integrators would often bid on the same premises job, and quote turnaround times and cable lead times were key determinants in establishing the winning bidder.

Cablers passed these segment pressures directly to Corning and other suppliers AT&T and Spectran. While Corning and AT&T devoted a large percentage of their fiber capabilities to single mode, Spectran owed its existence to the multimode market. Spectran used attractive pricing, rapid quote turnaround, and competitive lead times to attract business.

Waveguides at Corning Incorporated

Corning, Inc., in 1990 was composed of four primary sectors, Specialty Glass and Ceramics, Communications, Laboratory Services, and Consumer Housewares. Specialty Glass and Ceramics marketed over 40,000 specialty materials, including eyeglass materials and auto-emission filters. The Communications sector produced optical fiber, opto-electrical components for fiber networks, video display glass, and liquid crystal displays. Laboratory Services provided clinical testing, life-science research, and environmental testing services. Consumer Housewares produced such well-known products as Corning Ware, Revere Ware, and Corelle dinnerware.

In 1989–90, the Communications sector contributed approximately 21% to Corning's revenues and 37% to its profits, increases of over 35% in both categories. A significant contribution to corporate profits came from optical waveguides. Corning's quality and delivery had consistently provided a significant profit margin on this product.

Corning developed the first technically feasible optical fiber in 1970. The company then worked for eight years refining the technology and developing a proprietary low-cost manufacturing method. Despite years of only moderate interest from telephone companies and cablers, Corning funded the research and, in 1979, built a manufacturing plant in Wilmington. The plant operated for three years producing only samples and small orders for pilot projects before its first major order was received, which followed the deregulation of the telecommunications industry in 1982.

At that time, MCI announced plans to build a nation-wide fiber-optic network and ordered one hundred thousand kilometers of fiber from Corning. The order, ten times larger than any prior one, was for a new type of single-mode fiber that was still experimental at the company. To meet MCI's requirements, therefore, Corning moved a new generation of fiber technology from the lab to the plant floor, installed new production equipment, and embarked on one of the largest plant expansions in Corning's history. By 1986, sixteen years after proving the commercial feasibility of optical fiber, Corning's fiber-optics operations were running twenty-four hours a day and turning a profit.

The MCI order was quickly followed by others as competition in the telecommunications industry developed. In 1983, Corning funded the largest expenditure request in its history, $100 million, to expand the Wilmington plant to meet rapidly increasing demand and install Corning's fifth generation of fiber-optic manufacturing technology. Corning's dedication to its new technology and its willingness to invest allowed the company to compete with larger rivals such as AT&T and "Japan, Inc.," to become a world leader in waveguide manufacturing. In 1991 Corning Communications, having initiated a "total quality" effort to measure the performance of all business and manufacturing processes to determine competitive capabilities, was pursuing the Baldrige Award.

The initial growth phase, fueled by the needs of long-distance companies, had appeared endless, and to remain an industry's technological leader, Corning had averaged changes in production machinery every 12–24 months. In the second half of 1986, however, as Corning continued to increase its production capacity, the initial growth stopped. The market for long-distance lines was saturated, and increasingly customized fiber-optic, especially multimode, orders from the cable industry changed the demands on Corning's waveguide plant. By 1990, these new demands were not optimally satisfied by the manufacturing and information systems at the plant. By early 1991, construction to again increase the size and capacity of the plant substantially had begun, and this effort required the attention of everyone in the factory to maintain existing production levels.

Mike Jordan, planning and scheduling supervisor, had briefed Bob McAdoo on the complexity of production scheduling at the Wilmington plant: "In making waveguides, the process is different from standard production like making automobiles. With cars, ten Chevy engines and ten Chevy bodies make ten Chevy cars, with some quality reworking. Here, in optical waveguides, we can mix ten batches of the same chemicals under the same conditions with the same computer-controlled processes. Sometimes we'll get seven batches that can be sold; sometimes we'll get ten. Each batch will differ slightly from the other batches. For example, the maximum length of optical fibers will vary as bad sections are cut out. Glass-geometry precision will differ slightly from batch to batch. So we don't know how many saleable end products we'll get because of differences in selection yield. We also don't know how many end products will be Oldsmobiles and how many will be Chevys due to the distribution of characteristics. Luckily, we can substitute Oldsmobiles for Chevys here. Customers will take a higher quality cable for the same price. But this substitution costs us money. Selection, distribution, and substitution complicate the planning process."

Manufacturing waveguides required highly exact, computer-controlled systems, but the early emphasis on standard fiber products with few modifications for the long-distance companies had resulted in a system limited to keeping costs low while maintaining efficiency and high quality. The system was designed to control manufacturing at each step of the production process (Laydown, Consolidation, etc.). The primary function of the information system was to identify equipment and process problems in each individual production stage.

The tight controls coded into the system allowed few modifications in the product or production process. To get around the product and process controls, a small percentage of the plant's production was run as "experimental" products. Each production process had to be individually "tricked" into letting new products move through the system. The products were moved manually through the entire production process with computer overrides at each step. For example, new or customized products with diameters or lengths that were different from standard fibers required engineers to override set specifications in the Draw and Measurement systems. Since all fibers looked essentially identical to the naked eye, special fiber reels were identified with colored dots and batch numbers to flag them as requiring special processing. The manual intervention was not only time-consuming and labor intensive, but also prone to human error.

Computer overrides often conflicted with standard costing information and with constants in production algorithms. Thus costs could not be accumulated on special orders and new products. Inappropriate algorithm constants resulted in incorrect production information, and reported yields exceeded actual process inputs.

Information was captured by the system on each of the individual processes but was used to control only that process. No information was passed along by the system to the next production stage. Operators even keyed in reel identification numbers manually at each stage. This division of production information resulted in a vertically oriented information system that employees called, along with the associated computers, "stovepipes" of information. Each stovepipe was monitored and controlled by a separate staff (the stovepipe's "feudal lord"). Computers stored highly summarized information on products completed and in inventory.

The stovepipe infrastructure of the current system did not allow potentially useful information to be shared across production stages. The different systems had dramatically different field definitions and sizes, which offered little opportunity to integrate the data across the stovepipes. For example, measurement information from the OLS stage could not be used to eliminate later quality checks or to determine sampling strategies in the Measurement stage. The systems provided no means of feeding information forward or backward in the production process. Information on fiber defects discovered in later process steps required manual intervention, communication, and correction. Information gathered in prior stages, such as diameter measurements and usable fiber lengths determined in Draw, were unavailable to Measurement technicians, who might spend hours searching reels for a long usable fiber. Consolidating information from the different systems resulted in unacceptable delays in providing production information. In short, the stovepipe systems did not allow the plant to maximize the use of its capital-intensive equipment.

Designed to meet high demand for a few products, the system did not track work in process. All orders were matched to inventory. However, when a relatively stable supply of a few products had moved through the system, supervisors had been able to coordinate production based on inventory levels.

As the number of products multiplied and became more customized, and as customers demanded shorter lead times, a "Sneaker Patrol," the plant's production and scheduling staff, had become responsible for determining what was in the plant and adjusting production

schedules in an attempt to meet customer orders. The 4-week production plan listed the number of blanks of each product type to start. As orders came in or were canceled and as the yields changed in the production process, the Sneaker Patrol made schedule revisions. Currently, numerous daily schedule changes and comprehensive changes are made weekly to the 4-week plan.

Pressure to increase responsiveness can be seen in the fact that, in 1988, Corning fiber salespeople put pressure on Wilmington to respond in less than one day with delivery and cost information for customers; in 1991, they were pressuring Wilmington to respond in less than four hours. In 1991, Wilmington had a several-hour goal and monitored performance to meet that goal.

All changes, which were based on information that was often two days old, were projected by hand. Most information was gathered and transmitted by the production staff, the Sneaker Patrol, walking through the plant with clipboards and changing the colored and numbered dots on different carts of fiber reels. This process was being stretched to the limit as the Wilmington plant continued to add new fiber products and prepared to add additional capacity.

Mike Jordan, who as planning and scheduling supervisor, was also head of the Sneaker Patrol, explained how the process was being stretched: "A customer was buying multimode product of long length. This is not a standard product, so we have to begin a 'yellow-dot experiment,' where the particular yellow dot indicates 'produce long-length multimode.' The customer calls back in a few days and says he doesn't want the long-length. Because we can't waste good in-process fiber, I have to go out and take off the yellow dot from this particular experiment and produce this in-process fiber for stock. The next day, the same customer calls and says he wants a different band-width multimode. I then have to run out again and find some in-process fiber of that band width by looking around the plant and then put a yellow dot on that to indicate the length the customer wants. Can you imagine this happening many times each day? It does!"

The same information gathered for scheduling was used to quote order lead times to customers. Quoting a lead time one or two days longer than a competitor could lose an order. Missing a deadline or shipping incorrect product violated one of Corning's top cultural values. Currently, a significant percentage of customer orders were for shipment in less than 5 days, but the plant took over 6 days to complete most of the orders, even though the production process required significantly less time. All other delays were caused by the logistics of moving between operations (a minimal amount of time) and scheduling conflicts and inefficiencies.

Mike O'Koren, the Wilmington plant manager, described the plant as computer intensive but reliant on "people intervention" and "customized people processes:" "The customers are wanting more one-of-a-kind orders with shorter lead times. Our record of error-free shipments and past turnaround time have made customer service a competitive advantage. Maintaining this advantage is crucial to our success. Right now we don't have a system in place that allows us to shrink lead times. The only way we do it now is with what people do in their heads. We promise orders based on what we think is on the shop floor. We've been stretched pretty thin. As our volume increases and the number of product choices multiplies, the people system is going to break down."

Reliance on customized people processes and mutual production adjustments between feudal lords and the Sneaker Patrol had created a large informal communications network in the plant. Production processes had evolved to conform to this network.

Jordan estimated that the plant could accept orders for 10% more fiber a month if quote times could be reduced through the scheduling of a "made-to-order" manufacturing system. He explained that, in the information environment he envisioned, he could be much more effective: "I want to be able to sit at home or in the office and, on the PC, identify what fiber is in stock or anywhere on the floor. Now I have to check what is in the inventory or on the floor to see what is there. Today we have almost zero visibility about ware in process."

Jordan hoped, however, that any new systems wouldn't be as difficult to implement as the last systems project with which he had been involved: "Although this is my vision for fast response to our customer requests, the last information system project I was involved with, ATLAS, left me with a healthy dose of skepticism. ATLAS has worked out great, but not without some pain. Now we can see all orders, which customers place through the sales force at corporate, in 5 minutes. Before ATLAS, it took over 24 hours for us to get an order. I felt the project was badly undersourced. The system was being designed for multiple uses in multiple divisions. Coordination between all parties was difficult. Senior management in our sector didn't buy in initially, and without that pressure brought to bear, the project stagnated. It didn't work until we at Wilmington held our ground, insisted on getting the resources required, and fought for the project to be completed the right way. After we at Wilmington started kicking, the guys at corporate got involved and insured that corporate IS [Information Systems] put the resources on the project for our sector. We learned a great deal during ATLAS, and it is a real lifesaver now. I just wonder if new systems will be as difficult to implement."

On a recent visit to the Wilmington plant, McAdoo had spoken with O'Koren about the effect of the proposed new information system on the people who composed the informal communications network. O'Koren thought the new system would provide tremendous benefits to customers, but he was less enthusiastic about the effect on plant personnel:"Many people have done nothing but act as information transmitters in this network since the business was started. They feel very threatened. I think they're going to have to learn new jobs."

McAdoo noted that, as O'Koren was speaking, a large fish on his PC's aquarium display had turned and eaten several smaller fish.

THE APPROPRIATIONS REQUEST

The decision to request $5 million to revamp waveguide manufacturing had not been straightforward. On the one hand, the waveguide project had always been a high-risk, high-return project. Historically, large appropriations requests had been granted, and they had paid off. On the other hand, the configuration and timing of the local-loop market appeared as uncertain as the long-distance market had in 1970.

Tom LaGarde, manager of IS at the Wilmington factory, had been heavily involved with the preparation of the request. He discussed with McAdoo how the implementation effort would be managed: "At the highest level, we have a review board consisting of senior managers at corporate that meet twice a year to make sure the project is not out of sync with the company. We have been asked to submit appropriation requests twice a year after the initial request is approved. As we present each request, we have to establish where we've been and where we are going and establish how much money has been spent and what will be needed. We brought in Global Analysis, a Big Five consulting firm, because we felt our corporate IS group, though talented, did not have the experience for this type of project. We're using a computer-based tool to plan, track, test, and manage the project tool that connects each project person. There is a great deal of technical risk beyond the sheer size and complexity of the project. We have no experience with the relational database technology, which has to provide rapid and flexible access to great quantities of information. The other dimension of technical risk is the finite-forward-scheduling component which has never been developed before. We will break the project into seven teams of 5–7 people from about five organizations: contract programming houses, Global Analysis, corporate Engineering and IS, Digital, and the Wilmington factory. As for my organization, I'll have to provide support for the project. At the same time, the plant must have other information needs met. Combine this with a major plant expansion and the plant at capacity, and the difficulties inherent in the implementation become clear."

McAdoo picked up the appropriations request sitting on his desk to read through the body of the proposal. He knew he had to make a case to William Cunningham, manager of the entire Communications sector, to invest this much money on an information system. Furthermore, $5 million would require approval at the chairman level. Would changing the way information was managed at Wilmington convert a factory designed to produce standard products into a flexible manufacturing facility? Were there other, better, alternatives to FMS? McAdoo and his staff had considered the option that Corning not put any more money into waveguides. They had also looked for, but not found, some other way to fix the current problem. The staff believed in FMS; after all, they had spent the last year in intensive analysis and design. But did they understand the industry forces, and did these forces require the type of strategy suggested by FMS? Finally, would the system work? How, given the ATLAS project delay and cost, could he recommend an information-systems project of this magnitude of this strategic importance?

McAdoo wanted to make sure his staff had thought through the issues carefully before he made a decision. Did his staff have answers to the myriad of important questions? Sighing, McAdoo got up and started the long walk to the meeting with his staff. He would then have the weekend to think things over, but on Monday he had to meet with Cunningham and make a recommendation on FMS.

Case Study Questions

1. Use the competitive forces and value chain models to analyze the Corning Telecommunications Division. What competitive forces did Corning have to deal with? What were the strategic advantages of switching to a flexible manufacturing system for optical waveguides?

2. What were the problems with Corning's existing manufacturing system for optical waveguides? How serious were they? What management, organization, and technology factors contributed to these problems?

3. What management, organization, and technology issues had to be addressed to implement a flexible manufacturing system successfully?

4. What were the dangers and risks of this project?

5. What criteria would you use to determine whether Corning should invest in this project?

6. Should Corning make the $5 million investment in the new flexible manufacturing system? What other alternatives are available?

Glossary

Acceptance testing: Provides the final certification that the system is ready to be used in a production setting.

Accountability: The mechanisms for assessing responsibility for decisions made and actions taken.

Ada: Programming language that is portable across different brands of hardware; is used for both military and nonmilitary applications.

Adhocracy: Task force organization, such as a research organization, designed to respond to a rapidly changing environment and characterized by large groups of specialists organized into short lived multi-disciplinary task forces.

Administrative controls: Formalized standards, rules, procedures, and disciplines to ensure that the organization's controls are properly executed and enforced.

AI shell: The programming environment of an expert system.

Analog signal: A continuous wave form that passes through a communications medium. Used for voice communications.

Anti-virus software: Software designed to detect and often eliminate computer viruses from an information system.

Application controls: Specific controls unique to each computerized application.

Application generator: Software that can generate entire information system applications; the user needs only to specify what needs to be done and the application generator creates the appropriate program code.

Application software: Programs written for a specific business application in order to perform functions specified by end users.

Application software package: Set of prewritten, precoded, application software programs that are commercially available for sale or lease.

Applications portability: The ability to operate the same software on different hardware platforms.

Arithmetic-logic unit (ALU): Component of the CPU that performs the principal logical and arithmetic operations of the computer.

Artificial intelligence: The effort to develop computer-based systems that can behave like humans, with the ability to learn languages, accomplish physical tasks, use a perceptual apparatus, and emulate human expertise and decision making.

ASCII: American Standard Code for Information Interchange. A 7- or 8-bit binary code used in data transmission, microcomputers, and some large computers.

Assembly language: A programming language developed in the 1950s that resembles machine language but substitutes mnemonics for numeric codes.

Asynchronous transfer mode: Networking technology that parcels information into 8-bit "cells," allowing data to be transmitted between computers of different vendors at any speed.

Asynchronous transmission: Low-speed transmission of one character at a time.

Attribute: Piece of information describing a particular entity.

Backward chaining: Strategy for searching the rule base in an expert system that acts like a problem solver by beginning with a hypothesis and seeking out more information until the hypothesis is either proved or disproved.

Bandwidth: The capacity of a communications channel as measured by the difference between the highest and lowest frequencies that can be transmitted by that channel.

Bar code: Form of OCR technology widely used in supermarkets and retail stores in which identification data are coded into a series of bars.

Baseband: LAN channel technology that provides a single path for transmitting text, graphics, voice, or video data at one time.

BASIC (Beginners All-purpose Symbolic Instruction Code): General-purpose programming language used with microcomputers and for teaching programming.

Batch control totals: A type of input control that requires counting transactions or any quantity field in a batch of transactions prior to processing for comparison and reconciliation after processing.

Batch processing: A method of processing information in which transactions are accumulated and stored until a specified time when it is convenient and/or necessary to process them as a group.

Baud: A change in signal from positive to negative or vice-versa that is used as a measure of transmission speed.

Behavioral models: Descriptions of management based on behavioral scientists' observations of what managers actually do in their jobs.

Bit: A binary digit representing the smallest unit of data in a computer system. It can only have one of two states, representing 0 or 1.

Bit mapping: The technology that allows each pixel on the screen to be addressed and manipulated by the computer.

Bottom-up approach: In the history of artificial intelligence, the effort to build a physical analog to the human brain.

Briefing books: On-line data in the form of fixed-format reports for executives.

Broadband: LAN channel technology that provides several paths for transmitting text, graphics, voice, or video data so that different types of data can be transmitted simultaneously.

Bugs: Program code defects or errors.

Bureaucracy: Formal organization with a clear-cut division of labor, abstract rules and procedures, and impartial decision making that uses technical qualifications and professionalism as a basis for promoting employees.

Bureaucratic models: Models of decision making where decisions are shaped by the organization's standard operating procedures (SOPs).

Bus network: Network topology linking a number of computers by a single circuit with all messages broadcast to the entire network.

Business driver: A force in the environment to which businesses must respond and that influences the direction of business.

Business process: A set of logically related tasks performed to achieve a defined business outcome.

Byte: A string of bits, usually eight, used to represent one number or character stored in a computer system.

C: Powerful programming language with tight control and efficiency of execution; is portable across different microprocessors and is used primarily with microcomputers.

Cache: High speed storage of frequently used instructions and data.

Case-based reasoning: Artificial intelligence technology that represents knowledge as a database of cases.

Carpal tunnel syndrome (CTS): Type of RSI in which pressure on the median nerve through the wrist's bony carpal tunnel produces pain.

CD-ROM: Compact disk read-only memory. Read-only optical disk storage used for imaging, reference, and database applications with massive amounts of data and for multimedia.

Cellular telephone: Device that transmits voice or data, using radio waves to communicate with radio antennas placed within geographic areas called cells.

Central processing unit (CPU): Area of the computer system that manipulates symbols, numbers, and letters and controls the other parts of the computer system.

Centralized processing: Processing that is accomplished by one large central computer.

Change agent: In the context of implementation, the individual acting as the catalyst during the change process to ensure successful organizational adaptation to a new system or innovation.

Channels: The links by which data or voice are transmitted between sending and receiving devices in a network.

Choice: Simon's third stage of decision making, when the individual selects among the various solution alternatives.

Class: Feature of object-oriented programming so that all objects belonging to a certain class have all of the features of that class.

Classical model of management: Traditional descriptions of management that focused on its formal functions of planning, organizing, coordinating, deciding, and controlling.

Client/server model: A model for computing that splits the processing between "clients" and "servers" on a network assigning functions to the machine most able to perform the function.

Coaxial cable: Transmission medium consisting of thickly insulated copper wire. Can transmit large volumes of data quickly.

COBOL (COmmon Business Oriented Language): Predominant programming language for business applications because it can process large data files with alphanumeric characters.

Cognitive style: Underlying personality disposition toward the treatment of information, selection of alternatives, and evaluation of consequences.

Combinatorial explosion: In computer processing, the overload that results when trying to test more rules to reach a solution than the computer is capable of handling.

Competitive forces model: Model used to describe the interaction of external threats and opportunities that affect an organization's strategy and ability to compete.

Compiler: Special system software that translates a higher-level language into machine language for execution by the computer.

Compound document: Electronic document that consists of differing types of information acquired from separate sources such as graphics, database, spreadsheet, and text-based programs.

Computer abuse: The commission of acts involving a computer which may not be illegal but are considered unethical.

Computer-aided design (CAD): Information system that automates the creation and revision of designs using sophisticated graphics software.

Computer-aided software engineering (CASE): The automation of step-by-step methodologies for software and systems development to reduce the amount of repetitive work the developer needs to do.

Computer-based information systems (CBIS): Information systems that rely on computer hardware and software for processing and disseminating information.

Computer crime: The commission of illegal acts through the use of a computer or against a computer system.

Computer generations: Major transitions in computer hardware; each generation is distinguished by a different technology for the components that do the processing.

Computer hardware: Physical equipment used for input, processing, and output work in an information system.

Computer matching: Processing control that matches input data to information held on master files.

Computer mouse: Hand-held input device whose movement on the desktop controls the position of the cursor on the computer display screen.

Computer operations controls: Procedures to ensure the programmed procedures are consistently and correctly applied to data storage and processing.

Computer software: Detailed preprogrammed instructions that coordinate computer hardware components in an information system.

Computer virus: Rogue software programs that are difficult to detect and spread rapidly through computer systems, destroying data or disrupting processing and memory systems.

Computer vision syndrome (CVS): Eye strain condition related to cathode ray tube (CRT) use, with symptoms including headaches, blurred vision, and dry, irritated eyes.

Concentrator: Telecommunications computer that collects and temporarily stores messages from terminals for batch transmission to the host computer.

Connectivity: A measure of how well computers and computer-based devices communicate and share information with one another without human intervention.

Connectivity audit: A method for examining amount of connectivity an organization has by examining five areas of connectivity such as network standards, user interfaces and applications.

Control aids: Capabilities that allow the user to control the activities and functions of the DSS.

Control unit: Component of the CPU that controls and coordinates the other parts of the computer system.

Controller: Specialized computer that supervises communications traffic between the CPU and the peripheral devices in a telecommunications system.

Controls: All of the methods, policies, and procedures that ensure protection of the organization's assets, accuracy and reliability of its records, and operational adherence to management standards.

Conversion: The process of changing from the old system to the new system.

Conversion plan: Provides a schedule of all activities required to install a new system.

Cooptation: Bringing the opposition into the process of designing and implementing the solution without giving up control over the direction and nature of the change.

Copyright: A statutory grant which protects creators of intellectual property against copying by others for any purpose for a period of 28 years.

Core systems: Systems that support functions that are absolutely critical to the organization.

Counterimplementation: A deliberate strategy to thwart the implementation of an information system or an innovation in an organization.

Critical success factors (CSFs): A small number of easily identifiable operational goals shaped by the industry, the firm, the manager, and the broader environment that are believed to assure the success of an organization. Used to determine the information requirements of an organization.

Customization: The modification of a software package to meet an organization's unique requirements without destroying the integrity of the package software.

Cylinder: Represents circular tracks on the same vertical line within a disk pack.

Data administration: A special organizational function for managing the organization's data resources, concerned with data planning, information policy, maintenance of data dictionaries, and data quality standards.

Data bus width: The number of bits that can be moved at one time between the CPU, primary storage, and the other devices of a computer.

Data conversion: Process of properly transcribing data from one form into another form for computer transactions.

Data definition language: The component of a database management system that defines each data element as it appears in the database.

Data dictionary: An automated or manual tool for storing and organizing information about the data maintained in a database.

Data element: A field.

Data flow diagram (DFD): Primary tool in structured analysis that graphically illustrates the system's component processes and the flow of data between them.

Data management software: Software used for creating and manipulating lists, creating files and databases to store data, and combining information for reports.

Data manipulation language: A language associated with a database management system that is employed by end users and programmers to manipulate data in the database.

Data quality audit: Survey of files and samples of files for accuracy and completeness of data in an information system.

Data redundancy: The presence of duplicate data in multiple data files.

Data security controls: Controls to ensure that data files on either disk or tape are not subject to unauthorized access, change, or destruction.

Data workers: People such a secretaries or bookkeepers who process and disseminate the organization's paperwork.

Database: Collection of data organized to service many applications at the same time by organizing data so that they appear to be in one location.

Database administration: Refers to the more technical and operational aspects of managing data, including physical database design and operation.

Database management system (DBMS): Special software to create and maintain a database and enable individual business applications to extract the data they need without having to create separate files or data definitions in their computer programs.

Debugging: The process of discovering and eliminating the errors and defects--the bugs--in program code.

Decision-support systems (DSS): Computer systems at the management level of an organization that combine data and have sophisticated analytical models to support semistructured and unstructured decision making.

Decision tables: A graphic in the form of a table that portrays the conditions that affect a decision; used for documenting situations in which the decision process is highly structured.

Decision trees: Sequential tree-like diagrams that present the conditions affecting a decision and the actions that can be taken. The branches represent the paths that may be taken in the decision-making process.

Decisional roles: Mintzberg's classification for managerial roles where managers initiate activities, handle disturbances, allocate resources, and negotiate conflicts.

Dedicated lines: Telephone lines that are continuously available for transmission by a lessee. Typically conditioned to transmit data at high speeds for high-volume applications.

Descartes' rule of change: A principle that states that if an action cannot be taken repeatedly, then it is not right to be taken at any time.

Design: Simon's second stage of decision making, when the individual conceives of possible alternative solutions to a problem.

Design: Stage in the systems life cycle that produces the logical and physical design specifications for the systems solution.

Desktop publishing: Technology that produces professional-quality documents combining output from word processors with design, graphics, and special layout features.

Development methodology: A collection of methods, one or more for every activity within every phase of a development project.

Digital image processing: Technology that converts documents and graphic images into computerized form so that they can be stored, processed, and accessed by computer systems.

Digital scanners: Input devices that translate images such as pictures or documents into digital form for processing.

Digital signal: A discrete wave form that transmits data coded into two discrete states as 1-bits and 0-bits, which are represented as on-off electrical impulses. Used for data communications.

Direct access storage device (DASD): Refers to magnetic disk technology which permits the CPU to locate a record directly, in contrast to sequential tape storage that must search the entire file.

Direct cutover: A risky conversion approach where the new system completely replaces the old one on an appointed day.

Direct file access method: Method of accessing records by mathematically transforming the key fields into the specific address for the records.

Direct file organization: Method of storing records so that they can be accessed in any sequence without regard to their actual physical order on storage media.

Distributed database: A database that is stored in more than one physical location. Parts or copies of the database are physically stored in one location and other parts are stored and maintained in other locations.

Distributed processing: The distribution of computer processing work among multiple computers linked by a communication network.

Divisionalized bureaucracy: Combination of many machine bureaucracies, each producing a different product or service, under one central headquarters.

Document imaging systems: Systems that employ digital image processing to store, retrieve, and manipulate a digitized image of a document, allowing the document itself to be discarded.

Documentation: Descriptions of how an information system works from either a technical or end-user standpoint.

Domestic exporter: Global strategy characterized by heavy centralization of corporate activities in the home country of origin.

DOS: Operating system for 16-bit microcomputers based on the IBM Personal Computer standard.

Downsizing: The process of transferring applications from large computers to smaller ones.

Drill down: The ability to move from summary data down to lower and lower levels of detail.

DSS database: A collection of current or historical data from a number of applications or groups.

DSS software system: DSS component that permits easy interaction between the users of the system and the DSS database and model base.

EBCDIC: Extended Binary Coded Decimal Interchange Code. Binary code representing every number, alphabetic character, or special character with 8 bits, used primarily in IBM and other mainframe computers.

Economic feasibility: Determines whether the benefits of the proposed solution outweigh the costs.

Edit checks: Routines performed to verify input data and correct errors prior to processing.

Electronic calendaring: Software that tracks appointments and schedules in an office.

Electronic data interchange (EDI): Direct computer-to-computer exchange between two organizations of standard business transaction documents.

Electronic mail: The computer-to-computer exchange of messages.

Electronic market: A marketplace that is created by computer and communication technologies which link many buyers and sellers via interorganizational systems.

Electronic meeting software: Software designed to enhance the productivity of face-to-face meetings or of meetings among participants in scattered locations.

Electronic meeting system (EMS): Collaborative GDSS that uses information technology to make group meetings more productive by facilitating communication as well as decision making. Supports meetings at the same place and time or in different places and times.

End user: Representative of a department outside of the information systems group for whom information systems applications are developed.

End-user development: The development of information systems by end users with little or no formal assistance from technical specialists.

End-user interface: The part of the information system through which the end user interacts with the system, such as on-line screens and commands.

End-user software: Software tools that permit the development of applications by end users with little or no professional programmer intervention or that enhance the productivity of professional programmers.

Enterprise analysis: An analysis of organization-wide information requirements by looking at the entire organization in terms of organizational units, functions, processes, and data elements; helps identify the key entities and attributes in the organization's data.

Entity: A person, place, or thing about which information must be kept.

Entity-relationship diagram: Methodology for documenting databases illustrating the relationship between various entities in the database.

Entrepreneurial structure: Young, small firm in a fast-changing environment dominated by a single entrepreneur and managed by a single chief executive officer.

Environmental factors: Factors external to the organization that influence the adoption and design of information systems.

EPROM: Erasable programmable read-only memory. Subclass of ROM chip that can be erased and reprogrammed many times.

Ergonomics: The interaction of people and machines in the work environment, including the design of jobs, health issues, and the end-user interface of information systems.

Ethical no free lunch rule: Assumption that all tangible and intangible objects are owned by someone else unless there is a specific declaration otherwise and that the creator wants compensation for his work.

Ethics: Principles of right and wrong that can be used by individual's acting as free moral agents to make choices to guide their behavior.

Executive support systems (ESS): Information systems at the strategic level of an organization designed to address unstructured decision making through advanced graphics and communications.

Expert system: Knowledge-intensive computer program that captures the expertise of a human in limited domains of knowledge.

External integration tools: Project management technique that links the work of the implementation team to that of users at all organizational levels.

Facsimile (FAX): Machine that digitizes and transmits documents with both text and graphics over telephone lines.

Fair Information Practices (FIP): A set of principles originally set forth in 1973 that governs the collection and use of information about individuals and forms the basis of most U.S. and European privacy law.

Fault-tolerant computer systems: Systems that contain extra hardware, software and power supply components that can back the system up and keep it running to prevent system failure.

Feasibility study: A way to determine whether a solution is achievable, given the organization's resources and constraints.

Feedback: Output that is returned to the appropriate members of the organization to help them evaluate or correct input.

Fiber optic cable: Fast, light, and durable transmission medium consisting of thin strands of clear glass fiber bound into cables. Data are transmitted as light pulses.

Field: A grouping of characters into a word, group of words, or complete number.

File: A group of records of the same type.

File server: Computer in a network that stores various programs and data files for users of the network. Determines access and availability in the network.

Floppy disk: Removable magnetic disk primarily used with microcomputers. The two most common standard sizes are 3.5-inch and 5.25-inch disks that are made up of polyester film with magnetic coating.

Focused differentiation: Competitive strategy for developing new market niches where a business can compete in the target area better than its competitors.

Formal control tools: Project management technique that helps monitor the progress towards completion of a task and fulfillment of goals.

Formal planning tools: Project management technique that structures and sequences tasks, budgeting time, money, and technical resources required to complete the tasks.

FORTRAN (FORmula TRANslator): Programming language developed in 1956 for scientific and mathematical applications.

Forward chaining: Strategy for searching the rule base in an expert system that begins with the information entered by the user and searches the rule base to arrive at a conclusion.

Forward engineering: The final step in re-engineering when the revised specifications are used to generate new, structured program code for a structured and maintainable system.

Fourth-generation language: A programming language that can be employed directly by end users or less skilled programmers to develop computer applications more rapidly than conventional programming languages.

Frame relay: Shared network service technology that packages data into bundles for transmission but does not use error correction routines. Cheaper and faster than packet switching.

Frames: Method of organizing expert system knowledge into chunks, but the relationships are based on shared characteristics determined by the user rather than a hierarchy.

Franchiser: Firm there the product is created, designed, financed, and initially produced in the home country, but must rely heavily on foreign personnel for further production, marketing, and human resources.

Front-end processor: Small computer managing communications for the host computer in a network.

Fuzzy logic: Rule-based AI that tolerates imprecision by using non-specific terms called membership functions to solve problems.

Garbage can model: Model of decision making that states that organizations are not rational and that decisions are solutions that become attached to problems for accidental reasons.

Gateway: Communications processor that connects dissimilar networks by providing the translation from one protocol to another.

General controls: Overall controls that establish a framework for controlling the design, security, and use of computer systems throughout an organization.

Gigabyte: Approximately one billion bytes. Unit of computer storage capacity.

Global culture: The development of common expectations, shared artifacts, and social norms among different cultures and peoples.

Graphical user interface: The part of an operating system that users interact with that uses graphic icons and the computer mouse to issue commands and make selections.

Graphics language: A computer language that displays data from files or databases in graphic format.

Group decision-support system (GDSS): An interactive computer-based system to facilitate the solutions to unstructured problems by a set of decision makers working together as a group.

Groupware: Software that recognizes the significance of groups in offices by providing functions and services that support the collaborative activities of work groups.

Hacker: A person who gains unauthorized access to a computer network for profit, criminal mischief, or personal pleasure.

Hard disk: Magnetic disk resembling a thin steel platter with an iron oxide coating; used in large computer systems and in many microcomputers.

Hardware controls: Controls to ensure the physical security and correct performance of computer hardware.

Hierarchical data model: One type of logical database model that organizes data in a treelike structure. A record is subdivided into segments that are connected to each other in one-to-many parent-child relationships.

High-level language: Programming languages where each source code statement generates multiple statements at the machine-language level.

Hypermedia database: Approach to data management that organizes data as a network of nodes linked in any pattern established by the user.

Immanuel Kant's Categorical Imperative: A principle that states that if an action is not right for everyone to take it is not right for anyone.

Implementation: Simon's final stage of decision making, when the individual puts the decision into effect and reports on the progress of the solution.

Implementation: All of the organizational activities working toward the adoption, management, and routinization of an innovation.

Implementation controls: Audit of the systems development process at various points to make sure that it is properly controlled and managed.

Index: A table or list that relates record keys to physical locations on direct access files.

Index server: In imaging systems, a device that stores the indexes that allow a user to identify and retrieve a specific document.

Indexed sequential access method (ISAM): File access method to directly access records organized sequentially using an index of key fields.

Inference engine: The strategy used to search through the rule base in an expert system: can be forward or backward chaining.

Information architecture: The particular form that information technology takes in a specific organization to achieve selected goals or functions.

Information center: A special facility within an organization that provides training and support for end-user computing.

Information partnership: Cooperative alliance formed between two corporations for the purpose of sharing information to gain strategic advantage.

Information policy: Formal rules governing the maintenance, distribution, and use of information in an organization.

Information portability: The sharing of computer files among different hardware platforms and software applications.

Information requirements: A detailed statement of the information needs that a new system must satisfy; identifies who needs what information, and when, where, and how the information is needed.

Information rights: The rights that individuals and organizations have with respect to information which pertains to themselves.

Information system: Interrelated components that collect, process, store, and disseminate information to support decision making, control, analysis, and visualization in an organization.

Information systems department: The formal organizational unit that is responsible for the information systems function in the organization.

Information systems managers: Leaders of the various specialists in the information systems department.

Information systems plan: A road map indicating the direction of systems development, the rationale, the current situation, the management strategy, the implementation plan, and the budget.

Information work: Work that primarily consist of creating or processing information.

Information workers: People in the labor force who primarily create, work with, or disseminate information.

Informational roles: Mintzberg's classification for managerial roles where managers act as the nerve centers of their organizations, receiving and disseminating critical information.

Inheritance: Feature of object-oriented programming in which a specific class of objects receives the features of a more general class.

Input: The capture or collection of raw data from within the organization or from its external environment for processing in an information system.

Input authorization: Proper authorization, recording, and monitoring of source documents as they enter the computer system.

Input controls: Procedures to check data for accuracy and completeness when they enter the system, including input authorization, batch control totals, and edits.

Installation: Systems life cycle stage consisting of testing, training, and conversion; the final steps required to put a system into operation.

Institutional factors: Factors internal to the organization that influences the adoption and design of information systems.

Intangible benefits: Benefits that are not easily quantified; they include more efficient customer service or enhanced decision making.

Integrated Services Digital Network (ISDN): International standard for transmitting voice, video, and data to support a wide range of service over the public telephone lines.

Integrated software package: A software package that provides two or more applications, such as spreadsheets and word processing, providing for easy transfer of data between them.

Intellectual property: Intangible property created by individuals or corporations which is subject to protections under trade secret, copyright, and patent law.

Intelligence: The first of Simon's four stages of decision making, when the individual collects information to identify problems occurring in the organization.

Internal integration tools: Project management technique that ensures that the implementation team operates as a cohesive unit.

International information systems infrastructure: The basic information systems required by organizations to coordinate world-wide trade and other activities.

Interoperability: The ability of a software application to operate on two different machine platforms while maintaining the identical user interface and functionality.

Interorganizational systems: Information systems that automate the flow of information across organizational boundaries and link a company to its customers, distributors, or suppliers.

Interpersonal roles: Mintzberg's classification for managerial roles where managers act as figureheads and leaders for the organization.

Interpreter: A special language translator that translates each source code statement into machine code and executes it one at a time.

Intuitive decision makers: Cognitive style that describes people who approach a problem with multiple methods in an unstructured manner, using trial and error to find a solution.

Iterative: Process of repeating the steps to build a system over and over again.

Jukebox: A device for storing and retrieving many optical disks.

Key field: A field in a record that uniquely identifies instances of that record so that it can be retrieved or updated.

Kilobyte: One thousand bytes (actually 1024 storage positions). Used as a measure of microcomputer storage capacity.

Knowledge and information-intense products: Products that require a great deal of learning and knowledge to produce.

Knowledge base: Model of human knowledge that is used by expert systems.

Knowledge engineer: Specialist who elicits information and expertise from other professionals and translates it into a set of rules, frames, or semantic nets for an expert system.

Knowledge work systems (KWS): Information systems that aid knowledge workers in the creation and integration of new knowledge in the organization.

Knowledge workers: People such as engineers, scientists, or architects who design products or services or create new knowledge for the organization.

Knowledge-level decision making: Evaluating new ideas for products and services, ways to communicate new knowledge and distribute information.

Knowledge-level systems: Information systems that support knowledge and data workers in an organization.

Legitimacy: The extent to which one's authority is accepted on grounds of competence, vision, or other qualities.

Liability: The existence of laws that permit individuals to recover the damages done to them by other actors, systems, or organizations.

Local area network (LAN): Telecommunications network that requires its own dedicated channels and that encompasses a limited distance, usually one building or several buildings in close proximity.

Logical design: Lays out the components of the information system and their relationship to each other as they would appear to users.

Logical view: Representation of data as they would appear to an application programmer or end user.

Machine bureaucracy: Large bureaucracy organized into functional divisions that centralizes decision making, produces standard products, and exists in a slow-changing environment.

Machine cycle: Series of operations required to process a single machine instruction.

Machine language: Programming language consisting of the 1s and 0s of binary code.

Magnetic disk: A secondary storage medium in which data are stored by means of magnetized spots on a hard or floppy disk.

Magnetic ink character recognition (MICR): Input technology that translates characters written in magnetic ink into digital codes for processing.

Magnetic tape: Inexpensive and relatively stable secondary storage medium in which large volumes of information are stored sequentially by means of magnetized and nonmagnetized spots on tape.

Magneto-optical disk: Optical disk system that is erasable. Data are recorded by a high-powered laser beam that heats tiny spots in the magnetic media.

Mainframe: Largest category of computer, classified as having 50 megabytes to over 1 gigabyte of RAM.

Maintenance: Changes in hardware, software, documentation, or procedures to a production system to correct errors, meet new requirements, or improve processing efficiency.

Management control: Monitoring how efficiently or effectively resources are utilized and how well operational units are performing.

Management information systems (MIS): Computer systems at the management level of an organization that serve the functions of planning, controlling, and decision making by providing routine summary and exception reports.

Management-level systems: Information systems that support the monitoring, controlling, decision-making, and administrative activities of middle managers.

Managerial roles: Expectations of the activities that managers should perform in an organization.

Master file: Contains all permanent information and is updated during processing by transaction data.

Megabyte: Approximately one million bytes. Unit of computer storage capacity.

Megahertz: A measure of cycle speed, or the pacing of events in a computer; one megahertz equals one million cycles per second.

Memory aids: In DSS, capabilities to update and refresh memory, including databases, views of data, work spaces, and libraries.

Microcomputer: Desktop or portable computer with 640 kilobytes to 64 megabytes of RAM.

Microeconomic model: Model of the firm that views information technology as a factor of production that can be freely substituted for capital and labor.

Microprocessor: Very large-scale integrated circuit technology that integrates the computers memory, logic, and control on a single chip.

Microsecond: One millionth of a second.

Microwave: High-volume, long-distance, point-to-point transmission in which high-frequency radio signals are transmitted through the atmosphere from one terrestrial transmission station to another.

Middle managers: People in the middle of the organizational hierarchy who are responsible for carrying out the plans and goals of senior management.

Migration: The ability to move software from one generation of hardware to another more powerful generation.

Millisecond: One thousandth of a second.

Minicomputer: Middle-range computer with about 10 to 650 megabytes of RAM.

MIS audit: Identifies all the controls that govern individual information systems and assesses their effectiveness.

Model: An abstract representation that illustrates the components or relationships of a phenomenon.

Model base: A collection of mathematical and analytical models that can easily be made accessible to the DSS user.

Modem: Device for translating digital signals into analog signals and vice-versa.

Module: A logical unit of a program that performs one or a small number of functions.

Muddling through: Method of decision making involving successive limited comparisons where the test of a good decision is whether people agree on it.

Multimedia: Technologies that facilitates the integration of two or more types of media such as text, graphics, sound, voice, full-motion video, or animation into a computer-based application.

Multinational: Global strategy that concentrates financial management and control out of a central home base while decentralizing production, sales, and marketing operations to units in other countries.

Multiplexer: Device that enables a single communications channel to carry data transmissions from multiple sources simultaneously.

Multiprocessing: An operating system feature for executing two or more instructions simultaneously in a single computer system by using more than one central processing unit.

Multiprogramming: A method of executing two or more programs concurrently using the same computer. The CPU only executes one program but can service the input/output needs of others at the same time.

Multitasking: The multiprogramming capability of primarily single-user operating systems such as those for microcomputers.

Nanosecond: One billionth of a second.

Network data model: A logical database model that is useful for depicting many-to-many relationships.

Network operating system: Special software that manages the file server in a LAN and routes and manages communications on the network.

Network topology: The shape or arrangement of a network.

Neural network: Hardware or software that attempts to emulate the processing patterns of the biological brain.

New information architecture: An arrangement of the organization's hardware, software, telecommunications, and data resources to put more computing power on the desktop and create a companywide network linking many smaller networks.

Node: Each of the devices in a network.

Object code: Program instructions that have been translated into machine language so that they can be executed by the computer.

Object-oriented database: Approach to data management that stores both data and the procedures acting on the data as objects that can be automatically retrieved and shared.

Object-oriented programming: Approach to software development that combines data and procedures into a single object.

Object-oriented software development: Approach to software development that de-emphasizes procedures and shifts the focus from modeling business processes and data to combining data and procedures that create objects.

Office activities: The principal activities performed at offices; these include managing documents, scheduling and communicating with people, managing data, and managing projects.

Office automation systems (OAS): Computer systems, such as word processing, voice-mail systems, and video-conferencing systems, that are designed to increase the productivity of information workers in the office.

On-line processing: A method of processing information in which transactions are entered directly into the computer system and processed immediately.

On-line transaction processing: Transaction processing mode in which transactions entered on-line are immediately processed by the computer.

Open systems: Software systems that can operate on different hardware platforms because they are built on public non-proprietary operating systems, user interfaces, application standards, and networking protocols.

Open Systems Interconnect (OSI): International reference model for linking different types of computers and networks.

Operating system: The system software that manages and controls the activities of the computer.

Operational control: Deciding how to carry out tasks specified by upper and middle management and establishing criteria for completion and resource utilization.

Operational feasibility: Determines whether the proposed solution is desirable within the existing managerial and organizational framework.

Operational-level systems: Information systems that monitor the elementary activities and transactions of the organization.

Operational managers: People who monitor the day-to-day activities of the organization.

Operations: In DSS, logical and mathematical manipulations of data.

Optical character recognition (OCR): Form of source data automation in which optical scanning devices read specially designed data and translate the data into digital form for the computer.

Optical disk: Secondary storage device on which data are recorded and read by laser beams rather than by magnetic means.

Organization (behavioral definition): A collection of rights, privileges, obligations, and responsibilities that are delicately balanced over a period of time through conflict and conflict resolution.

Organization (technical definition): A stable formal social structure that takes resources from the environment and processes them to produce outputs.

Organizational culture: The set of fundamental assumptions about what products the organization should produce, how and where it should produce them, and for whom they should be produced.

Organizational impact analysis: Study of the way a proposed system will affect organizational structure, attitudes, decision making, and operations.

Organizational models: Models of decision making that take into account the structural and political characteristics of an organization.

OS/2: Powerful operating system used with the 32-bit IBM/Personal System/2 microcomputer workstations that supports multitasking, networking, and more memory-intensive applications than DOS.

Output controls: Ensure that the results of computer processing are accurate, complete, and properly distributed.

Outsourcing: The practice of contracting computer center operations, telecommunications networks, or applications development to external vendors.

Packet switching: Technology that breaks blocks of text into small fixed bundles of data and routes them in the most economical way through any available communications channel.

Page: Small section of a program, which can be easily stored in primary storage and quickly accessed from secondary storage.

Parallel processing: Type of processing in which more than one instruction can be processed at a time by breaking down a problem into smaller parts and processing them simultaneously with multiple processors.

Parallel sensor system: A machine consisting of many nodes that each act as a processor feeding information to a hierarchy of higher-level nodes.

Parallel strategy: Conservative conversion approach where both the old system and its replacement are run together until everyone is assured that the new one functions correctly.

Parity: An extra bit built into the EBCDIC and ASCII codes used as a check bit to ensure accuracy.

Particularism: Making judgements and taking actions on the basis of narrow or personal characteristics.

Pascal: Programming language used on microcomputers and to teach sound programming practices in computer science courses.

Patent: A legal document that grants the owner an exclusive monopoly on the ideas behind an invention for 17 years; designed to ensure that the inventors of new machines or methods are rewarded for their labor while making widespread use of their inventions.

Pen-based input: Input devices such as tablets, notebooks, and notepads consisting of a flat-screen display tablet and a pen-like stylus that digitizes handwriting.

Personal information manager: Packaged database tool designed to support specific office data management tasks for an information worker.

Phased approach: Introduces the new system in stages either by functions or by organizational units.

Physical design: The process of translating the abstract logical model into the specific technical design for the new system.

Physical view: The representation of data as they would be actually organized on physical storage media.

Pilot study: A strategy to introduce the new system to a limited area of the organization until it is proven to be fully functional.

Pixel: The smallest unit of data for defining an image in the computer. The computer reduces a picture to a grid of pixels. The term *pixel* comes from *picture element*.

PL/1 (Programming Language 1): Programming language developed by IBM in 1964 for business and scientific applications.

Pointer: A special type of data element attached to a record that shows the absolute or relative address of another record.

Political models: Models of decision making where decisions result from competition and bargaining among an organization's interest groups and key leaders.

Post implementation: Final stage of the systems life cycle in which the system is used and evaluated while in production and is modified to make improvements or meet new requirements.

Primary activities: Activities most directly related to the production and distribution of a firm's products or services.

Primary storage: Part of the computer that temporarily stores program instructions and data being used by the instructions for use by the CPU.

Printer: A computer output device that provides paper "hard-copy" output in the form of text or graphics.

Privacy: The claim of individuals to be left alone, free from surveillance or interference from other individuals, organizations, or the state.

Private branch exchange (PBX): Central switching system that handles a firm's voice and digital communications.

Process specification: Describes the logic of the processes occurring within the lowest-level bubbles of the data flow diagrams.

Processing: The conversion of raw input into a form that is more meaningful to humans.

Processing controls: Routines for establishing that data are complete and accurate during processing.

Product differentiation: Competitive strategy for creating brand loyalty by developing new and unique products and services that are not easily duplicated by competitors.

Production: The stage after the new system is installed and the conversion is complete; during this time the system is reviewed by users and technical specialists to determine how well it has met its original goals.

Production or service workers: People who actually produce the products or services of the organization.

Professional bureaucracy: Knowledge-based organization such as a law firm or hospital that is dominated by department heads with weak centralized authority; operates in a slowly changing environment.

Program: A series of statements or instructions to the computer.

Program-data dependence: The close relationship between data stored in files and the software programs that update and maintain those files. Any change in data organization or format requires a change in all the programs associated with those files.

Program security controls: Controls designed to prevent unauthorized changes to programs in systems that are already in production.

Programmers: Highly trained technical specialists who write computer software instructions.

Programming: The process of translating the system specifications prepared during the design stage into program code.

Project definition: Stage in the systems life cycle that determines whether or not the organization has a problem and whether or not the problem can be solved by launching a system project.

Project management software: Software that facilitates the development, scheduling, and management of a project by breaking the complex project into simpler subtasks, each with its own completion time and resource requirements.

PROM: Programmable read-only memory. Subclass of ROM chip used in control devices because it can be programmed once.

Protocol: Set of rules and procedures that govern transmission between the components in a network.

Prototype: Preliminary working version of an information system for demonstration and evaluation purposes.

Prototyping: Process of building an experimental system quickly and inexpensively for demonstration and evaluation so that users can better determine information requirements.

Pseudocode: Method for expressing program logic that uses plain English statements rather than graphic symbols, trees, tables, or programming languages to describe a procedure.

Query language: A high-level computer language used to retrieve specific information from databases or files.

RAM: Random access memory. Primary storage of data or program instructions that can directly access any randomly chosen location in the same amount of time.

Rational model: Model of human behavior believing that people, organizations, and nations make consistent, value-maximizing calculations within certain constraints.

Rationalization of procedures: Streamlining of standard operating procedures in order to maximize the advantages of computerization and make information systems more efficient.

Record: A group of related fields.

Reduced instruction set computing (RISC): Technology used to enhance the speed of microprocessors by embedding only the most frequently used instructions on a chip.

Reference model: A generic framework for thinking about a problem.

Register: Temporary storage location in the ALU or control unit where small amounts of data and instructions reside for thousandths of a second just before use.

Relational data model: A type of logical database model that treats data as if they were stored in two-dimensional tables. It can relate data stored in one table to data in another as long as the two tables share a common data element.

Repetitive stress injury (RSI): Occupational disease that occurs when muscle groups are forced through the same, repetitive actions often with high impact loads or thousands of repetitions of low impact loads.

Report generator: Software that creates customized reports in a wide range of formats that are not routinely produced by an information system.

Representations: In DSS, conceptualization of information in the form of graphs, charts, lists, reports, and symbols to control operations.

Request for Proposal (RFP): Detailed list of questions submitted to vendors of packaged software or other computer services to determine if the vendor's product can meet the organization's specific requirements.

Resource allocation: Determination of how costs, time, and personnel are assigned to different activities of a systems development project.

Responsibility: Accepting the potential costs, duties, and obligations of one's decisions.

Reverse engineering: The process of taking existing programs, file and database descriptions and converting them into corresponding design-level components that can then be used to create new applications.

Ring network: Network topology in which all computers are linked by a closed loop in a manner that passes data in one direction from one computer to another.

Risk assessment: Determining the potential frequency of occurrence of a problem and the potential damage if the problem were to occur. Used to determine the cost/benefit of a control.

Risk Aversion Principle: Principle that one should take the action which produces the least harm or incurs the least cost.

ROM: Read-only memory. Semiconductor memory chips that contain program instructions. These chips can only be read from; they cannot be written to.

Rule base: The collection of knowledge in an AI system that is represented in the form of IF-THEN rules.

Rule-based expert system: An AI program that has a large number of interconnected and nested IF-THEN statements or "rules" that are the basis for the knowledge in the system.

Run control totals: Procedures for controlling completeness of computer updating by generating control totals that reconcile totals before and after processing.

Satellite: Transmission of data using orbiting satellites to serve as relay stations for transmitting microwave signals over very long distances.

Schema: The logical description of an entire database, listing all the data elements in the database and the relationships among them.

Secondary storage: Relatively long-term, non-volatile storage of data outside the CPU and primary storage.

Sector: Method of storing data on a floppy disk in which the disk is divided into pie-shaped pieces or sectors. Disk storage location can be identified by sector and data record number.

Security: Policies, procedures, and technical measures used to prevent unauthorized access, alteration, theft, or physical damage to information systems.

Segregation of functions: Principle of internal control to divide responsibilities and assign tasks among people so that job functions do not overlap to minimize the risk of errors and fraudulent manipulation of the organization's assets.

Semantic nets: Expert systems that use the property of inheritance to organize and classify knowledge when the knowledge base is composed of easily identifiable chunks or objects of interrelated characteristics.

Semiconductor: An integrated circuit made by printing thousands and even millions of tiny transistors on a small silicon chip.

Senior managers: People at the highest organizational level who are responsible for making long-range decisions.

Sensitivity analysis: Models that ask "what-if" questions repeatedly to determine the impact of changes in one or more factors on outcomes.

Sequential file organization: A method of storing records in which records must be retrieved in the same physical sequence in which they are stored.

Sociotechnical design: Design to produce information systems that blend technical efficiency with sensitivity to organizational and human needs.

Software: The detailed instructions that control the operation of a computer system.

Software controls: Controls to ensure the security and reliability of software.

Software metrics: Objective assessments of the software used in a system in the form of quantified measurements.

Software package: A prewritten, precoded, commercially available set of programs that eliminates the need to write software programs for certain functions.

Software re-engineering: Methodology that addresses the problem of aging software by salvaging and upgrading it so that the users can avoid a long and expensive replacement project.

Source code: Program instructions written in a high-level language before translation into machine language.

Source data automation: Input technology that captures data in computer-readable form at the time and place the data are created.

Spaghetti code: Unstructured, confusing program code with tangled logic that metaphorically resembles a pot of cooked spaghetti.

Spreadsheet: Software displaying data in a grid of columns and rows, with the capability of easily recalculating numerical data.

Standard: Approved reference models and protocols as determined by standard-setting groups for building or developing products or services.

Standard operating procedures (SOPs): Precise, defined rules for accomplishing tasks that have been developed to cope with expected situations.

Standing data: Data that are permanent and affect transactions flowing into and out of a system.

Star network: Network topology in which all computers and other devices are connected to a central host computer. All communications between network devices must pass through the host computer.

Storage technology: Physical media and software governing the storage and organization of data for use in an information system.

Stored program concept: The idea that a program cannot be executed unless it is stored in a computer's primary storage along with required data.

Strategic decision making: Determining the long-term objectives, resources, and policies of an organization.

Strategic information systems: Computer systems at any level of the organization that change the goals, operations, products, services, or environmental relationships to help the organization gain a competitive advantage.

Strategic-level systems: Information systems that support the long-range planning activities of senior management.

Strategic transitions: A movement from one level of sociotechnical system to another. Often required when adopting strategic systems that demand changes in the social and technical elements of an organization.

Structure chart: System documentation showing each level of design, the relationship among the levels, and the overall place in the design structure; can document one program, one system, or part of one program.

Structured: Refers to the fact that techniques are instructions that are carefully drawn up, often step-by-step, with each step building upon a previous one.

Structured analysis: Method for defining system inputs, processes, and outputs and for partitioning systems into subsystems or modules that show a logical graphic model of information flow.

Structured decisions: Decisions that are repetitive, routine, and have a definite procedure for handling them.

Structured design: Software design discipline, encompassing a set of design rules and techniques for designing a system from the top down in a hierarchical fashion.

Structured programming: Discipline for organizing and coding programs that simplifies the control paths so that the programs can be easily understood and modified. Uses the basic control structures and modules that have only one entry point and one exit point.

Structured Query Language (SQL): The emerging standard data manipulation language for relational database management systems.

Subschema: The logical description of the part of a database required by a particular function or application program.

Supercomputer: Very sophisticated and powerful computer that can perform very complex computations extremely rapidly.

Support activities: Activities that make the delivery of the primary activities of a firm possible.

Switched lines: Telephone lines that a person can access from his or her terminal to transmit data to another computer, the call being routed or switched through paths to the designated destination.

Switching costs: The expense a customer or company incurs in lost time and resources when changing from one supplier or system to a competing supplier or system.

Synchronous transmission: High-speed simultaneous transmission of large blocks of data.

System failure: An information system that either does not perform as expected, is not operational at a specified time, or cannot be used in the way it was intended.

System flowchart: Graphic design tool that depicts the physical media and sequence of processing steps used in an entire information system.

System residence device: The secondary storage device on which a complete operating system is stored.

System 7: Operating system for the Macintosh computer which supports multitasking and has powerful graphics and multimedia capabilities.

System software: Generalized programs that manage the resources of the computer.

System testing: Tests the functioning of the information system as a whole in order to determine if discrete modules will function together as planned.

Systems analysis: The analysis of a problem which the organization will try to solve with an information system.

Systems analysts: Specialists who translate business problems and requirements into information requirements and systems.

Systems design: Details how a system will meet the information requirements as determined by the systems analysis.

Systems development: The activities that go into producing an information systems solution to an organizational problem or opportunity.

Systems life cycle: Traditional methodology for developing an information system that partitions the systems development process into six formal stages that must be completed sequentially with a very formal division of labor between end-users and information systems specialists.

Systems study: Stage in the systems life cycle that analyzes the problems of existing systems, defines the objectives to be attained by a solution, and evaluates various solution alternatives.

Tangible benefits: Benefits that can be quantified and assigned monetary value; they include lower operational costs and increased cash flows.

Technical feasibility: Determines whether a proposed solution can be implemented with the available hardware, software, and technical resources.

Technostress: Stress induced by computer use whose symptoms include aggravation, hostility towards humans, impatience, and enervation.

Telecommunications: Communication of information by electronic means, usually over some distance.

Telecommunications software: Special software for controlling and supporting the activities of a telecommunications network.

Telecommunications system: Collection of compatible hardware and software arranged to communicate information from one location to another.

Telecommunications technology: Physical devices and software that link various hardware components and transfer data from one physical location to another.

Teleconferencing: Ability to confer with a group of people simultaneously using the telephone or electronic mail group communication software.

Terabyte: Approximately 1 trillion bytes; unit of computer storage capacity.

Test plan: Prepared by the development team in conjunction with the users; it includes all of the preparations for the series of tests to be performed on the system.

Testing: The exhaustive and thorough process that determines whether the system produces the desired results under known conditions.

Time sharing: The sharing of computer resources by many users simultaneously by having the CPU spend a fixed amount of time on each user's program before proceeding to the next.

Top-down: An approach that progresses from the highest most abstract level to the lowest level of detail.

Top-down approach: In the history of artificial intelligence, the effort to develop a logical analog to how the brain works.

Total quality management (TQM): A concept that makes quality control a responsibility to be shared by all people in an organization.

Touch screen: Input technology that permits the entering or selecting of commands and data by touching the surface of a sensitized video display monitor with a finger or pointer.

Track: Concentric circle on the surface area of a disk on which data are stored as magnetized spots; each track can store thousands of bytes.

Trade secret: Any intellectual work or product used for a business purpose that can be classified as belonging to that business provided it is not based on information in the public domain.

Traditional file environment: A way of collecting and maintaining data in an organization that leads to each functional area or division creating and maintaining its own data files and programs.

Transaction cost theory: Economic theory that states that firms exist because they can conduct marketplace transactions internally more cheaply than they can with external firms in the marketplace.

Transaction file: In batch systems, the file in which all transactions are accumulated to await processing.

Transaction processing systems (TPS): Computerized systems that perform and record the daily routine transactions necessary to the conduct of the business; they serve the operational level of the organization.

Transborder data flow: The movement of information across international boundaries in any form.

Transform algorithm: Mathematical formula used to translate a record's key field directly into the record's physical storage location.

Transmission Control Protocol/Internet Protocol (TCP/IP): U.S. Department of Defense reference model for linking different types of computers and networks.

Transnational: Truly globally managed firms which have no national headquarters; value-added activities are managed from a global perspective without reference to national borders, optimizing sources of supply and demand and taking advantage of any local competitive advantage.

Tuple: A row or record in a relational database.

Twisted wire: Transmission medium consisting of pairs of twisted copper wires. Used to transmit analog phone conversations but can be used for data transmission.

Unit testing: The process of testing each program separately in the system. Sometimes called program testing.

UNIX: Operating system for microcomputers, minicomputers, and mainframes that is machine-independent and supports multiuser processing, multitasking, and networking.

Unstructured decisions: Nonroutine decisions in which the decision maker must provide judgement, evaluation, and insights into the problem definition; there is no agreed-upon procedure for making such decisions.

User-designer communications gap: The differences in backgrounds, interests, and priorities that impede communication and problem-solving among end users and information systems specialists.

User interface: The part of the information system through which the end user interacts with the system; type of hardware and the series of on-screen commands and responses required for a user to work with the system.

Utilitarian Principle: Principle that one should take the action that achieves the higher or greater value.

Utility program: System software consisting of programs for routine, repetitive tasks, which can be shared by many users.

Value-added network (VAN): Private, multipath, data-only third party managed networks that are used by multiple organizations on a subscription basis.

Value chain model: Model that highlights the activities that add a margin of value to a firm's products or services where information systems can best be applied to achieve a competitive advantage.

Very-high-level programming language: Programming language using fewer instructions than conventional languages. Used primarily as a professional programmer productivity tool.

Video display terminal (VDT): A screen, also referred to as a cathode ray tube (CRT). Provides a visual image of both user input and computer output.

Videoconferencing: Teleconferencing with the capability of participants to see each other over video screens.

Virtual private networks: Inexpensive telecommunications over public phone lines with computers and software creating an illusion of a private network for a company.

Virtual reality systems: Interactive graphics software and hardware that create computer-generated simulations that provide sensations that emulate real-world activities.

Virtual storage: A way of handling programs more efficiently by the computer by dividing the programs into small fixed or variable-length portions with only a small portion stored in primary memory at one time.

Voice input device: Technology that converts the spoken word into digital form for processing.

Voice mail: System for digitizing a spoken message and transmitting it over a network.

Voice output device: Converts digital output data into spoken words.

Walkthrough: A review of a specification or design document by a small group of people carefully selected based on the skills needed for the particular objectives being tested.

Wide area network (WAN): Telecommunications network that spans a large geographical distance. May consist of a variety of cable, satellite, and microwave technologies.

Windows: A graphical user interface shell that runs in conjunction with the DOS microcomputer operating system. Supports multitasking and some forms of networking.

Windows NT: Powerful operating system developed by Microsoft for use with 32-bit microcomputers and workstations based on Intel and other microprocessors. Supports networking, multitasking, and multiprocessing.

Word length: The number of bits that can be processed at one time by a computer. The larger the word length, the greater the speed of the computer.

Word processing: Office automation technology that facilitates the creation of documents through computerized text editing, formatting, storing, and printing.

Word processing software: Software that handles electronic storage, editing, formatting, and printing of documents.

Workflow management: The process of streamlining business procedures so that documents can be moved easily and efficiently from one location to another.

Workstation: Desktop computer with powerful graphics, mathematical processing, and communications capabilities as well as the ability to perform several complicated tasks at one time. Often used in scientific or design work.

WORM: Write once, read many. Optical disk system that allows users to record data only once; data cannot be erased but can be read indefinitely.

Name Index

United States Companies Index

Foreign Companies Index

Subject Index

Value-added network, 231–232
Very large-scale integrated circuit,
   117–118
Very-high-level programming language,
   165
Videoconferencing, 234
Virtual private network, 231, 487
Virtual reality system, 359–362
Virtual research institute, 336–337
Virtual storage, 153–154
   page, 153
Virus. *See* Computer virus
Voice input device, 134
Voice mail, 234

Voice output device, 135
Voyage estimating decision support
   system, 43

W

Walkthrough, software, 306
Wide area network, 230–231
Windows, 158–159
Windows NT, 157
Wireless transmission, 222–223
Wizard system, 52
Word length, 118

Word processing, 38, 343–345
Word processing software, 166
Workflow management, 346–347
Workflow system, 345–349
Workstation, 38, 121, 357
   computer-aided design, 124–125
   microcomputer, compared, 124–125
   representative, 121
Write once, read many (WORM), 130

X

XCON, 416

Photo Credits